THE CHRISTIAN FOUNDATIONS OF CRIMINAL RESPONSIBILITY

A Philosophical Study of Legal Reasoning

THE CHRISTIAN FOUNDATIONS OF CRIMINAL RESPONSIBILITY

A Philosophical Study of Legal Reasoning

by

J. M. B. Crawford

and

J. F. Quinn

Toronto Studies in Theology
Volume 40

The Edwin Mellen Press
Lewiston/Queenston/Lampeter

Library of Congress Cataloging-in-Publication Data

Quinn, John (John F.)
The Christian foundations of criminal responsibility: A philosophical study of legal reasoning / John Quinn and J.M.B. Crawford.
p. cm. -- (Toronto studies in theology ; v. 40)
ISBN 0-88946-979-2
1. Criminal intent--History. 2. Criminal intent--Religious aspects--Christianity--History. 3. Criminal liability--History. 4. Criminal liability--Religious aspects--Christianity--History. I. Crawford, J.M.B. II. Title. III. Series.
K5066.Q56 1990
345'.04--dc20
[342.54]
90-5638
CIP

This is volume 40 in the continuing series
Toronto Studies in Theology
Volume 40 ISBN 0-88946-979-2
TST Series ISBN 0-88946-975-X

A CIP catalog record for this book
is available from the British Library.

The Edwin Mellen Press
Box 450
Lewiston, New York
USA 14092

The Edwin Mellen Press
Box 67
Queenston, Ontario
CANADA L0S 1L0

The Edwin Mellen Press, Ltd.
Lampeter, Dyfed, Wales
UNITED KINGDOM SA48 7DY

Printed in the United States of America

In Memoriam

F. Stewart McNeilly, Department Chairman
and
Penelope Palmer, Faculty

late of the Department of Moral Philosophy,
The University of St. Andrews, Scotland.

Dear friends and companions, be remembered.

CONTENTS

***

"To the Courteous Reader"

"If thou findest in this
work any small errours,
be pleased to excuse it,
being the first that hath
adventured in this untrodden
path. And your good acceptance
may further encourage me to
continue.

Your faithful Servant,
J.W."

Taken from
A Treatise . . . concerning the Office and Authorities of Coroners and Sherifes by John Wilkinson, of Bernards Inne, Gent.
(London, 1657)

PREFACE

THE PURPOSE of this work in legal research was to discover the principal intellectual sources for that amiable concept in the criminal law which is variously known as *intention* or *mens rea*. As one delved more and more in the legal garden, one slowly began to see that the common law use and development of *mens rea* owed an unstated, and, perhaps, even an unseen debt to various Christian writers. Christian thinking had a strong appreciation for human beings, and saw the person as the centre of worldly existence. Christianity created and provided the forms of judgment wherein one moved from this earthly world into a heavenly world. The end of a person's life was fulfilled by and through a union with God. One hoped for God's mercy and grace in order to gain salvation; but the act of living, and the act of cooperating with God's grace and mercy was a personal act. Christian thinkers generally regarded what one did to be of importance towards one's heavenly end. In that way, one's existence was not illusionary. What one did had value of a real kind.

Key to Christian thinking was personal responsibility. What, then, was the person? The two concepts of intellect and will were those which expressed both human dynamism and human tension. Human dynamism might serve to concentrate the mind on asking from whence did human action spring? In what way is this action a human action? Is there some general concept, based upon some formulated principle, in which questions about human action can be formulated and then examined? When a priest administered absolution, what was he absolving? One may say that an animal has a mean disposition, but one does not absolve the animal; a person may have a mean disposition, but one can absolve that person and ask that a penance be performed, with the hope that one might overcome one's weaknesses, even when those weaknesses seemed to be dispositional.

All falling from grace through sin was not a matter of the mind only. One could know the good, yet not follow it, as St. Paul counselled. The dynamism of action was intimately involved with the tension of knowledge, especially knowledge which could not move one to action. One might say, "I know the good," but it did not follow from that state of knowledge that one would then do the good. One can recall the rich young man from the gospels, who, upon being told that he should sell all that he possessed and give his wealth to the poor, took leave of Christ as a much sadder man, unable to divest himself of his wealth. The Christian believed that one needed to have both the good of the intellect and the good of the will. Knowledge could be detailed and intricate, but it could be the wrong kind of knowledge. Action could be vital and intense, but it could be the wrong use of the human will. These two equipollent concepts – the will and the intellect –, which are conceptually distinct, nevertheless were intertwined in Christian thought, and each had its place in the scale of values which led to human perfection through grace. One had to have the proper moral code, and one also had to create the proper moral disposition in accordance with that Christian code. The road to Christian perfection involved containing the dynamism of the will and the power of the mind.

As with any central concept, it will not be found to be expressed in one simple phrase or code. For us today (as, no doubt, for those tomorrow), the language of the Christian past, from the age of the Fathers to that of the Schoolmen, is a language separated from us. The modern languages of psychology, psychiatry, and science, do not work easily within the confines of the older language which spoke about intellect and will, or the heart, or divine commands. One must now return to the older language, which expressed Christian concepts, with a sense of patience. One must be willing to give a bit and to read, as the older English law texts from the sixteenth century did say, with a sense of charity ("...reader, in your charity excuse our misprints with your eyes..."). When one does this, one may come to understand that Christian thought did have a great concern for an individual, and did have (certainly in theory, in spite of religious excesses) a conceptual fundament upon which human rights could exist and be defended.

If it were the case that *this* person was to be *judged*, as well as *loved*, by God, then *this* person had to be real, and had to be the foundation upon which any judgment concerning his salvation had to be made. On the other hand, if one had to be held responsible for one's acts, then, in theory and in principle, there had to be a way by which it could be determined that one did, in fact, do this act, or permit that omission. One could not be judged by default, nor could one be made guilty for what one did not do, or did not know, or could not do, or could not have known. The soul, with its conceptual distinctions of the will and intellect expressed by the fact of one's personhood and existence, could not be held to account for what it did not do. Christian thought believed in the integrity of the person. The integrity of the person was a real relationship between God and a person. That real relationship was believed to be founded upon Christian grace and virtue, which the believer lived and practised. At the heart of Christianity was mercy, expressed through the confessional. By confession, one directly told God, either through the confessional, or through private accusation, that one had sinned. The sins were real; one held oneself to be responsible for their commission; one hoped for God's mercy through absolution, or through private confession.

Christian theology developed broad categories of excuse whereby a penitent might be excused for his sins, or, for that matter, might be seen not to have sinned at all, however much the penitent may have accused himself of being a sinner. Conditions were set down to guide a confessor so that he could determine whether a pentinent had sinned, and whether the penitent were contrite of heart and mind. In the finest sense, moral theory developed whereby one could be held to standards of virtue deemed to be real and over which one could exercise a sense of responsibility. By stating that the voluntary is a real concept, and by affirming that intellectual powers truly are powers of human expression over which one could exercise control and direction, both value and protection were given to human endeavors and actions. The theory underlying Christian virtue was that one could, in fact, direct one's actions and exercise control over one's life.

In moral theory formed by these assumptions, one can see that the life of the person is of highest value. There can be no collective, as with a bee hive or an ant hill. Even monastic life, which may seem to be a collective, is not that; it is, to the contrary, a personal expression of mind and will whereby one voluntarily enters into communal life, and will accept its rules. The person is not lost; rather, one has a community of persons.

The common law had rich theoretical soil from which to grow. It possessed a rich language of the will and of the intellect, and a language which could express the subtle interworkings of human passions. It had a very practical understanding of fallen human nature, and it could even be argued (though outside the scope of this research) that the language of Christian moral theory is far more pliable than psychoanalytic language of our own time. Any legal theory growing up with these linguistic beginnings would possess a complex conceptual base. Such a foundation would permit it to develop fine understandings of human action, and to address the different ways in which action and responsibility would lend themselves to legal description.

As the common law left its earlier Christian roots, its development was never fully excised from Christian belief. The grand names in English law were, at the same time, grand churchmen. Sir Edward Coke (d.1634) or Sir Matthew Hale (d.1676), for example, were equally at home then in writing about theology and philosophy. Hale, as we have suggested, could be viewed as the last scholastic mind in the common law, as Hegel might be viewed as the last schoolman in philosophy. What one may wish to keep in mind is that law, as a subject, has matter of its own to advance. A simple distinction may be made, to distinguish the foundations of the law (for our work it would be the criminal law) from the advance of the law, with its content and those propositions which express that content. For instance, of the somewhat new crime of *bail jumping*, one could say that there are propositions which express its legal content, whilst, at the same time, there are the theoretical foundations of the statute which are based upon an understanding of the legal concept of, "*to do something knowingly*." The content of a proposition on *bail jumping* is the statutory prohibition itself, which expresses the law. Underlying that statute are the legal foundations which permit the making of such a law, namely, that the law embodies a philosophical understanding of what it means to act *knowingly*.

As the common law developed its criminal sanctions, it did so by drawing upon that tradition of the will and the intellect, and the person in general, which was embodied in Christian theories. Common law held that one could be responsible for wrongs, and gave a rubric whereby wrongs could be adjudged of and attributed to the wrongdoer. In good part, Christian theory gave impetus to much of what police powers of a common law state would express to be crimes against the realm. In the period now, when many criminal statutes have been decriminalized, we may be seeing the de-christianizing of the criminal law. Whether in substance that be the case or not, it can still be argued that the underlying concept of criminal intention expresses and embodies much of what a Christian tradition of will and intellect and person gave to the common law.

A powerful element to be located in Christian thought is that the person is more than any national state in which he or she lives. In this way, the Christian roots of intention can serve to be a foil against modern law-making, wherein legislatures create a plethora of crimes in which the intention of the agent is of unconcern to the legislature, it desiring to engage in social engineering. So often one will read that an intention is presumed because an act was done. *Actus reus* then embodies intention, giving prosecutors an easy burden of proof to discharge. What is bothersome about this style of law-making is that it fits the human person into a legislative mold, and that is, if excesses grow, but another way to displace the person and to dilute the development of a viable concept of legal and moral responsibility. In Christian theory, with its understanding of moral guilt, one first had to commit the offence before one could be condemned for the offence. If one did not intend to sin, then it would be wrong to condemn one as a sinner.

A further issue is this. When one permits the state to remove intention from the law, one gives over to the state itself what will or will not be taken to be an exercise in personal responsibility. The fictional category of a statute, made by the legislature in its law-making capacity, is seen or thought to be more real than the intention of the agent under that law or statute. The worry which Herbert L. Packer expressed in his article, "*Mens Rea and the Supreme Court*, [1962: The Supreme Court Review, edited by Philip B. Kurland, (The University of Chicago Press, 1962), pp. 107-152] has substantial foundation for any legal theorist, or for any practising defense attorney. "Yet the constitutional question remains. Faced with the hard case that inescapably poses the issue, is there any basis for a constitutional doctrine of *mens rea*? Given the erosion of *mens rea* in traditional criminal law it takes some temerity to assert that due process now requires a constitutional doctrine of *mens rea* to be fashioned. But the suggestion that it does is less temerarious than it would be if these questions had been given due consideration by the courts. As we have seen, they have not. And the Supreme Court itself bears prime responsibility for having sanctioned the erosion of *mens rea* in what can be restrainedly described as an intellectually unsatisfying way. Strict liability in the criminal law is irrational, in the substantive due process sense of that word. *Mens rea* as extended to include negligence as a mode of culpability ought to find its way into constitutional doctrine" (pp. 151-52).

If *intention* is not thought to be a real category for describing human responsibility, then what is a real category? Aristotle, in the *Nicomachean Ethics*, stated that if an action did not originate from within the person, then it was either an involuntary action or a non-voluntary action, and one then would appeal to circumstances in order to explain human movement. If one removes the voluntary from the course of an explanation, one is then left, variously, either with external elements whereby to explain what occurred, or with internal compulsions to explain human actions. A theory of action which presents intellect and will as the real predicates of human action, and thus human responsibility, may be seen to be a golden legal defense of the value of the person against the power of the state.

To write more than this would be to step outside of the confines of a *Preface*.

CHAPTER ONE

The Early Christian Councils

In this chapter, by the sparing use of historical sources, we wish to show how the concept of criminal responsibility has developed in the common law. The logical form of intention was never given to the law pure and simple. Legal systems have all wrestled with the problem of how to assign guilt for actions and deeds; some systems are harsh, some systems are lenient. Intention will emerge as a candidate for assigning guilt for crimes. We may distinguish between the logical form, i.e., how the language is constructed to express that one is responsible for an act or criminal omission, and what is assigned, i.e., that one did a criminal act. The crimes will vary, but they are distinct from the requirements for establishing guilt in a criminal act. By appealing to the development of a concept through the centuries one may be able to discover for oneself that the components of intention may look to be simple enough, but upon examination of those components one may find that when each element within the concept is examined no simple logical operator emerges; instead, an unclosed and developing concept emerges. It would be a simple hope that one might entertain, wishing for a simple isolation which a formula could give: namely, that the logical form of intention is to assign guilt, while those actual crimes themselves which are committed serve to act as variables within the formula. One may be guided by such a hope, but it has not yet been realized in a final form.[1]

We have no doubt that one may isolate "intentional" elements in a statement, as when we say that one must have an intention in order to be deemed responsible for one's act, and/or the consequences of his act–or even once removed, when we come to the law of Agency wherein the acts of an agent are taken to express the mind of the principal, and thus actions which the principal himself would do, ratify or approve. One philosophical difficulty may be how to determine that any sentential arrangement actually does express an intentional quality. In a graphic way, one might ask how a sentence pictures an intention. A large part of the common law concerns itself with refining intentional language, of separating *obiter dictum* from Black Letter pronouncements of what the law is and what is the right and proper construal of a legislative sentence, statute, act, ordinance, or what is the proper reading of a case holding. Determining the what of intention, and the range of intention, is not a simple act of locating something; it is, rather, a complicated act of understanding of what something may be, and the range over which it dominates.

The earlier sources for the common law notions about responsibility derive in great part from the theological systems of the early Middle Ages. On this, we believe this note can be made. It does not muddle our discussion if this claim is advanced: that the two systems of law, theological and civil, have the same aims in mind, though their specific problems be different. Each system places a requirement upon an agent to determine if he is or is not responsible for his meritorious acts. The term "meritorious" should not bother us. One is "meritorious" when he obeys a speed limit, or does not intentionally kill another person. A theological system, such as was advanced in Judeo-Christian religions, is a legal model (in part). An agent is related to God by his meritorious acts. It is assumed that an agent can act meritoriously. If we argue that one cannot act meritoriously, then there is little need to pursue the analogy. One does not fault a robot for its mistakes because the mistake is part of the robot; it is not in addition to the robot. The robot turns left rather than right not because it is a mischievous robot but because its mechanical and electrical components cause it to turn left. In awkward English one would say that the robot has "leftness" as an essential part of its "robotness," just as one's television set is not to be described as being malicious because it will not transmit B.B.C. 2. It will not transmit on that frequency because it cannot receive that frequency.

If we take both systems, civil law and theological law, as models of some society or other (one is the earthly society, and the other is the heavenly society), we may compare the common elements in each system. We use the word "system" in a very loose sense to mean that the requirements for meritoriousness in one set of beliefs may, at the same time, correspond in great part to the requirements for meritoriousness or rectitude in the other system. The requirements for a moral act, in a religious system like Christianity, may have many elements in common with a full-blooded intentional act under the civil law (its criminal branch). We may be asking of the requirements of each questions which could be common to both systems.

We labor this point because we think one can be put off unnecessarily by both of two questions. One may attempt to ascertain that the common law is little more than a subset of medieval canon law; or, one may argue that the common law is so different in aim that it is to create confusion if one asks whether the common law has theological roots. In the first instance one often tries to champion a cause. In the second case one tries to stress differences to such a point that no comparison can lie. We think both positions are extreme, and do not think either helps one that much.

A theological system may embody modes of excusing which a common law legal system does not embody. We cite one instance. Christian theology makes a claim about one's ability to act by stressing the fallen nature of man. It is advanced that a man cannot be the author of good acts in a supernatural sense. At this point the problem becomes doubly complicated. If a man cannot author good acts, what does he author? He moves his arm, he can walk, he can talk, he can compose a sentence, or listen to what others have said; how, out of all of these specific actions, does one arrive at the notion that one cannot author a certain kind of act, namely, a theologically good act? Must there be some other conceptual element superadded to the concept of a human act which experience itself will not give? If one cites a list of actions attributable to a man, how does one know that the list is incomplete or, if not incomplete, how does one arrive at a class of actions, and the requirements for them, which transcend an empirical list?

If it is a requirement for the doing of a good act that one receive "grace" in order to do a good act, has not one claimed that in order to understand the empirical order of events (the class of actions and events which are or can be contingently the case) one must step outside of that empirical order and come to see that order by means of some prior model, the model itself not contained in the order of events? At this point one system (a religious system which is based upon certain tenets) departs from a legal system which would not require a trier of fact and of law to possess such a religious belief, or uphold a prior set of assumptions, in order to be able to try facts and law. One system, apparently, is assumed to be value-free. The common law requires only that a man know the nature and quality of his acts, and be able to perform his duties in a reasonable manner. But what man is, is not defined. One would not be met with a theological definition that in order to be a man under this legal system, one must be a man who had a fallen nature, and only that class of individuals are included in the legal system. The common law would not accept as an excuse *qua* excuse that the reason *A* killed *B* was the fact that *A* was a fallen son of Adam who could do no better. The law would, through its official machinery, inquire if *A* were sane, it would inquire if he understood the nature and quality of his act (which was the killing of *B*), but it would not inquire into his theological beliefs in which it was stated that man, because possessed of a fallen nature, could naught but sin, unless aided by supernatural grace.*

Such would be a difference between the two systems. What is central to both systems is man. A question central to each system may be: can a man be responsible for his actions, whether at civil law, or religious law?

If each system embodies common questions about kinds of human behavior and action then it stands to reason that we will find borrowings from one system to the other. Medieval canon law developed out of refinements from Roman law, but Roman law had little connection with English common law. While the canonists moved to codification, the common lawyers stressed the piece-by-piece nature of litigation. The aims of the canon lawyer will be to make clear how, within a theological system

---

* We do not doubt that a civil law system could incorporate religious beliefs, and then embody those excusing conditions which are prevalent in the religious law the civil law incorporated. But common law, as it has refined itself of its religious presuppositions and inheritances, tends towards religious neutrality. We wish only to maintain here that the common law advances one standard of excusability, whilst religious law of the Judeo-Christian tradition might advance a different standard of excusability.

which holds a man responsible for his religious acts, a man can be said to be responsible or how a man can be excused. For the legal philosopher the elements which constitute the concept of responsibility under *both* systems may be of interest, since the common element to both systems is man.[2]

What would an adherent do to fulfill the requirements of each system? System One may specify a set of simple rules, which, when known, an adherent is expected to follow (as one might follow the rules of a private club). System Two may have a set of rules the contrary of System One (one might imagine an Anarchists' Club in which the sole rule was not to be bound by any rule which any other private club might embody). Or System Two, in a less radical form, may be a set of rules which are somewhat different from System One, but which obligate one to follow rules, much as System One obligates one to follow its rules. If one viewed believers in this way—as if each were a member of a private club in which each club had its own set of rules—one might argue that the common ground between different believers would lie not in what set of rules each followed or believed, but in how each member assigned responsibility for human acts. If responsibility were no more than what a rule dictated, then any system devoid of that rule would preclude making comparison between the systems. No rule would entail no responsibility (as when a legislature decriminalizes an act). But if a comparison is between not rules, but in what manner responsibility is to be found and predicated of an actor, then it may be possible to compare System One with System Two, however different in content may be the rules of the two differing systems.

It is at this point that we think it may be worthwhile to see the development of early common law from within the world of medieval moral and religious theory, and to ask how medieval notions of human behavior may have influenced notions of criminal responsibility at common law.

We may, to state the case another way, test any legal system by presenting questions to the fundamental assumptions of the system. If our sense of a defense to a charge is to challenge the workings of the system itself, then, as we stated earlier in this chapter, it may be important to consider if being a fallen man does influence or affect our status as defendants.[3] If a system holds us to be responsible for our actions, but at the same time holds that that responsibility, as the word is normally understood, is a chimera or is a logical impossibility within the axioms of the system, then, plainly, one is not responsible for his actions because the system by its logical stop excludes responsibility as a viable notion. Were one to espouse seriously the doctrine of predestination, and take the doctrine in the strong sense to mean not only that God knew what would be the case, but caused the case to be the case, then it would be odd for a theologian to introduce the notion of human responsibility for human acts. What would a human be, save for an act predicated upon the movement of a creature? The creature would always be described in passive terms, i.e., an act was done of it. Responsibility is an active notion, unless one wants to present an existential metaphor that man, no matter what he does, is damned!

By like reasoning if one advances for serious consideration that no man is responsible for a criminal act because every man is predetermined by prior conditions to his act, and those prior conditions are beyond his self or personal control, then one has attacked a fundamental assumption of the criminal law: namely, one has said that responsibility does not follow upon a voluntary act because a voluntary act is a self-contradiction. If every criminal act is a determined act, then one denies that an act could be an intentional act. The concept of intention embodies in its elements that one could choose, that the exercise of choice was voluntary, and that one was not forced, coerced, or under duress to act, and that one could have refrained from what one did. One may wish to argue that the barest meaning of "to choose" need only mean that a range of possibilities be evident, as the possibilities within a predetermined mathematical series, to an agent. But have we avoided a conceptual snarl by excluding free will in the strong sense? We think not. If we mean by "to choose" that one chooses from amongst a predetermined range, what of the act of choosing itself? That act must be unforced. If it is not, then the act itself of choosing must entail that it is an action brought about by some other power than the actor choosing, and if this is the case then one is not talking about an actor, but one is talking about an agent through whom an action is exercised. We are not trying to locate an empirical finding about human behavior, e.g., does the motor mechanism of choice rest in this or that part of the brain. We are analyzing a concept, that of "to choose," and are inquiring about what logical states are excluded by the concept. We are arguing that "to choose" excludes, in the strongest sense, "it was determined for."

If an actor is one in whom action originates, and the origination of his action is not predicated of some other, then the locus of choice will be the actor. If, on the other hand, the locus of action is in some other than in the actor himself, then the actor is transformed into an agent, and his actions are those, in the strongest sense, of another.

We are not trying to unravel, for instance, what might be contained in the concept, *prohairesis*,[4] as used by Aristotle in his moral theory. Not only may one have much difficulty in attempting to state precisely what Aristotle means by the concept in conjunction with what he means by voluntary and involuntary, but there seems to be no easy mapping from the Greek onto the common law notion of "will." The common law notion of will derives from a Christian context wherein the concept of "will" is foreshadowed by the concept of non-recurrence. For the traditional Christian each and every act of an actor was unique and non-repeatable. Christianity knows nothing of the doctrine of recurring forms, which, in theory at least, would maintain that what distinguishes A from A' would be a point in time. Christian thought would not advance a doctrine of similarity and return because its notion of final judgment precluded that the same agent could be twice held in jeopardy for his actions. It would be theoretically possible that if A failed (let "A" be some person at time "t") and were judged to have been sinful, it could, nevertheless, be argued that his guilt and sinfulness was not the final state of his being. It could be advanced that A at time t_1, could at some future time be A', at time t_n and $A \neq A'$. For the Christian theologian this amounted to a contradiction in terms. The theory of eternal return precluded a final judgment about the status of A. The Christian doctrine of will was linear, and it precluded recurrence (even in theory) of human actions. An individuating feature of an act of will for Christian theology was not only the time at which an act occurred, but that the act occurred in addition to the time of its occurrence. The future was open, non-recurrent, and unique without the possibility of recurrence. Forms did not originate within a cyclic universe, or within cyclic movement; forms originated in the mind of God, were insubstaniated in matter, and, together, were an expression both of God's freedom (to create from nothing) and intelligence (to direct to a final end, which was Himself). Although Christian notions of the voluntary have in their history an Aristolelian notion of an internal human power, Christian thinking provided a different model of the universe in which the volitional occurred, and a different model for volitional action: grace aiding nature to attain a supernatural end.

The common law can accommodate both concepts of will at the practical level. We dwell upon the distinction at length because, from our reading of the sources of the common law, we believe that it is not the Greek model of will which is being advanced when accounting for human responsibility for an action. Each account of will requires that an actor give his reasons for his action, if at all possible; and each account of will does permit extenuating circumstances to be advanced to excuse or exonerate an accused. One theory of will does not stress the notion of "free," while the other theory does stress such a notion.[5]

We would like to turn now to an examination of texts from which the concept of intentional action matures. Most of the texts concern killing of another, in some form or other. The general categories will contrast killing which is permitted and deemed to be licit, and killing which is wrong and is condemned. The dominant notion will be a twinned one: it will combine "to excuse" and "to be responsible for." There will be no single doctrinal constant; in place of a doctrinal constant there will be various notions about the nature of intellect, will, and human nature. There will emerge, also, a pattern about what it means to excuse one so that what one did, even if wrong in itself, would not be held to be a deliberate wrong pursued by an actor. No single or uniform doctrine of excusing existed in these early texts, even though some later writers like Plowden or Covarruvias write as if St. Thomas Aquinas developed a uniform doctrine of excusing. He did not, and we have listed in the appendix a range of citations from his writings to show where he treated the topic of *to excuse*, but did not develop a uniform doctrine of excuses. Little analytic writing about what the concept "to excuse" entailed exists in early common law writing. It is a topic which has become of interest only for later legal writers, and even there little formal writing exists on the subject.[6]

The simple legal case is as follows. There exists a rule, and *D* is alleged to have transgressed that rule. The simple relationship which exists is between a law and the following of it. But the simple statement of the case also embodies philosophical questions one may wish to consider. What are the *bare* conditions for the proper observing of the rule or law? Is that rule obvious in its address, or is the follower of the rule assumed to know more than what the rule itself states? Must *D* also know the habits and customs of the community in which the rule exists, if he is to follow the rule correctly? Does a simple reading of the rule, or hearing of the rule, address itself in such a way that the content of the rule is self-evident so that no possible contingent case may void the rule? Will the ordinary man understand, upon reading or hearing the rule, that it applies to him; and that it applies to him not only in *this* present situation, but that it applies to him in all possible situations? Further, will the rule embody those conditions which serve to excuse under the rule? For instance, although all vehicles are forbidden in the public park after sundown, one doubts if patrolling vehicles are forbidden in the park after sundown. How then is any actor to know, after having been apprised of the law, what conditions may excuse under that law? A law, for instance, may require *D* not only to *know* that 'x' was wrong, but also require that *D* wilfully do 'x.'[7] If the Crown or a prosecutor fails to demonstrate both elements of the offense, then *D* may be acquitted. But how is one to know this?

The historical development of degrees of criminal culpability will show how competing models develop, and how the concept of culpability was both enlarged and made more precise by the advance of those models.[8] We will make only this one observation about our sources. Most of them have not been commented upon, and those few which have (Bracton, Glanvill, Coke and Hale) have received little, if any, analytic dissection. It may be to the tribute of the common law that, after all is said and done, it is a practical discipline not in need of great theoretical dissection. We very much doubt if any legal or moral philosopher would be persuaded by the latent wisdom of such an assertion.

The earlier theological decrees regarding homicide served to complete a double task. Any person who caused a death did so on a double plane. He caused the death of a person in the civil realm; he also removed the deceased from the sphere of religious good works, and this was a serious removal since it presented the deceased to the judgment of God, not something lightly to be brought about. The difficulty which we have removed from our present approach to criminal responsibility is that we do not add to a criminal act that the accused must be religiously forgiven. He must purely and simply be dealt with by means of the criminal process. During a plea in mitigation, if the accused has been found guilty of his crime, it does reward counsel to demonstrate to the court that the accused regretted what he did, and is properly disposed to reform himself; but this is not a necessary ingredient in our criminal process for it to work effectively.* The earlier pronouncements of the Councils had to meet the double task, both of condemning wrongful temporal actions, and, at the same time, extending conditions whereby the criminal, who was also a sinner by the force of his serious crime, might be shrived. Conditions for mitigating the guilt of the penitent were more severe, and the penitent, as well as his confessor (or bishop, if the crime were so theologically serious for his sole consideration to dispense a penance or not), had to meet bilateral conditions. The confessor had to assure himself that the penitent demonstrated a sorrow for his sin, and the penitent had to know for himself that he had, in fact, transgressed religious law. It had to be determined that he had, as a penitent, serious matter to confess; that he knew that the matter was serious and grave; and that he accused himself of having freely sinned and violated religious law. The relationship between the penitent and his confessor (in the best sense of the word) was that of an accused who, voluntarily moved himself to confess,

---

* Jurisdictions which have adopted determinate sentencing practices view punishment as a fixed tariff which the accused pays by serving a fixed sentence for a crime. Very little is left to judicial discretion or favor. The court may step outside of the standard sentence, and award a longer sentence, but this is meant to be the exception and not the rule. The expression of contriteness will not reduce a fixed sentence. At best, contriteness may persuade a court not to exceed the standard punishment for the offense. [*Cf. State v. Oxborrow*, 106 Wn. 2d. 525, 723 P. 2d 1123 (1986) securities scheme given 10-and 5-year concurrent sentences, not 0-90 days or 0-12 months. Oxborrow had defrauded investors of $58 million.]

and the confessor, as a judge, voluntarily granted or withheld absolution. Both the confessor and penitent pledged themselves to act honestly, God being their witness.[9]

The early models for homicide[10] come to us through the Councils of the Church, and appear as Council pronouncements. The form of these pronouncements is not one of extended, analytical argument; to the contrary, the form is that of a rule, or a directive, announced. We are not concerned with their historical force, and we draw upon these early models mainly to show how from the simple statements about homicide there developed a complicated and refined concept which the courts used to assign guilt to an accused, and which the accused used to defend himself against criminal guilt.[11] For the believing Christian the center to his doctrine was to locate responsibility for sin and for faults. Attempting this location was to attempt a delicate balance. If one totally condemned the world and the flesh, then one fell into heresy, for it had to be maintained that God created a good, although fallen, world. If one claimed that the intellect of man was totally corrupted, one fell into heresy again because Christian doctrine claimed to illumine the intellect against all falsehood. If the intellect were fully corrupted, how then could it be expected to distinguish truth from falsehood? If one located the cause of sin and fault totally in man's corrupted will, then one faced a heresy again: how could a good act, which the will impelled a man to accomplish, issue forth from a totally corrupted will?[12] Within the limits of a belief proposition, the heresies can be seen as excesses, or paradoxes, within fideism. The common law would deal with puzzles of this sort, but in secular form.[13] What may have been stopped by an appeal that such a holding (in a theological debate) might be heretical could, in the common law, become a fashion which the courts adopted as part of the conventional wisdom. The reasonable man would become the ordinary man who rode the Clapham omnibus. Common law would assume that a man has both volitional and intellectual faculties. The oft-quoted example is of a will: one need not make one, but if one does, one must prove that the will was made of one's own volition without any coercion; one also must observe the rules for the making of a will, for instance, if one makes a bequest to *A*, one must be sure that *A* has not signed as a witness to the will. If he has, the bequest is void at law.

Theological models of early Council pronouncements may serve as examples of argument forms for later common law developments. Both were illustrative within a legal framework of acceptable and non-acceptable cases. In the common law one turned to past decisions to find guidance for present decisions, the theory there being that legal judgments must be universalizable in theory if such judgments are to be guides for legal behavior.[14] That a judgment might be universalizable stemmed from the assumption that "all men" were thought to be equal under the law, and that what might be derived from particular cases concerning this or that man would affect the class of "all men." Embodied in common law reasoning was a belief that the universal was virtually contained in the particular. This man, Jones, was bound by the force of this law or statute or custom which was a general expression of what should or should not be observed. The restriction put upon a plaintiff in an action might arise from the form of the action itself. If the plaintiff in a civil action did not issue the correct writ with its correct language, he might therefore lose his power of legal redress;[15] but all this serves to show is that a universal right of redress had to be circumscribed by a general manner or form of action so that a universal notion – an injury or claim – might be channelled into some general form, and thence expressed to the court as a certain wrong or harm which, because it was now possessed of a correct legal form, could be adjudicated. We doubt if the courts entertained this procedure in order to resolve any conflict between the linguistic triad of what relation obtained in a universal-general-particular classification. The general form of a complaint or plea or writ served to give flesh and bones to a universal right of redress in whatever was the present problem for judgment before the court. It was not an exercise in logical analysis, whatever logical assumptions were assumed.

From the assumption that "all men" was a class to which the law applied, the model for the early lawyers was the common case. The concept of the *common case* is not without its logical flaws. Be it remembered that any common case at law is a case which has been constructed out of language. It is a little linguistic engine or device, and not an object like a stone or the sea. The common case is a constructed case, not a given case. Any who try to marshall cases for persuasive purposes in a legal brief find that *the* difficulty is to show how case One bears an example to case Two, when the facts of One are dissimilar to the facts of Two.[16] What must be jettisoned from one case to make it comparable to another case for legal force? How broad may the resemblances be which nevertheless will permit one to claim a family resemblance exists or obtains between this case and that case?[17]

Any person may come into a court of law and plead for his defense his own individuality and the individuality of the case itself, concluding that only he himself has the right to judge himself.[18] If law were a comparison of particulars *qua* particulars, such a defense would be a sound defense by the very notion of what it is to be a particular, which is, by definition, unique. Such a defense rejects the concept of a common case. The rejoinder which the common law has given to this defense is that an offence under the law may arise precisely because human action (omission or commission) may be viewed as a series of moves under a legal network, and the reasons one offers when in a court of law for his move, or lack of move, will serve to fit one into the legal network, as guilty, or exclude one from the legal network, as innocent.

The ground for comparisons in a *common case* concept rests in this double way. Common law accepted the force of genus-species reasoning. It also accepted that reasons could be given for action or omission, and that from an evaluation of those reasons offered by a defendant in a criminal action, the judge and jury would make an assignment of guilt or innocence. In the main, the juries were triers of fact and the judges determiners as to what the law was which would apply to those jural facts determined by the jury. If a reason cannot be offered for an action, then a paradox is created: namely, an agent does an act, or refrains from doing an act, but at the same time cannot explain to himself why he acted or failed to act. This, for the common law, was another way to describe a man as mad, or to say that he was an idiot, or closer to our times, that a man was functioning as an automaton, or was frenzied, or, simply put, was not fully in control of his actions. Ought one then to say that human actions as such are ultimately so solitary and unique in quality that no legal system can arise to embrace those actions under canons of prescribed control?[19] The epistemological assumptions of "common case" reasoning at law are that no action is so hidden or unique that it cannot be viewed by the law. The underlying assumption to this belief may be that if an action can be known to its agent, then the agent can describe aspects of his actions by stating his reason for his actions.

In no way do we think that a legal monist, or anarchist, has been easily routed. He makes a strong objection against the unanalyzed legal assumption that solitary events may be compared. To know, in an ultimate sense, why this man killed his wife may require that one be this man who killed his wife. But the law has never admitted to being that precise, and it has admitted that common moral qualities can be discussed. The giving of reasons constitutes the art of legal argument out of which legal guilt or innocence ensues.

The logic of the common case embodies an assumption that particulars can be talked about; they can be freed from their very particularity by reason and speech. For instance, one can talk about "this chair" and the force of one's locution can be understood, and acted upon, as in, "Will you sit in this chair?" Even if we were to admit that the force of language is not related to objects, the common law would not be troubled. One may perceive, and one may speak about what one perceives, necessitating no conjunction of speech to perception. Yet if one did understand the sentence, "Will you sit in this chair?" and did in fact sit upon this chair, the mysterious world of the legal monist would dissolve by the simple fact that an instruction had been brought about in a([n] assumed) world of solitary and mysterious particulars. This particular chair becomes, by force of the question, this-particular-chair-to-be-sat-upon, or this-particular-chair-not-to-be-sat-upon. Were it a solitary and mysterious particular no person could direct our, or his own, or any other's attention to it by use of an illocutionary proposal, such as, "Will you sit in this chair?"

If simple directions can be expressed by the use of such simple locutions, then it is argued that reasons can be given for actions. The common case is no more a mysterious concept than that of a chair. This object can have attention directed to it by means of an unlimited number of sentential modes; likewise, out of the singularity and particularity and uniqueness of human actions one can, for legal purposes, devise common classes of actions and cases which may be looked upon and understood. As we might qualify our question, "Do you wish to sit on the blue chair to your right, or the red chair to the left?" so one might talk about the death of a person as accidental, or by design, or by natural causes; all of these in turn are subject to further possible refinement, as our question about which chair to sit upon may be refined and made more precise. By what physical or mental process one's sentence arises, or by what physical or mental process *and* what scientific conditions must obtain in order for there to be a world in which chairs can be talked about, may present endless perplexities for a thinker; but the law was not concerned about metaphysics. Why this world? For the common law it would have been: That there is a world.

The Council of Ancyrani, 314 A.D., under Pope Silvester I, concerned itself with homicide in the following way. Question twenty-two of the Council, "*ex interpretatione Isidori Mercatoris,*" was *De his qui volentes homicidium fecerunt*?[20] The reply given at the Council was to the effect that if the killing were a voluntary killing then it was absolutely the case that a penalty should be assigned against the act; but if the killing were an involuntary killing, then one should be deemed to be not guilty of culpable homicide, but should, nevertheless, perform some kind of penance because a human life had perished.[21] If a penitent in the course of his confession admitted to causing the death of a person, but claimed, in good conscience, that the death resulted involuntarily on his part, then his confessor could absolve the penitent; the action confessed would not have been matter which was considered to be grievous or mortally sinful. If, on the contrary, the penitent had admitted to killing another, and admitted that his own act was a voluntary act, a requirement in the chain of seriousness for the elements of a sin, then one had a different matter. In both cases the same result was evident: some other had been killed. The distinction rested not upon the "matter" of the act, as, for instance, Lady Wootton[22] has suggested should be the sole concern of the court (thus ridding the court of the problem of determining if an accused had formed a criminal intention), but upon the "form" of the act: did the penitent freely elect to sin? The model is not, necessarily, of a penitent coolly sitting down to deliberate whether or not to kill some other; the model is that a penitent, within the framework of a penitential system, could distinguish for himself between what he did, and thus for what he may be held responsible for bringing about, from what happened to him, and for which he may, or may not, be held responsible. Whether an act was voluntary or involuntary served as the test to distinguish between culpable and non-culpable. A penance was recommended by the Council of Ancyrani in the instance of involuntary homicide because a penance might cause the penitent to strive to be more careful; such a penance also might serve to assuage any lingering guilt or remorse a penitent had for having been involved, even though involuntarily so, in the death of another being.

We have introduced the terms "matter" and "form" of an act to help with explication. As explanatory terms they were not employed until later in the development of moral theory by canonists. Leeming suggests[23] that Stephen Langton was the first to have employed the concept in sacramental theology, but mentions that William of Auxerre used the term during the same period, the early thirteenth century. Langton's death is given as 1228 A. D. In language not scholastic, Leeming suggested that the early Church theologians, such as Tertullian, Cyprian, Cyril of Jerusalem, Gregory of Nyssa, and St. Ambrose of Milan, laid the foundation for such a distinction between matter and form, but without developing pre-existing Aristotelian categories. He said, and we quote, "...nevertheless it is clear in their minds that there are in a sacrament the two things, the material element and the verbal."[24] The terms themselves find their way into the common law, its criminal tradition, when the law employs the distinction between the objective matter of a crime, its *reus*, from its subjective element, the *mens rea* of the crime. One can admit that a general comparison can be made between the "matter" of a sacrament, and the *reus* of a crime, and the "form" of a sacrament, and the intentional element in a crime.[25]

The force of the Council of Ancyrani continues to serve as a criminal model in penitential reasoning when one reads that it was referred to as a guide by Pope Zacharias (741-747 A.D.), in his seventh letter, or Epistola

VII, the title of which was, *"Zachariae papae ad Pippinum maiorem domus regiae, itemque ad episcopos, abbates et proceres Francorum."*[26] Two of the questions set for guidance concerned homicide: XXIII, *"De his qui homicidium sponte perpetrant?"* and XXIV, *"De his qui homicidium non sponte perpetrant?"*[27] The direction of Ancyrani was followed, and no distinctions were introduced in the papal response to either of the questions.[28] In the Carolingian edicts of 789, during the reign of Pope Hadrian the First (787-794 A.D.), we read under the "Capitvlare Aqvisgranese" a general condemnation of homicide in the "Titvli Capitvlorvm" at LXVII, *"De homicidiis."*[29] A man's life may only be taken by command of law, *"...nisi lege iubente."* The distinction between culpable homicide is protected by the force of the law, and it is assumed that the law may command acts and make those acts, even if they are the killing of another, legitimate when done under the cloak of the law. Law confers legitimacy to actions.

The Council of Moguntinum, the first session, held under the papal reign of Leo IV (847-855 A.D.), and itself held in 847 A. D., sets out a more detailed reply to two questions, XXII, *"De homicidiis?"* and XXIII, *"De homicidiis non sponte commissis.?."*[30] The general statement of the Council of Ancyrani was followed, with reference made to guidance from other Councils.[31] Illicit killings were to be punished by excommunication, *"...sine conscientia iudiciis occiderit."* The distinction is maintained between voluntary and involuntary killings. Force is given to the concept of crime and penalty, when the language of the response tells us that one may not return to the civil community until a penance is completed. We are also informed that illicit killing merits an excommunication and a severe penance.

The interesting distinction which obtains at this Council is between what now would be murder and manslaughter, or intentional and unintentional death. It is suggested, as an example, that a master could kill his servant girl by an excess of zeal (*"...de domina quae per zelum ancillam suam occiderit..."*) but that he might not have intended to kill her when he was punishing her so. It would appear from this example that a distinction is being forced, or developed, either between what the agent himself intended, or between what was thought to be done or achieved (as when one says he wishes only to punish a person) and what actually is achieved when it is something other than what was desired (the one punished dies as a result of the punishment).[32] It would be to extend this early distinction too far if one were to attempt to apply it to the complicated situations of fact in modern criminal law.[33] The response of the Council initiates the distinction between an end which an agent may by design achieve, and an event which might come about as an accident. If the latter, then a mild penalty is attached to such a happening, a penalty of 50 days. What was brought about involuntarily would, if one were attached, suffer a mild penalty. We preserve such a distinction to this day. When one causes the death of a driver or pedestrian in an automobile crash it can be argued that one could have foreseen that such might have happened, but the courts generally assess the consequences of the act by means of a fine and do not involve themselves with the question of whether or not the defendant intended to cause a victim's death. The latter finding is open to the court, but it is seldom used.[34]

The general force of the distinction between degrees of seriousness which the Council enunciated serves to impress upon one that a standard of care ought to be evident to a person, and that from such an appreciation one can distinguish between an act which was fully willed producing consequences which a reasonable man would expect, and an act which was brought about involuntarily or by accident, even if harmful consequences flowed from it. In both instances a certain harm ensued, and for each such classification of harms a penalty would attach, stressing that some reasonable standard of behavior ought to be observed in the community, or a reasonable standard of care ought to be attempted in the community. The harms which result are not to be thought of as neutral if the harms concerned the loss of life (or matter equally serious). When one could conjoin a harm, the death of that man, with the voluntary conduct of the defendant which brought about that harm, then a heavy penalty is attached because a defendant had brought about a serious effect which need not have happened. In an accident, which the Council termed an action brought about involuntarily, it can always be questioned whether or not the accident *should* have happened. One is left with two alternatives, the first being that what happened did happen without any design or control on the part of the defendant, and was truly not only an involuntary production on his part, but was a production which in no way could he have avoided. The scholastics of the thirteenth century would analyze such an event as that brought about by ignorance on the part of the defendant, *and* the ignorance was that for which he was in no way culpable; it was not an ignorance brought about deliberately by himself, as one might speak of an act or an attitude springing from bad faith.[35] The other side of the alternative would be that what was caused involuntarily could, in some way, have been avoided if the agent had been cautious, or had taken precautions to prevent it. The type of ignorance which attached to the notion that one could have taken precautions to prevent can be shown by an example from modern tort law. In most medical malpractice suits, unless gross negligence obtains from the onset of the case, it will be an adequate defense for a physician to argue that what he did was within the medical standards of the community. We do not mean to mix the fields of tort law and criminal law. But in this instance it may be easier for one to see how culpable and non-culpable ignorance are viable legal categories for a medical defendant, in much the same way that for the medieval theologian such importance was attached to various kinds of ignorance if such ignorance was to serve as an adequate defense to the charge that one had sinned, and would be held responsible, or not, for his sinning. The modern defendant in a malpractice suit faces terrestrial seriousness, in the form of a massive monetary award against him for damages should he lose.[36]

The twenty-third response of the Council of Moguntinum preserved what the Council of Ancyrani had announced. Voluntary homicide, which is a killing arising from a deliberate or voluntary intention, is condemned. During Tudor times one will see that the common law made a distinction between unintentional killing and killing which one brought about by chance-medley (or chaud-medley). The killing under chance-medley, deriving from *24. Hen. 8.c.5.* (and then repealed by *9 G. 4. c.31*), appears to be intentional, but arising from an affray or sudden act of self-defense negates the intentional aspect of the act. Much like the notion of "double-effect," the intention of the agent is to defend himself, primarily, and that another is killed is secondary. We have cited the Latin text in a footnote at the end of this chapter.[37] It is, also, outside the scope of our aim to discuss how one would have proved, in early canon law, how facts in a killing might lead to the distinguishing of the voluntary from the involuntary. It is enough for our purposes here to note that those conceptual distinctions were a part of the moral literature.

Pope Hadrian II, 867-871 A.D., through the Council of Worms (Wormatiense) in 868 A.D., developed the following distinctions with regard to homicide, as well as preserving earlier pronouncements. The Council set down a serious penalty for any person who kills a priest ("*Qui sacerdotem morti voluntate tradiderit...*").[38] The next rule, XXVII,[39] harkens back to the Old Testament, and recapitulates Deuteronomy 20, to the effect that in a time of war, unless one acts from intentional hatred ("*...odii meditatione...*") or greed ("*...vel propter auartiam paganum occiderit...*), killing does not merit a penance. Both canons, twenty-six and twenty-seven of this Council, stress the notion of the voluntary in a deed. When one encounters a construction such as "*voluntate tradiderit*" and "*odii meditatione*" the force of them is to italicize the agent in the act, and to remind one that what flowed is a consequence freely originated from the agent. The use of "*meditatione*" carries with it a cognitive geography: that what was entertained or known or exercised was done so with thought, or by design, or because of an intention.

Canon XXVIII introduces[40] insanity and unsoundness of mind as a condition which ought to mitigate the imposing of a penance. The condition is interesting because it calls attention to the state of the agent as one who may do a harmful act, and, to all appearances seem to be voluntary, but the voluntariness is prohibited by his being "*insaniens*" or "*irrationabile*." Such reasoning will find its way into the common law in Bracton.[41]

Canon XXIX attempts to develop the category of an event.[42] The stress of the canon is upon the order of necessary happenings over which one might have had no control ("*...dum ille operi necessario fortassis incumberet...*") and which does not arise from any intention, or from negligence, on the part of the agent (as when one fells a tree, and some other is killed by the falling tree). In modern law, such a death would be a death by misadventure; or it may be viewed as a non-culpable homicide (as in a motorway accident). What the canon attempts to relieve of an agent are the following predications. The death of a third party was not related to the state of the will of the actor, thus there is no agency because of will. The causal conditions which brought about the death of the third party were not intended by the actor, thus there is no intentional agency. In general language one would say that the defendant did not prepare a trap into which the unwary human victim had entered.

The illustration of a man killed by a falling tree abounded in medieval philosophy and moral theory. It seemed to have been that kind of example which was thought to present clearly the notion of a non-negligent act. An agent did not cause the event; to the contrary, the event happened. If an agent had caused the event, (in the strong sense of "cause"), it would had to have been the case that the agent willed what he did–as with an intentional murder–or, barring that it was an intentional act, the agent would have had to have been reckless or negligent in some fashion–preventing what might have happened by having had some notion or expectancy that what actually did happen would have been likely to have happened.

The Council of Triburiense, 895 A.D., is concerned with a number of criminal matters, and we shall have to refer to them in passing rather than to treat of the Council in detail. We reduce a great part of the text to footnotes in Latin quotation only to show that there is a continuity of thought without the addition of much new matter or criminal distinctions.

The thirty-sixth canon[43] of the Council preserves the tree example, but elaborates a bit more on distinctions (and the case now concerns two brothers). The qualifying clause attempts to spell out that one did not want in any way or manner the death of the other: "*Quia non voluntate, non incuria illius, non denique consensu, nec ullo suo mortem incurrit reatu....*" The tree simply falls and the other is killed.

The canon closes with a sensible observation or exhortation, that little of joy comes from crime either for the just man or for the evil man, "*Quidam de sapientibus ait: Premit insontes debita sceleri noxia poena iustusque tulit crimen iniqui*," and then proceeds, in the thirty-seventh canon, to discuss accidental death of an infant, which can happen often ("...*ut saepe contingit...*"). The example shows one that infanticide is not being talked about; what is being described is another event which happened, although some negligence might have arisen on the part of the mother. A mild penance can be given to the mother, but the father ("...*homo qui caldarium pependit...*") is not involved in the act, as such, and may rest with a peaceful mind.[44]

The force of the example is that we are given a distinction between death which may be caused deliberately and a death which may result from some event, and the reason for the event being a possible case owed to one's negligence and lack of care. An appreciation for the force of events is shown, but a distinction is made between events which purely happen, as the tree falling, and a child dying. We have seen that homicide can result from one willing to kill another; we have seen that homicide can come about because one has expressed an excess of "zeal" in the disciplining of a slave or servant; we have seen that death can come about because of an event in nature; now we see that death can come about, and, for the most part, it appears to be an event within the course of nature, but the "nature" here has been a set of conditions set up in a household, and that set of conditions may have been other than they were. That they could have been other than they were permits the canon to ascribe negligence to the mother. In medieval moral theory this category will be transformed into "ignorance which is concomitant with an act," and it will be assumed by care and diligence one could obviate this category in one's behavior, and therefore obviate the harms which would ensue from such behavior.

It is a trying category because it appears to predicate responsibility on what one, at the moment, did not know or cause, but upon a failure for not acting properly. A risk must be "reasonable," and it is assumed that reasonable risks are within the capacity of agents to bring about. It is not that one permitted *phi* to happen; it is not that one willed *phi* to happen; it is not that one intended a counter-condition to be the case. The force of the objection is that one should not have let such a condition happen because, from the enlightenment of practical and human experience, one should have been aware that such might happen, whether in fact it would or not. The closest analogy one has is to insurance underwriting, when an underwriter anticipates in the preparation of an assured's policy what may be the scope of the foreseeable risks the company should underwrite and which the assured should reasonably expect to be insured against. One cannot insure against every risk; but one must not underinsure.[45]

Had the example been altered slightly to a mother allowing her child to be tended by an inexperienced baby sitter, all other parts of the example holding, one might have a mother faced with criminal negligence. One may not employ as a defense that one assigned away one's natural rights and obligations. A defense through agency, i.e., that the servant was at fault and not the master, must be a reasonable defense.[46] Although a baby sitter might be absolved of her negligence (or even found to be negligent), the parent(s) could be found guilty of having taken a reckless disregard for life, and what might have been simple negligence for them would be transformed into criminal negligence.[47]

By its fifty-second canon the pronouncement of Ancyrani was followed, and we have cited the Latin of this canon in a footnote to show the similarity of expression and feeling to the earlier pronouncement. No models of important novelty are added in the present expression.[48] Stress is put upon voluntariness throughout the pronouncements of this Council, from the fifty-second through to the fifty-fifth pronouncement. What penance is given depends upon the presence or absence of voluntariness, given expression to in the fifty-second canon. It is left to practical religious wisdom to determine the volitional state of a penitent at the time of the commission of his sin. Such a determination does not necessarily reveal a lack of preciseness on the part of the Council. The question often is how to provide a scale of practical wisdom and it is a practice in modern criminal law[49] to leave the practical nature of a finding open to a jury and not to a rule or scale, i.e., was one two-tenths voluntary and eight-tenths involuntary? is a formulation it would be hard to follow. We do not possess a mathematical scale for human actions. We may be able to measure speed or distance or mass, but we are not able to measure voluntariness and involuntariness.

In passing, we wish to say that the fact that we do not possess a mathematical scale by and with which to measure accurately the voluntary or the involuntary (as one might measure blood pressure), does not mean that we are plunged into an abyss of imprecision or of darkness. It may be that there must be a distance between what we describe and the vehicle by and through which it is described, as if to say that language itself is a limit upon the act of knowing.

We must remember, also, that we do live in a culture which has embraced technology. We believe that language is precise and can be made more precise, as measured by our advances in science. We believe that we not only can make exact locations in the world, but also that we can exactly create worlds as a result of the clarity of scientific language. Language is both power and exactness for us. What then of human actions? Why can we not make these exact kinds of locations there?

Human actions seem to fall outside of a technological network. To some, like the reductionist, this is not so. A human being is just a more complete robot, and time will reveal how the complete robot ultimately operates. "Why is this so?" is reduced to, "How is this so?" But intentional explanations of human actions, with their awareness of human character and its past, do not lean to the reductionist's camp. Like all essentialism, a single flaw is perceived in its formulation. The essentialist states that any formula about the real world is as real as the real world. But if wishes be as horses, then all beggars would ride like kings. That an object may exist, and that an object does actually exist, are convertible metaphysical notions one makes at his peril.

Essentialism and reductionism look to formulas to displace the real. Carried to a logical extreme, both seem to believe that there can be presented some formula which will displace the real. When that habit of mind comes into the law, it turns to codes to understand human conduct and not to human conduct to understand human conduct. A good law, or a sound law, becomes a law which the law-making powers have artfully constructed, and into those legal categories human actions somehow fit. One will often observe (and we do not say this necessarily that it must be a feature of criminal codes) that the intentional elements of the criminal act are either over-broad, or they are diminished excessively. A crime is defined in very general fashion.[50] An underlying criticism of such statutory constructions is that they do not reflect human nature or public expectations, but rather are harsh crimes and may even be petty in their scope and effectiveness. *Mens rea* is extraordinarily diminished, or may take on the meaning of "know" in a tort sense, and *actus reus* will be accentuated so that a mere doing becomes the essence of a crime.

In the course of legal experience, however, we find that one proposes reasons for his actions. A simple causal explanation will not account for a motive, for a goal, for an intention, for a hope, for a desire, or for a change (as in, "I decided to wear brown this season and not pinstripes"). If we wish to utter a trivial metaphysical statement of the form that change (of whatever kind) involves a transition from what may be the case to what is the case, we have done so by excluding that "what may be the case" can only be a case at all because one designs that it be the case rather than some other end be a possible case for consideration. To exclude that one considers, is to exclude a world of locutions which are part of our common language. If we hold that such a host of locutions are accidental and are nominative only (they are only names which we use in discourse but the names relate to no internal condition or situation), then how odd it is to explain any state of affairs. One's explanation of some state of affairs could always be rejected by an appeal to the theory that language is only used and does not convey what is the case outside of itself. One uses a sentence, and the world does what it does. Any explanation (even of itself) would be little more than an accidental conjunction of a sound or sign with an event. Even when one believed that he might have explained, one would be haunted, at least in theory, by the persistent doubt if he could *know* that he had explained some event or other, even if the event were so simple an event as knowing whether or not one had used a sentence correctly.

If we admit that some aim or other can be a possible case then we are assuming that action for which a human being is to be held responsible is an act for which a reason can be given by him for its doing or production. A theory of "potency" and "act" at the level of human discourse is a theory which suggests that what now is the case – for example, some dispute in court – is a production which need not have been the case. If one were forced to do this, and only this, then the defense of necessity or duress might obtain, and, by the force of such a defense, it might be argued that because an agent was only a causal feature in a set of features (Bloggs was just a cog in the wheel of events) he was absolved of human responsibility.

The first aspect of an intentional description is that one can offer a reason for what action he proposed to himself.* How one causes himself to act may not admit of a simple description. One may appeal to simple human experiences to show this condition. When one writes a letter he may have intended to say one thing, but, when finished, notices that he omitted to say what he had intended to say, or said it poorly and unclearly, or said it clearly. How one physically directs himself, or how one sententially produces sentences upon the page in the form in which they appear, may admit of no final and exhaustive situation (i.e., moving from some general explanation of the form, "all 'x's do such and such, and this 'x' did such and such in this instance"). If what one did at this moment did follow from some general explanation, then one's human actions would be a function of that general explanation. One could argue that responsibility then would not be a feature of what some "x" did; rather, it would be a feature of the general explanation (as with the example of the defective medicine). The failure of the prescribed tablet resulted from a failure to follow the formula correctly when preparing the tablet. Liability would be attributed to the wrong formula having been followed.

A second aspect of an intentional description is that one may be able to account for his actions by means other than an appeal to causal presentations. If an appeal is made totally to a causal explanation of what one did, it is arguable if any reason at all has been provided for what one did.[51] It is a variant of the defective tablet case. One did this (whatever it may be) because one is so constructed, and things so constructed act in this way and not in that way.

The twofold approach of an intentional explanation suggests that one may propose an end, and then one may accomplish that end (if there are no internal contradictions to prevent an accomplishment). Crimes of aiding and

* We do not want to suggest that a little man inside of a person "proposes" projects to be done or aims to be reached. What we do with the language of intention is to understand why an agent acted, and our assumption is that one can, if only to himself, ascertain why he did this rather than that. The standard way we propose a consideration to ourselves is in question and answer form. But the question and answer form (an arbitrary feature of a non-necessary language form) is not the action itself. It mirrors our understanding of an action.

abetting preserve this distinction.[52] One aspect of the crime is to aid, while a further aspect is to take steps to abet – what had *D* in mind, and what steps took he in execution?* This locution is somewhat awkward. What the court inquires after is what the accused had in mind, and then what overt acts the accused did to bring about effecting the plan or design. Unless the Crown clearly shows that the accused had in mind *and* in fact did bring himself to perform elements of the forbidden act, then there is not a case for the accused to answer, and the defense may move for a dismissal of the charges.

A recent example may serve to illustrate the two-tiered nature of criminal intention. Although this case which we cite was to be controlled by *Smith* [1961] A. C. 290, but now would be controlled by Section 8 of the *Criminal Justice Act* 1967, the example is appropriate here:

> The law of murder and manslaughter is set out in sections 198, 199 and 202 of the Penal Code of Kenya. A person who by an unlawful act or omission causes death is guilty at least of manslaughter; and if the act is done with malice aforethought, he is guilty of murder. Malice aforethought is established where, *inter alia*, there is 'knowledge that the act or omission causing death will probably cause the death of/or grievous harm to' another person; and in section 5 of the Code 'grievous harm' is defined as including anything likely seriously or permanently to injure health or any organ. The Crown...submits...that 'knowledge'...does not mean actual knowledge, but means...the knowledge that a reasonable man would have of the probable consequences of his acts and omissions.[53]

Returning now to matter from the Council of Triburiense, one will note how the fifty-third canon appears to leave room for the category of accidental death; but it also adds, by way of a cautionary gloss on the text (which appears as a note in the text), that if the death is other than accidental ("...*sed casu contingente occiderit*...") a legal penalty would then fit ("...*ut sequenti subinfertur capitulo*...").[54] Of interest for the common law is *that* such

---

* In no way do we mean to suggest that an accused is required to give evidence and thus prove his innocence. It is for the Crown or the prosecution to prove the elements of a criminal charge, and, if those elements are not proven, the charge fails. If, however, the accused does take the stand in his own defense, then his testimony serves to rebut the charges of the Crown or prosecution through suggesting that some other reasonable explanation can be given of the acts of the accused, according to the evidential canons in criminal law that one need succeed in his case by meeting the burden of reasonable doubt.

a distinction does appear, and is submitted for penitential consideration. We have reproduced the text in a footnote, but shall comment no further on it. The fifty-fourth canon of the Council follows Ancyrani, and we have reduced it to a footnote only for the sake of consistency in this text.[55] Its matter was stated in that portion of our text on the Council of Ancyrani.

When we come to view the Council of Namnetense, A.D. 895, following upon the Council of Triburiense, we find little legal theory, but we do find what may be called a judicial statement about punishment for crimes. The seventeenth and eighteenth canons state respectively, *"De poenitentia homicidii voluntario" and "De poenitentia eius quo non volens fecerit homicidium."* It is not within the scope of this study to relate crimes to punishments. Such has little formally to do with the concept of intention. The bearing upon the common law is that both canons reveal an attitude of mind which assumes that to have a law one must, of necessity, have a concomitant punishment. It is an attitude which follows us to recent times.[56] In the practical order of the governmental life of a commonwealth it may be the case that crimes must have assigned to them subsequent punishments or fines; but in the logical order, considering law *qua* law, there may be no need to make this conjunction. One may have a law of conscience, the punishment for having broken or transgressed a law a simple knowledge that one had done so, and a related consequence that one was displeased by one's own sense of failure. The "punishment" would simply be that one knew that one had violated the law; there would be no need to add a punishment on to the fact of the transgression. We cite this as an instance only to dispute the claim that a law necessarily entails a subsequent punishment. It does not, but it may.

One has to search behind the pronouncements of the canons to discover if any legal theory be present in their expressions. One is not presented with reasons why a certain act is forbidden,[57] and one may observe that if an authority deems itself above question or examination, it may then issue pronouncements which offer few reasons for its proposals.

The Council of Trosleianum, A.D. 909, need not concern us greatly. Its statements concerning both lying and homicide, and its extended metaphor that lying kills the spirit, ("...*Os quod mentitur, occidat animan...*"),* are obvious in their force. One may see here a model for oaths in a court of law, but we would not suggest that this Council is a common law source for oaths. It is to be remembered that Christians were enjoined against taking oaths. On a theological scale, deliberately to lie, or deliberately to murder, were both morally grievous in the eyes of God, each, as it were, killing one's spirit because each was a mortally sinful act against God's moral law.

The long thirteenth question from this Council (running nine full elephantine pages) illustrates the Pauline model for responsibility. We author our actions (as when we tell the truth), and we can, therefore, be held responsible for what we say, and equally can be condemned for lying. One's mind, just as one's public actions, should be in accord with the law. Neither should one lie nor should one deliberately kill. The underlying thread throughout the Question is that our public actions (I move my hand) are brought about by our private powers (it is the person who moves his own hand). The extended metaphor, then, is that lying (which originates privately in one's mind) is akin to killing (which is a public act), and thus both are grievous acts because both have their source in the person who wishes to transgress the moral law.

In passing, we would observe that what one can extract from the Council of Trosleianum is a strong rationalistic flavor for human actions. If God is the author of man, and God is held to be rational, then man, in his image, must be rational and must be able to control his own actions.[58] The unanalyzed assumption of the common law is that a man is thought first to be held responsible for what he does, and only afterwards thought to be excused from what he did.

There is little need for more citations from the Councils. We have used them here for the purpose of showing how they contained models for legal behavior, even though the legal behavior was within a religious system. We have attempted to argue that it does not matter what system holds models or exemplars of legal behavior; the models themselves are of value for philosophical analysis. We are not examining whether a certain system is

* *Ibid*., p. 774. Question XIII, "*De Homicidis & mendacibus*," extends from pp. 767-775.

true. One may play an absurd game, and at the same time see that the rules of the absurd game are not themselves absurd. The common law, in its earliest formal expression through Bracton, absorbed models for legal behavior from what was then present. The models were, in great part, to be found both in religious writings and in canonical pronouncements.[59] It is for the historian to demonstrate the possibly direct influence of one set of writings from one period upon writers of a later period. We have assumed that there is a philosophical relationship between earlier legal models and later legal models, and we believe that there is enough good case law extant to show that the medievals were accepted as guides, in some aspects of legal theory, in our early decisions.[60]

The early Councils appear to have stressed the term "voluntary" for the test of a responsible act. If we turn to Roman military law one notices there, unless it is a penalty of the strictest liability (wounding whether with intent to wound or not), that the voluntary was the test for a violation. The Councils seemed to have preserved such a legal operator, and it seems possible that one could argue that a linguistic model for voluntary action, within a well-defined legal context, is set forth for us in military law. The comparison is not to be made between the similarities of military to civil or canon law. The similarities rest in the use which a common term took to convey responsibility within a legal framework.[61] The legal framework may act as a guide for a key term, such as was "voluntary," so that one can come to see what such a term ranges over.

We wish to close this excursus into the past without dwelling further upon sources from the various Councils, or discussing citations from Gratian (in the text of Antonio Contii which we have employed). It is enough for us to appreciate that the *Corpus Juris Canonici,** as well as Councils and Synods, and the great body of writings of the medieval canonists and theologians, were models for the growth of early common law. The common law had a ready fund of models from which to develop notions of the voluntary, or to

* Comprised of the *Decretum* of Gratian (1140 A.D.), the *Decretals* of Gregory IX (234 A.D.), and *The Sext* (1298 A. D.). For commentaries on the Canons with regard to intention, one may consult: *Kanonistische Schuldehre von Gratian bis auf die Dekretalen Gregors IX* by St. Kuttner (Città del Vaticano, 1935).

ask what degree of ignorance may serve to excuse, or to determine how responsibility may be assigned for human acts and omissions. Law, however, does not (generally) move rapidly. Most legal development is slow over time.* If one is to control human society, one must realize that it is through time that the wisdom of laws is perceived. Legislative codifiers (who want rapid change) may disagree, but the history of the criminal law is rather much this: laws rapidly made soon die by long disuse. Law is that curious admixture of the theoretical and the practical, which needs time and wisdom to measure its workability.

* Even the modern legislative practice to construct new criminal codes, in order to improve the operation of criminal law, does not overcome the fundamental problem faced by law: namely, how to apply the law precisely? The particulars which surround a case are more complicated than we realize. There is no simple statute to insure that every case will be a simple case.

Endnotes Chapter 1

1. We are against attempting too facile a comparison between the common law and medieval canon law systems, in which a claim is advanced that one system emerged from another, as might a butterfly from a chrysalis. Some who have had great knowledge of and acquaintance with the common law, such as the late Richard O'Sullivan, Q.C., K.S.G., of Middle Temple, have argued that the common law grew out of the rich soil of medieval moral theory, indicating that Thomas Aquinas was of powerful influence upon early common lawyers. *Cf.*, *The Philosophy of the Common Law*, to be found in: *Current Legal Problems* (Stevens & Sons, Ltd., 1949), pp. 116-138; also, *Natural Law and Common Law*, to be found in: *Transactions of the Grotius Society* (vol. 31, 1946), pp. 117-138. However, we wish to stress one other side of the equation: that is, one must also attend to the workings of the common law as they are found, and from their use then determine what they mean and contain.

2. *Roe v. Wade*, (1973) 410 U.S. 113, and *Doe v. Bolton*, (1973) 410 U.S. 113, illustrate how the legal definitions from one legal system do not necessarily fit the legal definitions of another legal system. It was as if a fetus was a "person" under the meaning of the term as embodied in the Fourteenth Amendment of the United States Constitution. The theological definition of a person did not map on to the constitutional definition of the word person, yet the word was used in each legal system; i.e., it is used in canon law, and it is used in constitutional law. *Evans v. Ewels* [1972] 2 All ER 22 shows (in a simpler vein) how the range of the word "person" under section 4-a of the Vagrancy Act 1824 was made more precise by being limited to meaning only a sexual part of one's body, and not the body in general. Each instance shows that a concept is precised.* Of interest to a legal philosopher is how a concept is precised in different legal systems.

* *"precised," v. i., meaning: to make precise or definite.*

3. One may consult *Predestination, Grace and Free Will* by Dom M. John Farrelly, O.S.B. (London: Burns & Oates, 1964) wherein its author attempts to defend the thesis that Divine foreknowledge does not causally predestine. *Cf.* Chapter 5, "Grace and Free Will," pp. 152-216, and Chapter 6, "God's Sovereignty and Man's Freedom," pp. 217-307. One may also read, for instance, how St. Prosper of Aquitaine (*The Call of All Nations* [London: Longmans, Green and Co., 1952]) can puzzle over why some are saved by grace, and others not. This is discussed in Book One, beginning with the nature of and distinction between animal will and human will, progressing to grace as a cause of supernatural actions in man. In the translation of P. De Letter, S.J. Chapters One through Twenty-five, pp. 26-88 cover the material. Final human responsibility for one's acts and actions seems not to be possible unless grace is given freely to all, a paradox which bothers predestination theorists.

4. One may consult W. F. R. Hardie's *Aristotle's Ethical Theory* (Oxford: At The Clarendon Press, 1968), especially chapters viii, "The Distinction between the Voluntary and the Involuntary," pp. 152-159, and ix, "Choice and the Origination of Action," pp. 160-181. One may also consult Sir Alexander Grant's note on the matter of the voluntary and involuntary in his edition of the Ethics, *The Ethics of Aristotle* (London: Longmans, Green, and Co., 1874), vol. 2, p. 25, of E. N., Bk. III, Chaps. lv-v. The concept of "free choice" in the E. N. does not entail that an actor possesses a quality of free will; he may only be free from restraint, and thus may choose. Thomas Marshall's *Aristotle's Theory of Conduct* (London: T. Fisher Unwin, MCMVI) at Chapter III, "The Conditions of Moral Conduct: Freedom, Choice, and Responsibility," pp. 142-183 offers a good analysis of Book III, Chapters 1-5 (1109, b27–1115, a3) of E. N. Marshall suggests that *prohairesis* does not correspond to the English word "Will." "Aristotle has no word to express the state of consciousness of a person acting under such circumstances [a free agent doing something not contemplated by him at the time of action], who would, nevertheless, certainly be said to 'will.'...With the question of the freedom of the will, as a practical question, Aristotle does not concern himself. He assumes (with the rest of the world) man to be the uncontrolled cause of his own actions, bodily and mental" (p. 173). One may also consult *The Ethics of Aristotle* as edited and commented upon by John Burnet (London: Methuen & Co., 1900), Book III, "The Will.–Courage, Temperance," pp. 108-162, his introduction to the Greek text, as well as his footnotes and gloss to the text. L. H. G. Greenwood's *Aristotle: Nicomachean Ethics, Book Six* (New York: Arno Press, 1973, a reprint of 1909 Cambridge U. P. edition) gives a helpful gloss on *prohairesis* at pp. 40, 49, 55, 175 and 178. Ackrill, in his edition, *Aristotle's Ethics* (London: Faber & Faber, 1973), renders "voluntary" in this way: "Since that which is done under compulsion or by reason of ignorance is involuntary, the voluntary would seem to be that of which the moving principle is in the agent himself, he being aware of the particular circumstances of the action" (IIIIa, 21-23, p. 78: *Nicomachean Ethics*, book III.1). J. E. C. Welldon, *The Nicomachean Ethics* (London: Macmillan and Co., 1897) renders the same passage in this way: "When we speak then of an action as voluntary or involuntary, we must have regard to the time at which a person performs it. The person *whose actions we are considering* acts voluntarily; for in actions like his the original power which sets the instrumentality of his limbs in motion lies in himself, and when the origin of a thing lies in a person himself, it is in his power either to do it or not to do it" (p. 59). F. H. Peters, *The Nicomachean Ethics* (London: Kegan, Paul, French & Co., 1886) renders the passage as follows: "In applying the terms voluntary and involuntary, therefore, we must consider the state of the agent's mind at the time. Now, he wills the act at the time; for the cause which sets the limbs going lies in the agent in such cases, and where the cause lies in the agent, it rests with him to do or not to do" (p. 59). Sir David Ross in his *The Nicomachean Ethics* renders the passage in this way: "Both the terms, then, 'voluntary' and 'involuntary,' must be used with reference to the moment of action. Now the man acts voluntarily; for the principle that moves the instrumental parts of the body in such actions is in him, and the things of which the moving principle is in a man himself are in his power to do or not to do" (p. 49) [London: Oxford University Press, 1969]. A more expanded version of the passage is provided in *The*

Nicomachean Ethics, Robert Williams (London: Longmans, Green, and Co., 1869): "And, moreover, the terms voluntary and involuntary are predictable of our acts not in the abstract but only in the moment of action. And in cases such as these a man at the moment of action does act voluntarily; for his limbs are the instruments by which the act is done, and the efficient cause of their motion is his own volition. And, where the efficient cause lies in ourselves, it is in our power to do the act, or not to do it" (p. 60). The translation of St. George Stock, *The Nicomachean Ethics* (Oxford: B. H. Blackwell, 1897: Second edition, revised) follows rather much the rendering given by Williams, and appears on pp. 43 and 44 of Stock's text. His summary of Book III is most helpful, pp. 40-43, especially his diagram illustrating the conditions under which an "act" occurs.

5. W. E. G. Floyd, in his *Clement of Alexandria's treatment of the problem of evil* (Oxford University Press, 1971) makes a helpful statement about *prohairesis* (choice) and *autezhousion* (in one's own power, free) when he says this of Clement:

> Throughout Clement's writings, **προαιρεσις** =*Prohairesis* ("choice") and **το αυτε ξουσιον** = *To Aute Chousion.* ("in one's own power, free") are, for all intents and purposes, synonymous. Yet, to the educated Alexandrian ear, they were loaded terms with very different philosophical overtones. The first was an Aristotelian term which is defined as follows: "Choice may be called either thought related to desire or desire related to thought; and man, as an originator of action, is a union of desire and intellect." [*Eth. Nic.* vi.2, 1139 b5-7] **προαιρεσις** =*Prohaireses* describes moral purpose or will in the fullest sense and involves both an element of desire for an ultimate end and an element of deliberation in a choice of the means – means which lie within our power. The second term (**το αυτε ξουσιον** =*To Aute Chousin*) was *unknown* [italics mine] to Aristotle and emerged into common Greek usage with the Stoics, specifically Chrysippus (c.208-281 B.C.), to suggest a similar moral responsibility. (p. 29)

The difficulties inherent in framing *the* Christian doctrine of Will for Clement of Alexandria are dealt with in Chapter II of Floyd, "The Gnostic Polemic II: Determinism," pp. 24-40.

6. The late J. L. Austin's essay, "A Plea for Excuses," from *Proceedings of the Aristotelian Society, 1956-57*, was a seminal essay, but little has gone on since then in the law. Legal excuses remain, for the most part, uncharted. See also: *The Abuse of Casuistry, A History of Moral Reasoning*, by Albert R. Jonsen and Stephen Toulmin, (University of California, 1988), which gives an excellent account of casuistry as a form of moral reasoning.

7. In *Lim Chin Aik v. R.*, [1963] 1 All ER 223, the conviction of *D* was quashed because, although he had wilfully acted, he did not knowingly violate Singapore law.

8. It is not our intention to repeat the literature on the subject, nor to exhaust adjacent fields on the subject, such as criminal responsibility in canon law. On the latter one may consult *Ignorance In Relation To The Imputability Of Delicts* by Innocent Robert Swoboda, O.F.M., J.C.SL. (Washington, D.C.: The Catholic University of America Press, 1941) for an adequate survey of canonical law. The two-part article by Albert Levitt, "The Origin of the Doctrine of Mens Rea" (17 *Illinois Law Review*, pp. 117-137, and pp. 578-595) is adequate for early Old Testament law on the subject, as well as early Christian notions on the subject, and need not be restated here. It should be read in conjunction with "Phases in the Development of Criminal Mens Rea," a two-part article by H. D. J. Bodenstein (*The South African Law Journal*, Pt. 1, Vol. 36 [1919], pp. 323-349, Pt. 11, Vol. 37 [1920], pp. 18-34) which presents fuller historical documentation.

9. Although it is a later citation than those with which we are concerned, one may cite this passage from the Council of Trent to show the juridical nature of confession. "If anyone says that the sacramental absolution of the priest is not a judicial act, but is the mere ministry of pronouncing and declaring that the sins of the person confessing are remitted, provided only that he believes himself absolved even if the priest gives absolution in jest and without a serious intention; or if anyone says that the confession of the penitent is not required so that the priest can absolve him, let him be anathema." The citation is from the session of the Council, November 25th, 1551, and is cited in an English translation in *The Church Teaches* (St. Louis, Missouri and London: B. Herder Book Co., 1955), which was a translation of various Council pronouncements as prepared by the Jesuit Fathers of St. Mary's College, St. Mary's, Kansas. The Latin references in the work are to Denzinger: *Enchiridion Symbolorum*, page 307 of the translation, paragraph 808 of the Council, and page 919 of Denzinger.

10. We have used the following edition to cite Council and Papal texts: *Conciliorvm Omnivm, Generalivm et Provincialivm, Collectio Regia* (Parisiis, MDCXLIIII) in 37 volumes. We shall cite the volume, page, and Council of this edition throughout. We have also consulted *Decretorvm Canonicorvm Collectanea* (Parisiis, Apud Iacobum Puteanum sub insigni Samaritanae, M. D. LXX.), and shall cite this text by page, listing it as: *Decretorvm*, page ___. We mention this to our readers because each edition of these early documents is, generally, a unique edition, and the making of locations of the citations is often difficult when ones tries to match one edition to another. (The same is true of law reports in different editions, as *Law, Lawyers and Legal Citations*, by C. J. Rees, Esq., Librarian, Supreme Court Library, Royal Courts of Justice, in the *New Law Journal*, August 5, 1976, at page 799, aptly demonstrates.)

11. Swoboda observed (*op. cit*) that the "...Church...always taught that knowledge and the will to transgress the law form the necessary internal or moral elements of all sin. Against the legalistic views of the Jews and Gnostics the early Fathers and ecclesiastical writers expressly taught that the mere objective violation of law did not constitute moral guilt without the deliberate consent of free will" (p. 14). He cited Matt. XV, 19; Matt. XXIII, 27; Matt. V, 28; Matt. XII, 34: also, St. Augustine, *De Vera Religione* (Migne,

vol. 34, p. 133) "*Usque adeo peccatum voluntarium est malum, ut nullo modo sit peccatum, si non sit voluntarium,*" and Tertullian, *De Poenitentia* (Migne, vol. 1, page 1232), cap. 111. We cite this to suggest that there was a developed notion about intellect and will which could be taken over by the common lawyers, and shall cite evidence in support of our assumption when we have reason to quote from Plowden in *Reniger v. Fogossa* (4 Edw. 6, Easter Term).

12. Richard Hooker, in his *Of The Lawes of Ecclesiastical Politie* (London: The Works, 1676), saw the dilemma which the denial of reason presented at the cost of the elevation of will. Truth both had to be known *and* good works to be done. If truth could not be known, how then would one judge that what he did was, in truth, *the* truth? *Cf.* The Third Book of Ecclesiastical Polity, pp. 138-139, *op. cit.*

13. Each legal situation involves one in taking some view of the facts of the case. The "facts" are not neutral datum, however much the term suggests. The courts then take a position that once the facts of a case have been established it follows that the duty of the court is to enunciate the law which applies to those facts (or apply such law as those facts permit). But "intellect" and "will" are not "facts". They are sophisticated concepts, historically inherited, and used in a court. How one views those concepts will determine how one sees "facts" in a case dictated by one's precedent view. One such case, important even though a State Supreme Court case from the United States, is *State v. White* [60 Wn.(2d) 551, September 1962]. The defendant appealed his conviction for murder. Part of the assignment of error which he alleged in his brief for the appeal was that the court, in first instance, had not understood the force of his defense of irresistible impulse, and that it had constrained his defense by a rigid use of the M'Naghton rule on insanity, a defense permitted in the State of Washington. The Supreme Court of the State saw what the defendant had advanced, and stated the issue in these terms, "It is contended that if a man does not have control over his own behavior, he has no free will and cannot be blamed for his misbehavior" (p. 589). St. Augustine could have phrased the question! But the court would not accept irresistible impulse as a defense. It claimed the defense was unclear as a viable legal concept; and that if it admitted the defense crime might not deterred. It found that M'Naghton as a rule "...better serves the basic purpose of the criminal law—to minimize crime in society" (p. 592). That White could not control himself, which later evidence and a retrial showed, was of no concern to the court. Its statement of the problem, however, could have been taken from an early Church Council. At law, without fear of theological heresy, it might well have been an admissible finding of fact that *D* could not control himself and did act out of impulse. But the law would not permit such a finding (p. 593). It could not see such "facts."

14. We do not intend to convey the impression that early common law decisions were guided in great part by turning to reported cases. Reported cases were in their infancy, as the fine work by L. W. Abbott shows: *Law Reporting In England 1485-1585* (University of London Legal Series: University of London, The Athlone Press, 1973). It is not until one reaches

the late 18th century that law reporting becomes dependable and skilled. Furthermore, the plentitude of texts on the criminal law do not come to us until the beginning of the 19th century with *A Treatise on Crimes and Misdemeanors* by William Oldnall Russell (1819), running into many editions, and then the more detailed and somewhat analytical writing of James Fitzjames Stephen, as in his *General View of the Criminal Law* (London: 1863). A review of the *Bibliotheca Legum Angliae*, compiled by John Worrall (London: 1788), shows less than two pages (84-85) of "Criminal and Crown Law," listing them together, the only text of the period being the somewhat rare three-volume work of Henry Dagge, *Considerations on Criminal Law* (London: 1774). One had Blackstone, Serjeant Stephen's *Commentaries*, and Wooddeson's *Lectures*, as well as Deacon's *Criminal Law*. Some may have attended Sir Robert Chambers' lectures on English law, 1767-1773, at Oxford, who held the Vinerian Chair after Blackstone; however, Chambers' lectures remained in manuscript until published in 1986 by Thomas M. Curley (University of Wisconsin, 2 Volumes).

15. One may consult *Forms of Action at Common Law*, by F. W. Maitland (Cambridge, 1909); or *A History of Legal Institutions*, by A. T. Carter (London: Butterworth & Co., 1902), especially Chapters XXII and XXIII, pp. 199-221, "Criminal Trials and Criminal Jury," and "Civil Process and Civil Jury"; also, *The English Legal Tradition*, by Henri Levy-Ullmann (London: Macmillan & Co., 1935).

16. "Clearly then to argue by example is neither like reasoning from part to whole, nor like reasoning from whole to part, but rather reasoning from part to part, when both particulars are subordinate to the same term and one of them is known. It differs from induction, because induction starting from all the particular cases proves...that the major term belongs to the middle, and does not apply the syllogistic conclusion to the minor term, whereas argument by example does make this application and does not draw its proof from all the particular cases." Analytica Priora 69a (McKeon translation), as cited at page 1, *Introduction to Legal Reasoning*, Edward Levi (Chicago).

17. One may recall Judge Simeon Baldwin's early criticism of the case-book method of teaching law, when, in 14 *Harvard Law Review* 258, he said of a case-book: " It is in substance a series of fragmentary discussion of particular topics, interspersed with fragmentary portions of opinions from reported cases....No science can be learned purely from particulars. The universals must be studied to discover what the particulars mean and whence they sprang."

18. "As he stood before Judge Gesell, Ehrlichman continued to proclaim his innocence. He told the court, 'I believe I am the only one who really knows whether I am guilty and, your honor, I am innocent of each and every charge'" (from the report by Robert Siner, *International Herald Tribune* [Paris edition], August 1st, 1974, p. 1). Siner gave an account of the sentencing of Mr. John Ehrlichman, former Chief Domestic Adviser to former United States President, Richard M. Nixon, to a 20-month-to-five-year sentence pronounced by U.S. District Court Judge Gerhard Gesell, of Washington, D.C.

19. We do not wish to moot this. No doubt an imaginary world populated by such creatures of the imagination could, possibly, devise a legal system of strict liability. It would be odd, however–perplexing, even–to claim that one knew that such a legal system did (in theory) exist, but at the same time to maintain that one could not know the reasons for his actions.

20. *Conciliorvm*, Tomus Secundus, M.DC.XLIV, p. 59.

21. *Ibid.*, "XXII: *Qui voluntarie homicidium fecerint, ad poenitentiam quidem iugiter se submittant. Circa exitum autem vitae, communione digni habeantur. Eos vero qui non voluntate, sed casu homicidium fecerint, prior quidem regula post septem annorum poenitentiam communioni sociauit secundum gradus constitutos. Haec vero humanior definitio, quinquenni tempus tribuit*" (p. 66).

22. One may consult her *Crime and the Criminal Law* (London: Stevens & Sons, 1963), the fifteenth Hamlyn Lecture, especially Chapter Two, "The Function of the Courts: Penal or Preventive?" pp. 32-57 which suggests that intention, as a question in a criminal defense, ought to be minimized, if not abandoned in English criminal procedure. One should incline towards the facts, and away from subjective qualities and their ascertainment. Her criticism of diminished responsibility as a viable and logically sound procedure was expressed in "Diminished Responsibility: A Layman's View," *The Law Quarterly Review*, Vol. 76 (April 1969), pp. 224-239.

23. *Cf.*, *Principles of Sacramental Theology* by Bernard Leeming, S.J., (London, New York, Toronto: Longmans, Green and Co., 1955) at pp. 403-407, "The Matter and the Form in the Sacraments." Also, A. Michel, art. "Matiere et Forme," in *Dictionnaire de theologie catholique*, ed. Vacant, Mangenot (Paris: Amann, 1903-52), vol. X, (1928), col. 346-349. Also, Chapter II, "Matter and Form of the Sacraments" in vol. 3 of *Moral and Pastoral Theology* by H. Davis, S.J., (London: Sheed and Ward, 1945), pp. 9-13. Davis cites the decree of Pope Eugenius IV [1431-1447] to the Armenians [given 22 November 1439] which stated that all "Sacraments are constituted of three elements: by things which are the matter, by words which are the form, and by the person of the minister" (p. 9). This would bring the usage of the terms late on into the early renaissance.

24. *Op. cit.*, p. 404.

25. In his discussion of duress in *Lynch v. D. P. P.* [1975] 1 All ER 913, R. A. G. O'Brien in "Compelled to Abet Murder" observes, "The concept of *actus reus* and *mens rea* was developed in our [English] criminal law from the conditions laid down by the moralists for the commission of mortal sin. Grave matter is the *actus reus* and full knowledge and full consent are the elements of *mens rea*....In Canon Law it [duress] will be found under the heading of "metus." In the Code, it is stated that "metus" diminishes the imputability of a delict where the act is intrinsically wrong; in other cases it takes away guilt altogether: Canon 2205 paras. 2 and 3 (*Law & Justice*, No. 48/49, Trinity/Michelmas Terms, 1975, p. 87).

26. *Conciliorvm*, Tomus Decimus septimus, M.DC. XLIV, p. 374.

27. *Ibid.*

28. *Ibid.*, p. 384: "*XXIII: De his qui homicidium sponte perpetrauerunt in XXI[I], capitulo Ancyrani Concilii continetur: Qui voluntarie homicidium fecerunt, poenitentiae iugiter se submittant, perfectionem vero circa vitae exitum consequantur. XXIV: De his qui homicidium non sponte perpetrauerunt, in eodem Canone XXII. capitulo continetur: De homicidiis non sponte commissis, proior quidem definitio post septem annorum poetnitentiam perfectionem consequi praecepit, secunda vero quinquennii tempus explere.*"

29. *Conviliorvm*, Tomas Vigesimus, M.DC. XLIV, p. 4, and the response at p. 34: "*LXVII: Item vt homicidia infra patriam, sicut in lege Domini interdictum est, nec cause vltionis, nec auaritiae, nec latrocinandi, non fiant; & vbicumque inuenta fuerint, a iudicibus bostris secundum legem ex nostro mandato vindicentur; & non occidatur homo, nisi lege iubente.*" One may note that the principle is enunciated here that death brought about by the command of the law and in accord with the law is non-felonious homicide. One may intend to execute a prisoner, but, acting with legal accord, the intention is not a criminal intention.

30. *Conviliorvm*, Tomus Vigesimus Primus (Ab anno DCCCSVII. ad annum DCCCLV), M.DC.XLIV, p. 578, "Tituli Capitulorum."

31. *Ibid.*, pp. 589-560: "*XXII: In Concilio Ancyrano, cap. 21.* [the listing should be cap 22] *de homicidis ita scriptum est: Qui voluntarie homicidium fecerint, poenitenti quidem iugiter se submittant, perfectionem vero circa vit ixitum consequantur. In Concilio vero Agathensi, cap. 37. de homicidis & falsis testibus ita legitur: Itaque censuimus homicidas & falsos testes a communione ecclesiastica submouendos, nisi poenitenti satisfactione crimina admissa diluerint. Item in Concilio Agathensi, cap. 62. scriptum est de his qui feruus extra iudicem necant: Si quis seruum proprium sine conscientia iudicis occiderit, excommunicatione vel poe nitentia biennii reatum sanguinis emundabit. Item in Concilio Eliberitano, cap. 5. scriptum est, de domina quae per zelum ancillam suam occiderit: Si qua femina furore zeli accensa flagellis verberauerit ancillam suam, ita ut intra certium diem animam cum cruciatu effundat, eo auod incertim sit voluntate an casu occiderit: si voluntate, post septimum annum: si casu, per quinquennii tempora acta legitima poenitentia, ad communionem placuit admitti. Quod si vero intra tempora constituta fuerit infirmata, accipiat communionen.*"

32. One finds an interesting and later parallel on this very point when one reads the Act of Assembly as passed in the Colony of Virginia in 1662. "At a Grand Assembly holden at James-City by Prorogation, from the 17th of September, 1668, to the 20th of October, 1669, in the 21st Year of the Reign of our Sovereign Lord King Charles II. No. 1, *An Act about the Casual Killing of Slaves*: Whereas the only Law in Force for Punishment of refractory Servants resisting their Masters, Mistresses, or Overseer, cannot be inflicted on Negroes, nor the Obstinacy of many of them, by other than violent Means suppressed: Be it Enacted and Declared by this Grand Assembly, and the

Authority thereof, That if any Slave resist his Master, or others by his Master's Order, correcting him, and by the Extremity of the Correction should chance to die, such Death shall not be accounted Felony, but the Master, or that other Person by his Master appointed to punish him, be acquit from Molestation, since it cannot be presumed, that prepensed Malice which alone makes Murder Felony, should induce any Man to destroy his own Estate." (Printed at: London, Printed by the Order of the Lords Commissioners of Trade and Plantations, by John Baskett... MDCCXXVIII), p. 91. We have cited the copy which is held by the Library at Lincoln's Inn.

33. One could, however, see its application in modern criminal cases. In *State v. Frazier* 339 Mo. 982, 98 S.W.2d 707 (1936) *D* struck the deceased on the jaw, and did not know that the deceased was a hemophiliac. The charge could be reduced from murder to manslaughter, arguing that the fight arose from an "excess of zeal" and that the defendant had not intended to kill his victim. The assault in this case could be taken as wilful and premeditated and felonious, as it was held by the court; the unintended outcome could be argued in mitigation. The appellant in this appeal case was convicted of manslaughter. "2416. (2239) *Manslaughter.*–351. Whoever unlawfully kills any human being without malice, express or implied, either voluntarily, upon a sudden heat or involuntarily, but in the commission of some unlawful act, is guilty of manslaughter..." (Burns Ann. Indiana Stat. (1926)) may show the force of the mitigation from the side of the agent. *He* did not intend to kill, etc. and one looks to his state of mind or being ("zeal" or "frenzy" or "excitement") to mitigate his act, as in the servant girl example.

34. The dangerous driver is a problem to the law. Generally the notion of "dangerousness" is denied by a driver when he faces a charge. He claims that he was acting reasonably, and, in the last analysis (unless one is dealing with a drunken driving charge, which presents a different issue than what we wish to show here), the public policy of the law is to assume that people drive, and do not drive *and* want to murder others. Lord Hailsham, in an *obiter dictum* in *Hyam v. D. P. P.* [1974] 2 All ER 39 at 55c remarked, "The reckless motorist who is guilty of manslaughter, but not murder, is not at least ordinarily aiming his actions at anyone in the sense explained in *Director of Public Prosecutions v Smith.* If he were, it is quite possible that, as in *Director of Public Prosecutions v. Smith*, he might be convicted of murder."

35. In Q.vi, Art. 8 of the *Summa Theologiae*, 1a2ae, Aquinas speaks of such ignorance as "affected ignorance" and offers this example. "Ignorance is *consequent* to the will to the extent that the ignorance itself is voluntary. This happens in two ways....The first way occurs when the act of the will is brought to bear on the ignorance, as when one wills not to know in order to have an excuse for sin, or so as not to be turned away from sin..." (from the translation of John A. Oesterle, *Treatise on Happiness* [Englewood Cliffs, N.J.: Prentice-Hall, Inc., 1964, third edition], p. 79). It may also be found in Volume 17 of St. Thomas Aquinas, *Summa Theologiae*, translated by Thomas Gilby, O.P., and entitled "Psychology of Human Acts" (London and New York: Blackfriars & Eyre & Spottiswoode, 1970), p. 33 in S.T.1a2ae.6,8, "Does ignorance render an act involuntary?" We cite this as but one of numerous examples one can find in the better-known medieval authors.

Albert Magnus, in his *Compendium Theologiae Veritatis* (Strassburg, [Johann Pruss], 1489), is concerned with the will and sin and ignorance; Stephen Langton, as cited in Powicke's book on him (Oxford, 1928), which used the Cambridge manuscript from St. John's College, Cambridge, is shown to deal directly with the matter of affected ignorance in F. 173^{v}.21, "*de ignorantia affecta*," as well as other discussions of ignorance as the cause of sin, etc. Alexander of Hales discussed the matter at length in his *Summa*, volume 3, *De Malo* (1930, Qaracchi edition). In a more easily obtainable edition of Albert Magnus, one may consult his *Compendium Theologicae* (LVGDVNI, Sumptibus Ioannis Champion, in foro Cambij., M.DC.XLIX), referring to Book III, "De Malo in genere," pp. 193-264. Duns Scotus asked "*Utrum peccatum primi hominis fuerit ex ignorantia*?" (Libri II, Distinct. XXII, Quaestio Secunda at Vol 2, pp. 353-354) in his *Questiones Quolibetales* (ex quatuor voluminibus) *scripti Oxoniensis Super Sententias* [Venetiis: Typis Abbundij Menasolij, 1680], proceeding to distinguish three types of ignorance, i.e., ignorance prior to an act, ignorance concomitant with the act, and ignorance following after an act. The value of this area for the legal scholar is that it presents him with very detailed modes of excusing, and a legal defense, at the least, is a mode of excusing (as is ignorance).

36. One may notice how the concept of "ignorance" is used in modern tort law. We shall cite two cases. One will illustrate that what happened (the harm) could not have been reasonably avoided, although it could have been extraordinarily avoided: namely, there had been some arcane research conducted on the matter which one, possibly, could have known about. The second case illustrates that the "standard of care" need only be reasonable, and that if it embodies risks, even though criticized by the medical community, those risks may be taken if they seem to be reasonable risks. The first case is *Roe v. Ministry of Health* [1954] 2 All ER 131. A glass ampule which contained nupercaine, which was administered for a spinal anesthetic, was contaminated because it had been immersed in a phenol solution, and, unknown to all in the surgical theater, it was not realized that a phenol solution could penetrate the molecular flaws of the glass ampule, thus causing a contamination of the nupercaine which, in turn, when injected in a lumbar puncture could cause spastic paraplegia in the patient. Since none of the medical community was apprised of such a possibility occurring, the Court of Appeal was unanimous in holding that the Ministry was not negligent. The second case is *Moore v. Lumley and the Governors of St. Bartholomew's Hospital*: 19 July 1975, unreported, before Mr. Justice Thompson. There is, however, an adequate report of the case in the *British Medical Journal* for the 20th of December 1975, as well as a partially adequate report of the case in the Annual Report, 1976, of The Medical Defence Union (3, Devonshire Place, London, W.1.), pp. 23-25. Their report is flawed because they do not give the name of the litigants properly, although they do give an adequate summary of the case. The facts of the case are: The plaintiff suffered from varicose veins since the age of 18, and was now 57. He was treated by the *Fegan* technique, which was the technique of compression sclerotherapy. The technique was not without its hazards, but in spite of hazards the technique was thought to be an excellent one for treating varicosities. The alternative to this technique of injections was surgery, and this the plaintiff did not desire. The plaintiff suffered

complications after his third treatment of injections, and brought suit against the doctor (the operator in the injections) and the hospital. Judgment was against the plaintiff, on the grounds that the technique, although possessing some risk, was not hazardous. The opinion of Mr. Justice Thompson was, to the effect, that no doctor "...is negligent merely because there is a body of opinion taking a contrary view [against the treatment he prescribes]." Nor is it every mistake which imports negligence. In the words of Lord Justice Scott [*Mahon v. Osborne*: (1938) 2 KB, p. 14], "the standard of care the law requires is not insurance against accidental slips," col. two, p. 715, of the B. M. J. statement of the case, *Medicolegal*, "Hazards of compression sclerotherapy," pp, 714-715. *Cf.* also *Whitehouse V. Jordan and Another*, L. R. (Times) 5 December 1979 (C.A.), p. 13; also, *Chatterton V. Gerson and Another*, L. R. (Times) 6 February 1980, (QBD).

37. *Ibid.*, p. 590: "*XXIII: In Concilio Ancyrano cap. 22 scriptum est de homicidiis non sponte commissis, prior quidem definitio post septennem poenitentiam perfectionem consequi praecepit; secunda vero quinquennii tempus explere.*"

38. *Conciliorvm*, Tomus Vigesimus Tertius (Ab anno DCCCLXVII at annum DCCCLXXI), Concilium Wormatiense, p. 101: "*XXVI: Qui sacerdotem morti voluntate tradiderit* (the construction of '*...voluntate tradiderat...*' stresses the voluntariness of the act), *carnem non comedat, nec vinum bibere praesumat: ieiunet autem usque ad vesperam, exceptis testis diebus atque dominicis. Arma non sumat, & ubicumque ire voluerit, nullor vehiculo deducature, sed propriis pedibus proficiscatur.*" The rest of the text sets out penalities, penances, and fasts to be observed.

39. *Ibid.*, p. 101: "*XXVII: Qui odii meditatione, vel propter auaritiam paganum occiderit, quia non leui vitio committitur, vt homicidam conuenit poenitere: quando quidem nec exteris gentibus, nisi oblatam pacem respuerint, bellum est populo antiquo penitus inferre praeceptum.*"

40. *Ibid.*, pp. 101-102: "*XXVIII: Si quis insaniens aliquem occiderit, si ad sanam mentem peruenerit, leuior ei poenitentia imponenda est, quam ei, qui sana mente tale quid commiserit. Cui quamuis poenitentia sit imposnenda, quia ipsa infirmitas causa peccati, licet fortassis occulta, contigisse creditur, tantum tamen leuior, quam ei qui sanus aliquem occiderit, quantum inter insanum & samun, irrationabile & rationabile, constat esse discriminis.*"

41. One may consult Bracton's *On The Law And Customs Of England*, translated by Samuel E. Thorne (Cambridge, Mass.: The Selden Society and The Belknap Press of Harvard University Press, 1968) in volume two, "Of Pleas of the Crown," in the calendar entry for: *Of homicide through misadventure and accident*, p. 384, from which we quote: "...a crime is not committed unless the intention to injure exists,...as may be said of a child or a madman, since the absence of intention protects the one and unkindness of fate excuses the other."

42. *Ibid.*, p. 102: "*XXIX: Saepe contingit, ut dum quis operi necessario insistents arborem incidit, aliquis subtus ipsam veniens deprimatur; & idcirco*

[very often the case] si voluntate vel negligentia incidentis arborem factum est, ut homicida poenitentiae debet omnino submitti. Quod si non voto, non incuria illius, non denique scientia contigit, sed dum ille operi necessario fortassis incumberet, iste insperatus occurrens, sub arborem improuisus deuenit & syb ipsa, nemine valente penitus adiuuare, suppressus est, incisor arboris homicidae procul dubio non est comparandus."

43. *Conciliorvm*, Tomus Vigesimus Quartus, (Ab anno DCCCLXXII ad annum DCCCCIX), Concilium Triburiense (under Pope Formosus, 891-895 A.D.), p. 662: "*XXXVI: Si contingat duos fratres simul arborem succidere, siue in silua, siue* ['u' = 'v' throughout] *quocumque loco, & cadente arbore, alter alteri, Fuge vel caue dixerit, & ipse stans, siue fugiens, subtus ipsam arborem deuenerit, & mortuus fuerit, superstes frater, innocens de morte defuncti diiudicetur. Quia non voluntate, non incuria illius* [= neither reckless or careless], *non denique consensu, nec vllo suo mortem incurrit reati: sed dum ambo insisterent operi necessario, incautus & insperatus casu arboris depressus est*, [the tree simply and unexpectedly falls], *nemine penitus adiuuare valente. Hanc eamdem statuimus diffinitionem de ceteris similibus, siue cognatis, siue nulla proximitate coniunctis* [and this should hold over to other examples where one has no intention to bring about a wrong and is in no way connected to what is brought about, i.e., one is not a cause of a criminal event]. *Istam diffinitionem tenuere patres nostri apostolici vire: ideo eorum exempla sequentes, per futura tempora inuiolabilem eam custodimus, & posteris nostris sequendam transmittimus: quia graue peccatum est, & nostro ministerio contratium, innocentem opprimere, & securum crimine, scienter criminosum habere.*" One can notice that "scienter" carries over from this Council to the common law ("...*scienter criminosum habere*").

44. *Ibid.*, p. 663: "*XXXVII: Si quae mulier, ut saepe contingit, infantem proprium prope ignem collocauerit, & alius, qui caldarium super ipsum ignem pependerit, & aquam infuderit, atque aqua ipsa per ignem seruens egreditur, & infanti superfunditure, & propterea mortuus agitur: mater infantis, propter negligentiam, iudicio sacerdotum poeniteat, & homo qui caldarium pependit, securus permaneat. Simili modo de ceteris similibus, quae saepe diuerse solent euenire, & iudicamus, & esse volumus.*"

45. We do not want to dwell upon the nature and extent of occupiers' liability (already extensively treated by P. M. North in his book, *Occupiers' Liability* [Butterworths, 1971]) but one can draw upon that area of the law for comparisons here. Chief is to determine what is entailed by the concept of liability. It rests upon the notion that risks can be anticipated, and thence prevented, as was expressed in the recent case from the House of Lords in *British Railways Board v. Herrington* [1972] 1 All ER 749, holding that the Board had not acted with reckless disregard towards a six-year-old child who had trespassed upon its land (a railway) and who suffered an injury; nevertheless, the Board had failed to act with due regard to humane considerations, and were, under the circumstances, culpable. As in the case of the mother in the citation from the thirty-seventh canon, similar reasoning was applied in *Herrington*. The House of Lords assumed that the Board would assume that small children might play near their electrified line, and would have taken precautions against the trepass of children. In other

jurisdictions the tort notion of maintaining an "attractive nuisance" might indict a defendant in a similar case, i.e., he should have known "x" condition would attract harm.

46. *Cf., Tesco Supermarkets, Ltd v. Nattrass*, H. L. [1971] 2 All ER 127.

47. In *R. v. Charlotte Smith*, (1865) 34 L.J.M.C.153; L. & C. 607, Blackburn, J., in a case concerning homicide by neglect, observed, "To render a person who has the charge of another criminally responsible for neglect, such as is alleged in this case, there must be, on the part of such person, a duty arising from the helpless character of the person who is under control. Such a duty, for instance, arises in the case of those who have charge of infants, invalids, or lunatics." We have extended his observation to suggest that if one appoints a defective agent, knowingly, the defects of the agent will not be a defense for the principal in a charge of criminal negligence.

48. *Ibid.*, p. 671: "LII: *Placuit nobis de homicidiis non sponte commissis, his inferere, quod in Ancyrano sancto Concilio, capite vigesimosecundo legitur, ubi dicitur: De homicidiis non sponte commissis, piror quidem diffinitio post septennem poenitentiam perfectionem consequi praecepit: Secunda vero, quinquennii tempus explere. Modus autem huius poentientiae in episcoporum sit arbitrio, ut secundum conuersationem poenitentium, possint & extendere tardantibus, & minuere studiose festinantibus*."

49. Under the *Criminal Justice Act 1967*, proof of criminal intent is no longer given in the form that a jury *must* assume that *D* intended the natural consequences of his acts. The language of the Act is now as follows: Section 8, provides that, "A court or jury in determining whether a person has committed an offense,

(a) shall not be bound in law to infer that he intended or foresaw a result of his actions by reason only of its being a natural and probable consequence of those actions; but

(b) shall decide whether he did intend or foresee that result by reference to all the evidence drawing such inferences from the evidence as appear proper in the circumstances.

David Napley, in his commentary upon the Act, stated that, "The section, however, does nothing to clarify whether, and to what extent in particular crimes, intent or foresight is required to be proved," p. 29 of *A Guide to Law & Practice under the Criminal Justice Act 1967* (London: Sweet & Maxwell: 1967), an observation which later decisions (from 1967) would puzzle over, and upon which we shall comment in the section on modern case law.

50. There are hosts of examples: Washington Criminal Code 9A.44 ff. wherein intent is seldom a defense to the charges of any kind of sexual contact. One may read the *Commentary On The Immorality Act* (Act No. 23 of 1957) by Hardie and Hartford (Cape Town: Juta & Co., Ltd., 1960), to observe how offenses of the strictest liability are cast, diminishing *mens rea* almost totally. The classic case, of course, is: *R. v. Larsonneur* (1933) 97 J.P. 206 (C. C. A.), the police, having arrested D., caused her to be found in the

United Kingdom, her presence thereby being an immigration offense. Paradigm cases for offenses of this kind may be older counterfeiting or uttering cases in which the offense is complete when *D* "knows" the coin to be false, no matter how innocently he acquired the coin or note. Elizabethan recusant statutes functioned much the same; one offended if one "knew" that a priest was about the land.

51. *Cf.*, *Free Action*, by A. I. Melden (London, 1961), Chapter Nine, "Motive and Explanation," wherein the author argues that causal explanations and explanations by an appeal to motive are not logically interchangeable pp. 83-104.

52. *R. v. Clarkson and others*, [1971] 3 All ER 344. Citing *R. v. Coney* (1882) 8 QBD at 557 "...to constitute an aider and abettor some active steps must be taken by word, or action, with the intent to instigate the principal, or principals" this court held that presence was not enough to convict a person of aiding and abetting, but (at 347), "It must be proved that the accused intended to give encouragement; that he *wilfully* encouraged."

53. *R. v. Sharmpal Singh* [1962] A. C. - Privy Council - 188, p. 196. The defendant was accused of homicide, it being claimed by the Crown that he had caused the death of his wife by acts of violence on his part during sexual concourse with her.

54. *Ibid.*, p. 671: "LIII*: Si quis filium suum (quod absit) non sponte, sed casu contingente occiderit, [*iuxta homicidia non sponte] secundum homicidia sponte commissa poeniteat, ut sequenti subinfertur capitulo.*" By contrast, Roman military law could be severe, *"De milite, qui commilitonem suum vulnerauit. 22 Miles, qui commilitonem suum gladio vulnerat, caput amittit."* "*A soldier who wounds a comrade*. 22 A soldier who wounds his comrade with a sword shall be beheaded." Taken from the Military Law from Ruffus, the text and translation appearing at pp. 154 and 155 in *Roman Military Law* by C. E. Brand (Austin & London: University of Texas Press, 1968). That one wounded a fellow soldier, and not with what intention one may have wounded, comprised the offense; thus the *actus reus* directed the penalty–the wounding itself–and it would not matter if the wounding had been by accident, by negligence, or by intention.

55. *Ibid.*, p. 671: "LIV*: De his qui voluntarie homicidium fecerint, Ancyrano sancto Concilio, capite vigesimoprimo legitur: Vt poenitentiae quidem iugiter se submittant: perfectionem vero, id ist, communionis Christi gratiam circa vitae exitum consequantur, etc.*" The fifty-fifth canon simply sets out penalties for intentional homicide ("*Si quis sponte homicidium fecerit...*"), and there is no need to reproduce the text here since nothing of major change is added to a voluntary act.

56. One need only consult Edward Poste's introduction to Gaius (*Gaii: Institutionum Iuris Civilis Commentarii Quattor*, or *Elements of Roman Law By Gaius* [translation and commentary by Edward Poste; Oxford: At The Clarendon Press, M.DCCC.LXXV]), p. 5, wherein he states: "The essence of every Law is the injunction or prohibition of some given act and the menace

menace of an evil in the case of non-compliance. Every law, that is to say, is at once Imperative and Punitory; it is only Imperative by being punitory." Poste would then have assumed, no doubt, on this notion of "imperative," that the expression "2+2=4" would not be imperative, since no penalty attaches to the expression. We prefer to use the model that from an understanding of the law, one follows the law; Poste, and other voluntarists, assume that the force of the law is that one is moved by a force (i.e., the penalty) other than the legal proposition itself. We are not Austinians, and do not embrace a command theory of law. The logical priority which a criminal law should possess is that it is first a law, and then that it commands. The relationship is not "p and q"; rather, the logical relationship is "If p, and p, then q." Such a relationship permits one, in theory, to argue that the justification for law as law rests in its reasonableness. The justification for a punishment, following upon a transgression of the law, may be its effectiveness within a just standard. One must separate the conceptual elements. If one does not then a claim is advanced that any description of a law must, at the same instance, be a description of a punishment concomitant with the law. This, we suggest, is a logical fallacy.

57. We reproduce the Latin canons from the Council of Namnetense from *Conciliorvm*, Tomus Vigesimus Quartus, p. 685, for the sake of consistency: "XVII: *Si quis voluntarie & per insidias hominem interfecerit, iugi se poenitentiae submittat. Et si hoc publice actum constat, si laicus est, a communione orationum quinquennio remoueatur: post quinquennium, tantum in orationum communionem recipiatur, non autem offerat, non corpus Domini contingat. In quo perdurans quatuordecim annis, tunc at plenam communionem cum oblationibus recipiatur. Si quis de industria & per insidias occiderit hominem, ab altari meo euelles eum, vt moriatur, dicit Dominus*." One will observe that no reason is given for the penitential assignments; they are simply given. "XVIII: *Si quis casu* (as an accident) *non volens homicidium perpetrauit, quadraginta diebus in pane & acqua poeniteat. Quibus peractis, biennio ab oratione fidelium segregetus: non communicet, nec offerat. Post biennium in communione orationis offerat, non tamen communicet: post quinquennium ad plenam communionem recipiatur. Abstinentia ciborum in arbitrio sacerdotus maneat*." This policy finds itself in judicial sentencing under common law procedures when a sentence is left to the discretion of the trial judge. It is also reflected in magistrates' practice when reasons for decisions need not be given. The "reason" rests in the office of the judge (or in the sacerdocy); namely, because one holds a dignified office it is therefore assumed that he knows how to judge properly whether or not one gives reasons for his judgment. Its lack of logical force is self-evident.

58. *Ibid.*, XIII, "*Qua sententia cum sub interminatione prohibeatur (i.e. Gen., 9.) homicidium, tamen ne quis insipientium putet animan hominis in sanguine constitutam, quae immortalis est, & quae ideo sic appellature, quasi anaema, it est a sanguine longe discreta, nouerit sanguinem animarum typice intelligendum ipsum vitale, quo vegetantur, & sustentantur, & viuunt homines in carne per animam. Non enim sanguis hominis ad substantiam animae creditur pertinere: quamuis alibi legislator dicere videatur: Anima omnis carnis in sanguine est.* (Levit.17) *quod non ideo dictum est, ut hoc sit anima, quae est proprie spiritalis substantia: sed quod per sanguinem anima, ut diximus, typice*

significetur, per rem scilicet visibilem res inuisibilis, sicut & illud: Petra autem erat Christus, (I.Cor.10) *non quia hoc erat, sed quia hoc significabat. Quo sensu & illus intelligendum est, quod sequitur*: Quicumque effuderit humanum sanguinem, fundetur & sanguis illius....*Ergo cum ille qui occidit sanguinem non effuderit, quomodo eius sanguinem Dominus effusurus est*?" We would add that the argument is novel in one regard. It suggests that by the fact of existing one is a human being. Theories of brain-death would reject this kind of thinking, substituting in its place an activity or arrangement theory of human behavior; i.e., to be human one must have a brain, and, having a brain, it must perform in a specified way and at a specific level if its owner is to be deemed human. Would there, however, then be a valid difference between a man who decided to sleep all of his life, and Karen Quinlan, who was rendered permanently unconscious as a result of drug poisoning (*Matter of Quinlan*, Superior Court of New Jersey, Chancery Division, November 10, 1975, Muir., 348 A 2d, 801, and overturned March 31st, 1976, by the Supreme Court of New Jersey, Hughes, C.J.)?

59. Our aim is not to present an analysis of Latin models, but for some of the early sources of common law one, of necessity, must turn to the legal Latin of the period. In his edition of Bracton: *Selected Passages from the Works of Bracton and Azo*, edited for the Selden Society by Frederic William Maitland (London: Bernard Quaritch, 1895), Maitland has cited in his second appendix, pp. 225-235, the texts both of Bracton and Bernard of Pavia on the subject of homicide. It is Maitland's claim, with which we see little to disagree after having viewed the texts, that the language of Bracton on the subject is taken mostly in style and content from what Bernard of Pavia wrote in his own *De homicidio voluntario vel casuali*. One may refer to Maitland's text which appears in an interleaved printing, one line of Bernard with the same line beneath it of Bracton. The similarity of Latin is hardly coincidental. In such a case one can safely assert that the early scholastic texts did influence early writers of the common law; what one cannot demonstrate, without greater textual analysis and without more historically accurate texts (since so much is yet in manuscript), is the extent of the influence. We do have enough early case law to show that scholastic writers were cited in legal decisions, and that early scholastic categories–such as degrees of ignorance–were accepted in the common law.

60. One may turn to so dissimilar a source for legal theory as the Council of Basil, [*Conciliorvm*, Tomus Trigesimus Primus, (A.D. 1433), edition of M.DC.XLIV, Parisiis], p. 147, where, during its discussion under what species the Holy Eucharist may be received, we encounter a strict liability model about the nature of ignorance and the law, which model will appear in Plowden's report of *Reniger v. Fogossa, pp. 19-20, volume one of The Commentaries or Reports of Edmund Plowden* (London, 1816). The language of the Council, from p. 147, states this on ignorance: "*Nec potest dicere quod ignorantia excusaret ecclesiam a sacrilegio, & contemptu, & per consequens a damnatione, quia ut alias dictum est, ignorantia iuris, in his quae sunt necessaria ad salutem, cuiusmodi sunt praecepta diuina & Christi, non excusat*." This in turn is traced back to Aquinas. He seems to have been a voluminous source both for canonists and for legal writers, Plowden citing him in *Reniger V. Fogossa*. The common heritage reveals itself in a central notion as was *if*

ignorance excuses, and we tend to find a common reflection of the common notion in the common lawyers, in the canonists, and the theologians of the period. Sir Paul Vinogradoff, in his *Roman Law in Medieval Europe* (Third Edition, with a preface by F. de Zulueta, Oxford, 1929) suggested (pp. 117-118) that the only test for the influence of Roman law in England was to find in it maxims which had passed into juridical thinking. We think the same holds for scholastic legal models which did, in fact, pass into our legal heritage. Plowden is one example.

61. We make the following citations from Brand (*op.cit.*, footnote 50). One will notice how "voluntary" functions in various legal contexts. Military Laws from Russus:

"De militibus castra vel urbem prodentibus, aut custodiam negligentibus 36 *Si quis, cui custodia vel vrbis vel castrorum credita fuerit ea prodiderit; aut, quum ea defendere posset, praeter* voluntatem [emphasis ours] *praesidis sui, vel extra necessitatem ad vitae periculum tendentem, inde recesserit; capitis supplicio damnabitur.*" "Soldiers who betray a camp or city, or neglect their defense. 36 If any person to whom the custody of either a city or camp has been entrusted betray such a trust, or when able to defend them withdraw from them without authority of his commander, or without necessity in the form of compelling danger to his life, he shall be condemned to the punishment of death" (pp. 160-161). Note: We would modify the translation to include the force of "*praeter voluntatem*" which signifies that one, of and by his own will, did act without authority.

"62 *Si quis conuictus fuerit semetipsum hostibus dedere* voluisse, [emphasis ours] *ultimo supplicio subiicietur...*" "62 If any person is convicted of having wished to surrender himself to the enemy, he shall be subject to the supreme punishment...." Again, the force of "voluisse" is that one has moved himself of his own will, and the range of "wish" in the translation is more "one desires to...." pp. 168-169.

"64 ....*Qui denique sponte transfugerit, & reuersus fuerit; ad totem vitae tempus seruus esto.*" "62 ....If he voluntarily [*sponte*] deserts to the enemy and is brought back, he shall be a slave for the rest of his life" pp. 168-169.

From the *Corpus Juris Civilis*, Modestinus' *Punishments, Book 4*, one reads, (11) "*Et is; qui volens transfugere adprehensus est, punitur,*" is rendered as "Any person who, intending to desert to the enemy is apprehended, shall suffer death" pp. 174-175.

Military Affairs, Book 1, of Arrius Menander:
"(3) *Temporarium exilium voluntario militi insulae relegationem adsignat, dissimulatio perpetuum exilium.* [Any person in temporary exile who voluntarily enlists incurs the penalty of relegation to an island; if he conceals his condition, he is liable to perpetual exile.]
"(5) *Reus capitalis criminis voluntarius miles secundum divi Traiani rescriptum capite poniendus est...*" [A volunteer guilty of a capital crime shall suffer death, according to a rescript of the divine imperial Trajan....]

CHAPTER TWO

Cicero and St. Augustine

A legal philosopher need not be bothered excessively by a system of law which excludes certain actions from punishment. One may criticize the system socially, i.e., stating that it is obvious that one class within the society is benefiting unjustly by a certain privilege, but such a move within a legal system does not baffle or confuse. It can be listed plainly as an exception or an exemption, and most games provide us with models of exception or exemptions. Much of early common law held exemption or exception moves in its legal rules, as the benefit of clergy did show.

One need not be bothered, either, by the forms which legal punishments take, or by what is legally punished. One may confer names as he pleases, and, by an extension of such an attitude, one may punish what he pleases unless one adheres to a legal belief which maintains that punishments are a necessary extension of law, and those laws which exist are of a necessary number dictated by a necessary order in the world. It would be a type of rigorism embodied in a severe natural law theory of law that would state that the number of laws in existence would be a necessary and not an accidental number of laws, and the punishments attached to that necessary number of laws would themselves be necessary punishments. Lawmaking would have to it no contingency; all lawmaking would be viewed as that which must necessarily be the case.

Even were one to hold to such an excessive naturalism in legal theory (to which natural law theory can lend itself), a legal philosopher might not be bothered by what forms punishment took for laws infracted. He might object to the existence of such punishments, but that is a different question from what we wish to consider. What ought to concern a legal philosopher, and what does concern us in this chapter, is the manner, and whatever justification was advanced (either implicitly or explicitly) for that manner, in which an accused was brought within the boundary of legal guilt or innocence. If all within the legal system are not guilty (of crime, or of some crime) from the onset, then one can state that the legal system admits that some may be guilty while others may be innocent. How is such an assignment of legal value made? One may appeal to another legal system in which all were guilty (in some form) and none (save two persons) were innocent. Christian law held that all were born with and into sin, save for some theologians who argued, as did, for example, Duns Scotus, that Mary, the mother of Christ, and Christ Himself, were born free from sin. Removed from a matter of belief, and transformed into a matter of legal statement, one has a legal system in which all are guilty but in which two legal exceptions to guilt are tolerated. In the common law system, however, no such wide-ranging assignment of guilt was made over its members; thus, the question of how guilt or innocence was proved is of importance for philosophical consideration, and by a selection of leading texts we hope to demonstrate how intention became the central concept in this demonstration. There developed a legal concept which could protect or judge an accused; but as with many concepts it stands in "such disparitie / As is twixt Aire and Angells puritie."

The use of a term does not assure that it denotes a concept marking out clearly what are and what are not the conceptual borders of the term. The use of "intention" comes early into common law; but the marking off of clearly defined limits comes late into the common law, if at all. One can turn to various chapters of Peter Abelard's *Ethics*[1] to note that "intention" is that device which determines if an act possesses an ethical quality and is not simply a neutral act. Just what intention is, or signifies, is not that precisely stated. It may be a psychological quality; it may mark some operation of the human will; it may rest in some aspect of the human intellect. The term may also be modified, suggesting that "it" is not only some ontological quality, but a quality possessing a certain attribute or property. An intention may be "good" or it may be "bad." The relationship between the term "intention" and what that term signified was often assumed to be known; namely, one's intention is what the term signified. We would remark that such is a circular argument, but legal reasoners, as well as early theological moralists, seemed little disturbed that they did not specify exactly what was an intention. Kenny has suggested that the terms *consensus* and *intentio* were used as synonyms by Abelard in his *Ethics*, and that the terms denoted a state of mind of an agent and not desire.[2] If, however, *desire* were to mean only a blind impetus, we would agree with him; but if desire connotes an object which is desired, then it would seem that one could "intend" what one "desired." At one place Abelard states:

> God is said to be the power and judge of the heart and the reins, that is, of all the intentions [*quarumlibet intentionum ex affectione animae uel infirmitate seu delectatione carnis prouenientium*] which come from an affection of the soul or from a weakness or pleasure of the flesh.[3]

Our minor differences may be resolved if one were to assume that when "intention" is used, it is referring to a rational movement of the soul, and is therefore presumed to pertain to one's rational faculties.[4] It is not our wish, either, to individuate faculties by stating that the will has one location, and the intellect some other location. Such individuation of concepts seems to create rather than diminish perplexity. It is sufficient for conceptual analysis to distinguish between the use of terms.[5]

Medieval parlance preserved a distinction between willing and knowing, casting the distinction in the language of a faculty psychology (which to us now seems bothersome). What was preserved by the distinction was the distinction between "knowing that one could do 'x'", and, "knowing that one could do 'x,' whereupon one then did 'x' (or then x-ed)." Knowing that I can "x" does not compel me to "x-ing." One may then be ready to admit that from a distinction in how terms can be used, it would be fallacious to attempt to derive empirical functions or to make locations. That I can speak about "the will" does not demonstrate that some entity exists which corresponds to my use of the term, "will." It does, however, become important for the law to preserve a distinction between "intention" as a term which has a cognitive usage, from "intention" as a term which has a volitional usage, and to appreciate that one usage does not equal the other usage.[6] An accused may know that the act he did was wrong at law, but it may have been an act which he did not voluntarily do, and it is voluntariness which is the central element to be proved if he is to be found guilty. Equally, it may be that the accused voluntarily did an act, but did not know that his act was criminal, whereupon the central element in the crime which the Crown must prove is that the accused knew that his act was a criminal act. The nature of a criminal defense may vary greatly as to how intention is viewed. Does it mean "know," and only know; or does it mean "will," and only will?

We need not first turn to Bracton to see the use of intention in relation to the assignment of guilt. Quite apart from the conciliar sources and the *Corpus Juris Canonici*, we do have other records of the use of intentional language. Plucknett[7] cites a passage from the laws of Aethelred II (although the passage he cites is, he says, only to be found in one manuscript, 1008 A.D.), in which this relationship is made obvious, and we reproduce a part of it here:

> And if it happens that a man commits a misdeed involuntarily; or unintentionally, the case is different from that of one who offends of his own free will, voluntarily and intentionally; and likewise he who is an involuntary agent of his misdeeds should always be entitled to clemency and better terms owing to the fact that he acted as an involuntary agent. Careful discrimination shall be made in judging every deed, and the judgement shall always be ordered with justice, according to the nature of the deed, and meted out in proportion, in affairs both religious and secular; and, through the fear of God, mercy and leniency and some measure of forbearance shall be shown towards those who have need of them. For all of us have need that our Lord grant us his mercy, frequently and often. Amen.[8]

There was to be found, certainly, a tradition in which the will was spoken of as a free and spontaneous faculty. One may return to the writings of St. Augustine, among other Augustan theologians, to appreciate the tradition. When one comes to the early medievals one finds that the notion of the will, as a freely moving faculty, became highly developed in the literature. For Anselm of Canterbury[9] the notion of "will" is expressed as the free act of love a creature shows for God, modelled on a concept of deity in which God freely creates and freely loves His creation. Hugh of St. Victor (d.1141), often called *Alter Augustinus*, presents us with a highly developed language of will, and we quote a passage from *De Sacramentis* which bears directly upon a definition of will:

> XXIV: *What free will is*:
>
> For spontaneous movement or voluntary desire is free will; free, indeed, in this, that it is voluntary, but will in this, that it is desire. But the power itself and the aptitude of the will is the freedom whereby it moves in either direction, and it is said to be the free choice of the will. Now moving voluntarily and being born by spontaneous desire, this is to choose with power and to judge with freedom, in which free will consists.[10]

We note a further refinement of this definition when Hugh of St. Victor moves from the sphere of a general model (the model just stated concerned not only will in general, but will as it pertained to angelic creatures) to man specifically, stating:

> IV: *On free will*:
>
> The movement of the mind is in the will.... In the movement of the mind alone is there free will; in the movement of the body and of sensuality are those things which follow free will. For thus was the disposition of nature, for the voluntary movement of the mind was desire, free in the voluntary, will in desire. The mind, therefore, moves by itself, and is the first movement of the will. Therefore, the movement of the mind is always justice or injustice....For in that the mind moves, it moves by freedom, because it moves voluntarily and moves by itself, and to it belongs the fact that it moves, either to merit, if it moves well, or to blame, if evilly.[11]

Coupled to this notion of the will was a position holding that human activity springs either from knowledge or from ignorance, and both such states or privations were conditions for which one himself was responsible. Ignorance was viewed as a vice,[12] and, at the same time, it was viewed as a cause of action. In a defense one alleges, often, that he did not know that such and such was the case or could have been the case. For the medieval theologian that would not have constituted a defense. The specific charge to be answered was to remove any trace of fault on one's part for having been ignorant, and thence for having acted in accord with such ignorance.

We cite Hugh of St. Victor because he was a, if not the, leading sacramentalist of his time who ranked with Abelard. We have omitted his chapters on Natural and on Written Law because they do not concern us directly. But we wish to make reference, in passing, that in *De Sacramentis*, Book II, Part XIV, Questions 1 through 9, he stresses an intentional aspect to the operation of penance, stressing that merit is attached to one's state of will. The will was viewed by him to be the author and commander of works; so the category of a good but will-less act would have been meaningless.[13]

It is not our concern to review or develop a medieval concept of the voluntary. In itself that would require a separate book, or books. We do wish, however, to suggest that the concept of the voluntary was not an isolated notion found only in a few writers, or that it was an isolated legal notion, which it was not. However, to discover how "voluntary" or "intention" functioned in early legal argument at the common law one needs to draw upon some of the sources of the period, and then, by assumption, to see how the term reflects the similarity of other usages of the period. Of course, a legal sentence should be self-sufficient, and it should be looked at in its own sentential and legal setting. But such legal purity seldom exists, if for no other reason than that the law is such a borrower of common ideas, and it is to the force of major common ideas that we must often turn for help. We have chosen some leading medieval texts about the will and about the nature of the voluntary and the involuntary. Both of these areas embrace questions about ignorance, its nature and causes. But medieval texts in themselves do not possess any magical clarity on how key terms are to be used or on how precise their meaning is. The medieval mind, if that is not a metaphor too wide of the mark, possessed both a logical clarity and a penchant for presenting intellectual models as if those models were empirical facts about human or angelic behavior. It takes only a short look at Aquinian epistemology, to cite but one of many possible examples, to see that the relationship between the known and how it comes to be known is explained by the use of various models of behavior, beginning with a generalized notion about objects, and then a model as to what sense knowledge means, then on through a series of "extractor" models of mind which show the intellect moving from the sensible particular, up through a phantasm, through various phases of intellect, and finally to a "something" which is at rest in the mind as the thing known.

This kind of model analysis is foreign to us, but yet we are at home with it. One experiences both a tension and a satisfaction in reading such an analysis. We do create models (of atomic behavior, of computer programming, of physiological input when speaking about the function of the brain) but we tend to want to ground them more on "fact" and less on inspiration as to what a fact should be. The medieval presented everything together; we want to analyze everything, but we do not want it all together. Thus we offer this mild "caution" about the use of the term "voluntary" and its related terms. We have to free the term from its many functions. It was at home in theological discourse, as when it was asked if the angels' act of disobedience was a voluntary act; it was at home in moral discourse, which any appeal to Abelard reveals; it was at home in general religious discourse about man (in general) when questions were asked about man's sinfulness and if it were voluntarily caused; it was at home in formal mental analysis, as when Aquinas commented upon portions of the *Nicomachean Ethics* and Aristotle's use of the term "voluntary"; it was at home in the wide-ranging discussion of medieval writers about the nature of ignorance. The concept of the will admitted of no simple reduction of term to faculty. It was a complicated concept, and for the major writers (Abelard, Magnus, Aquinas, Scotus, Pullen, Bonaventure, Ockham, Langton) no simple view of their use of the term follows.

When, therefore, the concept of "voluntary" enters into the common law it does not enter as a single uniform concept to which a lexical clarity can be assigned. It is a multi-layered term, and it is a metaphor. Like many multi-layered terms or metaphors, a single term was often made to do too much; and overwork kills the spirit and dulls the fineness of the mind. When "intention" begins to be used as a pivotal term it is asked to do too much, and little philosophical refinement attends its use. The law may be able to slight on the fineness of analysis, but the philosopher may not; if he does, he courts danger. Since there was no clear tradition about how the term "voluntary" was to be used (because it had many usages), one could not return to the bulk of medieval writing and claim that it meant only this and not that; one will witness the force of the law and not its conceptual refinement. It first controls; afterward it may, perhaps, explain.

Plucknett suggested that between the years 1113 and 1118 there occurred an outburst of legal writing in England.[14] We wish to turn to some of the writing of that general period to show how the notion of "intention" finds its way into the developing common law. It will be the only period of the common law where theological, philosophical, and legal influences permeate one another. After the time of Bracton, save for some reflections by Coke, Hale and Hawkins of a religious nature, the law will not be so close to other conceptual sources. By looking at some of the instances of the use of "intention" in *Leges Henrici Primi* one may gather how the concept began to function in our legal system.[15] It is a larger source for the early legal use of the work than was Glanvill.

An important rule of evidence is given early on in the *Leges* which suggested that evidence should be given, and after given it should then be judged. Legal evidence was not a private issue; thus its conjunction to intention would imply that the accused would present his reasons for an act (or serious omission), and that about his actions there would be a public nature. The passage reads as follows, and we shall cite the translation of it only:

> 5, 7a: Nothing shall be done in the absence of an accuser; for God and our Lord Jesus Christ knew Judas was a thief, but because he was not accused, he was therefore not cast out, and whatever he did among the apostles remained credited to the dignity of his office.[16]

And we read a little later on in the same chapter,

> 5, 9a: No one should be judged or condemned before he has lawful accusers personally present and the opportunity to offer a defence for the purpose of clearing himself of the charges.[17]

The growing concept of a legal defense would be that reasons would be given, within the ambit of an accepted legal framework, for the actions or omissions of an accused. What underlies such a theory is the assumption that what an accused does is thought to be his act, and that his act may be seen as what is public, which would be the action itself, and what is private, which would be his reasons for his actions. No theory of irrationalism is espoused in such a doctrine of legal evidence. It may be granted that odd reasons might have been advanced for the doing of, or refraining from doing of an act, such as demonic possession, or witch-spell casting, but that is only to observe that a legal system accepted as a rational or legal explanation for an action other than what we would accept in the present day. We need only cast our minds back to that period after the Second World War when many an accused claimed that he had been bewitched by the political doctrine of Communism to explain why he was not a "good" citizen at some time in his life. His excuse, or reasons, often served as an effective plea in mitigation, if not even as a complete defense against a charge of political disloyalty. Even so barbaric a method of trial as trial by battle was not revoked in England until 1819 under the statutes of 59 Geo. III, c. 46.[18]

The aim of the *Leges* was to foster a judicial attitude that legal guilt should follow upon one's voluntary responsibility for his acts. Guilt ought not to be forced: "A confession extracted by duress or fraud is invalid."[19] The prevailing Christian notion at work in the shaping of these early laws is, more or less, that to be a man is to be composed of both body and soul. The unity of the principles is expressed in the existence of a human being, and he is neither to be thought of as solely spirit, or as solely corporeality. Just how the composition worked was left open to serious disputes, and these disputes, in themselves, do not concern us here. We mention, in passing, that no unified medieval theory about human behavior issued forth, which numerous conciliar condemnations and clarifications were to show. Some writers thought that the body was an expression of a world-soul, while some thought that each man possessed his own unique soul. However the different positions with regard to the nature of the soul, and its union to the body, were resolved, what appeared to develop is a concept of human nature which held that each man was unique, and thus uniquely responsible for his moral actions or omissions.[20] There existed, however, some conditions which would excuse him from fault, but those we will discuss later when we discuss ignorance and the law.

It is when one turns to 5,28b of the *Leges* that a clear statement about intention occurs, but, at the same time, we would caution against assuming that its clarity is also conceptually helpful. We meet with a simple statutory declarative: "A person is not to be considered guilty unless he has a guilty intention."

Levitt[21] states that Maitland had correctly traced the use of the phrase [*Reum non facit nisi mens rea*: 5,28b of the Downer text] to St. Augustine of Hippo, having found its "source" when Sir James Fitzjames Stephen did not,[22] himself an eminent historian and practitioner of criminal law in the nineteenth century. Such an omission on his part alone ought to tell one that the historical roots of the concept of intention are not a matter of simple historical location, or that its roots possessed a persistently vivifying force as might the living force of a ritual. Its roots had simply been lost. What one fears is that if its roots were lost then, too, its conceptual framework might have been lost. We make this extended *caveat* because of certain comments we now wish to make about the Augustinian roots of intention.

We prefer to suggest, and argue mildly, that an attempt to locate "intention" in one of the sermons given by St. Augustine, and then to argue, from its location, that the common law doctrine(s) of "intention" stem from that historical location is to import into the common law more than the evidence will permit. The method should be that one should be willing to admit conceptual links into a growing tradition, but one should view the "links" as parts of a living tradition each moment of which in some way recapitulates what precedes it. The Augustinian tradition grew out of a rich Roman tradition in which law, rhetoric and philosophy all had powerful parts to play. We do not intend to show, as in a biography, how St. Ambrose, himself steeped in Roman culture and learning, may have transferred Roman learning to St. Augustine when, as a young scholar, Augustine was a pupil of St. Ambrose. So much of early Christianity was formed by legal minds, thereupon converted to Christian beliefs, that one assumes that Roman culture was transmitted to the early church in that way. The doctrines and edicts and papal letters of the early councils show how much Rome had permeated early Christian culture, especially after the time of Origen, who himself believed that Christian education needed to model itself after pagan education, but in a manner fitting to Christian beliefs.[23] It is telling that the early location made for intention rests in a sermon rather than in a legal work. We think there is a reason for it in such a form; the doctrine took a Roman form, a concept expressed in the literary form of the time – a church sermon. The tradition of the Senate had not been surpassed; it had been embellished by a growing political body, as was the early Church. One may turn to Cicero's *De Inventione* to appreciate that legal analysis might occur in other than legal form.

The phrase, "*Ream linguam non facit, nisi mens rea*," occurs in Sermon 180 of St. Augustine's collected sermons.[24] The body of the sermon discusses oaths and lying, which we have appended in a free translation of our own to the Latin text and have placed in the chapter endnotes. The sermon is both compressed and foreign to us now. What seems to be a simple example, the asking of a question whether it rains or not in this place ["*Pluit in illo loco*?"], has a complicated import due to the compression of the Latin. The compression is made even more complicated because the example should be seen from within Augustine's own thought. One is not dealing with a simple grammatical example; rather, one is dealing with an example produced by a philosopher and theologian and functioning within a system of his assumptions. The early Christian believers were seriously troubled by oaths; the gospels had counselled against the taking of oaths; but there seemed to be occasions either when one should be able to take an oath and not violate Christian teachings, or when oaths had been taken and were not in violation of Christian belief. But to take an oath also meant for one to tell the truth. What conditions bound one so that an oath would be truthful? Two problems then presented themselves: the nature of an oath, and the conditions when an oath was truthful.

Why is an oath of special value? In this sermon the underlying belief is that God is perfect and cannot deceive. Christian believers are called upon to be like God the Father, both perfect and without any taint of deception. The further assumption which this sermon draws upon and elucidates, coherent with the general spirit of Augustinian philosophy, is that the human person is directed to be one in all that it does. Human character should have to it a unity, and should not be at odds with itself ("Si discutiat homo quoties juret per totum diem, quoties se vulneret, quoties gladis linguae se feriat et transfigat, *quis in illo locus invenitur sanus*?" [italics ours]. By taking seriously the command or injunction not to lie or to deceive, one preserves a wholeness of the body and soul. By being unwilling to take oaths, the Christian is reminded that when he gives his word, he gives his word in the same fashion as God gives His word, and to do so is a serious act. When an oath or affirmation is false, the falseness does not rest in the words themselves, but in the uttering of them, since words are a production of the mind or soul ("*verbum procedit ex animo*"). If the soul is bent upon wickedness ("*nisi mens rea*"), then productions which emanate from the soul will, by necessity, be false and wrong. To the Christian this is wrong for the reason that God, often depicted as *logos*, and the model of human spiritual perfection, is mocked by an imperfect human act. The imperfection occurs when the human *logos* produces the false word, revealing a heart set in deception.

The simple example of asking some person if it has rained or not gives us two possibilities. One may answer rashly, but without deception, or one may answer deliberately, with an intent to deceive the listener. This latter act is, for Augustine, a dreadful act. It represents the mind out of order with the world, but paradoxically so. The mind has created a sentence, which is real, but that real thing is perverted against itself and is made with the purpose of deceiving. It is made doubly damning when, having fashioned a sentence by which to deceive the listener, the producer then avers that what he has said is true, and he declares it to be so by swearing that the sentence is true. The Latin sentence shows Augustine's strong dislike for this double act of deception: "*Videtis quam ista detestanda sit bellua, et de rebus humanis exterminanda*?"

Why we hesitate to justify a common law theory about intention based upon this single passage is that to do so would require that one carry into such a justification an Augustinian psychology about human nature in general, and this the common law does not. What Augustine wished to stress in his 180th Sermon was how a corrupted will could produce in evidence that which caused perjury. We know that the respondent answered "yes" to the question which had been put to him regarding rain not because he truly knew in fact that it had rained, but because it served his own secretive purposes to claim an oath that he truly knew that it had in fact rained.

It is not our concern to undertake either to present a synopsis of Augustine's religious philosophy, or to attempt to make it coherent or to defend it. To accept, at face value, that a single phrase from a body of sermons (which occupy 1700 folio columns in the standard edition[25]), is to make too bold a claim for a central theory of the common law. However, seen in a religious background which was concerned about man's propensity for sinfulness because of his fallen nature, and given the stress of early Christian philosophy upon the corrupted will of man, when one reads of *mens rea* within the context of Augustinian philosophy, it is possible for one to appreciate that this simple notion as to what relationship occurs between mental acts and public acts is, in fact, a complicated notion serving to account for human responsibility. Central to Christian belief was that one was responsible for one's acts, that one knowingly could sin. Paramount in the scale of perfection was a will subjected to God by obedience. The guilty mind, the criminal mind, was a result of willfulness, and to be willful was another way to create without regard to consequences. A lie is a wrongful creation.

Augustine was concerned to hold that knowledge was obtainable and that what was obtained was certain and reliable. It was not a question about doubting the existence of *a* or *the* sensible particular (a position not even attributable to Cicero in his *Academica*[26]), it was a question of whether one could gain personal knowledge, which Augustine would have expressed as knowledge of "the truth," and he argued that one could in Book Three of *Contra Academicos*.[27] It was also a predominant, even if curious, feature of Augustine's thought that he held that the will determined all that one did naturally, and that the will, when the cause of evil, was not itself another cause within a series of other efficient causes. Gilson has presented a cogent synopsis of Augustine's voluntarism, and we need not reproduce it here.[28] A possible distinction one could make in the Augustinian use of the concept of will would be to distinguish between the will as a force or cause and the product of a force or cause. It may be an acceptable distinction, but it contains little legal force. One might wish to argue by a form of measurement, suggesting that a heinous act reveals a heinous will, if such a distinction were made viable in law. But such an argument from proportion contains a fallacy which simple case law recognizes. Two acts could be done by two different defendants, and each act judged to be heinous, but one act could be done by a child, not knowing what he did was vicious or wrong, while the other act could have been caused by the hardened criminal. Each act, as an act, did great harm; but to argue from the harm done to the state of mind of its perpetrator is to indulge in a leap of faith and not of logical necessity.

We do not wish to give the impression that "intention" then was a vacuous notion. It was not. We wish only to argue that what Augustine may have meant by its use does not restrict its use totally. He was a student of Cicero's thought,[29] and we may turn to one of his writings to gain, more or less, a neutral guidance about intending and human acts. In *De Inventione,*[30] Cicero makes some sensible statements about, and an analysis of, various forms of legal pleas. We accept the truism that little of Roman criminal law influenced our common law origins, as Levitt and others have suggested.[31] Our purpose in turning to Cicero is to look for standard forms of use of legal notions, and it will be our contention that those common usages passed into Christian theological writing, through Tertullian, Ambrose, and Augustine, and then were transmuted into vehicles for Christian religious concepts.

We will recall from the previous chapter that the concept of the voluntary, as expressed in various conciliar canons, did not specify that one "intended." The grounds of responsibility rested upon voluntariness, and then upon what practical judgments a confessor might make about the guilt or innocence of his penitent. The grounds, we suggest, for determining the guilt or innocence of a penitent would rest upon what reasons he offered for what he did. In the *De Inventione* we read of a legal analysis of possible reasons for actions, and these we wish to consider before we return to conclude our analysis of the *Leges*.

The problem which one faces if he remains with an Augustinian analysis of error, or of falsity, is that the analysis for an inordinate act, such as perjury, returns one to a complicated theory about the will. Unless one accepts the Augustinian analysis of will, and how it causes all human acts, one will never ascertain the reason for an action. If God is the source of all truth, and if the human will is a corrupted and fallen power, then to account for criminal acts one must present all criminal law within the context of Christian theology and its assumptions about human nature. The common law has not such a rigorous precision, however admixed it is and was with Christian assumptions about human behavior.

Augustine's voluntarism, holding that the will (and whatever is entailed by his concept of it) is responsible for all human action, presents the legal philosopher with two distinct problems. One is the problem of meaning. Is there a consistent Augustinian position about the will? The other is this: admitted that there may be *the* Augustinian position, what conceptual clarity does it give to a legal concept and operator such as intention? One's feeling is that we are encumbered with two notions which, in the end, do not help us to "explain" a human action in a legal context. The common law may have had vestiges of Augustinian voluntarism, but these vestiges are not recrudescences very much alive in the common law. We are willing to admit that intention may have been borrowed by the early legal writers and statute draftsmen, and it may have been used without much historical appreciation. Its occurrence in the *Leges* indicated this. Even if one turns to a closer source for the usage, adverting to Ivo,[32] perhaps the immediate source for the usage of intention in the *Leges*, one needs to enlarge upon the occurrence of the term by making an appeal to accepted legal usages for the voluntary. One such source we have traversed by reading from the Councils.

We wish now to turn our attention to Cicero's *De Inventione*.[33] Although Augustine may have invented a new explanation to account for the nature of voluntary action, he did not invent the accepted usages of the term "voluntary." The term possessed a rich usage in the Latin language, and had been part of Roman law. When Cicero in *De Inventione* discourses about the nature of legal pleas, he gives us, perhaps, a hitherto unappreciated legal and rhetorical lexicon by use of which one may disentangle what is meant by "the voluntary" in its various forms. His method is not to present us with a secret entity or power which is called "the will."[34]

For legal philosophy, central legal notions may be understood in one of two ways. They may be understood as concepts, pure and simple, and then tested for their clarity and consistency. What will be the agreed upon test will depend upon what one accepts to be the aims of a legal system. A legal system need not pass a strict logical test to determine whether or not it functions as a serviceable legal system, and for this reason we do not specify what kind of test(s) one might use to judge a legal system. The aims of a consequentialist, or some variety of utilitarian, will not be the aims of a natural lawyer. Each system of legal theory may, most likely, be content to function with certain sets of unanalyzed primitives within the system. Present-day common law is able to function with its magistrates' courts in which a magistrate reaches his decision without need to offer reasons for that decision. The common law rules of procedure protect the litigant by permitting him to file for a new trial in a higher court should he wish, but if he does not file for a new trial, even though the magistrate did not offer reasons for his judicial finding, the litigant is then bound by the finding of the magistrate's court. One might find such to be illogical; but it is perfectly functional, and largely acceptable to many litigants. Trying to fit a meta-legal grid or matrix upon a legal system in order to establish if the system is a "good" or "proper" system is to forget that legal systems, in part, dwell in the practical order; and there are many avenues to the practical. But one may look at the central concepts of a legal system and try to see if they are understandable; or ask if so many exceptions are made to a single understanding of the central concepts because, it is discovered, no central concepts exist within the system as a whole.

On the other hand, one may eschew a purely logical approach to legal analysis for the sake of turning to a linguistic analysis of the law and its central notions. For the moment, by use of passages from *De Inventione*, we wish to attempt the second approach. We wish, too, to show that "intention," in whatever linguistic presentation it is clothed, whether it has been used to signify "will" or "motive" or "intent" or "wish" or "aim" or "purpose" or "cause" or "design" or "foresight," is made the more evident when it is seen functioning in some accepted legal context, as is presented by Cicero. The early legal linguistic usage demonstrates that one is not searching for a hidden entity, an "intention," as might be suggested by the appearance of the word in a bare statutory pronouncement such as the *Leges*. The linguistic history we wish to draw upon may free us from a search for hidden entities.*

* We are aware that there is a sacramental use for the term intention. For example, the Cambridge Manuscript of the *Questiones* of Stephen Langton (*The New Scholasticism*,

De Inventione was divided into two distinct books, both of which concern the practical art of legal rhetoric. The work has been referred to as a pleader's book. It is, for our purposes, a study in practical argument forms which one would employ in a court of law. For a modern student coming to the Bar such a work would appear to be a blend of evidence and practical exercises. For the legal philosopher the book contains a vast quantity of samples of "how to make oneself clear," in a vein reminiscent of Peirce's popular essay, "How To Make Our Ideas Clear."[35]

The following examples and usages occur in *De Inventione** which are of interest about intentional use of terms, and we cite them.

When reference is made to an interior sense, we encounter language of this style: "Memory is the firm mental grasp of matter and words." ("[*m*]*emoria est firma animi rerum ac verborum perceptio*." D.I. (I) vii, 9, pp. 20-21.) When Cicero draws a distinction between "act" and "fact" we read the following: "Every subject which contains in itself a controversy to be resolved by speech and debate involves a question about a fact, or about a definition, or about the nature of an act, or about legal processes." ("...*aut facti aut nominis aut generis aut actionis continet quaestionem*." D.I. (I) viii, 10, pp. 20-21.) Asking further questions about an "act" we read, "There is a controversy about the nature or character of an act when there is both agreement as to what has been done and certainty as to how the act should be defined, but there is a question ...about how important it is...." ("*Generis est controversia, cum et quid factum sit convenit, et quo id factum nomine appelari oporteat constat*...." D.I. (I) ix, 12, pp. 24-25.) About legal deeds we read, "It is

---

Volume IV (1930), p. 224, the article by Alys L. Gregory) records this usage of intention: Cd. 191: *Vtrum intentio baptizantis vel baptizati sit necessaria in baptismo*. One may read Chapters 14 and 15, "The Doctrine of Intention" and "Presumption of Intention" in *Principles of Sacramental Theology* by Bernard Leeming, S.J., (London: Longmans, Green and Co., 1956) to appreciate that this was a (somewhat) standard use of the term to mean "comply with." The modern business equivalent is revealed in the doctrine of agency, as, "Did the insurance agent comply with the aims of his Principal when preparing the insurance policy for the assured?" Aquinas speaks about "De Intentione" in S.T. 1a2ae, 12, 1, and there the term has wider than sacramental use only.

* We will cite from the work as follows: D.I., either part I or Part II, and give the paragraph and page number. A citation will then appear at: D.I. (1) {para (ix)} 36, pp. 72.

purgatio when the deed is acknowledged but *intent* is denied; it has three parts, ignorance, accident, necessity." ("*Purgatio est cum factum conceditur, culpa removetur. Haec partes habet tres, imprudentiam, casum, necessitatem.*" D.I. (I) xi, 15, pp. 30-31.) The same passage continues, "*Deprecatio* is used when the defendant acknowledges that he has given offence and has done so intentionally, and still asks to be forgiven; this can rarely occur." ("*Deprecatio est cum et peccasse et consulto peccasse reus se confitetur et tamen ut ignoscatur postulat: quod genus perraro potest accidere.*") One attempts to shift the criminal charge by "...transferring to another either the act or the intent or the power to perform the act...[e]ither the cause or the act itself is attributed to another." ("*Remotio criminis est sum id crimen quod infertur ab se et ab sua culpa et potestate in alim reus removere conatur...[s]i aut causa aut factum in alium transferetur.*")

Cicero shows other cases where "intent" may need to be construed, and he turns to written documents to discuss this matter.

> -In one case it seems that there is a variance between the true words and the intent of the author.... (*Nam tum verba ipsa videntur cum sententia scriptoris disdissidere...* [D.I. (I) xiii, 17, pp. 34-35].)
>
> -The first class [of case] is said to be concerned with the letter and the intent.... (*Quare primum genus de scripto et sententia...* [*loc. cit.*].)
>
> -What more certain proof of his intent could the author of the law have left than the statement which he wrote himself with great care and pains? Therefore, if there were no written documents we should be in sad need of them to learn from them the intent of the law giver.... (*Quod enim certius legis scriptor testimonium voluntatis suae relinquere potuit quam quod ipse magna cum cura atque diligentia scripsit? Quodsi litterae non exstarent, magno opere eas requireremus, ut ex eis scriptoris voluntas cognosceretur...* [D.I. (I) xxxix, 70, pp. 114-115].)
>
> -'A controversy over the letter and the intent occurs when one party follows the exact words that are written, and the other directs his whole pleading to what he says the writer meant. The one who bases his defence on the intent will sometimes show that the intent of the writer always had the same end in view and desired the same result, at other times he will show that the writer's purpose has to be modified to fit the occasion as a result of some act or event. (*Ex scripto et sententia controversia consistit, cum alter verbis ipsis quae scripta sunt*

> *utitur, alter ad id quod scriptorem sensisse dicet omnem adiungit dictionem. Scriptoris autem sententia ab eo qui sententia se defendet tum semper ad idem spectare et idem velle demonstrabitur; tum ex facto aut ex eventu aliquo ad tempus id quod instituit accommodabitur* [D.I. (II) xlii, 122, pp. 290-291].)
>
> -*Loc. cit.* at 123, But there is another kind of argument brought forward by advocates of the intent in which the wish of the writer is shown not to be absolute, i.e., having the same weight for every occasion and for every action, but it is argued that his wishes ought to be interpreted to fit the occasion in light of some act or some event. (*Aliud autem genus est eorum, qui sententiam inducunt, in quo non simplex voluntas scriptoris ostenditur, quae in omne tempus et in omne factum idem valeat; sed ex quodam facto aut eventu ad tempus interpretanda dicitur.*)

In one very long passage, the body of which we cite here Cicero shows the other side of the argument when one wishes to adhere to the letter of the law. The argument proceeds in this fashion:

> It is not right for us to argue about the intent of one who left us a clear indication of his intent in order that we might not be able to dispute it; that much inconvenience would result if it should be established as a principle that we may depart from the written word. For those who draw up a written document will not feel that what they have written will be fixed and unalterable, and judges will have no sure guide to follow if once they become accustomed to depart from the written word. Therefore if the object is to carry out the wish of the writer, counsel will urge that it is he rather than the opponents who adhere to the writer's wishes; for one gets much closer to a writer's intent if one interprets it from the writer's own words than one who does not learn the writer's intention from his own written document which he has left as a picture, one might say, of his own desires, but makes one's own inferences.
>
> (*Si aliud sensisse scriptor, aluid scripsisse dicetur, is qui scripto utetur haec dicet: non oportere de eius voluntate now argumentari, qui, ne id facere possemus, indicium nobis relinquerit suae voluntatis; multa incommoda consequi, si instituatur ut ab scripto recedatur. Nam et eos qui aliquid scribant non existimaturo id quod scripserint ratum futurum; et eos quo indicent certum quod sequantur nihil habituros si semel ab scripto recedere consueverint. Quod si voluntas scriptoris conservanda sit, se, non adversarios, a voluntate eius stare. Nam multo propius accedere ad scriptoris voluntatem eum qui ex ipsius eam litteris interpretetur quan illum qui sententiam scriptoris non ex ipsius scripto spectet, quod ille suae voluntatis quasi imaginem reliquerit, sed domesticis suspicionibus perscrutetur* [D.I. (II) xliv, 128, pp. 296-297].)

We wish now to turn to other passages in the work which illustrate Cicero's thoughts about human actions. To this point one can see that a document is said to embody an intent of its author by asking us to look to its purpose, or its time of construction, or to the simple construction of the sentences themselves, arguing here that an author is able to express his feelings and intentions and desires by use of sentences. The word "intentio" never appears. What word does appear is either a form of "voluntas" or "sententia," or a construction from legal phraseology itself, when he said "culpa removetur" to mean that criminal intent has been denied (at D.I. (I) xi, 15, p. 30). The rare occurrence of a form of intention does appear in this way,

> ...after that one may use the most effective argument, a comparison of the act and *purpose* [italics ours] of the opponents with the letter of the law, showing what was written, what was done, what the judge has sworn to do. (*...postea, quod vehementissimum est, facti aut* intentionis [emphasis ours] *adversariorum cum ipso scripto contentione, quid scriptum sit, quid factum, quid iuratus iudex* [D.I. (II) xliii, pp. 292-295].)

This is the form of intentio which one will read in some medieval* uses of the word at the time of Bracton. But "intention" seldom occurs, and its few occurrences never appear to signify a "criminal mind." When Cicero, in those rare occasions, does employ "intentio" (in some form) it appears to mean design or purpose. One might argue that it has some association with a blend of formal and final causes, but Cicero never develops such a notion.** If one is considered to be free of guilt, the phrase we read, or a form thereof, is "*quod absit a culpa*," which is rendered simply as "because he is free of guilt."***

Cicero makes a general statement about the nature of argument, telling one how arguments are formed and from what they are drawn. He tells his reader that "All propositions are supported in argument by attribute

---

* Cap. 13, "*De differentia inter volunatem & finem & intention*; Cap. 16, "*Vtrum omnis actio ex intentione & fine pensetur.*" *Sententiarum Pars II* of *Petri Pictauiensis*, Roberti Pulli (Paris: ed. of Hvgonis Mathou'd, M.DC.LV).

** Were this an important notion in *De Inventione* one would have assumed that "intentio" in this form would have made regular appearances throughout the work, and it is plain that it does not.

*** From p. 268, D.I. (II) xxxiii, 101.

of persons or of actions" (D.I., p. 70). He holds that "purpose" ("*consilia*") is an attribute of a person (*loc. cit.*). His definition of purpose is: "*Purpose* is a deliberate plan for doing or not doing something." ("*Consilium est aliquid faciendi aut non faciendi excogitata ratio*." D.I. (I) xxv, 36 p. 74.) He says (*loc. cit.*), that "The attributes of actions are partly coherent with the action itself, partly considered in connection with the performance of it, partly adjunct to it and partly consequent upon its performance." He joins the class of person and action when he speaks about the category of *Manner*, and we cite him directly:

> *Manner*...is the category under which one inquires how and in what state of mind the act was performed. Its parts are intention and lack of intention. How we seek to calculate one's intention from the acts which one performed secretly or openly,* by the use of force or by persuasion. Lack of intention, on the other hand, is related to justification, the sub-heads of which are ignorance, accident and necessity, and to emotions, such as annoyance, anger, love and the others belonging to the same class. (*Modus autem est in quo, quemadmodum et quo animo factum sit, quaeritur. Eius partes sunt* prudentia et imprudentia [emphasis ours]. Prudentiae *autem ratio quaeritur ex eis, quae clam, palam, vi, persuasione fecerit.* Imprudentia *autem in purgationem confertur, cuius partes sunt inscientia, casus, necessitas, in affectionem animi, hoc est, molestiam, iracundiam, amorem et cetera quae in simili genere versantur* [D.I. (I) xxvii, 41, pp. 78-81].)

It is to be noted, and we have the terms emphasized, that the state of mind Cicero reports is spoken of by use of "imprudentia" or "prudentia," and that in its positive sense the term connotes: foreseeing (a rare use), good sense, sagaciousness, practical judgment, discretion, acquaintance with a thing, knowledge of how to do, and even a meaning of "statesmanship." We are not given a doctrine about a hidden something, an intention. When intention is referred to in this context, it is the notion of intention which is calculated from an act, a sense which did come into common law use early on. One does not have the presence or absence of a bare intention. One looks to assign reasons for actions.** All of these observations on the part of Cicero

* The translator states that "acts performed openly as characterized by violence, passion and daring, secret acts by deceit, fraud, etc."

** He says (*loc. cit.*, p. 81) "*Result* is the outcome of any action; in this connexion it is customary to inquire what happened after each thing, what is happening, and what will tend to develop a central point about legal argument: that "an argument seems to be a device of some sort to demonstrate with probability or prove irrefutably (D.I. (I), p. 83).

When he comes to speak about the cause of human acts he uses language of this kind:

> The cause of an act falls under the heads of impulse and premeditation. An impulse is what urges a person to do something without thinking about it, because of some feeling or emotional state: examples are love, anger, grief, intoxication, and in fact every state in which the mind seems to have been so affected that it could not examine the act with care and deliberation, but did what it did from a certain mental urge rather than from reflection.
>
> (*Causa tribuitur in impulsionem et in ratiocinationem. Impulsio est quae sine cogitatione per quandam affectionem animi facere aliquid hortatur, ut amor, iracundia, aegritudo, vinolentia et omnino omnia in quibus animus ita videtur affectus fuisse ut rem perspicere cum consilio et cura non potuerit et id quod fecit impetu quodam animi potius quam cogitatione fecerit* [D.I. (II) v, 17, pp. 180-181].)

The same passage continues,

> Premeditation on the other hand is careful and thoughtful reasoning about doing or not doing something. It is said to have been present when the mind seems to have avoided or sought something to do or not to do for a definite cause; if an act is said to have been performed because of friendship, etc.
>
> (*Ratiocinatio est autem diligens et considerate faciendi aliquid aut non faciendi excogitatio. Ea dicitur interfuisse tum, cum aliquid faciendi aut non faciendi certa de causa vitasse aut secutus esse animus videbitur; si amicitiae quid causa factum dicetur, et. [loc. cit].*)*

The portion is remarkable for its definiteness. He continues his instructions to the prosecuting counsel and tells what must be done to make reasons

happen." ("*Eventus est exitus alicuius negoti, in quo quaeri solet quid ex quaque re evenerit, eveniat, eventurum sit.*")

* In a like vein, one reads in *De Officiis, Book I. viii* (27), "But in any case of injustice it makes a vast deal of difference whether the wrong is done as a result of some impulse of passion, which is usually brief and transient, or whether it is committed willfully and with premeditation (*...an consulto et cogitata...*); for offenses that come through some sudden impulse are less culpable than those committed designedly and with malice aforethought (*...quae meditata et praeparata inferuntur...*)." *Cicero XXI De Officiis,* [translated by Walter Miller, (Loeb Classical Library, 1975)], pp. 27-29.

evident. The next paragraph begins in this way, and with it we will close our citations on the matter of premeditation:

> For no one can be convinced that a deed has been done *unless some reason is given why it was done* [italics ours].[36] Therefore the prosecutor when he says that something was done on impulse, will be under the necessity of dilating upon that passion and, as it were, agitation and state of mind, with the full powers of his thought and expression, and of showing how great is the force of love, what powerful mental agitation arises from anger or from any of the causes by which he claims that the defendant was urged to commit this crime. Here pains must be taken that it may not seem strange that a mind disquieted by such passion should undertake some crime.
>
> (*Nam nihil factum esse cuiquam probatur, nisi aliquid quare factum sit ostenditur. Ergo accusator, cum impulsione aliquid factum esse dicet, illum impetum et quandam commotionem animi affectionemque verbis et sententiis amplificare debebit et ostendere quanta vis sit amoris, quanta animi perturbatio ex iracundia fiat aut ex aliqua causa earum, qua impulsum aliquem id fecisse dicet* [D.I. (II), v, 19, pp. 182-183].)

A few lines down, at the close of the instruction, Cicero states that the prosecutor should be able to explain mental disturbance, and to offer parallels illustrating that crimes can be committed from impulse.

The language he uses is,

> This can be done by citing examples of those who have done something under a similar impulse and by collecting parallels and by explaining the nature of mental disturbance.
>
> (*Hic et exemplorum commemoratione, qui simili impulsu aliquid commiserint, et similitudinum collatione et ipsius animi affectionis explicatione curandum est ut non mirum videatur si quod ad facinus tali perturbatione commotus animus accesserit* [*loc. cit.*].)

Linking his instruction that reasons must be given for actions, he makes a sensitive distinction by stating that a deed and the reason for a deed are conceptually distinct:

> The result is deceptive when the matter turns out[37] differently from what the defendants are said to have expected; for example, if one be said to have killed a person other than he wished to kill because he was misled by resemblance, or suspicion, or false description; or to have killed a man under whose will he did not inherit, because he thought that he would be an heir under that will; for (the prosecutor will say) we should not judge *his intent* [italics ours] by the result, but consider with what intent and hope his mind set out a career of

crime; the pertinent fact is the purpose with which anyone performs an act, not what success he attains.

(*Eventus autem tum fallit, sum aliter accidit atque eit qui arguuntur arbitrati esse dicuntur: ut, si qui dicatur alium occidisse ac voluerit, quod aut similitudine aut suspicione aut demonstratione false deceptus sit; aut eum necasse, cuius testamento non sit heres, quod eo testamento se heredem arbitratus sit. Non enim ex eventu cogitationem spectari oportere, sed qua cogitatione animus et spe ad maleficium profectus sit considerari; quo animo quid quisque faciat, non quo casu utatur, ad rem pertinere* [D.I. (II), vii, 23, pp. 184-185].)

One may appreciate that the notion of transferred malice,* at times denominated as oblique intention, is not a novel notion. There is a great similarity between the conceptual content of the passage just cited and its modern counterpart, revealed in *Latimer*, as distinguished from *Pembliton*. We pause here, however, to warn against too facile a comparison. The broad conceptual notes of the concept bear similarity, but not identity. The modern doctrine, it needs to be urged, is to be accepted with some reserve, and some writers have stated this warning.[38] Edwards[39] believes that Lord Coleridge was less than clear when he attempted to distinguish *Latimer* from *Pembliton*. The language of section 20 of *Offences Against the Person Act*, (24 & 25 Victoriae, Cap. 100) is cited below, and may provide the reason for the presumed distinction between the two cases. It will be remembered that the defendant in *Latimer*, with his belt buckle, took aim at *A* but hit *B*, the barmaid, by mistake, yet wounded her seriously. It all occurred in the midst of a tavern brawl. In section 20 we read:

20. Whosoever shall unlawfully and maliciously wound or inflict any grievous bodily Harm upon any other Person, either with or without any Weapon or Instrument, shall be guilty of a Misdemeanor...

One was under no mental obligation to oneself, in order to violate the provisions of this statute, to specify against whom one had intended to direct his violence; it was enough, simply, to direct violence against any person whatsoever. If the violence arose within a context deemed to have been

---

* The term "general malice" was first used in *R. v. Hunt* (1825) 1 Mood 93. Use later favored "transferred malice" to denote the same legal concept.

unlawful (as would be a pub brawl), then the *actus reus* of the crime was satisfied if some person were subjected to grievous bodily harm.

Pembliton, having been decided twelve years earlier in 1874, concerned a fight, during which the defendant hurled a stone at *A* but hit, not *B*, but a window and broke it. He was charged in the indictment under the *Malicious Damage Act* (24 & 25 Victoriae, c. 97, s. 51). The concept of general or transferred malice, upon reserve,* was held not to apply to the facts of the case, the jury having found that the defendant threw the stone intending it hit some person and not intending to break or strike a window. Since the jury found as a *fact* that the defendant did not willfully intend to strike or break a window, the court then accepted that finding of fact and adjudged that the law in question, which required an accused under the statute to have wilfully intended to damage property, had not been abridged. Blackburn, J., offers one a clearer reading of the problem in the case than does Lord Coleridge, C. J., and we will close by citing a short excerpt from Blackburn, J.:

> Can this man be considered, on the case submitted to us, as having wilfully broken a pane of glass? The jury might perhaps have found on this evidence that the act was malicious, because they might have found that the prisoner knew that the natural consequences of his act would be to break the glass, and although that was not his wish, yet that he was reckless whether he did it or not; but the jury have not so found, and I think it is impossible to say in this case that the prisoner has maliciously done an act which he did not intend to do.[40]

There are numerous passages from *De Inventione* which may be cited to show that Cicero intended guilt to be found for a criminal act only after reasons for acts or omissions had been given by or had been elicited from the accused. The giving of reasons could occur when the prosecutor had advanced an argument which could not be defended, or when counsel for the defense offered an excuse which could not be met by the prosecutor. We do not think it furthers our comparison here to advance his every Latin usage which might revolve around the concept of an intent. We have excluded one usage of "intentio" which is: The charge is. This rendering occurs at *De*

---

* *Pembliton* was decided in the Court for Crown Cases Reserved.

Inventione, II, xxvi, 79, p. 244, and appears in this way: "*Accusatur* (He is brought to trial). *Intentio est: Iniuria sororem occidisti* (The charge is: "You killed your sister without warrant."). It is obvious that *intentio* is not being used in that way either in Augustine or in the *Leges*.

If the argument is advanced that *De Inventione* represents a rather young Cicero, and, perhaps, an unreflective usage of key legal terms (which we think is an ill-founded argument with regard to legal usage, nevertheless), one may fortify the worth of the comparison by turning to the late and mature Cicero which appears in his *Topica* (composed, it is assumed, in 44 B. C., a short while before his death). In section XV of *Topica* he proceeds to discuss "...efficient forces which are called causes."[41] Having made various distinctions which may pertain to various concepts of cause, there appears in section XVII a long statement about cause in relation to an intended act, and we reproduce it here in full because of the force it has upon the roots of criminal intention:

> XVII. But of the causes which are not uniform in operation, some are evident and others are concealed. Those are evident which affect our impulses or judgment; those that are controlled by fortune are concealed. For since nothing happens without cause, this is exactly what Fortune is, an event which is the result of an obscure and unseen cause. Again these results which are produced are partly *unintentional*, [italics ours] and partly due to our own volition. The unintentional are the product of necessity; those in our own volition are accomplished by design. To illustrate, throwing a weapon is an act of the will, but hitting some one unintentionally is the act of Fortune. This distinction supplies the beam which you use to prop up a weak case in your pleadings: 'Perchance he did not throw the weapon, but it slipped from his hand.' Mental agitation belongs with acts performed in ignorance or lack of foresight. For though such a state of mind is voluntary – for these conditions yield to reproof and admonition – still they produce such violence of emotion that acts which are voluntary seem sometimes to be necessary and certainly unintentional.
>
> (XVII. *Sed tamen earum causarum quae non sunt constantes aliae sunt perspicuae, aliae latent. Perspicuae sunt quae appetitionem animi iudiciumque tangunt; latent quae subiectae sunt fortunae. Cum enim nihil sine causa fiat, hoc ipsum est fortuna, qui eventus obscura causa et latenter efficitur. Etiam ea quae fiunt partim sunt ignorata partim voluntaria; ignorata, quae necessitate effecta sunt; soluntarsia, quae consilio.* [Note:

Hubbard states, and we include, this footnote to this passage: "*After* consilio *The MSS. have* Quae autem fortuna, vel ignorata vel voluntara (What is accomplished by Fortune is either unintentional or voluntary): bracketed by Schuetz (1804 edition).] *Nam iacere telum voluntatis est, ferire quem nolueris fortunae. Ex quo aries subicitur ille in vestris actionibus: si telum manu fugit magis quam iecit. Cadunt etaim in ignorationem atque imprudentiam perturbationes animi; quae quamquam sunt voluntariae--obiurgatione enim et admonitione deiciuntur--tamen habent tantos motus, ut ea quae voluntaria sunt aut necessaria interdum aut certe ignorata videantur* [*Topica*, XVII, 63-65, pp. 430-431].)*

The legal grammar of Cicero employs intentional operators. If responsibility is to be assigned to an agent for what he did, then one looks for verbs which show a conative or volitive disposition. The transition from an affective source or disposition to an esoteric quality, in part, reveals itself in Augustine when he centers human responsibility in the Will (as any number of his major writings reveal). But we think it would be a mistaken judgment to argue that Augustine invented an "intentional" operator by which to account for, or with which to assign guilt to, human failing. He remained within the volitive tradition however much he hypostasized the Will as a faculty.

One may cite two works of St. Augustine in which, if one were to argue for intention as a concept central to his ethical theory, intention plays a relatively small part in the language of the works. Reviewing *De Mendacio* and *Contra Mendacium Ad Consentium*[42] will reveal how little the word

---

* The passage itself has reference to a fragment of *The Twelve Tables* (Loeb edition by E. H. Warmington: Heinemann, 1967), fragment 24 on p. 493: "If a missile has sped from his hand, and the holder has not aimed it..." ["*Si telum manu fugit ma* (*gis quam iecit*)..."]. One may also read in St. Augustine's *De Libero Arbitrio Voluntatis*, Book One, Chapter IV, the following parallel: "E. If to murder means to kill an man, murder can occur sometimes without sin. For when the soldier kills an enemy or the judge or official puts a criminal to death, or when, [italics ours] *by chance, a man unwillingly or unwisely lets a weapon escape from his hand, I do not think that these men sin when they slay a man*. Augustine: I agree." (English edition by A. S. Benjamin and L. H. Hackstaff [New York: Bobbs-Merrill Company, Inc., 1964], p. 9). Evodius, a few lines down in section 27, uses this language: "The law is not at all wrong to punish the man who willfully and knowingly murders his master," an example of language not known to Augustine, and derived, it appears, from his study of Cicero. One may also refer to *The Institutes of Justinian*, Lib. iv, Tit. xviii, D. 5.34., pp. 505-506 for passing reference to the same passage from the *Tables* in the edition, Latin-English, prepared by T. C. Sandars (London: Longmans, Green, and Co., 1883 [7th edition]).

"intentio" is used throughout the two treatises, yet it could be argued how appropriate would be that term, were it a developed ethical concept which functioned as the pivotal term of a system, to function as a central metaphor or vehicle when discussing so deliberate an act as "lying."

It is clear that for Augustine the example of lying, as well as blaspheming, provided a strong model for that kind of human activity in which one course of action contradicted another course of action.[43] The extra-mental and public, that statement which one might assert (although Augustine did not confine lying to utterances; one could lie by silence), could be in conflict with the intra-mental and the private. The danger latent in this model, we would suggest, is to attempt to equate the concept of intention with that of the act of lying. As a concept, "intention" in part grows out of the Christian heritage which condemned lying. But that is not the whole of the concept. One can observe, as we hope the examples from Cicero indicated, that Roman law contained many rhetorical models of what reasons for an action or legal omission might be presented to exculpate or legally to blame. To lie might be one of a member of a legal set of acceptable candidates only.

By undertaking textual examination–permitting one in part to examine St. Augustine's theory of mental operations–it should be noted that the sentence which immediately precedes "*Ream linguam non facit, nisi mens rea*," is "*Interest quemadmodum verbum procedit ex animo*." The "*verbum*" is a production "*ex animo*." The falsity of a lie rests in the ability of the soul to produce what is not the case. The production is not the center of the lie. Were it, then one would have a reader-card theory of truth, wherein the proposition or utterance would be akin to a reader-card, and the state of affairs (in the world) would, or would not, correspond to the sentence on the reader-card. In part this is so, since what is produced may not be a correct printout of what actually is the case. Yet we should recall that Augustine has turned the example around once again; he has stated that what is actually said does, actually, correspond to what is the case; however, one has nevertheless told a lie.

His is not a rhetorical trick. It has its foundation in the early theology of Christian belief wherein "God" was believed to be true and one throughout his triune processions. The Son was believed to be the Word which progressed from the Father. If the "Word" did not represent the "mind" of the Father, then the procession could not be "true" owing to the difficulty that what found its origin in the Father would not, however, represent the mind of the Father. We are not attempting to argue for the logical coherence of the doctrine of the Trinity, and we trust that our statement of it (in part) is not obscure. For the Christian it would appear that he wanted to model himself after Christ (in all ways), who Himself was an expression of the Will of the Father. It is for this reason, we suggest, that Augustine wanted to model the inherent structure of a lie not in what was produced but in how it was produced. His expression reflects the mind of early Christian speculation. To cite but one early source we may turn to Lactantius (250-325 A.D.) who himself gave expression to such early theorizing when, in chapter 49 of the *Epitome of the Divine Institutes*,[44] we may read:

> He that knows not Christ is for ever alienated from truth and from God....He who acknowledges not the Son cannot acknowledge the Father. This is wisdom, this the mystery of God. It is through the Son that God has willed it that He should be acknowledged and worshipped....Yet it must not be imagined that there are two Gods: Father and Son are *one*. For since the Father loves the Son, and assigns all things to him, and since the Son loyally obeys the Father, and wills only what He wills, so great a fellowship cannot be disrupted, so that they can be spoken of as two, in whom substance and will and faith are one – the Son through the Father, the Father through the Son. One honour must be paid to both, as to one God; and it must be so divided through two worships that their very division may be overcome by a bond that cannot be broken. Nothing will be left to him who divides the Father from the Son, or the Son from the Father.

From a reading of St. Augustine's two treatises it is apparent that he treats of lying by considering what is logically prior and what is logically posterior in a lie. It is not what is produced which is the artifact of a lie, as might be a proposition or an utterance or a label; the essence of a lie consists of the willingness of an agent *to produce* a lie. Augustine offered an intentional analysis of a lie. The modern counterpart in the criminal law is the law which governs various types of criminal attempts.

Were he to have concentrated only upon a material fact, the "that" which was produced, his definition would not have possessed a logical completeness. A material happening may be explained as an instance of a miscalculation, as an accident, as a simple mistake, as that which was done through non-culpable ignorance, as that which was done outside of the control of an agent, or as an act done by inadvertence,[45] among the list of possible reasons (or explanations) for the occurrence of Ø. But willing to lie will not admit of these exempting moves; one has to admit that a lie was intended, and afterwards decide (because of duress, or necessity, or human frailty) whether ø-ing will be excused.

We may be accused of having begged the question by stating that the analysis of lying which Augustine made was itself an intentional analysis of lying, but we can see little other room for some other analysis of his account of lying. One may disclaim the beliefs which Augustine propagandized; one may fault him for failing to distinguish, with appropriate seriousness, the degrees of culpability to be attached to lying, but such would be to miss what he did say. If one produces, it is assumed that one intends to produce. That statement, we are aware, needs to be offered in a restrictive sense. A poet, or an artist, or a writer, or a scientist, may claim that he did not intend to produce <u>this</u> particular "x" (whatever it be: a fact, a sentence, a composition, an experiment), and what he did produce he may argue, as in the *Ion*, happened and he knows not how. That we are able to make any human production at all may, in itself, be an ontological mystery, just as the fact of any universe whatsoever may be an ontological mystery: we have no fact, nor any theory, which will bring us outside of the given. That there is a given molecular arrangement in the universe, at any moment, no fact in the universe, or the history of it we imagine, will yield. An infinite series will not yield a "why" outside of the series (in a final sense); the creationist closes fact in mystery. Why this fact? Because of a fiat. Why a fiat? One ends with the unanswerable.

The catch in such a puzzle is that one may offer some reason to himself on why he did this or that. One may say little more than, "I intend not to answer," and one has, by such a locution, given an intentional account for what one has refused to do. We are aware that some extremely difficult cases can arise from a wide use of the concept of "intentionally to produce,"*

* The model which comes to mind, and *Ion* may be the impetus for such a model, is the problem which present-day analysis may provide. One can call such an example the problem

but, for the moment, we wish to argue from the restrictive application of the notion. Augustine's assumption– and it is open to logical question–is that "to produce" entails "to intend to produce." At law it is sound law. The bank

---

of the residue of an act. Let us offer this example, in no way unusual (as a clinical example, but highly unusual in commonplace life), of the liar. Assume that *A* has told a deliberate falsehood, and, when caught in it, admits that he lied. Assume further– as if it were a clinical experiment–that *A* is asked if he did lie, and if he knew that he did lie. He answers, "Yes." If he shows remorse for what he had done, as might be argued from the *Nicomachean Ethics* (Book III), one could conclude that his action was both voluntary and involuntary. It was, it would seem, voluntary in that he produced it; it was involuntary in that he showed regret for what he had done, and would not have shown regret, or the like, for what he had done, if what he had done had been fully within his control. But this is still not an exhaustive account of compulsory or involuntary act. It may be that we have to use the model of hypnosis. An analyst might argue that at some time in the life of the patient the patient suffered some harm in a room of this type, and that when in a room of this type, rather than to recall to mind the harm he suffered and subject himself to emotional anguish, the patient simply refuses to face reality in any simple way; the act of lying provides for the patient the escape he needs from reality. What has been produced by the analyst is an explanation of an action, the explanation itself a residue not to be perceived in the ordinary intentional explanation when *A* simply stated that he lied, and knew that he had lied. What the residue model provides is an account of an action which the agent does not, and, possibly cannot, give. The hard philosophical question arises when one wonders if a single case of this kind can then be extrapolated to fit *any* intentional action? The fundamental problem it touches is: How complete must an explanation be to be considered to be a complete explanation?

The difficulty is further compounded when one sees that two questions are being considered in the one problem. One is first-inquiring if such a concept as the "residue of an act" is a valid concept, or whether it is purely a depiction of the imagination. Philosophical error may be brought about when one moves from the hypothetical "let us suppose *x* to be the case" to "and it is a case one must answer." If one admits that the hypothetical case is of value (without analyzing the test for "value"), then one faces an empirical difficulty of locating the concept, i.e., are there accounts of actions in the real or extra-mental world which lend themselves to the features of a concept which speaks about the residue of an act? The famous case is that of Dr. Morton Prince who treated Miss Beauchamp and her five separate personalities, a case which the law would presently classify under a form of automatism. What happens in rare cases such as these is that the burden of deciding what to do with them in any classificatory sense is thrown upon the jury for them to accept the testimony of the defendant, or his assigns, as "fact." [One may refer to Chapter 10, "Automatism and Drunkenness," pp. 165-182 in Nigel Walker's book, *Crime and Insanity in England* (Edinburgh: The University Press, 1968), volume one, to read how unsatisfactorily such is treated by the common law at present.] The criminal law will, at the very least, permit a defense to certain charges by means of either an appeal to diminished responsibility on the part of the defendant, or an appeal to automatism. One has not solved the conceptual problem; one has only, at law, permitted a utilitarian solution by which the jury, or judge alone (in certain cases), may render a verdict of Not Guilty by reason of diminished responsibility or automatism. The philosophical problem remains as to what constitutes a full and final explanation of an intentional action.

robber can be charged not only with actual robbing of the bank, but he may be charged as well with intending to rob the bank: conspiracy.

Augustine was, as we have indicated, able to solve for himself how an intentional action could, at the same time, be an action that an agent might now wish for, and he did this by claiming that the will was corrupted by lust. As a concept, "lust" embraced more than simple venery. He spoke about the "chastity" of the mind with regard to lying. We need not pursue the implications of the notion here since it is not germane to any argument about intention.

When one reads the two treatises on lying one notices the first, and earlier, treatise does not employ "intentio" other than once when it occurs in the phrase, "*addita etiam intentione vel salutis tuende....*"[46] The operative verbs in *De Mendacio* are verbs which concern speaking, enunciating, producing, thinking, willing, or verbs which directly state that one has lied, as in "*os autem quod mentitur, non corpus, sed animam occidit*" (col. 494 of Migne).* None of the verb constructions which Augustine employs are directly intentional; one must read an intentional reference into the verbs, and such an interpretation of his text means that one must seek other than a primary meaning for his employment of verbs in standard grammatical constructions. This would be clearly to distort the obvious.

Contra Mendacium followed some twenty-five years after Augustine's first treatise on Lying. Although he considered *De Mendacio* to be complicated and somewhat unclear – as we are told in his *Retractationes* (1, PL 32.630) – he permitted it to remain. The latter work, *Contra Mendacium*, for which there is no need here to summarize, represented a mature Augustine, and appeared near to the time of his *Sermons*. What is of concern in the work is that it reveals a use of the term "intentione" which was absent

---

* "*Mentior, itus*" occurs throughout the first text. It is a verb which directly means to lie, or to cheat, to deceive. It is not an intentional compound in which the intentional aspect of the verb must be conjoined to the primary sense of the verb, as in "One intends..." + "...to lie" = "*Mentior.*" One would use some form of "intendo, did, tum and *sum*" if one wished to call attention to a distinct act of the mind, as in "*Intendere animum, to direct one's thoughts* or *attention to* any thing."

from the earlier work. It also provides us with a link from one period of use to the period of the *Leges*.

The value of reviewing the Latin text of *Contra Mendacium* is that it reveals the addition of a newer grammatical apparatus. Not only are the standard verbs present, such as willing, desiring, planning, lying, obtaining, knowing, thinking, causing, and the like, but we read how the concept of *an* intention is stressed and pointed out independently of the other forms used in verbal discourse. Augustine develops the metaphor of speaking the truth from one's heart, "*Qui loquitur veritatem in corde suo* [PL 40.526]." It is a metaphor drawn from Scripture, and it implies that the very act of telling the truth is an act whose "truthfulness" lies hidden from the world but is known to God, since God knows the full content of a man's soul. The echo of such a concept may have been the warning given by Christ that adultery may be committed in a man's heart only should a man fully entertain the desire to transgress the moral law, circumstances only, in the main, preventing him from acting fully in accord with his desires. The devoutly consummated wish ranks in seriousness with the full-blooded act.

He then proceeds to close the portion (Chapter 6 at section 14: PL 40:527) in which the metaphor of the heart is developed by quoting from Psalm xiv, 3: *Qui non egit dolum in lingua sua.* The effect is, from the prior clause, that if one speaks the truth from his heart then "...he has no need to deceive with his tongue." The force of the Latin, by use of "egit" and "dolum," is to tell the reader that if one has taken care to listen to his own conscience or voice of his heart, then he need not labor to construct with care and deceitfulness a lie to be spoken. The phrase is compressed, but it carries in its language the force of to do with careful but deceitful deliberation; deliberation being that activity of the soul which is private and known only to one's private self.[47]

Beginning at Caput VII [PL 40:527] one may observe the Latin occurrences of intention. We shall cite the sentences seriatim:

> Caput VII.–*Mendacium nulla velut bona* intentione [emphasis ours] *admittendum.*
>
> *Aut enim licebit utrumque pari ratione defendere, ut ideo haec non esse dicantur injusta, quia ea facta sunt* intentione [emphasis ours] *qua deprehenderentur injusti, aut si sana*

doctrina nec propter inveniendos haereticos vult nos cum feminis impudicis saltem corpore, non mente, misceri, profecto nec propter inveniendos haereticos vult a nobis saltem voce, non mente, aut immundam haeresim praedicari, aut castam catholicam blasphemari [PL 40:528].

18. *Interest quidem plurimum, qua casua, quo fine, qua* intentione [emphasis ours] *quid fiat: sed ea quae constat esse peccata, nullo bonae causae obtentu, nullo quasi bono fine, nulla velut bona* intentione [emphasis ours] *facienda sunt* [PL 40:528 at 18].

Caput VIII. – 19. *Peccatum esse ex* intentione *aliud alio levius; non tamen faciendum levius, quod saepe alterius generis peccato gravius est* [PL 40:529].

There is a use of "intendens" from the New Testament which is cited by St. Augustine (Galatians, vi. 1) in which "delicto" appears:

Fratres, et si praeoccupatus fuerit homo in aliquo delicto, vos qui spirituales estis, instruite hujusmodi in spiritu mansuetudinis, intendens *te* [emphasis ours] *ipsum, ne et tu tenteris* [PL 40: 537].

Multum autem fatendum est propinquare justitiae, et quamvis re ipsa nondum, jam tamen spe atque indole animum esse laudandum, qui nunquam nisi hac intentione [emphasis ours] *mentitur, qua vult prodesse alicui, nocere autem nemini* [PL 40:541 at Caput XVI].

Sed nultum est ut iste in tantum perseveret affectus, ne intentione [emphasis ours] *desit effectus* [PL 40:543 at Caput XVIII].

The path of the arguments is plain enough for one to see. The intention of an act determines the quality of the act when one speaks of human actions and qualities. The definition of a good act is that a good intention is present. "[I]ntention" functions here as that aspect of a human production which the agent controls. Augustine is not concerned with non-subjective qualities, as in "kindness which kills." The aunt may do a good deed by leaving an inheritance to her grandson, and the inheritance may be the cause of his self-destruction. The effects of a good act do not concern Augustine; in fact, he takes a very hard attitude towards those who would argue from conceived effects to a change in a cause, as when one might argue that unless such and such were done (unless one lied to an enemy but for the achievement of a possibly good end) harm might ensue. In both treatises on lying he will not permit a lie to be told so that good may result. The moral quality which a human act possesses flows first from what the agent intended, or what Augustine at times refers to as what one conceived in one's heart. There is a mild doctrine of "effects" when effect means what effect the agent himself desired. The force of a good act rests in what the agent wills himself to do; if his willing is good or virtuous (meaning that the cause of the aim or the intention arose from a good will), then should the results of the act fail to match the hopes or expectations which launched the act, the agent is not at fault.[48]

The term "intention," when it makes its appearance in our legal literature through the *Leges* and in Bracton, comes to us with a rich past. It is a cluster-concept which requires care to separate out its various and different strands; it is also a metaphor, used by Augustine, when drawing upon biblical tradition, for the secretness of the heart and for the secretness of why men act. The notion stands variously for aims, purposes, goals, ends, foreseeings, wishes, or for that final hope that one might entertain as a reason for doing what he did. There is nothing precise about the term; it is not an H_20 term, nor is it a precise term as, for example, in Greek tradition one might be able to distinguish a wish (*boulsis*) from a desire (*orexis*). Nor does the term, in its early appearance in Augustine, offer any clear rule on how one might distinguish, conceptually and grammatically, "what one wanted to do" from "one should have realized the following consequences would have followed from what one did." There is no foresight test contained in the elements of "intentio." One may equally be referring to the subjective aspect of a human act *or* to the objective aspect of a human act. Augustine places the logical priority on the intention of the doer, asking him to inquire of himself his true reason for doing this act. One may assume that this was a minor flaw of early moral and legal writing not to have qualified the term rigorously. One may have need to make the logically unconvincing reply that in matters of moral and legal reasoning one seldom sees so clearly.

In the next chapter we shall show how these early rich roots of responsibility began to work in the common law. One sees, if one is willing to look, how the wisdom within the various traditions grew into the criminal law, no rigid rule of selection evident at any one time. The law drew upon philosophical sources when it adopted the language and arguments of the scholastics, who, in turn, had drawn upon Plato, Aristotle, the early Fathers, and the pronouncements of the Church. We will begin by inquiring where Bracton brought the criminal law with his early notions of intention.*

* Please refer to the Addendum, this chapter, for references to Ivo of Chartres.

Endnotes Chapter 2

1. In the edition of Peter Abelard's *Ethics*, edited and translated by D. E. Luscombe (Oxford Medieval Texts: Oxford, At The Clarendon Press, 1971) Abelard at one (of many) instance states, "For God thinks not of what is done but in what mind it may be done, and the merit or glory of the doer lies in the intention, not in the deed." Near the end of the same paragraph he states, "...yet, through the diversity of their intention [*per diuersitatem tamen intentionis*], the same thing is done by diverse men, by one badly, by the other well" (pp. 28-29).

2. *Cf*., *The Anatomy of the Soul*, by A. J. Kenny (Blackwell, 1973), pp. 136-137.

3. *Op. cit*., "*Why works of sin are punished rather than sin itself*," p. 41.

4. Our concern is not to dispute how certain key Latin words are used by Abelard, but to make only what appears to be a common sense observation about use here.

5. We admit that medieval philosophers were interested in faculty psychology. They were also concerned with locating spatially the functions of the soul. One may read at length in Edwin Clarke's, *An Illustrated History of Brain Function* (Oxford: Sandford Publications, 1972), especially in Chapter 3, "Medieval Period: The Cell Doctrine of Brain Function," pp. 10-51. Dr. Clarke convincingly shows that the medievals were concerned with making empirical and spatial locations in the brain which expressed rational and volitional operations of the soul.

6. One may confer the classic case of treason, *R. v. Steane* [1947] K. B. 997. One may contrast the decision in *Steane* with the submission, and later the decision in *Hearst*. *Steane* held that the defendant did not intend to do the acts he was charged with because of duress. Glanville Williams criticized the judgment. In *The Mental Element in Crime* (Jerusalem: Magnes Press, 1965) he says, "...Steane should have been acquitted by reason of the defence of duress, and not because he lacked intent to assist the enemy" (p. 23). In *United States of America v. Patricia Campbell Hearst* we read in the trial brief for the United States, on page 14, "One who acts under duress, or later performs protagonistic acts because he feels menaced, acts as intentionally and knowingly as the law requires. (9) *footnote*: The person who is forced to rob a bank knows what he is doing and intends to do the acts which result in the harm proscribed, but the law *excuses* his acts as a matter of policy, because, just like entrapment, they were not at his own instance." IN THE UNITED STATES DISTRICT COURT FOR THE NORTHERN DISTRICT OF CALIFORNIA, CRIMINAL NO. 74-364-OJC, February 3rd, 1976. We would caution that if one holds a strictly cognitive or intellectual notion of intention, then Hearst follows; but if one holds a voluntarist theory of intention, then Steane follows. We have cited these two cases to show that the dispute between the two poles has not yet been resolved.

7. *Edward I and Criminal Law* by T.F.T. Plucknett (Cambridge University Press, 1960), p. 61, from the translation of Miss A. J. Robertson of VI Aethelred 52, *Laws of the Kings of England* (1925), p. 107.

8. In *The Treatise on the Laws and Customs of England commonly called Glanvill* [*Tractatus de legibus et consuetudinibus regni Anglie qui Glanvilla vocatur*], the edition prepared by G. D. G. Hall (London and Edinburgh: Nelson's Medieval Texts, Nelson, 1965), one finds no intentional operator used in the classification of crimes. The jurisdiction of the law is divided into civil and criminal, and matters pertaining to crimes are stated, and forms of penalty assigned. Under "Criminal Pleas" [*De placitis criminalibus*], pp. 171 onwards, the form of the action(s) is stated, how an accusation is to be made, what sureties may be demanded, and how the criminal is to be convicted. Under "Homicide," p. 174, no evidential guidance is given.

9. *Cf.* Chapters 72 and 73, "The Soul which despises the Supreme Being will be eternally wretched" and "Every human soul is immortal," pp. 80-81 in the *Monologion*, edited and translated by Jasper Hopkins and Herbert W. Richardson (London: SCM Press, 1974).

10. From, *Hugh of Saint Victor On The Sacraments of The Christian Faith*, translated by Roy J. Deferrari (Cambridge, Mass.: The Mediaeval Academy of America, 1951), p. 85, Book One, Part Five, "On the creation of the Angels, and on free will...."

11. *Ibid.*, *De Sacramentis*, Book One, Part Six, Question IV, p. 96.

12. *Cf.*, *ibid.*, "How ignorance is a vice," pp. 137 onwards, Book One, Part Seven, Question XXXII, of *De Sacramentis*.

13. *Cf.*, *ibid.*, p. 414, "VI. That good will alone suffices, if the opportunity for operating is not given."

14. *Cf.*, *A Concise History of the Common Law* by Theodore F. T. Plucknett, (London: Butterworth & Co. (Publishers) Ltd., 1956), Chapt. 14, "Professional Literature," pp. 252-289.

15. The edition which we have employed for quotations is that which had been prepared and translated by L. J. Downer, Leges Henrici Primi, (Oxford: At The Clarendon Press, 1972), and we shall quote from it throughout.

16. *Leges*, p. 87.

17. *Ibid.*

18. *Ashford v. Thorton*, 1 Barn & Ald. 405 appears to be the last appeal from murder to invoke this method of trial.

19. *Leges*, p. 89, section 5, 16a. It should be recalled that Pope Innocent III, on 24 August 1215, condemned the Magna Carta by issuing a Papal Bull

which declared that, King John having been impelled to enter the agreement and to sign it because of force and fear, the document was void. One may consult *Magna Carta* by G. R. C. Davis, published by The Trustees of the British Museum, 1971, p. 29, or the *Selected Letters of Pope Innocent III*, as edited by C. R. Cheney and W. H. Semple (Edinburgh: Nelson, 1953).

20. It is interesting to turn to some of the spiritual writers to see how the responsibility concepts developed. It should be impressed upon one that a spiritual act, such as meditation, was just as "full" a human act as was walking or talking. William of Saint Thierry could write, "So is it with the *intention* in comtemplation or in prayer (italics ours). If the understanding of reason or of love has not received something definite from you that it can quickly put before itself where its affections can rest and its attention find an object, and where it can pour out the fruits of its devotion, then contemplation grows faint, prayer waxes cold, attention falters, understanding becomes weak, and reason can do nothing" (pp. 72-73 of *Prayer* in *On Contemplating God* by William of Saint Thierry, translated by Sister Penelope CSMV, volume 3 in the Cistercian Fathers Series [Shannon, Ireland: Irish University Press, 1971]). One may also refer to his *De Natura Corporis et Anima* (Migne: P. L. 180, col. 707). It cites a typical twelfth-century position of the common mind on the matter: "[T]he philosophers of this world defined the soul as a simple substance, distant from the matter of its body, the organ of its members, having the power of life. The doctors of the church, on the other hand, define it thus – a spiritual substance particular to each individual, created by God, vivifying, rational, immortal, and able to turn to good and evil" (as cited on p. 12 of *An Introduction to the Cistercian De Anima* [London: Aquin Press, 1961] by G. Webb).

21. "The Origin of the Doctrine of Mens Rea," p. 117, *op. cit.*

22. *Cf.*, *A History of The Criminal Law of England*, volume II, (London: Macmillan and Co., 1883), p. 94, Chapter XVIII, "Criminal Responsibility." In his *A General View of The Criminal Law of England* (London and Cambridge: Macmillan and Co., 1863) Stephen makes mention only of Bracton as an early source for the definition of homicide (p. 41) and does not trace his sources back further than that.

23. *Cf.*, Christopher Dawson, *The Crisis of Western Education* (London: Sheed & Ward, Ltd., 1961), Chapter One, "The Origins of the Western Tradition of Education," pp. 3-12.

24. *Opera Omnia*, Volume Five, *Sancti Aurelii Augustini*, Sermon 180 appears on p. 972 (Paris edition, 1841). From Caput II (pp. 972-973) of this edition we have taken the Latin text, and set it down here.

Caput II. – 2. Juratio licet a Deo usurpata, homini tamen fugienda. Perjurium quot modis contingit. *Invenimus enim jurasse sanctos, jurasse primitus ipsum Dominum, in quo non est omnino peccatum.* Juravit Dominus, et non poenitebit eum: Tu es sacerdos in aeternum, secundum ordinem Melchisedech (Psal. cix. 4). *Aeternitatem sacerdotii Filio cum juratione promisit. Habes etiam*, Per memetipsum juro, dicit Dominus (Gen. xxii. 16). *Et illud juratio est*, Vivo ego dicit Dominus (Num. xiv. 28). *Quodmodo homo per Deum, sic Deus per se ipsum. Non est ergo peccatum jurare? Durum est hoc dicere: et quoniam diximus Deum jurasse, quam blasphemum est hoc dicere ? Jurat Deus qui peccatum non habet: non ergo est peccatum jurare: sed magis peccatum est pejerare. Fortasse quis dicat non esse proponendum de Domino Deo jurationis exemplum. Deus enim est, et forte illi soli competit jurare, qui non potest pejerare. Homines enim falsum jurant, vel cum fallunt, vel cum falluntur. Aut enim putat homo verum esse quod falsum est, et temere jurat: aut scit vel putat falsum esse, et tamen pro vero jurat, et nihilominus cum scelere jurat. Distant autem ista perjuria, quae due commemoravi. Fac illum jurare, qui verum putat esse, pro quo jurat: verum putat esse, et tamen falsum est. Non ex animo iste perjurat; fallitur, hoc pro vero habet quod falsum est; non pro re falsa sciens jurationem interponit. Da alium qui scit falsum esse, et dicit verum esse- et jurat tanquam verum sit, quod scit falsum esse. Videtis quam ista detestanda sit bellua, et de rebus humanis exterminanda? Quis enim hoc fieri velit? Omnes homines talia detestantur. Fac alium, putat falsum esse, et jurat tanquam verum sit, et forte verum est. Verbi gratia, ut intelligatis, Pluit in illo loco? interrogas hominem; et putat non pluisse et ad negotium ipsius competit, ut dicat, Pluit: sed putat non pluisse; dicitur ei, Vere pluit? Vere, et jurat; et tamen pluit ibi, sed ille nescit, et putat non pluisse: perjurus est. Interest quemadmodum verbum procedit ex animo. REAM LINGUAM NON FACIT, NISI MENS REA,* [emphasis ours]. *Quis est autem qui non fallatur, etsi noluit fallere? Quis est homo cui non subrepat fallacia? Et tamen juratio ab ore non discedit, frequentatur: plura sunt plerumque juramenta, quam verba. Si discutiat homo quoties juret per totum diem, quoties se vulneret, quoties gladis linguae se feriat et transfigat, quis in illo locus invenitur sanus? Quia ergo grave peccatum est pejerare, compedium tibi dedit Scriptura, Noli jurare.*

The Translation:

It is lawful for one to take an oath if the practice is directed by God, notwithstanding the fact that it may be hastened by men (I will also speak about) *perjury and how it may take place*. We do find examples of the saints taking oaths, and we also find that our Lord himself had taken an oath which was in no way sinful for him to have taken. *Our Lord took an oath, and it did not displease him* (to take the oath, when he said): *You are a priest forever, according to the order of Melchisedech* (whereupon Psalm 109 is cited which reads: "Thou are a priest for ever in the line of Melschisedech"). With an oath He promised the eternity of the priesthood to his Son. You also know from Scripture, Our Lord did say, *I have taken an oath upon my very own self* (whereupon Genesis xxii. 16 is cited, which reads, "Once more the angel of the Lord called to Abraham out of heaven; and he said, This message the Lord has for thee: I have taken an oath by my own name to reward thee for this act of thine, when thou wast ready to give up thy only son for my sake"). And here is another example of the taking of an oath, *I am the living God, says the Lord*, (whereupon this passage from Numbers xiv. 28 is cited: " Such was the Lord's message to Moses and Aaron: Will this thankless multitude never cease complaining; must I hear nothing but lament from the sons of Israel? Tell them this, As I am living God, the Lord says, the very words you have used in my hearing shall come true; your bones shall be left to die in this desert"). How a man does this is through God, just as God does this through himself. But is it not a sin to take an oath? This is a hard question to answer, and for this reason. We have said that God himself has taken an oath, and does it not seem as though we have blasphemed by having spoken in this way? God, who is without sin, has taken an oath: therefore it would follow that it is not a sin to take an oath: but rather what is greatly sinful is for one to commit perjury. Perhaps one may say that an example of oath-taking by our Lord before God has not been proposed. For as He is God, then perhaps He alone is capable of taking an oath, because he is incapable of committing perjury. Men, however, are capable of swearing falsely, by concealing matters, or by letting matters be concealed.

Either a man believes that something is true when it is actually false, and rashly swears an oath: or he knows or he believes what is false, but yet he nevertheless swears that it is true, and nevertheless with wickedness he affirms an oath. These perjuries are to be kept in a separate class, and there are two things I wish to mention. Let him take an oath who believes it to be true, for he swears by this: what he believes to be true, which is, however, false. Such falsehood does not proceed from one's soul; it has escaped one's notice, that one has uttered as true what was in fact false; but not knowing that such was false, one takes an oath.

Here is another example: of one who knows something to be false, yet he says that it is true: furthermore, he takes an oath (as it were) that it is true; even though he knows it to be false. Do you appreciate that such a monster must be detested, and be removed from human affairs ? And who wants this to be done? All men who detest such matters.

Consider a further example. A person believes something to be false, but nonetheless by oath affirms it to be true, and there is the chance that it may be true. Freely put, so as to be understood, one puts this question to someone, "Does it rain in this place?" That man happens to believe that it has not rained, but, to cause a difficulty, [*et ad negotium*] by coincidence, just as he speaks, it does rain: but he does not know that it has rained; however it is remarked to him, "It is really raining now, isn't it?" Truly it is raining, and he affirms it: however, although it is actually raining, he himself does not truly know that, and he even believes that it has not rained. He is a perjurer. What is important to observe is how the word proceeds from our soul. One does not produce guilty speech unless one has a guilty mind. Who is there however who has not deceived, yet at the same time has not wished to deceive? Who is the man who has not come forward with this fallacy? Nonetheless, swearing an oath ought not to run counter to our speech, and this is commonly understood: there are many matters which require an oath, rather than mere talk. If a man becomes frustrated how often he swears throughout the day, how often he feels vulnerable, how often he is severely critical of himself, what part of him then is sane? Because it is therefore a grave sin to commit perjury, holy Scripture offers to you this restraint, Be unwilling to take oaths.

25. *Op. cit.*

26. *Cf. The Academics of Cicero*, translated by James S. Reid (London: Macmillan & Co., 1880), pp. 7-11 of his introduction.

27. *Cf.*, St. Augustine, *Against The Academicians*, translated by Sister Mary Patricia Garvey, Mediaeval Philosophical Texts in Translation, No. 2 (Milwaukee, Wisconsin: Marquette University Press, 1973), 4th edition, Book III, pp. 50-83.

28. *The Christian Philosophy of St. Augustine*, by Etienne Gilson (London: Victor Gollancz Ltd., 1961), Chapter II, "The Elements of the Moral Act," esp. pp. 127-136. The author states on page 134, and we quote, "If the will is the active force which calls forth sensation, it is also the force which causes rational knowledge....But whatever the degree of knowledge we attain, it is always determined by an impulse to investigate which has its origin in the will." *Cf.*, also, Chapter II, "The Nature of the Soul," in *Augustine's Psychology*, by T. J. Parry (published dissertation of the University of Strassburg: Borna nr. Leipzig, 1913). Parry presents a strong picture of Augustinian voluntarism, pointing out that one use of "intention" is as "intentio peragendi," meaning of the Will in action. He cites Chapter 3 of *De immortalitate Animae* of Augustine for this usage.

29. *Cf. Rhetoric at Rome*, by M. L. Clarke (London: Cohen & West, 1966), Chapter 14.

30. *De Inventione*, translated by H. M. Hubbell, Loeb Classical Library, volume No. 386 (London: Harvard University Press & William Heinemann Ltd., 1968).

31. Levitt, *op. cit.*

32. We shall refer to Migne's edition of *Sancti Ivonis, Opera Omnia* (Parisiis: 1889), and shall cite from his *Decreti Pars Decima* (which encompasses columns 689-746, and is titled *De Homicidiis*) and *De Homicidio*, Book VIII of *Panormia* (which encompasses columns 1303-1322 in Migne).

33. We shall make all of our citations from the edition prepared by H. M. Hubbell: *De Inventione*, Loeb Classical Library (London: William Heineman Ltd., and Harvard University Press, 1968). We shall simply cite the page of Hubbell's text when making citations hereafter.

34. Grant argues that Cicero appears to have possessed no profound understanding of Aristotle's *Nicomachean Ethics*. Even if one admits the point one may yet conjecture with some reasonable force that the edition of the *Nichomachean Ethics* which was prepared by Andronicus of Rhodes, and known to Tyrannion, a learned friend of Cicero, could be facilitated to the Latin tongue. The concept of the voluntary would not have been a strange notion to Cicero, and he could easily have gained an understanding of it, for legal use, from his reading of the *Nicomachean Ethics*. One may consult *Andronici Rhodii, Ethicorum Nicomacheorum, Paraphrasis* (Oxonii:

MDCCCIX), pp. 92-141 concerning 'sponte' and 'de voluntate.' This is a reprint of the edition by Daniel Heinsius, MDCVII (Lugduni Batavorum).

35. One may read William James' gloss on the piece in his own *Pragmatism*, Chapter Two, "What Pragmatism Means," (Longmans, 1908), pp. 46-47.

36. One may read such a position recently argued in moral philosophy by the late Arthur E. Murphy in his *The Theory of Practical Reason* (LaSalle, Illinois: Open Court Publishing Company, 1965), edited by A. I. Melden, in Chapter Two, "Practical Reasons As Grounds for Action," pp. 24-56.

37. One may refer to the English case *R. v. Latimer* (1886), 17 Q.B.D. 359 to observe how two different legal systems, as are Roman law and common law, may yet share a similarity in legal reasoning. In *Latimer* the defendant, *D*, had been involved in a pub brawl. During the course of the brawl he took aim at *A*, hoping to hit him with his belt, and hit *B*, the barmaid, who he did not intend to hit. He injured *B* gravely. In a reserved judgment, Lord Coleridge, C. J. stated, "It is common knowledge that a man who has an unlawful and malicious intent against another, and, in attempting to carry it out, injures a third person, is guilty of what the law deems malice against the person injured, because the offender is doing an unlawful act, and has that which the judges call general malice." He distinguished the case from *R. v. Pembliton* (1874) L.R.2 C.C.R.119, showing that intent in *Pembliton* differed and did not guide in *Latimer*. The language of the Malicious Damage Act, 1861, s.51 controlled *Pembliton*, but did not control *Latimer*, in the determining of the requisite intent for the crime.

38. In *Criminal Law* by Smith and Hogan (London: Butterworths, 1969) one reads this caveat: "It is important to notice the limitations of this [namely, the doctrine of transferred malice in the criminal law of common law jurisdictions] doctrine. It operates only when the *actus reus* and the *mens rea* of the *same* crime coincide. If D, with the *mens rea* of one crime, does an act which causes the *actus reus* of a different crime, he cannot, as a general rule, be convicted of either offence" (p. 45). (Even this caveat, we would advance, needs further refinement.)

39. In *Mens Rea in Statutory Offences* by J. Ll. J. Edwards (London: Macmillan & Co. Ltd., 1955), the author, on pp. 12-16, criticizes the legal clarity of the supposed principles underlying the decision of the court in *Pembliton*.

40. Present commentary, with intent upon recommendations for statutory revisions of the *Act*, may be read in *Working Paper on Offences against the Person* (London: H. M. S. O., August, 1976) as prepared by the Criminal Law Revision Committee, pp. 40-45, paragraphs 100-117, "Wounding, Grievous Bodily Harm and Actual Bodily Harm." Edwards (*op. cit.*), p. 15, cites from the case comment (1886) of 2.L.Q.R.536 on *Latimer*: "Questions of this kind have given abundant exercise to Continental Writers on the theory of criminal responsibility. The comparatively rough methods of our own

criminal jurisprudence are perhaps sufficient for the common purpose of justice."

41. We will cite from the edition of H. M. Hubbell throughout, which also contained the *De Inventione*. The passage in this instance is from *Topica*, XV, 58, p. 425.

42. We have used the Latin texts which are printed in J. P. Migne's *Patrologia Latina* (Paris, 1865), 40.487-548; the editions run consecutively, D.M. then C.M.A.C. The English translation of each text we have consulted appears in volume 16 of The Fathers of the Church (Edited by Roy J. Deferrari [New York: Fathers of The Church, Inc., 1952]), "St. Augustine: Treatises on Various Subjects." *Lying* (*De Mendacio*) is translated by Sister M. S. Muldowney, S.S.J., Ph.D., and appears on pp. 47-110 of that volume; *Against Lying* (*Contra Mendacium Ad Consentium*) was translated by Harold B. Jaffee, Ph.D., and is printed on pp. 113-179. Both translators used the text as prepared by J. Zycha, *Corpus Scriptorum Ecclesiasticorum Latinorum* 41 (Vienna, 1900), but this edition was not available to us. However, both translators consulted Migne.

43. It will be recalled that in Sermon 180 the passage from Scripture upon which St. Augustine was commenting was James, 5:12, wherein we read, "But above all, my brethren, do not bind youselves by any oath, by heaven, by earth, or by any oath at all. Let your word be Yes for Yes, and No for No; if not you will be judged for it." When one turns to the *Contra Mendacium*, which was written by Augustine late in his life and was a treatise against the Priscillianists, who, among other matters, felt that lying was itself justified at times to aid the spread of religious doctrine, in Chapter 16 (from the English edition, *op. cit.*, of Jaffe, p. 167) we read, "Let your speech be 'Yes, yes'; 'No, no.'" which citation, in this instance, is taken from St. Matthew at 5:33-38, wherein one reads, "Again, you have heard that it was said to the men of old, Thou shalt not perjure thyself; thou shalt perform what thou hast sworn in the sight of the Lord. But I tell you that you should not bind yourselves by any oath at all: not by earth...nor by Jerusalem....And thou shalt not swear by thy own head....Let your word be Yes for Yes, and No for No." One reading is that Christ has condemned Pharisaical evasions which appeared to permit one to perjure oneself as long as an oath was not taken directly in the name of Yahweh. St. Matthew 23: 16-22 indicates how serious it was, for the believing Christian, to make and take an oath, "And the man who swears by heaven swears not only by God's throne, but by him who sits upon it."

44. The text was edited and translated by E. H. Blakeney (London: S. P. C. K. Press, 1950) and the English appeared on p. 97. The Latin text appears on p. 34, and we cite it accordingly: "*...quem qui ignorat a veritate ac Deo semper alienus est....Qui Filium non agnovit, nect Patrem potiut adnoscere. Haec est sapientia, et hoc mysterium summi Die. Per illum se Deus et agnosci et coli voluit....Nec tamen sic habendum est, tanquam duo sint Dii. Pater enim ac Filius unum sunt; quum enim Pater Filium diligat, omniaque ei tribuat, et Filius Patri fideliter obsequatur, nec velit quidquam nisi quod Pater, non potest utique necessitudo tanta divelli, ut duo esse dicantur, in quibus et substantia, et voluntas, et fides una est. Ergo et Filius per Patrem, et Pater per Filium. Unus est*

honos utrique tribuendus tanquam uni Deo, et ita dividendus est per duos cultus, ut divisio ipsa compage inseparabili vinciatur. Neutrum sibi relinquet, qui aut Patrem a Filio, aut Filium a Patre secernit."

45. Note Austin's analysis of *R. v. Finney* (*op. cit.*) in section 6 of, "A Plea for Excuses."

46. In Migne, at column 313, Caput XX, the context in which "intentione" occurs is the following: "*Fides enim appellata est in latina lingua ex eo quia fit quod dicitur: quam manifestum est non exhibere mentientum. Quae eise minus vilator, cum ita quisque mentitur, ut ei nullo incommodo nullaque pernicie credatur*, addita etiam intentione *vel salutis tuende,* [emphasis mine] *vel pudicitiae corporalis: violatur tamen, et res violatur in animi castitate atque sanctitate servanda.*" It is rendered in this way by Sister Muldowney: "For, faith has received its Latin form from the fact that what is said is done. Hence, it is evident that a person who is lying does not show faith. Even though this faith be violated in a smaller degree, when a person lies under such circumstances that, without bringing inconvenience or damage to another, he is believed and that he even has the intention of protecting the health or bodily chastity of another, nevertheless, faith is violated, and this is likewise done even in preserving the chastity and holiness of the soul" (p. 106, *op. cit*).

47. We do not want to engage in biblical commentary on the matter of the Psalms, nor of Augustine's understanding of the text herewith under question. When we come to review the various English translations of this passage (Psalm 14, or 15, depending upon how it is catalogued; we read it as Psalm 14), we have a wide range of English terms to chose from for the act of lying, or the act of harming one's friend or neighbor. The Authorized Version speaks of "backbiting" but that is not a term we use now with the force it may have had centuries ago. The Knox translation renders the passage in this way," ...one whose heart is all honest purpose, who utters no treacherous word, never defrauds a friend, or slanders a neighbor..." (rendered as Psalm 14, p. 483 of *The Holy Bible*, published by Burns & Oates, London, [5th edition], 1965).

The Latin which may have been used by Augustine we take from *Collectaneo Biblica Latina*, Vol. 1, "Liber Psalmorum: Iuxta Antiquissimam Latinam Versionem Nunc Primum Ex Casiensi Cod. 557" as edited by D. Ambrosio M. Amelli, O.S.B. (Fridericus Pustet: Romae, Ratisbonae et Neo-Eboraci: MCMXII). The text, however, reads, "*Ambulans immaculatus et operans iustitiam. Et loquens veritatem in corde suo. Non fraudauit in lingua eius neque fecit proximo suo malum et improperium non accepit super proximos suos.*" The compression which Augustine's citation gives is, in this Latin text, expanded. But the force of the Psalm remains in spite of the change of text.

In the citation, from Migne, Augustine uses "dolum," a term which is replete with legal and moral meaning. It has the force of evil intent, wrongdoing with a view to the consequences (as opposed to simple negligence); it may mean fraud, or deceit, or guile. A recent and discursive treatment of *dolus, culpa* and *casus* may be found in Part Three, entitled "Philosophical Aspects," of Professor David Daube's *Roman Law* (Edinburgh: At The University Press, 1969). That portion covers pp. 129-175, and it will show how various degrees of negligence functioned in Roman law. Daube reads "*dolus*" as meaning "evil intent." He makes the observation that "evil intent" in Roman law differed from "evil intent" in Greek law. For the Greeks it functioned in the criminal law, and entailed that one was of a slothful, immoral disposition (for whom ignorance could not be an excuse because one's own slothfulness was the cause of the ignorance), while for the Romans "*dolus*" was a function of the civil law, and concern was not for retribution but for compensation and payment of damages, as in Delicts or Contracts. *Dolus* was a term of wide meaning. One may refer to *Roman Law and Common Law* by Buckland & McNair (Cambridge: At The University Press, 1936), Chapter X, "Delict and Tort" (pp. 300-307, section 4: Dolus) to appreciate how rich and unsimple the concept was in Roman law. One simply assumes that such rich nuances would have been appreciated by St. Augustine, who modelled so much of his writing after Cicero. The translation from the Hebrew by Mitchell Dahood, Vol. 16, *The Anchor Bible*, Psalms 1-50 (New York: Doubleday, 1966) gives a different rendering, and hence changes the force of "dolus." Dahood's translation reads: "...He who walks with integrity and practices justice, // and speaks the truth from his heart, // He who does not trip over his tongue, // Who does no wrong to his fellowman, // and casts no slur on his neighbor." He translated the Psalm as number 15. The portion rendered "...trip over his tongue..." Dahood argues is in account with the Hebrew habit to form denominative verbs from parts of the body; also, that the text ["*rgal 'al* l^{e}sn"] is both problematical and does match a later Psalm XXXIX ("...I will heed my steps lest I stumble over my tongue...") for its consistency of imagery. Dahood's text is on pp. 83-85.

48. One fruitful illustration of this notion about moral acts and their effects can be taken from the novel of L. P. Hartley, entitled *The Shrimp and the Anemone* (Putnam & Co. Ltd.; 1944, Faber & Faber Ltd., 1975). In the first chapter the two children, Eustace and Hilda, observe that a shrimp was clutched by a sea anemone. The dialogue is telling, "It was a shrimp, Eustace decided, and the anemone was eating it, sucking it in. A tumult arose in Eustace's breast. His heart bled for the shrimp, he longed to rescue it – but, on the other hand, how could he bear to rob the anemone of its dinner? The anemone was more beautiful than the shrimp, more interesting and much rarer. It was a 'plumrose' anemone....If he took the shrimp away, the anemone might never catch another, and die of hunger. But while he debated the unswallowed part of the shrimp grew preceptibly smaller....He made up his mind to release it. But how?...But Hilda cut him short...'I've got it,' said Hilda....The shrimp lay in the palm of Hilda's hand, a sad disappointing sight. Its reprieve had come too late; its head was mangled and there was no vibration in its tail. The horrible appearance fascinated Eustace for a moment, then upset him so much that he turned away with trembling lips. But there was worse to come. As a result of Hilda's forcible interference with its meal the anemone had been partially disembowelled; it could not give up its prey without letting its digestive apparatus go too. Part of its base had come unstuck and was seeking feebly to attach itself to the rock again....'I wish we'd let them alone,' sobbed Eustace. "What would have been the good of that?' demanded Hilda,...'We had to do something,' Hilda

continued, 'We couldn't let them go on like that.' 'Why couldn't we?' asked Eustace" (from pp. 9-11 of Chapter One).

ADDENDUM

Ivo of Chartres

A metaphor which might be used to describe the growth of early common law notions of criminal responsibility might be the metaphor of the coral reef. Within the freshly growing common law a central body of notions begins to impress itself on the common law's growth and development. One is not speaking about the relation of parts within an organic whole, which concept suggests that what is growing is developing out of a preordained design in which what is expressed as a final cause properly reveals what was contained within the formal cause. The example is more of the relation of elements to one another, as the parts and shadings of the sky make up the sky. There is a blend both of the accidental and of the substantial. How the patterns form themselves is accidental; but that they are parts of the sky in its cloud formation, and not parts of the earth, or of the water, reveals a substantial nature which changes. One need not inquire further to ask if one is inquiring after a hidden substratum which is the ultimate composition of the sky; that is a theory, from among possible theories.

The process of judging, of determining if this man be guilty or innocent, sprang up in the common law from borrowings from canon law, medieval theology, moral customs and religious customs, and all of the legal customs present (as a force) in England.[1] Like a coral reef, the growth of the law, in its smaller parts, began to shape and to form what one knows as the common law. Early on the common law developed as a respect for written judgments,[2] for oral argument (but not as we know it now[3]), and for a consistency. The consistency would not possess a uniformity such as the continental canon law writers would give law; the consistency would be more the application of broad general principles, akin to transcendentals, and less like strict formal canonical rules. A judgment would seek to be fair; an accused would be given some kind of fair hearing; a charge would be openly heard, generally, and openly discussed. Reasons would generally be given for decisions. In this way, legal principles of the common law were transcendental in nature, they were not to be found codified in a single instance, but were to be found at work in the movement of the law.

It is, however, a matter of historical fact which we need not record that the criminal law was the slowest of all of the common law to change and to make itself humane. Centuries would pass from the time of Bracton before the criminal law would reach the humaneness we now associate with it, and we will not concern ourselves with an historical analysis of this change.

Ivo of Chartres died in 1117 A.D. The authorship of the *Leges* is thought to date from 1113 or 1114 A.D., with a *terminus ad quem*, suggested by Downer,[4] to be 1118 A.D. The influence of Ivo can be found throughout the *Leges*, but it would be outside of the scope of our argument to locate the textual strands of one text to be found within another text; it should be left to the textual scholar to demonstrate such manuscriptal influences.[5]

Mention needs to be taken, however, that the common law had a tradition from which to draw upon for the purpose of developing a legal structure under which assignments of guilt or innocence could be made. It is true, of course, that legal guilt was not a neutrally pure legal concept; it was admixed with the moral beliefs and customs of English society, as reflection upon any number of leading cases will reveal.[6] The early writings of the canonists and moralists provided much material which a growing legal structure like the common law could incorporate. Criminal charges in themselves carried a natural stigma. It was assumed that to break the law was to perform a wicked act. Not only did one cause a harm, but one's criminal act was viewed as act worthy of condemnation.[7] Penalties for crimes, apart from their cruelty and physical hideousness, were both to the community and to God. If one slayed a religious minister, for instance, one was judged to be a religious *and* civil outlaw both to God and to man, and both had to be appeased.[8] Such harmony of disparate worlds may seem natural to the medieval mind which believed in a balanced harmony between the realms of matter and the realm of the spirit, which the literature and theology of the age show us, and it may seem strange to us now; but it should be remembered that blasphemy, for instance, is still actionable at common law as a misdemeanor.

The *Leges* preserves many of the common cases which were to be found in medieval theological writing. The cases of the tree falling upon the unwary passerby, the mother who rolls over in her sleep and accidentally smothers her child, the accidental wounding or non-purposeful wounding* or killing of an innocent third party, the dangerous trap which, set for animals, catches a person, and other such standard cases find themselves in the fabric of the *Leges*. What is lacking from this early compilation is any conceptual analysis of what, for instance, is meant by "Will" or "Purpose" or "Mind" or "Cause." For such, as well as other key concepts, one must borrow from the literature of the period, and even that literature is not uniform in its employment of terms. It is the fine reading which makes the terms precise. One such instance is to determine what is meant by Mind. Each major medievalist has a different theory about how Mind** operates and what its nature is; for the legal scholar must draw upon the broad classifications of the period. The literature on this period, from the eleventh through to the fifteenth centuries, is yet sparse; and the texts, many of which are of major figures, are yet unedited.[9]

It would be an unwise reading of the *Leges* to require of it a conceptual refinement it does not possess. As a skeletal structure it possesses avenues and branches upon which developing legal notions could grow, and then develop towards a maturity. If one wishes to make legal locations, the work can be used as something of a common law Pausanias, showing how certain rudimentary legal operators had found themselves in a budding legal structure. Degrees of guilt would operate within the legal structure;[10] an adjectival method would begin to function in which "mind" would have to be qualified as being a "guilty mind" to which guilt was assigned. The language may appear to seem unnecessarily Platonic, speaking as one would about the realm of the mind and the realm of the body, but it should be recalled that the early moral apparatus was Augustinian in nature; an Aristotelian refinement of terms would not enter into the literature of the

---

* A distinction between "accidental" and "non-purposeful" might entail this reasoning. An accident may have been avoidable or not (by care or means taken by the agent), while a non-purposeful happening means that the event was out of control of the agent, and he could not have reasonably taken precautions to prevent its happening.

** *'Intellectus'* is how we have rendered Mind. The Latin concept has a wider range than our present term "mind," but is suitable here.

age until approximately 1215 A.D., when that corpus was made available to the scholars at Paris, and elsewhere in the young universities.[11]

The notion of a mental intention enters the common law from mixed sources. The *Leges* uses the language of intention, but it does not refine that language. We read, for instance,[12] that "No one is obliged to make amends for his own child whom he did not kill intentionally,..." Again we read, "If anyone, while he is endeavouring to separate persons fighting among themselves, is killed, though innocent, either intentionally or through the negligence of the disputants, the one who slew him shall pay amends...."[13] Differences in the quality of an act are reflected by use of this mental distinction, "But there shall be some difference of result depending on whether someone asked the man who is killed to join him in the task, or whether he came of his own volition...."[14] The sole use of "*intendit*" occurs in this passage, when we read, "...[W]here a man intends one thing and something else results (where what is actually done is the subject of the accusation, and not the intention) the judges shall...fix a compensation...."[15] At section 72, 2b of the text, following upon a statement that homicide (72,2) can be committed either by accident or by design (*consilio*), we read of the use of "*possibilitatem*" to mean "intention," as in, "The intention of the penitent when doing a good work," but the meaning of the term in post-classical Latin is taken generally to indicate that one has the power to undertake to do, and it should be read as a dispositive noun, one taking a clue that it is feminine in gender (*possibilitas, atis, f.*). It is not normally associated as a synonym for *intentio*. We will find that the early law follows along the pathway of sacramental theology on the general notion of intention by accepting variants of the notion that an outward deed is itself an expression of inward state of mind. The sacramental refinement of this general notion is well known to theological writings; its logic, however, was not well known, or well formulated by early common law jurists, and, we would suggest, many of our modern difficulties, both with the range and scope of *mens rea* and *actus reus*, stem from too easily accepting what were general theological notions, which worked in one sphere, and forcing them to work in another sphere without determining how one sphere, the sacraments, differed from another sphere, the law.[16] The language which will describe a serious act, such as homicide, will (for the most part) be volitive language, and will not be a special language which picks out a mental state or depicts a mental event. When Ivo of Chartres speaks of homicide, he speaks of it in terms of the Will.[17] He does, it is to be admitted, make reference to a guilty mind, but he does so within the context of lying, and not of killing.[18] It is the early volitive tradition, with its adherence to Augustine, and later Augustinian interpretation, which first finds its way into rudimentary notions of intentional acts.

When we turn to Bracton's *De Legibus* we enter a period of the common law in which religious sources are drawn upon for the purpose of transmuting them and making from their impetus a legal tradition outside of theology. This period of the common law, like the history of the inception of the Inns of Court and of English legal traditions, is marked by obscurity. The obscurity arises from our not possessing clear and precise texts, from not having clear and precise editions of major theological writers, and from not having records which can easily tell one what happened during the period. One assumes that the community of scholars was small and intimate enough for their writings to be known, and we buttress such an assumption by trying to show various textual similarities to be found in a writer, or, if one cannot locate direct textual similarities of language, then one may search for similarities of tone or sentiment or style in argument. For the legal philosopher the method is both helpful and useful, but he should not make the method of the legal historian and textualists his own method. The two ways of seeing a text are different. The legal philosopher hopes to withdraw an argument and its implications from a text; the legal historian is content, very often, with locating a source[19] for a concept.

ADDENDUM NOTES

1. In his brief account of the roots of intention from Anglo-Saxon times, Professor Plucknett shows how diversified the early roots are which impinge upon criminal responsibility in the common law, drawing upon Anglo-Saxon laws, French sources, early Penitential writings, as well as formal theological writings, to form a growing law. Cf. Chapter III, "The Criminal and Intention," in *Edward I and Criminal Law* (Cambridge University Press, 1960). He recapitulates what Levitt, *op. cit.*, had said, in part, in 1917.

2. A concise account is provided in *The Oracles of the Law* by J. P. Dawson (The University of Michigan Law School, 1968) in Chapter I, "The Growth and Decline of English Case Law," pp. 1-99, especially section 5 thereof, "The Case Law of the Year Books," pp. 50-65. The fullest account is in L. W. Abbott, whom we cited earlier.

3. 1907, 7 Edward VII, c.23, *Criminal Appeal Act.*

4. *Op. cit.*, pp. 34-37, "The Dating of the *Leges*."

5. The edition of Ivo of Chartres which we have consulted is that prepared by Migne in the series *Patrologia Latina* (Vol. 161, vol. 1 thereof, listed as 161:1, PL), Paris, 1889, *Saeculum XII Sancti Ivonis, Carnotensis Episcopi, Opera Omnia.* In his bibliographical apparatus it is unfortunate that Downer does not list the sources for his secondary references, and, from his edition of the *Leges*, it is difficult to determine from what written text he is citing when referring to an historical influence upon the *Leges*. For example, Downer suggests that the immediate source for 5,28b, "*Reum non facit nisi mens rea*," of the *Leges* is to be found in [Ivo] *Pan* viii.111. If one turns to the *Panormia* of Ivo as printed in Migne, one will discover that the collation is of no help to locate to what passage in particular Downer had referred. Ivo authored two texts on the topic of *Homicide*. One text is entitled, *Decreti*, and it is a canonical collection of commentaries upon what we now know as the *Decretals*. In Migne, *Decreti Pars Decima* (PL, 161:1, col. 689-746), the tenth part concerns homicide, and its full title is: "*De homicidiis spontaneis, et non spontaneis. De parricidiis, et fratricidiis. Et de occisione legitimarum uxorum, et seniorum, et clericorum. Et quod non omnis hominem occidens homicida sit; et de eorum poentientia.*" The work discusses killing, and it examines the conditions which cause a killing to be lawful as opposed to those conditions which render a killing to be unlawful, and hence sinful. The traditional language of the Will is preserved suggesting that a voluntary and unlawful killing is serious and sinful, while an involuntary, non-felonious, homicide is excusable. One can observe that there is a refined and existent framework from which to draft a legal code. One may also observe that Ivo consistently defers to the major writings of St. Augustine, some of which we list in brackets taken from Ivo's text, "De Homicidius" [*Epistola ad Publicolam; Epistola ad Marcellinum; De Civitate Dei; Quaestionum in*

Exodus; Contra Cresconium Grammaticum; Ad Macedoniam; Ad Donatum; Ad Laetarium; Super Joan.; Quaestionum super Num; De libero arbitrio; Quaestionum in Leviticum; Quaestionum evangeliorum]. The linguistic influence, therefore, of Augustine is apparent, the text of Ivo in this treatise revealing how the Will is that faculty by and through which a consideration of criminal and moral responsibility rests. Ivo also, as the title indicates, draws upon the various pronouncements of the Councils of the Church to indicate how degrees of seriousness are assigned to immoral acts. He cites with approval the broad condition by which criminal conduct may be excused which the Council of Worms stated: that the insane are not morally responsible for their acts. ["Cap. 154, (of the present text): *De insano si homicidium perpetraverit. Ex eodem, cap.* 7 (counc. Vorm, c. 28).] But throughout this treatise on homicide, Ivo does not use the language of "intention" directly. If an act occurs in which the question of moral or culpable responsibility is moot, he asks if the action is voluntary; and the form which the inquiry takes is to use "sponte" or "voluntate" in some form or in some nominal construction, as in, "sponte comisso" [at col. 734] or "*Qui voluntarie homicidium fecerint...*" [at col. 730]. This construction and language are consistent with the use we saw from the Councils, and from Augustine and from Cicero. When we come to the *Panormia*, in the edition of Migne, it is not to writing on Homicide that we turn, which occupies the beginning of Book 8 (col. 1303-1318), but to the question entitled, *De Juramento Licito et Illicito* (col. 1325-1334), at Cap. CXI, wherein Ivo considers this question: "*De eo qui jurat falsum quod verum. August. De. Verb. serm. 28*" (col. 1331-1332). The "rain" case is again discussed, as it was by Augustine, and of it Ivo says, "*Dicitur enim vere pluit, vere et jurat, et tamen pluit ibi, sed ille nescit, et putat non pluisse, perjurus est. Interest quemadmodum verbum procedat ex animo. Ream linguam non facit, nisi rea mens.*" There is no further commentary upon the matter, and, one may notice, by referring to the text of Migne both for Augustine and for Ivo, that the text is a fairly close reproduction of the Augustinian text which we reproduced in Chapter 2. It should be noted that Ivo's reproduction of Augustine still locates an intentional act (in relation to the taking of an oath) to the knowing telling of a falsehood by an agent. There is no isolated mental quality to be found in his text which would be considered an "intention" *per se*.

6. In *Pillans v. Van Mierup*, 3 Burr. 1663 (1765), Lord Mansfield held, in part, that a moral duty was ground enough for the enforcement of a civil contract. In *Hawkes v. Saunders*, 1 Cowp. 289 (1775), he reaffirmed the position, holding that the moral duty itself was the consideration in a contract. The House of Lords, however, in the case of *Rann v. Hughes*, 4 Brown P.C. (1778), held that Lord Mansfield was mistaken in his understanding of the doctrine of consideration in the law of civil contracts, and stated by way of correcting him, "It is undoubtedly true that every man is by the law of nature bound to fulfil his engagements. It is equally true that the law of this country supplies no means, nor affords any remedy, to compel the performance of an agreement made without sufficient consideration." This is not a lesson easily learned. In the mid-1970's, Burmah Oil, because of a fall in the English stock market, was forced to sell much of its North Sea oil holdings. The market rose in mid-1976; now that same oil company

undertook a law suit against the purchaser of those same stocks, because they were forced to sell the stocks at an unjustly low and unfair price.

7. *Leges*, 61, 18, p. 199 (Downer edition).

8. *Leges*, 66, 1, p. 209.

9. The major work of the period with regard to its moral concepts and its psychological notions (as to how the soul "functions") is still D. Odon Lottin's *Psychologie Et Morale Aux XIIe Et XIIIe Siecles*, as published by Abbaye Du Mont Cesar (Louvain, Belgique, 1949) and J. Duculot, its editor, at Bembloux (Belgique). There is still not a published text of Stephan Langton's works, and one must be a manuscript scholar to be able physically to read the script of the text, a copy of which is at St. John's College, Cambridge. Legal philosophy and jurisprudence from 1100 to 1500 is a subject which is not even in its infancy; it is, at best, in a fetal stage of development.

10. *Leges*, sections c.90 ff.; c.91 ff.; c.92 ff.; c. 93ff. and c. 94.

11. *Cf. Aristotle in the West* by F. Van Steenbergen (Louvain).

12. 88, 8: "*Nemo ipsius suum infantem reddere cogatur quem uoluntarie non occidit...*" (pp. 272-273 of Downer).

13. 90,1: "*Si quis dum inter se dimicantes diuidere satagit ex industria uel incuria decertantium occidatur innocens reddat eum qui occidit quamuis rixam non incepit*" (pp. 278-279 of Downer).

14. 90,6b: "*Distantis uero sit si quis eum ad opus suum rogauerit et si sponte aduenerit...*" (pp. 280-281 of Downer).

15. 90, 11d: "*...ubi homo aliud intendit et aliud euenit (ubi opus accusetur, non* uoluntas [emphasis ours])*...iudices statuant...*" (pp. 284-285 of Downer).

16. *Cf. Principles of Sacramental Theology*, by Bernard Leeming, S.J., for a clear statement of the notion of sacramental intention. One may consult Chapter Fourteen, "The Doctrine of Intention," pp. 435-461, and Chapter Fifteen, "Presumption of Intention," pp. 462-496 (London: Longmans, Green and Co., 1955).

17. At Cap. 39, when speaking about punishment, Ivo replies that a punishment accrues to the type of act, "*Si quis voluntarie homicidum fecerit, ad januam ecclesiae catholicae semper subjaceat, et communionem in exitu vitae sua recipiat. Si autem non ex voluntate, sed ex casu aliquo homicidium fecerit, prior canon septem annis agere poenitentiam jussit, quinque secundus mandavit*" (*Decreti Pars* X, at col. 702, [PL, 161:1], Paris, 1889). The language is familiar from the early Councils when the severity of a penance was to be determined by how fully a penitent had consented to an act. If one did an act "*ex casu*" then such precluded that one had acted from evil premeditation, and may, or may not, have been careless. It could be open to question if by

accident also entailed that one's moral character (as in culpa) may have contributed to the accident. It may have been an "accident" but one which resulted from "carelessness"; or it may have been an accident, pure and simple.

18. *Cf. De Mendacio*, PL, 161:1, cols. 1333-1338, *op. cit.*

19. We wish to reduce to a footnote an example of what we mean. When Professor Maitland pioneered in developing early English legal history he produced a number of valued texts, and made comparisons from historical sources in order to throw light upon a legal past clothed fairly much in darkness. When he edited selections from the writings of *Azo and Bracton* (Selden Society, vol. 8, 1894, as published [then] by Bernard Quaritch, 1895: London), he had, by use of an appendix, attempted to show that Bracton's attitudes towards homicide were, in part, found to have been derived from an exposition on the subject by Bernard of Pavia. By the method of textual comparison, Maitland reproduced the text he had of Bracton, and the text he had of Bernard of Pavia, over pages 225-235 of the volume. The text for Bernard was that which had been prepared by E. A. T. Laspeyres, and it was entitled, *Bernardi Papiensis Summa Decretalium*, printed at Ratisbonae by G. Iosephum Manz, MDCCCLXI, even though Maitland listed the publication date as 1860. In the text of Laspeyres Titulus X is to be found in Liber V, and it is entitled, "De homicidio voluntario vel casuali," pp. 219-224. In the edition which we consulted one can observe that a final text has yet to be produced of Bernard's text, so much textual apparatus of variant texts there is to be found reduced to footnotes by Laspeyres. What Maitland did, and we need not reproduce it here, was to show how passages from Bracton (in the impoverished edition which Maitland had of the text in 1894) matched in style (somewhat) and in tone what had been composed by Bernard of Pavia on the subject, and he concluded that from Bernard the major subject matter of Bracton on homicide had been derived.

The portion of Bracton to which Maitland refers is now to be found in the superb edition prepared by Professor Thorne of Harvard (Harvard University Press and The Selden Society, 1968) at folio 120, and it is entitled "The crime of homicide and the divisions into which it falls" [*De crimine homicidio et qualiter dividitur*], occupying that portion of *De Legibus* which is concerned with Pleas of the Crown, beginning on p. 340 of the Thorne edition.

If we note that Bernard of Pavia died in 1191 A. D., the textual influence is plausible. The composition of *De Legibus* is thought to date from the 1250's, and its emendations place it near to 1268-1277, when, it is supposed, the redactor(s) gave us the book we now have. But this is a matter for the textualist to decide. With the death of Raymond of Pennafort at 1275 A.D., and considering the time of the composition of *De Legibus*, another textual scholar, F. Schulz, argued that Raymond of Penafort (*his spelling*) was the derivative influence for Bracton's position (in folio 120) on homicide. In

The Law Quarterly Review (July, 1945, pp. 286-292), Schulz argues his thesis by presenting the Latin texts of both Bracton and Raymond de Penafort. He used the Woodbine edition for Bracton; while for Raymond he used the edition of 1603, which we shall cite properly, and an unpublished manuscript: Bodleian MS. *Selden Supra 87* (Summary Catalogue no. 3475) which, in folios 5 through 46, contained the *Summa de casibus* of Raymond and was, in this manuscript, a copy which was written in England in the late 13th century.

The edition from Rome is dated 5 November 1603, and its proper title, not given by Schulz is: *Svmma* Sti. *Raymundi de Peniafort Barcinonensis, Ord. Praecicator. De Poenitentia et Matrimonio*, Cum Glossis Ionnis De Friburgo (Nvnc Primvm in lvcem edita), Roma sumptibus Ioannis Tallini. The next edition we consulted was that which Schulz did not like because he claimed that it confused a reader by incorporating into the text of Raymond commentaries other than his own which he cited or used. This is the Veronae edition of MDCCXLIV, *Ex Typographia Seminarii, Apud Augustinum Carattonium*, and its title is: *Sancti Raymundi de Pennafort*, Ordinis Praedicatorum, *Summa*, which was a revision of the edition of MDCCXX. It may be a matter of personal taste, but this edition is not confusing. It puts into scare quotes that material which Raymond used, and, by citing material in this way, it saves the reader the necessity of having to use a Vatican Library to find material. The edition is, we would urge, therefore of much use.

The judgment which a legal philosopher may wish to make about the historical research of both of these scholars is that it does show that common law concepts did not originate solely from within the method of the common law itself. No doubt both Bernard of Pavia and Raymond of Pennafort are writers from whom Bracton, or his redactor, may draw, and one must bear this historical influence in mind. It does not close the case. The state of manuscript research into this sphere of medieval scholarship is in its infancy. Schulz states that there existed other manuscripts in the hands of private collectors which he could not locate (p. 290). In an adjacent area, Bernard Leeming, S. J., could remark, in his *Principles of Sacramental Theology* (*op. cit.*), on an important issue which concerned differences on the validity of sacramental administration in medieval theology that "The present position of studies in mediaeval canon law and moral theology does not permit an exact estimate of the number and influence of followers of the various positions..." (p. 537). We are just now having edited and put into print texts of major writers of the Middle Ages, and the condition of medieval legal texts is, at the very least, a century behind in scholarship that of medieval theological and philosophical texts. Such an influential follower of St. Thomas Aquinas as was Bernard of Trilia has only now come to be printed: *Quaestiones Disputatae de Cognitione Animae Separatae*, Ad Fidem Codicum Edidit by Pius Kunzle, O. P. (Fribourg: Editionis Francke Bernas, 1969).

This edition is superior to that of the 1965 Pontifical Institute edition. What the historical research in law does do for the legal philosopher is to show him how much one world, that of medieval canon law and theology, influenced and fostered a newer world, which was the early common law.

Schulz argues, and we do not wish to pursue the matter in this study, that the position taken by Maitland, with regard to the influence of Bernard upon Bracton, must be abandoned in light of Raymond's *Summa de casibus*. We prefer to use both texts to demonstrate that the medieval tradition was a living tradition, and, as such, one can assume that both (and other authors too) exercised an influence upon the development of the concept of homicide in *De Legibus*.

CHAPTER THREE

Aquinas, Bracton, and the Medieval Sacramentalists

Many years ago, in fact, just after the Second World War, there existed a magicians' supply shop in Los Angeles, California, by the name of *Merv Taylor's*. It was a shop known for its high class equipment, carrying on the tradition of a great shop, *Thayer's*, which had closed during the war, having been a fixture for professional magicians for decades. *Taylor's* had one hallmark: his equipment was finely made, but simple. At work in most of his illusions or devices was one simple principle, and the results were always spectacular to behold. One of his famous tricks was called "*Multum in parvum*." It consisted of a small shot glass from which the magician appeared to pour endless amounts of liquids into several larger tumblers, and then the entire amount into a large tumbler, and thence to cause it all to disappear! The entire piece of equipment cost an illusionist only $37.50.

Not to belabor false analogies, nor to construct the same, one could view the development of our early criminal law principles as a study in "much from little," and with great economy and simplicity. The difference, certainly, is that the beginnings do not disappear in the end, as did the liquids in the illusion. Our principles have become refined, and the body of our criminal law has been enlarged greatly from what it once was; but even this may be a matter of opinion. There were more crimes in the eighteenth century for which one could suffer penalties than there now are; however, trial processes in our own age tend to be more complicated, as well as fairer, and the body of current law *seems* to possess a complexity greater than it once did. But this is another topic for some other paper. It could equally well be argued, perhaps, that modern law tends towards simplicity and precision – mark the reforms in the law of property in 1925 – and though greater in number of statutory instruments, nevertheless, is actually simpler to work with.

What we observe, to use the historical present tense, from the time of Bracton is that the common law begins to grow out of a canonical and legal tradition which used remarkably few leading principles. Guilt for a crime, however assigned, or if gained through torture like the hideous *peine forte et dure* (Statute of Westminster 1, 1275) which permitted the accused to be pressed under weights until he pleaded "Guilty" or "Not Guilty," needed an admission of the accused. That admission was founded upon a theory of human nature: i.e., that an accused knew what he did, and that he assented to do what he did. The canonists balanced the human equation between the movement of the intellect and the movement of the will. Medieval theological and philosophical theory[1] did little to discuss at length the cause(s) of madness. It was acknowledged that one could go mad and be insane,[2] but such observations played little part in the formal development of the law. A cause might be assigned to account for the madness; the accused may have been considered to have been possessed. On the other hand, from the point of view of theory, it may have been argued that the *matter* had not been predisposed to accept a human *form*, and thus the madness of an individual may have been accounted for in that way without appeal to the instigation of the devil. The insane were excused at law.[3] If an accused were simply a Poor Tom, then he might be excused as one might excuse an infant. We hesitate to compare Poor Tom to an animal, for, although Coke likened madness (later) to raging like an animal, one must, nevertheless, not forget that animals were considered to be responsible for their actions (during a period of our common law).[4] One did not become an animal (as when a man changes into a werewolf); for, if one did actually become an animal, it would have entailed (for the medieval mind) that a man was no longer a man. This is not a distinction without a difference, nor is it a tautology. The medievalist needed to preserve a real distinction between what was called animal behavior and what was called human behavior. One could liken Poor Tom's actions to those of an animal; but Poor Tom was yet a man because, it was urged, Poor Tom at some time (possibly) could again become a moral agent, which an animal could never become. Furthermore, Poor Tom, even with his moral faculties and his rational faculties suspended, possessed an immortal soul, and an animal did not. The analogy was a part of medieval and Renaissance understanding. We need only turn to Donne's amorist inclinings to read how the imagination and understanding of an Elizabethan poet and lawyer preserved this mixture, as in

> The soule with body, is a heaven combin'd
> With earth, and for mans ease, but nearer joyn'd.[5]

The law takes over this preservation and, however variously it understands or misunderstands the nature of madness, that a man be mad and not be thought to be the same as an animal follows into the logic of the law. Poor Tom, for all that, was always a man for the law.

If a theory of legal responsibility developed, it developed out of a prior theory *that* one was always to be considered as a moral agent, save when excusing conditions (sleep, unconsciousness, lunacy, possession [i.e., that one should, at least, try to unpossess a person, even if the rites for such unpossession might, finally, cause the person to be burned, the logic persisted that one should be brought back to a human state so that, even in death, one could behold God]) were thought to prevail. Moral agency, as we have suggested, arose or could be predicated of a person, owing to the interaction of Intellect and Will. Much ink would be spilled to argue which was the nobler faculty, the Intellect or the Will, and the force of such arguing would be spent mildly in developing legal theory as to what constituted the atomic elements of a law. Was a legal proposition a law because it appealed to a command, or was it a valid legal proposition, and thus binding upon a subject, because it appealed to one's reason? One strand of the theological argument, thus transmuted into legal theory, would advance the claims of the Will and thus of Edict and Parliamentary pronouncements and enactments, while another strand of the theological theory, woven into legal speculation, would advance the rights of Natural Law and thus of Constitutional or (Contract) theories of law.[6]

It may be advanced that the writings of Raymond of Pennafort influenced Bracton's formulations of the law on homicide, and that textual comparison will show (as Schultz attempted) how textual passages are mirrored in Raymond's treatise. *Liber Secundus*[7] of Raymond's *Svmmae* sets forth textual similarities, which does support Schulz partially. For our purposes the chapter shows that Raymond may have been one of a number of models available to Bracton; the state of scholarship for that period (1200's) is not well advanced, as we said in our previous chapter. In the *De homicidio* itself, one can note how the atomic elements for legal responsibility appear. It may be asked if the homicide were an "accidental" killing, or was it from "necessity," or was it "deliberate" and "voluntary." Did one give over to killing without wicked deliberation (*...odij meditatione* [T:149, Col. 1])? Is one moved to sorrow for what he has done? These, and other citations, flow on from the tradition of canonical writers. Degrees of seriousness are sketched out, the recurring cases presented, e.g., accidentally being hit by a stone, or the falling tree cut by the woodsman, concluding that "*...quod homicidium voluntatiu semper est mortale peccatum, & enorme...si quis voluntate*" (T:159, Col. 2).

Raymond preserves the distinction, from Augustine, between spiritual and corporeal homicide [T:145, Cols. 1 & 2]. Although the notion may seem strange to us now, it did seem reasonable, and moving, to the early canonists, and, in fact, it found its way into Elizabethan drama.[8] We will recall that the distinction, earlier in theology, concerned the interior act of the soul, namely, one must not lie. Lying, though it may not be perceived by some third party, is yet seen by God, and such seeing, it was thought, by God Himself was to see the soul as it was: a lying soul was a soul which had suffered a spiritual death, just as Christ saw the High Priests as they truly were, "Whited Sepulchres." The force of such belief, and its resultant logic, would fortify the integrity of an oath; one would not lie if one believed and knew that God was one's witness. The transference in Elizabethan drama, to cite but a single instance, would show the audience how an outward effect, or the possibility of an outward effect, could serve to stand for the interior state of an agent. Hamlet, upon sheathing his sword and deciding not to kill Claudius the King at prayer, then reasons (3.3.90 ff),

> Up, sword, and how thou a more horrid hent,
> When he is drunk asleep, or in his rage,
> Or in th'incentuous pleasure of his bed,
> At game, a-swearing, or about some act
> That has no relish of salvation in't,

> Then trip him that his heels may kick at heaven,
> And that his soul may be as damned and black
> As hell whereto it goes;...

The King, however, which Hamlet did not know, had not repented:

> KING [*rises*]. My words fly up, my thoughts, remain below.
> Words without thoughts never to heaven go.

Had Hamlet killed Claudius then he would have been guilty of the terrible crime of spiritual homicide. Claudius' act of praying is a lie because his actions are moved by wrongful intentions, purposed to deceive, as Claudius' refrain revealed, "Words without thoughts never to heaven go."

Raymond (T:148, Cols. 1 & 2) notes the four modes of killing: "*Facto quatuor modis, scilicet iustitia, necessitate, casu, & voluntate.*" We shall not dwell upon the gloss at length – it is far too long a text – but we wish to note that Raymond does appeal to *intention* to ground the goodness of an act. He says (T:149, Col. 2) with regard to sorrow for an act that it turns upon a proper goodness of mind ("*...bonarum enim mentium est, ibi culpam agnoscere, vbi culpa no est...*"). If that which happens from necessity, in which an agent has not turned his mind to it to bring it about (or rejoice in it even, "Ah, glad the old bag died!"), did not have an "*intentionem corruptam*," then moral condemnation should not fall upon the penitent. One's interior state of mind is pure, and to one's inadvertent act* (such as cutting down the tree) no guilt should accrue. The words which operate through the text for the purpose of determining guilt are "*voluntate*" or "*propter intentionem corruptam*" or a killing which is not done "*justitia.*" Although a killing may be "*sponte,*" it may have been commanded, as a soldier killing another soldier in battle. If the command is lawful, and granted that one himself does not possess a wickedness of will, the killing which results is just because it is done under the cloak of the law.

---

* "Inadvertent act" may appear to be an awkward construction. That which one does is not "inadvertent." One turns to cutting down the tree. The consequence is what one does not foresee, or encompass, or imagine, or design, or plan for. But in cases such as this, one generally speaks about the entire act, the meaning of which to be taken to mean that one acted, *and* there were consequences, but one had not desired those consequences, nor had any knowledge that they would come about, so that the total action, i.e., cutting down the tree, is described as an inadvertent act.

We are not so much concerned with arguing that one text may have influenced another text, as Schulz[9] argued, as we are to demonstrate the form(s) growing in our early common law to convey intention.

When we search for the logical structure of intention as it is thought to be embodied in Bracton, or Raymond of Pennafort, or in early case law, one finds that one must provide more than a ramiform stem, as, for instance, is provided by Sir James Fitzjames Stephen in his *History of The Criminal Law of England.*[10] His schematum is helpful, and it does fall within the tradition of many of the texts on ethics (of an earlier period[11]) which presented a subject *as if* it were a tree; for instance, like the Arbor Bigamiae,[12] a tree-like drawing showing the degrees of impermissible marital relationships. Obviously, what the trees or tabulations do not do (we are not prejudging that they are not *able* to do) is to present an analytical examination of their logical or schematic content. The diagram may give one a form to follow, as did a mood and figure in a syllogism, but the logical forms which intention could take had not been thoroughly tabulated, nor premises examined to answer the question of whether such premises were true primitives of a system, or were, rather, conclusions from premises the truth of which was itself in need of examination and analysis.

There appeared to be a common form of scholarship, a community of thought, circulating in the Middle Ages. We can isolate parts of the transmission, as did Schulz, by locating sentential similarities from one author to another, e.g., Raymond of Pennafort upon Bracton, and/or (to follow on Maitland's extended argument in *Bracton and Azo*)[13] the force of Bernard of Pavia upon Bracton. But even here one cannot rest in simple isolated texts. Of these authors one can ask, Shall they serve as if they were first premises in an historical demonstration? and serve solely so? It is unlikely that we can rest there *if* we argue from the force of a tradition, something living and viable within and upon a scholarly community. If we rest only with Raymond or Bernard, like the argument from motion, we find that they, as authors, do not contain themselves without need of any other. One finds that one must turn to an adjacent and living tradition: that of the various books of penitentials (*Liber Poenitentialis*). From recent scholarship it can be demonstrated that Robert of Flamborough, *circa* 1205 A. D., through his *Liber Poenitentialis*, exercised influence upon other canonists and theologians of the period.[14] Flamborough's book was intended to guide confessors, and it was not, as were the larger Summas of the period, a speculative textbook concerned with difficult topics in theology; e.g., the existence of God, or the nature of the Will, or the justification for the immortality of one's soul. When one turns to Albert Magnus, or Aquinas, one finds that the logical form of a claim, i.e., what are the constitutive elements (say) of an interior act,[15] is examined in conjunction with its logical content, and the form of the examination embodies the argument(s) of an objector, a statement of what position is thought to obtain, and then a rejoinder in which the propriety of the position is justified by an appeal to formal logical argument and to (what is thought to be) the proper use of leading authorities. Flamborough is not arguing in this way; in fact, it is less an argument he is presenting than a statement of how one should view penitential matters. What one does extract from his *Liber Poenitentials*, however, is a usage of language, in tone and in meaning, which will have found its way into the early language of legal estimation and codification, as one reads in Bracton, for instance, in the distinction branched to depict differences of degree of seriousness in regard to homicide.

In Book III of the *Liber Poenitentialis* one can read that "intention" is functioning as a key wòrd to express an interior state of mind ordered towards a proper understanding of a sacramental state. Flamborough speaks of "*De intentione ordinantis*"[16] and the opening sentence is clear in its statement that intention determines a sacramental act, which we quote:

> 84. *Intentio ordinantis est de substantia ordinis, ut scilicet intendat facere id quod ecclesia intendit facere in cujuslibet ordinis collatione.*[17]

So important is the conjunction of correct speech (or sacramental formula) with the intention of the priest (or, in this case, of the one who administers the sacrament of baptism in accordance with the mind of the Church) that Flamborough states what will not serve as a valid baptism, as these passages may illustrate. We add, that he warns against obvious sacramental omissions,[18]

> 85. *Sed, licet intentionem rectam habeat, multotiens tamen multa omittit.*

And then he cites various examples,

> *Verbi gratia, in baptismo sunt aqua et verba haec: 'Ego baptizo te in nomine Patris et Filii et Spiritus sancti. Amen.'*

sets what should be the case or the rule, and these examples of misrule or invalid baptisms (and thus show how a sacrament, in general, can be rendered invalid).

> *Si ergo aliquis immergat in quocumque alio liquore quam in aqua, non baptizat.*
>
> *Item, si mutet verba et dicat 'Ego immergo te,' vel 'intingo,' non baptizat.*
>
> *Item, si truncat verba dicendo 'Ego baptizo te in nomine Patris,' nisi plus addat, non baptizat.*

The rule is a general one, and he states it in this way to account for cases he may not have included,

> *Item, si corrupte proferat verba sponte et ex certa scientia, cum sciat et possit recte proferre, vel si sic proferat ut errorem introducat, non baptizat. Oportet igitur ut forma verborum sit integra, perfecta et ordinata.* Item dico in aliis sacramentis (emphasis ours).

The labor of refining these early declarations about instrumental causality would fall upon the later scholastics, and we need not develop their notions here. It is enough to state that Flamborough has advanced a simple notion of instrumental causality, and, to this day, it is found in the workings of the law. When one takes a solemn oath, calling God as his witness (in most cases), one creates speech (one's own words) which stands for, or is an instrument of, the state of one's mind. Simply put, this is the doctrine of sacramental intention, and Flamborough gave instances of it when he cited improper ministrations of a sacrament.

We draw upon this early sacramental language to suggest that it seemed reasonable for early legal writers to draw upon. It was not an arcane language, although it was a difficult language, many different theologians holding different attitudes as to the *precise* meaning of sacramental intent. Early common law borrowed heavily from a religious moral past, and one doubts if it could have been otherwise, the past being what it was. Logically, there is no need for a replication of or borrowing from the past; but the movement of human life is, more often than not, a movement from what was the case to what may be the case, shaped by the past. Human inventiveness is seldom *de novo*: linguistic traditions are carried over into what is originated or invented, however submerged be the workings of the linguistic roots and past of a language.

To what extent one can construct a linear map of which texts influenced which later authors, Firth is guarded in his claims, stating through his critical edition that, at present, the manuscript tradition cannot support overly large claims. He tells us that the *Libri sententiarum* of Peter Lombard, as well as the works of Peter Cantor, *Summa de sacramentis et animae consiliis*, and of Robert Courson, *Summa*, are not cross-indexed against possible parallels with Flamborough's prose either because the textual study is incomplete, with no critical edition of an author yet printed, or, at present, there seems no close relationship to compare. The state of definitive legal editions is worse yet. Bracton was only recently completed by Professor Thorne. Other early legalists, such as Thomas Langton or Ralph de Hengham, are in manuscripts only, and which of those manuscripts are the critical manuscripts scholarship has not revealed.

One observes, in *Liber Quintus* of Flamborough,[19] that its author is concerned, as were the early Councils of the Church, to assign fairly and justly to a penitent the penances he would have to undertake for certain sins. To the model penitent of the *Liber Poenitentialis* (just as to the model student in St. Germain's *Dialogues between a Doctor of Divinity and a Student of the Common Law* [*circa* 1523]) there are put by the confessor model questions, the purpose of which is to ascertain the penitent's sorrow for his sins, as well as the degree of seriousness of each sin.

We need not examine the treatise in detail. However, we wish to draw upon certain topical portions which may be important to our own understanding of the evolution of "intention" at law, and, in this way, portions of the *Liber Poenitentialis* may be helpful to one in an attempt to gain an understanding of certain root legal concepts.

It was patently evident that Flamborough possessed a language of intention, revealed in his sections on sacramental intention. He appeared to restrict intentional language to human acts in which emotion or compulsion did not hold sway. When one administered a sacrament it was assumed that one administered it with a proper disposition. One would not baptize *rashly*; one would not absolve *in anger*; one would not ordain *compulsively*; one would not celebrate Mass *contumeliously*. The order of the sacraments was an order of the mind; an intentional order in which the sacrament, as a sign, revealed the state of mind of its ordinand, and so confirmed by a valid ritual. Each sacrament had a certain matter (water for baptism; oils for chrism; bread and wine for Eucharist, and the like); each sacrament had a certain (verbal) form. The sacramental form brought one to a cognitive order of existence. It was not the Will, *per se*, which denominated and distinguished each sacrament one from the other, as well as marked out what were valid from what were invalid sacramental administerings; rather, it was the specific sacramental formula, as properly understood by the minister or priest or bishop, which distinguished a sacrament from the others, and determined its validity in administration. Flamborough is clear on the matter, as we trust these few selections did reveal and demonstrate. "[U]nderstand," in this instance, should entail: understand *and* properly perform, as in the concept of a performative utterance. It is no good for a minister simply, *in se*, to "understand" a sacramental formula without, at the same time during its enactment, speaking that formula correctly. Were he to "understand," but to speak incorrectly, it could then be advanced that the sacrament had been administered incorrectly or invalidly.

The causality for sacramental efficacy is, for Flamborough, an intentional causality. The intention of the priest, coupled with proper matter for the particular sacrament, constituted proper sacramental administration, all other matters being equal. The "link" between the private world of an agent, and the public world of ritual (as in sacramental form), was to be found in the intention of the agent, and the expression of his intention was through the vehicle of the rubric of sacramental form: its proper matter, and its proper language.

Why then does that same kind of intentional clarity not carry over into penitential matters? The answer to this question may be found in the act of sinning itself, and as seen by Flamborough's ideal confessor. One may, also, have to introduce an axiom common to Christian theology: if the intellect were at fault for sin, then, mirroring in some way its Divine Author, He Himself would be at fault for sin in the world, and such an assertion was simple heresy for a Christian believer. The fault, which Augustine of Hippo argued, lay in the Will of man; it was the Will which produced an act, and also which desired an end. To sin was both to produce an act (to consent and to do) and to seek a wrongful end, that object of desire which was a wrongful object to be desired, "object" here being used in the very loose sense of an attainment one sought or seeks. The *Liber Poenitentialis* continued on in that strong Augustinian tradition of the Will as the root of wickedness.

By turning to the language of Flamborough's advice one can observe that it is to the language of the Will, and not to the language of the mind, that he turns to state human failings. The human will is not a simple compulsive or non-cognitive faculty. To have advocated such would have been in bold contrast to the developed rational tradition from Augustine, through Gregory of Nasianzus (of the *De Animae*) to St. John of Damascene (of the *De Fide Orthodoxa*). The human will was a rational appetite; it was not thought to be an involuntary response. One may not understand how early Christian writers justified such a conception, nor agree with their understanding of the voluntary; we state only that they did claim such an understanding of the Will.

Flamborough asks, to take some instances, if a killing were: "*Si quis voluntarie homicidium fecerit....*"[20] The stress is upon "voluntary." He speaks again of "*Si quis casu non volens homicidium perpetraverit...*,"[21] again stressing the volitive nature of an act, and not its simple intentional nature, as he would have spoken of sacramental administration as possessing a proper or fit "intention."

One is constantly asked to consider the character of the penitent, and in this regard Flamborough uses dispositive predicates to ask about his penitent. Did the sin arise because of jealousy, or from greed, or from lustfulness, or from anger, all of which center upon some defect of Will?

One of strong character wills not to be jealous, nor lustful, nor violent, nor avaricious. An act, such as homicide, is to be determined whether or not "*..de homicidio sponte commisso...*,"[22] and that verbal form occurs frequently throughout the treatise. Did the agent act of his *own free will*? The confessor is then instructed to look for signs of the penitent's sorrow for his sinful acts. Flamborough, with regard to serious sins, uses the verb "lugeat," which suggests that one deplores, or bewails, or laments his past sinful actions. Verbs of this sort show that Flamborough wants the ideal confessor to recognize in the penitent signs that the penitent is voluntarily repulsed towards sin. The confessor is not to seek whether a penitent "knows" only that what he did was wrong; that would be a simple intentional state. On the contrary, to know that an act is deplorable is not the same as to deplore an act which one knows to be deplorable. The latter state brings with it the full movement of the Will towards contrition.

Because the giving of absolution is a practical judgment, Flamborough asks the priest to determine if the case is a doubtful case or not. If "*eo quod incertum sit sif voluntate an casu occiderit*," the nature of the penance will turn on determining whether "*si voluntate*" is the case or whether "*si casu*"[23] is the case. An act done with full and free commission of one's will is, of the degrees of seriousness, the most serious, and, as such, deserves a graver penance.

There is, then, a sufficient tradition connecting Christian medievalists one with the other that Bracton could draw upon. What we do not observe in the Bractonian presentation of culpability is any minute or detailed analysis of human faculties, as we observe in the writings of the various theologians (writing in an Augustinian tradition) up to the twelfth and thirteenth centuries; nor do we observe the detailed conceptual model analysis of human faculties which early scholastic Aristotelians will present in their effort to explain various modes of human behavior. One is left to *assume* that Bracton drew upon the religious corpus about him, and one cites certain leading authors to show how reasonable it appears to make these assumptions that the period did influence his compilations of the law which is concerned with human culpability and criminality. One seeks out the traces, some authors more than others showing stronger trace elements in Bracton.

When we come to view that portion of Bracton's *De Legibus* in which he discusses the crime of homicide,[24] one has to accept that his (Bracton's) claims do not justify or explain all that he (Bracton) hopes will be justified or explained. Bracton asks both *what* is homicide and *why* it is so called: "Hence we must see what it is and why it is so called, its various kinds, and the punishment imposed."[25] Thorne notes that this definition follows, in the main, from the *Summa de casibus* of Raymond of Pennafort at ii, 1,1. One will recall that Raymond's statement read as follows, and we shall cite from *De homicidio* at *Tit*. 1 of Liber Secundus, the first paragraph, using the Tallini text:

> *In prima parte dictum est de quibufda* [the Verona text reads: *quibfdam criminibus* at page 137] *criminibus, quae principaliter Deum committuntur; in hac secunda parte de ijs, quae proximum specialius committuntur, agendum est: & primo de homicidio. Videndum ergo quid f(s)it homicidium, & vnde docatur; quae eius species, qua poena homicidae puniantur, & quae dispensario fiat erga clericum homicidam* (T: p. 145).

There is an undeniable parallel in what Bracton set out and in what Raymond had written.

Bracton accepts that a distinction rests between spiritual and corporal homicide, but he chooses to develop only the meaning of corporal homicide, which he states to be "...the slaying of a man by man."[26] The stress is not upon the man dying, but upon how his death was brought about. This is made clear, but without a reason for the distinction, when Bracton says, "If it is done by an ox, a dog or some thing it will not properly be termed homicide."[27] The victim is killed (bodily), and his death is something which the other, as agent, causes. But cause is not a simple empirical connective, as in A stabbed B, and B died. The cause of a victim's death can be brought about by word (in three ways) and by deed (in four ways). One turns to some state of the agent to determine the nature of the agent's act. Beneath the historical circumstances which surrounded the actual making of law and custom[28] a fundamental mental principle runs through common law, following it to our most recent decisions of this day: namely, however embodied and expressed, responsibility for a criminal act rests in an agent's state of mind. Criminal guilt is, although a tortured and difficult process (perhaps) to determine by trial, that which indicates or symbolizes a guilty mind of the agent. The criminal law will keep returning to the agent, even in a modified form when the "law" assumes that an agent "should have foreseen" the "natural consequences" of his act. That formula, however, must be struck down in cases of insanity, which return to the state of an agent's mind: that he could not form a criminal intent (for whatever reason), and thus his "mind" could not contain "guilt" for his act. These are general principles, but as general principles they are rooted early on in the common law. Bracton has drawn upon the sacramental tradition, and upon the moral tradition of the canonists, the yeast of both traditions at work in his early codification of the criminal law. The sacramental tradition was concerned to establish *that* a sacrament, by means of its matter and form, *could* be administered properly, and it did so (in part) by developing the doctrine of sacramental intention which was present in twelfth- and thirteenth-century theological writings about the nature of a sacrament. The moral and canonical tradition needed to establish *that* a penitent *could* sin, and also that he *could* be sorry for his sins. This double-sided aspect of sin (its commission and its contrition) involved both cognitive and volitive elements: one knew that one sinned, and one willed not to sin again. The power, in part, rested in the agent to know what he had done (and, by implication, what he could do) and what he should do. By knowing, he could dispose himself to act, the two broad principles which serve to form a conception of what is a unified human act, and to which some concept of responsibility might attach.

Bracton's divisions of the crime of homicide provide us with little new conceptual analysis. His analysis is fairly much an accepted following of earlier theological divisions, save that he does bring into his criminal division the statement that the mind of the offender, in some way, determines the nature of the act. The link between design and execution rests in the intention of the agent, and Bracton speaks of it in this way:

> But it is homicide if done out of malice or from pleasure in the shedding of human blood [and] though the accused is lawfully slain, he who does the act commits a mortal sin because of his evil purpose. But if it is done from a love of justice, the judge does not sin in condemning him to death, nor in ordering an officer to slay him, nor does the officer sin if when sent by the judge he kills the condemned man. But both sin if they act in

> this way when proper legal procedures have not been observed.[29]

The "intention," if one attends to the Latin text, is not the intention of *mens rea*; it is the concept of intention which is qualified by a volitive use of a participle as an adjective, i.e., "*corruptam*" tells one the nature of the intention, "...*propter intentionem corruptam*." The notion of "corruption" followed on in the tradition of St. Augustine of Hippo, that the will, as a human power and faculty, was the seat of human corruption.*

We are not trying to make much of little; but we are concerned to argue that if one accepts the notion of intellect that mind cannot help but know what is presented to it, then (within Augustinian theory) evil (within its many manifestations) must spring from the human will. The priority of value within the causal depiction of a human act will be to attribute to the will the power of being a first cause (however difficult it may be to account for such a notion without at the same time encountering logical paradoxes), and, as a first cause, it *may* or *may not* embody what it ought to follow (namely: the

---

* The notion of corruption of the human will is rife with conceptual problems. It need only be suggested here that the "corruption" tradition attributed to St. Augustine of Hippo may have indicated various internal problems about the concept of will, none of which indications are lucid or without difficulties. On the one hand, corruption may indicate a *design* flaw, i.e., that the will, as a faculty, was so designed that it contained within itself the seeds of its own errors, in much the same fashion that a piston engine may not be a rival for a rotary engine, or a Weber carburetor may not rival fuel injection for performance. If the will is seen to be both a power and faculty, what if the power is flawed, and what if the faculty is flawed? What kind of performance will be given? For St. Augustine, the will was part and parcel of man's fallen nature, hence his flawed nature. Imperfection was part of the will, just as genetic imperfection might be part of a gene.

On the other hand, corruption might be considered as a *capacity* limitation. The reason why corruption is to be found in human behavior is because the will always falls short of attainment, just as a small bore racing car might not be able to exceed the performance of a large bore racing car. The capacity of one is greater than the capacity of the other. Whatever the smaller vehicle attains will always be less than what a larger vehicle could attain.

The logical difficulties inherent in any conception of a *flawed* or *imperfect* will is that whatever is done by will will always be done by and with a *flawed* or *imperfect* will. The elements of which a flaw or imperfection consist do not magically come in and out of play by luck. Those elements are more akin to a harmful gene recessively being the case, than to the contrary appearing as the possibility that the number seven might appear on the first throw of the dice. Imperfection is a flaw *inherent* in this concept of the corruption of the will, and it is not an accidental quality which could, at some time hence, be apparent if certain conditions obtain (like rain on a summer's day sent to spoil the day).

One is left with the old question, which certainly perplexed many theologians: how can an imperfect will reach for perfect acts?

good). In any case, if one is to have a notion of criminal responsibility (derived, as it can be seen, from a notion of theological rectitude) which is coherent, it makes no logical sense to punish, or to extract any form of retribution, if, hypothetically, a theory of human acts is advanced which holds that human acts are non-rational in origin. It must be argued that although the will may not follow what ought to be the case by seeking the highest good, nevertheless, rationally it will follow after *some* good which is desired to be the case. An evil act (and, by force of similitude for Bracton, a criminal act) must be a rational act.

A mis-emphasis seems to occur when (in theory) one confuses that "one may elect to do" with "one should have done." In general, to argue for criminal responsibility it is not common to have as a part of a theory a developed concern why an agent may do less than what he can do, or should do. We are aware, however, that the law will entertain capacity hearings to determine if one is sane, or if a child has the capacity to appreciate the meaning of a criminal statute under which he is charged.[30] It is when one turns to a theory of excuses or exemptions under the law that one will then concentrate upon the question of why an agent did less than he should do. The roots of the assumption for us in this culture may be Pauline: that one tries for the good, but does evil, even against one's will. That is a mystery we are not attempting to solve here.

The principle had been part of common discourse of the period that "intention" determined how a human act was to be viewed. But such viewing, if we may press that metaphor, embodies a two-step distinction. First, what made a human act meritorious or not was that such a act had to be a human act, and the humanness of an act rested upon an intention. An intention, however, possessed an adjectival quality: namely, the *intentio* was either a good intention, or it was a bad intention. We can recall to mind that Abelard himself had carried forth the distinction that intention was the arbiter of virtue in these words, "...*quod intentio sola separat*."[31]

If we may, we wish to issue a caution at this point. When we are discussing various mental distinctions using certain mental predicates, we are aware, and hope our prose reflects this state of awareness, that we are not talking about a robot. One must read the writers from the Middle Ages with a certain giving spirit; it is all too easy to hold them up to ridicule at a surface level, and this often reveals that one does not understand the force of their own writings. They were not talking about "human machines" which one assembled from parts like a "will" and an "intellect" and other such components. The mind of the medieval scholar, with all due respect for his religious assumptions (as well as having an awareness of them), was set upon distinguishing what was presented to him. In the writings of the period, from Peter Lombard (whose *Liber Sententiarum* dates from 1150 A. D., and was the chief theological work of the Middle Ages upon which all scholars commented at some time or other during their writing careers) to John or Joannes de Bromyard, an English Dominican of the late fourteenth century (*Summa Praedicantium*) and follower of Aquinas, the aim of the writings was to *distinguish*. In language fitting to our own time we would say that, in the main, those older writers wrote the philosophy of mind. The Latin into which they cast their thoughts lends itself to one, generally, reading the works in English now, to assume that Latin nominatives indicated substantive conceptual states, so that one spoke of "the" soul, as if one were to speak of "the" goal-post. Such an understanding of their Latin is a misunderstanding, and if one wishes to understand what they did write one should appreciate that the writing of the period of the Middle Ages reveals a developed sense of linguistic subtlety (often only discovered when one must render into English what they wrote in Latin).

The force of the great church Father, Augustine, transmitted itself, certainly, to Peter Lombard, and, we assume, Lombard would have been known to Bracton, either in the full textual sense, or (as we speak of knowing Freud in the twentieth century without having labored through all that he has written) known to Bracton by general consensus of commentaries made by other writers. When Lombard asked "*Quid Sit Peccatum*," which is *Distinction* 35 of Book Two of his *Sentences*'[32] he refines the notion of *malice* by showing that sin, in itself, consists not solely of malice of will, but also of a capability and power to do that which is contrary to law. The Latin reads as follows:

> *Ex prima defcriptione aftenditur peccatu effe voluntas mala, fiue locutio & operatio praua, id est, actus malus tam interior quam exterior: ex altero vero tantum oftenditur effe actus interior. Voluntas enim, vt in fuperioribus dictu eft, motus animi eft; actus*

> *ergo interior eft. Ambr. quoque in lib de Paradifo ait, Quid est peccatum, nisi legis diuinae praeuaricatio, & celeftium inobedientia praeceptorum? Ergo in praeiaricante peccatum eft, fed in mandante culpa non dictio non fuiffet. Non confiftente autem preccato, no solum malitia, fed etiam virtus fortaffe non effet: quae nifi aliqua malitiae fuiffent semina, vel fubfiftere, vel eminere no poffet. Ecce praeuaricationem legis & inobedientiam definit Ambrofius effe peccatum.*

There is sufficient theological framework extant that Bracton could, by simple substitution, read "crime" for "sin." He appears to have codified (at 340) current theological notions relating to the capacity to sin, the requirements for sin, and what might be necessary to distinguish wrongful acts from non-culpable and (even) virtuous acts. Of note is that the objective legal order in itself is not the last step in the chain of legal guilt. There is, yes, a legal order, and against that order one measures the rightness or wrongness of acts which one does. But if one stopped there only with an objective order one would have had early on a strict liability theory of criminal guilt at work in our common law, and this we had not. Bracton still turns to the "heart" of a man. He does not demonstrate *how* guilt is to be established; no method is given, but he states *that* the intention of the agent must act as the last step in the criminal process in which guilt is to be determined. The model which comes to mind for determining guilt is still the model of the confessor and the penitent, and that there be guilt, that one can find in oneself a remembrance of the elements of a criminal commission on the part of oneself, Bracton turns to intention. Intention is that which an agent produces to cause a change. The change may be towards a proper end, and thus no crime has been committed; the change may be towards an improper (illegal) end, and thus a crime may have been committed. But, and this is where he twins law and morals, if one acts well exteriorly (as with a judge sentencing a man to death) while interiorly (by taking malicious delight in entertaining a wicked purpose) one acts as the devil's own, then one has sinned. The criminal law, for the most part, does not look that deeply to human intentions.*

---

* By carrying over an Augustinian concept of the will of man as the source of human wickedness, Bracton could ask about the interior 'side' of an act. The interior side of act is not necessarily a cumbersome phase, as one can understand when he, to himself, might resolve to "attempt" to do something, although never doing something. Exteriorly the "attempt" does not

We wish, however, to pause here to comment upon Bracton's turning from legal stipulations, i.e., his divisions of homicide into excusable at law in contrast to what is not permitted by law–to his moral and religious stipulation in the phrase, "...he who does the act commits a mortal sin because of his evil purpose."

Until now we have argued that the concept which we have come to know in our criminal law as criminal intention has been a concept which, mixed and rich in its sources, has been rooted in a language which centered upon the Will. We have also argued that the dominant feature of that concept has been to stress both its rationality and its freedom. In no wise have we meant to suggest that what medieval and late Renaissance theologians were to call the "mystery" of the freedom of the Will was in any way "solved" by its early common law borrowers. Bracton does not present us with any theory of the Will in the *De Legibus*. If any theory is to be found, it is assumed that the reader (of the time) has enough religious association to know what Bracton is talking about; and for one engaging in philosophical retracings, one must take hints, as it were, from the text itself, and attempt to make associations with what seems to be reasonable connections with the religious and moral tone of the age. In part we have tried to follow this method by showing how linguistic echoes can be found which lead one back to other texts of the period which seem to be germane and pertinent. The

---

show through in the act, although one might observe that an agent was trying hard. But an agent might never have tried at all, yet might have resolved to "attempt" to try. (Stuart Hampshire remarked, "The subject is in the best position to judge what his attitude or sentiment is or was; for the subject usually knows directly and without inference what he was thinking at the time, and therefore can know whether the content of his thoughts was such as to exclude the sentiment imputed" [*Freedom of the Individual*, Chapter 5, "Determinism and Psychological Explanation: A Postscript" (London: Chatto & Windus, 1975), p. 130].)

As if one needed more support–which we believe one does not–that the period was sensitive to the language of intention, one may refer to the *Sententiae Divinitatis* (written between 1141 and 1147 by an author unknown to us) to read:

> ...three things are needful that this [Eucharistic] change should come about: Order, action, intention. Order, that there should be a priest; action, that those words should be said; intention, that he should utter them with the intention that the bread and wine should be changed into the true flesh and blood. For if he utters them to instruct a deacon how to consecrate, no change is produced *(Die*, Ein Sentensenbuch der Gilbertschen Schule, ed., B. Geyer, in Beitrage, VII [Munster, 1909], cited by Bernard Leeming in *Principles of Sacramental Theology*, *op. cit*., p. 438).

common historical assumption about Bracton in the face of the scant evidence for his textual sources has been that he was a theologian who knew the early law, and that both forces of learning appear in mixed and confused fashion in the *De Legibus*. Apart from the difficulty (even now) of the text itself, one must fill in the blank spaces in his writing by finding and drawing upon sources which he may have known (in a general sense) or drawn upon actually himself, or were both drawn upon and known by his redactors.

May we show how, for Bracton, the human will functions in the same way both for legal culpability and for moral and religious culpability by contrasting a modern statement (from our own age) against will which would suggest (though not with Bracton in mind) that the human will cannot function as a harmonious and unified concept if it be mixed with legal and religious guilt. The statement (of theory) which we have in mind is that made by Lord Russell[33] when he said,

> Praise and blame, rewards and punishments, and the whole apparatus of the criminal law are rational on the deterministic hypothesis, but not on the hypothesis of free will, for they are all mechanisms designed to cause volitions that are in harmony with the interests of the community, or what are believed to be its interests. But the conception of 'sin' is only rational on the assumption of free will, for, on the deterministic hypothesis, when a man does something that the community would wish him not to do, that is because the community has not provided adequate motives to cause him not to do it, or perhaps could not have provided adequate motives. We all recognize this second possibility in the case of insanity: a homicidal lunatic would not be deterred from murder even if he were certain to be hanged for it, and therefore it is useless to hang him. But sane people, when they commit a murder, usually do so in the hope of escaping detection, and it is this fact that makes it worth while to punish them when they are detected. Murder is punished, not because it is a sin and it is good that sinners should suffer, but because the community wishes to prevent it, and fear of punishment causes most people to abstain from it. This is completely compatible with the deterministic hypothesis, and completely incompatible with the hypothesis of free will.

The journey itself would take volumes if one were to examine, by the critical methods of our times, what leading medieval writers thought was *the* nature of the Will in opposition to *the* nature of the Intellect; one must content oneself with a simple statement of the issue, and we shall try to do so here. Against the backdrop of their concept of God as a perfect, omniscient, omni-benevolent and omnipotent being, of whom they knew more by way of revelation, faith and personal belief than they did by reason, argument and design, the medieval mind was obsessed by two general problems: that man could sin and be held responsible for his sinful actions, and that God could know that man could sin but, at the same time, was as deity in no way responsible for the fall of man and for his subsequent human transgressions.

There appeared to be a central theme: that, in some fashion, man was responsible for his sins, a point taken from Revelation and a belief in the Final Judgment when Christ would appear as final judge, the parousia St. Paul speaks of in his first epistle to the Corinthians in the fifteenth chapter. The religious belief in the physical resurrection of the human body gave force to a moral belief that human deeds, and human failings, had consequences in the physical world for which an accountability was due. The good of human acts was not interred with one's bones; it arose when one arose again from the dead and would be used to mitigate, by the doctrine of good works, the evil which one had done in his past life. Howsoever strange this may appear to the legal philosopher,* for the medieval mind the doctrine of resurrection made concrete for that mind that one's actions were both one's own, and that, to them, merit or demerit attached everlastingly through good works or sin.

In contrast to the considerations of Lord Russell, Bracton, as with any other medieval, could not accept that one's actions under the criminal sanction would be conditioned in a way which would preclude the freedom of one's will.[34] If that were so, or if that were thought to be the case, then no merit, nor demerit, could attach to a human action precisely because that action was not a human action. The dominating hypothesis for Bracton, and for most medievals, would have been that, in some way (however mysterious or unexplained), one himself had to decide (without overriding compulsion, which would then serve to lessen the power of one's will) what one would do,

---

* In a plea of mitigation in a modern trial one does state to the judge prior to the administrating of sentence that the accused is possessed of some merit and character, and one often does so by stressing the good qualities apparent in the accused's past.

or would not do, as to choice. One could have before oneself the terrifying image of eternal damnation (as had Dr. Faustus, for instance, in Christopher Marlowe's play), but if that image did not paralyze one's will and paralyze one with fear, then one was not relieved of responsibility for his actions. Could one's will, however, be overborne by fear to such an extent that it could permit one to argue that it was not the person who acted criminally, but was some aspect of his physical creature which acted? It is a hard position for the criminal law to admit for two reasons. First, as a theory in and of itself, how then does one account for actions predicated of a person, but not by the person? Secondly, the practical problem: will juries accept into evidence that one's voluntary powers can be suspended (as they seem to be in hypnosis), but that one is fully conscious and is not hypnotized, yet one is moving as would any other conscious person move, save for the fact that one's will is abated, or over such a power one does not have personal control?[35] There is a further problem for the law. Assume that indeliberate actions can be accounted for, in which the power of the voluntary seems not to be operable in the person; this question then arises: Are we advancing an insanity defense, but under a newer guise? We seem to want to say, "I was not myself, but I was not insane." It may be too fine a distinction for law.

What then is a mortal sin, and how does it relate to the common law? For the purpose here of legal analysis, it is the difference within a legal system between crimes of a serious nature, and crimes of a less serious nature. A number of common law jurisdictions carry over the distinction between a felony and a misdemeanor, and then make even further distinctions by talking of the "grade" of the felony, as when it is said that murder is a Class A felony, or that manslaughter in the first degree is a Class B felony, or assault in the third degree is a Class C felony. When one spoke of mortal and venial sins, two distinctions were thought to obtain in religious law. It was thought that a definition could attach to each sin, setting out a definition of the sin, and then setting forth obvious examples of such sins. The second distinction (much like the obverse of a coin is to the reverse of a coin) pertained to the state of the agent himself: namely, he had to fulfill within himself certain subjective conditions. Just as only a perceiver has immediate knowledge, only the agent and God (because of God's omniscience) were presumed to know fully whether those conditions were present (fulfilled) or absent (unfulfilled). It was assumed that one could know the nature and quality of one's act; or, in a milder sense, it was assumed that one could be aware of what one had done so that one had matter to present in a confessional, there and then to permit the penitent and the confessor to determine if one had sinned at all. It may have been possible, as when a confessor artfully extracted the conditions under which a penitent had sinned, to establish if those conditions were present at the time when the penitent sinned, or to remove some of the possibility of self-deception on the part of the penitent; but the *actual* state of knowledge that the penitent may have had when he *actually* sinned was, finally, known only to himself, if it was known at all, as an agent. A certain order of discretionary relief obtained to protect the penitent against himself, and this rested upon the side of the confessor to distinguish, for the sake of administering absolution, a penitent who may have sinned truly, from a penitent who merely (but painfully) scrupled over committing sin, which, in fact, had not truly been the case in spite of the penitent's guilt. In the latter instance it was a condition of the sacrament of penance that a penitent would be bound by the finding of the confessor. The reason for such a religious condition was for the sake of letting the penitent put his conscience to rest, rather than endlessly worrying over the worth of his contrition. When the priest stated that he, the priest, had absolved, the penitent was supposed to leave the confessional feeling and believing that he, the penitent, had been absolved fully and truly. The rhetorical device was effective; when counselling a scrupulous penitent the confessor could say, in words to this effect, "You are truly absolved, and you must believe this; for, if you do not, you doubt your Faith, and, by your presence here in the confessional, I know that you do not doubt the teachings of your Faith. It is a teaching of your Faith that I can absolve you. Go in peace."

When this religious theory transferred itself into early common law, as we see in Bracton by his reference to mortal sin, it did not do so by listing sets of penitential conditions or by giving a penitential analysis of matter of gravity. It was enough, simply, to make mention of a religious stipulation, which Bracton herewith did. The reference to a "mortal sin" signified both exterior and interior states. There was something to be known; and there was a way in which the knowing could occur, and thus be knowing of a sinful kind.

Bracton, in a compressed form, uses the language which bespeaks of interior conditions for a human act. It is language which for us at present is moderately strange because it is a form of language which tends to give the impression that hypostatized entities or faculties are being depicted or spoken about. We think it can be said, though, that medieval writers, although giving the appearance of speaking about hypostatized entities, were not in fact committing the fallacy of concreteness (which Whitehead was wont to call such hypothesis). It may have been a simple case that Latin, as a form of expression, lent itself to such apparent hypostatization because of its case structure. Medievals, by force of their understanding of the nature of first and second intention, were generally careful to distinguish those sentences which referred to objects from those sentences which referred to constructions of language, or *ens rationis*.

"[M]ortal sin" as a category of rebuke occurs freely throughout medieval theological treatises. Philosophically one may read the appellation in neutral form to mean: it is forbidden, or it is thought to be serious. But however one wishes to read the usage, when an act was deemed to be or have been mortally sinful, it meant that certain conditions were present, and, also, that certain excuses did not obtain. When Bracton, for instance, speaks in this way of homicide he has made reference to a standard case from medieval writing. We will quote him, and then show what case is instanced:[36]

> Of necessity, and here we must distinguish whether the necessity was avoidable or not; if avoidable and he could escape without slaying, he will then be guilty of homicide; if unavoidable, since he kills without premeditated hatred (340) (341) but with sorrow of heart, in order to save himself and his family, since he could not otherwise escape [danger], he is not liable to the penalty of homicide. By chance, as by misadventure, when one throws a stone at a bird or elsewhere and another passing by unexpectedly is struck and dies, or fells a tree and another is accidentally crushed beneath its fall and the like. But here we must distinguish whether he has been engaged in a proper or an improper act.

We wish, first, only to analyze this portion, and then to continue on with what remains of the text.

In order for an act to be thought mortally sinful it had to possess certain elements. What one did had to be serious; one had to know that what he did was serious; and one had to consent freely to his doing what was serious.[37] The guide was religious, the Church defining in its teachings what was or was not sinful. It was assumed that one then *knew* what one ought to do. The broad moral definition and hortation was "do good; avoid evil" and this had its roots, certainly for a lawyer, in Roman law: *primum non nocere*, avoid causing harm. But how then does one move from an act prohibited by law to committing a mortal sin, as Bracton asserts?

The move is accomplished by the apparent twinning of concepts. If the social order did not violate the canons of the religious order, then what one did socially one also did with religious approval, save for the broadly unimportant area of neutral human acts. If one were commanded to do good, one was also commanded by the voice of conscience to seek the good. A social order inherently wrong (and for medieval thinking this was a state of affairs almost impossible because it was thought that some social order, however bad, was better than no order at all) was an order which one would not, voluntarily, seek (if one sought the good). It could also be said that a social order which was inherently wrong would be one, *ipso facto*, which would not possess a valid legal order—but one could object to this statement on one of two grounds. It may be empirically the case that most observed social orders, fitting such a description, were not possessed of valid (i.e., justly ordered) legal processes, but it would not guarantee that some social order might not be just, although apparently unjust. One might object to communism as a social theory that it was considered to be unjust, but it could (and very often does) possess a sound legal order. The second objection is trivial, but possible: one could imagine a social order in which, as a hobby, all followed just procedures but in their heart of hearts all were unjust. To that set Bracton would say they sinned mortally because they had no love of justice (340).

We are not suggesting that the social order of society did, in some necessary manner, follow a set of beliefs thought to be divine. What we are suggesting is that the text of Bracton, where he introduces the concept of a mortal sin, does so as a measure by which a social act (in this instance, a legal act) can be judged privately. One may, within the set of one's beliefs, observe that one's acts have a double side to them, and it is the presence of such double-sidedness which prevents one from interpreting Bracton solely as a lawyer who set down legal stipulations and legal theory pure and simple. He did not, as the text tells us.

It is from the insight from the text that Bracton is writing, often from the dual view of lawyer and of theologian (in that he borrowed theological texts), that one must first unravel his religious assumptions with regard to law before one can appreciate his "pure" legal concepts. One will not, with the state of the manuscript tradition what it is, find sources for every section in *De Legibus*; even to suggest this seems to deny Bracton's status as a writer. He did not beg, borrow and steal every line; indeed, very far from that. But his touchstone for legal theory appears, the more one examines his texts, to have sprung from the developed religious ideas of the period. In the range of the word "religious" we wish to include writings which were theological, philosophical (as, for instance, is the *Summa Theologiae*), or canonical, as were the various commentaries upon Gratian. The writing of the medieval period ranged over all categories without much distinction, save for such treatises which dealt directly with philosophical or logical commentary.

Bracton does not set out to "prove" his stipulations. His notion of the voluntary, as opposed to a quotation from Lord Russell which we wished to cite as a comparison for sake of contrast, was that as an expression of the Will (of man) it functioned both in civil and criminal law, and it also ruled in matters of conscience (as the appeal to the concept of mortal sin illustrates). Not only did one have a common world of legal and religious propositions of law running side by side (to employ a metaphor), each however possessing an identity of its own, but one also had a common power which ranged over and was requisite to each system: the Will. It was the "will" which directed a man to act legally; it was the "will" which directed man to act religiously. In modern law we see such track theories of law. In the United States of America, or in Australia or Canada, there are laws which affect each state or province separately, and one is bound by them; there are laws, too, which are federal in nature, and are distinct from the laws of a state or of a province. The double division is clearly understood by an appeal to American law. Each state is sovereign in the union, and, precisely as an independent state, possesses its own distinct set of laws; but as a member of a federation (the "united" states which make up "America") the federation itself has a set of laws known as Federal Laws. The independent states possess their own courts and procedures; the federal government possesses its courts and its federal procedure. Though there may exist some similarity between the procedures of the two systems, each is a distinct system, and the features of one do not bear any controlling influence upon another. Bracton seemed familiar with the two worlds of law, and, like so many of the period in other writings, moves freely from one conceptual sphere to the other.

How Bracton viewed the operation of intention is found in a number of steps which one must isolate from and comment upon in his text. There is no proper order for this analysis that we can perceive, so we shall begin by isolating his appeal to canon law, which tells one not what intention be (as one might give a formula for a chemical or isolate an enzyme which causes and induces a convulsion), but advances a concept of necessary condition for a licit act. The theory which Bracton uses is one which goes by the shorthand name of *versari in re illicita*.[38] It follows the common law to this day, but not in that Latinized form, as a modified form of a doctrine of natural or probable consequences, and in tort law functions under the doctrine of "foreseeability."

The Latin text of Bracton (341) reads as follows, "*Sed his erit distinguendum utrum quis dederit operam rei licitae vel illicitae*" and Thorne renders it as, "But here we must distinguish whether he has been engaged in a proper or an improper act" (341).

It appears to be the case when a canonical or theological notion is grafted on to law that the canonical or theological roots are lost (or submerged), and that what remains is a conclusion from a set of discarded premises. There may be an interesting sociological explanation for such vanishings or submergences, but the simple fact that one can observe of legal reasoning is, often, such reasoning attempts to be economical and sparse (barring the obvious exception). Law or "the" law, functions within the world of practical and conventional wisdom; its sources, when one comes to examine them at a later date, are woven into the fabric of law, and the distance which time represents never lets one get close enough to the fabric to be able to observe the separate and individual strands which make up a larger legal pattern. By the time of Plowden, (1571), notions which were in full flower in continental and civil law were reduced to an abbreviation, one reason being that canonists and civil lawyers were not cited as a matter of form in common law.[39] But although they were not cited, this did not entail that they were not used, or that their legal understandings were not employed. Very often they were. Canon and Civilian law principles would continue to hold force in English canon law.

Versari in re illicita served as a concept through and by which one could both ascertain the guilt of a penitent and mitigate that guilt. It is unnecessary for us here to give a detailed historical analysis of the growth of the concept, save to list some leading writers in footnote form. The concept itself, and the writers who embraced and developed it, are sufficient matter for a separate study. The logical form of the concept is very well expressed in this citation from Aquinas. It is a long citation, but it contains the nub of the notion, and we consider it best to preserve the quotation *in toto*. Aquinas is discussing homicide, and the question he puts for our consideration is: *Is somebody who kills another by accident guilty of homicide*? In his *Reply* to the objections he states, and we quote (*Summa Theologiae*, 2a2ae. 64, 8):

> In Aristotle's definition [*Physics* 11, 6. 197b18. *lect* 10], chance is a cause that acts without a personal agent intending it. Simply speaking, therefore, accidental happenings are neither intended nor voluntary. And because every sin is, as Augustine says [*De Vera Religione*, 14, PL 34, 133], voluntary, it follows that accidents as such cannot constitute sins. What is not willed or intended as such may nevertheless be incidentally willed or intended. We may incidentally cause something by removing the obstacle against that thing happening [Aristotle, *Physics* VIII, 4 255b24. lect 8]. It follows that somebody who does not remove such occasions of homicide* as he could and

* At this point we find that the translation of Rickaby is far more clear, and we wish to cite it. Rickaby says, "Hence he who does not remove the conditions from which homicide follows, supposing it to be his duty to remove them, incurs in a manner the guilt of wilful homicide; and this in two ways: in one way when, being engaged upon unlawful actions which he ought to avoid, he incurs homicide; in another way when he does not observe due

> should remove will in some way be guilty of voluntary homicide.*

The quotation from the principal text continues,

> This can come about in two ways – when a person engages in nefarious activities which he should not have engaged in, or when he does not take due care. This is why the law lays down [*Decretals of Gregory* IX; V, 12, 23. RF 1, 157 (R. F. = *Corpus Juris Canonici*, 2nd edition by E. Richter, E. Friedberg, Leipzig, 1879, a two volume edition in which the *Decretals* is printed) and Gratian in the *Decretum* 1, 48, 49. R. F. 1, 197-198] that if a man engages in legitimate activities and uses due care, he is not guilty of any homicide that may ensue; if, on the other hand, he engages in illicit activities, or even fails to take due care in some legitimate enterprise, he is guilty of any homicide that may occur.

The body of the reply bears weight upon the first objection and answers to it. The objection, with its answer, we will now cite:

> First, It would seem that somebody who kills another by accident is guilty of homicide. For we read in *Genesis* [Genesis 4, 23-24, Lamech said the following to his two wives (Ada and Sella), '...note my saying well. The man that wounds me, the stripling** who deals me a blow, I reward with death. For Cain, sevenfold vengeance was to be taken; for Lamech, it shall be seventy times as much.' The Hebrew text states 77 times, the Septuagint Greek has 490 times, and the Latin text can mean either number] that Lamech killed a man when he thought he was killing an animal and that he was in consequence accounted a killer. Therefore a man who kills another by accident incurs the fault of homicide.

---

precaution. And therefore, according to the Civil and Canon Laws, if one is engaged upon a lawful action, taking due care therein, and homicide follows from it, he does not incur the guilt of homicide. But if he is engaged upon an unlawful action, or being engaged upon a lawful one, neglects to observe due precaution therein, he does not escape the charge of homicide, if the death of man follows from his doing" (pp. 48-49, *op. cit.*).

* S. T. 1a2ae, 6, 3: "*Can there be voluntariness without any act?*"

** Our concern here, as throughout this study, is not with the meaning of theological belief, nor its justification, nor with its textual explication. Our reason for saying this is, in this instance, that the biblical text which is cited does not speak directly of a killing by accident. It may be (unless Aquinas' medieval objector possessed a Latin biblical translation which is now lost to us) that one would have to "infer" accidental killing from the introduction of "stripling" into the text, reasoning that a youth passing from boyhood into manhood could not, or would not likely possess sufficient malice or meanness of character to kill deliberately.

The reply to this first objection is as follows: 1. Lamech failed to take sufficient care to avoid homicide, and therefore incurred the guilt of homicide. This first objection and reply (even though its biblical force is less than textually accurate) should be read in conjunction with the third objection and reply, both of which we cite:

> 3. Distinction 50 of the *Decretum* contains many canons which impose penalties for accidental homicide [Gratian, *Decretum* 1, 50, 4-8. R. F. 1, 178-180]. But it is only fault that renders a man liable for punishment. Therefore he who kills a man accidentally becomes guilty of homicide.

The Reply is:

> [3. *Praeterea, in* Decretis,[4] *inducuntur plures canones in quibus casualia homicidia puniuntur. Sed poena non debetur nisi culpae. Ergo ille qui casualiter hominem occidit, incurrit homicidii culpam.**]
>
> *Piana: *reatum*
>
> The canons impose penalties on those who take another's life accidentally in the course of doing something illicit or of not taking sufficient care. [3. *Ad tertium dicendum quod secundum canones imponitur poena his qui casualiter occidunt*, dantes operam rei illicitae (emphasis ours) *vel non adihibentes diligentiam debitam.*]

The body of the article, as was the custom with medieval disputation, cites a text favorable to itself; in this instance the text cited to support the Reply which Aquinas made was taken from St. Augustine, and is as follows:

> ON THE OTHER HAND, Augustine writes [*Epistola* XLVII, *ad Publicolam*, PL 33, 187] *There can be no question of our being held responsible for any evil that may perchance result from some good and lawful action of ours.* Homicide may, nevertheless, accidentally result from people doing something good, and it cannot therefore be held to be their fault. [SED CONTRA *est quod Augustinus dicit ad Publicolam*, Absit ut ea quae propter bonum ac licitum facimus, si quid per haec praeter nostram voluntatem cuiquam mali acciderit, nobis imputentu.[5] *Sed contingit quandoque ut propter bonum aliquod facientibus homicidium consequatur casualiter. Ergo non imputatur facienti ad culpam.*][42]

To instance what Aquinas means (and what is meant) by an action the doing of which is unlawful, his second objection and response makes clear, both of which we cite:

> 2. According to Exodus (21, 22-3), 'When men strive together, and hurt a woman with child, so that there is a miscarriage, and

> any harm follows, then you shall give life for life.' But this can come about even though there is no intention to kill. Therefore accidental killing can make a man guilty of homicide.[43]

To the response to the second objection one must be aware that Aquinas is considering *rational* human acts, as the body of his discussion throughout Question 64, "De Homicidio" (S. T., 2a2ae. 64,1), indicates. We give this warning because to quote out of context, especially in so vast a work as the *Summa Theologiae* with its many self-references, may mislead a reader as to the force of a Reply (or to the assumptions which the Reply assumes are known from earlier portions of the text). A rational act, for Aquinas, involves one in a conscious and deliberate act. In this light his Reply assumes that a reader knows that deliberately to cause an abortion or to procure an abortion is, for Aquinas, an incident of an act which clearly at law is unlawful, and would be known as such to an agent so attempting or doing.:

> 2. A person who strikes a pregnant woman is doing something wrong [and it is to the Latin text itself that one must turn to appreciate that Aquinas is talking here about a wrong in itself: "...*quod ille qui percutit mulierem praegnantem* dat operam rei illicitae;...], so that if either the woman or the fetus dies as a result, he will be guilty of the crime of homicide, especially since it is so clear that death may result from such a blow.[44]

One may observe from Bracton's use of language, "*dederit operam rei licitae vel illicitae...*," that this format is common to the statement of the question. His linguistic formulation accords with that given by Aquinas to the same maxim. We have typed the phrase in italics throughout.

Versari in re illicita[45] (and its cognate forms), if considered within a legal framework, was an unrefined causal statement which asserted that from causes flow certain effects. The legal concept which the maxim embraces is that from what is lawful, only the lawful should obtain or result. If other than that, say the unlawful obtains, then one was to return to considerations other than the agent himself. One investigated intervening causes, such as necessity, or duress, or chance, or, in very general terms, that cause which did not attach to the will of an agent. By definition, if one was pursuing that which was lawful, and one was acting lawfully, but what resulted from one's lawful actions was some harm or some consequence which was deemed to be unlawful, it could not then have been anything unlawful which the agent himself brought about. The simple model for early law, no doubt derived from religious tradition (in part), was that from good only good should flow. But a fact of practical life was that harm often flowed from human actions. How then was one to account for such harm (or evil, or unlawfulness)?

The simplest model for Bracton, consonant with Canon and Civil theories, was to inquire after the aim of the agent. Bracton set out his legal theory with this assumption: If an agent intended (and one need not inquire at this point what were the requirements for an intention) to do what was lawful, then what effects flowed from the acts of the agent should themselves be viewed as effects, or conditions, condoned by the law.

Let us offer a simple example from life of this age. If I am crossing in a zebra crossing, and am well into pacing across the roadway by using a zebra crossing, all oncoming road traffic must stop and give me the right-of-way. Oncoming vehicles owe to me a legal duty to stop and to permit me to cross the road. The Road Traffic Act defines this clearly and simply.

Consider then that a pedestrian is crossing the roadway in a properly designated zebra crossing. Midway he is struck down, and injured, by an approaching automobile. If one stops at this point in the example (even though it may be viewed either as an example from the law or torts, or as a statutory crime of negligent homicide) one may argue that the driver of the vehicle is guilty either of a tortious act or of a criminal act, or both. We wish only to consider the example in light of criminal law.

The elements of our legal set are simple. A driver, "p," has struck and injured a pedestrian, "q," at a zebra crossing. If we appeal to the simple Bractonian formulation, that of considering the "lawfulness" of the act of the agent, then we can conclude that the agent brought about an unlawful act. Because what the agent was doing–i.e., striking a pedestrian in a crosswalk while the pedestrian was lawfully crossing–was unlawful, any consequences which flow from the action of the agent are themselves to be considered as unlawful. The example forces us to invert its elements to show how the same situation at law could be considered as a lawful situation. It would be done in this way.

Had the driver of the automobile stopped his car for the sake of permitting the pedestrian to cross (safely), then the stopping of his car would have been a lawful act flowing, as it were, from his knowledge and understanding of the traffic code which stated that a driver is commanded to yield the right-of-way to pedestrian traffic in zebra crossings. The "not-yielding" (let us assume for sake of the example here) resulted from an intention of the driver (to continue driving on) to do what, in this *legal* context, was illegal. Thus, the driver of the vehicle in this example instances *versari in re illicita*. His intention to continue driving onwards was, by law, an intention which the law forbade by force of the rule regarding pedestrians in zebra crossings. The consequences, at law, are deemed to be punishable (by fine, by imprisonment, by official rebuke in a Court of law), and, in this case, "q," the injured pedestrian, may have a right at law to redress his injury, pain and suffering, and be awarded general and special damages against "p," who drove the automobile.

We have not moved to consider excuses at law, or exemptions from the law. When we ask what will serve as an excuse, or when we ask what will be an instance of an exemption from the law, it calls for an answer wider than we wish to consider here. Our interest here is solely to consider the bare and simple elements which the statement Bracton (and even Aquinas) produced may contain for legal analysis: "*...distinguendum utrum quis dederit operam rei licitae vel illicitae.*" On its face it appears to be a notion which will strictly contain the limits of liability for an act (and we say this without involving the reader with modern notions in tort law as to how we now may limit liability for actions). What Bracton has produced is a legal container in which some limit for liability may be placed.

In the Bractonian analysis of criminal liability the first element we have sought to isolate has been to ask what function was served by the maxim itself–*versari in re illicita*? We have asked this question because we believe it to be the key question for ascertaining an answer as to what makes an action legal under the law. For the moment we have not wished to consider how the philosophical or religious concepts of "will" or "soul" may function for Bracton because we do not think these are first principles within his system. His formal model is that of legal action. He is concerned with assigning criminal liability for a criminal act. The criminal wrong is understood as such by asking what relationship an act bears to its cause. If the cause is tainted by criminality, then the act produced by the agent will be a criminal act. In the strongest sense, "*illicita*" comes about when the agent forms an intention to do wrong. Our movement is from the realm of the infra-mental to the realm of the extra-mental, from the aim which is posited by a formal cause, to its achievement as is revealed in a final cause. The achievement in this instance is the forbidden act. Bracton does not tell one how the act is brought about or produced. He is not, as was St. Augustine, involved in legal psychology to postulate how an action may proceed "*ex suo animo*." Nor is Bracton concerned with the possible epistemological problem whether one can have actual knowledge of oneself intending to do something. Bracton's only concern, we believe, is to state that if one does intend an act, the identity at law which will attach to that act (its legal description) will be given to that act by the nature of the agent's intention. If, however, the entertaining of the intention itself is forbidden by the law, but yet one intends nonetheless to intend and produce an act under governance of that proscribed intention, then one has engaged in an illicit act. To engage in an illicit act is, by definition, to have committed a crime.

What we derive is that intentional description under Bractonian analysis involves two steps in its understanding. First, one must understand that an agent can intend some act; secondly, one must understand if that act is permitted or not. If one took only the second element to the exclusion of the first element, one would be describing tortious acts only (which often abandon any *mens rea* concept, or entertain a different burden of proof to establish *mens rea*). For example, it is the fact *that A* struck *B* in a crosswalk which is the forbidden element in the tort of negligence, not what *A* actually intended when he struck *B* in the crosswalk. For Bracton, both elements which we have indicated must be present for legal guilt to attach to a criminal act or omission.

We should now like to discuss the concept of "omission," referring to the *Summa Theologica*, 1a.2ae.6.3., "Can there be voluntariness without any act?"

The reason why the concept of omission is important to *mens rea* is that it permits the law to impose duties upon a member of society, and thus permits the law to hold that there may be a class of wrongs which spring from the concept of duties within one's control.[46] If, for instance, a landlord is negligent in not keeping his fire escapes in good repair, and, subsequently, there is a serious fire on his premises in which the death or injury of a tenant ensues, the landlord may be charged with a form of criminal negligence for not having repaired the fire escapes. That the fire escapes were *not* repaired may, for sake of consistent legal theory (excuses and exemptions aside), be viewed as a positive legal proposition that the landlord did *not* intend to keep the fire escapes in proper repair. His "not doing" is as positive an act at law as his doing, and here, by appeal to an early concept of Will to account for omission (as well as other matters), one may show how the common law grafted on to itself through Bracton, and subsequent legalists, a coherent theory which will account for omission at law.

Aquinas, in the instant article, states, and we quote,

> To be voluntary means to spring from the will. Now one may come from another in two ways. One, directly, when it proceeds from it precisely as agent, thus heating from fire. Two, indirectly, when it proceeds from it precisely as not acting, thus a shipwreck from loss of helm.
>
> Notice, however, that the result of a lack of action is not always to be brought home to the non-acting agent, but only when he could and should have acted; thus if the steering had broken down or he were not responsible the helmsman is not charged with the loss of the ship.
>
> Now there are cases when by its resolve and action the will can intervene to break the inertia with respect to willing and acting, and sometimes ought to do so. Then it can be held responsible, for the not willing and not acting are in its charge. *Thus there can be voluntariness without an act* (italics ours), sometimes without an external act though with an internal act, as when a person wills not to act, sometimes, however, without even an internal act, as when he does not will to act.[47]

Aquinas reinforces the position he developed in the Reply in the three articles following it, and, for sake of brevity, we have reduced them, Latin and English, to a footnote.[48] Our concern is not to develop or defend an Aquinian theory of Will; only to draw upon it for sake of illuminating some Bractonian assumptions. In conjunction with this article, one may refer to the *Summa Theologiae*, 1a2ae, Question 71, article 5, "Does every sin involve an action?"[49] The Article itself involves a long commentary on the sin of omission, but, without centering upon its theological topic, one may take the

Article to be a moderately concise statement of how an omission may involve an act of the will; hence, to omit may mean to intend to omit. We have placed pertinent portions of the Article, both Latin and English, in a footnote.

We have stated that we believed that the first element to be isolated in an analysis of Bractonian criminal liability was the element which concerned the licitness of an act, and an expression of that element was to be found in how the expression "*versari in re illicita*" functioned (in its various sentential forms). Bracton's employment of that legal formula, taken from a large range of canonical instances, caused one to turn to the agent's Will to determine if one were to be adjudged guilty of a criminal act.

But Bracton expands upon the notion by requiring us, at times, to advert, not to consequences for the sake of determining criminality, but to how an act was brought about. He states, and we quote, "But if he was engaged in a lawful act and did not employ due care, liability will be attributed to him."[50] It is not an unusual comment upon an example (since it occurs following upon an example concerning the flogging of a pupil); it serves to illustrate, in this compressed treatise of Bracton's, that one adverts to *how* a consequence was brought about, as well as to one's intention, to ascertain criminal liability. What may seem unusual in the observation is that from the realm of Will the text has turned to the realm of instrumentality, seeming to complicate what at first appears simple and clear. We think that one can make sense of this introduction of instrumentality without distorting Bracton's text, or its sense.

What one notices in a medieval text such as this is how a balance was attempted within the four categories of causality, explanatory ways in which to account for phenomena and events. Bracton correctly identifies the necessary element in the chain of criminal responsibility to be intention, but he does not, as (for instance) did Abelard, rest there only. Bracton stresses the material side to an act; one not only intends, one also brings about what he intends. The balance of causal notions may be seen in this way. To intend, pure and simple, rests within the sphere of formal causes. When the intention is executed, then one has reached a final cause. But two other causal elements must link together formal and final causality, if a full explanation is to be offered of a completed human act (in these terms). One must *be able* to bring about, and one *must* bring about. Efficient causality is the power to bring about; material causality is the bringing about *by means of*, as in, I have the power to walk to the store (am not incapacitated) and I do walk to the store (because my feet move me there).

Material and efficient causality, if one draws upon them for legal analysis here, provide one with a ground for two questions: Did the agent possess the capacity to bring about..."x," and in bringing about "x" did he "ø" properly? If we advert only to intention to establish criminal liability or criminal guilt, then a legal system is "paved with good intentions" or it imports strict liability (as in *Morissette* or *Lambert* before the United States Supreme Court overruled them).[51]

Any number of examples serve to show why a theory of criminal liability must pose the two questions we have mentioned. Criminal liability (in the common law, at least) does not rest between two extremes; it rests between "not guilty" and "guilty by reason of...'a'..." where "a" is a variable which some category within the system fills. A choice of selected examples may uncompress what we have stated.

If a surgeon operates, and the patient dies, we may ask a number of questions of the matter. Did the surgeon intend to kill the patient? If the answer is, No, he did not intend to kill the patient, we can turn from intention directly to inquire of other aspects surrounding the death of the patient. Was the patient the cause of his own death, i.e., was he in such a medically poor condition that no surgeon at all could have saved him? One turns to a material condition (the poor health of the patient) to relieve the surgeon of responsibility. But what if we have neither a criminal intention on the part of the surgeon to cause death, nor a material condition on the part of the patient which was the cause of death? What if we have a condition brought about because of the doctor himself, i.e., that he was inebriated when he operated, or used non-sterile instruments, or used untrained nurses as surgical assistants, or failed to perform adequate tests beforehand to determine if the patient might have suffered any toxicity from the anesthetic? Questions of this form skirt an appeal to direct criminal intention (because in every instance *D* could with all honesty reply that he had not intended to kill the patient); to the contrary, we are asking about the care used by the agent when he produced an act from which a harmful consequence flowed.

The criminal law is replete with examples wherein a lack of due care entailed criminal responsibility. A police officer may be in hot pursuit of a felon, but, while firing a pistol or rifle at the felon, may kill an innocent bystander. If a jury found that the officer acted without due care for life or limb, he could face criminal charges. A soldier, or a government official, may follow the orders of a superior officer or official, only to find that he, having followed those orders, committed a crime and the defense of superior orders does not obtain.[52] An officer may attempt a lawful arrest of a suspect, only to discover that the arrest was unlawful, and now he faces a wrongful arrest charge, or a charge of malicious prosecution. The key in these examples (as with a whole family of such examples) is that the defendant, although in a lawful pursuit, undertakes the act without due care.

To undertake without due care is not, we shall argue, to find evidence of a criminal intention carried over into an act. We are not arguing that one cannot criminally intend, and thus look to the act and its consequences to find evidence to support the charge that *D* did form a criminal intention. One can and does. But what Bracton introduces when he speaks of due care is a turn upon a problem which occupied medieval theologians: it was the problem of the nature of ignorance, and its classification.

Not to attend with due care is a form of ignorance. This is a most complicated topic in medieval theology and philosophy, and it occupied major writers greatly. Not only, for example, do we find the major writings of Aquinas occupied with the question, we find also his lesser writings occupied with the question.[53] Ignorance was said to be antecedent to an act, concomitant with an act, or consequent upon an act, and to what degree one could establish that the act of *D* sprang from his ignorance, and his ignorance was that for which he could not be held accountable, then one excused another from the harmful consequences of his act, or from the act itself.

In the case of the example with the surgeon and the patient who died, to exclude due care by an appeal to ignorance, one would have to establish that "not knowing" was a privation which carried with itself no legal penalty or necessity. If the patient (say) died from the anesthetic (i.e., anaphylactic shock wherein one's air passages are cut off by a gross swelling of the tongue), one might ask if the surgeon had taken (or caused to be taken) a full medical history of the patient. If he said that he had not, although he would in fact have been ignorant of the fact that the patient was allergic to an anesthetic agent, "ignorance" of that kind would not be considered to be absolving of his responsibility as a surgeon to have taken (been required to take) due care.

If the patient had died as a result of the surgery itself, then the lack of the skill revealed by the surgeon could be viewed as a form of ignorance for which he may or may not be responsible. If, during the course of making an incision, the operator severed an artery one could ask if the artery *qua* artery was unusual (e. g., during the course of a gall bladder operation one must distinguish with care the hepatic artery from the common bile duct), or did the operator fail to determine the origins and termination of the two structures? If the vessel were not unusual (i.e., in an unexpected location in the anatomy) then the question of due care arises. If he attempted to shunt normal exploratory procedures in the furtherance of a desire to speed the operation, then he failed to exercise due care (the proof being that the patient died, or suffered a greater harm as a result of the operation and the faulty surgical procedure). The surgeon's ignorance (of the artery) brought about by a shortcut taken by the surgeon is not a form of ignorance which would excuse him from liability or criminal negligence.

The medieval writers went to elaborate lengths to illustrate the kinds of ignorance, and it is not within the scope of this chapter to pursue them in detail. The classifications are, at times, not that clear. The force of the topic does, however, relate to criminal law when we ask if there are conditions which do excuse a defendant, and we have already excluded his intention. In modern criminal law we will be concerned with non-intentional states which do, nonetheless, produce harm, as in reckless acts, or in harms caused through negligence. One should qualify the descriptions, to avoid confusing categories from Tort law with Criminal law, by speaking of criminal negligence or recklessness if the harm pertains to criminal law.

To attempt to belabor the symmetry which may be thought to obtain between the four broad causal categories and a budding criminal law would be an exercise in legal archaeology of questionable merit. One should be aware from reading Bracton that he drew heavily upon medieval sources; one should, however, be guarded in making too-generous attributions towards development from one field to another. It shows through clearly from the text of *De Legibus* that intention was of paramount importance for the assigning of criminal guilt; but it was not a sole principle of law without limit. Other legal principles come into force for Bracton, one of which was the legal principle of "due care" which imposed the condition upon an actor that he bring about what he intends with care and caution. Implicit in such a principle is both a respect for the skill of the agent, and a respect to be exercised for the patient (or any third party). From the seeds which we find in *De Legibus* for this principle will grow, over the centuries, an important legal concept.

Endnotes Chapter 3

1. *Summa Theologiae,* 1a. 1, 1, in which article one asks, "Is another teaching required apart from philosophical studies?" How the distinction intertwines, and what relationship each part has to each, one may read in an interesting excursus into the matter, seen in "Ratio and Revelatio," Chapter Three, of *Sacra Doctrina: Reason and Revelation in Aquinas*, by Per Erik Persson, translated by J. A. R. Mackenzie (Oxford: Basil Blackwell, 1970), *cf.* pp. 267-297.

2. *Cf. Medieval Minds: Mental Health in the Middle Ages*, by Thomas F. Graham, Chapter Three, "Abelard to Aquinas," pp. 60-76.

3. It is not until we come to Timothy Bright's, *A Treatise of Melancholie* (London: Thomas Vautroller, 1586) that we begin to have separate writings concerned with the physical basis for mental ailments. Bright's work, in its title, states that the book is one "Containing The Causes thereof, & reasons of the strange effects it worketh in our minds and bodies: with the phisicke cure, and spiritual consolation for such as have thereto adioyned an afflected conscience...." It was the first book by an English physician on mental illness. One may also read Sir Geoffrey Keynes' *Dr. Timothie Bright 1550-1615*.

4. *Cf. Liability for Animals* by Glanville Williams (Cambridge, 1939).

5. *To the Countesse of Huntingdon* (p. 122), *John Donne* in the edition of John Hayward (Penguin Books, 1970).

6. We need not belabor our reader here with bibliographical accounts of this well-known legal distinction in legal theory. One may consult *The Nature of Law* by T. E. Davitt (St. Louis & London, 1951) for an account of the volitive vs. the cognitive tradition in early medieval law. For two recent accounts of problems which arise from strict utilitarian accounts of law we suggest, *English Law and Moral Law* by Professor A. L. Goodhart (London, 1953) and "The Model of Rules" by R. M. Dworkin, *The University of Chicago Law Review*, Vol. 35, No. 1, 1967. In no way do these simple divisions exhaust theories of what the nature of law is. For instance, laws might be seen to be little more than codified cultural expectations (as with the U. C. C. in the law of contract).

7. *Svmma Sti. Raymvndi de Peniafort* (Romae Sumptibus Ioannis Tallini), with Book Two beginning at p. 145, "De homicidio." The Verona edition, 1744, is an easier edition from which to cite. We shall simply abbreviate by putting 'V' for the Verona edition, and 'T' for the Tallini edition, putting a page number after the initial so that one can cite the portion of the text we have glossed.

8. One such instance which comes clearly to mind is from *Hamlet*. In Act 3, scene 3, one will recall that the King, Claudius, is at prayer (3.3.35ff):

KING. "O, my offence is rank, it smells to heaven,
It hath the primal eldest curse upon't,
A brother's murder. Pray can I not,
Though inclination be as sharp as will,
My stronger guilt defeats my strong intent,
And like a man to double business bound,
I stand in pause where I shall first begin,
And both neglect."

Hamlet, of course, does not know what the interior state of the soul is to Claudius himself. When Hamlet enters the stage, with intent to kill Claudius, he sees Claudius at prayer, and this causes Hamlet to think and say, (3.3.75 ff):

HAMLET. "Now might
I do it pat, now a'is a-praying –
And now I'll do't, [*he draws his sword*] and so a'goes to heaven,
And so am I revenged. That would be scanned:
A villain kills my father, and for that
I his sole son do this same villain send
To heaven....
Why, this is bait and salary, not revenge.
A'took my father grossly, full of bread,
With all his crimes broad blown, as flush as May,
And how his audit stands who knows save heaven?
But in our circumstance and course of thought,
'Tis heavy with him: and am I then revenged
To take him in the purging of his soul,
When he is fit and seasoned for his passage?
No." [*he sheathes his sword*]

9. Comparing Schulz's article with the texts, and now with the availability of Thorne's majestic text and translation of Bracton, one is moved to admit that a strong similarity of text exists between Bracton's text on homicide (120 folio, pp. 340 onwards in Thorne) and Raymond of Pennafort's *De Homicidio*. If anything, such similarity (which was not unusual in medieval authors) shows how living and viable was the canonical and penitential tradition of the Middle Ages upon the law.

10. *Cf.*, Vol. III, Ch. xxvi, p. 19 (London: Macmillan and Co., 1883). We have simply reproduced his diagram and herewith attached it. We have also attached his English version of it, taken from Stephen's *A General View of The Criminal Law of England* (First edition, 1863, London & Cambridge: MacMillan and Co.), a volume, we are sorry to state, which is impossible to obtain.

BRACTON ON HOMICIDE:

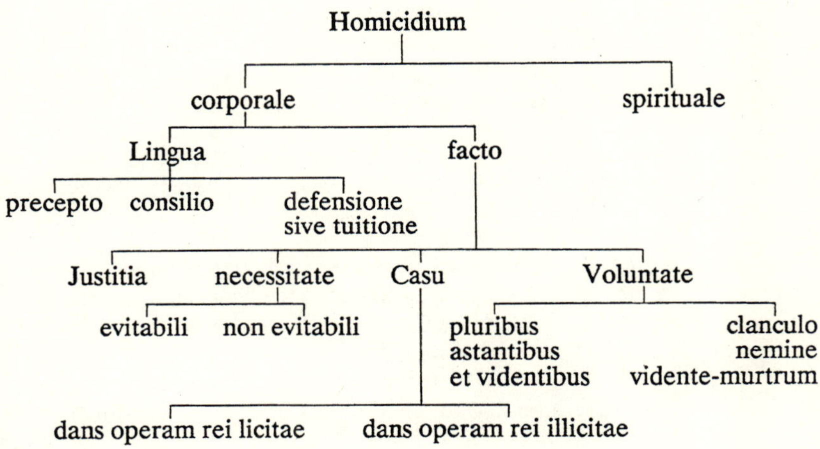

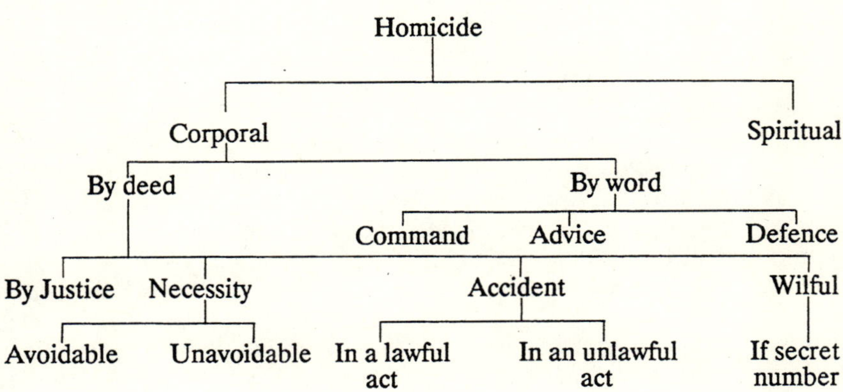

Of the division into Voluntate as "*pluribus astantibus et videntibus*" against "*clanculo nemine vidente-murdrum*," Stephen himself, in the 1883 edition in which the Latin branch appears, states (and this makes clear why his 1863 edition of the *Criminal Law* omits the distinction which his Latin tabulation cited):

> The distinction between voluntary homicide in the presence of witnesses and in the absence of witnesses is not only a distinction without a difference, or with only an accidental difference, but it is also open to the remark that if there are no witnesses it is impossible to say whether the homicide was *necessitate, casu*, or *voluntate*, (in Bracton's sense of the word) [*History of the Criminal Law of England*, Stephen (1883), vol. III, pp. 29-30 of Ch. xxvi].

11. In any antiquarian library of theology and philosophy, one may find any number of examples from early volumes in which schemata are employed to depict concepts. A standard example of this method may be found in a work by Joannie Stierio, who, when depicting the powers of the soul ("*De Anima Rationali*"), produced two charts entitled "*De Intellectu*" and "*De Voluntate*" which were intended to show the nature and extent of their power and operations [*Praecepta Physicae, Editio Tertia*, (Ex Officina Rogeri Daniel, almae Acadamiae Typographi, 1647), pages 60-62].

12. A common teaching device (for example) employed by many legal and theological writers on marital law was the *Arbor Bigamiae*, a chart which illustrated what parties may, or may not, marry because of the degree of blood relationship deemed to exist between them. In the *Summa, Avrea Armilla*, (page 587), by Placentius [a.k.a. Bartholomaeo Fumo Villauren], a chart is produced to illustrate the degrees of consanguinity which are deemed to be permissible and impermissible in marriage, [the edition of 1591, Antverpiae, apud Petrum Bellerum]. One may consult the popular work of Henrici Cardinalis Hostiensis [the edition of 1544, (Lugduni)], page 57 of the chapter, "*De bigamis non ordinandis*" in which the *Arbor Bigamiae* is reproduced. In the *Tribunal Confessariorum, et Ordinandorum*, by Martin Wigandt [Venetiis, 1733, Apud Nicolaum Pezzana], a work of moral theology, one may see the "*Arbor Consanguinitatis*," at page 719, which depicts such relationships (which we have reproduced here). It was a common device to be found in many of the Renaissance and Elizabethan texts, and was not special to any author. Even to this century the style carried over into legal writing, as witnessed by Douglas A. Stroud's *Mens Rea* (London: Sweet & Maxwell, 1914), who constructed a ramiculated diagram of criminal excuses in Chapter One of his work, "Excuses From Conviction of Crime" (page XXXVI).

SVMMA,

AVREA ARMILLA NVNCVPATA,

CASVS OMNES AD ANIMARVM CVRAM ATTINENTES BREVITER COMPLECTENS.

A Reuerend. P. F. Bartholomæo Fumo Villauren. Placentino, Ord. Præd. ac Hæreticæ prauit. Inquisitore, edita.

Summarijs, singulis titulis præfixis, aucta; Decisionibusque Sacros. Concil. Trid. in marginibus annotatis illustrata, Triplici adiecto Indice.

Omnia hac postrema editione castigatiora reddita.

ANTVERPIAE,

Apud Petrum Bellerum.

M. D. LXXXXI.

Cum Gratia & Priuilegio.

Typus graduum Consanguinitatis.

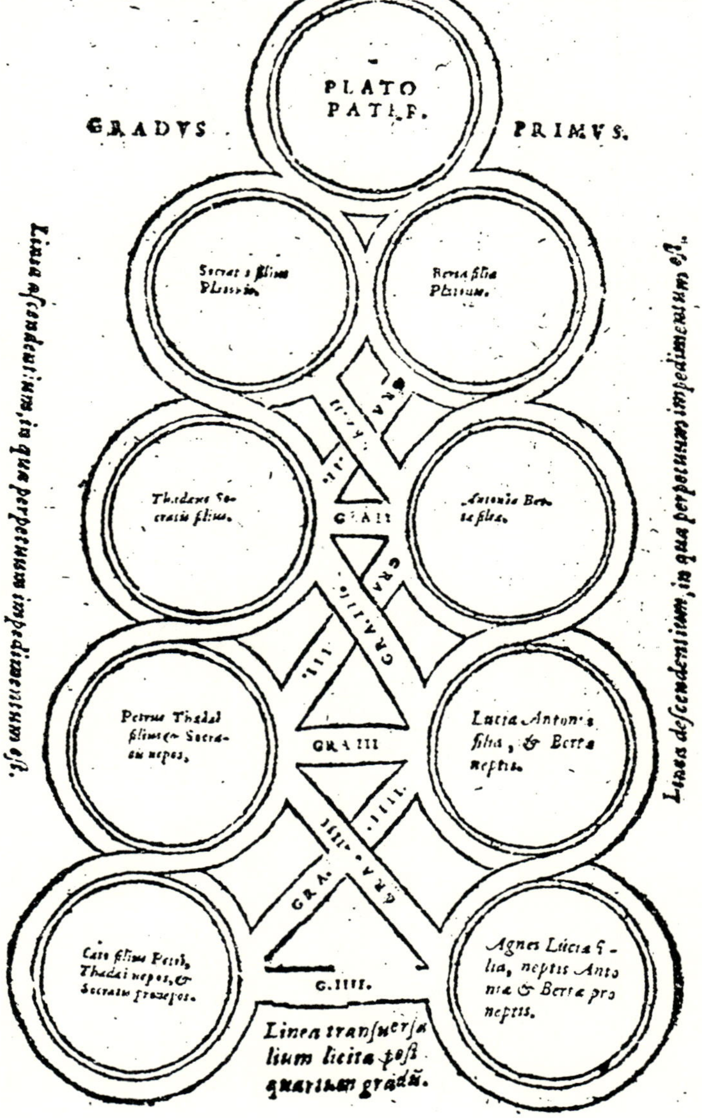

TRIBUNAL CONFESSARIORUM, ET ORDINANDORUM

DECLINATO PROBABILISMO, COMPLECTENS ſtylo brevi, clara, ac firma Sententia, omnes uſitatiores materias Theologico-morales juxta probabiliora, ac inconcuſſa Dogmata Angelici, ac Quinti Eccleſiæ Doctoris, D. THOMÆ AQUINATIS Ordinis Prædicatorum, ejuſque invictiſſimæ Scholæ:

SERVIENS OMNIBUS THEOLOGIS MORALIBUS, potiſſimum iis, qui ſive pro animarum cura, aut Ordinum ſuſceptione, ſive pro imponenda Theologiæ Moralis ſtudio coronide, vel defendendis Theſibus moralibus methodo Thomiſtica arguere, examinare, aut reſponſa dare cupiunt. Ipſis etiam pœnitentibus, cuiuſcunque ſint conditionis, perutile ac neceſſarium.

Opera, ac ſtudio

R. P. MARTINI VVIGANDT

Ord. Prædic. SS. Theologiæ Magiſtri, ejuſdemque in celeberrima, & antiquiſſima Univerſitate Viennenſi Doctoris, ac quondam ſtudii Generalis in Conventu Primi Moderatoris, ſeu Regentis.

EDITIO CÆTERIS CLARIOR, ET CORRECTIOR, A R. P. FRANCISCO VIDAL *gemino Tractatu Propoſitionum Damnatarum, & Bullæ Cruciatæ aucta.*

VENETIIS, MDCCXXXIII.

Apud Nicolaum Pezzana.

SUPERIORUM PERMISSU, AC PRIVILEGIO.

Arbor Consanguinitatis.

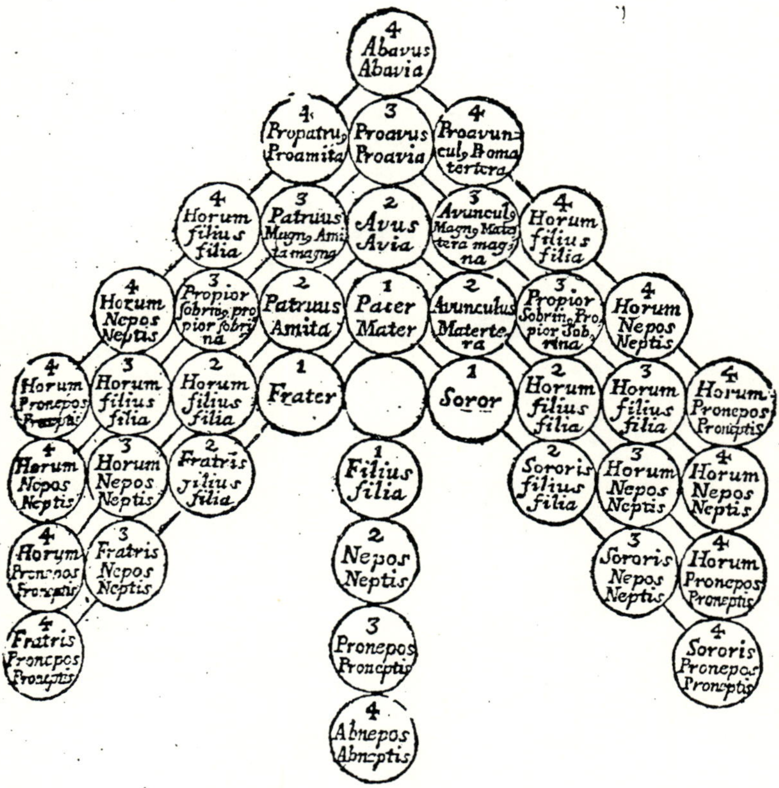

In cellâ vacuâ se fingit positum, qui de suâ cum altero cognatione quærit.

13. (London: Bernard Quaritch, 1895), pp. 225-235, where both Bracton and Bernard are reproduced line for line (which we indicated earlier).

14. The critical edition of this writer has now been edited by J. J. Francis Firth, C.S.B., and is entitled: *Robert of Flamborough, Canon-Penitentiary of Saint-Victor at Paris* (Toronto: Pontifical Institute of Mediaeval Studies, 1971). In the prolegomena to the critical Latin text of Flamborough, Firth remarks that this penitential differed from that of writers before it because this text included "...in it the new canon law of the decretists and of the decretals, that law which had been developed in the school and rendered effective by papal initiative throughout the Church. Alan of Lille had quoted some of the new decretals in his penitential, but only those which involved matters of public order, such as ecclesiastical burial. It seems that he and others hesitated to bring to bear upon the conscience of a penitent the rigid formalities of this new law as it was expounded by the canonists in their commentaries. Insofar as can be determined at the present state of research, Flamborough was the first to make available to confessors in a short, readable, comprehensive work the new law of the decretists and of the decretals, organized in a practical way for solving cases of conscience. For the first time this juridical offshoot of the Gregorian Reform extended its influence beyond synods and church courts and was put at the service of the ordinary confessor, through whose ministry reform measures could now present a more insistent appeal to the individual conscience.

"Flamborough's manual was soon followed by others in which similar use was made of the new law: the penitentials of Paul of Hungary, of Saint Raymond of Pennafort and of many others" (pp. 17-18).

For a further commentary upon how the *Decretum Gratiani* affected early Medieval church law, one may be referred to the study of Stanley Chodorow, entitled: *Christian Political Theory and Church Politics in the Mid-Twelfth Century: The Ecclesiology of the Gratian's Decretum*. It was published by the University of California Press, 1972.

15. For example, S.T.I., Q xix, all of the articles, "Of the Good and Evil of the Interior Act of the Will" of Aquinas, or *De Natura Boni*, Cap. 2 *De voluntario et involuntario* by Albert Magnus (Opera Omnia: Tomus xxv Pars 1, *De Natura Boni*, Primum Edidit Ephrem Filthaut, O.P.[Monasterii Westfalorum in Aedibus Aschendorff, 1974]), pp. 26-29, paras. 59-70, as examples of analysis in depth of a concept.

16. *Ibid.*, p. 107.

17. *Ibid.*

18. *Ibid.*, p. 108. All of these citations are from section 85, p. 108.

19. The fifth chapter of his penitential book is entitled, "De Homicidio," covering pp. 209-228, which is Cap. ii of that chapter, as edited by Firth. It spans paragraphs 242 to 270 thereof.

20. *Ibid.*, paragraph 263 of p. 225.

21. *Ibid.*

22. *Ibid*, paragraph 265, lines 76-79, of section xi, "De homicidio pro vindicta facto." The following paragraph, 266, of section xii, sets out the contrast, which its language reveals: "*De homicidio non sponte commisso*."

23. *Ibid.*, section xviii, "*Si domina ancillam per iram occiderit*," paragraph 273, p. 228. In passing, this lenient attitude towards the killing of slaves survived in common law until the middle of the nineteenth century; but we are seldom creatures beyond the mores of our own times.

24. We cite Volume Two of *On The Laws and Customs of England* as translated and revised by Professor Samuel E. Thorne of Harvard (Selden Society and The Belknap Press of Harvard University Press, 1963), and shall henceforth cite it simply as: Thorne, II, giving the pages from the volume. The portion on homicide is taken from *De Placitis Coronae*, pp. 340-342, entitled: *The crime of homicide and the divisions into which it falls.* [*De crimine homicidii et qualiter dividitur.*] We will cite the English translation in the body of our text, and place the Latin original in the footnotes.

25. *Thorne, op. cit*, II, p. 340: "*Et under imprimus videndum de homicidio, quid sit homicidium, et under dicatur, quae eius species, et qua poena homicidiae puniantur.*"

26. *Ibid.*: "*Et est homicidium hominis occiso ab homine facta.*"

27. *Ibid.*: "*Si enim a bove, cane, vel alia re, non dicetur proprie homicidium*".

28. We are not concerned here to develop historical justifications for how common law principles evolved through their various historical stages, as, for instance, Professor Kaye might have been in his articles on the early history of murder and manslaughter (L.Q.R., July, 1967) which involved him in actually reading early court records in manuscript form. Even Stephen (p. 29) in volume three of his *History of the Criminal Law* (*op. cit.*) confesses that he does not understand Bracton's distinctions between homicide as *lingua* and homicide as *facto*, although he does understand the divisions under deed. For the philosopher it is sufficient *that* distinctions were attempted showing that even in early criminal codification stress is upon what an agent does, however opaque the distinctions seem. Opacity is, and has always been, a major legal hazard in the development of the law, as dissenting judgments demonstrate.

29. Thorne, p. 340. The Latin text reads thus:

> *Istud autem homicidium si sit ex livore* [in the tropologic sense the second-order meaning of the term is: *envy, spite, malice, ill-will*] *vel delectatione effundendi humanum sanguinem, licet ille iuste occidatur, iste tamen peccat mortaliter propter intentionem corruptam. Si vero hoe firt ex amore iustitiae, nec peccat iudex ipsum condemnando ad mortem, et praecipiendo minstro ut occidat eum, nec minister si missus a iudice occidit*

condemnatum. Et peccat uterque si hoc fecerint iuris ordine non servato.

30. *Cf.*, *State v. Q.D.*, 102 Wn.2d 19 (1984) at 25: "Frequently, the same facts required to prove mens rea will be probative of capacity, yet the overlap is not complete. Capacity to be culpable must exist in order to maintain the specific mental element of the charged offense. Once the generalized determination of capacity is found, the State must prove beyond a reasonable doubt that the juvenile defendant possessed the specific mental element."

31. In *Ethics*, by Peter Abelard (translation D. E. Luscombe, Oxford), one reads in the *Te Ipsum*, p. 28: "It is indeed obvious that works which it is or is not at all fitting to do may be performed as much by good men as by bad men who are separated by their intention alone."

32. Our edition is: *Magistri Sententiarvm Libri IV*, Petro Lombardo Episcopo, edited by F. Robertis VVianti (*Lvgdvni*, Sumptibus Claudij Landry, M.DC.XVIII), pp. 210-211. In the citation we have preserved the original spellings. Read "s" for "f", and "v" for "u" (in some words).

33. From *Horizon*, Vol. xvii, 97, 1948, the article entitled "Sin," p. 14. Also to be found as Chapter vii, "Sin" (pp. 89-99) in Russell's book, *Human Society in Ethics and Politics* (George Allen and Unwin Ltd., 1954), p. 97.

34. Aquinas, in his *Summa Theologiae*, 1a2ae, Q. 6. art. 6, at least considers the question in this fashion, but gives an answer to it which is both confusing and unconvincing. The question is put by him thus, and we cite Blackfriars text (London: Eyre & Spottiswoode, 1970: Volume 17 of the series) "Does fear render an action simply involuntary?" [*Utrum metus causet involuntarium simpliciter*?]

35. We have current cases where the court permits a consideration that one's will was overborne because of fear or duress. Consider, *R. v. Hudson*, and *R. v. Taylor*, [1971] 2 All ER 244, *re* the question whether threats had overborne the will of a juror, causing him to testify falsely. However, in *U.S. v. Hearst* 1976) (9th Cir.)__F.Supp__, the court did not accept the defense that the defendant had been "brainwashed," making her seeming voluntary actions actually to be involuntary, or non-voluntary, actions. The civil law of marriage will permit the contract to be vitiated if the will of one of the parties to the contract has been overborne in some fashion (which nullifies consent to the union).

36. Thorne, *op. cit.* *Necessitate, quo casu distinguendum erit utrum necessitas illa fuit evitabilis vel non. Si autem evitabilis et evadere posset absque occisione, tunc erit reus homicidii. Si autem inevitabilis, quia occidit hominem sine odii meditatione in* (340) (341) *motu dolore animi, se et sua liberando cum aliter evadere non posset, non tenetur ad poenam homicidii. Casu, sicut per infortunium, cum aliquis proicit lapidem ad avem vel animal et alius transiens ex insperato percutitur et moritur, vel si quis arborem inciderit, et per casum arboris aliquis opprimatur, et huiusmodi. SED HIC ERIT DISTINGUENDUM*

UTRUM QUIS DEDERIT OPERAM REI LICITAE VEL ILLICITAE [capitals, ours]

37. Aquinas expressed the difference between *mortal* and *venial* sin by means of a comparison, and we shall cite his text. We shall cite the fine English translation of the late Joseph Rickaby, S.J. [*Aquinas Ethicus*, Vol. 1 (London: Burns and Oates, Ltd., 1896), pp. 208-209], and shall cite the Latin text from the Latin-English edition prepared by John Fearon, O.P., entitled *Sin*, which is volume 25 of the *Summa Theologiae* in the Blackfriars series (London: Blackfriars, 1969), pp. 42 & 44. "The difference of venial and mortal sin follows upon the diversity of inordination that enters into and makes up sin. For there is a twofold inordination: one by the withdrawal of the principle of order another where the principle of order is maintained, but some inordination occurs in what follows upon the principle. Now the principle of all order in morals is the last end. Hence when a soul is disordered by sin to the extent of turning away from its last end, that is, from God, to whom it is united by charity, then is the sin *mortal*; but when the disorder stops short of turning away from God, the sin is *venial*....For in speculative matters he who errs in principle is beyond the reach of persuasion; but he who errs indeed, but adheres to first principles, may be recalled by the aid of those same principles. And so in matters of conduct, he who by sinning turns away from his last end, suffers a fall that is, so far as the nature of the sin goes, beyond repair, and exposes himself to be punished everlastingly. But he whose sin stops short of turning away from God, is under a disorder that by the very nature of the sin admits of repair; and therefore he is said to sin *venially*, because he does not so sin as to deserve never-ending punishment."

The Latin text reads as follows: "*Differentia autem peccati venialis et mortalis consequitur diversitatem inordinationis, quae complet rationem peccati. Duplex enim est inordinatio: una per subtractionem principi ordinis; alia qua, salvato principio ordinis, fit inordinatio circa ea quae sunt post principium. Principium autem totius ordinis in moralibus est finis ultimus,* [and this is deleted by Rickaby: *qui ita se habet in operativis, sicut principium indemonstrabile in speculativis, ut dicitur in* Ethic (*Ethics*, VII, 9. 1151a16-17)]. (The passage to which Aquinas refers is rendered by Ackrill in his translation of the *Nicomachean Ethics*, 1151 a, 15-20, p. 143 [Faber & Faber, 1973] as follows: "For virtue and vice respectively preserve and destroy the first principle, as the hypotheses are in mathematics: neither in that case is it argument that teaches the first principles, nor is it so here – virtue either natural or produced by habituation is what teaches right opinion about the first principle. Such a man as this, then, is temperate; his contrary is the self-indulgent.")

With regard to moral order, Fearon notes, in his gloss on the text, and we quote, "By moral order, St. Thomas means a sequence of moral decisions. In this sequence, intention of ultimate end or goal not only preceded choice of means chronologically, but also determines which possible human actions are apt means" (p. 42).

The Latin text continues, "*Unde quando anima deordinatur per peccatum usque ad aversionem ab ultimo fine, scilicet Deo, cui unimur per caritatem, tunc est peccatum mortale: quando vero fit deordinatio citra aversionem a Deo, tunce est peccatum veniale....Nam in speculativis qui errat circa principia, impersuasibilis est: qui autem errat salvatis principiis per ipsa principia revocari potest.* [Fearon adds to the Latin text, "The author has in mind science which would be deductive, rather than science in the sense of empirically attempting to verify a hypothesis.] *Et similiter in operativis qui peccando avertibur ab ultimo fine, quantum*(42) (44) *est ex natura peccati, habet lapsum irreparabilem: et ideo dicitur peccare mortaliter aeternaliter puniendus. Qui vero peccat citra aversionem a Deo, ex ipsa ratione peccati reparabiliter deordinatur, quia salvatur principium: et ideo dicitur peccare venialiter, quia scilicet non ita peccat ut mereatur interminabilem poenam.*"

38. I. R. Swoboda, O.F.M., J.C.L., published his dissertation on the subject of imputability, *Ignorance in Relation to the Imputability of Delicts* (Washington, D.C.: The Catholic University of America Press, 1941), and it offers a reasonably clear canonical history of certain canonical maxims, one of which is the notion of *versari in re illicita.* As an early study, however, some of his sources are inexact, and some of the writing less than clear analytically.

39. If one compares the early editions of Plowden, *1571 Les Comentaries...* (In Aedibus Richardi Tottelli, Octobris, 24, 1571), or *Cy enfuont certeyne Cafes Reportes...* (Anno 1584), or *Vn Report fait per vn vncerteine...* (In Aedibus Richardi Tottelli, 1584) with the later English edition in two volumes of 1816 which we have previously cited, one finds that the English editor found it necessry to make apparent Plowden's Civil references to Bartholus or Covarruvias.

40. One may note that Suarez's *De Legibus* appears in London, 1679, from the press of J. Dunmore, T. Dring, B. Tooke, & T. Sawbridge.

41. Herewith appended is a reproduction of the Latin text which we employed, taken from Volume 38 (2a2ae, Q. 63-79) of the *Summa Theologiae* as prepared and translated by Marcus Lefebure, O.P. of the Dominican Chaplaincy of the University of Edinburgh (Blackfriars, 1975), and entitled *Injustice.*

"*articulus 8. utrum aliquis casualiter occidens hominem incurrat homicidii reatun*

RESPONSIO: Dicendum quod, secundum Philosophum6 casus est causa agens praeter intentionem. Et ideo ea quae casualia sunt, simpliciter loquendo, non sunt intenta neque voluntaria. Et quia omne peccatum est voluntarium, secundum Augustinum,7 consequens est quod casualia, inquantum hujusmodi, non sunt peccata. Contingit tamen, id quod non est actu et per se volitum vel intentrum, esse per accidens volitum et intentum, secundum quod causa per accidens dicitur removens prohibens.8 Unde ille qui non removet ea ex quibus sequitur homicidium si debeat removere, erit quodammodo homicidium voluntarium.

Hoc autem contingit dupliciter: uno modo, quando dans operam rebus illicitis, quas vitare debedat, homicidium incurrit; alio modo quando non adhibet debitam sollicitudinem. Et ideo secundum jura,9 si aliquis det operam rei licita: debitam diligentiam adhibens et ex hoc homicidium sequatur, non incurrit homicidii reatum. Si vero det operam rei illicitae vel etiam det operam rei licitae, non adhibens diligentiam debitam, non evadit homicidii reatum, si ex ejus opere mors hominis consequatur.

AD OCTAVUM sic proceditur:1 I. Videtur quod aliquis casualiter occidens hominem incurrat homicidii reatum. Legitur enim *Gen.*,2 quod Lamech credens interficere bestiam interfecit hominem, et reputatum est ei ad homidicium. Ergo reatum homicidii incurrit qui casualiter hominem occidit.

I. Ad primum ergo dicendum quod Lamech non adhibuit sufficientem diligentiam ad homicidium vitandum; et ideo reatum homicidii non evasit."

42. *Ibid.*, Latin, p. 44, English, p. 45.

43. *Ibid.*

> "2. Praeterea, *Exod.* dicitur, *si quis percusserit mulierrem praegnatem, et aborsum fecerit, si mors ejus fuerit subsecuta, reddet animam pro anima.*3 Sed hoc potest fieri absque intentione occisionis. Ergo homicidium casuale habet homicidii reatum."

44. *Ibid.*, Latin, p. 46, English, p. 47. The complete Latin reply to the objection is as follows:

> "2. Ad secundum dicendum quod ille qui percutit mulierem praegnantem *dat operam rei illicitae*; et ideo si sequatur mors vel mulieris vel puerperii animati, non effugiet homicidii crimen; praecipue cum ex tali percussione in promptu sit quod mors sequatur."

45. A simple example from the period of the logic of the maxim at work is this case from *Pleas of the Crown, The Eyre of Northamptonshire, 3-4 Edward III*, (Selden Society, 1981, Volume 97 [printed 1983]), p. 164: "Simon Osbern was arrested for killing Nicholas fitz Simon...27 July 1328. The jurors...say...Simon and Nicholas quarrelled on the way to a tavern....A fight broke out between them and Nicholas struck Simon in the head and knocked him down. Simon got up and straightway fled as best he could....When Simon saw that Nicholas would kill him with that staff and that he must defend himself or die, he took a small pole-axe and struck back at Nicholas and hit him in the head, so that he died on the spot....Wherefore they say that Simon killed Nicholas in self-defence and not in felony or malice aforethought. And they say expressly that if Simon had not so defended himself he could not have avoided being killed."

46. We would distinguish, however, "omission" from "recklessness" as the latter term was expanded in *Caldwell* [1981] 1 All ER 961. *Cf.*, *Divergent Interpretations of Recklessness*, NLJ, March 25, 1982, pp. 289, 313, and 336, Glanville Williams. To omit means one knows but does not act upon that knowledge; to be reckless, as Lord Diplock expanded the notion in *Caldwell*, means to be ignorant of, yet to be deemed responsible for such ignorance. The concepts differ.

47. S.T., 1a2ae., 6.3. We append the Latin text of the article.

"RESPONSIO: Dicendum quod voluntarium dicitur quod est a voluntate. Ab aliquo autem dicitur esse aliquid dupliciter: uno modo directe, quod scilicet procedit ab aliquo inquantrum est agens, sicut calefactio a calore; alio modo indirecte, ex hoc ipso quod non agit, sicut submersio navis dicitur esse a gubernatore, in quantum desistit a gubernando.

Sed sciendum quod non semper id quod sequitur ad defectum actionis reducitur sicut in casuam in agens ex eo quod non agit, sed solum tunc potest et debet agere. Si enim gubernator non posset navem dirigere vel non esset ie commissa gubernatio navis, non imputaretur ei navis submersio, quae per absentiam gubernatoris contingeret.

Quia igitur voluntas volendo et agendo potest impedire hoc quod est non velle et non agere, et aliquando debet; hoc quod est non velle et non agere imputatur ei quasi ab ipsa existens. Et sic voluntarium potest esse absque actu; quandoque quidem absque actu exteriori cum actu interiori, sicut sum vult non agere; aliquando autem etiam absque actu interiori, sicut cum non vult agere" (p. 14 of Volume 17, entitled Psychology of Human Acts, translated by Thomas Gilby, O.P., [Blackfriars, 1970]).

48. *Op. cit., supra*:

"I. Ad primum ero dicendum quod voluntarium dicitur, non solum quod procedit a voluntate directe sicut ab agente, sed etiam quod est ab ea indirecte sicut a non agente."

"Hence: I. That is defined as voluntary which issues from will, not only directly as acting, but also indirectly as not acting."

Summa Theologiae, 1a2ae. 6,3

articulus 3. utrum voluntarium possit esse absque omni actu

AD TERTIUM sic proceditur:1 I. Videtur quod voluntarium non possit esse sine actu. Voluntarium enim dicitur quod est a voluntate. Sed nihil potest esse a voluntate nisi per aliquem actum, ad minus ipsium voluntatis. Ergo voluntarium non potest esse sine actu.

2. Praeterea, sicut per actum voluntatis dicitur aliquis velle, ita cessante actu voluntatis dicitur non velle. Sed non velle involuntarium causat, quod opponitur voluntario. Ergo voluntarium non potest esse actu voluntatis cessante.

---

1 1a2ae. 71, 5 ad 2. *De malo* II, I ad 2. II *Sent* xxxv, 3.

3. Praeterea, de ratione voluntarii est cognitio, ut dictum est.2 Sed cognitio est per aliquem actum. Ergo voluntarium non potest esse absque aliquo actu.

SED CONTRA, illud cujus domini sumus dicitur esse voluntarium. Sed nos domini sumus ejus quod est agere et non agere, velle et non velle. Ergo sicut agere et velle est voluntarium, ita et non agere et non velle.

RESPONSIO: Dicendum quod voluntarium dicitur quod est a voluntate. Ab aliquo autem dicitur esse aliquid dupliciter: uno modo directe, quod scilicet procedit ab aliquo inquantum est agens, sicut calefactio a calore; alio modo indirecte, ex hoc ipso quod non agit, sicut submersio navis dicitur esse a gubernatore, in quantum desistit a gubernando.

Sed sciendum quod non semper id quod sequitur ad defectum actionis reducitur sicut in causam in agens ex eo quod non agit, sed solum tunc potest et debet agere. Si enim gubernator non posset navem dirigere vel non esset ei commissa gubernatio navis, non imputaretur ei navis submersio, quae per absentiam gubernatoris contingeret.

Quia igitur voluntas volendo et agendo potest impedire hoc quod est non velle et non agere, et aliquando debet; hoc quod est non velle et non agrer imputatur ei quasi ab ipsa existens. Et sic voluntarium potest esse absque actu; quandoque quidem absque actu exteriori cum actu interiori, sicut cum vult non agere; aliquando autem etiam absque actu interiori, sicut cum non vult agere.

I. Ad primum ergo dicendum quod voluntarium dicitur, non solum quod procedit a voluntate directe sicut ab agente, sed etiam quod est ab ea indirecte sicut a non agente.

Voluntary and Involuntary

article 3. can there be voluntariness without any act?

THE THIRD POINT:1 I. It seems no[a]t. For that is voluntary which proceeds from the will, from which nothing proceeds except through some act, at least that of the will itself. Hence given no activity there is nothing voluntary.

2. Again, just as a person is said to will by an act of will, so when the act is over he is said not to will. A not-willed effect is involuntary, the opposite of voluntary. Therefore there cannot be anything voluntary when willing stops.

---

1 1 1a2ae. 71, 5 ad 2. *De malo* II, I ad 2. II *Sent* xxxv, 3.

a The teaching of this article lies behind the moral treatment of sins of omission: 1a2ae, 71, 5.

2 Arts. 2 & 3 above.

3. Besides, knowledge is essential to voluntariness, as we have seen, 2, and knowledge involves activity. Hence voluntariness cannot be present without some activity. Hence voluntariness cannot be present without some activity.

ON THE OTHER HAND that over which we hold mastery is said to be voluntary. And we are the master with respect to acting or not, and to willing or not. Acting and willing are voluntary. So also is not acting and not willing.

REPLY: To be voluntary means to spring from will. Now one may come from another in two ways. One, directly, when it proceeds from it precisely as agent, thus heating from fire. Two, indirectly, when it proceeds from it precisely as not acting, thus a shipwreck from loss of helm.

Notice, however, that the result of a lack of action is not always to be brought home to the non-acting agent, but only when he could and should have acted; thus if the steering had broken down or he were not responsible the helmsman is not charged with the loss of the ship.

Now there are cases when by its revolve and action the will can intervene to break the inertia with respect to willing and acting, and sometimes ought to do so. Then it can be held responsible, for the not willing and not acting are in its charge. Thus there can be voluntariness without an act, sometimes without an external act though with an internal act, as when a person wills not to act, sometimes, however, without even an internal act, as when he does not will to act.[b]

Hence: 1. That is defined as voluntary which issues from will, not only directly as acting, but also indirectly as not acting.[c]

Summa Theologiae, 1a2ae. 6, 4

2. Ad secundum dicendum quod *non velle* dicitur dupliciter: uno modo prout sumitur in vi unius dictionis; secundum quod est infinitivum hujus verbi *nolo*; unde sicut cum dico, *nolo legere*, sensus est, *volo non legere*; ita hoc quod est, *non velle legere*, significat *velle non legre*; et sic *non velle* causat involuntarium. Alio modo sumitur in vi orationis; et tunc non affirmatur actus voluntatis; et hujusmodi *non velle* non causat involuntarium.

3. Ad tertium dicendum quod eo modo requiritur ad voluntarium actus cognitionis sicut et actus voluntatis, ut scilicet sit in potestate alicujus

---

b Note that a mere 'negation' of willing is not enough, a 'privation' of a willing that could and should be is required.

c To avoid ambiguity, it should be observed that many manualists change St. Thomas's terminology. They treat his distinction between the direct and indirect voluntary as that between the positive and negative voluntary. They call willing something for itself directly voluntary, and willing something which results from it, as when a therapeutic operation causes an abortion, indirectly voluntary. This is the celebrated *voluntarium in causa* which looms large in casuistry. On this see 1a2ae. 77, 7. 2a2ae. 43, 3; 64, 7 & 8; 150, 4.

considerare, et velle; et agree; et tunc sicut non velle et non agere, cum tempus fuerit, est voluntarium, ita etiam non considerare.

Voluntary and Involuntary

2. 'Non-willing' has a double meaning. First, when taken as a single term, *non velle*, the infinitive of *non volo* or *nolo*, not to wish or to be unwilling. So that if one says, 'I am unwilling to read,' one can be taken to mean, 'I am willing not to read,' so that willing not to read and not willing to read are equivalent: in this sense 'not-to-will' causes involuntariness. Second, when taken as a sentence, and then no act of will is posited: in this sense 'to will not' does not cause involuntariness.d

3. Voluntariness requires an act of cognition by the same token that it does an act of will; certainly the ability to consider, as well as to will or act, should lie in a person's power. Hence just as not willing or not acting are voluntary on occasion, so also is not considering.

49. From the body of the Reply we cite the following portions:

Reply: This question arises with regard to sins of omission, and from the fact that there are varying opinions about them. Some [Note: Aquinas does not name them] hold that every sin of omission involves activity, either internal or external. An internal action is involved when one decides not to go to church at a time when he should. An external action is involved when a man busies himself with other matters either during church-time or just before church-time and is thereby unable to attend.

In many ways this latter situation is equivalent to the former, for if a man sets his mind to one course of activity which excludes another, then he also chooses to omit the latter unless he is unaware of their incompatibility, in which case he could be guilty of negligence. Others hold the opposite point of view, saying that a sin of omission does not necessarily involve activity, for the mere fact of not doing what one is bound to do is a sin.

Both opinions contain an element of truth. If we consider in the sin of omission that which directly and properly pertains to the concept of sin, sometimes the sin of omission is accompanied by an internal act, e.g. when a man chooses not to go to church; sometimes, however, it is not accompanied by any act, either internal or external, e.g. when a man just simply does not think either of going or not going at a time when he should be going to church.

However, if we consider in the sin of omission the causes or occasion of the omission, then the sin of omission must of necessity include some act.*

* In the language of insurance, an insurance underwriter will often ask, when reviewing the policy of an assured, if the risk is worth the company taking. For example, it may be that the assured has been involved in a series of accidents for which, at law, a court has deemed that he was not legally responsible; nevertheless, an underwriter may ask if the assured possibly caused the accidents, however unintentionally they were caused. Did the assured brake his

For there is no sin of omission unless one omits to do what he is capable of doing (italics ours). When one decides not to do what he can do there is always an accompanying reason. And if it is beyond his control, there is no sin, e.g.. when one cannot go to church because of illness.

However, if the reason for the omission is within his control it is a sin. The reason for the omission, insofar as it is voluntary, must include at least an internal act of the will.

Sometimes the choice directly involves the omission, as when a man chooses not to go because it would be too much trouble. In this case the choice is properly associated with the omission. Since the nature of sin involves free will, the desire for the sinful constitutes the sin.

Sometimes, however, the choice directly involves the reason for the omission: whether the thing chosen is concomitant with the omission (when one chooses to indulge in recreation at a time when he should be in church), or whether it precedes (when one chooses to stay up late at night and fails to arise in time for church)" (p. 19 of *Sin* (Vol. 25), [Blackfriars, 1969]).

A coherent and analytic presentation of what Aquinas means exactly by his various writings on Will, and its relation to human actions and omissions, is a study yet to be done, and it is outside of the range of this study.

Summa Theologiae, 1a2ae. 71, 5

"RESPONSIO: Dicendum quod quaestio ista principaliter movetur propter peccatum omissionis, de quo aliqui diversimonde opinantur.

Quidam enim dicunt quod in omni peccato omissionis est aliquis actus vel interior vel exterior. Interior quidem, sicut cum aliquis vult non ire ad ecclesiam quando ire tenetur. Exterior autem, sicut cum aliquis illa hora qua ad ecclesiam ire tenetur, vel etiam ante, occupat se talibus quibus ab eundo ad ecclesiam impeditur.

Et hoc quodammodo videtur in primum redire: qui enim vult aliquid cum quo aliud simul esse non potest, ex consequenti vult illo carere, nisi forte non perpendat quod per hoc quod vult facere, impeditur ab eo quod facere tenetur; in quo casu posset per negligentiam culpabilis judicari. Alii vero dicunt quod in peccato omissionis non requiritur aliquis actus: ipsum enim non facere quod quis facere tenetur peccatum est.

Utraque autem opinio secundum aliquid veritatem habet. Si enim intelligatur in peccato omissionis illud solum quod per se pertinet ad rationem peccati, sic quandoque omissionis peccatum est cum actu interori,

---

own car suddenly, thus "causing" [bringing about the conditions] for a third party driver to rear-end the assured's car? Is the assured, if he has several fall-down cases on his medical claims, one who tends to race about, or is he in a profession or avocation which exposes him to above-average risk of injury? Aquinas is arguing, here, for stronger notions of fault than what an insurance underwriter might argue when considering whether or not a policyholder's policy should be renewed or not. But the "form" of the reasoning is similar: namely, each asks if one has contributed to the chance of risk of harm, and each asks if what the party contributed to the risk was non-negligent, negligent, or even deliberate.

qut cum aliguis vult non ire ad ecclesiam, quandoque vero absque omni actu vel interiori vel exteriori, sicut cum aliquis hora qua tenetur ire ad ecclesiam nihil cogitat de eundo vel non eundo ad ecclesiam.

Si vero in peccato omisionis intelligantur etiam causae vel occasiones omittendi, sic necesse est in peccato omissionis aliquem actum esse. Non enim est peccatum omissionis nisi cum aliquis praetermittit quod potest facere et non facere. Quod autem aliquis declinet ad non faciendum illud quod potest facere et non facere, non est nisi ex aliqua causa vel occasione conjuncta vel praecedente. Et si quidem causa illa non sit in potestate hominis, omissio non habet rationem paccati: sicut cum aliquis propter infirmitatem praetermittit ad ecclesiam ire.

Si vero causa vel occasio omittendi subjaceat voluntati, omissio habet rationem paccati: et tunc semper oportet quod ista causa, inquantum est voluntaria, habeat aliquem actum, ad minus interiorem voluntatis.

Qui quidem actus quandoque directe fertur in ipsam omissionem; puta cum aliquis vult non ire ad ecclesiam, vitans laborem. Et tunc talis actus per se pertinet ad omissionem: voluntas enim cujuscumque peccati per se pertinet ad peccatum illud, eo quod voluntarium est de ratione peccati.

Quandoque autem actus voluntatis directe fertur in aliud, per quod homo impetitur ab actu debito: sive illud in quod fertur voluntas, sit conjunctum omissioni, putta cum aliquis vult ludere quando ad ecclesiam debet ire, sive etiam sit praecedens, puta cum aliquis vult diu vigilare de sero, ex quo sequitur quod non vadat hora matutinali ad ecclesiam."

50. "*Sed si dabat operam rei licitae et non adhibuit diligentiam debitam, imputabitur ei*" (Thorne, *op. cit.*, p. 341).

51. *Morissette v. U.S.*, 342 U.S. 246 (1952); *Lambert v. California* 355 U.S. 225 (1957).

52. Military law is replete with examples wherein superior orders is not a valid defense to capital crimes.

53. *In passim* one may refer to his various works. In the *De Malo*, 3.6., he asks whether ignorance can be the cause of a sin. In the next question, 3.7., he asks whether ignorance is a sin. In the following question, 3.8., he asks whether ignorance excuses sin, or diminishes it. In his *Commentary on the Sentences*, at 2-22-2-1, he asks if ignorance is a sin. At the subsequent chapter, 2-22-2-2, he asks whether ignorance excuses sin. Common to these excursions is a style of question which seeks to establish what kinds of conditions will excuse an act when the defense for the harm done by the act is a defense of ignorance. The conclusion to be reached was to answer, Is the Defendant guilty (in any shape or form) for his ignorance, or is such ignorance permissible at law? Our statement here is an immediate simplification of an area in medieval thought which is unbelievably complex and detailed, but it is a subject outside our frame of reference.

CHAPTER FOUR

Fleta, Britton, and Early English Case law

Just as the legal historian may answer questions of time with a reserve of caution, as in the question, "When, precisely, did the Inns of Court begin?" so also must the legal philosopher answer certain questions concerning the development of legal principles in early common law with just as great a reserve of caution. It is one question to ask how principles historically influenced the development of the law, and this we do not ask; it is another question to ask what were the principles which were present, in actual or viral form, and this we do ask. But to search for a line with clear and distinct borders as to what was a heavenly principle, and what was an earthly principle, at common law, will not be found. Early common law moved with some ease between heaven and earth, within a world of custom and all of its elements, and within a world of moral and religious beliefs. One has not a simplified appeal to a bold chalk mark across a chalkboard to mark off one sphere from the other, as a medieval Pope might divide the earth into East and West, and let earthly princes sail to either realm and obtain all that they wished.

We have some broad historical facts to which we can appeal. After the *Decretum* canonists sprang up to develop law in its various sectors, and they were able to draw upon the theoretical foundations developed by medieval theologians. Canon lawyers, however, would proceed to develop legal principles and would not do "legal theology." The list and scope of both published and unpublished works is long, and far beyond the scope of this study.[1] The broad theological teachings of the Church would serve to guide canonists and legal scholars on the Continent, and very much of the published legal work would be done with, or under, Church approbation. The Civilians would develop Roman law in accordance with Church beliefs.[2]

Common law would develop with a blend of nominalist and realist principles. Cases would be decided by judges, and each case would be *this* case; however, though each case was a particular "this," some kind of harmony would be sought so that one would not be thrown into judicial randomness. The "realist" side to the law would strive for justice; the "nominalist" side to the law would work through case by case to conclusions. The case law of the period, from the Plea Rolls, is compressed and sparse, and it would seem that a common judicial habit of mind, formed from local traditions and customs, put its impress upon the formation of early case law.[3] The judgments which the Courts rendered were abrupt and undetailed,[4] as any examination of the Plea Rolls and records of the various Eyres will demonstrate. How certain key terms of law serve to function is left to personal understanding. One can puzzle over the logical force of such key terms in the cases. There is no system of case law, as we have come to understand the system of case law in our time. One works with passages and with scattered cases, and from their reading one may intuit key legal concepts which control early legal reasoning. The early law shows us a vocabulary growing, as the forms of action themselves grew. New causes of action bring about new demands upon a language to provide for legal distinctions. The early language draws from the religious language of the period, for that language was rich in its distinctions, and had a long application in penitential directions.[5] Religious language, such as a theologian might employ, would contain complex sets of distinctions, and then explanations of such distinctions, which the law, in the main, would not. Where a theologian might distinguish between "intention" and "motive" (that one does not necessarily include the other), the law will not be that exact. Passages in Bracton bear this out.

Bracton speaks of an appeal for malicious arson and robbery.[6] Thorne's translation of the passage is as follows:

> If one in the course of a riot or during a civil disturbance commits arson, wickedly and feloniously, either through enmity or the sake of spoil, let him be punished by capital punishment.

> I say "wickedly," because accidental fires or those caused negligently and without evil are not so punished....*

It is a simple passage, but it yields, we would suggest, some complicated transformations. If one uses the language of motive by which to understand extensions of the passage, motive can be read in two ways. It may mean that one acted out of spite, and also while spiteful one formed an intention at law to act unlawfully. But the passage may also be read without any appeal to motive. It may mean that one simply and clearly broke the law knowingly.

When one looks closely at the Latin text, some of the Latin uses permit various inferences of meaning. The adverb, "*nequiter*," may mean, when translated into English, a state of character, as when it might be said of one who acted *wickedly* that he so acted because he possessed a wicked nature or disposition or character. But the adverb may also direct us to what was done, as when something is badly done. The adjective, "*nequam*," also permits various interpretations. When Bracton speaks of, "without evil intent" ("*non mala conscientia*"), two distinct senses may be given of the usage. On the one hand, it may refer to the actual intent needed to commit a serious crime, which one may call the substantive use of the phrase. On the other hand, that same phrase may mean that only one with a wicked disposition would commit a felony, which one may call the adjectival use of the phrase, since it describes a state of character.

Language which appeals to motive may be proper to understand a criminal act. A criminal act may permit two fundamental questions to be asked of it. One may ask how it was that such a dreadful act could be committed, and an appeal to motive may serve as an answer. But if one were to ask solely how an act was brought about, an appeal to the concept of a criminal intention serves to answer that question. One may postulate that motive and intention are separate concepts, but one should also be aware that motive and intention may overlap. In the passage cited from Bracton (*supra*), "*nequiter*" serves to indicate both motive and intention. While motive

---

* The Latin text, p. 414 of Thorne, reads: "*Si quis autem turbate seditione incendium fecerit nequiter et in felonia, vel ob inimicitias vel praedae causa, capitali puniatur sententia. Nequiter dico, quia incendia fortuita vel per negligentiam facta et non mala conscientia, non sic puniuntur.*"

and intention may be distinct concepts logically, it is possible that a term or a phrase may express them indifferently, without a conceptual conciseness or clarity. In this passage one may argue that *mens rea* is the predominating concept, but its use is as a cluster concept which may permit, at some times, the inclusion of motive into its parsing. It may mean that one possessed both a wicked character and did intend (a usage one finds in modern revised codes of criminal law).* The status of one's character would provide a ground for motive, while an appeal to the voluntary ("*sponte*") would provide the intentional grounds for the act.

The overlapping of motive and intention shows through in a number of Bracton's texts. In the section in which he has discussed the crime of homicide and its subdivisions,[6] one reads: "*Pro homicidio vero iustitiae iusta et recta intentione facto*," which is a clear case of the presentation of the intentional requisites of an act *without* any appeal to a motive behind or accompanying an act.

One may argue, by way of constructing an argument, that Bracton does assume that intention differs distinctly from motive when he permits "necessity" to negative intent, as when he says,

> Of necessity, and here we must distinguish whether the necessity was avoidable or not; if avoidable and he could escape without slaying, he will then be guilty of homicide; if unavoidable, since he kills without premeditated hatred but with sorrow of heart, in order to save himself and his family, since he could not otherwise escape [danger], he is not liable to the penalty for homicide.[8]

But his reasoning is not all that clear, since the passage, as well as others, shows that if the act is legally permissible, so must the state of mind accompanying the act be legally and morally without taint. If Necessity forced an agent to act (kill in self-defense, or throw cargo overboard), the act can yet be tainted if the agent takes malicious delight in the other's death or the other's loss of cargo. One may explain this intertwining of concepts of

---

* *Cf. Washington Criminal Code* [1975 1st ex.s. c260 9A.04.110.]. In this title, unless a different meaning is plainly required, (12) "Malice" and "maliciously" shall import an evil intent, wish, or design to vex, annoy, or injure another person. "Malice may be inferred from an act done in wilful disregard of the rights of another, or an act wrongfully done without just cause or excuse, or an act or omission of duty betraying a wilful disregard of social duty."

motive and intention by suggesting that no hard and clear distinction was apparent to Bracton between a separation of a system of law from a system of morals. This can be seen when, speaking of war, Bracton says, " If it is unjust he who kills will be liable; if just, as a war in defence of the *patria*, he will not, unless he acts with evil intent. [*nisi hoc fecerit corrupta intentione*]."[9]

There would have been little difficulty for legal theorists after the time of Bracton[10] to answer a charge that they failed to distinguish with care and clarity a system of laws from a system of morals. The relation of an agent to a legal proposition would be much the same as was the relation of the existence of the world to God. Because it was thought (for the most part) that the order of the world was the case because of the internal order of God, and from objects one could argue to the existence of God, so, by parity of reasoning, it would be odd if, of adherence to a legal proposition (in criminal law), it could be asserted that the agent was lawful by publicly obeying the force of the criminal law, but privately withheld obedience to the law by force of malice (which only the agent could know) secretly resolved. The public good, which was law, should express the private good, which was morals, just as the public order of the world expressed the private order of Deity. If a human act were conceptually to be described as a fully constituted human act, then both spheres of human behavior, exteriority and interiority, would of necessity have to be joined in a unitary act. Bracton does, within the tradition of natural law, rightly advance the proposition that an "evil intent" (motive) can vitiate the value of a legal act. Elevated to theological speculation it could be said that if God were omniscient it would be improper to claim that He knows contradictions approvingly; i.e., that a man's public act was proper (the domain of law) while the interior conditions precedent to the act were improper (an evil motive). To preserve a consistency between acts and intentions, what a man did (under the circumstances described) would amount to a lie, and such would have been assumed to be morally wrong in the eyes of God. It was one man doing, as it were, two different acts, but simultaneously. To predicate of "A" both "p" and "-p" would produce a contradiction, and an act done from evil motives, yet apparently good in public eyes, would be thought to be contradictory. The position was consistent, as a meta-legal position, for a system of conduct which made the thought of adultery as deserving of punishment as serious as if one actually did commit adultery.

Reasoning of this kind with regard to the essence of a legal system does not move us now (or generally does not move all of us) because we view systems as constructions, in much the same way that one can view geometric systems as constructions from consistent and well-defined axioms. For Bracton, however, as for most natural lawyers, the fundament of a legal system was its parallel, in some ways, with the nature of God.

Let us explain this assumption, briefly. If God possessed a true and non-contradictory self-identity then what He did would be an expression of His true and non-contradictory self-identity. Were it the case that He could know one thing, but do exactly the other, then two (and, perhaps, more) problems would arise for the Christian theologian. One problem would be that God would directly be the author of evil because, it could be argued, if doing and knowing were not one, He could know the good, but do less than the good. Manicheism, and other such dualisms in which "good" and "evil" were coeval principles, had long been condemned by the Church. The second difficulty would be that if the acts of God were not true expressions of Himself one would thereby introduce a contradictory element into His very nature, and this Christian theology would not permit, God being the source and author of all truth. If one follows this belief and carries it over into the province of law one may argue that following the law is akin to God doing an act; that act, on the part of God, expresses His true nature; therefore, when an agent acts lawfully, it is assumed that his public expression (by following the law) reveals his own interior nature (a mind properly informed wishing to follow the law.)

The Middle Ages gave witness to legal systems *qua* legal systems without at the same time being exercises in meta-legal logic upon theological presuppositions. It would be a mistake for us to convey the impression that every bit of medieval law was an expression of theocratic law. It was not, as any number of statutes show us.[11] What is important to our argument, however, is to appreciate what indebtedness early criminal formulations and theory had to theological and canonical writing of the period, and we believe this to be instanced clearly in Bracton's twinning of moral and legal concepts (which, at times, are incarnate within one word as it functions on both levels).

The formula, then, for the voluntary as a ground for criminal guilt finds its expression in Bracton's *De Legibus*. The language of the various appeals in the *De Placitis Coronae* show that the Will, in some way, is the ground upon which criminal guilt is built. If it can be shown that one acted "wickedly" or "maliciously" or "premeditatedly," and that the action sprang from within control of the agent as a voluntary action, as an action over which he could exercise reasonable control, then the machinery of guilt and responsibility can function by bringing to bear the collective legal condemnation of the criminal sanction upon the defendant.

The early law itself shows how "malice" was used adjectivally. Criminal law writers of the present day suggest the "malice" can be distinguished in civil use from criminal use: "Malice in criminal law means intention or recklessness...; but malice in the law of tort, or express malice, means improper motive, that is, any motive that the law does not approve of."[12] One notices, however, that in Bracton the distinction is not that apparent; if apparent, it is virtually, rather than actually, so. Drawing upon an early case of replevin, a civil action for recovery (in this instance, for recovery of straying farm animals), we read:

> A man has brought Replevin against another for an ox and forty geese, tortiously....The plaintiff is a great lord, and very evilly disposed; and whereas my hedge was good enough, he, in malice, broke it down and drove in his beasts.

To the objection that, "He ought to fence the place; and if any beasts come in for want of fencing, one ought, by custom of the country, to drive them out, and not impound them," the reply of the defendant was,

> The place was fenced with a hedge according to custom, and you in malice made a break in the hedge, and drove in your beasts...[13]

Notwithstanding that the action is for replevin, one may note from the language of the defendant that from *his* point of view the noble lord had acted, not only from spitefulness and iil-motive, but also had fully intended to cause property damage. The word "malice" functions in that incarnate manner (as we had earlier suggested) here by twinning both aspects of motive and intention. For technical reasons one may, of the instant case, suggest that "motive" only is to be read because the case, properly, was not a criminal case, but we doubt if this is to rebut the incarnation of concepts in any strong way.

One may advert to early civil cases for the purpose of showing how flexible certain key terms were. There is, however, a good body of criminal cases, and commentary, to which one may turn to trace the growth of key criminal concepts. We have a body of cases from the Year Books of Edward I which may be studied, some of which were presided over by Ralph de Hengham who, prior to his appointment, had written a number of legal Summas. In his *Magna Hengham*[14] we observe that in the second chapter, Hengham cites as a separate offense "(15) *melletis*." The term means "Chaunce medley" or an "affray," stemming from twelfth-century usage.[15] What is interesting is to note that early on a distinction was recognized between designing to do (a crime) and happening to commit a crime. Selden, in the text, observes, and we quote:

> (15) *Melletis*] *Glanvil* and *Bracton* have *de Meletis* for suddain affrais or dislikes; the word is so us'd too in *Regiam Majest. lib. 1. cap. 3.* and hence our CHAUNCE MEDLEY, corrupted oppos'd against FORETHOUGHT FELONY, as MANSLAUGHTER with us, against MURDER. See *Skene ad citat. loc. & de verb. Signific.* But CHAUNCE MEDLEY is in *Stamford* otherwise. *Skeen* interprets *Chaud melle* by *Rixa* in the Civil Law.[16]

One should appreciate that even with the introduction of a distinction between designed versus sudden human acts, the question always before the court will be how to "prove" that the distinction obtains. Considering here as we are only the theoretical components of a legal distinction, one faces little problem with the burden of judicial proof. It is enough for our purposes to note *that* a distinction found its way into the common law between *kinds* of human acts in which the question of the *degree* of control one may or could exercise was admitted as a valid question for legal solution. What becomes apparent upon serious philosophical reflection is that the notion, very often, was intuitive; what were assumed to be the conceptual elements of (say) a voluntary act, as opposed to any lesser human act such as an involuntary act, were not defined clearly at length (as the same kind of question might have been developed through an extended argument by a medieval theologian). In order for one to arrive at some clear understanding of how sound legal principles came to develop, and to accommodate sound sets of workable distinctions within the criminal process, one is required to review the early case law, and from such a review attempt to formulate what principles seemed to have evolved. Nevertheless, early case law tends to be compressed, and this very compression tends to obscure a simple statement of legal principles; moreover, the cases themselves tend to express principles in an enthymematic fashion which leaves a legal theorist to wonder over what assumptions were suppressed to lead to this obvious conclusion expressed in the judgment of the court. Reaching a coherent statement as to what were *the* dominant sets of legal principles in a growing legal system (as was early common law) is an inductive process, and fraught with the hazards of any inductive undertaking. Whatever theory arises finds itself limited not only by the set of facts which the court finds or admits, but the theory is also limited by what interpretation the court places upon the facts. The older medieval notion seems apt: that consistency is found far from the particular; general principles may be consistent; applications of general principles not. It is a caveat only; not a rule.

From a report of cases in the Court of Common Pleas for Michaelmas Term, 31 Edw. 1.,[17] one may observe that Hengham's J., brother on the Bench, Roubury J., found that injury did not necessitate criminal intention.

> One John brought his writ of Trespass, and complained of W., that he had maimed him, to wit, cut off one of his fingers &c.–W. said that he was not guilty.–The Inquest said that he had cut off one of his fingers.–It was adjudged by Roubury that he (John) should recover his damages.

In *Hyam v. Director of Public Prosecutions* H. L. [1974] 2 All ER 41, it may be recalled that Lord Diplock, delivering his dissenting judgment on behalf of the judicial House, stated on page 64 of the instant judgment,

> I have found no trace of the actual expression 'grievous bodily harm' being used before 1803, by writers of the law of homicide or by judges, to describe what was a sufficient evil intention to constitute that 'malice aforethought' that was the badge of murder. Apart from minor piecemeal exceptions of assaults in particular circumstances which had been made

> felonies by earlier statutes, until the passing of Lord Ellenborough's Acts [43 Geo 3 c 58, 1803], assaults, however serious their physical consequences, were classified as no more than misdemeanours unless they resulted in death.

Our early Year Books, although not intended to be ruling case citations as one finds in much later case law,[18] show how a certain consistency permeated the development of common law in its statement of assumed, but never doctrinally stated, first principles. Lord Diplock held that it was consistent in *Hyam* not to let "intent" mean "statutorily constructed intent," as *per* Lord Ellenborough's Act. To read intent in such a way departed from the spirit and course of earlier common law holdings. One could, although the noble Lord did not, support the position he developed by an appeal to cases earlier than those cited in the body of his judgment.

One need not argue that some early decisions did not follow the forethought principle, or natural consequence principle. An act may have had probable natural consequences, but it need not be viewed by the court then as the court in our own day might have viewed natural consequences (prior to the *Criminal Justice Act*, 1967). Nor need a court follow a forethought principle, as the Year Book case we have cited demonstrates. American courts tend toward a stricter construction of the probable and natural consequences of an act than do English Courts (presently), because English Courts, as we have stated in the body of our writing, are controlled by the spirit of the *Criminal Justice Act*, 1967, section 8 (b) of the Act.[19]

The early Year Books show that distinctions obtained, as between murder and manslaughter, but that little technical elaboration followed when the distinction was introduced. If the case were one of manslaughter, one reads the following: "Spigurnel answered that the statute [with reference to its application to the present case, one regarding rape] did not allow it except *in the case of manslaughter* [italics ours]."[20] The standard phrase when manslaughter is indicated is simply, "de mort de home."

From *The Pleas of the Crown* before Spigurnel, J.,[21] we do find recorded a phraseology which speaks of the state of a subject, but which does so only as a report (of a criminal action) and not as an analysis of a volitional state. We read, "...and she said that the said Ralph had ravished and ruined her against her will...," "...and they presented that the said Ralph had ravished her against her will...,"[22] language of a kind which one finds in present day cases of rape.[23] Of various killings one might read, "Three men were indicted for the death of a man who was murdered." If guilt were found, as in the instant case, one reads, "The Jury said that only one was guilty of the deed, and that the other two were not guilty of the deed, *nor of assent to it*" (italics ours),[24] the latter disjunctive phrase serving to indicate some kind of intentional finding from the facts of the case.

As other times one will have to read further than the indictment to find why the charge was (say) one of manslaughter. We read in a case that Richard and William were indicted for manslaughter, and, in the facts of the case, we see that one John, brother to Richard, had done the killing: "Richard made an unsuccessful attempt, and the thief knocked him down; Richard cried out, and his brother John came up, and struck the man on the head, in the consequence of which he died." In his judgment, Spigurnel, J., noting that John was not twelve years old when the killing occurred, stated, "If he had done the deed before his age of seven years, he should not suffer judgment; but if before his age of twelve years he had done any other deed not involving the loss of life or limb, and against the peace, he should not answer, because before that age he is not with the peace"[25] (A.D. 1302).

Early criminal case law tends to observe rules and formulae to announce legal findings, in marked contrast to theological writing of the same period which considered not only hypothetical cases, and citations from leading historical authorities, but also engaged in a detailed analysis of why and/or how "A" may have Φ -ed. The law did not. A simple narrative of the facts, for the most part, was given; then a finding was made, and judgment announced. If a principle were at work it would be stated in some ancillary and compressed form in the body of the case. In a note upon a case of 1302[26] we read,

> Note, if a man attacks another with premeditation or in any other manner, the value of the weapon belongs to the justices' clerk as his fee, and shall be paid to him immediately.

It is assumed that one can determine if an act were done with premeditation; no analysis is given of various meaning which could attach to the term. At other times, as some of the cases in law Latin illustrate, age will protect (as in endnote 26 of this chapter). We read that a boy shot an arrow and, it is to be gathered, by mischance, killed a woman. Because of his age he is adjudged not to be guilty of a felony, but the thing from which the arrow is glanced is declared a deodand.[27] Or, as with the law French, so one will read in Latin the use of legal formula which states that a victim in rape was taken against her will. The defense of the accused, fortunately accepted in this ancient case, was the consent of the victim. The text reads,

> *Item, presentatum fuit per duodecim de Y. quod H. Rapuit quamdam puellam, et N. et eam duxit ad manerium suum in eadem villa, et eam cognovit carnaliter contra suam voluntatem.*[28]

The case continues to the extent that it is to put to the jury to decide. We read,

> Duodecim. *Nos dicimus quod ipsa rapiebatur vi per homines domini Hugonis. Justiciarius. Fuit ne Hugo consentiens ad factum vel non*? – Duodecim. *Non. –Justiciarius. Cognov-erunt ne eam carnaliter*? – Duodecim. *Sic. [Justiciarius]. Muliere invita vel consentiente*? – Duodecim. *Consentiente. – Credo quod deberet hic quod tamen post defuit. – Justiciarius. Domine Hugo, quia ipsi vos acquietant, nos vos acquietamus.*

The findings are simple, by modern methods of law. But at the time it was also simple in comparison to any section of an authoritative religious or legal treatise which discussed in what way one's will could be overpowered. The exercise reveals that in matters practical, as in criminal law (for the most part), one assumes much of what directs the case. Such has its virtues; but it also has its deficiencies, one of which is to hide or obscure first principles upon which a decision may have been founded, and this kind of obscurity follows *mens rea* formulations up until the writing of this work. One may simply assume *that* one's will could be overpowered, and then admit such an assumption into a system of legally permissible excuses, only to find that the assumption itself is unclear, the unclarity revealing itself when the definition calls for greater precision (as the *Hearst* case revealed when the center of the dispute between the prosecution and defense was to what extent it could be claimed that one moved about [walked, talked, continued in companionship with one's abductors] but yet moved without recourse to intention, i.e., did not intentionally participate in a bank robbery, or did not intentionally fire an automatic rifle). How the common-sense legal assumption is refined will dictate how a jury finds.

A further analysis of a common-sense legal assumption may reveal that an assumption is so stated that it will not admit of refinement, save for a slight technical refinement in its minor premises. When looked upon in analytic detail one may find that the conceptual form of the assumption is such that it does not admit of a meaningful counterexample, as when one claims that "voluntary" means "to spring from within." If the test of the voluntary is that it begins from within the agent, and only this, then a number of candidates are excluded from our consideration. The definition is either broad, and thus apt to be tautologous, telling one that action which is conscious is action which the agent does voluntarily; or the definition tends to be unnecessarily restrictive, and excludes such cases which may arise from fear, constraint, impulse, anxiety, moods, chemical changes which the human system itself manufactures, misjudgment (as when one thinks he has chosen freely but was, in fact, induced to take or to buy unknowingly), or mis-response (as when one believes that he is acting in accord with the wishes of his guest, but in fact, is fully irritating the guest unawares).

Common-sense legal principles function *as if* they are clear and primitive first principles within a legal system, without need of refinement; their refinement, and the patent need for such, arises when certain questions are answered wrongly. The test for "wrong" will be what sensitivity is shown for the knowledge of the time – why, for instance, premature codification of the common law is hazardous. The force of each concrete occasion should, in the best fashion, direct the formation of legal principles. *Hearst* was a case which bent many unquestioned assumptions and formulations about the nature of *mens rea*. If the definition will not permit one to consider if the definition does not obtain – however paradoxical it may be to assert this – then one is in danger of making the concrete instance fit the law; and, as we have argued in the first part of our work, to do so assumes that a legal system is fully and necessarily and unrestrictively well-defined. We think this is a logically unsound assumption. We also think genuine miscarriages of justice occur by adopting such an attitude towards legal reasoning.

It is a truism to assert that the criminal law grows by having to solve new problems and answer new questions. The legislature, in its law-making capacity, may make law; but the courts, in their interpretative capacity, both make law and make law work in a practical sense. The broad principles are laid down by the legislature, but it is for the courts to make those broad principles apply in particular cases. In this way, the courts have a residual but most important law-making capacity. They have a chance to develop legal principles, to refine them, and to apply them, and then to redefine them again when those general principles work awkwardly. The jurisprudence which develops through case law is that which grows out of response to particular difficulties which a particular case presents for resolution. Each newer case, however, may require the court to re-think accepted principles.

New questions may create new difficulties which old ways cannot answer. A simple sentence may illustrate two distinct and exclusive ways in which a legal position may be seen. Take this sentence: "I know that I lifted the book from the table, but for the life of me I do not know why I did so." If one stresses one aspect only, namely: *that* one acted (and knows it) but excludes *why* one acted (one cannot account with a reason why one so acted), one advances a strict on/off notion of intention. Such an on/off understanding of intention excludes any question about degrees of human action. On the other hand, if one were to view intention as a cluster concept, in which various conceptual components* are conjoined, then any formulation of that cluster concept in terms only of one element in the cluster would be a misformulation or misapplication or misunderstanding of the concept.[29]

The role of the legal philosopher is generally different from the role of the legal historian or law teacher. Although the legal philosopher will work with case law (unless he is trying to invent a totally new system of law—which is the model of the legislator who devises new laws), his aim is to question the logic of the case law with which he works. He puts to it the question: why this rather than that? He will search for the elements which may underlie legal reasoning or which seem to reappear in the bodies of

* We posit that the conceptual elements are dissimilar each to the other.

cases he analyzes, and he is at liberty to sustain his analysis on isolated legal principles and elements.

Some of these attitudes did find themselves into legal instruction, especially under the impetus of Dean Langdell of Harvard Law School, 1870. Langdell thought that one could locate the number of fundamental legal doctrines, and this could be done by selecting leading cases from the historical advance of the law.[30] The fallacy in the logic of this method is that it accepts as the fundament of the critical method the assessment of the professor of law. What seem to be "legal principles" are often little more than the critical impressions of the editor or compiler himself; lacking from these hornbooks of law was any underlying critical principle which served to justify the assumption that a law case, by itself, contained *the* critical principles whereby future decisions would be guided. One was given a multiplicity of impressive cases; what one was not given was a unifying principle whereby cases were to be selected and classified. The reasoning was circular, i.e., the justification that a single critical principle was at work in the cases was assumed by the cases included in the collections. By using "A" one proved "B"; and then by using "B" one set about to prove "A." But the logical form that a legal assumption might take was not isolated or analyzed.

The temptation is to assume that the body of the law contains any set of intuitively self-evident first legal principles. We have argued, and wish to continue to argue, that one must return to certain historical considerations, such as leading cases (without worrying if some preordained principle makes them so), leading writers or treatises, and in addition to an examination of these sources strive to see what critical principles are at work, and then set about to answer if they are fundamental legal principles. Pressing the legal philosopher is to determine the truth of the assumption made by the law that a relationship obtains not only between the facts of this case and a legal principle enunciated therefrom, but between that legal principle and other facts of future legal cases. It is not so much a puzzle about induction, although the conflict which inductive reasoning presents for logical analysis may appear, as it is a puzzle about a fundamental assumption of the law: that a legal formulation does, in some fashion, reflect or present the nature of things and of persons. To assert this position, however, does not close the issue. What it does is to set some boundary or some context to the statement of the problem which legal formulation(s) should meet, and, perhaps, even solve.

If one were to advance (what seems to be) a radical position and claim that between what is said in a legal proposition, and that state of affairs which is depicted by the legal proposition, there is no connection, then it appears that one would be saying that between legal propositions and persons or things, *in strictu senso*, nothing is signified.* We believe a legal philosopher may ask a further question about legal reasoning. He may ask to what does it apply, and whom does it affect? He may ask, all the more, whether the reasons advanced by (or contained in) the legal system are valid, or coherent, or sensible, or logical, and he then may propose ways and methods whereby to test for each of his questions. He may inquire why certain legal assumptions are made (by a system), and he may query if they work, or are workable, or are prudent, or are coherent. He may, then, judge the system, which we see to be the calling of a philosopher.

Without attempting to betoken the merits of *Fleta*, we do turn to it, however, to demonstrate how the logical strands of *mens rea*, or intention generally, appear in early common law.[31] Now that we have workable and scholarly editions of the text we are able to turn to the text to note how many of our accepted legal notions, which one easily can take for granted, came into being. As to the objection that the anonymous treatise does not preserve legal notions from the period in a state of untarnished historical exactness, one may reply that such is too much to ask of any text on early

* We do not want to step outside of our inquiry and be accused of making broad statements about language and the law. We wish only to assert what is a common-sense position about language and the law. Legal sentences and legal propositions, and the like, may not strictly describe human nature or contingent states of affairs. Legal language may not be a language of essences (i.e., describing the nature of a being or an entity). But legal language is a form of language under which persons are assumed to act, and by which persons are assumed to be directed. It is a language which compels, from compelling general social conduct, to compelling a lawyer to follow a certain procedural form when submitting a motion in a case. *We assume* (and this properly may be a question about law-making and the legislative) that legal language may be predicated of human nature and states of affairs. *How* such predication may be justified is a question we do not argue here. It would perhaps be a separate topic in itself. We wish only to tell the reader what assumptions we have made about legal language and states of affairs.

common law; moreover, if one argued in this fashion, and were to apply the argument to cases actually decided by judges, what then would one do with the many odd judgments which did not contain mainstream teaching or consensus? For the legal philosopher it is enough here that a record of legal opinion is given which preserves certain legal assumptions which were current, and which have been transmitted. Bracton, *Fleta*, Britton, *The Mirrour of Justices*, Fitzherbert, Staundford, Richard Crompton, among many others, serve to give, as distinguished trial counsel Mr. Louis Nizer once said in his autobiography, *My Life in Court*, a balance of probability to the truth, a balance towards the strength of the truth being the case in a given* situation when one finds certain notions appearing, again and again, in different and distinct situations. It is not *a priori* necessary truth; rather, it is a kind of logical appearance which tends to recommend itself rather than to disrecommend itself to practical reason, causing one to believe (most likely) that something is probably the case, akin to the balance of probabilities which govern evidence in jury findings in criminal law cases at common law.

One usage recorded by *Fleta* is the following:

> Should a man rashly attempt to devise the king's death or procure or incite or give aid or assent to the king's betrayal or the betrayal of the king's army, *although he should not have carried his intention into effect*,... (italics ours).[32]

The Latin for the italicized portion reads, "*quamuis voluntatem non perduxerit ad effectum*." One may note that the notion of "attempt" carries over a ring from Bracton, who, on the same subject, wrote:

> The crime of lese-majesty takes many forms, one of which is where one rashly compasses the king's death, or does something or arranges for something to be done to the betrayal of the lord king or of his army, or gives aid and counsel or assent to those making such arrangements, *even though what he has in mind is not carried into effect* (italics ours).

---

* Nizer had stated that cross-examination, when done with finesse and skill, tends, on the balance of probabilities, to extract the truth of what was the case. It is a practical judgment, and for that reason one appeals to a notion of "on the balance of probabilities." By extending his metaphor, we are suggesting that early records of the common law (cases, rolls, treatises, statutes), even with regard to their historical inexactitude at times, will, on the balance of probabilities, reveal more of the logic of the law of what is the case than what is not the case, upon prolonged examination. *Cf.* pp. 11-13, *Prologue*, of *My Life in Court*, by Louis Nizer (Garden City, New York: Doubleday & Company, Inc., 1961).

The Latin text in Bracton is: *"licet id quod in voluntate habuerit non perduxerit ad effectum."*[33] The parallel in notions is close enough to suggest that they share a common notion, *Fleta* using the form "*quamuis voluntatem*," while Bracton employed "*in voluntate habuerit*" to express an incompleted act. The Latin roots, in the samples of the text, suggest that a notion had been put into the mind by the agent himself (awkward as the restatement of the notion be in English). One had willed, and in willing had formed an intention to bring about, some end. Common to "Attempt" is that the agent had formed a design; moot to "Attempt" is whether the design can, in fact, be attempted. The text here assumes that one can form an intention "to do," and that a crime (under certain circumstances) can be completed at the moment of the mental formation (*in voluntate habuerit*, or *quamuis voluntatem*) of it. The Latin carries over with its sense that one has rooted a concept in the will, as distinct from a concept rooted solely in the intellect. We no longer speak in this way presently, and, when put into English prose, it appears that one is talking (simply and exclusively) about the philosophy of mind. One is not, but it is only by appreciation of the genuine grammatical form of the original statement (in Latin) which reveals a volitive emphasis which English usage does not reveal. This distinction will become clearer as more texts are cited. The Latin, and, at times, the French reveal that the evilness of an intention arises from a corruption of character; to speak of a corrupt intellect would have been an odd, if not an incorrect, usage of medieval notions of crime or sin. A wrong could be, and the language would tell one, an objective wrong (*culpa*, or even an accident in which personal harm was caused as *casus* embraced) or a wrong attributable to the intention of a subject (as *dolus* or *peccatum* indicated). When one modified a notion, as in "evil intent," the modification suggested that such a corruption sprang from the Will of the agent, and an explanation of such a corruption would stress how the Will, as a rational appetite itself, wrongly willed. The Will was also a less than rational appetite, but in Latin (at least), its non-rational use could be explained, as when one spoke of blind lust, or raging anger, and the like. We take time to expostulate upon this distinction because without it, "intention" pure and simple seems, purely and simply, an intellectual notion *only*; and we argue that it is not, nor have early common law writers seen it to be a purely cognitive notion. Because Intellect was thought to be able to consider any set of propositions (or concepts, if one wishes to stress the non-propositional powers and abilities of Intellect), then, as such, it would be to fail to understand the nature of Intellect to claim that one predicated responsibility of it for what it considered. To the contrary, responsibility, as a moral predicate (and, for that matter, as a legal concept), rested in the Will for what set of rational considerations it chose to act upon or under. However reified the language may be, in speaking about Intellect and speaking about Will, what is at stake is how properly to assign a role to a concept. Such a role here is the concept of "being responsible," and it was thought that Will, as the final arbiter of human action, occupied that role. To be finally responsible for an act brought one (in theory) into the realm of *praxis*; to shape one's character was a form of action (just as to undergo a change from potency to act was a form of action), and action rested within the power of the Will and not of the Intellect.

For a legal system developing out of the close of the Middle Ages one should not be surprised that the vocabulary of that emerging system would contain and reflect its theological and philosophical heritage. The various treatises on law from the early Renaissance show us these echoes from the Middle Ages, and it would be pleonastic to draw upon the large variety of legal texts to demonstrate the extent of this heritage. What may bother us in our generation is that we are not sympathetic, generally, to a philosophy of mind which speaks in terms of mental faculties. It strikes us as if parts of a computer are being described, while, all the same, the parts themselves are remaining hidden when, somehow, it is thought that they ought to be open to inspection. We tend, in our age of scientific demonstration, to reject metaphyscial demonstrations which appeal to conceptual distinctions *as if* these conceptual distinctions are real and instantiated.

We think it might be of greater profit to accept that our emerging legal system did borrow a faculty vocabulary, and that it did use it, preserving distinctions between intellection and volition, and, to understand how legal notions of criminal responsibility evolved, one must bear with those early notions. As late as 1696, in the manuscript by Chief Justice Hale, which we consulted and read in the British Museum, entitled *Tract Concerning the Law of Nature*,[34] one reads a treatise which abounds in scholastic distinctions and usage, preserving (even if critical of the distinction) the language which distinguished between the power of the Will and the power of the Intellect. Now, we may prefer to appreciate the distinction between modes of action without, at the same time, ascribing a particular mental faculty to account for the particular mode of action. Optative may differ from indicative without the need of postulating an optative faculty in opposition to an indicative faculty of mind.

To return then to *Fleta*, one may appreciate that it reflects a use of "attempt" similar to Bracton. One may intend to attempt, and both treatises are satisfied that the intentional portion of the crime has been fulfilled. They both are silent on that portion of a crime which one might now describe as *actus reus*. The actus reus of a prohibited action seems to be incorporated within an intentional description of the prohibited act; one does not find a separate portion dealing specifically with the non-intentional elements of a crime. It will be for later, and modern, writers to dwell upon this portion of a crime's elements, but even here *actus reus* is done in passing and without treatment in monograph form. [C. F., endnote 54, this chapter.]

Woven into the discussion of homicide in *Fleta* is a use of "intention" which is adjectival, which moves between legal use and moral use, and which demonstrates the volitional nature of a rational act. We shall attempt, by citing passages from Chapter 23, "Of Homicide," to demonstrate how all of these usages occur in *Fleta*.

The opening sentence of the chapter, "Of Homicide," uses intent as a cluster word. The sentence is, "Homicide is the slaying of man by man with evil intent," and it is to the Latin text that one must turn to see that "intent" is rendered from "*nequiter*." The term does not possess a logical preciseness (which we might expect now from key terms), suggesting, as it does, that one may be a man of bad character who did a condemned act. To translate the term as "evil intent" does not, thereby, render it epistemically clear. The vague meaning is that a wrong is done, and that the wrong may reflect the character of the agent, his baseness. "[*N*]*equiter*" is used to embrace "motive" in the text, and this passage will support such a reading:

> A judge, for example, slays in justice when he lawfully condemns, unless his intention is corrupt, [*nisi intencionem habeat corruptiam*], as, for example, if his judgement should be actuated by malice or delight in shedding human blood, [*ex liuore* (which may mean, in a tropical sense, *envy, spite, malice, ill-will*) *vel voluptate effundendi humanum sanguinem*], and in such a case, although the slaying be lawful, it is homicide and he commits mortal sin: but it is otherwise if he acts from love of justice, in strict conscientiousness.[35]

The early description of murder in which intention is the key concept makes an explicit distinction between law, as one system, and morals, as an element of a legal act. Although the legal act may be legal in a strict sense, i.e.; conforming with a legal code, and one may have adhered to the external form strictly which that legal code may dictate, it is still possible to fault that act morally. One could argue that the absence of a mental element, which omission is caused by the agent himself, may render the perfect legal act an immoral act. This permits one in theory to argue that an act may admit of two distinct descriptions, even though that self-same act is predicated of a single intention. By an agent intending to *phi* (ø), the same act of the agent may admit of two distinct, exclusive descriptions. Early common law, in its course of development, admitted of this common sense distinction. It admitted that there was a distinction between a moral act and legal act. By its use of language, the early common law might use the same term to admit of both distinctions, as when one reads "*nequiter*," or "*liuore*," and terms of like weight.

One may argue that moral predicates and legal predicates function in opposing ways one from the other. Because each has a different expectation and aim, they signify in mutually exclusive ways. In part this is true to say. It has been the case historically, especially with the criminal sanction, that a legal system is concerned with public acts and not, generally, with private acts.* One might argue that it would be too much for a legal system (like the

* A moral system is generally thought to be the conscience of the person and that which guides or polices one's acts. It is not a necessary truth that a legal system and a moral system cannot intersect – consider a theocratic legal system –, or a legal system which does not make the distinction between public and private face in human actions. Some may argue that a system like Soviet law blurs the distinction between the person and the state for the reason that the state is thought to embody the aims of the person. We believe, however, that one can logically distinguish a moral system from a legal system.

common law) to be concerned in its official capacity and through its machinery with the policing of strictly private intra-mental conditions. In the first place how could one enforce sanctions against thoughts? Legal predicates, then, would be seen as those which attach to public conditions. How one felt, what one believed, what one privately intended, would be classed as moral predicates.

Cast into a simple logical form it would mean that every act an agent authored would admit to two distinct logical descriptions. If a legal act were "p" and a moral act were "p-prime," then any relationship holding between "p" and "p-prime" would be non-necessary. One would come into the legal sphere by offering his reasons for an action: "I stole the automobile because...." The legal act would have been the taking of the automobile conjoined to what reasons the court might accept to excuse one from the act or not. What is stressed, to make it a legal matter, is the public nature, i.e., "the stealing of." The private nature of the act would be incorporated into the public act when it could be said that the reasons one offered, "I thought it was my car" were accepted by the court or not. The actions of an agent fit into what is publicly permissible or acceptable.

But the same action could be a moral action, "p-prime." One might be an adherent of a strict religious sect which did not believe in private ownership. But the problem which is perplexing is that criminal law (as an example) does not maintain a strict distinction between what an agent believes to be the case, and what the law states to be the case. The overlap is blurred when, to some criminal charges, it is material to know what the accused believed or thought was the case. To attempt a distinction between moral and legal predicates on the basis of extensionality only is a distinction which helps the law little, if at all. Some criminal charges are voided when one states that he truly believed "x" to be the case, as in the sections of *The Theft Act*, 1968.

We would wonder further if the distinction between moral and legal predicates on the consideration only of public and private realms is that strict. Most criminal offences require that a defendant acknowledge his guilt. It is not a necessary condition for the finding of guilt; but guilt, as such, functions as a judicial and prosecutorial device at trial. If an accused truly cannot admit guilt, then such could be advanced as a possible defense that the accused did not know that he had committed a crime. The ambit of the criminal sanction includes *mens rea*, which is to bring the accused within the boundaries of a criminal sanction, and also includes *actus reus*, which (as a modestly open-ended concept) includes not only the definition of the crime, and the legal circumstances which may surround a crime, but also the legal abhorrence which attaches to a crime. We are not arguing that a necessary condition for criminal guilt is that the accused himself believes that he is guilty. But it may be reasonable to consider, as a form of defense, if the accused understood if he himself did commit a crime. He may in fact have fulfilled the material conditions surrounding a crime's definition; but if he had no understanding of the formal conditions which attached one might argue from such a fact that the accused either did not know the nature and quality of his acts (as with a plea of insanity), or that the accused was without benefit of criminal knowledge (*scienter*), or that the accused (within the strict conditions of a legal system) acted from diminished responsibility, or that an accused acted without any awareness of what were the elements of an offense–acting out of ignorance–rebutting the assumption that he had committed a crime.[36]

Fleta uses a number of key terms to express criminal intention, as can be seen in the chapter dealing with homicide (Chapter 23).[37] The first sentence, it will be recalled, expressed "wilfully" by the use of the Latin term "*voluntate*." If an intention (*intentionem*) were corrupt, the sentence modified the word "intention" with the Latin adjective "*corruptam*," which modification served to indicate that an intention ("*intentionem*") in and of itself did not express malice or wickedness of mind. A corrupt intention was also expressed in this Latin usage by the expression "*animo corrupto*," which indicated that one's soul itself was corrupted or wicked. One may consider this passage for its multiple use of intentional terms:

> Wilfully, as for example, if a man, with corrupt intention, wickedly and feloniously slays anyone by deliberate attack, in anger or hatred or for the sake of gain: and if this is done secretly, it will be accounted murder.[38]

Save for the historical fact that murder meant a killing done secretly, the language of the sentence preserves the volitional aspect of intending. An intention is not synonymous with verbal formation; the text is not explaining how sentences which express legal intention were formed. What the text is attempting to indicate, and possibly explain by its appeal to an ablative notion of cause and of source, is that a crime *may* be accounted for by presenting a particular account of human action springing from the soul. An "*animo corrupto*" is a compressed way to account for an internal dissolution.*

The phrase "*in assultu premeditato*" reflects a twelfth-century usage* that one has premeditated upon his act. The assault is not spontaneous (like a tavern brawl might be). The assault is the expression of design; one has considered what could be done *and* one has consented to what could be done. As in the opening sentence to the chapter, "*nequiter*" is used; not to mean wicked intention but to mean only wicked. The cluster of words, then, which we are given to portray homicide tend to depict a corruption of

---

* One cannot but help to appeal to Aquinian notions of human faculties when examining this period. His influence upon writers was profound, and one finds later legal scholars in constant debt to Aquinas. If we choose to draw upon him as representative of much medieval theory, we cannot avoid how he saw the Will to be. Without trying to offer a unified theory of Will, his writings do appear to be consistent, in spite of whatever dilemmas they may now cause for us regarding how he envisaged his theory of will. Willing was a rational appetite (S.T.1a2ae. 8. 1). In the first answer of that same article he stated that the will is related both to good and evil. The actual desire for the good was the will in act, *voluntas*; and the will shrinking from evil was *noluntas*. In article 2, same question, he stated that the term "Will" "sometimes indicates the power of rational desire and sometimes its activity." Will was that power of the soul which linked the realm of the spirit and the realm of matter, and moved the suppositum, which was man, to an end. Intellect, of itself, *moved* nothing. How did will and intellect "move"? At S.T. 1a2ae 9.3 Aquinas says, "the mind brings itself from a potential to an actual knowledge of a conclusion by its knowing the premises: this is how it sets itself in motion. Likewise the will: it moves itself to willing the objects which are on account of the end because it wills the end." What we have to plug in is that he is depicting a faculty which *exists*. That a faculty does exist (actually) takes that faculty from the drawing board and puts it into the world. The question is not, How can what is unmoved then come to move? rather, the quesiton, is, How that which exists does move. In S.T. 1a2aw 78, 1, he asks how malice (*malitia*) is a cause of sin. One of the causes of sin may be a lack of order in the will (*ex defectu voluntatis*). "Malice" is an evil habit (E.N. 11,4.1105b19-28). In *Fleta* we could argue that an "*animo corrupto*" is an expression of the soul for a disordered end. The disordered end is to infringe the law (one meaning of law was the King's peace). So the phrase, in this text, is a shorthand expression indicating that the will has turned against a higher good, the law, and sought a lesser good, i.e., the disorder; which a crime reflects.

* *Premedit/ o*, with premeditation, 1192; *Premetior* (deponent), to measure out beforehand, *circa* 1180; to consider beforehand, *circa* 1180. From Medival Latin Word-List by J. H. Baxter and C. Johnson, (Oxford University Press, 1934), p. 325.

character and an entertaining of a wrongful design for some end. The language of the sentence is parallel to Bracton:

> *Voluntate, ut si quis ex certa scientia et in assultu praemeditato, ira vel odio vel causa lucri, nequiter et in felonia et contra pacem domini regis aliquem interfecerit.*[39]

When *Fleta* presents an analysis of a felonious act it is interesting to see what range of action and omission is shown in the example. If, when two were quarrelling, and one killed the other, then the following set of legal conditions seem to obtain:

1. There was an intention to kill said to be in those who were there and simply wished to kill, but did no deed,
2. Those who gave counsel were said to have an intention to kill,
3. Those who physically aided were said to have an intention to kill,
4. Those who physically involved themselves, i.e., involved themselves in some non-legal way in the affray.

Of "3" and "4" the distinction might have been between *active* v. *passive* participation in the affray,

5. The fighters themselves are found to be by *Fleta* guilty of intentional killing, one of the other.

The force of the example seems to be, however loosely framed, that non-legal actions which are felonious should not have the preoccupation of any one. "Bystander" cases are often a problem for the Courts (in our own century), and there seems to be no hard-and-fast rule. If a jurisdiction has a constructive malice statute, then the burden of rebuttal shifts to the defendant to prove that he was not involved in a conspiracy or an attempt; but the Court, or the prosecution, generally adverts to the nature of the crime itself. Bank Robbery will be treated with greater seriousness by the prosecution than will, say, bystanders at a legitimate prize-fighting match who cheer on a victor to "kill" his opponent, even if, in fact, it sadly happens that his opponent is killed by a blow. *Fleta* preserves and reflects the heavenly morality of the Middle Ages where, morally, the seriousness of an act rests not in its effect, but in the intention with which the effect was brought about.

The major observation one might make of *Fleta* is that it mixes intentional language. At times when criminal intention is spoken of, the language will be strictly volitive. But there are usages in the instant chapter ask if intention means an intention authoring an act, or whether intention means "premeditation," which, properly, is a cognitive term. When we read,

> He too, who slays in an unjust war, and likewise in a just war, if the intention is corrupt, [*dum tamen mente corrupta*], commits homicide,[40]

we should read this as we would have read "*corrupto*" in conjunction with "*animo*."

There is good sacramental usage to preserve *peccatum* holding both to mental and volitive spheres, and an appeal to a simple example may make this clear. If one does not actively entertain temptations, theologians were wont to say that they came and went, and had little to do with the Will. But if mental awareness has little to do with the Will, it does not follow that every form of rational consideration has nothing to do with the Will. The Will, it was accepted, was a rational faculty. If, however, one attended to the content of his own mental musing or temptations, theologians were of the belief that one was actively, volitionally, entertaining mental considerations. Intellect, purely as a faculty with its operations, excluded movement to a practical end; the sphere of "movement" (broad as is that notion) incorporated the Will. If from an action it could be said that neither the Will nor the Intellect was present, then it would have been argued that the movement was of a lower nature only, such as pure sense movement, or simple vegetative movement, or, as in sleep or in a coma, involuntary movement.

We directed our attention to *peccatum* for the simple reason that in a temptation to sin, as opposed to sinning actually, the only difference in description which one could provide for the elements of a temptation, as opposed to the elements of sinning actually, would be the consent of the agent. Consent was a serious and important category, and, for this reason, it was not sufficient only to demonstrate that one knew (some "x" or other); the importance, from a moral point of view (and, we would add, a legal point of view), was whether one did consent. Consent was a rational volitional act, or seen to be so for moral theory of the period. In *Fleta* we encounter, again and again, the consensual use of mental predicates, and this always leads one back to the will. Later legal usage will turn from this clear volitive use of language, and will, in turn, begin to speak about intention as a set of logically possible ends which might be achieved, had the agent properly considered them. Here the use of intention excludes the efficient condition which will provides, and the linguistic usage depicts intention as if it were only a relationship of a formal to a final cause. The error which this kind of depiction involves is that it removes from the defendant certain kinds of excuses which, we wish to argue, are genuine legal excuses which a common law court ought to entertain. As we had stated earlier, *Hearst* and other such relevant cases which involve compulsion, kinds of duress, and forms of automatism, are made difficult to defend to a judge or jury.

The textual parallels are so obvious between Bracton and *Fleta*[*] that one need not belabor citing them. Each work advances an intentional definition of criminal responsibility; the scope and range of such propositions are broad rather than microscopic in detail and assumption. When *Fleta* discusses "Murder" the chief element of the crime, other than its secretness, is a slaying "committed wickedly by men's hands" ("*occisio a manibus hominum nequiter perpetrata*"). The parallel text in Bracton (Thorne, p. 379) reads, "Murder is the secret slaying of man by the hand of man [whether those slain are known or strangers] [committed wickedly]." The text, it is suggested, is corrupted, thus its adjectival description "*nequiter perpetrata*" is bracketed by Thorne, the phrase having been omitted in some manuscripts. Bracton is, however, more precise when asking "What is called murder?" The text states why the "hand of man" phrase is included:

> The words 'by hand of man' are used to distinguish it from the case of those slain or devoured by beasts and animals which lack reason; such persons cannot be said to be murdered feloniously since animals which lack reason cannot be said to commit *injuria* or felony.[41]

---

* One may refer to the Selden text from which we cite to locate the parallels in text in Bracton. Richardson and Sayles cite the folio pagination of an earlier Bracton Latin text, and that pagination does not correspond to the (now) definitive volume which had been prepared by Samuel E. Thorne, and which edition we cite. But the folios are off only by one page, or two at most, and one can easily find the parallels by comparing Thorne with the Selden text. Where there is any doubt, we cite the page for the Thorne edition of Bracton. We wish to note, too, that Richardson and Sayles do not offer a propositional analysis or comparison between Bracton and *Fleta*; thus an atomic analysis of the sentences of each text will reveal larger differences between the two writers.

Even though the *Fleta* states that dead bodies should be examined to determine the cause of death (Chapter 25, "Of the Office of Coroners"), the text does not directly advert to the reason why a portion of a definition, i.e., "Murder," contains some of the elements it does contain.

That Bracton considers a reason why a definition contains certain particular elements to the exclusion of other elements is not an oddness of Bracton as opposed to *Fleta*. Each treatise rests the ascription of legal responsibility to intention (in whatever way "intention" is technically expressed). For Bracton, that one's intention is considered, permits a punishment to be assigned, or not. Whether we consider the theory successful or not, it was part and parcel of medieval religious theory that a punishment was made to fit the crime, and this tradition is easily demonstrated by turning to Bracton's *De Actionibus*. For Bracton, an action was "nothing other than the right of pursuing in a judicial proceeding what is due to one."[42] When kinds of punishments are considered they are considered in relation to the magnitude of an iniquity. Lesser crimes receive lesser punishments, but the magnitude of a crime turns upon its intentional elements.* Bracton says,

> Punishments are rather to be mitigated than increased. [Offences are committed intentionally, by impulse or by accident.] Robbers commit offences intentionally, by deliberation; those who are drunk, by impulse, moved by their drunkenness.[43]

And, a little later in the same text, when it is advanced that various offenses must be considered from seven points of view, we read this sentence concerning "Fortuity," i.e., one of the seven categories whereby the severity of a punishment can be determined:

> Fortuity, as where one does some act intentionally and with full understanding, as homicide, or does it accidentally....

---

* *Note*: The crime, *qua* crime, would be defined by statute or common law. That one had committed a crime would depend upon one's defense, i.e., whether or not one had formed the requisite intention for the commission of the crime. The relationship which obtains is between the crime as defined (statute or common law) and the agent acting under that definition. The objective element to any crime would be its definition; the subjective element would be whether or not one did commit a crime. In no way do we suggest that crime is purely a subjective category. It is not, and early common law was clear on the matter. *Nulla poena sine lege.*

> Depending upon this, his deed will be either felony or misadventure.[44]

Both treatises are strong in their treatment of intention, and both treatises offer us enough instances of non-intentional actions, that one can safely assert that each treatise mirrors the long tradition in Christian theology of treating intentional wrongs one might commit as reasoned acts of the will. There was theory enough developed to account for some kinds of human action which were not reasonable. *Fleta* speaks of that "innocence of mind" which protected a madman or child from legal guilt,[45] as did Bracton. In Bracton the text states, "as may be said of a child or a madman, since the absence of intention ("*innocentia consilii tueatur*") protects the one and the unkindness of fate excuses the other."[46]

These early treatises reveal that a theological tradition was taken over into them, and that a crime, like a sin, could only be attributed to human action if the action were fully human. If a being, like an animal, did not possess reason, the measure of punishment would be different from the measure of punishment meted to a person. An animal might be vicious, from its disposition; but its viciousness would be different in kind from any viciousness a person might be said to possess or display because of the difference in species. The early law developed from within a tradition of reason and will, and the measure of an act was the reasonableness it embodied. The language of the early legal writings confirms that the way in which criminal behavior was explained was that it was an act of the will. Many of the moral predicates assigned to account for transgression were volitive predicates, incorporating what one knew, but also expressing that what one knew fell under the control of one's will. The will moved one to a good. It was not a theory without application. Minimal conditions were assigned so that the law could distinguish grades of actions, as was the distinction between a madman, held to be non-responsible for an act, and the murderer, held to be responsible for an act.

Other writers, and case law, show how the tradition worked into the law. We are given the conclusions of a conventional wisdom borrowed from the theologians, leaving their involved and intricate arguments behind in the tomes of medieval theology. If we review Britton, for example, we find modest indications that commonplace assumptions were at work in the early common law. We draw upon the work not to show that it is an adequate historical recording of the law at work, but rather for the purpose of showing how commonplace notions simply entered the law writers' vocabularies. In the sixth chapter of the first book of Britton[47] we read what is now familiar to us concerning homicide:

> ...this felony may be committed under colour of judgement through malice of the judge [*par colour de jugement par male volunte de juge*], or under some other pretence, as by false physicians and bad surgeons, and by poison and sundry other ways, our pleasure is, that all those who have committed such secret felonies be indicted.

The double world which incorporated both the public expression of a crime, its act, and its private springs of action, the conscience of the person, is evident in Britton. Not all serious events were judged to be felonies, as death by accident made clear.[48] But such mischances were subject to deodand.

When speaking of treason, Britton compresses his description by stating that the crime "consists of any mischief, which a man knowingly does, or procures to be done" ["*Treason est en chescun damage qe hom fet a escient ou procure de fere a cely a qi hom se fet ami.*" is the full sentence in law French]. The conditions for "knowing" or "procuring" are not elaborated upon.[49] Chapter XI "Of Burglars"[50] preserves the distinction as to who may or may not be capable of committing a felony. But any analysis of the crimes, save for a procedural presentation on how appeals may be commenced, is lacking. Even the statement regarding homicide speaks simply as "and our will is, that those, who command aid or counsel others to kill [*qiu comaundent ou aydent ou conseilent de tuer la gent*] be indicted for this felony as well as the principle actors."[51] The language is broadly statutory, and possesses no philosophical or theological ampleness as one found in Bracton or *Fleta*. The text does, however, speak directly about the element of an offense resting in a *consent*. The passage in question concerns the escape of prisoners, and states,

> and if any gaoler be suspected of having consented to the escape, let him be taken and indicted for consenting to the felony; and if found guilty of consenting, let him have judgment of death.[52]

Inquiry could be made to determine if one had been wrongfully imprisoned, and the language of the text adverts to language which states, "who has imprisoned another or detained him wrongfully in his custody, or in our prison maliciously and wrongfully under colour of judgment,"[53] from: Chapter XIV, "Of Inlawry, or being restored to law." The treatise does make a passing mention in Chapter XXVI, "Of Appeals of Mayhem," to striking a knight without any provocation from the knight, but this is little more than to affirm what was a tradition in the law, that some actions, done in the heat of passion, were more excusable than other actions which might, as with treason, be done with cool premeditation. Britton embodies the assumptions which are found written in Bracton and *Fleta*, as well as statements of the law from case law. It is to a later age and later writers that one must turn for legal theory.[54]

Endnotes Chapter 4

1. One may consult the excellent bibliography at the end of Volume Two of the translation of Suarez's works in *The Classics of International Law* as edited by James Brown Scott (London: Wildys & Sons Ltd., 1964; and New York: Oceana Publications Inc.). The bibliography (pp. 869-890) lists the writers and/or works to which Suarez appealed in *De Legibus*, *Defensio Fidei*, and *De Triplici Virtute*, and one notices to how few English canonists he appeals. No reference is made to English case law, which appears to be the distinguishing feature of common law against Contintental theorists. One may also refer to the detailed study by S. H. Russell, *The Just War in the Middle Ages* (Cambridge University Press: 1975), in the bibliography (i-xi) of which are cited a large number of manuscript *Summas*, unpublished. Many manuscript *Summas* were in circulation (even if in few copies) which could have been read by lawyers and judges, and thus inform their legal thinking, but we are unable to detail (at present) what influenced whom.

2. Writers such as Azo, Bartolus, Narvarrus, Covarruvias, Hostiensis.

3. *Cf.*, *The Oracles of the Law*, by John P. Dawson, of Harvard Law School, (published by: The University of Michigan School of Law, 1968), Chapter One, "The Growth and Decline of English Case Law," pp. 1-99.

4. Or may even be lost. *Cf.*, Volume Two of Thorne's Bracton (*op. cit.*), p. 408, when the translator writes of a text in Bracton: "...as [in the Roll] of the last Eyre of Martin of Pateshull in the county of Lincoln in the tenth year of King Henry, among the pleas of the crown, [the case] of Gilbert, son of Archard and Alan Swade, who was beyond the age limit." No record of this case now exists.

5. *Cf.*, the remarkable able *Penitential Canons of Confession* (A.D. 963) and their clear use of language to determine how a penance is to be assigned to a confessed sin. These may be found in *A Collection of the Laws and Canons of the Church of England*, [edited by] John Johnson (Oxford: M.DCCCL) and printed by John Henry Parker (from the edition of M.DCCXX, London), Volume One, pp. 426-449.

6. Thorne, *op. cit.*, Volume Two, p. 41.

7. Thorne, *op. cit.*, p. 341.

8. Thorne, *op. cit.*, pp. 340-341, "*Necessitate, quo casu distinguendum erit utrum necessitas illa fuit evitabilis vel non. Si autem evitablis et evadere posset absque occisione, tunc erit reus homicidii. Si autem inevitabilis, quia occidit hominem sine odii meditatione in motu dolere animi, se et sua liberando cum aliter evadere non posset, non tenetur ad poenam homicidii.*"

9. Thorne, *op. cit.*, p. 342.

10. *Infra*, page 225. Although it is not our intention to present or to defend a system of natural law which would have been available to common law writers at, and after, the time of Bracton, it takes little effort to indicate that there existed a strong natural law tradition which common law writers (in its formative period to Plowden) could, with ease, have drawn upon. Excluding an analysis of the problem of whether it was the Will or whether it was the Intellect which was supreme in the making of law (a problem which divided natural law theologians equally), any number of sources were available to early legal writers on the matter of natural law. Sir John Fortescue's, *De Laudibus Legum Angliae* (second edition, with notes and English translation by John Selden: printed by Henry Lintot for Daniel Brown, at the *Black-Swan*, without *Temple-Bar*, MDCCXLI) presents the Chancellor as a strong natural lawyer. In chapter three of the instant work he tells the Prince (Henry) that all laws are holy, and lead back to God as their author. In chapter fifteen the Chancellor states that all human laws "are either the *Law of* (a) *Nature*, (b) *Customs*, or *Statutes*" (p. 28 of this edition). One would understand that by Nature one meant the world created by God which, at the same time, proclaimed His existence. Since law was intended to be reasonable, it would be assumed (for sake of argument) that Customs and Statutes would be under the guidance of human reason, which, in turn, would correct itself (and save itself from error) by an appeal to the natural order of the world. In the excellent edition of St. German's *Doctor and Student*, collated and prepared by the late T. F. T. Plucknett, and J. L. Barton (London: Selden Society, 1974), one may refer not only to the first dialogue, which occupies pp. 2-71 of that edition, and which is a discourse on the nature of law supporting, in the main, natural law assumptions, but one may also refer to the list of editions of both Canonists and Civilians to which St. German made appeal, most within a natural law tradition. Bracton's own account of what natural law is (Volume Two, pp. 26-27) as distinct from private law, civil law, and *jus gentium*, gives one a rather clear picture of what assumptions operate in the *De Legibus*. It is, for him, "a certain instinctive impulse arising out of animate nature by which individual living things are led to act in certain ways. Hence it is thus defined: "Natural law is that which nature, that is, God himself, taught all living thing." [*Ius naturale est quod natura, id est ipse deus, docuit omnia animalia*.]" He then proceeds to make a latinate distinction, stating, "The word 'quod' is then in the accusative case, the word 'natura' in the nominative. On the other hand, it may be said that the word 'quod' is in the nominative case, so that the definition will be this: Natural law is that taught all living things by nature, that is, by natural instinct" [*Ius naturale, quod docuit omnia animalia natura, id est per instinctum naturae*]. The twinning of moral and legal notions, with regard to natural law, is put by Bracton thus (pp. 26-27, Volume Two, Thorne), and it serves to substantiate the assumption that a human act must be unified, possessed of no disparity in its interior and exterior elements: "The world 'natura' will then be in the ablative case. This is what is meant when we say that our first instinctive impulses are not under our control, but our second impulses are" [...*primi motus non sunt in nostra potestate, secundi vero sunt*]. That is why, if a matter proceeds only as far as simple sensual pleasure, not beyond, only a venial sin is committed. But if it proceeds farther, to the contriving of something ["*ad aliquid componendum*"], as where one puts into practice what he has shamefully thought ["*ut exerceat quis quod turpiter cogitavit*"], it will

then be called a third impulse and a mortal sin is committed. And note that for the reason that justice is will ["*quod qua ratione iustitia est voluntas*"], taking into account rational beings only, natural law is impulse ["*ius naturale motus*"], in regard being had to all creatures, rational and irrational. There are some who say that neither will nor impulse may be called *jus, jus naturale* or *jus gentium*, for they exist in [the realm of] fact; "will or impulse are the means by which natural law or justice disclose or manifest their effect, for virtues and *jura* EXIST IN THE SOUL (*caps. ours*)."

Of "law" itself, Bracton says (p. 27 of Thorne, Volume Two) that "all *jura* are incorporeal and cannot be seen." [*Iura autem omnia sunt incorporalia et videri non possunt*]. The point here is that, as a cognitivist, one *knows* (through understanding and reason) law. The force of law is not a simple proposition; it is a proposition understood to be lawful. It is a simple but important distinction.

11. For instance, *The Consulado del Mar* (Code of Barcelona) dates from the 13th century, and is a set of maritime regulations only. When, at Chapter 287, "Of Cases of Recapture," titles "8," "9," and "10," we encounter the use of the term "voluntary," it is used without any theological significance, meaning simply, "without force or constraint" as in, "(8)...and shall afterwards abandon it [ship], voluntarily, and not from any fear or apprehension of any vessel coming upon him." This use of "voluntary" carries over to sections "9" and "10" of the act. The chapter relates to prize law. *Cf. Rule of Law* by R. W. Nice (N.J.: Littlefield Adams & Co., 1965), pp. 228-234, esp. p. 233.

12. *Criminal Law*, The General Part, by Glanville Williams (Stevens, 1953), p. 543. In the second edition (Stevens, 1961) the citation may be found on p. 697.

13. This case is to be found in the *Year Books* of Edward I, volume two, p. 64 (published by the authority of Her Majesty's Treasury, under the direction of the Master of the Rolls, 1864, Public Record Office, Rolls House, London). The law French for the above citation, p. 65, reads as follows: "*Un home porta le replegiare vers un altre d'un beof e xl. owes atort....Cely qe senpleynt est graunt semur e home de graunt malice la fit abatre, e enchasa lyenz sez avers, prest.*" Excluding the plaintiff's rejoinder, the text for the defendant continues, "*Que la place fut enclos de hay solum usage, e que vous par malice feystes un breke del hay, e vos bestes lyenz enchacates, prest....*"

14. "Radulphi De Hengham, Edwardi Regis 1, Capitalis *olim* Justitiarii Summae. Magna Hengham, & Parva, vulgo nuncupatae. ex vett. Codd. MSS. cum Cl. Seldeni Notis" (Londini: Typis E. & R. Nutt, & R. Gosling, MDCXXXVII), pp. 6 and 7.

15. "*Melleta*, 12c., c1320; *mesleta* 1221 melee, affray; *melletum* 1328, c 1327." From *Medieval Latin Word-List*, by Baxter and Johnson, (London: Oxford University Press, Humphrey Milford, 1934), p. 262.

16. *Op. cit.*, p. 7. The quotation is compressed. The work of "Skene" to which Selden refers is: Skene (Sir John): *De verborum significatione. The exposition of the termes and difficill wordes conteined in the foure buiks of*

Regiam Majestatem (Edinburgh, 1597). There is also a London edition of 1641. Skene also produced: *Regiam Majestatem. The auld lawes and constitutions of Scotland faithfully collected* (Edinburgh, 1609).

"*Rixa*" is not a term which carries over into common law discourse. The Latin word is *rixa*, *ae*, (f) and it means 1. a quarrel, brawl, dispute, contest, strife, or contention, and of rarer usage, 2. a battle contest. Other forms of the word signify to quarrel or to dispute, etc. (The root to the word is given as a wide opening of the mouth.)

In his *Introduction* to his translation of questions 22 to 30 of the *Summa Theologiae*, printed as volume 19, *The Emotions* (London: Blackfriars & Eyre & Spottiswoode, 1967), Eric D'Arcy states (pp. xxiv and xxv) and we quote (in part): "Since...the English word *appetite* fails to reproduce this dual aspect [i.e., that 'appetite' has an object in both what is pleasant or unpleasant], I propose to render *appetitus* and *appetitiva* as *orexis* and *orectic*. This has two advantages: first it may serve as a reminder that St. Thomas' *appetitus* has much the same meaning and scope as Aristotle's (όρεξις), rather than that of the English *appetite*; second, in modern psychology the terms *orexis* and *orectic* are used to distinguish the affective and conative aspects of an act from the cognitive....St. Thomas took the words from William of Moerbeke's Latin translations of Aristotle. In *De anima III* Aristotle divides the powers of the soul into the *logistikon*, the rational, and the *orexis*, the non-rational; then, within the non-rational, he divides the *aisthetike*, the sensory orexis, into *epithumetike* and *thumike*... Moerbeke rendered *thumike 'irascibilis'* and *epi-thumike* sometimes '*concupiscibilis*' and sometimes '*appetitiva*';...I therefore propose to translate *appetitus irascibilis* and *appetitus concupiscibilis* as *the spiritual orexis* and *the affective orexis* respectively."

We cite this longish footnote to suggest that "*rixa*" and "*orexis*" may have in common this root: action done under passion and without deliberation. "*[R]ixa*" may be derived in this way from "*orexis*." In the *E.N.* 1.2. 1, Aristotle employs the word to mean desire or propension.

When we turn to the use of "rixa" and suggest that it is related to the Greek '(όρεκτικός)' meaning "appetitive" (and in turn meaning action without rational deliberation and purpose), some continuity is provided in the history of the notion. We do not mean to be Procrustean, and we put this reading only as a suggestion. We are aware that one must not press the reading too far as if it solidly represents Greek legal theory; it does, and it does not. As was pointed out by J. W. Jones in *Law and Legal Theory of the Greeks*, "Perhaps the most important advance made by Aristotle was in his insistence that there may be intention without premeditation. Hitherto there had been a tendency to treat acts done in sudden anger as involuntary. Patroclus in the *Iliad* says he killed Amplhidamas 'unwillingly in anger' [xxiii.8], and Plato, while not prepared to say that acts done in sudden passion were excusable, thought they stood nearer to involuntary than to voluntary acts, especially if they were immediately regretted. It is, however, knowledge rather than forethought which to Aristotle is the test of liability. Children, and in Aristotle's view animals, can act voluntarily but not with forethought. [*E.N.* iii.2.2.] There need be no previous course of reasoning to stamp an act as intentional; sudden acts may be voluntary, and the intent may be simultaneous rather than prior to the physical movement. [As when we sit down or stand up. See *Mag. Mor. 17....*] Such choice as exists may lie only in the preference for acting to refraining, no other alternative being present to the mind. In this, Aristotle was only giving theoretical expression to a development which had already taken place in the courts, where plotting and scheming had come to be seen as but one, but not the only, form of intention" (pp. 272-273 Oxford: At the Clarendon Press, 1956]).

One may refer to the *Laws* of Plato, Book IX, where he presents his discussion on the voluntary and involuntary in the course of the discussion between the Athenian and Clinias.

We do *not* wish to suggest, however, that common law followed or paralleled the positions advanced in Greek criminal law. The force of what we have said in this endnote is solely to suggest that in the common law, from a Civilian (and also canonical notion, as we shall show) concept, a modest parallel may be found in the transformation of "*rixa*" into "*melleta*" or "*medleta*" into "Cha[u]nce-Medley." The "orectic" aspect of the notion was preserved, as one may instance Deacon's *Digest*. He states, "CHANCE-MEDLEY (or, as some choose to write it, *chaud-medley*) is where homicide is committed by a man upon a sudden affray in his own defence. In its former etymology it signifies a *casual* affray; in the latter, an affray in the *heat* of blood or passion; both of pretty much the same import – though the former is in common speech too often erroneously applied to any manner of homicide by misadventure; whereas it appears by the statute of *24 Hen. 8. c. 5.* [and repealed by 9. G. 4. c. 31.] and our ancient books, that it is properly applied to such killing only, as happens in self-defence upon a sudden encounter. *4 Bl. Com. 184*" (pp. 223-224 of *A Digest of The Criminal Law of England* by Edward E. Deacon [London: Henry Butterworth, 1836], volume one).

So described, "rixa" has, as a legal concept, a philosophical consistency which roots it in a sense of action springing from appetite. It is not our purpose to attempt to defend an Aristotelian interpretation of "intention" in relation to what the same concept may mean in common law through various stages of its development. One may see, by reference to some leading texts, how the term "rixa" preserved the meaning of unintended though voluntary action. Durandus (of St. Purcain, d. 1334) offers this definition of "rixa" in his *Repertorium Aureum Juris* (Venice: Henetijs per Baptistam de Tortis, 1494), folio 69 as:

"*Rixa* - De rixa agitur etiä tempore feriato." Which would mean that one while agitated or irritated for a time had brought about a death or had killed another while fighting with him. The verb "agito" indicates that one has been roused, unsettled, excited, disquieted; "ferio, ire" in its participle form means that one has killed by striking, or gave a death blow. Its Greek root, which obviates forethought in the act, is "(̔θουριος)," which means "impetuous", and "(θοριέν)", which means "to leap." We read the phrase to mean that in the heat of passion one, unintentionally, kills or injures, and this is in accord with "rixa" as it found its way into common law reference. To put "agito" into the passive form may indicate that the agent had the agitation befall him, as a mood or passing vexation. To use a verb passively, when it also has an active form, is to minimize its intentional and deliberate force, and to stress that a state or action is happening to the agent rather than that the agent is bringing about a description deliberately. We might say in English that one found himself to be angered by, rather than that one had intended to be angry at. Durandus's definition suggests an unintentional but impetuous act.

In English there is an ample study of Greek law from the view of "intentional" v. "unintentional" (one may consult: *Athenian Homicide Law* by D. M. MacDowell [Manchester University Press, 1963 and 1966], or the two-volume *The Administration of Justice from Homer to Aristotle* by R. J. Bonner and Gertrude Smith [New York: Greenwood Press, 1968 or the original edition from the University of Chicago, 1930 for the first volume, 1938 for the second volume], as well as early collected editions of such laws, i.e., *Leges Atticae...collegit, digessit et libro commentario illustravit* by Samuel Petitus [Parisiis: Sumptibus Caroli Morelli, 1635], cf. esp. Libert Septimus, "De Sicariis," pp. 504-526), and some studies on Roman criminal law, when one comes to the period of the Middle Ages, broadly from the time of the Decretals, one finds little mongraphical research in English. Not only is there little in English, the texts themselves must be consulted and this demands a specialists knowledge which few have. Most of our texts, apart from some reprints now being issued here and there, must be those of first instance. To close this extended endnote we shall list some sources which reveal how "*rixa*" was treated by some leading lawyers and theologians of the late Middle Ages into the Renaissance. Our listing shall be brief since, clearly, it is not a direct part of our own study. We would add that such a study yet needs to be done by some scholar.

For some of the medievals, "rixa" would be subsumed to "*ira*," and one might speak of an action done as a result of anger. Aquinas in S.T. 1a2ae, article 8 asks "What are the types of anger?" and in the second question and second response in the article speaks of anger which has a quick-tempered (*velocitatem irae*) quality. Other writers may speak about an action done spontaneously or voluntarily, as does Cardinal Hostiensis (d. 1271) in his *Summa Aurea* [Lugduni, M.D.LVI, or *Summa Hostiensis*, as the 1537 printing lists the work, printed at Venice by Iacobus Giunta] in the body of his question, *De homicidio voluntario, vel casuali*, which embraces seven articles (folio 358 - folio 360; Liber quintus) in the Lugduni edition. The formula of "operam rei licitae" (359, col. one and col. two) is found at work in his third article "Homicidia quis dicatur." Resort is made to the voluntariness of the act and to the knowledge the agent possessed when doing the act to determine what punishment obtains.

Other writers will maintain "*rixa*" as a separate classification, as does Angelus de Clavasio (1411-1495) in his *Summa Angelica* (*Summa de Casibus Conscientiae*), a book which is akin to a modern law dictionary in which terms are listed alphabetically, and examples and explanations given. In our edition (Lyons, 1513) the reader is told that defending oneself when attacked is lawful, but to seek to be provoked, and thence to defend oneself, is mortally grievous. Angelus preserves the ingredient that a "motus animi" occurs, indicating that one is not under full rational control of oneself. One experiences "*animo effrenato insurgit impugnatem ad occiden*" which suggests that self-control has been lost. (The entry occupies folio cccciij-b to folio cccciiij-a.)

When one turns to other leading legal theorists of the period one will observe that actions which spring from involuntary causes, such as one might describe chance-medley, will, as actions, be assessed by considering to what extent they were voluntary and deliberate. In the *Explicatur Clement: si furiosus, de Homicidio, & Irregulariter*, of Covarruvias y Leyva (1512-1577, Spanish canonist) one finds that "*rixa*" is not a separate legal category for him; it would be madness, or involuntary action, in which a result occurred, and then the result would have to be assessed from the point of view of how responsible was the agent for his action. Covarruvias reaffirmed much of Aquinas' notions about the Will, and thus adverts to degrees of rationality when considering the punishment due for an act. It should be remembered that Aquinas tended toward an extreme rationalism in his teaching about the Will. The section on 'Anger,' from which we quoted earlier in this endnote, shows him to regard even anger as a form of a rational action seeking a rational end.

On the other hand, other canonists accepted "*rixa*" as a separate category, and included it in their writings or legal dictionaries or in books which were referred to as collections of cases on matters of conscience. Bartholomea Fumo, who died in 1545 and had been an Inquisitor of the Faith, wrote, *Summa Casuum Conscientia Aurea Armilla*. [In our own edition he is printed as: Placentinus, Bartholomaeo Fumo Villauren, Summa, Aurea Armilla nvncvpata Casvs Omnes ad Animarvm cvam attinentes breviter complectens....(printed at Antverpiae, apud Petrum Bellerm, in 1591).] His listing appears as follows, and we cite it here to end this footnote:

> "DE RIXA.
> *Rixa quid & quando mortale.*
> *Rixa filia irae importat contradictione in factis, quando ex ira aliqui se inuicem per eutiunt, non ex authoritate publica, sed ex voluntate inordinata; & ex sino genere peccatum mortale est, in eo, qui iniuste alterium aggreditur, quia nocumentum proximo contra charitatem infert. In eo autem qui se defendit, animo repellendi illa iam iniuriam, cum debita moderatione peccatum non est. Secus si cum animo vindictae, vel odij, vel excedit in moderamine, quia tunc peccatum mortale vel veniale est, secundum quantitatem odij vel excessus. Primi enim motus communiter veniales sunt, & imperfecta actus, vt saepe diximus*" (from p. 725 of the 1591 Antwerp edition).

Many other citations could be given, but they would serve to be an end in themselves, and would be outside of the scope of this work. Bartholomea Fumo's entry preserves the consistency of meaning which is found in all of the citations we have examined, and his seems to be the clearest and briefest, and hence we cite him.

To observe how the case law of the period operated on the Continent (from that period spanning the late Middle Ages and into the Renaissance) one may turn to the various Church courts and inspect their criminal findings. A fundamental abridgement of criminal law from its sources is to be found in the *Compendium libri quinti Senteniarum...in quo, praetermissa opinionvm varietate...verae practicae Criminalis...Iulii Cari. Milan.* by Galdericus Galinus (printed by Iacobum Lantonum in 1621), 340 pp. Another "text" book of the period is by D. Petri Follerii, entitled, *Canonica Criminalis Praxis* (printed in Venice by Bartholomaei Rubini in 1583). It treats of criminal topics, defining them, and making practical comments about various crimes. Of the same order is the text by Ludovicus Carerius, *Practica causarum criminalium* (or *Nova Cavsarvm Criminalivm*) which was printed at Venice in 1564. [Middle Temple Library holds a copy printed in 1569 at Lugduni.]

Giambattista Ziletti was an editor of a two-volume work of criminal opinion drawn from Baldus onwards, and the work is entitled: *Criminalium consiliorum atque responsorum tam ex veteribvs qvam ivnioribvs celeberrimis ivriconsvltis collectorvm*, and was printed at Venice, volume one, 1562 and volume two, 1560. (We have two separate editions, and it can be assumed that the "first" of each edition was printed in 1559-1560.) In the same vein, as a canonical work, is *Practica Criminalis Canonica*, a very simple *handbook* of criminal offenses compiled and commented upon by Juan Bernard Diaz de Luco, (Lvgdvni, Apvd Theobadvm Paganvm, M.D.XLIII. One finds that the *Decisiones Avreae, sev Definitiones, Qvaestionvm Controuersarum...ex variis S. Regii Consilii Cathaloniae* (printed at Fanco-fvrti Ad Moenvm: Cura & impendio Rulandiorum, Typis Matthia Beckeri, 1609) compiled by Ludovico a Pegvera considers the problem of "rixa" in its fourteenth decision: "*An homicidium secutum ex vulneribus in rixa illatis, sit poena ordinaria homicidii puniendum, vol extraordinaria arbitrio iudicis*" pp. 69-76 thereof.

17. *Op. cit*., Vol. One, Year Books of Edward I., p. 322. The law French reads as follows: "*Un Johan porta soun bref de Trespas, e senpleint de. W., quil luy avoyt mahayme, saver, coupe le un dey & c. – W. dist qe de rein coupable. – LENQUEST dist qil luy avoyt coupe le un dey – Agarde fut par Roubury qil recoverast ces damages de xl. livres....*"

18. *Cf*., "The Origin of the Year Books," pp. 268-273, in Chapter 14, of *A Concise History of the Common Law*, by Theodore Plucknett, 5th edition (London: Butterworth & Co., 1956).

19. *Cf*. Chapter 3, "Proof," pp. 28-35, in *A Guide in Law & Practice under the Criminal Justice Act* 1967, by (Sir) David Napley (London: Sweet & Maxwell, 1967). Note: one would now need to consult case law on the matter since the enactment of the Act.

20. *Cf*. p. 520, Appendix I, volume one, Year Books of Edward I, *op. cit*., as well as citations using the same phrase throughout the cases, pp. 496-526.

21. *Op. cit*., p. 496 ff. The criminal pleas date from A.D. 1303.

22. *Op. cit*., p. 506, "*...e ele dit qe meme cely Rauf encontre son gre lavoyt ravy e parieu...*" – "*...e presenterent qe meme cely Rauf encontre son gre la ravyt...*" A.D. 1302.

23. *Cf*., *Director of Public Prosecutions v. Morgan*, H.L. [1975] 2 All E.R.347, now overruled by *Howe and Bannister, H.L.*, [1987] *LRC (Crim.) 413*.

24. *Op. cit*., p. 508. The law French reads as follows (p. 509): "...[Pais] dit qe lun soulement fut coupable du fet, e les deux nent del fet, et de lassent; mes disseint qe les deux le [MS has 'ne'] enterrerent sanz vewe de Coroner."

25. *Op. cit*., p. 510. The law French is not important for the facts of the instant case. The standard phrase for manslaughter appears in the law French thus, "*Richard e Willeame furet enditez de la mort un home....*"

Regarding the phrase, "...he is not with the peace," its meaning was the he, John, was not a member of a tything. A tything was "in its first appointment, the number or company of ten men with their families, held together in a society, all being bound for the peaceable behaviour of each other" (*Jacob*, as cited in *Stroud's Judicial Dictionary* [3rd edition, volume four], Sweet & Maxwell, 1965. The reference to 'Jacob' is Jacob's Law Dictionary, 3rd ed.).

26. *Op. cit.*, volume one, p. 514. The law French is as follows: *"Nota, si home ensywt autre en assaut purpense ou en autre manner...."*

27. The Latin is taken from volume one of Year Books of Edward I, from the Appendix II, which contains Reports and Notes in Latin of Criminal Cases, Temp. Edw. I., on p. 529: *"Quidem puer J. de Burtone nomine, aetatis duodecim annorum, fecit infra quemdam damum, et sagittavit metam extra domum, et per infortunium quamdam mulierem R. nomine interfecit.—Justiciarius. Quia non est etatis duodecim annorum non est felo, sed bonus et fidelis.—Et quia se subtraxit, proclamatum fuit publice quod reveniret si vellet. Et quia le Hoke fuit occasio mortis Rose, eo quod sagitta glaciavit super eam, appreciabatur & c."*

The meaning of "Deodand" given in the *Termes of the Lawes of this Realme* (printed by Thomas Wight and Bonham Carter, at London, in 1598), a work attibuted to William Rastell, the entry for number 155 states, and we quote:

> "Deodande, is when any man by misfortune is slaine by a horse or by a cart, or by any other thing mooveth to further the death, then the thing that is cause of his death, and which at the time of his misfortune did move, shall be forfait to the king, and that is called Deodandem and that pertaineth to the kings Almener for to dispose in almes and deedes of charitie." [we have cited only the English, and not the accompanying entry in law French.]

John Cowell, in *The Interpreter* (London, printed for William Sheares, 1637) gives this definition:

> *Deodand* (*deodandum*) is a thing given or forfeited (as it were) to God for the pacification of his wrath in a case of misadventure, whereby any Christian soule commeth to a violent end, without the fault of any reasonable Creature.

This is more in accord with the treatment of *Deodandvm* in Lib. I, Cap. 12 of *Les Plees Del Corone by William Stavndford* (Londini: Ex Typographia Societatis Stationariorum, *Anno Domini* 1607), pp. 20a-21a. Cowell contains the standard references to Britton, Staunford, Bracton, and Fitzherbert. Why the concept of "deodand" is interesting is that it provided a link to the Old Testament, and to the dual nature of law and morals (as we wrote upon earlier). If one returns to Exodus 21, verses 12 ff., one observes this text: " Whoever kills a man with intent to kill, must pay for it with his own life. But where there was no malice aforethought, and God provides the occasion ["Provides the occasion"; literally, "delivers him into his hand." This could mean a chance encounter, followed by a murder in hot blood, which would be classed as manslaughter; *cf.*, 1 Kg. 26. 23. But accidental killing may be meant (*cf.* Num. 35, 22, 23; Deut. 19. 4), the accident being represented as a Providential interference], he shall be allowed to find refuge in such place as I shall appoint for thee." The force of the chapter reveals that fines may be paid by one (under certain stipulations of law) to compensate for a loss. (We have cited, with commentary, from *The Holy Bible*, published by Burns & Oates, London, 1965, p. 67.)

28. This particular case comes from Alfred Horwood's edition of the *Year Books*, which we have cited; but the instant case is taken from the manuscript of W. [Gulielmi] Fletewoode, and is a report of cases from the Cornish *Iter.*, dating from criminal trials of the reign of Edward I. This case comes from manuscript "A," but is not dated. Horwood says, in his Preface,

> The absence of the name of the Justice and the surname of the prisoner in the case at pp. 529-532, and ignorance of the year when the trial took place, have placed an obstacle to a reference of the proceeding. But this case presents the distinct and important fact that a prisoner who was a knight refused (because he was a knight) to be tried by the ordinary jury, and claimed to be tried by his peers (*per pares meos*, p. 531); and that his claim was at once allowed by the Justice, who must be presumed to have understood what the law was in such case, and who, by his iteration of the prisoner's phrase (*per vestros pares*) may be supposed to have had in view, and to have recognized the prisoner's appeal to, the "judicium parium" of Magna Charta" (page xlviii, of Volume One, *op. cit.*).

The case itself is cited in *Appendix II* of the volume, and is to be found in manuscript "A" only, which was held by Lincoln's Inn. One can assume safely that the case dates from the very early 1300's. William Fleetwood was Recorder of London during the time of Queen Elizabeth I. Middle Temple Library holds a single copy of his *Annalium tam regum Edwardi quinti*...etc., [London: 1579].

29. One may consider *R. v. Hadfield* (1800), 27 St.Tr. 1281 (or, later, *M'Naughton's case* (1843) 10 Cl. and F. 200). In *Hadfield*, the great advocate Thomas Erskine tried to change our legal perceptions of what it meant to be insane at law. On pp. 1307-1330, Erskine argued the case. His defense was that a human act must include not only the conceptual element, i.e., that one acted, but it must also include a question: Why did one act in that fashion? For Erskine, an intentional act combined two elements: *that* and *why*. Did they not, he reasoned, then one could not advance the defense of insanity. A single sane moment could obliterate an insanity plea. There are elements of an act which make one seem normal (tying one's shoe, being able to walk without hesistancy, discoursing on simple matters, and the like), yet these single instances of apparently sane conduct are not to be used to prove sanity. *Hadfield's* case was resolved by putting the defendant into what one now would call "preventive" detention. Erskine's arguments in the case were many decades ahead of the conventional wisdom of the law in 1800 regarding

insanity. The defendant was spared capital punishment by reason of insanity, but was to remain in detention because of his insanity.

By drawing the mind of the court to see a problem afresh, Erskine was able to show that the limits heretofore placed upon an understanding of the operation of a legal notion were limits which needed to be expanded. To a new problem, to which newer questions are put, the law may grow. One takes an older concept (such as madness) only to discover upon legal analysis that it is not a simple black or white notion, but it is a notion which contains many other elements which only the presentation of the novel case may extract. The legal concept, which was thought to have precise boundaries, is now seen or understood to be open-ended.

30. A brief but adequate account of Langdellianism in the law may be read in *The Ages of American Law* (Storrs lectures on jurisprudence; 1974), by Professor Grant Gilmore (Yale University Press). Chapter 3, "The Age of Faith" (pp. 41-67), gives an account of Langdell's scientific enthusiasm that scientific principles could be introduced in the teaching of law, and that one could develop a "legal method" as this quotation from his own *Cases on Contracts* (1871), and cited by Gilmore at page 43 reveals:

> [T]he number of fundamental legal doctrines is much less than is commonly supposed; the many different guises in which the same doctrine is constantly making its appearance, and the great extent to which legal treatises are a repetition of each other, being the cause of much misapprehension. If these doctrines could be so classified and arranged that each should be found in its proper place, and nowhere else, they would cease to be formidable from their number.

We would agree with the assumption, and we think it is a good guide for both the teaching and analysis of the law. We do not think, however, that it has been put in practice. Most case law books are notoriously deficient in instruction in analytical method, or in setting out a procedure whereby a student (or any person, for that matter) can progress in developing a measured understanding of how to read a case with analytical thoroughness. Most of the hornbooks throw at the student an undigested collection of cases–determined by the editor to be "leading cases"–and the student, by dint of Socratic intuition, is left to discover for himself why these are leading cases, and what (if any) are the guiding principles whereby judicial wisdom decided each case. It is a misuse of scientific method when no critical or analytical guidance is given or presented.

31. The editions of *Fleta* we have used are these. For direct textual proofings we have turned to the edition of Selden, which appears as: "*Fleta* seu Commentarius *Juris Anglicani* sic nuncupatus, sub Edwardo Rege *primo* seu circa annos abhinc CCCXL, ab Anonymo conscriptus, atque & Codice veteri, autore ipso alinquantulum recentiori, nunc primum typis editus." Subjungiture etiam Joannis Seldeni ad Feltam Dissertatio Historica. Londini, M.DC.XLVII. This is the first printed edition of the work. For the textual exactness and translation we have used that edition prepared for the Selden Society, *Fleta*, Volume II, Prologue, Book I, Book II, edited and translated by

H. G. Richardson and G. O. Sayles (London: Bernard Quaritich, 1955), which appears as volume 72 for 1953 in the series. We have also used volume 89 for 1972 of the Selden Society edition of *Fleta*, which is Volume II, Books III and IV, prepared by H. G. Richardson and G. O. Sayles (London: The Selden Society, 1972). We have consulted David Ogg's edition of: Ioannis Seldini *Ad Fletam Dissertatio* (Cambridge: At the University Press, 1925).

32. Fleta, Volume II, Richardson and Sayles (1955), *op. cit.*, p. 56, Chapter 21, "Of the Crime of Lese-Majesty".

33. Thorne, *op. cit.*, p. 334.

34. Unpublished, Harlean manuscript 7159, British Museum.

35. *Fleta*, *op. cit.*, p. 60 (Vol. II). The sentiment, certainly, is old. Seneca detailed such a repugnant emotion when he spoke of Hannibal's delight when he saw a trench flowing with human blood. Seneca thought such was cruel emotion. *Cf.*, *On Anger*, Book Two, v. 3-vi. 1, p. 177 of Volume One of Seneca's *Moral Essays* (translated by J. W. Basore, Heinemann, Ltd., 1970).

36. *Cf.*, *Henderson v. Morgan*, 49 L.Ed. 2d 108. *D* did not understand that to a plea of guilty to a second degree murder charge a necessary element in the charge was an intent to cause death. *D*'s guilty plea was thus not a voluntary plea under the circumstances.

37. P. 60, volume II.

38. *Op. cit.*, p. 60, which Latin texts reads: "*Voluntate, vt si quis animo corruptio in assultu premeditato, ira vel odio vel causa lucri, nequiter et in felonia aliquem interfecit, quod si occulte fiat pro murdro habebitur.*"

39. Thorne, *op. cit.*, p. 341:

> By intention, as where one in anger or hatred or for the sake of gain, deliberately and in premeditated assault, has killed another wickely and feloniously and in breach of the king's peace.

40. *Fleta*, C.23, p. 61.

41. The Latin text from Thorne, p. 379, reads:

> *Item a manu hominum dicitur ad differentiam eorum qui a bestiis et animalibus quae ratione carent occiduntur vel devorantur, et qui non possunt dici murdriti in felonia, quia animalia quae ratione carent non possunt dici fecisse iniuriam neque feloniam.*

42. Thorne, *op. cit.*, p. 282.

43. *Ibid.*, p. 299. The Latin text reads: "*Et poenae potius molliendae sunt quam exasperandae. Delinquunt latrones proposito per factionem. Ebrii, impetu per ebrietatem cum ad manus vel ferrum pervenitur.*"

44. *Ibid.*, "*Eventus, ut si ex voluntate et conscientia certa fecerit quis aliquid, sicut homicidium, an ex eventu...Et secundum hoc aut erit felonia aut infortunium.*"

45. The texts themselves are these.

Fleta: "...deed should not be deemed felony, because they were not actuated by an intention to slay, but by the equity of the law they are to be entirely absolved, because a crime is not committed unless the desire to harm is present, just as may be said, moreover, of a child and a madman, for innocence of mind protects the one and the mischance of the deed excuses the other. With crimes, *regard should be had to the intention and not to the consequence* [italics ours], and it matters nothing whether a man slays or furnishes the occasion of death. Intention and purpose distinguish crimes: and theft is not committed unless there is a desire to steal."

The Latin texts reads: "*In istis autem casibus et similibus non debet reputari felonia, eo quod occidendi anomo premissa facta non fuerint, set omnino sunt de iuris equitate absoluenda, quia crimen non contrahitur nisi voluntas nocendi interueniat, secundum quod dici poterit insuper de infante et furioso, cum vnum innocencia consilii tueatur et alterum infelicitas facti excuset. In maleficiis autem spectari debet voluntas et non exitus...Voluntas enim et propositum distingunt maleficia: furtum vero non committitur sine affectu furandi* (p. 80, Book I, C.31).

The pertinent portion from Bracton (p. 384 of Thorne) is bracketed, but it does read as follows: "It is will and purpose which mark *maleficia*, nor is theft committed unless there is an intent to steal." ["*Et voluntas et propositum distingunt maleficia, et furtum non committitur sine affectu furandi.*"] But *not* bracketed, and immediately following, is, "In crimes the intention is regarded, not the result." ["*In maleficiis autem spectatur voluntas et non exitus.*"]

46. Thorne, *op. cit.*, p. 384. Thorne also footnotes this excuse, to madness or to infancy, to the Digest [48.8.12], which reads: "*Infans vel furiosus si hominem occiderint lege Cornelia non tenentur, cum alterum innocentia consilii tuetur, alterum fati infelicitas excusat.*"

47. We have consulted the text of *Britton*, The Second Edition, by Edm. Wingate (London: Printed by the assignes of John Moore, Esquire, Anno 1640, and have employed the French text and translation of, *Britton*, Volume I, by Francis Morgan Nichols, M.A. (Oxford: At The Clarendon Press, MDCCCLXV). Selection is from Nichols, p. 34.

48. Nichols, *op. cit.*, p. 39, Chapter VIII, "Of Accidents."

49. Nichols, *op. cit.*, p. 40, Chapter IX, "Of Treason."

50. *Ibid.*, p. 42, which reads: "Infants under age, and poor people, who through hunger enter the house of another for victuals under the value of twelve pence, are excepted; as are also idiots and madmen, and others, who are incapable of felony." It may be argued that one has an example of an appeal to "necessity" here in the inclusion of "poor people" taking less than 12 pence.

51. *Ibid.*, p. 34, Chapter VI, "Of Homicides."

52. Nichols, *op. cit.*, p. 44, Chapter XII, "Of Prisoners." Nichols records, as a note, a note which appears in the 'N' manuscript, and we cite it to show how far the notion of consent was taken.

"Note, that for a felon slain in prison judgment of homicide shall be given. For though he was lawfully condemnable for the felony, yet it is necessary that it pass by judgment. For we ought not to hold them absolutely felons until the law has condemned them." The force of the note is that an intentional killing could occur even if one had not acted out of malice, but had acted wrongly according to the prescriptions of the law. This could be taken as an early example of constructive malice, the guard thinking he had the right to kill a felon, but, at law, he did not possess that right until the court passed formal legal judgment upon a felon. One can notice this regal theme developed by Shakespeare in *Richard III*, when Richard wrongly causes the death by drowning of the Duke of Clarence, as if it were ordered by the King.

53. Nichols, *op. cit.*, p. 48. The law French, in part, is: "*...ou en nostre prisoun par colour de jugement par malice et a tort....*"

54. In Schad V. Arizona, 111 S.Ct. ____, 59 USLW 4762, 49 CrL. 2277 (1991), the United States Supreme Court, in a sharply divided opinion, Mr. Justice Souter for the majority labored to justify that the *actus reus* of premeditated murder and the *actus reus* of felony murder are insubstantial distinctions, and that a jury may return a verdict of guilty when a defendant was accused *either of* murder in the first degree, *or* felony murder (when a death occurs in the commission of a felony, as robbery in this case). "We see no reason, however, why the rule that the jury need not agree as to the mere means of satisfying the *actus reus* element of an offense should not apply equally to alternative means of satisfying the element of *mens rea*."

Mr. Justice White (joined by Marshall, Blackmun, and Stevens, JJ) wrote an enlightened dissent which, with respect, demonstrated that the majority was confused in its reasoning. Now, as then, *actus reus*, as well as *mens rea*, prove to be difficult concepts upon which many a judge, since the time of *Fleta*, had stumbled.

CHAPTER FIVE

Covarruvias, Early English Textualists: Staundford Plowden, and Marowe

Only in fundamental textbooks does one come to the definite close of one epoch, and the definite opening of a newer epoch, a literary device which has come to be an accepted part, perhaps out of necessity, perhaps out of a need for marshalling documentary material with some ease and facility, of historical genre. A student will read about the "Renaissance and the Reformation," or read that the vicegerent of Henry VIII in 1535 issued injunctions to the universities at Cambridge and Oxford which did require them to cease conferring degrees in canon law[1]; but the law, accordingly, does not end its peculiar methods because an historical period has been defined, or an historical fact has been dated. The force of the logic of legal reasoning carries over from one period to another, as an examination of the case law and early legal writings will reveal.[2] In this chapter we shall concentrate on the expression which intention, in its manifold forms, assumes in some of the earliest writers of the common law, both from cases and texts. We shall see that a legal notion begins to operate, while at the same time the buttress for that legal notion tends to be less observed, or less evident, as when one might observe the vault of a great hammerbeam ceiling without being conscious of the support which the flying buttresses give directly to the ceiling. The reporters and early textualists were less concerned with directing one's attentions to fuller statements which analyzed the nature of Intellect, or Will, or Appetition, than they were with stating in their reports and texts the use of a concept, as when it might be said that D wittingly did, or D wilfully did, or the D simply caused the death of P. Correspondingly, the language used in certain statutes to express aspects of intentional guilt was concise.[3]

A review of early statutory construction, although without the purview of this monograph, will reveal that legal pivots, such as "malice" or "wilfully" or "cause," were used in a simple declarative sense not involving technical explanations of their use within a statute. One may turn to William Rastall, Sergeant at Law,[4] to gather many examples from his collection of the statutes indicating such a simple and direct use of language in legal construction. One should note, too, that statutory construction (which often embraces a meta-legal aim for its political ends) does not permit one to say easily that "the law" is this or that necessarily, as when one might urge that the court "always" excused the idiot or the one who fell into madness;[5] plainly, this was not always the case, as the various statutes on Treason indicated. By acquaintance with a large range of case law one may urge that the common law did strive for consistency through its judicial operation, but one should avoid entertaining an unwarranted assumption that the common law necessarily reflected consistency. There is some measure in Holmes' remark that "consistency is the hobgoblin of petty minds."

We shall turn now to the considering of basic, linking legal texts of our early common law period. In William Staundford's *Les Plees Del Corone*, 1557, we have an early exposition of the criminal law in England. The value of the text for this analysis is that the text presents a link from the Middle Ages from the time of Bracton. Staundford's book is replete with citations from Bracton's *De Legibus*, and we shall cite from his use of Bracton. As for the purpose of the book itself, in his opening chapter the author puts the matter directly to the reader as to the purpose of a book on Pleas of the Crown. He says,

> *Plees del Corone, sont les plees queex conteignont loffences faits encounter law coron & dignitie le Roy. Per que pur le mieux entendement de eux, est requisite a veyer queux sont les dites offences. Et puis de la maner coment ils serront pledus. Et darreynement de la maner coment ils serront triers & judges.*[6, 7]

It would be unwise of us to overlook an obvious trait of early legal writers in general, and of Staundford in particular, which was their adherence to the "word" of the law, and their striving then to make clear what the language of various statutes meant, as well as to provide a rule for the interpreting of statutory language. In Staundford's abridgement of *Fitzherbert*[8] a reader is made aware with what care, and caution, statutory language is approached. Passage after passage measures the extent of a legal power (which a King, or some lesser person, may be said to possess) against the language of the law, or the language of a statute, which confers such a power. The natural expression of this kind of legal precision came to be known early on in the common law through *Heydon's* case which interpreted statutes narrowly.[9]

In that portion of Staundford's text to which we wish to direct attention, one will observe that Cap. 3 begins with: "*Felony du mort du home*."[10] The text of the edition of 1607 reproduces the statute of Henry VII concerning Conspiracy, but cites the wrong regal notation, giving 3. H. 7, ca. 13 for the statute when the correct citation should be Cap. 14. Cap. 13 concerns long bows. The statute is introduced, without exposition, simply by the heading of "*Ou conspiracy de tuer home serra felony sans act, ou auter rien fait*." The language of the statute is clear, and we doubt if it requires commentary at length, save to observe that it is a statute concerned with prohibiting certain mental acts of a subject. The statute declares: "Conspiring to destroy the King, or any Lord Councellour or great Officer shall be felony." The statute empowers the King, or whom he directs, to *enquire*, to question a subject on the matter of what the subject had thought. If, in the course of such an enquiry, it is discovered that any subject did "make any confederacies, cö-passings, conspiracies, imaginatiös w' any person or persons, to destroy or murder the king or any lord of this realme, [etc.]," then if any be found guilty by this inquiry, "if such misdoers be foüd guilty by confession, or otherwise, that the said offence bee iudged felony."[11]

Evidence for the felony would have to have been some overt act of entering into a confederacy, or, one assumes, testimony to the effect that one would be implicated in the felony. One need but reflect upon *Sir Walter Ralegh's case* (1603) to appreciate that at that time an accusation could displace actual proof of an overt act.[12] The model for the statute seems to draw upon an old confessional model: one should be pure of heart, and one should not make plots. The making of a plot to overthrow or murder the

King, and others of such esteem, touches too closely of Satan plotting against God and his creation. Like the unforgivable sin against the Holy Spirit, so is the heart of a subject intent upon treason or murder of the King. The statute preserves these religious roots.

Staundford reproduces the modes of homicide according to Bracton. Measured against the modern text which Thorne has prepared (and which we have employed), the minor variants within the text of Staundford itself compared to Thorne's text of Bracton do not call for extended commentary. A commentator, we would expect, is called upon to accept the spirit of the law and not the letter of the law when comparing the Bracton in the *Pleas* with the Bracton of our own age. The fundamental distinctions and divisions are preserved in the *Pleas* of 1607. There Thorne, from the benefit of many manuscripts, reads:

> Corporal homicide is where a man is slain bodily, and this is committed in two ways: by word or by deed. By word in three ways, that is, by precept, by counsel, and by denial or restraint. By deed in four ways, that is, in the administration of justice, of necessity, by chance and by intention. In the administration of justice, as when a judge or officer kills one lawfully found guilty. But it is homicide if done out of malice or from pleasure in the shedding of human blood [and] though the accused is lawfully slain, he who does the act commits a mortal sin because of his evil purpose.[13]

Of course, any citation one makes from Bracton's *De Legibus* should carry with it the caveat which Thorne himself issued, "It is evident that we have Bracton's great book only in corrupt form, but many texts have come down to us in worse [form]."[14] As we have indicated, the text which Staundford offers we have placed in endnote 13.

We know that Staundford intended his text to contain a presentation of the older authors, some abridgement of their texts, and an adequate presentation of pleas of the Crown, or criminal matters which would fall under the jurisdiction of the crown, and hence be punished by force and prerogative of the State.[15] What is easy to overlook is how the *Plees* embodied the legal assumptions and principles of an older age. The Middle Ages did not end, nor did the Tudor period simply begin; Staundford shows the truth of this in page after page of his *Plees*. The criminal principles of the common law were formed out of older principles; some principles which directly found themselves transcribed in the *Plees*, and, by indirection, can be found at work in the earliest records of our case law. Let us offer a direct instance of this claim.

Staundford speaks about licit and illicit killing. In Lib. 1, at folio 12-a (of the edition we have employed), we read this transcription from Bracton. Since we have cited Bracton's text earlier, we shall, in this case, cite Staundford's text. It reads:

> *Sed his distinguendum est, vtrum quis dederit operam rei licitae, an illicitae.*

The doctrine, if that be not too strong a word, of the licitness of intentions is introduced, its purpose to be used as a legal tool and concept by and through which a killing may be excused or condemned. Staundford continues, and asks after what comprises an illicit intention. The text states:

> *Vt si lapidem proijciebat quis versus locum, per quem consueuerunt homines transitum facere, vel dum insequitur quis equum, vel bouem, & aliquis a boue, vel equo percussus furerit, & huiusmodi. Hic imputabi' ei.*

We may refer to Thorne's text (p. 341) for a fuller text. But the matter of each is the same, and in each we see carried on a tradition which harkens back to the early Fathers of the Church. Staundford's *Plees* state that liability is imputed to the agent. That is the case because, as the text informs us, it is assumed that one should have known better. We are not given an analysis of liability in terms of negligence, or recklessness, or strictly premeditated intent; only a general anatomical statement, to the effect that if one knows that he might cause a harm or an injury (owing to the nature of the circumstances, e.g., a common pathway, commonly travelled), and then acts in a way to bring about such a harm or injury, then liability may be imputed to him. The text of Bracton which Thorne presents[16] carries over "illicitae" by opening the sentence, "*Si illicitae, ut si lapidem*" while the text of Staundford assumes that one will carry over an "illicitae" from the previous sentence,[17] although as an editorial device a marginal caption is given, simply as "Illicite."

The Latin verb which appears in the text is "*imputabit*," and it carries over the force of having to reckon, to account for, and to ascribe to, to measure an account (as when one makes a financial entry). The text itself suggests that the illicitness of the intention of the agent is constructed from the force of events, and questions which could be put to describe those events. Is it commonly known that men use this footpath? Is it common knowledge that one ought not to chase large farm animals across pedestrian footways? If a harm has been caused by an agent, and if the agent cannot give a lawful excuse, then the events which the agent brought about will be viewed as events which have unlawfully been brought about. The categories of legal excuse were given earlier in the text of Staundford, as they were in Bracton: killing by privilege of law ("*Justitia*"); death brought about by necessity ("*Necessitate*"); death which was inevitable ("*Inevitabilis*"); death from an accident, which accident was unavoidable and not the result of carelessness ("*Casu Infortunium*"). Constructive malice, which has since been rejected as a category of criminal liability in English criminal law by force of Section 8 of the Criminal Justice Act, 1967,[18] is, nevertheless, a way to account for a criminal act when, as a defense, the accused suggests that he did not intend the consequences which ensued.[19] The theory underlying constructive malice was that an action which had produced a harm needed to be accounted for within a legal framework which would either tolerate the harm done, or condemn the harm done. In this instance the framework into which an explanation would fit would be the framework of the criminal law.

Staundford speaks of licit intention drawing directly upon Bracton's example. Thorne rendered Bracton's text as:

> But if he was engaged in a lawful act, as where a master has flogged a pupil as a disciplinary measure, or if [another is killed] when one was unloading hay from a cart or cutting down a tree and the like, and if he employed all the care he could, that is, by looking about him and shouting out, not too tardily or in too low a voice but in good time and loudly, so that if there was anyone there, or approaching the place, he might flee and save himself, or in the case of the master by not exceeding mean and measure in the flogging of his pupil, liability is not imputed to him.[20]

Brought into sixteenth and seventeenth-century common law is the medieval doctrine of *versari in re illicita*. The *Plees* enunciates intentional language, stating that the licitness of the intention, in conjunction with the *actus reus* of the offense, will determine (in great part) whether criminal responsibility and subsequent criminal guilt should be attributed to *D*. It will be for later writers, East, Hale, Hawkins, to expand upon this inclusion when the criminal textbook develops as part of the legal literature. The assumption underlying Bracton, and at work in Staundford, is that a legal world of some kind does exist. Human actions and omissions and confederations and elaborations are to be seen within the domain of an existing legal world. It would be a wrong reading of these early writings to assume that they were attempts at hypothesizing a legal world (as Sir Thomas More may have hypothesized the world of *Utopia*); the sense of human action and possibility is realist and practical, and the early legal writings are not concerned with the subtlety of a presumed counter-example or counter-case which one did find in large numbers in the Replies and Responses ("*Sed Contra*" and "*Responsio*") of medieval disputations and treatises. To import legal skepticism to the various books on *Pleas of the Crown* is to misread seriously. The world of "*Cogito*" and its doubts was not part of criminal reasoning. It was not that the law doubted its principles; it is that it strived, through its early authors, both to state the principles at work in the law, and then, in later and longer works, to elaborate upon its principles.

Staundford carries over to the sixteenth century, and also into the seventeenth century by force of the many editions of his work, principles which come from Bracton, and *arguendo*, from the predominating medieval theologians and moralists. The portion of "*Felony du mort du home*" of the first book of the *Plees* introduces one, at folio 12a and 12b, to language which has been customary to us, as when we read about what the "voluntary" entails when spoken of in conjunction with killing: "*Voluntate, vt si quis ex certa scientia, & insultu praemeditato, ira vel odio, vel causa lucri, inequiter & in felonia, contra pacë domini Regis aliquem interfecerit.*" Familiarity with the literature of the period, and its history, tells one that the definition restates the language of the voluntary, and its relationship to the language of deliberation and intellection, a theme recurrent in medieval disputes. We are not being asked to understand how a brain, a physical organ, can be possessed of and, simultaneously, direct neurological movement.[21] We are being asked to understand and employ a concept, *that* one can will, and *that* one can deliberate, and *that* one can entertain an intellectual relationship to a particular.

It may be observed that the *Plees* which Staundford compiled from earlier sources did reveal a growing legal grammar which reflected a rich assortment of legal distinctions whereby excuses and exemptions and responsibility could be assessed and evaluated. The wealth of legal categories showed that the criminal law could deal with a wide range of human failings. The law could ask after "imaginings," as in, "*Quaunt home face compasser ou imaginer law mort nostre Seignor le roy*."[22] It cited ways in which a crime could be brought about, as when the 1557 Statute of Treason is cited, part of its language stating, "*made treason, petit treason or misprisiö of treason, by words, writing, ciphring, deeds or otherwise*."[23] When asking after the nature of a killing, the language of the *Plees* carries with it the examples which are found even in the early Councils of the Church, and which have been cited in earlier chapters herein. The range of the legal questions embrace such considerations as, Was the killing done out of justice? or out of necessity? or was it an inevitable killing? or was there some degree of human responsibility? or was one absolved of all human responsibility? or did the killing come about by accident? or by misadventure? or was it a killing because of provocation? and was the provocation itself enough to excuse? or to blame? or did the killing happen against the wishes, or aims, or intentions of *D*? or to the contrary? or should it be asked how free was the agent? or was he an idiot? or a madman? or one temporally abandoned by reason? or did he premeditate upon the crime? or confederate? or plot? or retain an agent to kill? The *Plees* reflected and embodied a rich garden of legal differences.

If we return to so early a book as *The Boke of Justices of Peas*[24] we may see how legal distinctions with regard to responsibility, and degrees of guilt or culpability, were being incorporated into the budding common law. Few citations are needed from this short book to show that the medieval tradition regarding intention, and its relationship both to action and guilt, was a force in the development of criminal liability. The following citations demonstrate that the presence or absence of intention served to indicate the severity of a crime:

> C/-Also ye shall enquyre of all maner of felons bycause some of thë ben more heynouse thenne some as murdre &

> manslaughter / murdre is npnprely where a man by malice purpësed lieth in a Wayte to slee a man and accordynge to that malycyous entent and purpose he sleeth hym so that he whyche is slayne maketh no defence ayenst hym / for yf he doo it is manslaughter and no murdre / the offence of thys murdre is more heynous than the offence of other felons for yf the kynge graunt hym a pradon of all maner of felonnyes it auayleth him nought for murdre but yf it make expresse mencyon of murdres / & the statute therof is. Anno. xiii. Richardi. ii. ca. primo.

One may argue, without distortion to the text (but respecting that "murdre" proper carried here the sense of stealth and secret) that "malycyous entent and purpose" permits a distinction between a formal cause (the "malycyous entent") and a final cause (the "malycyous purpose"). The text itself from which we are quoting does gloss the side of the page to indicate a paragraph heading. It moves from what we have quoted, with the citation of "Murdre and manslaughter," to a definition of "Chaunce-medely." The definition, one will note, omits any appeal to intention, or to purpose, or to maliciousness (in any form, either substantively or adjectivally), stating simply:

> C/- And mäslaughter is where two men or mo mete and by chaunce medely they fall at affray so that one of them sleeth an other is but felonie in hym selfe and therfore if any persone be defectyf in this wyse make your presentement accordynge. vts.[25]

An echo can be heard from the early *Placita Corone Coram Spigornel*[26] when *The Boke* defines the elements of criminal rape to be:

> C/- ...rape is where a man rauissheth or taketh a mänes Wife wydo we or mayde ayëst her Will & hath to do with her ayest her Will how be it that she asseet after Warde yet it is felony....[27]

The same text defines "robberye" by an appeal to planning by *D*, stating,

> C/ - There be also felons that contryuyth takynge awaye of mennes goodes as roberye and thefte robberye is where a man lyeth by the kiges hygh Waye to market Towne in woodes diches or in any other secrete places where by they comen forth by and robbeth theym.[28]

The deed is spoken of a "mallapertnesse of the dede." The deed's gravity is intentionally described when we read,

> Also yf there be ony man that brenneth his neighbours hous maliciously by dae or by nygth it is felonye.

To see that the force of "wilfully" means to bring about, or actively to permit ("*actively*" ranging over commission and also omission), we may refer to the citation in *The Boke*[29] regarding "eschapes of felons" wherein we read,

> C/ - Also yf ony Sheryf Gaoler or any other persone have letten Wylfully eschape ony felon it is felony..../ & yf a felon eschape out of the kepinge of any gaoler ayest his Will it is fynable the fyne is an.

The "*Indicatament feloniae*"[30] we read of intentional language, although cited in Latin. For that done "*vi et armis*" we read, "*& felonice ut felo dni regis ïsidiand & insult pmeditat ctra pacë*," the gist of which is that the act was done with full knowledge of its doing. One may refer to *Anno Duodecimo Henrici Septimi*, Cap. VII, to the case of James Grame who murdered Richard Tracy, his master, to appreciate how the language of indictments in *The Boke* corresponded to the language in criminal cases of the period (*circa* 1497/8 A.D.). We have reported the case in the endnote below.[31] Other Latin terms will speak of "*mala pcogitatiöe*" to indicate the element of felonious intent[32] in *The Boke*.

We reproduce below a rare edition of *The Boke for a Ivstyce of Peace*, 1534, to show how the language of this work preserved the language of intention in various aspects; i.e., its strictly cognitive aspect, as where one plans, and its strictly volitional aspect, as where one brings about. We shall let the texts here stand without further comment.[33] It may be assumed that the notion of *actus reus*, which may be read *both* as the non-intentional elements of a crime, *and* its material limits, was embodied in the notion of a judicial power, i.e., that a Justice had the "power" to inquire after the nature of a crime. By assumption, we could argue that an inquiry is of some kind or other, of some limit or other, if only to limit the nature of one crime (say, robbery) from some other crime (say, murder). We reproduce folio pages from the Berthelet text of 1534.

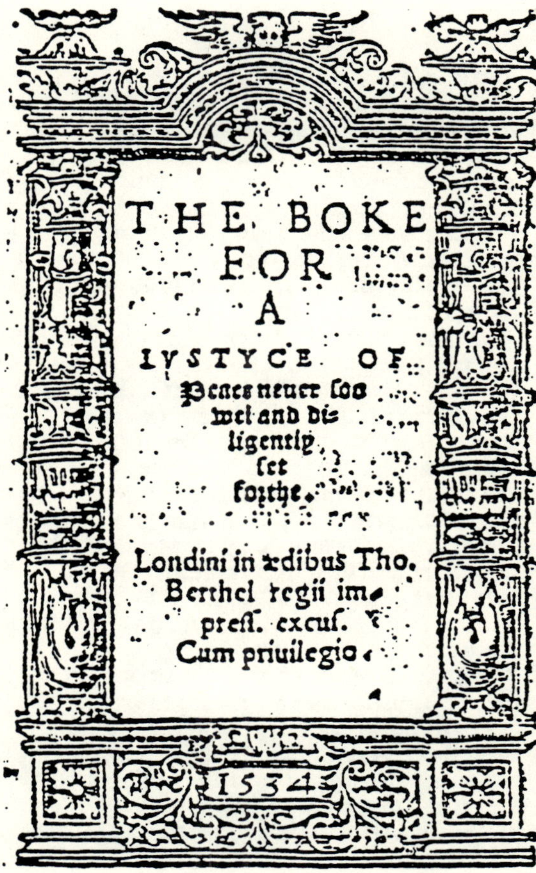

THE BOKE
FOR
A
IVSTYCE OF
Peaes neuer soo
wel and di-
ligently
set
forthe.

Londini in ædibus Tho.
Berthel regii im-
press. excus.
Cum priuilegio.

1534

baple. An. 25. H. 8. Ca. 14.

Markettis in churche yardes. ¶ Also ye shall enquere of all them that kepe any fayres, or markettes, in churche yerde, or in any other holy place, where any sekyng is: and howe longe they haue continued therin, the statute therof is of Edwarde the thyrde made at wynchester. And also in the statute made at wynchester, the. 13. yere of E. 1. it was defended, that feyers shulde no more be kepte in churche yardes.

Côuterfai kynge of coyne. ¶ Ye shall enquere of them that counterfeyt the kynges coyne, or if there be any false money and payment made therwith. And of thē that brynge false money into this realme, or that counterfeit the coyne of an other realme, whiche by the kynges sufferaunce is currant within this realme, ye shall doo vs to were. And of them that clyppe, washe, fyle, or other wyse falsyfie the money of this realme: And this semeth to be highe treasone, for the statute sayth, that he is a traytour to the kynge and his realme, Anno. 3. H. 5. statuto scdo. Capit. 6. et 7.

Galy half pens. ¶ And the same. iii. yere of the sayd kynge, it was ordeyned, that galyhalfpens, suskyns, dodkyns, and all money of Scotland shulde be all put out, and who that maketh, byeth, coyneth, or bryngethe into this realme galyhalfpens, suskyns, and dodkyns, shall be punysshed as a felon, and he that taketh or payeth suche money, shal lose an. C. s. wherof the kynge shall haue the one halfe, and he that wyll sewe the other halfe. And that Iusty=

tes of peace in euerye shyre of this realme, haue power to inquire therof, to here, and determyne the same.

¶ Also of theym that slee theyr mayster, that is for to say theyr soueraygne, as monke his abbotte or priour, wyfe her husbande, seruaunt his mayster, or any, vnder whose obeisaunce he is: the cause is, the mayster hathe to hym more truste than to a stranger. Vide statutum inde Anno. 25. E.3.cap.2. Of suche as sleye theyr soueraine.

¶ Also Justices of peace haue ful power and auctoritie in their sessions to enquire of trayterous murderers & murders of poysonynge as well as of the counterfeytynge of coyne of any outwarde royalme, suffred to ronne and go within this realme by the kynges assente, and to make proces therupō by capias only: for poysonnyng is adiudged and deemed as high treason by act of parliament made Anno. 22.H.8.cap.9. Poysonnynge.

¶ Also ye shal inquire, if any men be slayne or murdered by the day, whether the murderer be taken by the townshyp, where the deth or mourder was doone: for if he be not, the towneshyp shalbe amerced. An.3.H.7.cap.1.

¶ Also ye shall enquere of all them, that cast any bylles into any mans howse, in the whyche bylles is conteyned, that if the same person brynge not a certayne somme of money, or lay it at a certayn place & howre, his house shalbe brent, and the money be not there layd, the house is brent, this is highe treason, The statute therof is An.8.H.6.cap.6. Thretes to brēne a mās hous

Murder and manslaughter. ¶ Also ye shal enquere of al manˉ of felonies, bycause some of them ben more heynous thā some, as murder and manslaughter. Murder is proprely where a man by malyce prepensed lyeth in awayte to slee a man, and accordyng to that malycious intent & pourpose, he sleeth hym, so that he, whiche is slayne, maketh noo defence ayenste hym, for if he do, it is manslaughter and no murder, the offence of this murder is more heynous than the offence of other felonies: for if the kyng graunt hym a pdon of all maner of felonies, it auayleth him nought for mourder, but yf it make expresse mencion of murders. And the statute therof is, Anno. 13. R. 2. Cap. 1.

Chaunce medeley. ¶ And manslaughter is, where two men or mo mete, and by chaunce medley they fall at affray, so that one of them sleeth an other, it is but felony in hym selfe, and therfore if any person be defectiue in this wise, make your p̄sentment accordyng ther.

Rape. ¶ Also ye shal ēquire of rape. Rape is where a man rauyssheth or taketh a mans wyfe, wydowe, or mayde ayenst her wyll, and hath to do with her ayenst her wyl, albeit that she assent afterwarde, yet it is felony, and without the kynges charter make mencyon of rape, it auayleth hym nought. The statute therof is westm̄. 2. Cap. 34.

Robberie. ¶ There be also felons, that contryue takyng away of mens goodes, as by robberye and theft. Robbery is where a man lyeth by the kynges hygh waye to market townes, in

wods

woddes, dyches, or in any other secrete places, where people come forth by, and robbeth them, albeit that he taketh away but the value of a peny, or lesse, it is felony, for the malapertnesse of the dede and ieoperdie that a man is in of his lyfe, where it so take away from his person causeth the offence to be greater, than if it had ben theuyshely stollen.

¶ Thefte is where a thefe stealeth a mannes goodes in his chaumber or in his close, or any other place, yf the value passe .xiii.d. it is felony, and if it be not passynge the value of .xii. d. it is but petyte larceny, or brybery: for the whiche he shal not dye, but make a fyne to the kyng: but if it can be found at diuers tymes, that he hath taken goodes of that value and more, than he shall dye therfore. Thefte.

¶ Also if there be any man, that burneth his neyghbours howse malyciously by day or by nyght, it is felony. Also of them that breake howses by nyghte, to the intente to robbe, though they take nothynge a way, it is burgulary, which in it selfe is felony, bycause the lawe gyueth noo colour to breake a mannes howse by nyght. Burgularie.

¶ Clerkes conuict of petite treason, wylfull murder, or robberies done by or nere the high way. &c. shall make no purgation, except they do fynde .ii. sufficient sureties, euery of them hauynge landes or other heredytamentes of chartertholde of enheritance to the yerely value of .xx vi.s. viii.d. or els be worthe .xx.li. in mouable substance, eche of them to be bounde Clerkes conuicted.

It is not surprising to read a developed vocabulary in which mental and volitional conduct is modified in a number of ways in the course of a sentence, when speaking of an act done "maliciously," or that conduct was "wilful." If one refers to the *Mirour for Magistrates*[34] one will read a vocabulary of rhyme well suited to express machinations and evil designs, offering rich modifications in the adjectival presentment of human vices. What one does not find in such a vast collection of common rhyme is a justification for the use of pivotal terms which describe wickedness – nor ought one to expect such from poetry; but what the collection does reveal is that a language was sufficiently formed to accommodate complex descriptions of human conduct. It is but a short space from there to the world of Elizabethan drama, part of which depicted in complex ways the complex failings of the human condition, to appreciate that common law notions of legal responsibility and criminality were developing within, and out of, a fertile linguistic world.

The language of these various early treatises concerned with criminal offenses is both a language which is simple and direct, and also a language which incorporates complex notions from medieval theology. The medieval origins are by time and use suppressed, much like the roots of any language to the common eye and ear, and one is left with, as it were, conclusions. The supposings and premisses which may have led to various conclusions are to be inferred, which inferences this monograph has attempted in part. The reason for a term being used in a certain way may be divided into, "The reason for...," which is lost through time and custom, leaving us with, "...used in a certain way." Deliberately do we hesitate to make a simple distinction between "denotation" and "connotation." We wish to argue more deeply than what these notions signify. We wish to argue that a term may grow from within a tradition, as does the term "Will," and that the term comes to be used in a conclusive way, almost an enthymematic way, forcing one to think back to what the premises might have been so that, in turn, one can arrive at some comprehensive understanding of how, and why, the term is used. The "method" for such discovery is more literary in its mode than it is scientific; each new text, with each newer and fresher reading of key terms, renders newer conclusions about a common matter. One may ask how a term can come to be an entonic term, a word or concept which appears to generate much action and meaning of a strained sort. And one is brought back to the texts of the period in search of a tradition which gave such energy and tension to a key or pivotal term. The late Friedrich Waismann entertained what we believe to be a proper concept about philosophical activity when, with regard to language, he urged an open-minded model for and of its use, and warned against making easy nets in which all linguistic activity could be caught and confined.[35] Linguistic usage is not this simple, as present linguistic theory is revealing (and which literary critics have appreciated for a long time). We may see (or hear) a term used; but language carries along a context, so variegated and complex (and unobtrusive and unconscious) that it would be a simple man who thought that simple propositional analysis exhausted the range of use of a term. Perhaps – and we stress "perhaps" – an omniscient mind could embrace fully the nuances of language in its legal usages, but that is to assume that history could be viewed as both closed, and complete by an omniscient observer; by definition, therefore, excluding human research and enterprise, and thus of little practical use. Man is more a metaphor than a simple problem which may be solved.

From that brief aside let us return to the texts at hand. It was advanced in Putnam's study[36] that the text of *The Boke*, 1506, served as the base upon which Fitzherbert's treatise, 1538 (and later editions), grew. The 1574 text bears out the claim.[37] It was also advanced by Putnam, and the text of such edited and prepared, that the reading given by Magistri Thome Marowe at Inner Temple in 1503 was "the first systematic exposition of the procedure and powers of the justices, based on extensive knowledge of the law and practice on the subject." However, "Apart from Year books and material connected with the Inns of Court, there seems to be no reference to Marowe in legal literature till half a century after his death. Fitzherbert's failure to mention the *De Pace* in any of his works is the more mysterious inasmuch as a copy was probably produced at his own Inn in 1516 or 1517, and as Marowe was arguing frequently in the courts at Westminster after his call to be serjeant."[38] The chapter of *De Pace* which is of concern is the Twelfth Lecture (*Duodecima Lectura*): "*De feloniis inquirendis coram Justiciariis pacis*," contained on pages 375 to 383 of Putnam's edition. The two lawyers to take cognizance of Marowe were Brooke[39] and Fleetwood.[40] Other writers from later periods do cite Marowe, some of whose texts are not indicated in Putnam's study.[41]

Putnam constructed her text of *De Pace* from eleven manuscripts to produce the law French edition contained in her study of 1924. We are chiefly concerned with chapter twelve of *De Pace* which inquires after the nature of felonies; we are not concerned with the intricate and disputed legal historical question regarding what, exactly, were the powers of the Justices of the Peace, matter outside of the scope of this study. We agree with Putnam that *De Pace* was kept alive by a manuscript tradition indigenous to the Inns of Court, and reference in our endnote to an instant case may confirm that tradition when the Law Lords, during the course of oral argument, required a manuscript citation of an 1816 case to be produced in evidence.

In *Mort de home* Marowe sets out four categories of homicide. Although Bracton is not mentioned by him, Putnam suggests[42] that it is the Bractonian classification he is advancing: death by misfortune, suicide, manslaughter by chance-medley, and murder. The text reads as follows from *De Pace*:

> *Mort de home est auxi enquerable par lez iustices de pease & ceo poet estre fait en iiii maners, scilicet, par mysfortune; sicome home est occise par chaunce de vne mure gismaunt sur lay on par thonder ou ature maner dez chaunez, en toutz ceux casez ceo nest enquirable deuaunt Justices de peas, ou si home soit felo de se lou home tua luy mesme, ceo nest enquirable deuaunt Justices de peas. Mes de manslawghter ils poient enquerer & ceo serra entendre lou home tua vne autre par chaunce medle il est enquirable deuaunt eux. Le iiii*[te] *est murdre & ceo est lou home par malice prepense gitta en agaite & tua ascun home, cetst auxi enquirable deuaunt lez Justice & cetera.*[43]

The contrasts are simple enough. Death can occur without human intent; i.e., from nature, as by, lightning or a construction accident, a wall or roof falling upon one. These are common enough examples from the Fathers, when they spoke about trees falling upon passersby. When the inquiry presses to manslaughter one is given the example of chance medley, which tradition was fairly well-defined. The sentence which states that murder is brought about through *malice prepense* brings one back to the time surrounding Bracton, as well as embodying the expression of intention which can be read in the early cases from Bracton to the time of Marowe himself. We will consider some cases from the early courts and rolls, but first will cite and comment upon the text of *De Pace* which concerns murder (*mort de home*). The text is to be found on pages 378 to 379 in the Putnam edition; we will provide our own translation of the law French. The text continues:

> *Et nota que en mort de home lentent de celui que fait le mort ne fait le felony come il fait de Theft come est auauntdit & etc.; quar si home entende de bater ascun person & en cell baterie il tua vne ature, ceo est felony nient obstante son entent ne fut de luy occider. Mes en ascun cas de mort de homme lentent ferra le felony; sicome vne home dona a vne autre corrupt vitaille al entent de luy oue cest vitaille de poysoner & murderer & il deuia de maunger ou boire de ceo vitaille, ceo est felony. Mes sil ne sauoit le corrupcion ne entend luy poysoner al temps quaunt il luy dona, ceo nest felony & issint lentent en ceo fait le felony & etc.*

The notions which the law French embody rest near to being a legal shorthand for more expanded legal notions. Since we assume that Marowe was giving a Reading or Lecture at Inner Temple, we may be guided by the custom of the Inns, and we may assume that his audience had completed dinner, and that the utter barristers, who were students, were preparing to take notes. The examples which occur in this portion of his text (as well as other portions) would have been jotted down, and the student himself may have embellished the text with his own case citations or examples. Working within this background, the text can, without distortion, be expanded into sensible English.

Marowe offers us an extremely compressed and complex comparison when, at the opening of the sentence, he says that "*mort de home*" is different from "Theft." Why is this so? It is for this reason; his statement embodies the notion, Where is the crime to be found? Does "stealing" rest in the goods, or in the agent who steals the goods? If an owner picks up his bales of goods and carries them a certain distance, how does this differ from one who does not own the goods but who does the same as the owner with regard to the goods, namely, picking them up and carrying them away? The case which had perplexed judges at the latter part of the fifteenth century was *Carriers Case*, Y.B. 13 Edw. IV, where *D*, who was hired to carry goods to one place, promptly carried them to some other and different place, and seized the contents he was carrying. He was charged with committing a felony. The case was decided in 1473, but not without causing great differences among the Bench. The law concerning theft has always been perplexing* because one is always at odds in trying to isolate the larcenous element in the criminal act so that a criminal charge can be laid against *D*. Thus Marowe pressed a subtle point on his listeners, almost in a way worthy of a Socratic question: to wit, *where* is "theft" to be found, as opposed to, *where* is "murder" to be found? Does one simply apply a definition to an act of an agent? But what in the definition is to be applied to what? How is a criminal location made? What is it which makes that book *your* book, and not *my* book? Certainly it is not the "bookishness" of the book which renders it your possession and not my possession. It is not simple location which supports one's claim to possession. The book could rest just as easily on the table of the thief as of the owner.

Yet Marowe advances another element in his comparison. He wishes to argue that "intent" or "intention" does not by itself define the felonious elements of a crime. It will be seen that he assumes that a crime has to it a certain material element which brings the crime outside of what the agent aims at or wishes for. But Marowe advances this by example, and not simply by definition. The student needed to see that some forms of actions were different, however hard it was to put those differences into neat *a priori* descriptions. The lawyer must work through experience; and the assumption here is that the world of the particular is more complex, and more difficult to embody linguistically, than meets our mind's eye. With this prologue let us offer what the text states:

> We should take note of this distinction. When a person has been killed, the intent of the one who killed him is not only what makes the matter felonious, as, for instance, the intent of an agent in theft is what makes the matter theftous. This should be made clear for you by considering this example.
>
> If *D* claims that he intended only to strike *A* and no one else, yet by means of his blow strikes, and kills even, some innocent third party, it will be no defense for *D* to claim that he had not intended or aimed at this innocent third party. *D* is guilty of a felony even if he did not want to kill this unknown person.

---

* The *Theft Act* 1967 and the legal difficulties it has produced reveal that an exact statement as to what are the elements of a theft yet eludes us.

> We may take another case where intent is an ingredient in the determination of felony. Consider the man who knowingly gives a person food which is poisonous, with the intention to poison and cause the death of that person. But, by chance or good fortune, the victim avoids eating any of the poisonous food. What then? *D* is still guilty of a felony.
>
> But let us consider the facts of this same case but in a different way. Assume that *D* not only does not know that the food is poisoned, but also that *D* has no criminal intent to poison his guest. What shall we say if *D* gives this food to his guest? Has *D* committed a felony? No, he has not committed a felony. In this instance his intent does protect him against the possible charge of having committed a felony.

That this kind of case had suasive power in sixteenth-century legal reasoning will be seen when in Plowden, *The Queen v. Saunders and Archer* (1576) 2 PI. 473, the facts of the case materially embody many of the elements Marowe put forth for consideration seventy or so years earlier.

What is interesting to note about Marowe's language is that he moves from an adjectival description, *malice prepense*, to use of strict intentional analysis. In Theft it is the element of intention which makes taking larcenous, while in murder the element of intention is one element only in the elements of the crime. The example he gives is the use of "intention" to convey the object of intention. It will be no defense to the charge of felony to state, "I intended to strike A but not B." The law, as Marowe expounds it (and which his students were assumed to understand), forbade all criminal striking, or criminal assault; hence the material element of the definition, and which may be subsumed to the *actus reus* of a criminal commission or undertaking. In later legal language we have come to know what Marowe has spoken of as "oblique intention" or "indirect intention" or "constructive intent." The felony murder rule, or constructive malice (operable in some common law jurisdictions, but not in England), is embodied in the distinction Marowe makes.

The other portion of the example shows how intention may excuse, and there Marowe shifts to demonstrate the two ways in which a common example may be entertained. The reason why *D* is guilty in the first poisonous food example is that *D* is attempting to kill; the element in attempt is intentional. The case could equally have been made more complicated by *D* thinking that the food was poisonous, when, in fact, it was not. The example shows why it is to intent that an appeal is made in order to determine the guilt of *D*. We have a number of modern counterparts of this example, especially in narcotics enforcement where, often, the court will rule that it is immaterial to *D*'s guilt whether the sacks of contraband were heroin or sugar at the time when *D* "attempted" to sell the items to an undercover narcotics agent.

The closing part of the example shows that if an agent is devoid of criminal intention, and of criminal knowledge (truly not knowing that the food was poisonous; and, we assume, not having brought about the poisonous conditions by ignorance or culpable oversight[44]), then the elements for a felonious commission are not present in *D*, and a felony cannot be charged of or attributed to him.

In accord with Bracton, and most of the medieval moral theory we have considered, Marowe finally isolates guilt within the existence of intention itself. The logical primitive for legal guilt is the guilty intention itself. At this point, as we saw in Bracton, the guilt of the law and the guilt of moral stain are one. It will be recalled that Bracton saw this moment as the act which only the heart could know and which only God could judge. The example makes clear what Bracton may have meant when he said, "In crimes the intention is regarded, not the result."[45] Illustrating such a legal preconception is this case from the *De Pace*:

> *Item en auncien temps lentent en murdre oue vne notorious act fait de perfourmer mesme le murdre fut felonye coment que il ne fist le murdre en fait, sicome en cas vne garcoun voile auer tue son master quaunt il fut endormant & come il voillet auer scie son gutter, il gisoit sur luy cy dure que il mesme vigiloit & eschape ceo, & ceo fut aiugge felony en le garcoun et vncore le master fut en vie.*[46]

He is talking about murder by stealth where the very act of murder as criminal rested in its being planned, which concept was later embraced by treason, and which, in some early cases from the Rolls, we can read of malice as being treasonous when related to a killing. The two following cases show such a usage.

1. ...there came by night the aforesaid Richard Pope and William del Idel, the said John's servants, lying in wait feloniously like felons of the king and premeditating assault against the king's peace and his crown and

> dignity....And Richard struck the aforesaid John Carpenter, while John was lying asleep on his bed, with an axe and feloniously and *treasonably* [italics ours] struck him on his head...and he dealt him a mortal wound...from which he died.[47]

2. ...Richard Gyse and Robert Cook, servants of the said William de Cauntelo, came there feloniously as felons, and with *treason aforethought* [italics ours] they slew William De Cauntelo as he sat there on his bed, dealing him various mortal wounds.[48]

The passage from Marowe may be rendered:

> Note this: that in older times when one planned to commit a vicious crime or act, it was the intent itself to murder which was viewed as felonious, even though the actual murder had not in fact been performed. Take this example on the point. A young lad connives to take the life of his Master whilst his Master is asleep. But this clumsy lad, during the course of the attack, awakens his Master who thus escapes from harm. Did the lad commit a felony? Yes, he did, even though his Master suffered no bodily harm.

The passage carefully brings Marlowe's audience from a world in which the elements of a crime embrace *actus reus* and intent, to a world in which the nub of criminal guilt coincides with the nub of moral guilt: an agent intending, although the harm may never actually come about, to commit a criminal act. Move down through time as we will, the early books of the Justices, and this germinative Reading of Marowe in *De Pace*, show how the medieval world which Bracton embodied did serve to fund the growth of criminal concepts in the common law. The fundamental principle upon which criminality is founded for us finds its roots in the medieval principle, cited throughout this study, that man is the maker of his acts by force of his knowledge and his will.

We find Marowe's text of such importance for one major reason. It serves to refute the contention, advanced from time to time by some writers, that the early criminal law employed *mens rea* in a strictly adjectival fashion, and did not employ the term, and its adjuncts, in any substantive fashion. Marowe, by his analysis of felony by appeal to an agent's intention, clearly shows that the elements for criminal liability, and an analysis thereof, were transmitted in the early legal literature of the period. He also revealed that intention was not simply a grammatical term to reveal rebuke or disapproval.

It was a term which was employed to analyze the elements of a criminal act. Like the age of which it was a part, intention permeated early common law writings, each writer drawing in part upon a common medieval heritage which found itself in the culture – a commonality of spirit which the late Nicolai Berdyaev, with reference to the Russian spirit, referred to as *sobernost*, a prevailing, shared, cultural communality of spirit. The growing criminal law, *circa* the 1500's, revealed a commonness of legal principles in much the way that the carvings upon diverse churches and cathedrals in England revealed a common art form; and, as with any member in a species, commonality did not produce uniformity or sameness, nor did individuality produce chaos or unrelieved uniqueness.

When one turns to examine the 1574 edition of *First the booke for a Justice of peace*, one will discover that it is a replication of the 1534 edition (which pages were reproduced herein), save for some mild modification of spellings, and for the fact that the edition was produced by Richarde Tottyl at Temple Barre.[49] What is demonstrated is the force of "*The Boke*" over the sixteenth century in England, in various editions and abridgements and improvements, containing fairly much what is to be found in the very earliest 1506 editions. When one reads that the text is, "Newely imprinted and corrected," one should understand not that the text has been revised (as are our editions of law texts now, e.g., Salmond, Russell, Chitty, etc.), but that the text has had added to it recent statutory enactments. In most other ways Tottyl's text of 1574 is akin in most of its parts to Wynkyn de Worde's, *The Iustyces of Paes*, 1510 [Beale, T-132], like its progeny, printed in *'Fletestrete com[m]orante[m] in signo solis.'*

We wish now to draw examples from case law. Our purpose is not so much to force an unnatural conjunction between the early writers of the various "*bokes*" or "Abridgements" as it is to demonstrate that the common law had developing a workable set of pragmatic principles, to which later writers would strive to give formality. But even to our own day the force of the law, as the courts abjure, is not the texts but the decisions made by the courts on the cases they hear. Save from some leniency in jurisdictions in the United States of America, it is not customary to cite for the purpose of legal authority a textbook on the law written by a living author. The legal universe of early common law was the community and legal fellowship of the Inns. Without any pre-established analytical guide the cases from the courts seemed to present a wholeness of opinion and judgment, and, without any rhetorical exaggeration intended, such is the greatness of the common law.

It is not possible to cite all of the cases which may bear upon points of this study. We choose some which will serve to illustrate that a young legal vocabulary was concerned with a wide range of conceptual distinctions, and out of which concern legal liability could be justly apportioned.

It had been a moot point in theology, and certainly as old as the *Nicomachean Ethics*, Book III, as to how one could be made to do what he would not do. At law a defense of *duress* may be lodged. Here is how early common law saw that defense.[50] In modern language the claim is that a "hold harmless" agreement between *A* and *B* is void at law because such was executed under duress.

> And John, while not acknowledging that the deed had been made at the day and place mentioned in the said deed, says that he ought not be barred from his action [for damages for personal injury] by the aforesaid deed, for he says that Thomas by force and arms took him, John, at Handsworth, and imprisoned him so that he made the aforesaid deed under duress of imprisonment (*duriciam prisone*] and various threats of life and limb and by reason of the fear of death [*propter metum mortis*], wherefore he prays judgement whether he ought to be barred from his action by the said deed, etc....the jurors likewise came and, chosen and tried by consent of the parties, they say on their oath that John, at the time when the aforesaid deed was made, was seized by Thomas de Chaourches and kept under detention by Thomas and taken away entirely against his will [*omnino contra voluntatem*], and he was go greatly menaced in life and limb that through fear of death and to save his life he made the aforesaid deed and, if he had refused to make the said deed, Thomas would have killed him.

The instant case is of interest because it reveals how the defense of Duress may have moved a jury. The case leaves open–because such is not an essential element for its finding–how the Will is moved, or what is meant by Will. As with so much legal reasoning in a court, a jury (or a judge, if sitting without the benefit of a jury) looks towards believableness, and this is a matter of practical judgment which the extended process of a trial at common law may reveal. At no one point during the course of the trial is the "guilt" or "innocence" of an accused to be located.* The cumulative effect of damaging omissions, contradictory testimony, hesitancy, mis-answered questions, weights the scales toward or from a probable verdict in which probable doubt convicts or acquits the accused. It will be for subtler cases to inquire after the "movement of the will." It is enough to see that the common law did accept such a finding, and did not restrict such to cases of rape only (where one was taken against one's will).

In a later case, consistent with the notion from the above-mentioned case, we read, in *R. v. Bradshaw and Pytheous*,[51] how,

> A priest called Bredsha and a woman were indicted for poisoning, to wit, the woman was principal, and the priest as accessory by reason of his command.

We believe a better rendering of the text would be, "...and the priest as accessory *through reason of* his commanding [her]." We put the law French below (endnote 51) for the convenience of the reader. It is doubtful if such cases provided a clear statement of principle which would distinguish between the range of intentional actions and of non-intentional actions and what relationship such classes bore to criminal charges. Such cases did not serve to explain how the Will functioned, or could fail to function; rather, such cases served to indicate that the law would accept as a finding of fact that an accused acted from Duress, or out of Necessity, or under Coercion.[52] The categories had an *ad hoc* quality to them because of the difficulty inherent in extending a general notion to include a specific range of actions. It is for this reason that we have suggested that the court tends to make a practical judgment when these defenses appear, and the practical judgment leads it to consider if what is asserted by the accused in a criminal action is to be believed. Those specific questions which a philosopher or a theologian (then) might have asked are not inquired after in the judgment of the court. It is not concerned with the subtlety of how and in what ways or by what procedure one can be said to deliberate or to will.[53] These early cases admit that guilt will not be a finding when certain coercive and restraining conditions obtain. That certain kinds of conditions, such as torture, were

---

* Save of course for that one moment where an accused may simply admit that he is guilty, and confesses such guilt in an open court.

excluded admits only of the historical strangeness of the criminal sanction and how undeveloped may have been the legal sensibilities of the epoch. The criminal law, with its roots in vengeance, was the last primarily to crave after the unbloody world of gentlemanly rebuke.

The formula for the charges in the early cases is quite standard. We will continue to read variants of, "*ex malicia sua precogitat*."[54] Very early cases, which do not have any element of murder or manslaughter, are stated directly, without much complication or circumlocution. A simple and direct statement of the facts of a case can be found in the Forest Eyre Rolls or Forest Inquisitions.[55] These thirteenth-century cases speak of poachers, and the like, as evildoers (*malefactores*); it may, for example, be "proved that Robert the son of William of Loewick is guilty of evildoing to the venison" ("*Postea convictum...est culpabilis de malefactis venacionis*").[56] The same cases may advance a plea in mitigation, as for instance, "Afterwards it is witnessed that William the son of Henry carried the said venison under coercion and against his will..."[57] ("...*coactus et inuitus...portabat*..."). The volume prepared for the Selden Society by D. M. Stenton, *Rolls of the Justices in Eyre, Being The Rolls of Pleas and Assizes For Lincolnshire 1218-9 and Worcestershire 1221*, shows a range of cases marked by Bracton himself which demonstrate a language rich in making criminal distinctions. The volume of the *Pleas* reports a wide range of killings, robbings, and the like, and in language other than simply *A* hit *B*. For instance, we may read,

> The jurors suspect Hawisa, the mother of Richard, Alice's husband, that they killed Alice by her counsel and wish [...*per consilium et voluntatem suam eam occiderunt*...], and likewise Christina, Hawisa's nurse, and Christina's daughter named Margery....The jurors also suspect the husband, Richard, that she was killed by his command, because he hated her by reason of a certain Gloucestershire girl, whom he took to wife soon after Alice's death, and whom he still has.[58]

It is a rather clear statement of facts, as well as being a clear statement giving possible reasons for actions.

It is when we come to Plowden's Reports that we begin to observe how an explanation functions as more than a bare statement of facts, and begins to function as an explanation of the facts. We are presented with what we associate in a modern law report – a distinction between facts, law, and judgment.

Plowden's *Commentaries* may be employed to show how the principles of the criminal law which are to be found in the writings of Marowe, the various editions of the *Boke*, and its revisions, and in Staundford, were a common feature of the legal milieu. The *Reports* are a source which show the meeting of various worlds of thought: the common law itself, the continental tradition (of Civilian and Canon thinkers), and the intertwining of philosophical principles in legal argument.[59] It may be advanced without any distortion that in Plowden one will find a clearer statement of incipient legal principles than one will find in the early manualists' restatement of Bracton and other early legal writers. Although Staundford contained a compendium of legal principles garnered from earliest common law writers, what does not appear in his compendium is any critical presentment of those principles, whereas in Plowden one observes the legal process at work, and one observes how principles are applied and extracted. This may have been the case because his work was to be used by students at the Inns for their study and preparation for advocacy.

What we would choose to call the legal beauty of Plowden's *Reports* is that they reveal an inheritance of common ideas with concern for legal responsibility from diverse sources. One example is that Plowden offers a clear report of how the notion of *versari in re illicita* functions, which, it will be recalled, is that notion of legal culpability that the harmfulness of the consequences of an act is thought to originate within the wrongful intention of the agent. If, however, it can be believed that the agent's originating intent was not evil in itself, or contrary to law, then whatever harmful consequences may yet nevertheless flow from his originating intention should not be thought of as harmful consequences he intended. The intention "p" should not be considered to entail by force of necessary implication the consequences "q" which follow. The case in which the distinction occurs is *The Queen v. Saunders and Archer* (1576) 2 Pl. 473.

John Saunders was charged that he had "voluntarily and feloniously killed and murdered" (473) his infant daughter, aged three years. From a confederate, one Alexander Archer, Saunders had bought from him the poisons *Arsenick* and *Roseacre*, with the original intent to poison his own wife, Eleanor Saunders. The "motive" for the killing was love; John Saunders wanted to take another wife. The poison was to be mixed into some apples which were then to be roasted and later eaten. When Saunders discovered he had killed his own infant he pleaded that he had no malice against her, and was innocent. His wife, unknowing of the poison in the apples, had fed them to her little daughter, who died from the poisoned fruit.

The Court listened to his case with care, as well as to consider his defense that the death of his daughter was a non-intentional result of an accidental poisoning not within the design or aim or purpose of his criminal intent. He pleaded, simply, that he had not sufficient *mens rea* for the charge of murder. Plowden reports,

> ...But at last the said Justices, upon Consideration of the Matter...were of the Opinion that the said Offence was Murder in the said *John Saunders*. And the Reason thereof (as the said Justices and the Chief Baron told me [i.e., Plowden himself]) was, because the said *John Saunders* gave the Poison with an intent to kill a Person, and in the giving of it he intended that Death should follow. And when Death followed from his Act, although it happened in another Person than her whose Death he directly meditated, yet it shall be Murder in him, for he was the original Cause of the Death...[474].

The Court took care to distinguish between two kinds of actions. One species of actions could be those done through ignorance, and the fact of the ignorance was innocent in itself. This would have borne the name *actio ex ignorantia*. But a second species of action could be that done *ignoranter*, where the fact of the ignorance would not relieve the agent of culpability, as in actions done while drunk, which actions produced harmful consequences whether known or remembered by the drunken agent. Here the defense of ignorance would not obtain, because, it would be argued by the Crown, the state of ignorance was brought about deliberately and voluntarily by the agent. We will cite briefly from Plowden on the matter. In the present case the Court gave the following example:

> But if a Man prepares Poison, and lays it in several Parts of his House, with an Intent to kill Rats and such Sort of Vermin, and a Person comes and eats it, and dies of it, this is not Felony in him who prepared and laid it there, because he had no Intent to kill any reasonable Creature [474a].

But the same example can be taken, as does the Court, to make the matter criminal:

> ...when he lays the Poison with an Intent to kill some reasonable Creature, and another reasonable Creature, whom he does not intend to kill, is poisoned by it, such Death shall not be dispunishable, but he who prepared the Poison shall be punished for it, because his intent was evil [474a].

One can observe that the concluding sentence of the opinion of the Court gives example to *versari in re illicita*; i.e., that the harmfulness of the consequences carry into themselves the originating harm of the agent's intention, itself forbidden by law. We know that this notion clearly brings one back to Bracton in *De Placitis Coronae* wherein he distinguished between acts which were proper and improper, and intentions which were lawful or wicked, in the title: *De crimine homicidii*.[60]

The element of *versari in re illicita* was clearly embodied in Bracton, and we have commented upon it. But the notion, in Plowden, is drawn not only from his references to Bracton, but also from his references to leading canonists of his own age, one such being the eminent Spanish canonist, Diego de Covarruvias y Leyva (1512-77 A.D.) himself a disciple of Doctor Navarrus (Martin Azpilcueta, 1491-1586 A.D.), outstanding moral theologian and canonist who distinguished himself as a professor of law at Salamanca and Coimbra.[61]

In the *Commentaries* if one turns to the case of *Reniger v. Fogossa*, (1550), 1 Pl. 19, the defense submitted by Serjeant Pollard on behalf of his client is of interest because of the medieval notions it embodies, both directly from Bracton, and from its appeal to Covarruvias.

Anthony Fogossa was a foreign merchant whose goods were shipped aboard the vessel *St. Maria de Togma*. Because of a storm the Master of the ship, one Manuel Lopez, was compelled to cast into the sea a great part of his valuable cargo (which belonged to Fogossa). Fogossa was suing for the recovery of his lost cargo which had been jettisoned. To jettison cargo during a storm assumes that the act of jettisoning was voluntary. The question remained, Was this act of jettisoning the cargo a voluntary act for which the Master of the ship should be held responsible at law?

The facts of the instant case were as classic as if they had been transcribed from the *Nicomachean Ethics*, Bk. III, at 1110a, 9-11, which states:

> It may be debated whether such actions are involuntary or voluntary. Something of the sort happens also with regard to the throwing of goods overboard in a storm; for in the abstract no one throws goods away voluntarily, but on condition of its securing the safety of himself and his crew any sensible man does so. Such actions are mixed, but are more like voluntary actions.

During the course of his pleadings on behalf of Fogossa, Serjeant Pollard advanced a fourfold argument which, in his own words, did state:

> ...four Causes, *viz.*, the Avoidance of a greater Mischief, Necessity, Compulsion, and involuntary ignorance, can severally by themselves excuse a Man from the Charge of breaking the Law [at 1 Pl. 19a-20].

In the body of the report of the case, as the notes of the 1816 English edition of the *Commentaries* indicate, Pollard not only freely draws the attention of the Court to portions of *Deuteronomy* (chap. 19, v. 4, 5, 6, i.e.,, accidental killing embodying no wrongful intention) and to Aristotle, but reference is made to the "Civilians," Bartholinus (of Sassoferrato [1313-56 A.D.], an Italian jurist of great rank) and Covarruvias, with especial reference made to that work of Covarruvias's entitled, "*Si Fvriosvs, Rvbrica De Homicidio*."[62]

Covarruvias was a pupil of Martin Azpilcueta (1491-1586 A.D.), known in legal literature as Doctor Navarrus. It is outside the interest of this monograph to attempt to trace or make historical linkages between one author and another. We believe this is the proper province of the historian of ideas. But we do believe that one should point to some of the tradition. Through Navarrus and Covarruvias there developed a literature which analyzed both intention and ignorance. It would be artificial to put rigorous divisions upon the material these writers wrote because they easily moved from one mode, such as theology, to another mode, like law. The firm divisions which we accept now did not exist for writers of law and jurisprudence in this mid-Renaissance period. A category could as easily be at home operating in a legal treatise as it could in a moral treatise. Both of these writers, and others, drew upon much of what Aquinas had developed in the body of his writings on the subject of ignorance, and of intention.[63]

A brief perusal of the catalogues for the Inns and for the great universities of the period will show that the writings of the Italian and Spanish jurists and canonists were held by the libraries, and were known, and were cited in law reports and writings. That a canonist or a jurist discussed "intention" or "ignorance" would not have been a topic unique to his treatise, nor unique in its style of treatment. The canon lawyers tended to hand down what a Master may have said, and the Master may have been some earlier thinker, like Covarruvias, citing Doctor Navarrus (Martin Azpilcueta), or both men citing an earlier and deservedly acknowledged Master, as was Thomas Aquinas (1224-74 A. D.). For sake of making reading easier we shall place Aquinas' writing on ignorance in an endnote, as we have previously.[64] By appeal to the body of writings of Doctor Navarrus one will observe that "*ignorans*" and "*ignorantia*" occupied much analysis.[65] Navarrus argued that ignorance may have a fourfold division; i.e., an ignorance which was "*crassa*," or "*affectata*," or "*probabilis*" (a justifiable ignorance; e.g., a non-physician would not likely possess knowledge of skilled medical matters), or "*inuincibilis*" (an ignorance assumed to be so overpowering that it served to excuse or absolve). These divisions were further refined, commented upon, developed into cases, and transmitted through the literature (to be found variously in theology, law, philosophy, advocacy, and in case law), so that one during the course of a trial, could make reference to the various writings on the subject of "ignorance" and one's reference be understood in light of the traditions of the age.

Covarruvias followed in the same tradition. When one is referred to "*De delinquentibus ignoranter*" (tom. 1. Par. 3 at 3 & 4), what Pollard is telling the Court in the course of his oral argument is that the Court should take cognizance, while considering the merits of *Reniger v. Fogossa*, of the traditional arguments concerning ignorance, and its use as a legal (and moral) category to excuse or to exculpate an agent from legal guilt. Pollard could easily have cited Bracton, but the attention of the Court was drawn to a continuing tradition viable then during the fourth year of the reign of Edward VI (1550 A.D.). The section referred to in "*De delinquentibus ignoranter*" at sections "3" and "4" concern drunkenness and how that state may or may not excuse one if charged with killing a third party. One would inquire if that had been one's primary intention (*"vbi ea intentione se inebriauerit, vt ebrius" De Delinquentibus ignoranter*, [para. 3, p. 557-b]), and what ensued would be judged in the light of the original voluntary act: namely, drinking to become intoxicated.

The gravity of the consequences would vary *in legal estimation* (or *moral estimation*) with consideration of the agent's original intent. Though *D*, while intoxicated, may have killed *P*, the Court may think that the act of killing was possessed of less seriousness than if *D*, while sober, had done the same act with full premeditation. The canonists' arguments (and found argued in our courts to the present day, as the appeal in *Majewski* revealed)[66] might be twofold. One could inquire after the reasons of how the state of inebriation was brought about, i.e., did the agent voluntarily sit down and drink, and become intoxicated, or was he deceived into drinking party punch which he thought was free of liquor or harmless (as in a college prank at a college party with a non-drinker); or was he drinking, but was unconcerned, or unobservant (each state different), as to what he was drinking, *whereupon* consequences followed? The state precedent to the intoxication could be analyzed in greater detail. Then one comes to the state *whereupon* consequences follow.

That state itself could be analyzed. If *D* was intoxicated, but through no fault of his own, but then did kill *P*, it could be argued that his killing *P* was not premeditated (could not form a requisite criminal intent); or, though intoxicated, he still should have exercised some degree of self-control (i.e., either should have become aware that he was coming under the influence, and then stopped drinking further; or, even if under the influence, he must have had some degree of self-control). If one called the state of the agent before drinking state "A," and the state of the agent drinking state "B," and what he did while intoxicated as state "C," one might argue that each of his distinct personal states was brought about by him by force of what he knew and what he did not know. If one remained in state "A," one remained in that state for such and such a reason, or reasons. Those reasons might be complete and sufficient to account for what one was doing, or they might be incomplete, and not account for what one was doing; hence, a certain ignorance is admixed with one's knowledge. Thus for state "B" or for state

"C." From this complex picture the Court may be enabled to form some judgment about why *D* did "x."

A simpler picture could be given by appeal to a mechanical model. In English we do not speak about "states of ignorance." We eschew, generally, using abstract nouns in such a way that they account for action. We prefer to use verbs to account for action. There is a case, however, where we do use nominatives to account for action, and this is in the language of computer programming. If we consider a simple triad of "program-computer-output" we might have a present-day model for "ignorance-agent-action."

Were one to analyze a computer operation one could "excuse" the computer failure at various stages throughout its operation. One could inquire after the program itself, i.e., the particular matrix and its circuitry. If program "A" is plugged into the computer, but program "B" was the program which should have been plugged in, then the fault is a simple fault. Disconnect program "A"; connect program "B." But the error could be more complicated than that of a simple wrong input. The program itself could be ill-framed. Then one would inquire after more complicated explanations, e.g., was it a mechanical failure, such as wrong wiring, or poor fluid connections at "on-off" junctions? was it improperly made (e.g., greatest care was needed to punch out the micro-circuits to exact micro-dimensions, and these circuits were too large)? or is the program illogical?

This analysis could be run at each stage of the "program-computer-output" model until the error was found, and then a reason provided for why there was an error in the first place. In much the same way the medieval moralists attempted to analyze the conditions of knowledge prior to a human act. If one assumed that one acted from reasons, then those reasons could be analyzed to determine if they were sound grounds for action (within a legal or moral context). If the reasons were unsound, were tainted of "ignorance," then the moralist would inquire after the ignorance attached to the action. He would seek after the "program," and see what there was about this "program" which brought about this specific response, or action. Did the fault rest with the knowledge itself?–the "program model"? Did the fault rest with the agent?–the computer model, with inquiry after Will and Intellect and material dispositions? Or did the fault rest with what was done?—the "output" model? The particular moral shorthand for such analyses of ignorance was to speak of kinds of ignorance: there might be ignorance which was antecedent to an act; or ignorance which was concomitant with an act; or ignorance which was consequent to an act.

From the admission of a general category of "to-be-ignorant" the moralist would then discuss the fourfold relationship which could be obtained. The "kind" of ignorance would be analyzed. The powers of the agent would be analyzed (in terms of Will and Intellect and dispositions). Why the agent acted under or because of ignorance would be analyzed. Then an attempt would be made to determine if and how an excuse might obtain or not. Various moralists might provide various interpretations—for instance, a strict cognitivist, who argued that responsibility rested only in "knowing" that something was wrong, might argue for a different degree of moral or legal responsibility than might a voluntarist, who argued that the human Will was weak, or deceived (i.e., given the wrong good to seek after), or was forced, or was muddled. There was a tradition, however unclearly enunciated or unclearly formed, to which moral and legal argument could appeal in an attempt to excuse an agent or pardon an agent for an act, and that was the tradition which maintained that certain acts of an agent can be excused because of ignorance. What kind of ignorance, brought about in what manner, whether ignorance *simpliciter*, or "his ignorance" (that not only could one speak of "ignorance" as simple abstraction, but one also reinforced that abstract category by conjoining to it a pronomial element), would be dictated by the persuasiveness of the arguments of each thinker.

Thus, in the instant case, when Pollard (l. Pl. 19a) makes reference to "ignorance," he is arguing from within a fairly vigorous and acceptable legal and moral tradition. He stated,

> But where a man breaks the Words of the Law by involuntary Ignorance, there he shall not be excused. As if a Person that is drunk kills another, this shall be Felony, and he shall be hanged for it, and yet he did it through Ignorance, for he was drunk he had not Understanding nor Memory; but inasmuch as that Ignorance was occasioned by his own Act and Folly, and he might have avoided it, he shall not be priviledged thereby. And *Aristotle* says, that such a Man deserves double Punishment, because he has doubly offended, *viz.* in being drunk to the evil Example of others, and in committing the

> Crime of Homicide. And this Act is said to be done *ignoranter*, for that he is the Cause of his own Ignorance: and so the Diversity appears between a thing done *ex ignorantia*, and *ignoranter*. And therefore, as I said, where the Words of a Law are broken to avoid a greater Inconvenience, or by Necessity, or Compulsion, or involuntary Ignorance, in all these Cases the law itself is not broken.

The Court was moved by the conjunction of Pollard's four "Causes" (as he called them), and granted relief.

We would add, at this point, that it is a short step to argue that Pollard, as reported by Plowden, was familiar with the discussion of intention and the voluntary which was made by Covarruvias in the course of *De Homicidio* (the treatise in short title). In the second part of the opus, *De delictis & conatibus*" (pp. 531b to 539b), the various senses of killing are analyzed. The essential element in the act as criminal is stated as, "*Voluntarium homicidium est, quod dolo mala anima occidendi comittitur*" (tom. 1, pars 11, paragraph 1, p. 532a). His discussion draws heavily upon that of St. Thomas in the *Summa Theologiae*, 1a2ae, Question 72: *De distinctione peccatotum*, the gist of which is that an action is specified by its object (or in relation to its object). For Aquinas, for an act to be sinful it had to be a deviation from the law of God, the deviation itself had to be disordered ("*inordinatio*"), and the sinful act had to be a voluntary act. Drawing upon Aquinas, Covarruvias states,

> ...*interior vero actus semper distiguitur secundum finem; exterior autem materialiter Secundum obiectum, in quo exercetur; idcirco maleficia proposito fine non sunt distinguenda, nec commode' distinguuntur, ex idem vlterius constat, si actuum humanorum distinctionem exposuerimus* (533a, *op. cit.*).

He then cites the long question of Aquinas from the *Summa Theologiae*, "*De bonitate et malitia humanorum actuum in generali*," S.T. 1a2ae, Question 18 (in eleven articles), which serves to recapitulate the Aquinian moral tradition and its entailments. The state of the Will, at the time of the doing of an act, determines the nature and quality of the act with reference to the agent. This is not to diminish the material qualities of an act (its *actus reins*); but it serves to indicate that even a neutral fact can be made evil if the will of the agent so directs. Covarruvias affirms this proposition from Aquinas (which we cite from a modern text):

> Sins are differentiated specifically by the voluntary act rather than the inherent disorder. But voluntary acts are specifically distinguished according to their objects...it follows that sins are properly differentiated into species according to their objects.[67]

It is strong enough for purposes of argument here to suggest that Covarruvias restates an Aquinian notion of an intentional object, and that how the agent considers the object of his intention will indicate one aspect of the moral worth or wrong of his act. It is not a condition to be considered solely in itself, for it would make the assigning of a moral predicate only what the agent wished. The protection, however, that Covarruvias as a lawyer would have had would have been an appeal to what the law declared. It would not be that of a purely speculative case of the kind, How is a moral predicate discovered? Rather, it would be the case such that of the agent it could be asked, What did you intend? And his reply would be measured against what the law had permitted. If a curious intention were advanced, e.g., "I intended only to make a noise to scare my cat"–and the noise the agent made was to cause a bomb to explode in a crowded airplane, then his intention would be measured against his knowledge or ignorance. The Court could hear that such was his intention, i.e., to make a noise, but they could refuse to sanction it as a defense to (say) murder because such ignorance on the part of *D* would not be considered exculpatory.

For this reason a medievalist or a renaissant would consider "intention" in its relation to "ignorance," and "ignorance" in its relation to "intention." How the merit of an act turned upon the nature of an intent (*versari in re illicita*) would, in theory, be brought about by considering the conditions affecting the subject, and by determining if the subject appreciated the material facts (*the actus reus*) or material elements surrounding his intention. The law possessed a formal and defined element (its definition as a sanction) which could be known. If the subject did not know the law, and by his action revealed that he did not know the law, then interrogation could be directed to his ignorance, and his state of ignorance evaluated, i.e., was it reasonable, crass, invincible, affected?

It can be seen that a model of reasonableness is being advanced by such a use of balances. If one attended only to intention, to the exclusion of all other elements, criminal conviction would be impossible. On the other hand, if one attended only to the material elements of a crime, then acquittal would seldom be the case. But there are some cases (like Attempt, or Conspiracy) when one must not only inquire after the intention of the agent, *and* be aware of the material elements comprising the defined crime, but one must also inquire under what conditions, or from what considerations, the agent came to form an intention, and act because of it. If an agent formed an intention which, *by definition*, the law labelled as criminal, it is yet a licit defense to that criminal labelling that the agent did not know that the intention he entertained (and may have acted under) was criminal. At this point the ignorance of the agent, and the causes of his ignorance, become a proper subject for legal inquiry with the probative aim of possibly excusing *D*.[68]

It is evident that *Reniger v. Fogossa*,[69] as a case, revealed that ignorance in relation to a defense was understood well in early common law, just as the elements of criminal intent, or malice, were understood well by examples from *R. v. Saunders and Archer*. We wish to turn now to *R. v. Salisbury*, (1553) 1. P1. 100. In a recent English case the citation given from Plowden was as we have stated; but in the *Commentaries* the case is reported as *Matters of the Crown happening at Salop* (1553) 1. P1. 96a-101, of which *Salisbury* is one of the reported cases contained within the wider scope of the "*Matters*."[70]

The power of *Salisbury* is that it shows a grasp of the purpose of the criminal sanction: namely, to deter. Contrary to what was held in *R. v. Anderson and Morris* (cited in the endnote below), *Salisbury* disputes the contention that there can be honor amongst thieves or wrongdoers. The facts of the case are these. One John Vane Salisbury joined in an affray with his Master. His Master had lain in wait to kill a third party, but none of the servants of the Master, including Salisbury, knew of the criminal intentions of the Master. All were charged with murder. Salisbury appealed. We wish to cite (relevant) portions of the case since the logic of decision is contained in the presentation of the case.

The question given for resolution was:

> And at the End of the Evidence, the Inquest demanded of the Court this Question, *viz.* if so be in the Truth, *John Vane*

> *Salisbury* was in the Company of them, who of their Malice prepense killed him that is dead, and when he saw them combating together, took Part with them suddenly, and had not Malice prepense, and struck, with the others, him that is dead, whether this be Murder or Manslaughter in *John Vane Salisbury*. [1.P1. 97 (1553) at 100-a].

Lord Chief Justice Parker drew upon two broad principles which he made the basis for a legal decision (as we have indicated in the previous endnote). He believed that an enterprise, even if criminal, was bound by limits, just* as the enterprise of a company or corporation may be bound by limits, and if the company or corporation exceeds the limits of its incorporation, then it, or directors or agents of it, may be said to have acted *ultra vires*. Secondly, the Lord Chief Justice assumed that the conscience of the community would be outraged if the manslaughter verdict, of the instant case, stood–having in mind, no doubt, the furor which *D. P. P. v. Smith* [1961] A. C. 290 had caused when the decision seemed to affirm constructive malice or the felony-murder rule, or seemed to substitute a judicial fiction which would be the rule in the case rather than to accept the given testimony, and intentions, of the defendant. We would wish to suggest, with due respect for the verdict in *Anderson and Morris*, that *Salisbury* reveals a subtle understanding of the degrees of malice. The Court framed a careful and logical reply (which appears to have withstood the test of time). It said, and we quote:

> The Court answered, if *John Vane Salisbury* had not Malice prepense, but suddenly took Part with them who had Malice prepense, this is Manslaughter in him, and not Murder, because he had not Malice Prepense.

John Vane Salisbury had been arraigned, with others, upon an indictment of Murder for the killing of one Denbigh, who was a servant to a Doctor Ellis. The note which Plowden makes to the reader is a careful one. In it he raises the problem of a cognitive test: namely, how much must one know to be charged with sharing in the criminal intention of another? Plowden (at 100-a of 1.P1.97 [1553]) states:

> *Quod nota bene* (Lector) for I have heard this greatly doubted, *viz*, if the Master lies in Wait in the High-Way to kill a Man, and his Servants attend upon him, and the Master does not

---

* We wish to note that the *ultra vires* does not occur in the judgment. We have advanced the comparison, beginning at "just as the enterprise...."

> make his Servants privy to his Intent, and afterwards he, for whom the Master lies in Wait, comes, and the Master attacks him, and his Servants, seeing their Master fighting, take his Part, and all of them kill the Man, whether or no this should be Murder in the Servants, as it shall be in the Master, because they, without Malice prepense, took Part with him that had Malice prepense.

The Court took the law to be:

> ...that the killing of him is Murder in the Prisoners, if they killed him upon the Malice which they had against the Master, so that if you shall find that they had Malice against the Doctor, that Malice does in the Eye of the Law make the killing of him that was killed, who was the Doctor's Servant, and in his Company, to be Murder. And therefore you must take the Law so: *quod nota bene Lector* (*ibid*).

The Court had earlier instructed the jury, and the Court had used the language of conspiracy in its instruction: "You, Jurors, have heard the Evidence which has been given to prove the Prisoners guilty of the Murder whereof they are impeached, which Evidence proves that the Conspiracy was to kill Doctor *Ellis*, and the Malice prepense was against him, and not particularly against his Servant who is killed." The Court reasoned that the jurors might think that if the Servants did not know their victim, and entertained no direct malice against him whom they had killed, then, perhaps, the jurors might reason that murder should not be found. The instruction of the Court to the jurors displaces the defense of oblique intention or unintended victim. But the discharging of the availability of that defense did not discharge the problems which malice prepense presented.

The Court reasoned in steps. To prove the major premise, that malice against one is malice against all, this was stated by it:

> When a Man has Malice against another, and intends to kill him, and endeavours to put his Purpose in Execution, and kills one that resists his Purpose, it cannot be otherwise but that by Necessity of Reason he has Malice against all those who would defeat his Design, and that he would offer Violence to them that would defend the Person against whom his Malice is directed, rather than desist from his Purpose, and therefore if he kills them to whom he had before-hand intended to offer such Violence, this cannot be any Thing else than Murder [1.P1. 97 (1553) at 100-a and 101].

The minor premise is contained in the conjunction, which carries on directly after this passage:

> ...and so the Act declares his Intent before, and the Malice against the Principal begets in himself another Malice against those whom he presumes will resist his Purpose, which Malices are combined one to the other inseparably [1.P1. 97 (1553) at 101].

The reasoning is artful, declaring that "action speaks louder than words." It is a careful use, we would suggest, of judicial analysis of the facts of a situation, reasoning that servants are confederates because there is no economy in murder. One would kill those who would stop his design; but only one person was killed; therefore, it appears that all shared in the design, the proof being that they were alive.

The Court had advanced a careful statement as to what was Malice prepense, drawing upon the model of conspiracy. But conspiracy must be demonstrated by some overt act; if not, a conspiracy remains a thought only unacted upon. In this instance, upon the instruction by the Court on the law, the jury found that some were guilty. The findings of the jury are private. We do not have records to tell us how they determined as they did. Two were found guilty of murder; one was acquitted; and John Vane Salisbury was acquitted of murder by reason of his lack of malice prepense, but was convicted of manslaughter. He was, however, later reprieved.

If one compares the two cases, *Salisbury* against a modern case, *Anderson and Morris* [1966],[71] or similar cases, one may argue that *Salisbury* affords a better rule to follow (if the aim of the criminal sanction is to educate and dissuade the public against forming any kind of criminal confederation). *Anderson and Morris* seems to advance an *ultra vires* model (as we have suggested), and it has to it the logic of precision bombing in which the claim may be advanced that measured harm can be done without risk of excess harm being done. But the reality principle is often more forceful. Hospitals, in time of war, do get bombed, even if inadvertently; and, in pub brawls, persons do get killed. Is it not a better rule of law to dissuade one from begetting a harm, the consequences of which often cannot be controlled, than to protect one who has initiated a harm by finding in his favor because he, for some reason or other (or, perhaps, no reason at all), could not predict the extent of the harm he engendered?

It may be suggested, purely as a problem of philosophical interest, that *Salisbury* avoids the difficult issue as to what truly an agent intended, and that Parker, C.J., was sympathetic to such a difficulty when permitting the appeal in *Anderson and Morris*. Is it, however, a serious jurisprudential problem to consider if an agent can make known to himself what he himself intends? and then make known to a third party the fact of his first-party intention? The law assumes that *A* can declare himself to *B*; it does not assume that every person is an isolated monad, windowless within the world of surrounding monads.[72] If difficulties arise in an exchange (be it contracts, torts, trusts, various chancery matters, criminal law, insurance law, administrative law, marital law, the law of agency and principal, etc.) the difficulty, it is assumed, is that an exchange can occur, but in the occurrence of that exchange there may be difficulties of clarity one to the other. The law will not accept solipsism. The philosopher may. But we doubt if a legal philosopher could entertain solipsism with seriousness. He may, however, appreciate that the production of some human actions are shrouded in mystery, and hence simple, efficient cognitive explanations of human action (to which legal liability may attach) may be difficult, or even not forthcoming because of limits of explanation. But we doubt if this is to embrace legal solipsism. The difficulty lies within the human condition itself, that we progress from ignorance to knowledge – and this is not peculiar to the law. It may be added that a felony-murder rule had long acceptance in common law, and still does. Even section 8 of the Criminal Justice Act, 1967, it may be recalled, directs the jury, or judge without jury, to consider all of the facts surrounding the behavior of an accused in a criminal case before rendering judgment upon an accused. Is *Salisbury* so much different from *Anderson and Morris* if one applies the test of believability to the facts of each case? Did not the Court in *Salisbury* state the law clearly to the jurors, indicating that it might strain believability to suggest that the servants of a master were not joined in his enterprise, he willing to kill a third party, why then not be willing to kill any of his servants who did not aid him? Is murder so mannerly?

Each case indicates that a judgment upon the finding will be left to the practical assessment of the jury, or the judge. What is important is that some matter, other than a private whim of a legislative body (as arbitrary arrest, or death without due course of legal defense, or a terror squad randomly killing victims), is given to the Court or jury to decide upon. The scale of probability tips in one direction or the other; legal findings are not infallible nor are the members of a Court or jury omniscient. It would be to belabor a straw man to claim that the law saw itself as such. As *Salisbury* revealed some were guilty, some were acquitted, and the accused himself was reprieved. It may have been the case that one of the principals in *Anderson and Morris* had made an agreement with another not to cause grievous bodily harm to the victim of their intended violence. But no philosophical or jurisprudential problem of deep merit arises from this consideration. What does arise, as in both cases, is what a jury will believe to have been the case between those accused of a capital offense. In one case the jury found that the accused did not have malice prepense, and they grounded their judgment upon two premises. The accused had not confederated with the Principal in his malice; the accused acted out of the heat of passion. These seemed to be believable premises to excuse or to mitigate. In the latter case the Court chose to believe that an agreement, although criminal between intending felons, had limits, and that one of the parties to the agreement exceeded the limits of what was agreed; i.e., pulled a knife and killed the victim. The Court chose to view this killing as the single act of *A*, and not a conjoint act of *A* with *B*. We are left with what is to be believed. It could be advanced that *Anderson and Morris* does not extend a legal principle, but was a case so peculiar that it was a holding only for that particular set of facts. If a principle is to be extracted from it, it may be of dubious footing that criminal testimony with regard to what *a priori* limits were put upon a crime should be testimony to be weighed in court when given by principals charged with serious criminal offenses.

That malice prepense was not confined to the actual doing of a deed, or commission of an act, is shown by Plowden in the first part of *Matters of the Crown* (1553) 1. P1. 97. It is cited as *Griffith ap David's Case*.

The facts of the case are these:

> DIVERS Persons of the County of *Montgomery* were indicted for killing *Oliver ap David ap Hoel Vaughan*,...of Malice

> prepense, *viz.* some for giving the Wounds whereof he died, and *Griffith ap David ap John* and others for that they were present, aiding, comforting, and abetting the other to commit the said Murder. And they, who gave the Wounds to the said Oliver, and killed him, had fled and escaped, and *Griffith ap David ap John* and the rest were brought to the Bar [1.P1. 97 (1553)].

Plowden, at the close of the discussion of this case, with an added appeal of one *Morris Gittin* [1.P1. 98 (1553)] in which an accessory to a felony was at Bar, noted (on page 100 of the instant report) that the law on the point was unsettled in principle, and had changed in fact. The old law is cited in the case from *40 Book of Assizes 25* (which appears to have been from a copy of the book held by *Bromley J.*, as his personal manuscript), as well as citing Hill *7. H. 4. Coram Rege* (Hilary Term), wherein two cases from that term supported the old law. The principle of the older law, Plowden notes, revolved around a simple problem. If *A* was charged with killing, but escaped, and *B* was charged as an accessory, and did not escape, should *B* be charged and put to death? The logical problem was: what if *A* were recovered, tried, and acquitted? The older law enforced the logical principle of transitivity, i.e., if to have "a" and "b" one needed "a," but "-a" was the case (the accused fled and his guilt or innocence was undetermined), then it was thought unfair to find against *B* by affirming that "b" was the case. This was the language of the Court, set in an example (on p. 97 of the instant case):

> If *A.* is indicted for the Rape of a Woman and *B.* is indicted for that he was present and abetting *A.* to do it, now they are both Principals by Law, and if *B.* is arraigned, and found guilty in Inquest, and afterwards *A.* is arraigned, and by another Inquest acquitted, now Judgement shall not be given against *B.* because he could not be guilty but in respect that *A.* was guilty.

The cases which Plowden recorded as cited in the instant case held that Accessories could not be tried unless the Principals were indicted. The logical principle appears to be fair, that if the value of "a" cannot be determined, but the value of "b" depends upon what value is assigned to "a," then "b" should not be judged until the value of "a"' has been determined; and to determine "a" required a finding and judgment of the Court.

But Plowden, as teacher, warns the reader:

> So, *Note*, that at this Day those who are present and abetting, or ready to do the Act, are Principals as well as he that does it,

> and may be arraigned notwithstanding the other Principals are absent and not attainted (on p. 100 of the instant case).

The force to Plowden's warning is drawn from *Griffith*. Having considered the problem which transitivity posed, that "b" should not be judged unless a value to "a" has been found at law, the Court rejected such reasoning by a discussion, much sophisticated, of a distinction between "legal fact" and "legal deed." The Court said, on page 98,

> So that it cannot be well termed that they, who gave the Wound, are Principals in Deed, and the other Principals in Law, but they are all Principals in Deed, and in one same Degree.

We witness an interesting exercise in practical logic. The reason the Court offers for determining no difference in the degree of gravity between aiding, abetting, and commission, is given here:

> When many come to do an Act, and one only does it, and the others are present abetting him, or ready to aid him in the Fact, they are Principals to all Intents as much as he that does the Fact: for the Presence of the others is a Terror to him that is assaulted, so that he dare not defend himself, for if a Man sees his Enemy and 20 of his Servants coming to assault him, and they all draw their Swords and surround him, and one only strikes him, so that he dies thereof, now the others shall with good Reason be adjudged as great Offenders as he that struck him, *for if they had not been present he might probably have defended himself, and so have escaped* [italics our].

The Court continues further in its reasoning, stating,

> So that their Presence is the Cause of Terror, and Terror is the Reason that he receives the Wounds, and the Wounds are the Cause of his Death. And then inasmuch as both together, *viz.* the Wounds and the Presence of the others, who gave no Wounds at all, are adjudged the Cause of his death, it follows that all of them, *viz.* those that strike, and the rest that are present, are in equal Degree, and each partakes of the Deed of the other (on p. 98 of the instant case).

The case was difficult for the Bench to consider. Some of the Justices felt that the earlier principle should have been followed, that of "not *B* unless *A*," but the practical reasoning of the Court, through the remaining Justices, affirmed a change in principle, as the reasoning abovestated indicated.

In *Hales v. Petit*, Michelmas Term, 4 and 5 Elizabeth in the Common Bench, (1562) 1 Pl. 253,* Lady Margaret Hales was the plaintiff in the action of Trespass. She was also, of late, widow of Sir James Hales who had committed suicide. The defendant in the action was Cyriack Petit, who was successful. The case revolved on a technical point that the action for Trespass would be defeated because the plaintiff, Lady Margaret Hales, no longer had an interest in the land which was trespassed upon by the defendant's cattle. The plaintiff lost her interest in the land directly as a result of her husband's suicide. The Court expressed it thusly, on p. 256 of the instant case:

> By reason of the Felony [i.e., the suicide of Sir James Hales] aforesaid by the aforesaid *James Hales*, in Form aforesaid, perpetrated and committed, were totally forfeited and lost to the aforesaid late King and Queen, and the whole Right and Interest of the aforesaid *Margaret*, of and in the same Premisses were ended and extinct.

We have a modern counterpart of the same principle. In some property actions only the owner of the property may bring a legal action, and not the occupier. The principle, however, in *Hales v. Petit* was that Lady Margaret, wife of the late Sir James, had lost any interest in the property in question due to his suicide. We cite the case not to stress ancient property law; rather, we cite the case to illustrate with what care Plowden recorded the distinctions between certain kinds of acts which were deemed to be felonious. He sets down that Sir James "killed and murdered himself" (p. 257a). The drowning of himself was described as *felo de se*, and act in which one puts an end to his own existence deliberately.** Plowden said that he had heard only

---

* A record of the case, Plowden wrote, appears among the Records of Trinity Term, 3 Elizabeth, Rot [uli Parliamentorum] 921. Cf. pp. 224-226 for an account of the case in *Law Reporting in England 1485-1585*, by L. W. Abbott (University of London, The Athlone Press, 1973). *Hamlet*, Act v., Scene 1 burlesques the case, as the two Clowns, preparing to dig a grave, discuss death by drowning, when the first Clown wonders if it should be a Christian burial: "How can that be, unless she drowned herself in her own defence?"

** "*Felo de se*" per 4 Bl. Com. 189, as cited by Pollock C. B. in *Clift v. Schwabe*, 3 C.B.476, may embrace unexpected harm e.g., *A*, intending to kill *B*, pulls the trigger of the gun, but the gun, in discharging, explodes, and *A* himself is killed by the unexpected explosion, and *B* is not harmed; "...or commits any unlawful, malicious, act the consequence of which is his own death, as if attempting to kill another he runs upon his antagonist's sword; or shooting at another the gun bursts and kills himself."

Lord Dyer's reasoning on the case, who said that the case had five elements to it:

> First, the Quality of the Offence of Sir *James Hales*; secondly, to whom the Offence is committed; thirdly, what shall be forfeit; fourthly, from what Time the Forfeiture shall commence; and fifthly, if the Term here shall be taken from the Wife (pp. 260a-261).

The "quality" of the act was murder, not a simple killing, nor manslaughter.

> For Homicide is the killing a Man feloniously with Malice prepense, but Murder is the killing a Man with malice prepense (p. 261).

(The side-note in Plowden refers the reader to S. P. C. 18-b, which is Staundford's *Plees del Corone*, "Murder," cap. 10., of Lib. 1., which recapitulates Bracton and Britton on malice prepense.) In the instant case,

> And here the killing of himself was prepensed and resolved in his Mind before the Act was done. And also it agrees in another Point with the ancient Definition of Murder,* *viz.*, [*sic.*, Bracton 134 b; Britton, cap. 6; S. P. C. 12 e, and 17e] that *murdrum est occulta hominum occisio, nullo praesente, nullo sciente*; so that always he who determines to kill himself, determines by the Instigation of the Devil to do it secretly, *nullo praesente, nullo sciente*, lest he should else be prevented from doing it. Wherefore the Quality of the Offence is Murder (p. 261).

The stealthfulness of the act is no longer an aspect of the definition of murder for the common law. The definition does not make the distinction between the act as described (by law) and known by law. The Court may have answered that it would be unreal to expect that the agent did not know that what he was doing was forbidden. Yet the objection may be lodged, even if a mild objection, that to do what is forbidden does not entail that one knows what one is doing is forbidden.**

---

* Note: The French for pertinent portions of this text we take from the first edition of the *Commentaries*, 1571. "*Et quant al qualitie del offence q le offedour icy ad fait, il dit q il est en degree del murder, et nemy de homycide.s.manslaughter, car homycide est le occider de home feloniousment sans malice prepence, mes murdur est occider del home sur malice prepence. Et icy le occider de luy fuit prepense et resolue en sa ment deuaunt le act fait, et auxi il agree en aut point oue le auncient definicio del murder (folio 261).*

** The various manuals of the confessors were careful to preserve the distinction between the matter of the act (or action) which was sinful, and the penitent knowing that his own act (or action) was sinful. Aquinas, at S.T. 1a2ae.76, 4, *Utrum ignorantia diminuat peccatum* could see this distinction between matter done, and the subject doing, as a way to

To the second point the Court found that his death was an "Offence against Nature, against God, and against the King" (p. 261). Deciding upon the forfeiture, the Court passed to the fourth point regarding the death; namely, Time. It reasoned in this way:

> And...if one strikes another, so that afterwards he dies of it, the Indictment ought to say that he struck him feloniously. So that the Felony is attributed to the Act, which Act is always done by a living Man, and in his Lifetime, as *Brown* (Justice Anthony Brown in the case) said; for, he said, Sir *James Hales* was dead, and how came he to his Death? It may be answered by drowning; and who drowned him? Sir *James Hale*; and when did he drown him? In his Life-time. So that Sir *James Hales* being alive caused Sir *James Hales* to die; and the Act of the living Man was the Death of the dead Man" (p. 262).

The context of the reasoning saves one against a possible "Morning Star equals the Evening Star" confusion; i.e., is Sir James, when alive, equal to Sir James, now dead? What this selection from the judgment of the Court indicates is that the Court possessed a language with which it could intricately discuss the manner of a felony. One has only to cite the case to the Court on behalf of Lady Margaret (that the goods and chattels of her husband ought not to be subject to forfeiture) put by the Serjeant for the defendant. Here is a sample of Serjeant Walsh's reasoning, which we cite in part:

> And *Walsh* said, that the Act consists of three Parts. The first is the Imagination, which is a Reflection of Meditation of the Mind, whether or no it is convenient for him to destroy him, and what Way it can be done. The second is the Resolution, which is a Determination of the Mind to destroy himself, and to do it in this or that particular Way. The Third is the Perfection, which is the Execution of what the Mind has resolved to do. And this Perfection consists of two Parts, *viz.* the Beginning and the End. The Beginning is the doing of the Act which causes the Death, and the End is the Death, which is only a Sequel to the Act. And of all the Parts the doing of the Act is the greatest in the Judgement of our Law, and it is in Effect the whole, and the only Part that the Law looks upon to be material. For the Imagination of the Mind to do wrong, without an Act done, is not punishable in our Law, neither is the Resolution to do what Wrong, which he does not, punishable, but the doing of the Act is the only Point which the

---

excuse or extinguish a sin. Covarruvias (*op. cit.*) at *"De Delicitis & conatibus" Pars 1, section 2*, p. 532-b preserves the Aquinian teaching that ignorance may excuse.

> Law regards; for until the Act is done it cannot be an Offence to the World, and when the Act is done it is punishable. Then here the Act done by Sir *James Hales*, which is evil and the Cause of his Death, is the throwing himself into the Water, and the Death is but a Sequel thereof, and this evil Act ought some Way to be Punished (pp. 259, 259-a, and 260).

It was a long argument to dissuade the Court from connecting consequences, i.e., suicide should be punished in and of itself, and a suicide should not be linked to forfeiture of goods. The argument, however, did not move the Court. The subtle point of the defense was that the living should be punished as living; but the argument did not defease attainder. The report of the case states that Sir James Hales voluntarily drowned himself (pp. 254-a, 258). The discussion of suicide is ample, and the distinction is appreciated in the text between the agent and the patient, and that the act of suicide links these two aspects of a human act. It is the nature of a human act that a person may act upon himself, to his detriment, and the language of the judgment preserves this twinned aspect. It was not the case, certainly, that Sir James, when alive, was the same as Sir James, when dead. The subtlety of the Court's reasoning rested upon what view it took of a human act. The language of the Indictment gives us our answer:

> And the Indictment says, and may say, that he feloniously threw himself into the Water; for that which caused the Death may be said to be feloniously done. So that the Felony is attributed to the Act, which Act is always done by a living Man, and in his Life-time (p. 262).

We do not wish to dispute whether this instant case was "over-reasoned" in its analysis of suicide. Our purpose for citing the case was to show that the Court, then, was able to proffer subtle arguments, and that such a subtle style was part of the vocabulary and mind of the Court in some matters of criminal law.

To close, we wish to cite a case from the *Year Books* which possesses a poetic simplicity, containing as it does a simple statement and intuition of the doctrine of *versari in re illicita*. The general movement of this chapter has been to reveal, from older sources, that the common law was equipped in theory, however bare a statement of its theory may have been, to concern itself with the fineness of a human act from the standpoint of imputing or denying criminal intent. The accused in the case is not known.

ANONYMOUS

KING'S BENCH. 1498 YEAR BOOK 14 HEN VII. f. 14. Hil. 5.

HUSSY [C.J.] said that a question was asked of him, which was this: – A clerk of a church, being in a room, struck another with the keys of the church. And by the force of the blow the keys slipped from his hand, and went through a window and struck out a woman's eye. Should this be called mayhem or no? – that was the question. And to him it seemed that it should; for at the beginning this man had a bad intent.

Endnotes Chapter 5

1. *Cf., The History of the Canon Law in England*, by William Stubbs (p. 274), contained in *Select Essays in Anglo-American Legal History*, volume 1 (Wildy & Sons, Ltd., 1968), pp. 248-288.

2. One may also refer to the holdings of various great libraries in England to substantiate the hypothesis that medieval and Renaissance legal writing continued to exercise an influence upon our developing common law. For instance, *cf., Records of All Souls College Library, 1437-1600*, by N. R. Ker (published for: The Oxford Bibliographical Society *by the* Oxford University Press, 1971), p. 66ff., "List XVIII" which is the earliest list of law books of the library, revealing medieval and Renaissance authors; also, *cf.*, the holdings of the libraries of each of the Inns of Court to see the extent of medieval and Renaissance holdings in law. One may consult, to evidence the extent of the medieval and renaissance holding of legal texts, the *General Report to The King In Council from the Honourable Board of Commissioners on The Public Records* (Printed by Command of His Majesty King William IV, under the direction of The Commissioners on the Public Records of the Kingdom, MDCCCXXXVII). especially the chapters entitled, "Courts of Justice) (pp. 111-281), and "Inns of Court" (pp. 352-391). One may also consult the four-volume catalogue, *A Catalogue of the Printed Books in the Library of the Honourable Society of the Middle Temple*, C. E. A. Bedwell, Keeper of the Library (by Glasgow: University Press, 1914, and 1924 [the fourth volume]), to witness the presence of extensive medieval and Renaissance holdings in law. Such will be found, also, in the libraries of each of the other three Inns of Court, such as, for instance, the recent three bolume edition of: 'Catalogue of Manuscripts in the Library of the Library of Honourable Society of the Inner Temple Library' edoted by J. Conway Davies (Oxford University Press, 1972). One is aware, too, that available to the English legal scholar was not only the literature developing in England on law from the sixteenth-century, but that the Continent held vast legal resources which were available to the lawyers in the Inns. Great dictionaries of law which embraced Continental principles in legal definitions were of use to the English lawyer. For instance: *Lexicon Juridicum: Hoc est, Iuris Civilis et Canonici in Shola atque foro usitatarum vocum Penus* (Geneva: J. Stoer, 1615), a work attributed to John Calvin, and a legal dictionary which went through many editions, and from 1300 to 2000 pages in length. (The British Museum Catalogue records editions of: 1600, 1610, 1619, 1645 [*cf.*, Catalogue, Volume 4, p. 1016, columns 328-329, Calvinus (Joannes)].) Ample English legal dictionaries, ranking (say) with Calvin's in merit and depth, do not come until the middle of the 17th century, i.e., Cowell, Rastell (late 16th), Leigh, and the like.

3. It is not our chief concern to discuss intention in statute law, this having been done in 1955 in J. Ll. J. Edwards's study *Mens Rea in Statutory Offences* (London: Macmillan & Co., Ltd., 1955). One could argue, by appeal to the language of cases, that statutory concepts follow upon case law. Edwards argues that the legal adverb, "knowingly" is late in English legal

usage; but one could assert that the legal concept "to know what one was doing" was not a strange or novel concept when used to establish guilt, and one was aware of the medieval literature which existed on madness (*furiosus*) which exempted or excused an accused from guilt because the accused was assumed not to know what he had done. One may consult chapter III, entitled, "Knowingly" (pp. 52-97) in Edwards which shows how the adverb comes late into English statutory language. Examples wherein "wittingly" equals "knowingly" (and not to be found in Edwards' study) may be taken from: *The Laws of Q. Elizabeth, K. James, and K. Charles, the First, Concerning Jesuits, Seminary Priests, Recusants*, etc., Explained by William Cawley, of Inner Temple (London: John Wright and Richard Chiswell, MDCLXXX). (The work may be cited in short form, as *Laws against Recusants*, with Wing listing as: Wing-C-1651c.) *Stat*. v *Eliz.* cap. 1., s 2 (p. 33 of Cawley) states, "That if any person....shall by Writing, Cyphering, Printing, Preaching or Teaching, Deed or Act, advisedly and *wittingly*..." and later, (p. 34, Cawley), "...or by any Speech, open Deed or Act, advisedly and *wittingly* attribute..." (italics ours). Cawley does not gloss "wittingly" here, since it is assumed that from its use the word needs no comment. He does, however, in the same statute, put a gloss upon, "*Upon Purpose and to the Intent*" (p. 35) and states: "A was Indicted upon this Statute, and that of 13 *Eliz. cap* 2. of a *Praemunire* for aiding one B. *knowing* (italics ours) him to be a principal maintainer of the ...See of Rome." He continues by saying, "And it was held, by the greater part of the Justices, that the Indictment was insufficient, for want of those words (*Upon purpose, and to the intent, to set forth and extol the Authority*, etc.)," and continuing, states, "And *'contra formam Statut'* will not supply that defect, *Trin*. 20 *Eliz. Dyer* 363. Note, in the Report of this Case of the Statute of I *Eliz*. is mistaken for this of 5 *Eliz*. there being no mention of the intent in that of *Primo*. The intent is a hidden thing, and lies in the Heart, and therefore there must be some Overt Act or Speech which declares the intent; for the intent itself is not traversable, but that by which it is made manifest, as was judged in *Boothes* Case, Co. 5. 77." In his commentary upon Stat. xxvii *Eliz*. cap. ii., "An Act against Jesuits," Cawley, upon section six of that statute ["And every person...shall wittingly and willingly receive" (page 90)] says "And if we weigh the Grammatical construction of the words," one will conclude that "the receiving, relieving or maintaining of a Jesuit...and *know*n by the party to be such, is Felony," within the meaning of the Act. Here, the commentator takes "wittingly" to mean "knowingly." We shall have reason to cite from Cawley later because of his appeal to "intention" to explain the finding of an offense under a statute. His explication was, sadly, legal literature generally lost to us, no doubt owing to the rarity of his text. For an example of "wilful murder" one may turn to the language of 23 *Hen*. VIII, cap 1 (1532) which, in part, reads: "Be it therefore enacted by the King...That no person nor persons, which hereafter shal happen to be found guilty after the Lawes of this Land for any manner of petit treason, or for any *wilfull* murder of malice prepensed,...or for *wilfull* burning of any dwelling houses," as cited in: *A Collection of Statutes*, by Ferdinando Pulton (London: M. Flesher and R. Young, 1640 [S. T. C. number: 9331]), p. 506. *In Statutes Now in Use in the Kingdom of Ireland* (Dublin: printed for B. Tooke, 1678) the use of "cause" is to be found in the statute of 10 *Hen*. VII, cap xi (1495) in, "that was causer of that murder," p. 37.

4. *Cf., A Collection of all the Statutes, from the beginning of Magna Charta, unto this present yeare of our Lord, 1579*, by William Rastall, Sergeant at Law (London: Anno Domini 1579). One may refer to the listing Beale-S 66 (in *Bibliography of Early English Law Books*, J. H. Beale [Ames Foundation, 1926]). For example, with regard to murder or manslaughter (Rastell, 344-a), the Coroner is simply directed to inquire:

> And the Coroner uppon the viewe of the body dead should enquire of hym or them y had done that death or murder, of their abbettours and consentours. And whoe were present when the death or murder was don, whether man or womã,...

The conditions, or what legal exemptions ought or may obtain, are not stated. It would have been for case law to determine what legal custom should dictate in the matter.

5. *Cf.*, Rastell, *ibid.*, "Treason," 518-b (col. 2)-529-b (col. 2), esp. 521-a (col. 1), "And be it that if any person...shall happen to bee attainted & convicted of high treason by authority of parliament, or by the due course of y common lawes or statutes of this Realme, and afterwardes fall to madnesse or lunacy, that yet neverthelesse they shall have and suffer execution, there [sic] madnesse or lunacy not withstanding" (An.33.H.8.cap.20). Harsh as this sounds, it is law which obtains in some common law jurisdictions in the United States, modified, that if the accused (for felony) gain his sanity, he is liable to full penalty (e.g., Washington State). In the Criminal Code of Canada, Section 16, subsection (1), (2), (3), we read:

> "(1) No person shall be convicted of an offence in respect of an act or omission on his part while he was insane.
>
> "(2) For the purposes of this section a person is insane when he is in a state of natural imbecility or has disease of the mind to an extent that renders him incapable of appreciating the nature and quality of an act or omission of knowing that an act or omission is wrong.
>
> "(3) A person who has specific delusions, but is in other respects sane, shall not be acquitted on the ground of insanity unless the delusions caused him to believe in the existence of a state of things that, if it existed, would have justified or excused his act or omission."

Subsection (3) of the Code may appear to be as harsh as the statute under Henry viii.

6. The edition which we have consulted is: *Les Plees del Corone, Divisees in Plusors Titles & Common Lieux*, by Gvilliavlme Stavndford (Londoni: ex Typographia Societatis Stationariorum, Anno Domini 1607). For this edition the S.T.C. number is: STC-23224. [In legal citations his name is variously listed as: William Stavnford, or Staundford (the modern spelling), or Stanford, or Stamford.] We shall cite this edition simply as *Pleas*, Staundford, and use the folio pagination of the 1607 edition. The above-listed citation if from: *Pleas*, Staundford, Cap. l., folio 1a, "Cy commensa le Liure entitle les Plees del Corone."

7. We make mention here of an English abridgement of Staundford which is entitled: *A Vade Mecum and Cornu Copia. An Epitome of Master Stamford's Pleas of The Crown, With other Notes out of approved and good Authors of the same Argument*, by Wa. Young (London: Printed, *Anno Dom* 1660). In *Wing* this edition is listed under number Y-95. The edition which we have consulted is the above, although the directions in the edition tell one that, "The Committee of the House of Commons concerning Printing stated that the book, *A Vade Mecum*, could be printed as of May 26th, 1642." Citations which we shall make will be to the text of 1660, and we shall cite the work simply as *Vade Mecum*. In passing we wish to note that this is a modestly rare text, and, such the case, we shall make our citations ample in light of the few recorded copies of the text to be found in libraries.

8. In 1548, Sir William Staundford completed this exposition: *An Exposition of the Kings Prerogatiue, collected out of the great Abridgement of Iustice Fitzherbert, and other old Writers of the Lawes of England*, by the right Worshipfull Sir William Standford Knight, lately one of *the Iustices of the late Queenes* Maiesties Court of Common Plees (London: Printed for the Company of Stationers, 1607, *Cum priuilegio*). We shall cite this work as: Stanford's *Fitzherbert*, preserving the variant spelling "Staundford." The S.T.C. number for this edition is: S.T.C.-23218.

9. (1584) 3 Co. Rep. at 7b, 76 E. R. at 638. There is not a golden rule for interpreting statutes, and we do not wish to imply that Staundford, in Fitzherbert, gave one a simple rule or formula for so doing. What we wish to incline one to accept is that in the abridgement of *Fitzherbert* which Staundford composed one is made aware that the language of the law must be attended to with linguistic sensitivity, and that, in some respects, language itself put limitations upon the powers which law may confer. The difficult problem which statutes present is, in the main, outside of the purview of this study, but one may read an excellent and short statement of the difficulties of statutory interpretation in: "The Interpretation of Statutes" (chapter seven), pp. 96-104, in *Learning the Law*, by Glanville Williams, FBA, QC, (Stevens, 1969). Staundford's *Fitzherbert* discusses other than the interpretation of statutes. He takes care to present what other authors may have written, citing from Bracton, or Britton, or other writers of various books for directing Justices of the Peace; or he may cite statutory authority to explain how an action operates, such as "Trauers" ["Traverse"], for example, "Traverse to an Office, entitling the King to land by the attainder of another of Felony, treason, or premunire. 2 Ed. 6.8." (as cited in Pulton's *Statutes*, 1640, under "Traverse"), is commented on at length by Staundford to explain the purpose of the action; or he may gloss a legal term, as "catalla" or "felon" and explain what could be its various legal usages. An example of this kind of commentary at length is to be found in Cap. 16, *Corone*, folios 44b to 50a, of the 1607 edition of Staundford's *Fitzherbert*. Not found at length in the Abridgement is case law since case collections do not come into force until Plowden and Dyer made their collections of selected cases. One has an early model for legal analysis here. Staundford, for example, will begin with common usage, as when he says, "*Catalla* is a general word which comprehends as well Chattels mouable as not moueable," (folio 45-b), to its different particular uses.

10. *Ibid.*, Staundford, *Pleas*, folio 11a.

11. *Ibid.*, folio 11b.

12. *Cf.*, *Criminal Trials*, by David Jardine (1832) for an account of the case; or *History and Principles of the Law of Evidence*, by J. G. Phillimore (1850), p. 157ff.

13. Thorne, *op. cit.*, p. 340, "Pleas of the Crown," in Volume II of De Legibus.

To compare texts, we shall first reproduce the Latin text from Thorne, and then we shall reproduce the Latin text of Staundford's *Plees*, the 1607 edition. Thorne, p. 340-a, reads:

> *Sed corporale est quo homo occiditur corporaliter, et hoc dupliciter committitur, lingua vel facto. Lingua tribus modis, scilicet praecepto, consilio, defensione sive tentione. Facto quotuor modis, scilicet iustitia, necessitate, casu et voluntate. Iustitia, ut cum iudex vel minister reum iuste damnatum occidit. Istud autem homicidium si sit ex livore vel delectatione effundendi humanum sanguinem, licet ille iuste occidatur, iste tamen peccat mortaliter propter intentionem corruptam.*

From Staundford's *Plees* we read in Lib. l, folio 11b to 12a, "*Est enim homicid 'hominis occisio, ab homine fact.' Si auté a boue, cane vel alia re, nō dicitur npprie homicid': dicitur homicidum ab homine, & cedo quasi hominis cediū. Species homicidij sunt multae, nam aliud spūale, aliud corporale, de spūali vero ad presends non est dicend. Sed corporale est quo homo occiditur corporaliter, & hoc dupliciter committitur, lingua & facto. Lingua, tribus modis, s. precepto, consilio, defensione vel tuitione ["by intention"]: facto, quaturo modis, s. iustitia, necessitate, casu, & voluntate. Iustitia, vt cum iudex vel iustitiar̄, reum iuste danat̄ occidit. Istud autem homicidium si fit ex liuore vel delectatione effundendi humanum sangiunem licet ill' iuste occidat̄, iudex tū peccat mortalit̄, nppt̄ intentionē corruptā.*" [We have preserved the type font of the text, save to print 's' in place of 'f' (the older 's'), and have preserved the joint letter 'np'.]

14. *Henry De Bracton* by Samuel E. Thorne, on the occasion of the 700th anniversary of the death of Henry de Bracton, (printed by: The University of Exeter, 1970) p. 20. The warning which Thorne gives is not new to the labors of Bracton scholars. One need only refer to the essay, "The Text of Bracton," by Paul Vinogradoff to appreciate the textual difficulties which Bracton presented from the edition of Sir Travers Twiss, onwards. The essay may be found either in *The Law Quarterly Review*, April 1885, or in volume one of *The Collected Papers of Paul Vinogradoff* (Oxford: At The Clarendon Press, 1928), pp. 77-90. It is outside of our purpose to list the considerable literature on the subject.

15. *Cf.*, the preface of the text, "Lectore," of the *Plees*, folio A-ij.

16. *Ibid.*, volume II, p. 341 at f. 121.

17. *Ibid.*, *Plees*, Lib. 1, 12a at line C6.

18. *Ibid*. One will recall that *D. P. P. v. Smith* [1961] A. C. 290, was the verdict which served to occasion the remitting of the doctrine of constructive malice. The Home Office reprieved *D* in the instant case.

19. *Cf*., *State v. Bingham*, 40 Wn. App. 553 (1985) re: "premeditation."

20. Thorne, *op. cit*., volume II, p. 341. The text of Staundford reads as follows: "*LICITE. Si vero licite rei operam dabat, vt si magister causa disciplinae discipulum verberauerit, vel dum quis deponebat fenum de curru, vel arborem incidebat & hmidi, adhibuit dilegentiam quam potuit, s. respiciendo, & proclamando, nec nimis tarde, aut dimisse, sed tempore congruo & ita clamose, vt si aliquis ibi fuisset, vel illuc venisset, potuisset aufugere, aut sibi praecauere, non imputabitur ei. Idem iuris est de magistro non excedendo modum verberandi discipulum*." From Lib. 1, 12a, C - D. A simple case of an undefined intentional act may be this. *D* takes a shopping cart from the Sainsbury supermarket. *D*'s intention is take her groceries to her car. The shopping cart has a notice appended to it: "The Metropolitan police are liable to prosecute any person who causes an obstruction by carelessly leaving a shopping cart." *D*'s legal responsibility is larger than her immediate intention, i.e., to use the cart as a conveyance. *D* must also safely use the cart, and it would not (most likely) be an adequate defense to the charge of obstruction that she had intended *only* to deliver her groceries to her car. From the events, therefore a criminal intention is constructed, i.e., attributed to *D*.

21. Early writers, like M. Andreas Laurentius, in his *A Discourse of the Preservation of Sight* (1599) in the Oxford edition of 1938, did interest themselves in the workings of the brain as the chief organ of the body (*cf*. Chapter 1), but always as "the chiefe and principall seate of the soule" (p. 9 thereof).

22. *Plees* at 1a.

23. *Ibid*., at 4a and 4b, and also 11a.

24. *The Boke of Justices of Peas, 1506*, reproduced in: *Classical English Law Texts*, General Editor, P. R. Glazebrook (London: Professional Books Limited, 1972). One may read the Editor's introduction to the text (pp. iii-vii), which copy was produced from the sole surviving copy in England from the Library of Stonyhurst College, for listing of other editons of the work. One should also consult *Oxford Studies in Social and Legal History*, edited by Sir Paul Vinogradoff, Volume VII, "Early Treatises on the Practice of the Justices of the Peace in the Fifteenth and Sixteenth Centuries," by B. H. Putnam, Ph.D. (Oxford: At The Clarendon Press, 1924) in conjunction with *The Boke, 1506*. Note: No pagination exists in *The Boke*, but the citations are located e. g., "ca. primo."

25. *Ibid*.

26. *Year Book of Edward I*, Volume One, p. 497 ff.

27. *The Boke*, 1506.

28. *Ibid*.

29. *Ibid*., though a pagination is indicated by the signature "Bi" in the folio. We have indicated the caption, above, to correspond to the odd appearance of it in the text itself.

30. *Ibid*., at Ca. iv of the "folio."

31. As reported in Pulton (*infra*), p.430, we read: *"No lay person that doth murder his Lord or Master, shall have his Clergie*. Where abominable and wilfull prepensed Murders be by the Lawes of God & naturall reason forbidden, and are go be exchewed, yet not the lesse, many & diuers unreasonable and detestable persons, lacking grace, wilfully commit Murder, to the high displeasure of God, and contrary to all the Lawes abouesaid, and moreouer, against their naturall & obliged duty, wilfully commit prepensed Murder, in slaying their Master...in trust [hope] to eschew the perill & execution of the Law by benefit of their clery: In hope whereof, of late one James Grame, late of London yeoman, wilfully assented and prepensed the murder of one Richard Tracy Gentleman, then his Master, by him & his prepensed assent, the xix. day of February last past, at Brentwood...murdered and slaine, to the right perillous ensample of other euill disposed:...be it enacted, That the said James Grame, for the murder of the said Richard Tracy his late Master be attainted of the said murder as a felon that hath offended in pety treason,...& that the same James for...doing like murder have or ought to bee punished, and any priuiledge of his Clergy, or his demand for same, notwithstanding." Note: The case also stated, "...that if any lay person hereafter prepensedly murder their Lord, Master, of Soueraigne immediate, that they hereafter be not admitted to their Clergy..." revoking benefit of Clergy. Pulton noted that Stat 23. H.8.l. and l. Ed. 6.12. reaffirmed the force of this Statute. It should be appreciated that Parliament, temporal and spiritual, was in this case called upon to render a decision in a felony case, and as a result of the decision a Statute was enacted. (Obviously, 20th-century Parliamentary procedure would not do the same, respecting the distinction between executive and judicial matters) Citation taken from: *De Pace et Regni*...[by] Ferdinando Pvlton (London: Printed for the Companie of Stationers, An. Dom. 1610 [second edition]).

32. *Ibid*., folio xi, Ca. vii.

33. *Infra*, p. 301. This edition was auctioned at Bonhams, London, on November 26th, 1975, and its owner was gracious enough to permit us to have these pages reproduced for use in research. We are grateful both to the firm of Charles W. Traylen, Guildford, England and to his Principal, a distinguished Wall Street lawyer, for extending us the privilege to use and to reproduce an exceedingly rare text. There is a question whether the British Museum copy is the same as this copy. The 1574 edition of the "First The Booke for a Justivce of Peace" [printed by Richarde Tottyl, 1574, London] carries over the same language as the Berthedet text of 1534. The Tottyl

edition discusses murder and manslaughter, pp. 9 (b) – 10 (a). (The edition is listed in Beale as T-157, at page 129.)

34. *Cf.*, *A Mirour for Magistrates*, of Maister Baldwine, the edition of John Higins (Imprinted at London by Henry Marsh, being the asiigne of Thomas Marsh, neare to *Saint Dunstanes Church* in Fleetestreete, 1587). Any of the tales will serve to show that a full vocabulary existed to describe human gruesomeness. The tale of *The Lord Hastings* (folio 196-204) "...*vilanously murdered in the Tower of London* by Richard Duke of Glocester, the 13, of Iune, Anno 1483...," or "K. Richarde the iij...murdered his brothers children (1485)..." to his eventual downfall (folio 230-234), where it is interesting to read a portion of the closing stanza [sixth from the end of the poem, at folio 234-a]:

> The brand of malice thus kindling in my brest
> Of deadly hate which I to him did beare,
> Pricked mee forward, and had mee not desist,
> But boldly fight, and take at all no feare,
> To wyn the field, and Earle to conquere:
> Thus hoping glory greate to gayne and get,
> Mine army then in order did it set.

Whence we may observe how "malice" both serves to describe what is done through malice, and how "malice" serves to describe also that one acts by force of malice.

35. *Cf.*, "Language Strata," chapter iv, in *How I See Philosophy*, by F. Waismann (London: Macmillan, 1968), pp. 91-121.

36. Putnam, *op. cit.*, p. iv.

37. *First the Booke for a Justice of Peace* (Imprinted at Londö in Fletestrete, within *Temple Barre a the signe of the hand & Starre by Richarde Tottyl* (...), 1574). Note: This edition is 195 folio pages, plus The Table. It is listed in *Beale* as T-157 (Harvard: 1926), p. 129.

38. Putnam, *op. cit.*, p. 209.

39. *Ibid.*, pp. 210-211. Sir Robert Brooke in his "Abridgement," compiled before 1558, but not published until 1568, citing Marowe on Commission and Riots, as well as some of Marowe's court arguments.

40. William Fleetwood, of Middle Temple's manuscript of 1565, "The Office of a Justice of Peace..." was printed in 1658, giving reference to Marowe.

41. Indeed omissions to parallel antiquarian law texts may be a rule, and not an exception, owing to the state of antiquarian law holdings. Where Putnam p. 219 of her study, says: The earliest references that have come to my attention are in Fraunce, 'The Lawiers Logike' [1588 at 44] and in Cowell, "The Interpreter' [1607]," one has a case of not all texts being known or available to her. *Terms De la Ley* (attributed to Rastall), the edition of 1598 printed in London by Thomas Wight and Bonham Norton, makes reference to Marowe, "1.Ma.cap. 12" under the entry for "Rout," p. 175. William Fulbecke's "A Parallele or Conference of the Civill Law..." printed

by Thomas Wight at London in 1601 (first edition), makes reference to Marowe in the twelfth dialogue of the work, concerned there with "vnlawful assemblies, riots, routes, and forcible entries" (p. 83-b). The reference appears as: "Marr. lect 8." It is still not unusual for legal citations to be drawn from sole manuscripts. *Reference under s.48A of the Criminal Appeal (Northern Ireland) Act* 1968 (*No.* 1 *of* 1975) H. L. [1976] 1 All E. R. 937, when heard by the Law Lords required the manuscript copy of *Rex v. Thomas* because references to the case were inexact. The manuscript copy dated from 1816 of Bayley, J., and differed in detail from the case as it was printed in *Cases on Criminal Law* (3rd ed., 1964) of Turner and Armitage (Cambridge), or from its original appearance (1816) 4 M. and S. 441 (Maule & Selwyn's King's Bench Reports, 1813-17).

42. Putnam, *op. cit.*, p. 198. It could be argued, we believe, that Marowe was affirming a tradition, of which Bracton was a chief legal example, but which division of crimes, as we have seen, was not in statement unique to Bracton.

43. *Ibid.*, p. 378.

44. One may read a simple and clear discussion on degrees of ignorance in Book Two, Chapter One, of Francis Hutcheson's, *A System of Moral Philosophy* (Glasgow: R and A. Foulis, 1755). The merit of the discussion is its simplicity, contradistinguished from medieval discussions of the same topic which are detailed, extremely complicated, and do not lend themselves to easy English. The chapter is entitled: "The circumstances which increase or diminish the Moral Good, or Evil of Actions," contained in Volume One, pp. 227-237.

45. Thorne, *op. cit.*, vol. II, p. 384: "*In maleficiis autem spectatur voluntas et non exitus*," whereupon the text continues, "But here we distinguish between true cause [and cause in] misadventure, by animals which lack reason, or other movable things, which provide the *occasio*, as a ship, a tree that crushes, etc."

46. *De Pace*, p. 379.

47. This case appears in *Placita Coram Rege* as selection number 104, pp. 154-156, and is listed as "*Coram Rege Roll, no. 431* (*Michaelmas* [A. D.] *1368, m.65d," published as Volume 82 (1965)* of the Selden Society as: *Selections in the Court of King's Bench, Edward III* (volume VI), edited by G. O. Sayles (London: Bernard Quaritch). The Latin for the selection reads:

> *..secundo noctanter ibi venerunt predicti R. P. et W. del I., seruientes eiusdem Iohannis, felonice vt felones domini regis insidiando et insultu premeditato contra pacem domini regis, coronam et dignitatem suam....Et predictus Ricardus percussit prefatum I. C. cum quodam securi dum idem I. iacebat in lecto suo dormiendo felonice ed ceduciose super capud suum....et fecit ei vnam plagam mortalem...vnde statim obiit* (p. 155).

48. The second case appears in the same volume, p. 174, selection number 104, and is listed as "*Coram Rege Roll, no,. 459* (*Michaelmas* [A. D.] *1375, m.39* (*crown*)." The Latin text, p. 174, reads:

> *...R. G. et R. C., seruientes ipsius W.deC., felonice vt felones et sedicione precogitata prefatum W.deC. ibidem super lectum suum sedentem interfecerunt, dando ei diuersas plagas mortales.*

49. *Ibid.* The entry in Beale is T-157, and it is given as the last edition of this title to be printed by Richarde Tottyl.

50. *Placita Coram Rege*, Case 43, *Coram Rege Roll*, no. 355, (Hilary 1349 [A.D.]), m. 77, p. 68 (London: Selden Society, 1965), Vol. 82.

51. "*Vn priest appell B. et vn femme fueront indite de poisoninge s. la feme come principal et le priest come accessore per reson de son commandment....*" H. 23. H.8 Pleas De Corone, from *The Reports of Sir John Spelman*, vol. I (London: Selden Society, 1976), vol. 93, edited by J. H. Baker p. 48.

52. *Cf.*, "The Defence of Coercion," by J. F. Garner, LL.M. [1954], *Criminal Law Review*, pp. 448-450, who stated that it was difficult to draw the general principle as to what are the elements in the concept of "coercion" which then may be applied to any case. The defense has to it the quality that *this case only* is peculiar, and as a defense ought not to be extended to a range of cases.

53. *Cf.*, *The Elements of Law*, Part 1., Chap. 12, by Thomas Hobbes (in the Tonnies edition, second edition edited by M. M. Goldsmith [London: Frank Cass & Co., Ltd., 1969], which is concerned with what is deliberation, what is the will, and what is the voluntary, and the like, pp. 61-63.

54. *R. v. Weston*, K.B., 17 May 1536, p. 103 of *Spelman's Reports*, (Selden Society, 1976), vol. 93.

55. *Cf.*, *Select Pleas of the Forest*, edited by G. J. Turner (Selden Society, 1899), vol. 13, throughout the volume.

56. *Ibid.*, V(a), the body of *Pleas of the Forest in County of Northhampton Before William le Breton et alii, in the Thirty-Ninth Year of the Reign of King Henry* [25 June 1255], p. 30

57. *Ibid.*, p. 30.

58. Stenton, *Pleas of Crown*, At Worcester, 1221, case number: 1145, "Ricardus de Eghoe et Henricus Estrech 'occiderunt Aliciam uxorem Ricardi Estrech de Estwud' et fugerunt...," p. 562, Latin, and p. 563, English (London: Selden Society, Bernard Quatrich, 1934), vol. 53.

59. Plowden's work is interchangeably known either as *The Commentaries* or *The Reports*. We have employed two editions for these notes in this chapter. We have used, *Les Commentaries, ou les Reports de Edmunde Plowden vn apprentice de le comen Ley* [*In Aedibus Richardi Totttelli*. Octobris 24. 1571, imprinted at London in Fleetstrete within Temple Barre]; also, *Cy Ensuont certeyne Cases Reportes, per Edmunde Plowden vn Apprentice de le commen ley* [Anno 1584]; also, *Vn Report fait per vn vncerteine authour del part de vn argument del Edmond Plowden de Melieu Temple* [In Aedibus Richardi Tottelli, 1584]. We used the two-volume English edition of *The Commentaries* (London: S. Brooke, 1816). We have used the standard form of legal citation, i.e., "Pl." = Plowden's Commentaries, 1550-80 [per: Sweet & Maxwell's Guide to *Law Reports* and *Statutes*, Fourth Edition (London:

1962)]. Note: S.T.C. 20040 and 20049, and Beale R487, R486a, and R488 are the citations for the original edition used here.

60. *Cf.*, Bracton, vol. II, Thorne edition, pp. 340, 341, and 342.

61. If one refers to Doctor Navarrus, either the *Opera Omnia* (Venice, 1618), or the four-volume edition of his works, *Opervm Martini Ab Azpilcveta Doct. Navarri, Tomvs Secundus* (Romae, Ex Typographia Iacobi Tornerij, M.D.LXXX), the work entitled *De Finibus humanorum actuum*" will show to what extent both intention and ignorance (its nature and causes) related to human action as categories by and through which legal responsibility could be either attributed to an agent or excused of an agent. [Romae edition, *a fol.* 466 usque 496; Venice edition pp. 90 onwards.] His extended discussion on ignorance will be found in *De Poenitentia in Septem distinctiones a fol.* 497 usque 874, Tom. II, Romae edition, or in the Venice edition. Interestingly, Navarrus states, "*Intentio est actus voluntatis*" (*de fin. humanorum actuum*, @Numerus 2, Romae edition), which puts him in a volitive position concerning human responsibility for acts.

62. *Cf. Opera Omnia* (*Antverpiae*: Apud H. Verdvssivm, M.DC.XXVII), pp. 521-564, esp., *Secvdnae Relectionis*, Partis initium, *De delictis & conatibus*, beginning with Q.l, "Homicidium quid sit, & de homicidio voluntario," p. 531, as well as *Tertia Hvivs Relectionnis Pars*, beginning at p. 556, and cited by Pollard, "*De delinquentibus ignoranter.*"

63. How the categories of "ignorance" and "intention" separately and jointly may have functioned in the writings of the great medieval theologians, philosophers, canonists, and lawyers, is itself matter for long and extended research and analysis. The texts are difficult to locate; most would be in Latin; and all would require a medievalist not only who could translate Latin well, but who could analyze what he had translated with some philosophical freshness. An extended analysis of the two topics in medieval literature of "ignorance" and "intention" awaits a scholar, or scholars, to write the study.

64. Chiefly, one may refer to these titles for the body of his arguments on the topic. In the *Sentences* he writes at 2-22-2-1, "Whether Ignorance is a Sin"; 2-22-2-2, "Whether Ignorance Excuses Sin", in the De Malo he writes at DM-3-6, "Whether Ignorance can be a cause of Sin"; at DM-3-7, "Whether Ignorance is a Sin"; at DM-3-8, "Whether Ignorance excuses Sin, or diminishes it." One may refer to the body of the *Summa Theologiae* and of the *Summa Contra Gentiles* for some development of the same concepts. In all cases one will note that Aquinas draws upon what other writers had to say; e.g., quoting from St. Augustine of Hippo, from John of Damascus, from Origen, from the writers of the Gospels and Acts, and the like. In the same fashion did the canonists and civilians appeal to early authorities, and transmitted their arguments.

65. *Cf.*, Index Capitvm, *Opervm Navarri*, entries under *'Ignorans'* and *'Ignorantia,' Romae* edition, cited.

66. *D.P.P. v. Majewski* H.L. [1976] 2 All E.R. 142, i.e., self-induced intoxication is not an excuse in crimes of general intent.

67. *Cf.*, *Summa Theologiae*, Volume 25 (la2ae. 72, article 1 [London: Blackfriars, 1978]) as translated by John Fearon, O.P. The Latin text, p. 28

of this edition, reads: "*Et ideo peccata specie distinguantur ex parte actuum voluntariorum, magis quam ex parte inordinationis in peccato existentis. Actus...voluntarii distinguuntur specie secundum objecta. Unde sequitur quod peccata proprie distinguantur specie secundum objecta.*"

68. One may refer to *Morissette v. United States*, 342 U.S. 246 (1951) when the Court inquired into the state of mind which accompanied the material elements of the crime. The Court found that *D* did not design to steal and convert government property, contrary to 18 U.S.C. @641, because, upon inquiry and examination, it was found that *D* did not knowingly and wilfully do acts as unlawful. Because *D*'s ignorance was believable, he was acquitted.

69. *Cf.*, "Accomplices and Transferred Malice," by David Lanham, Jan. 1980, L.Q.R. 110 for a further view of Plowden, and others of the period.

70. The case in which the modern citation occurs is: *R v. Anderson and Morris* [1966] 2 All E. R. 644. This was a case which revealed what Lord Chief Justice Parker himself uttered during the course of his written opinion, "The law, of course, is not completely logical, but there is nothing really illogical in such a result, in that it could well be said as a matter of common sense that in the latter circumstances the death resulted or was caused by the sudden action of the adventurer who decided to kill and killed." The *facts* of the case were simple: *A* and *M* agreed to attack *W*. *A*, however, stabbed *W*. At the time of trial *A* was convicted of murdering *W*; *M* was convicted of manslaughter. The theory upon which the convictions turned was that *A* and *M* had a common design. *M* appealed his conviction for manslaughter. The Court of Criminal Appeal granted his appeal, and found that the jury had been misdirected in the Court of first instance. Parker C.J. rejected the theory in *Salisbury* on two grounds. He thought that it might not have been reported correctly (a constant bugbear to any legal historian), and, "it is in the opinion of the court quite clear that the principle [enunciated in *Salisbury*] is wholly out of touch with the position today. It seems to this court that to say that adventurers are guilty of manslaughter when one of them has departed completely from the concerted action of the common design and has suddenly formed an intent to kill and has used a weapon and acted in a way which no party to the common design could suspect is something which would revolt the conscience of people today." American law would most likely follow *Salisbury* and reject Parker's finding.

71. In *Regina v. Caton* (1874), 12 Cox 624, we read: "LUSH, J., said that the only question for the jury was whether the prisoner struck the fatal blow. If two men concerted together to fight two other men with their fists, and one struck an unlucky blow causing death, both would be guilty of manslaughter. But if one used a knife, or other deadly weapon...without the knowledge or consent of the other, he only who struck with the weapon would be responsible for the death resulting from the blow given by it." "His lordship...[said]...Caton was only answerable for his own acts, and not if the other man struck the fatal blow."

72. "(2) What is much more usual [*viz.*, when an agent performs an action] occurs when the agent knows quite a lot about what he is doing, but does not know enough and, in particular, doesn't know what turns out to be the crucial point in the business. He may know, for instance, that he is pointing a gun

and pressing the trigger, and yet be ignorant that the gun was loaded....It would be tedious to make a list of the sub-types of ignorance of this order – ignorance of the instrument, of manner, of amount, of degree and so forth. In any case Aristotle has done it [*E. N.* gamma 1, 1111a.]..." p. 48, *On Human Freedom*, by John Laird.

CHAPTER SIX

The Last Scholastic: Sir Matthew Hale

The medieval period of the common law comes to a natural end in the writings of Sir Matthew Hale, Chief Justice of the King's Bench, who was at once a great medieval philosopher and theologian. He embodied the spirit of former centuries.

When the *Historia Placitorum Coronae* found its way into print under the guidance and editorship of Sollom Emlyn in 1736, the English criminal law had there a work which ordered and defined and refined the elements of the common law. Hale did what Coke did not: he gave an architectural structure and ponderance to our criminal law. History records the death of Lord Chief Justice Hale to have been on Christmas Day, 1676, at the age of sixty-eight. He was a profuse writer, not only upon the law, but upon religion, philosophy, and science, with a large number of his manuscripts unpublished and held by the British Museum.[1] What causes him to be different to consider is that he was a jurist who was also a philosopher.[2]

The small legal handbook, *Pleas of the Crown,*[3] is a simple and methodical outline of the criminal law. The "method" of the book was common for the time, and has been seen in earlier authors: a simple, bare statement of the elements of an offense, drawing upon statements given by earlier and authoritative authors.[4] From the early chapters[5] one may glean that Hale observes that there are distinct elements or features to a criminal offense. One must consider the actor, asking after his capacities, faculties, and abilities; one must consider the nature of an act itself, asking if it be lawful or unlawful; one must look to the object of an action. The relationship, which is complicated, between the law and the separate elements of a criminal offense are not dwelt upon; they are merely stated. A simple extraction will show his method:

> *Manslaughter,*
>
> KILLING another upon a sudden falling out, or provocation, or unjustifiable act, manslaughter.
>
> 2. What a *sudden provocation*?
>
> Two strive for the Wall, and one kill the other, Manslaughter?
>
> 3. What *unlawful act*, whereupon Death ensuing will make Manslaughter?
>
> If the unlawful act be deliberate, and tend to the personal hurt of any immediately, *or by way of necessary consequence* [italics ours], death ensuing, is Murder.
>
> But if either such deliberation or intent of personal hurt be wanting, Manslaughter.[6]

To describe the elements of a criminal act, Hale will use a vocabulary known to us. He will also use certain key terms in broad ways, and one will be required, from the context of a term's usage, to make sense of the meaning of the term. This example may suffice to show our meaning. When one speaks of "malice," it is a term which encompasses (and often confusedly) a wide variety of meanings. But there are some usages of the term which are clear, as the context will show:

Mute, Paine fort & dure.

> NOW we come *to the Demeanor of the Prisoner* upon his appearance:
> And thereupon either,
> 1. He stands Mute.
> 2. He Pleads.
> 3. Or he confesseth the Fact.
> 1. What said a *standing Mute?*
> When he answers nothing at all: and then it shall be enquired, whether he stand Mute by malice or by the act of God.
> If it be by the act of God, then the Felony shall be enquired of, and whether he be the same person, as if he had pleaded not guilty.
> If by Malice, or if the Prisoner hath cut out his own Tongue, then he shall have Penance.[7]

The understanding plainly is, when speaking here of "malice," that *D* is ill-disposed to testify to the court, for whatever reason on the part of *D* (as opposed to *D* who may have been incapacitated by madness or by an act of God). The significance of "malice" is direct and unsubtle in this context. The usage here is different from a form of the usage here: that a felony by statute is that of "5.H.4.c. 5. Malicious cutting out Tongue, or putting out Eye, Felony"[8]; and one may be transported to a higher level of abstraction, as in, "For an intention of evil, though not against a particular person, makes a malice."[9] A simple statement of "malice" in this regard is given by Hale in the entry concerning *Petit Treason*:

> [such] Is confined by *Stat*. 25 *E*.3. to three *Particulars:*
>
> 3. Where a Servant, upon Malice taken during his Service, kills his Master after departure from his Service.[10]

The use of "malice" is not bothersome or complex in this common instance.

When one comes to the early usages of "intent" – early with regard to appearance in Hale's own legal writing and his usage of the term[11] – one has to observe the context in which it occurs, and from a sum of contexts come to estimate the range of the word. Some of the contexts suggest the following meanings. An "intent" is distinct from a consequence or an act:

> *Witchcraft*
>
> The Statute of 1 *Jac*. 12. the only Law now in force against it, and divides it into *two Degrees:*
>
> 1. Witchcraft in the *first Degree* made Felony without benefit of Clergy, including *four Species....*
>
> 2. *Consult, covenant* with, *entertain, employ*, feed or reward any Evil Spirit to any intent, (though no act be done thereupon).[12]

In the same title, Hale uses "intent" to mean "cause" or "urge":

> 3. Or to the intent to *provoke* any Person *to unlawful Love*; these Clauses come under the word [*taking upon*].[13]

In the language of *Burglary* Hale (in the *Summary*) uses "intent" in its simple meaning; to aim at an end, to effect a purpose:

> If the House be broken and entred [sic] with an Intent to commit a Trespass, as to beat the Owner, no Felony.[14]

Following upon the passage the usage is instanced again, "If with intent to commit a Rape," and stands without need of commentary. A similar usage is found in his statement regarding *Larceny*:

> 1. He that hath a Special property, as a Bailiff, etc., they are his goods *pro tempore*. A. bails Goods to B. and after *to the intent to* charge B. [italics ours] steals them from him, Felony in A.[15]

To describe an aspect of the "intent," Hale will preface it with an adjective:

> A man throws a Stone at another, which glanceth and killeth another, Manslaughter; and not Murther, because no *malicious* intent to hurt (italics ours).[16]

One will also meet other standard forms in which "intent" is embodied; for instance,

> If A. and B. having malice *praepense*, meet and fight...[17]
>
> The malice intended
>
> * to one, *egreditur personam*, and makes the death of another upon that malice, Murther, and qualifies the act in the same manner, as if it had had its due effect.[18]

"Intend" will vary in form. It will, from the sense of the sentence(s) in the *Summary*, variously mean "directed to or against"; or "intend" will itself mean a malicious intent. Generally, the sentences are clear in this short treatise.

We draw upon these few instances of how Hale employed certain key terms to show that it is to the text itself one must turn to understand key concepts. But there is a further reason. Often the charge is given that "intent," and any of its derivative forms, was imprecisely used, and given over to producing confusion. We question this assumption. It tends to confuse the inherent irrefrangibility of the concept with the use of a term. The term may be correctly used, as we believe Hale's brief usages in the *Summary* reveal; but his correct usage does not, by its formality, remove the conceptual difficulties inherent in *mens rea*.

Hale preserves certain usages which were common for the period, but which may not primarily be accepted usage now. When he speaks of "compassing," as in, "Compassing by bare words is not an Overt act,"[19] it is an intentional verb (which usage was known to Coke[20]). Where in current usage a trial lawyer would ask if *D* was conscious of what he was doing or attempting, etc., Hale will speak of an act done "knowingly" by *D*. It is a usage we preserve at law, but in ordinary discourse it is an awkward or stilted usage. "Knowingly" tends to embrace "intent," but it does produce this awkward locution: *D* knowingly did what he did not intend. One may knowingly open the latch to enter a room, but one may unintentionally have entered the wrong room or the wrong house. One ought not to equate

---

* But "intended" here means more "directed against."

"intend" with "knowingly" as if they are synonymous. They *may* be used synonymously; they are not necessarily synonyms.

"Knowingly" may in its usage embrace several distinct concepts, as these examples will show:

> A man keeps a Beast used to strike knowingly, and ties it not up, the Beast kills a Man, Felony by some, by others not, but a great Misdemeanour.[21]

Or the essential ingredient to make an offense may be knowledge:

> All Treason included Misprision: The Concealing of any Treason, is declared Misprision only by the *Statute* of 1 & 2 *Mar.c.* 10 *que induce auxi misprision.*
> But this in case of bare knowledge; for if knowledge and Assent, it is Treason: and though the Treason be by *Statute*, yet the concealing thereof is Misprision of Treason.[22]

For the offense of bringing into the Realm counterfeit money an element of the offense is that the money is "brought knowingly" into the Realm.[23] In this instance the text itself does not resolve the difficulty, i.e., that one "knowingly brings in false money knowing it to be counterfeit," as opposed to a broader reading, "that one brings in money knowingly" and it is discovered to be false. This possible ambiguity is found in a number of statutory examples, chief of which is the meaning of "possession," as when *D* is charged with being in possession of some forbidden substance or the like.

The chief meaning of "intent" in this early work by Hale is that an "intent" is the production of an evil, mainly a legal wrong,[24] or the production of a harm not permitted by law.[25] This is to give a simple logical scheme. The complications within that scheme begin to arise when one asks: If there are, what then are the ultimate constituents of action under the law? Broad as the formulation of the question is, it is not a question for a philosopher who does not possess a pedigree. Aristotle asked a question of this form when he asked what were the ultimate constituents of drama, which reply was that drama is the imitation of an action. It may seem to be unwise to ask after an "ultimate," but one may mitigate any sense of queasiness in a search after *ultimates* by replying that an *ultimate* may take the form of being *this answer* to *this question.* An answer may be revised in the light of further knowledge.

We make this preface because Hale thought that he had explained human action, and, perhaps, ultimately. One is required to turn from his formal statements on the law and to turn to his theorizings about human nature found in *The Primitive Origination of Mankind...according to The Light of Nature*.[26] The portion of the vast book which is of concern here is that section which was entitled, *De Homine*,[27] which fell into the accepted tradition of defining what was the nature of human nature. Hale set out to prove, in very broad ways, that truth was an accepted part of the Christian tradition: namely, that the truths of reason would find themselves to be in harmony with divinely revealed truths as contained in the Christian religion. The Middle Ages knew the debate well,[28] and its extremes.

Hale presented and developed a faculty psychology, explaining human action by appeal to these faculties and their powers. In a lesser work, which will not concern us, Hale believed that demons and devils could influence human action, but this statement provides no prolonged analysis (other than to affirm an accepted truth of Christian believers).[29] The key to understanding human nature was its rationality, and rationality presented itself through the operation of various human faculties. It was a standard presentation of human powers at home in a variety of scholastic treatises. In addition to the standard five senses which man possessed, he also possessed two internal senses:

> The internal Sense are of two kinds, *viz.*, 1. Such as concern perception of Objects: 2. Such as concern the motion of them as useful, or from them as noxious.[30]

The seat of organization, whereby the manifold of perception was made a unity, was the brain, "where it distinguisheth the Objects of the several Sensories."[31] His statement of how one knows is clearly within the tradition of the scholastics:

> The Phantasie, that in a way unsearchable unto us, 1. Creates the Images of the things delivered from the several Senses to the *Commune Sensorium*: 2. Compounds those Images into some things not unlike Propositions, though confusedly and indistinctly: 3. Makes particular applications of them one to another though still darkly and confusedly, whereby it excites the Appetite either to prosecture their attainment, or fly from them.[32]

From this depiction of how a person comes to gain knowledge of the world,* Hale proceeds to state how knowledge may become action:

> The Estimative Faculty, which is indeed no other than the last operation or composition of the Phantasie before-mentioned, whereby it concludes that this is a sensible good or a sensible evil, that it is attainable or feasible, or not attainable; that though it be good, yet sometimes it is not safe to be attempted by reason of the impendence of a greater sensible evil. This seems to be the dark and confused shadow of the decision of the practical Intellect in Man.[33]

We hope that we have not wrongly chosen to state the issue. We have said that Hale tells us "how knowledge may become action." The key to having a theory of responsible human action is that *D*, as an agent, may not only know what he did, but do because of what he knows. An action is a production, broadly; but a responsible human action must be a production to which responsibility can be ascribed. It seems to be beyond the bounds of

---

* Note: The intricacies of what may be the essence of the Estimative Faculty in its development and use in medieval philosophy is a topic far outside the field of this study, and is a topic of research unto itself. The importance of the concept, long ignored, was pointed out by J. Peghaire, in his seminal article, "A Forgotten Sense: The Cogitative, according to St. Thomas Aquinas," *Modern Schoolman*, XX (1943): 123-140, and 210-219. The notion of an internal estimative sense is not confined to Aquinas. It was used (but seldom formulated in detail) by a number of medieval writers. *Cf.*, J. F. Quinn's study, *The Historical Constitution of St. Bonaventure's Philosophy* (Toronto, Canada: The Pontifical Institute of Mediaeval Studies, 1973), especially Chapter Four: "Potencies of Human Knowledge," pp. 323-365, at pp. 335 ff, the discussion of Bonaventure's understanding of the estimative sense, and contrast of that understanding with that of Aquinas', pp. 337-338: "Since the useful or harmful qualities of sensible things are not apprehended either by the exterior senses or by the imagination, another interior sense is required for this operation. That sense is called *estimative* in the animals, because, in them, it is a natural instinct. It is called a *cogitative* sense in man, who estimates the useful or harmful qualities of sensible things in a discursive manner; so, comparing the particular values of sensible things, his sense of estimation is also called a *particular reason*....Though he does not use the names *cogitative sense* and *particular reason*, Bonaventure's description of the estimative sense in man is not much different from the one given by Aquinas, for Bonaventure maintains it is reason which decides whether or not to take delight in a good thing perceived through the senses. For both theologians, then, the sense of estimation is conjoined to the sense appetities, but it operates under the control of reason. Aquinas takes a different stand from Bonaventure, however, on the signification of *sensuality*. For Bonaventure, the name signifies an integral power unifiying both the cognitive and the appetitive potencies of a man's sensitive nature. For Aquinas, the name *sensibility* designates the totality of cognitive and appetitive potencies of sense in man, whereas *sensuality*, properly understood, stands only for his sense appetitites...(for) Aquinas, the *cogitative* sense is connected to sensuality in a way similar to the connexion between the practical intellect and the will in the action of free choice" pp. 338-339.

ordinary usage to attribute (unless metaphorically) responsibility to non-cognitive causes. One's blood is not responsible for its iron deficiency. To be responsible implies both that one can know, is able to know, how to act; and that one voluntarily produces or authors one's responsible act. Or, simpler yet, that in authoring a human act one can be said to know what one did, and one freely did it. How far the responsibility will extend, to what range of consequences, will vary with what degree of responsibility is accepted as feasible (both for the agent, and to be imposed upon the agent).

Hale links "knowledge" with "action" in the sentence which says, "This seems to be the dark and confused shadow of the decision of the practical Intellect in Man." It is not that Hale is denying that one can know without error; it is, rather, that he is *assuming* that between knowledge and action there may be a confused and dark side. The wish as promise is seldom the promise one may wish. Broadly, too, Hale gives some ground to believe that man has a moral faculty, if only to state that it is possible for one to perceive naturally correct or naturally evil states of affairs. A moral sense is, in some way, a natural human sense. The act of making a moral judgment, even in its simplest sense, is an interior act of the soul.

In passing, it does command the remark, however, that the theory of a natural inner moral sense, or an inner sense upon which one may ground or justify a moral sense, is itself a difficult theory to defend (and, in our time, an attitude of mind much removed from our common moral sentiment in the English-speaking world).[34] At this point in our exposition we are not concerned with presenting a justification of Hale's moral exposition and assumptions. His general understanding of moral foundations is, in the main, consonant with writers of his period, and, in this regard, Hale is a consistent and conventional figure.[35]

As his exposition of the faculties continues it parallels a standard Aristotelian understanding of human senses and their operations. He does draw a parallel between natural appetites (*Appetitus naturalis*) and the human will, which, for sake of harmony in a theory, links together the material and immaterial aspects of human activity. Linking these two disparate realms, Hale says:

> Now as to what Faculty or those Faculties that concern the pursuit or flight of what is thus propounded by the Phantasie or Estimative Faculty, they are generally two: The *Appetitus naturalis*, which bears some analogy to the Will in the Reasonable Nature; and the acts thereof are either prosecution of the Sensible Object propounded, if presented by the Phantasie and Estimative Faculty as good; or else aversation from it, if presented as evil[36]

Upon a rather general form of Aristotelianism, transmitted through the Schoolmen, one is given an explanation for human action (towards the naturally good, or from the naturally evil, as perceived) based upon a Christian understanding of human nature as a hypostatic union of soul and body.

We need not give a detailed analysis of Hale's presentation of the operation of the intellective nature of the soul. He himself says briefly:

> Now to give a brief Inventory of the Excellence of the Human Nature...
>
> ---
>
> In relation to himself I shall briefly consider these particulars:
> 1. The excellency of his Soul or intellectual nature in its nature, faculties, acts and habits....[37]

The object of intellection is, *"omne intelligibile,"* and this is a class of objects far wider than the class of objects which comprise the class of sensible objects.[38] One such "object" for the human intellect is, "10. The moral goodness and congruity, or evilness, unfitness, and unseasonableness of moral or natural actions, which falls not within the verge of a brutal faculty."[39] An effect of the object of understanding is for that object to radiate or transmit itself throughout one's character; i.e., understanding the beneficent may produce a beneficent disposition in an agent:

> Concerning intellectual Habits or the genuine effects of these acts in the understanding Faculty, and they are divers and diversly expressed by those that have treated thereof.
>
> ---
>
> 5. Prudence; which is principally in reference to actions to be done; the due means, order, season, method of doing or not doing.
> 6. Moral Virtues; as Justice, Temperance, Sobriety, Fortitude, Patience, etc., for these begin in the Intellect, though their exercise belong principally to the faculty of the Will.[40]

In harmony with many of the English writers of the period, the Will was the executor of an action, and, when one transposes this theory into the law to account for the action of *D* at law, it reminds one of the use of "voluit" in early Church law when the action of *D* was thought to embrace not only an aim he himself knew, but a corrupt exercise of his own will to achieve his aim. To speak of a "corrupt intention" was to describe the action of *D* incompletely; intention had to be an expression of both intellect and will.

Hale presents an ordered understanding of the Will:

> The Will therefore is that other great Faculty of the Reasonable Soul, and it is not a bare appetitive power as that of the sensual appetite, but is a rational appetite, and is considerable, 1. In its Nature, 2. In its Object, 3. In its Acts.[41]

From this portion of his treatise we wish to make some few large extractions. The connection between the philosopher and the criminal lawyer appears to be located in his descriptions of the Will. Of that faculty he makes the following assertion:

> 1. The Nature of the Faculty is that it is free, *domina suarum actionum*, free from compulsion, and so spontaneous, and free from determination by the particular Object, wherein it differs from the sensitive appetite, which though spontaneous, because moving from an inward principle, yet is, if not altogether, yet for the most part determined in its choice by the External Object. *But how far forth the Will is determined by the last act of the practick Understanding, or how far such a determination is, or is not consistent with the essential or natural liberty of the Will is not seasonable here to dispute* [italics ours].[42]

In the fashion of a judge, Hale puts aside the thorny issue of how to explain and justify the freedom of the will, but, equally, like a judge, he asserts and assumes that the will is free. From this assumption he is led to conclude:

> This liberty of Will, together with that other Faculty of Understanding, is that which renders the humane [sic] Nature properly capable of a Law, and of the consequence of Law, Rewards and Punishments; which doth not properly belong to the animal Nature, because destitute of these two Faculties.[43]

He then proceeds to state what is the object of the will, and the acts of the will:

> 2. The Object of the Will is not confined to a sensible Good, but is much larger, namely, such a Good as is compatible to an

> Intellectual Nature in its full latitude, such as are moral and supernatural Good.
>
> 3. The Acts of this Faculty are generally divided into Volition, Nolition, and Suspension: That division that herein better suits with my purpose are these, Election and Empire.
>
> 1. Election or choice, and this in reference both to means and end; for though the Schools tell us, that *Electio* is only *mediorum & non finis*, this is to be intended of the general end or good at large, and in its universal conception, for when several particular ends are in proposal, there it belonging to the Will a power of Election of these, as well as of the means to attain them.[44]

Stating that the body and its faculties may, in part, be subject to involuntary motion which is outside of the province of the will, Hale proceeds to depict how and in what ways the will does rule. The "Empire of the Will" may restrain the "motion of Appetite."[45] It is a compressed sentence which depicts this exercise:

> 1. Sometimes the very motion of the Appetite itself is restrained by the Empire of Will, so that a man doth not *appetere* that sensible good which otherwise he might or would, because he will not; and this is the most natural and noble regiment of the Will over the sensual Appetite.[46]

By the use of "*appetere*," which may mean "to desire earnestly," Hale seemed to indicate that a desire either had been extinguished, or that it had been prevented. The model given by the Latin verb here is that the will may either extinguish or diminish the force of a desire–or this is the reading we give to the passage.

The second example of the will in control is thusly stated:

> 2. Though it may fall out that the sensual Appetite may *appetere bonum sensibile*, yet the Will may and doth controll the empire of the Appetite in the execution of that appetition: As for instance, A man sees delicious fruit, and he desires it; in so much, that were there not a controll over the empire of his Appetite, it would command the Hand to reach it, and the Mouth to eat it: But the contrary command of the Will supersedes the command of the Appetite; the Appetite desires it, but the Hand is forbidden by the Will to reach it.[47]

What the illustration reveals is an echo of practical judgment, familiar to any reader of the *Nichomachean Ethics*, and, during the epoch in which Hale wrote, a text known to most moralists in England. The logic implicit here is not that the Estimative Sense has warned that "x" may be harmful; it is that an object is now seen as delectable, or as desirable, but the will does not convert what is seen or beheld as potentially or possibly a good *into* an actual good. A practical judgment, it may be recalled from the *Ethics*, can be resolved into two categories. The good may be seen as a good, and it is desired. It is assumed that if *D* were impelled, which is the force of "*appetere*," all that would prevent *D* thereupon from joining together a universal proposition with a particular proposition (i.e., *D* seeks after the [sensible] good; this "x" is a sensible good; therefore, the hand brings the fruit to the mouth) to effect a conclusion (which is the action itself) would be a warning from the Estimative sense that the good, as such, was not a good, but was, rather, a harm to be eschewed.

But Hale wishes to use the elements of a practical syllogism to show how the Will, after a good has been perceived as a desirable good, may elect to act towards the good, or may not act towards the good. The practical syllogism in and by itself does not, for Hale, author action in an agent. Can it? Hale would admit that an agent can be impelled, as a man driven by an uncontrollable desire; but Hale also wishes to argue that it is not a conceptual contradiction to assert that the will can control movement towards the sensible good (*appetere bonum sensibile*) if an agent will exercise such control. This is made clear, we believe, later on in the text:

> But the controll of the Will upon the Appetite in the reasonable Nature, is many times, and indeed most often done, not upon the account of a sensible evil felt or feared, which of it self were sufficient to determin the Appetite; but sometimes upon the account of such hopes or fear as fall not under a sensitive notice, as of the command or prohibition by God; yea many times upon a bare Moral account of the *indecorum*, unreasonableness, unseasonableness or utter unfitness of the thing it self, without any other motive of fear either of a present or future sensible inconvenience thereby; which Moral consideration can no way move the sensible Appetite, were it not for the Will, which being a rational Faculty is moved by it.[48]

The logic here is consistent with what was earlier said regarding the Estimative Faculty. If moral datum is not to be found in the sensible perception of objects themselves, then, according to Hale, the first ground for a moral predicate is to be found in the Estimative Faculty which "concludes that this ["x"] is a sensible good or a sensible evil."

The "link" between the sensible as good, and the good as moral, is to be located in the nature of the *phantasm*, which Hale calls "the Phantasie."[49] It will be recalled that he held that the second function of the phantasie was to render the perceived, as an image, into something not unlike a proposition. For coherence of theory, therefore, he provides a continuity between the perception of good or evil which the Estimative Faculty intuits – we may recall that the "Estimative Faculty,...is indeed no other than the last operation or composition of the Phantasie before-mentioned"[50] – and subsequent moral knowledge which is expressed by and through the construction of moral propositions which are the object of the human intellect.[51] In this way a moral proposition is not an imaginative invention unconnected with reality; quite to the contrary, a moral proposition is an expression of a fundamental moral principle, grounded upon a logically prior aspect of perception: namely, to avoid what is naturally harmful, and to seek what is naturally good, aspects of the real which are given directly in perception, and extracted by the Estimative Faculty when one comes to know what is contingently the case. (And, for sake of argument and presentation, it is defined that the "real" is not the content of a dream or phantasy, but is the extra-mental given in perception which, if one wished to attach a label to the theory, might be a form of realism.)

Hale makes a very strong statement as to the power of the human will ("*Imperium voluntatis*"), as the following excerpt will show:

> Now this *Imperium voluntatis* may be considered in relation,
>
> 1. To itself: It can suspend its own acting, either of electing or rejecting.
> 2. To the Understanding: Though it cannot suspend its perception, *omnibus ad percipiendum requisitis adhibitis*, yet it may suspend its decision or determination, or at least its *obsequium* to such decision.
> 3. To the Passions, which are as it were the Satellites *voluntatis*, and follow the command of the Will, where the Will acts according to its power and authority.
> 4. To the animal Spirits, and the Vessels in which they are received when designed to Motion, namely the Nerves and Muscles, these are all subject to the Empire of the Will, as to Local Motion of the whole Body or any part thereof,

> when the Spirits, Nerves and Muscles are in their dure and natural state.
>
> 5. To the sensual Appetite: And indeed herein is evident both the Empire and Sovereignty of the Will, and also the visible discrimination between the Humane Nature and Animal or Brutal Nature, and its preference before it. In the animal Nature it is evident that the sensual Appetite is that which hath and exerciseth the sovereignty and dominion over the spontaneous actions of the animal Nature, that commands the Foot to go, the Mouth to eat, and all other the spontaneous motions in order to a sensible good: But in Man the sensual Appetite is under the government of the Will and controlled by it, *at least when the reasonable Faculty is not embased and captived by ill custom or disorder.*[52]

It is readily apparent that this is a very strong statement of the power of the human will over itself and over the domain of human actions. In the fifth consideration we have put into italics what we deem to be Hale's explanation for the failure either of the will to control itself according to a rule, or to control the exercise of human appetites. If the Will is (apparently) such an ordered and rational faculty, why then does it fail in its exercise of proper self-control, or in properly seeking the good? If one stresses the rationality of the will, then is not one subject to the criticism which Hobbes advanced, namely:

> The Definition of the *Will*, given commonly by the Schooles, that it is a *Rational Appetite*, is not good. For if it were, then could there be no Voluntary act against Reason. For a *Voluntary Act* is that, which proceedeth from the *Will*, and no other. But if instead of a Rational Appetite, we shall say an Appetite resulting from a precedent Deliberation, then the Definition is the same that I have given here. *Will* therefore *is the last Appetite in Deliberating*. And though we say in common Discourse, a man had a Will once to do a thing, that neverthelesse he forbore to do; yet that is properly but an Inclination, which makes no Action Voluntary; because the action depends not of it, but of the last Inclination, or Appetite. For if the intervenient Appetites, make any action Voluntary; then by the same reason all intervenient Aversions, should make the same action Involuntary; and so one and the same action, should be both Voluntary and Involuntary.
>
> By this it is manifest, that not only actions that have their beginning from Covetousness, Ambition, or other Appetites to the thing propounded; but also those that have their beginning from Aversion, or Feare of those consequences that follow the omission, are *voluntary actions.*[53]

Hale would not accept the force of this criticism. It is to be recalled that he defined the Will[54] as "free," and that freedom embraced that the will was free from compulsion, that the will was spontaneous, and that it was free from the determination of any particular object (even, it may be assumed, the object of an appetite). Hale posits that it is within the gift of free will that free will may be abused; more a statement than an explanation of weakness of will. The underlying assumption, for Hale, is that when an agent does not make God the object of his intellect and will, then some lesser state of goodness obtains, and this lesser state is tainted with imperfection.[55] If the theory is embraced to its logical end, and if that is applied to legal reasoning, then a legal system has to be at once also a theocratic legal system (because the object of a properly willed act would be the good, and, by definition, only God is the highest good). Hale would call this "good" the "sovereign Good":

> Again, as to the power of the Will, it hath likewise Objects of Good answerable to the former distribution. 1. The subordinate Good of Moral Virtues, Honesty, Sobriety, Justice, Temperance, and all the train of Moral Virtues; these being united to the Will in their acts and constant habits, the Will enjoys a great Moral Good, tranquility of Mind, complacency and delight. 2. The Sovereign Good, which is the glorious God, reached after by the Will as the chiefest Good, and enjoyed in the manifestations of his Love, Favour, Presence, Influence, and Beneficence; this fills the vastest motions of the Will, fills it with Peace, Contentation, and Glory, and keeps it nevertheless in a perpetual motion, by returns of Gratitude, humble Love, Obedience, and all imaginable extension of its self for the Service, Honour, and Glory of that God that hath thus bountifully given to the Soul a power in some measure receptive of his Infinite Self....
>
> And now because Man hath a doubt state, namely a state in this Life in conjunction of the Soul with the Body, naturally dissolvible [sic]...[one is led to conclude that]
>
> 1. In this Life, the proportionable fruition of Man is that which is compatible to the state he hath here, namely [that man may exercise] dominion over his Passions and inferior Faculties, and the due placing, ordering, and moderation of them; a resignation of his Will to the Divine Will, and a dependance [sic] upon his Goodness, Power, and All-sufficiency: and from all these arise peace of Conscience, contentation and tranquility of Mind.[56]

From the point of view of possible application to a theory of law, and of human actions under the rule of law, Hale has espoused a double theory of Will. In the first instance the human will has a natural object, just as the intellect has a natural object. The will seeks after the good; the intellect seeks after the true, or truth. He casts his theory into the language of the period, redolent with scholastic usage and intonation, and for us in this age to use that language is as strange as if a modern singer is asked to sing Gregorian chant: it can be done, but self-consciousness may show through. In the natural state the human mind can discover and make law, and the human will can obey and command, both itself (in the regulation of personal moral behavior) and others (in obeying the prescriptions of a civil law).

Upon these purely natural operations may be added supernatural functions both for the Intellect and for the Will, and Hale would state that this comes about when man receives Divine revelation. At that point, the intellect and will, under the gift of Divine inspiration or Divinely revealed truth, seek after a higher object: God. The will seeks after God as the eternal good; the intellect seeks after God as the eternal truth. But these objects are given to humankind only through the gift of faith. They are not natural noetic objects, as may be a natural object like knowing that the tree is in the quad. Hale preserved the distinction between the natural order and the supernatural order of being. In this way, for theoretical consistency, responsibility for actions could be predicted for purely natural operations. With the gift of supernatural revelation would go a higher degree of moral responsibility because it was assumed that if God had revealed himself to man – God who neither deceives nor can be deceived – then, accordingly, the truth contained in that revelation would be of a greater purity and refinement than any moral or legal truth a polity might achieve without the benefit of Divine revelation.

As with the broad medieval synthesis it was assumed that human faculties, such as the intellect and will, were perfected by and through Divine revelation, with its attendant succors given through grace. Devoid of revelation, the intellect and the will functioned seeking their proper natural objects, the intellect seeking to know the true, the will seeking after the good, under whatever myriad forms the qualities of truth and goodness were presented. Thus, to our earlier question – Must a legal system (for Hale) necessarily be a theocratic legal system? – one can reply that he accepted a purely natural order because that order, in theory, could be the proper natural object of and for the exercise of the human faculties of intellect and will. Given the long argument presented in *Primitive Origination of Mankind*, one might assume that Hale would prefer that a common law system be directed by Christian principles; and, by appeal to historical knowledge, it was and is the case that Christian principles broadly informed the system of the common law. Is it logically necessary, though, that a theocratic system be generated from Hale's assumptions? We would argue, again, that it is not, because the fundamental assumption of Christian belief is that faith is "given" by God, and a gift cannot be compelled. Such being the case, it would be logically improper to formulate a necessary proposition (and its extensions as a legal system, or other) upon what is non-necessary, i.e., faith given by gift. Furthermore, if faith cannot be compelled, then the objects of that faith (its laws and decrees) cannot, logically, be binding upon one who does not naturally perceive those objects. It is to be preserved that the objects of faith were supernatural objects, known through belief, contrary to the world of natural objects which may be known through the natural exercise of one's human faculties. Granting, therefore, the assumptions which Hale espouses, that there is a difference between the natural and supernatural order of being, one could safely conclude that a legal system need not necessarily be a theocratic system. Inherent in this assumption are the seeds of tolerance.

Hale's preoccupation with the nature and function of the Will was not a sign of insularity on his part, nor was it a trivial theological obsession. The literature of the period was occupied with the nature and function of the will.[57] If some effective verbal expression could not be given concerning the nature and function of the Will, how then would law, be it civil or canonical or moral, justify that a man is to be held responsible for his voluntary acts? Hale possessed the peculiar qualification of having been a lawyer of outstanding reflectiveness, and also a philosopher and theologian who, as his published and unpublished treatises show, was concerned not only with stating what he thought the law to be, but also with presenting an organized statement as to what was human nature, and what was the nature of its powers, faculties and operations. One portion of his speculation revealed that he thought that the nature of will in relation to human acts needed to be understood if an effective and coherent theory of criminal law were to be devised under which one could be considered responsible for his actions or omissions. What we do not possess from Hale is a study which would have related criminal law to volition; we have only parts, as separate treatises, which must be joined, whereupon a coherent theory may (possibly) be formulated.

By turning to his unpublished treatise, the *Tract on Natural Law*,[58] one may read affirmations of what is found, in the main, in the published work, *The Primitive Origination of Mankind.* In the manuscript, the comparison between human and brute nature is put forth with the aim of justifying notions of control. Hale says,

> [95a] From the consideration of the dignity of the humane nature, specifical and appropriate to its selfe, ariseth that natural law which requireth that the due order and subordination of his faculties be observed that the Regent principle in him [control], namely his Soul and his Reason preside and govern [themselves] facultys, and be not commanded or governed by [impulse? or, lawlessness?], [and] that he keep the Reigns of his passions and sensual apetite [sic] in the hand of reason and moderate them according to the law of Nature which is the rule of his Reason, because although he doth not order himselfe, neither according to the Dignity nor order of his nature, but inverts it, going as it were with his heels upwards.
>
> He may observe in the Brutal nature the many of his same passions that are in Man as Anger, Revenge, Hatred, etc., in the irrascible part [and] love, delight, joy in the concupiscible [sic] part. And in the Brutes these are excited and acted in animal nature by a kind of necessary connexion between the object and the Passion, that they excite, and for the most part they exercise as fully and directly as the object or the phantasme thereof abide before them; for they [are not] under the regime of the Superior faculty, but are but the various habitudes and motions of the Animal Appetite which is the supreame [sic] Imperative faculty in the Animal nature.[59]

The statement is clear in the manuscript (however constrained the script) that there is an absolute difference between animal and human nature, and that the ground for the difference rests upon intellect and will. Given these two noble faculties, Hale believes that one has the ground for law because one has two separate operations, one which permits knowing, and another which permits choice to act upon what is known. After likening the conduct of brutes to replying to immediately given stimuli, Hale says of human nature,

> But in the humane nature the passions and sensual apetites [sic] are but inferior facultys, and in their just state and exercise [are] subject to the Empire of the Will at least as to the [direction], manner, time, season, and other circumstances of its Exertion.
>
> And when this subordination and the Exercises thereof are but suspended, Man is under a double offense against the Law of Nature that imbaseth and degradeth himselfe from the Dignity of his Nature to a Brutal Beast.[60]

This last sentence leads Hale to conclude that man then may become worse than a beast. When man becomes "bestial" one sees the following:

> A man on the other side whose lusts and Passions are once out of the Regiment and Discipline of reason because prodigious in his passions and Lusts improves [i.e., makes them more harmful, as one might "improve" the weapons of war by making them more destructive] his passions of Anger and hatred into Malice and envy, his passions of Love in [to] frenzy, invents enormous and unnatural Lusts and becomes insatiable in them.[61]

This description would have fitted with any of the descriptions of the enormity of vice which the texts in endnote 107 (*infra.*) might indicate, especially Senault or Montagu. He continues,

> So that happens with reason displaced and the natural order of the facultys of the reasonable Soul inverted as it happens by the extravagation [i.e., to exceed what is proper and reasonable] and displacing of the Animal Spirits in the Body from whence arise spasms and convulsions and distortions, and those terrible Symptoms that wholly disorder the operations and beauty of the Body and Mind. By which it appears that the keeping up of the Regiment of the reasonable Soul over the passions and lusts of the Animal nature, and the subduing of them to the Law of reason is part of that Law of nature which concerns the dignity and order of the human nature.[62]

Thus, by arguing from the notion of natural law, and from the nature of human nature, Hale concludes that it is reasonably apparent that a reasonable order in the world exists, and that from that order it is reasonable to conclude that human actions themselves must be reasonably ordered. The rule and measure for the concept of reasonable order is, for Hale, a theistic concept. Of law, he says,

> A law therefore I take to be a rule of morale Actions given to a Being endowed with Understanding and Will by him that hath power or Authority to give the same and exact obedience thereunto *per modum Imperii*, Commanding or forbidding such Actions under some penalty–expressed or contained in such law.[63]

The notion of natural law must, for Hale, include the "Supreme Legislator," and he argues in this way:

> Yet this rule of reason would not be a Law to him, unless there were some Superior that gave this Rule to him *per modum Imperii et sub ratione Legis*. For he [i.e., any person whatsoever] would be under no obligation to observe this rule of reason but only to himselfe and therefore may absolve himselfe by the Liberty of his will from the observing of that Rule and from all obligation to it.[64]

One may note, here, that an Ockhamist understanding of natural law is not being advanced. The creation of law is not exclusively within the domain of the will, but more reflects the Aquinian definition of law that law,

> was an ordinance of reason, directed to the common good, issued by the authority in charge of the political community, and promulgated to its subjects: *quaedam rationis ordinatio ad bonum commune et ab eo qui curam communitatis habet promulgata* (ST.la-2ae.xc,4.).[65]

By stressing the notion that law is "an ordinance of reason," the mind of that period would understand that law was not an invention, or an imaginative construct made solely by the force of will unconnected to the direction of natural law. In language closer to our own habit of mind we would distinguish a law of nature, founded upon the essence of an object, from a postulate or an hypothesis (each of which may help one discover or predict the nature of an object, but not necessarily so). Hale continues the paragraph, stating:

> As hee is Lord of himselfe So he would be Lord of that Rule which [throughout all was] the law of Reason, and keepe it or break it at his pleasure without giving account there of As any but himself.
>
> (6a) For though he remained a reasonable Creature, and is well acquainted with the rule of his reason, yet he remains a free and voluntary Agent and as to the Exercise of his Actions, and is Lord still of himself and them.[66]

The force of his objection is to illustrate that if reason is not measured against the natural law, then reason may be considered as the faculty which can invent any set of propositions (i.e., two systems, "L" and "-L," may in theory both be reasonable systems; but their reasonableness in and of themselves does not compel that one choose "L" to the exclusion of "-L"). Hale wishes to preserve the notion that a law must itself be measured against a pre-existing order, and that pre-existing order is not the limit of logical categories. A law must be logically coherent, but his is not the final measure of a law's lawfulness. The final measure of the authority of a law upon an agent is that the law mirrors or is in harmony with the will of God:

> Yet still the rule of reason simply considered (excluding the Authority of the supreme Legislator) would still be without the true formal nature of a Law, because tho' it were an excellent rule, yet it would indure [i.e., "endure" = *support* or *sustain*] no obligation upon him that hath it, but he might use or not use it at his pleasure, if hee can but deliver himselfe from the difficulties of other external supervisiant Government, Lawes or Penaltyes either by secrecy or power. Soe that every rule, nay the best of humane rules, The rule of reason itself considered abstractly from any superior Authority is not a law – or Rule *juncta cum Imperio*.[67]

The importance of his exposition of a notion of natural law is that he assumes that law is something which a man may know, and when a law is knowable, it follows, upon his reasoning, that the law may be obeyed. If one does not obey the law, then, for Hale, the fault rests primarily in the agent for not having disciplined himself to rule his human dispositions and inclinations. By appealing to a notion of natural law, Hale wishes to argue that law is not random or arbitrary, but is the law of a legal system which reflects the ordered mind of God. Whether one espouses this view or not, it is a consistent view, and it discharges a scholarly obligation that it has attempted, at least, to develop and present a coherent and systematic set of principles concerning the nature of civil law, and reasons for compelling obedience to the law. One may appreciate this effort without minimizing difficulties inherent in it.

In the Fifth Book of the *Tract*, Hale argued that the mind and the will of man gave true value to his moral actions, and, each under his control, a man was deemed to be responsible for his actions:

> And as before I observed that the true notion of God is the natural root of all those Lawes of nature that in special manner relate to God. So the true notion of the humane nature, and

the Constitution and value is the true fountain of those natruall [sic] Lawes that relate to a mans selfe wherein there are those *postulata* which almost all Mankind agree in, that are necessary to be promised to this purpose.

lst., That Man tho' he hath many of the frailities, [sic] affections and Lusts that are common to him and the animal Nature, yet he hath a specific dignity belonging to his nature far more Excellent than the common Animal nature[:] namely his reasonable Soul.

3rd., That that reasonable Soul ought to have the regiment and regancy [sic] over the Animal Lusts and Affections; otherwise in this life hee should have no prelation [i.e., *superiority, pre-eminence, dignity*] over the brutal and animal nature.

4thly., That although there may be accidental and adventitious proponeraces [? from "propane," as "to propose" or "to propound," or a variant of Scots law wherein a plea is made to a court, which may or may not be rejected before a final decree is given] that may give one man preformance [i.e., earlier rank] and prolation above another, yet essentially naturally and in the specifical Constitution all men are equal.[68]

What places man under this law, he concludes, is man's nature as reasonable and man's nature as voluntary, *and*, as a logical conjunct, natural law itself properly inclines the will and reason of man to what is reasonable and to what is a proper object of the will.

This last notion is adumbrated later in the *Tract*, when he states,

But the rational instincts [of man] have in them *formalem rationem Legis* being implanted in a creature ordered with understanding and will and therefore capable of Law.[69]

Although the powers of man may, in some ways, be necessitated – i.e., the mind if knowing, necessarily knows what it knows – Hale does not believe that necessary operations necessitate conduct:

That animal instincts are in their kind necessary and do for the most part absolutely determine the phantasy [i.e., "phantasm" as an epistemological concept] and Appetite to act conformable to them: But this rational instinct is still under the dominion of the Will in Man, And though it incline, persuade and move the Will to a conformity to it, it doth not necessitat [sic] or compell it: For the Will is essentially free and renders a man free to act or not, And therefore his conformity thereunto is truely [sic] and formally Obedience: And his disconformity thereunto is Sin: The Consequence whereof is guilt....[W]heras the rational instincts of the human

> nature tho' they perswade [sic] and incline the Will, yet are under the dominion of it.[70]

The conclusion of his prolonged argument is, broadly, that there is a natural imprinting in the soul by God upon the creation of each soul, and the proper and natural order of human existence is expressed by the natural appetite to moral rectitude. The argument is a kind of theistic intuitionism: that moral principles are imprinted upon the soul, and may be discovered (in some way) by reflection.

The last point which we wish to touch upon, and that in passing only, was that Hale thought that one need not steadfastly maintain that the Will was a distinct and separate faculty. He said early on in the *Tract*:

> And although possibly it may be true, that in the true method and Actings of the reasonable soul, and its proper and orderly motion, the Will being a reasonable Faculty should follow the decision of the Understanding – and possibly the Understanding and the Will are not so much two distinct faculties, but rather the Will is the Last Act of the Soul in things practical and as it were the confirmation of the Act of the Practical Understanding, Yet it is certaine wee Find in our selves a Power to suspend the decisions of Understanding, And sometimes we Act contrary to it, *video meliora deteriora sequor.*
>
> So that there is some kind of Regent Power in the humane nature that is free and opposite which we call the Will and the Liberty and Dominion thereof wherein the Soul Exerciseth, Whereby a Man hath within himselfe a Dominion over that which he doth, tho' it be *Regnum sub graviore regno*, namely the determing [sic] and Commanding power of Good.[71]

The picture which we have from these extracts is that Hale believed that there was an absolute difference in kind between animal and human nature; that human nature had within itself, because he believed it to have been divinely created, the seeds of its own moral wisdom and principles; that these "irradiated"* principles could be known upon reasonable reflection; that man was the master of his actions because of his intellect and will, and to fail to govern oneself was yet a fault for which one could be held responsible, save for the excuse which madness or infirmity permitted. Hale advanced a protective notion concerning conscience and the obligation to

---

* "irradiated" was a word used by Hale to account for moral principles impressed in the soul and diffusing themselves to the soul through the gaining of moral knowledge.

obey the law by stating that, "noe law can primarily and immediately oblige the conscience, but that of God."[72] It was but another way of stating that laws contrary to natural law, which was construed as an expression of God's will, were not laws at all, and, therefore, did not legitimately compel the obedience or adherence of the subject.*

It is evident that Hale did not accept that an appetite determined and compelled the will, but he did admit that the will could forsake control, and thus one could be driven by one's passions. We would not today tend to speak of "will" and "intellect" when describing human action, and one must appreciate that Hale did not wrongly concretize faculties but spoke of "will" and "intellect" with the understanding that any reader would appreciate that he was talking about man as one who may will, or may know. It is easy to overlook that Hale was not talking about disembodied faculties.

When one returns to law, by means of the *Placitorum Coronae*, having been acquainted with the wide theological and philosophical learning Hale possessed, one is aware then that a definite and fairly well-formed theory of human nature is at work in Hale's understanding of the criminal law, and what may be the duties and responsibilities of subjects under that law, and to that law. One may easily transpose the sentiment expressed in the *Tract on Natural Law* that "disconformity...is Sin: The Consequence whereof is guilt,"[73] with regard to the voluntary commission of a wrongful act to state that the voluntary infraction of the criminal law brings with it justified guilt and punishment. One may read "Sin" to mean offense within a legal system, i.e., a theological legal system.**

---

* A large portion of the *Tract*, Caput 8, 147a, ff. 198, concerns the theory of mind, and discusses how the intellect knows. The discussion of the agent intellect, phantasy (i.e., phantasm), and the relation of the known to the thing known, is at home in an Aristotelian-scholastic discourse of Epistemology, and we omit it here. The text is proof enough that Hale was familiar with scholastic epistemology. But the discussion bears little upon intention as such, and we have excluded it accordingly.

** A transposed reading of this kind of a term does not commit one to equating "sin" with "crime." In a meta-legal fashion one can say that a sin is an example of a kind of offense within a kind of legal system. We are prepared to accept such a meta-legal comparison. To produce the similarity one stresses the common features of each system for the assigning of guilt and responsibility for actions done under the legal system. This does not commit one to the position that all crimes are sins, or that legal and moral systems are one (to attempt to yield the conclusion that a legal system must necessarily embody a moral system).

We wish to turn, then, to consider the formal statements made by Hale with regard to the elements necessary for criminal offenses and their commission. In the second chapter of *Placitorum Coronae* he sets forth his formal understanding for responsibility under the criminal law:

> MAN is naturally endowed with these two great faculties, understanding and liberty of will, and therefore is a subject properly capable of law properly so called, and consequently obnoxious to guilt and punishment for the violation of that law, which in respect of these two great faculties he hath a capacity to obey: The consent of the will is that, which renders human actions either commendable or culpable; as where there is no law, there is no transgression, so regularly, where there is no will to commit an offense, there can be no transgression, or just reason to incur the penalty or sanction of that law instituted for the punishment of crimes or offenses. And because the liberty or choice of the will presupposeth an act of the understanding to know the thing or action chosen by the will, it follows that, where there is a total defect of the understanding, there is no free act of the will in the choice of things or actions.[74]

Because Hale admitted that the law of England excused one from culpability because of personal incapacity or personal defect, some of his analysis we wish to consider here for philosophical purposes. The general categories are broadly known (certainly from Hawkins' edition of *Pleas* of 1716, which pre-dated *Placitorum Coronae* by some twenty years). Hale put in an ordered list three general categories which may serve to excuse *D* from criminal liability: natural incapacity owing to infancy; accidental defects caused in *D* through 1) Dementia, 2) Casualty or chance, 3) Ignorance; and lastly, defects springing from civil causes, 1) Civil Subjection, 2) Compulsion, 3) Necessity, and 4) Fear.[75]

The core of his reasoning that infancy incapacitated an offender was the principle (or the assumption) that a youth of tender years did not know the difference between good and evil.[76] But one may educe from this statement a more manifest assumption: exercise of will and intellect is a *practical* exercise upon a content of information. An infant, though assumed to have such faculties in a potential state, cannot exercise them because he knows little to nothing, and certainly possesses no formal knowledge. If the root for punishing by means of the criminal sanction is that one both knows, and then elects to act contrary to what he knows (he ought to do), then, barring any reasonable excuse, *D* may be held criminally responsible for his acts. By assumption, then, a youth is held not to be able criminally to intend, or to be able, *formally*, criminally to commit. There may be the *material* elements present for the commission of or attribution of a crime, but a lack of knowledge *simpliciter* excuses. The latent assumption, therefore, by introduction of the category that infancy *per se* excuses, is that there must pre-exist a body of acceptable practical knowledge and social codes in order for it to be assumed that one has intentionally violated the criminal code of a society. The assigning of an age of consent, or an age of responsibility, will be a practical matter, estimated by the practical canons of the society.

Madness was a state of being which permitted of degrees. Partial madness (*dementia*) Hale found not to excuse *D* from criminal conduct because it was assumed that *D* had some control over himself. The statement given is this:

> Some persons, that have a competent use of reason in respect of some subjects, are yet under a particular *dementia* in respect of some particular discourses, subject or application; or else it is partial in respect of degrees; and this is the condition of very many, especially melancholy persons, who for the most part discover their defect in excessive fears and griefs, and yet are not wholly destitute of the use of reason; and this partial insanity seems not to excuse them in the committing of any offense for its matter capital.[77]

The assumption at work here is not that one is half sane, say from the hours of six o'clock in the morning until midday, and then becomes insane from midday until the following morning. Were that the case, it could be argued that such an insane state would excuse because any action done in such an insane state would be unintentional action at law. Hale says of the partial insanity he depicts (which we might now determine to be a depression of some kind):

> The best measure that I can think of is this; such a person as labouring un[der] melancholy distempters [sic] hath yet ordinarily as great understanding, as ordinarily a child of fourteen years hath, [and therefore] is such a person as may be guilty of treason or felony.[78]

One may question if this is an explanation on his part, or if it is an assertion of an assumption? Hale has not explained the state of *D* subjectively. He has assumed, we believe, that some forms of mental instability may be like a headache: there and present, but bearable; also, such a mental incapacity, though causing or influencing one's full adult powers to be less than flourishing, nevertheless does not so disable a person so as to render him irrational or incapable of willing. One may yet intend, but with diminished knowledge and foresight, appears to be the assumption at work.* Total madness excuses, and the authority for the proposition is taken from Coke's *Pleas of the Crown*, with the condition that the madness is absolute, and a total deprivation of memory. If, when mad, one becomes sane, and during a period of sanity does commit a crime, than one is culpable and made subject to punishment. However,

> If a man in his sound memory commits a capital offense, and before his arraignment he becomes absolutely mad, he ought not by law to be arraigned during such his phrenzy, but be remitted to prison until that incapacity be removed; the reason is, because he cannot advisedly plead to the indictment.[79]

The determination of sanity is a matter of fact for a jury to determine. If the phrenzy or madness (to preserve Hale's usage) is permanent, he then gives a direct statement why it should, as a mental condition, excuse one from culpability:

> Touching the great crime of *treason* regularly the same is to be said, as in case of *homicide*, such a phrenzy or insanity, as excuseth from the guilt of the one, excuseth from the guilt of the other: the reason is the same; he that cannot act '*felonice* or *animo felonico* cannot act *proditorie*,' for being under a full alienation of mind, he acts not *per electionem* or *intentionem*.[80]

Hale resorts to a logical scheme to describe criminal acts in his discussion of actions done through misfortune.[81] His description appears to differentiate actions done *from intention*, from those done voluntarily. It will be best to set down his own language:

---

* Note: The parallel here may come from the theology of the period. An assumption attributed to Luther was that man was so sinful that without the grace of God man could do no other than to sin. A contrary position was adopted by most branches of Catholicism: namely, that although man did fall from grace, the fall itself did not so corrupt his nature that he could not choose the naturally good. By parity of reasoning, Hale has suggested, at law, that a partial insanity is not to lose one's ability to understand or to will, an assumption within the same family that man after the Fall could yet seek the good, even if imperfectly so in his seeking.

> As to criminal proceedings, if the act, that is committed, be simply casual, and *per infortunium*, regularly that act, which, were it done *ex animi intentione*, were punishable with death, is not by the laws of *England* to undergo that punishment; for it is the will and intention, that regularly is required, as well as the act, and event, to make the offense capital.[82]

If this distinction between "will" and "intention" is seen within the background of Hale's own understanding of Will and Intellect, his distinction makes logical sense without, at the same time, committing one to a theory that criminal culpability is solely intentionality.

Hale had maintained that the Will could act by dint of moral propositions compounded by the understanding.[83] The object of the human intellect was that which was *omne intelligibile*, and one such class of objects would be moral propositions, or, as he phrased it, "The moral goodness and congruity, or evilness, unfitness, and unseasonableness of moral or natural notions."[84] The province of the Will was *not* to make moral propositions. They, if a causal explanation be needed, were compounded of the imagination and the intellect. But the will, in accord with the rationalness of a moral intuition, or a moral proposition compounded by the intellect, *may* perceive the rational quality of a moral good, and accordingly direct itself to act. Thus it would be linguistically improper for Hale, with these assumptions, to say that the Will forms an intention, i.e., that it reasonably makes a plan. One may refer to *De Homine*[85] in which he stated:

> Touching the thing called Reason, we must consider that it hath a double acceptation: It is taken for every conduct of any thing by fitting means to fitting ends, or the due and convenient ordering and adapting of one thing to another...viz., Active, Passive, or Mixt: 1. That I call Active Reason which from an inward intellective principle orders and disposeth; as the Watch-maker contrives, orders, and disposeth the several parts of the Watch, so that it excites a regular and useful motion: 2. The Passive Reason (which is more properly Reasonableness) is that order and congruity which is impressed upon the thing thus wrought; as in the Watch I see every thing moves duly and orderly, and the reason of the motion of the Balance is by the motion of the next Wheel, and that by the motion of the Spring–and the whole frame, order and contexture of the Watch carries a reasonableness in it, the passive impression of the Reason or intellectual *Idea* that was in the Artist: 3. The Mixt sort of Reason seems to be when a thing concurrs [sic] actively and from an internal principle, and (in things that have life) vitally, to the production of a reasonable effect; but yet *per*

> *modum instrumenti*, and in the virtue of a superiour direction of a reasonable agent....
>
> 2. But there is another kind of Reason which we call Ratiocination, or *Discursus rationalis*, which consists principally in these three things, though the two former without the latter make not up a compleat Ratiocination: 1. The simple apprehension of things themselves, which is done by images or representations thereof, made either by the Intellect, or by the representations made thereunto by Phantasie: 2. The compounding of the images or representation of things with an affirmation or negation; *this makes a Proposition* [italics ours]: 3. The composition of several Propositions among themselves, and drawing from them Conclusions; and this is called *Syllogismus*, Ratiocination or Discourse.

With regard to the Will, then, one must deduce that it is a rational faculty, but that the property of "rationalness" rests in the ability of the Will to recognize the rational elements in a proposition, because of which an agent may or may not act. The Will is rational in its ability to acknowledge rational propositions and purposes, appreciating that each may contain a rational element which the Will may, or may not, elect to act upon or acknowledge. This is not to "solve" the mystery or the difficulties inherent in a language of a faculty psychology which speaks of "intellect" and of "will." Our purpose is only to dispose of the rational claim which Hale makes by giving a rational disposition to his assertions. Within the framework of his assumptions, it seems to make sense to say that some kind of a relationship obtains between the Intellect and the Will; and it seems further apparent that the framework of that relationship must be within the grounds of rationality, a common element shared both by the intellect and by the will, but manifested in quite separate ways–just as one might say of different objects that they share in "color," but that each object manifests the common property differently (the lampshade may be red, while a sunset may be faintly pastel, but, by analogy, each depiction is colored and manifests the property of being colored in some way).

We have understood the grounds for the relationship between the Intellect and the Will to rest in rationality. To make sense of this relationship (not necessarily to solve its conceptual difficulties) it is best to understand the rational nature of the Will to mean that the Will is able to appreciate the rational elements in intellective processes and/or propositions it forms. Since both the Intellect and the Will are seen by Hale to be faculties of the human Soul, they could be described as having two grounds for a relationship. They may be thought of as "a" *R* "b," sharing a mutual and biconditional relationship, "*R*," through the soul. If "a" were the Intellect, and "b" were the Will, then the relationship of "a" to "b," and of "b" to "a," would be *via* the common ground "*R*" which they inhabit, i.e., both are expressions of operations of the Soul.

But there is a stronger way to express the relationship between one faculty and another. It may be to state that they both share in a common activity, i.e., both are "rational," and each, in its way, expresses rationality. We wish to state that one way of expressing rationality is to appreciate it, just as (by way of a simile) one who plays the piano and causes music to be made is appreciated by one who listens to music, and (in this instance) understands the music which has been played (as might a conductor, music critic, or one educated in the art of musical composition or playing). We want to use this extended simile to illustrate that though both are doing something different–i.e., one is playing and another is listening–both share in their understanding of a musical composition. For Hale, there would be a balance in this extended simile. As the Intellect is seen by him to be both active and passive, so the Will is both active and passive in that it may elect to act or refrain from acting. As the Intellect may err in its speculation, so may the Will err in its elections to act.

Where some writers of our own period might say the relationship of action to volition would be through the category of "trying,"[86] Hale would ground the *fact* of an action through the Soul: namely, since he deems Intellect and Will both to be faculties of the Soul, relationship of one faculty to the other is expressed in or by some further action of the Soul upon its members. The simple case for Hale is the proposition that something sweet is desirable, this "x" is sweet, therefore–barring some reason for restraint–the Soul, at the direction of the Intellect and the Will, moves the hand to pick up the sweet object to be eaten. One metaphor by which Hale described human actions was that of wheels within wheels; the action of one part is expressed and communicated to another part, an image which early deists appreciated.

The logical divisions Hale makes with respect to faculties and operations and powers of the Soul are just that: logical divisions. A human being is a total unity in which powers and operations express themselves through the agency of the Soul. One is therefore cautioned against concretizing the various faculties, inadvertently, then, to speak of them as if they were distinct and separate objects or operations (as an oil pump or a carburetor in an automobile engine have distinct and separate operations and functions). For Hale they are faculties and operations and powers functioning within the unity of the human soul. Such an attitude would stress the holistic view of human operations, in opposition to that human view which might view the human self as a collection and sum of operations (as might a robot be a collection of its parts). For Hale the human person is a *whole* in which there are parts. The human person is not a collection of parts out of which a whole emerges. The difficulty for a later reader, such as those of us of this century, is that when reading him and observing his partitive use of language – i.e., naming parts of the human person, as with Intellect, Will, Soul – it is easy to assume that he is speaking of distinct and finitely separate units, when, in fact, he is only using a language to refer to separate operations within a whole or human unity. For Hale the equation is not expressed thusly: from Soul + Body, how is a human unity formed? To the contrary, for Hale the human person *is* the unity of the soul *and* the body, which puts Hale in the family of the scholastic philosophers, who assumed the unit of soul and body, and does not put him into the school of Descartes, whom, it may be said, wondered how a unity could be produced[*] of soul and body.

If we may return again to the language used by Hale of act and intention (*supra*, endnote 82) it may now be understood that he uses the terms consistently within the framework of his own depiction of the faculties of intellect and will. One meaning of "intention" is that which pertains to the intellect *per se*: to form intellective propositions. But another meaning of "intention" is that rational good the Will elects to put into motion or to achieve. The term "intention" denotes both meanings. From the point of

* Or, if not produced, then logically justified and explained.

view of defense counsel what might make a sound intention not soundly intended would be an irrational, or uninformed, will. By appeal to Hale's understanding of Intellect and Will this defense objection would be a valid objection against the charge that *D* intended to *phi*. Any state of affairs may be able to be described intentionally; but it is a fallacy, akin to that of affirming the consequence, to assume that a state of affairs which permits of *some* intentional description necessarily was an intended state of affairs. One comes to know if the state of affairs was intentionally opted for, when, and only when, one has knowledge of the causes of the act, or action, so intentionally described. A material feature of any state of affairs is that such state of affairs may be described; and, furthermore, as so described, may be assumed to have been intended (on the assumption that a describable state of affairs may also be seen as an intentional state of affairs). But from this material assumption, a formal assumption is not yielded. The formal assumption is the knowledge of causes, and, until one knows the cause of *phi*, one does not completely know *phi*.

What the law depicts in our present time as constructive manslaughter, Hale describes by using the language of additional events upon the doing of an unlawful act, and that language possesses a history which is known to us from the Fathers. The cases set down in Chapter V bear examination because they show how distinct categories are employed to discuss the possibility of culpability.

The first case is a simple and common one, but we cite it for Hale's use of language:

> If a man do *ex intentione* and voluntarily an unlawful act tending to bodily hurt of any person, as by striking or beating him, tho he did not intend to kill him, but the death of the party struck doth follow...or if he strike at one, and missing him kills another whom he did not intend, this is felony and homicide.[87]

In modern language the law now expresses the concept as the doing of grievous bodily harm with intent to wound or harm, which offense is expressed in section 18, as amended by the *Criminal Law Act* 1967, schedule 3, Pt. III, of the *Offences Against the Person Act* of 1861. What Hale has incorporated in his description of *D* doing an unlawful act, voluntarily so, is a notion of responsibility for harm. If *D* puts into effect a harmful chain of consequences, then, if those consequences extend in their actuality outside of the intention of *D*, it is to be the case that *D* is to be held responsible for the harm, which, in this case, is the death of a victim. The underlying presumption is that one may not set an intentional limit upon a serious harm; *D* intended a harm, and it was a serious harm (inflicting injury), and it is not an allowable defense that *D*, in the doing of an unlawful act which caused a harm greater than he had expected. The force of the law is to protect the citizen or subject against unlawful harms, be they with mild but harmful consequences, or serious and unexpected consequences. Both outcomes are envisaged by the extension of the law. Any consequences which flow from the unlawful act are unlawful consequences; and it is not a requirement for the doing of an unlawful act that one take all of the possible consequences into consideration prior to the doing of the unlawful act. Since the consequences which flow from *D*'s unlawful assault are attributable to *D*, then it does not matter, for the sake of legal consistency, if the consequences are mild or serious in their extent; they are, *simpliciter*, consequences for which *D* is accountable because they are consequences which flow from his unlawful act which he did both *ex intentione* and voluntarily.

The next example takes rather much the same circumstance, but from it the notion of intention is lessened:

> So it is if he is doing an unlawful act, tho not intending bodily harm of any person, as throwing a stone at another's horse, if it hit a person and kill him; this is felony and homicide, and not *per infortunium*; for the act was voluntary, tho the event not intended; and therefore the act itself being unlawful, he is criminally guilty of the consequence, that follows.[88]

In the prior example the act done was seriously wrong from which further serious consequences flowed. In this example Hale wishes to preserve the element of wrongfulness by law, but a harmless intention. Is it a different case? Save for mitigating the intention, one is presented the notion of an action evaluated by force of a legal definition. In modern language the example constructed by Hale could be taken as one embodying recklessness, but one must express that with a caveat. Some embodiments of the concept express a subjective factor to be taken into account, as, for instance, "reckless" as used in section 1 of the *Road Traffic Act* 1972 which speaks of "Causing death by reckless driving." This category is contrasted, in the same Act, with "careless," as embodied in section 3 thereof:

> Careless, and inconsiderate, driving.
>
> If a person drives a motor vehicle on a road without due care and attention, or without reasonable consideration for other persons using the road, he shall be guilty of an offence.

In section 3 the test is an objective test, without reference to the subjective state of *D* at the time when the offense was committed – save for some truly unusual state of affairs which *D*, in defense, could present to the court for consideration; e.g., *D* was drugged and kidnapped, and put behind the wheel of the car, etc.

Hale, in the example (*supra*, endnote 139), may permit us to consider that *D* had acted recklessly, i.e., that *D* had created a harm, and was unconcerned as to what could have been the consequences of harm, be they serious, as with death, or be they innocent, as to have caused the horse to shy. In this example, contrary to the first example in which bodily harm was envisaged by *D*, one may say that, objectively, *D* was negligent, and the proof of his negligence is twofold. First, that he voluntarily committed a criminal offense; secondly, that however *D* may have depicted his own actions and measure of care, *objectively* a death ensued, that, *but for* the actions of *D*, would not have occurred. In that sense, *D* was reckless, and the test for recklessness in this example is an objective test: that, in fact, a death did occur. In the prior example, in which grievous bodily harm was occasioned *and* death resulted, the test for recklessness (because of the example) could be a subjective test; and, subjectively, *D* did intend bodily harm.

Does it matter then what intention *D* entertains if what *D* voluntarily does is criminal? The law moves on this point, and it moves with a certain uneasiness. In Tort law there has been, in this century, a great uneasiness about a doctrine of strict liability for unforeseen but caused harm, as the change from the doctrine of strict causal liability held in *Re Polemis*, 1921, to the notion of expectable or reasonable foreseeability of harms announced in

The Wagon Mound, 1961.* We appeal to recent Tort law only to suggest that the law is uneasy with doctrines of strict liability not admitting of reasonableness; but this is not to say that the criminal law does not employ strict liability constructions to secure prosecutions and convictions. It does.

What the legal philosopher must ask, however, is this: Is it reasonable to have constructive offenses where malice is attributable to *D*, when, in fact, *D* did not entertain the harm caused as an object of his intention?

It was not a defense to a criminal charge that *D* killed *Y*, but did so unintentionally, his true intention being to kill *X*. The logical move in legal theory was simple: *D* killed *Y*, who, like *X*, was of a legally protected class. It is not a defense to theft or burglary that one intended only to take Ten Pound notes, but, by accident, took Twenty Pound notes only. In some jurisdictions constructive felonies are absolute, as with Federal bank-robbing statutes in the United States; e.g., the driver of the car is as guilty of murder as the man he drove to the bank where the killing happened in the course of the commission of a Federal felony. In other jurisdictions, as in Great Britain, the law may mitigate an offense by requiring the judge and/or jury to consider all of the pertinent circumstances surrounding the act (as does the *Criminal Justice Act* 1967). Nonetheless, there is no hard-and-fast rule with regard to constructive offenses. If a justification, it may be that it is not an acceptable defense to permit *D*, because of his own ignorance, to plead that he meant only to transgress so much of the law, like a restaurateur who wanted only the meat without the vegetables. When a statutory wrong creates a harm, it necessarily embodies consequences which flow as a direct result of that harm having been voluntarily committed. The true "defense" is to be found in the language of Hale's case itself, "for the act was voluntary"; and, if the act was voluntary, *pari passu*, then *D* did not have to commit the act. He could have avoided the consequences by not having committed the proscribed act.

---

* The correct citations are: *Re Polemis and Furness v. Withy & Co. Ltd* [1921] 3 K. B. 560. *Overseas Tankship* (*U.K.*) *Ltd. v. Morts Dock & Engineering Co. Ltd.* (*The Wagon Mound*) [1961] A.C.

In the two cases, only the first follows the logical doctrine of *versari in re illicita*, but yet takes its force by adding that whatever consequences flow from a harmful wrongful act, *D* is to be held responsible for them, even for a death he might not have foreseen or desired. The justification for the reasoning (or assumption at law) is that harm cannot be "measured." Human bodies are fragile, and to initiate bodily harm is unwisely to take an unjustifiable risk. Such, properly, is to be reckless: namely, to be mindless or heedless as to consequences.

In the second case one is committing a forbidden act to which the law states other penalties may attach. It is a logically weak case, but it does have some justification that if *D* voluntarily creates a risk, out of which a greater harm develops as a consequence of the risk *D* had created, is it then reasonable to permit a defense of (some form of) ignorance on the part of *D*, even though he voluntarily assumed the (criminal) risk? May a wrongdoer profit from his wrong? The criminal law, generally, replies: No, he may not. Furthermore, although *D* did not intend the harm, not all of what we deem to be harmful need be intended. The reckless man, in the finest logical sense, does not intend the harm he causes; he intends only a particular harm, i.e., a bruised body, and not the natural result of his assault, the possible death of *V*. A self-induced ignorance is not a strong grounds upon which to base a defense against having brought about a criminal harm.

Although he does not use the word "harm," Hale does in the examples in his chapter on casualty and misfortune assume that a harm has to be explained, and that there are three ways in which a harm may occur and be unjustified at law. One may intend *phi*, and *phi* occurs. One may intend *phi*, but *psi* occurs, and *psi* and *phi* are both harms, but *psi* is a greater harm which could spring from the situation, and actually did. One may not intend *psi*, but *psi* occurs as a conjunct of the unlawful act *D* is committing, and it is a conjunct *D* brings about. All three cases are examples of harms having been brought about by *D*, the last of which is a "but for" situation accompanying *D*'s unlawful commission.

We wish now to turn to that class of actions which may be compelled, or may be done because of fear.[89] Hale seems to dismiss them out of hand, proffering an unreflective cognitive bias that there are simply some actions that one will not do, no matter what the case. Let us turn to his language, and then develop our discussion. He says,

> If a man be menaced with death, unless he will commit an act of treason, murder, or robbery, the fear of death doth not excuse him, if he commit the fact; for the law hath provided a sufficient remedy against such fears by applying himself to the courts and officers of justice for a writ or precept *de securitate pacis*.[90]

This is the obvious case that given menaces, one should consult with the police and assume that they will protect him. At best, it is a factual question about the nature and effectiveness of a police force in a given society. For Hale at this point has advanced not an argument but a remedy, and the effectiveness of the remedy depends upon the effectiveness of the police force. That *D* might give in because of reasonably grounded fears (for his own personal well-being, or that of his family, or even of an innocent and unknown third party) has not been disproved; *D* has only been rebuked, and to rebuke is neither to prove nor disprove.

The same example is taken a step further:

> If a man be desperately assaulted, and in peril of death, and cannot otherwise escape, unless to satisfy his assailant's fury he will kill an innocent person then present, the fear and actual force will not acquit him of the crime and punishment of murder, if he commit the fact; for he ought rather to die himself, than kill an innocent: but if he cannot otherwise save his own life, the law permits him in his own defense to kill the assailant.[91]

It will be noticed that a moral proposition is advanced to control an action of the will. This is paradoxical, for the force of the example is to ask if any state of affairs may so overpower the will of a person that he will act "out of fear" rather than to act out of consideration for a moral proposition or a moral good. What we have here is the Christian rationalist speaking, and it is a weak form of argument, even upon the principles advanced by Hale.*

---

* Note: It is not our intention here to recapitulate the tradition of the kinds of actions which are voluntary or involuntary, and if there are certain actions, no matter what force is put upon an agent, which yet are voluntary. If the key to attributing the predicate "just" to an action of a man is that such an action was done voluntarily (*cf.* Bk. V, Chap xii, *Nicomachean Ethics*: Justice and Injustice viewed in relation to the intentions of the agent), then to extinguish the cause of the voluntary will remove the act, or actions, from the sphere of the just or unjust with relation to *D*. His actions may reflect the justness or unjustness of him, or them, that may control him; but his own actions, *in se*, will not be just or unjust with regard to

The position which Hale takes in the citation given is reminiscent of the argument given in the first book of *The Laws*:[92] that the aim of the law is to inculcate in a man a fear *of* the law, and a fear *for* the law:

> *Ath.* And consequently each of us needs to be at once free from fear and filled with fear, the reason for these contrasted moods being as we have stated?
>
> *Clin.* Agreed.
>
> *Ath.* And when we intend to make a man immune from various fears, we achieve our purpose by bringing him into contact with fear, under the direction of the law?
>
> *Clin.* So it would appear.

We may argue that a man should embody a respect for and desire to be lawful, but not answered is the objection that fear may so overpower one that one could not act voluntarily, but, moved by fear, acted at the command of another. Hale seems to assume that to act out of fear means that one takes the object of fear as an object by which to justify one's action.

For Hale the object of human existence is *the good*. And God only is the total embodiment of that objective condition. Hale then assumes that man can be perfected only by and through union with God; any lesser category towards which one moves will, of necessity, not satisfy human desires and aims. If a man is moved by fear to harm another in a grievous way, then, Hale might reason, a man (in some way) has substituted some lesser object than God to satisfy himself: that is to say, one chooses, or prefers, some lesser condition.

But is this not to offer a reasonable approach to the Will, to assume that the Will necessarily follows the dictates of reason; e.g., necessarily it is

---

him. In the gloss upon Bk. V, Chap. xii, which was part of the corpus which paraphrased the *Nicomachean Ethics*, one reads this comment: "As was demonstrated in the previous examination, it is possible for a man to do unjust things without being himself unjust: a man will only be unjust when his action depends upon himself and there is no one to constrain him, and he knows and is not ignorant of all the surrounding circumstances....A man will only be just and his action will only be 'just dealing' in the true sense of the term when it is done voluntarily" [from *The Moral Philosophy of Aristotle...The Nicomachean Ethics*, and *...The Paraphrase Attributed to Andronicus of Rhodes*, by Walter M. Hatch (London: John Murray, 1879), the paraphrase at p. 283]. If, therefore, *D*'s action is involuntary, or non-voluntary, then a defense has been offered, or justified, for what otherwise would be regarded as a heinous act done out of fear.

wrong to kill an innocent man; therefore, necessarily one will not kill an innocent man? Fear then becomes an object which no man could entertain. But if Will relates to human character, and if moral virtue is a practice due to human character and habit, the only "excuse" for an action done through fear would be one's own weakness of character, and, for such a weakness of character, one would be held in blame. To have desired to have relieved oneself from any contingent state of suffering, at the expense of an innocent man's suffering, could not excuse, it is argued–reflective, certainly, of the sentiments of the Third Book of the *Nicomachean Ethics*.[93] Hale, in the chapter, "Of Homicide" reiterated this view:

> If there be an actual forcing of a man, as if A. by force take the arm of B. and the weapon in his hand, and therewith stabs C. whereof he dies, this is murder in A. but B. is not guilty.
>
> But if it be only a *moral force* [italics ours], as by threatening, duress, or imprisonment, etc., *this excuseth not* [italics ours].[94]

The first instance is where *D* becomes reduced to the category of pure, non-intentional instrumentality; but in the second instance it is assumed that if *D* considers the moral argument (or, to return to the earlier example, [*infra*, endnote 142], a physical forcing which does not reduce *D* to simple instrumentality, but presents *D* with a moral dilemma), to yield to its conclusion which, in turn, it is assumed directs his reason, and thus his will, is to yield to what is morally, and, here, legally unacceptable. The case however is not that pure.

If one returns to the *Nicomachean Ethics* (Bk. III, part 1)[95] Aristotle presents just such a case which he considers to be open to question, as does his commentator, Andronicus of Rhodes. The case is reported as follows:

> Actions, however, which are done under apprehension of evils greater than ourselves, or in order to gain some honourable end (as, for instance, if a tyrant enjoined the commission of some foul deed when he had our parents and children under his power, and in the event of our compliance they would be saved, and in the other alternative they would be put to death)–such cases, I say, raise an issue of dispute whether they are voluntary or involuntary.
>
> (Andronicus of Rhodes): There are, however, certain actions which are neither involuntary in the perfect sense of the form nor yet voluntary, but in a kind of intermediate position. Of this character are actions done under apprehension of evils

> worse than themselves, or in order to gain some honourable end. An instance of this kind would be a case where a tyrant enjoined some foul deed when he had power both over the agent himself and his parents and children, and was able to save them all – the victim and his friends, in the event of compliance, or to put them all to death in the event of refusal. Such an instance raises a question whether an act done under such pressure would be voluntary or involuntary.

Can it not be said that the form of the question will, greatly, indicate what will serve as an acceptable answer to that question? If, in questions about the nature of the action of the Will, a question takes the form, What be the proper object of the Will? then have we not answered the question already by assuming that the language of "proper object of the Will" is the proper form in which to cast our answer?

We had intimated that Hale revealed a strong tendency to use the assumptions of a Christian rationalist, and we say this for this reason. For Christian theology – and Hale certainly was an accomplished Christian theologian – the Will could be a stumbling block if, by counter-arguments, it could be advanced that there were a class of actions for which a man could not be held accountable. Following along in a general vein advanced in Book III, the first part, of the *Nicomachean Ethics*, was a tradition that a man was, in the end, responsible for his own actions. The concept of "grace" in Christian theology served to vindicate the proposition (and assumption) that no moral test would be presented to a man greater than a man's own capacities to withstand moral evil. New Testament teachings seemed to advance the general notion that Satan, the author of all evil, could not, for all of his power, overpower the Will of man to force a man to commit evil actions.

On the other hand, from that same Christian revelation, there was the fact of human failing and sinfulness. The apostles were men of demonstrated weakness, having fled Christ in a moment of great moral crisis; and Christ himself revealed natural human weakness in the account given of his crucifixion and death. How then were these human failings to be accounted for? One had the rule that one knew he must follow, as said St. Paul, but did not follow. The paradoxical nature of man did not admit of easy and complete description; nor, for that matter, of logical consistency. It would appear that the nature of man was better described by appeal to its inconsistencies than by an appeal to a logically consistent picture of human nature, untempered by human experience.

In Hale, therefore, one finds a curious inconsistency. He is aware, as a thinker, that the Will is not a maker of moral propositions; they fall within the province of the Intellect. He did, however, advance the notion of the Will that it was moved by the good. His own theological inclinations directed him in his belief, and assumption, that God was the highest good; and, therefore, that all men should seek after God. The belief occurs over and over throughout his moral and spiritual writings. What then of an action compelled by fear, or, as Hale refined the expression, of "moral fear"?

Hale the theologian, as well as Hale the advocate of the *Nicomachean Ethics* (3.i.), seems to speak for Hale the lawyer. Hale assumes that a moral proposition which forbids a class of actions because those actions are especially heinous will direct the Will in a moment of extreme crisis. If *D* chooses to take an evil course of action, then *D*, in effect, is sinning; and sin is a rational perversity of the Will. Were it not a perverse rational activity of the Will – and this is the nettle for the theologian – then there would be a class of actions, wrongful in themselves, for which one would not, however, be responsible. A rational Christian theology found this hard to accept. The obvious question was: How then would one be able *to know* when what appeared to be a human choice was truly not a human choice?

The historical period in which Hale wrote abounds in opinions by theologians on the matter of the relationship between sinful actions and the human will. An attempt to discuss the logical assumptions inherent in the topic by writers of that period is a topic far outside of this study. Of necessity we must be selective, mentioning only a few writers who would have been known to Hale on the matter.

Hale knew Richard Baxter as a friend, and it is not too much to assume that Baxter's *A Holy Commonwealth*[96] was known to him. Therein, Baxter wrote about "forced consent,"

> Man is a free Agent, and his Will cannot properly be compelled: If you threaten him with death, he may suffer it: It is supposed therefore that whatever he promiseth, he freely promiseth. We use[d] to say, a man is forced, when fear

> moveth him to consent: But this is not a proper force: It taketh not away the Liberty of the Will. He that consenteth, doth it to avoid some greater evil, which he thinks would else have befalen [sic] him; and it is his own Good that moveth him to it; [He that sweareth to his own hurt, and changeth not] is the person accepted of God, Psalm 15.4. If every incommodity would warrant men to break Covenants, no men would trust each other, and Covenants would lose their force.

The assumption here is that the nature of the rightfully spiritual man is to suffer gladly every kind of martyrological torture. But is this a proper rule for law? If by the simple means of hypnotism one may surrender himself to the agency of another, why then would not the more compelling means of torture itself, or the threat of great torture to innocent third parties, not arrest the liberty of the Will? The modern analyst could see in such urgings towards the promptings of heroic virtue the force of the superego, and, perhaps, an overly unreal estimation of human virtue.

From the same period a work of great learning, touching both law and morality, was Jeremy Taylor's *Ductor Dubitantium*.[97] He puts the same case for consideration under the heading, "Fear that makes our reason uselesse, and suffers us not to consider, leaves the actions it produces free from crime, even though it selfe be culpable." The example given is this:

> *Roberto Mangone* a poor *Neapolitan* travelling upon the Mountains to his own house, is seized on by the *Banditi*, a pistol is put to his breast, and he is threatned [sic] to be kill'd unlesse he will be their guide to the house of Signior *Seguiri* his Landlord, whom he knows they intend to rob and murder. The poor *Mangone* did so: his Lord was murder'd, his goods rifled and his house burned. The question is, whether *Mangone* be guilty of his Lords death.[98]

For his answer, Taylor cites from the *Nicomachean Ethics*, III.i., a portion known to us. In part, Taylor says:

> To this the answer is easy, that *Mangone* is not innocent; and though he did not consent clearly and delightingly to *Segiuri's* death, yet rather then die himself he was willing the other should.[99]

Taylor is appealing to Aristotle's notion that some actions are "mixed"; i.e., have to them elements both of the free and the constrained: "*These kind of actions are mixt, but they have more of spontaneity* and election in them then [sic] of constraint."[100] Taylor, however, seems *not* to have answered the case. He has cited a standard authority for the case. It is when Taylor begins to involve religious principles in his answer that the case is itself given a "mixt" answer.

Taylor resorts to a religious reply for the case:

> No Christian remaining a Christian is willing to offer sacrifice to *Daemons*, or to abjure Christ, if he be let alone: but he that in time of persecution falls away, not changing his heart, but denying his profession, this man is not *excus'd* by his fear, but *betray'd* by it.[101]

Taylor thereupon cites the *dicta* of Aristotle that some actions are so heinous that one must suffer death rather than to commit such heinous actions (N.E. Bk. III.i). But even this allusion is circumscribed:

> And because there are some things...*which are insufferable to humane Nature*, and therefore there is in laws assign'd a certain allowance of fear *qui potest cadere in fortem & constantem virum*, that is, in the case of danger of suffering the extremest evils, and our obedience to humane laws is excus'd in such cases, because no man is *ordinarily* bound by the laws to suffer a greater evil in keeping the law, then is threatned [sic] by the law it self to him that breaks them; therefore the law allows an omission of obedience in the fear of the greatest evils*.... But in Divine lawes it is otherwise, because no man can threaten or inflict on another an evil comparably so great as God does on them that break his laws; and therefore the lesse fear cannot be a reasonable excuse against a greater; and in all cases, the fear of man must yield to the fear of God. And therefore in the matter of a Divine Commandement, no fear of temporal evil is an excuse or warranty. Because we are taught to despise poverty and pain and death, and to doe all this chearfully and gloriously. And therefore this case of Conscience and it's [sic] whole dimensions are quickly measured.[102]

Taylor seems to settle upon the general religious maxim that there is nothing harmful which man can do to man which could match the wrathful vengeance of God. This is the first principle for the religious man: Be not afraid of them that can kill the body only. But Taylor then offers a more mitigating general principle which seems at harmony with civil law:

> But if in these or any other cases the fear be a surprise, sudden, and violent, and impetuous, that is, such that our reason is

---

* At this point in the text, Taylor refers the reader to Book III, Chapter l, Rule II (of the instant work): "Humane laws doe not oblige the Conscience to an active obedience, when there is an imminent danger of death, or an intolerable, or very grievous evil in obedience," the body of the *Rule*, pp. 26-31, of Book III.

> invaded and made uselesse, such as by a natural effort disorders all our faculties, such as that of *Arachne* in *Ovid* [Lib. 3. Metam.]...[or] such a fright as a hare or lambe are in when they are pursued by dogs and foxes, *Occupat obsessor sudor mihi frigidus artus, Caerulae aeque cadunt toto de corpore gutta* [*ibid.*], when nature is in a lipothymie [i.e., fainting or swooning], and our strengths are made extravagant, when we can doe anything in flying and nothing at all to consider; then our understanding cannot deliberate, and then our will does not consent, and then the effect is pityable but not criminal, but the fear it self possibly may be both. For sometimes our fear may be so great, that it fills all our faculties, and then there cannot be any deliberation; for that must be at leisure, and must look upon two objects. *Statius* [Lib. 5. Thebaid., omitting the Latin verse] well describes this kind of fear in the similitude of a hunted stagge...she hath no courage, no confidences, no hope of any thing; she dies if she stayes, but she cannot stay to consider so long; and when she runs, she dies too, and she hears the wolf at her ear, and sees him with her eye, and feels the teeth in her heart, and dies with fear. In such cases as these we are as men without reason, and therefore to be judg'd accordingly.[103]

Taylor, as we understand his Seventh Rule, appears to be unclear on how cases of fear might be resolved. He presses for the highest rule: that a man should not cause harm to another in order to prevent his own death. But he also admits, in his considerations of examples from Ovid and Statius, that one may be so overwhelmed by fear that one (properly) cannot be said to will. The consequences are heinous:

> Concerning degrees of fear which are lesse, such which leave us in a power to consider and deliberate, they may lessen the malice of the crime to which they drive, but cannot make the fact innocent.[104]

This is as if to admit that, as a principle in theory, if the Will be not totally extinguished in its natural exercise, then a degree of guilt attaches to the wrong done according to the measure and degree of the fear which impelled *D* to act contrary to his best Will. Thus we have two principles at work. The first is the noble religious principle, following on from the philosophical tradition of the *Nicomachean Ethics* that some actions are without excuse, that supererogation is expected of the Christian in face of extreme hardship or terror. The second principle, more in accord with the facts of human nature, states that it is possible for the faculties of man to be so overcome by a state of fear and terror so as not to function naturally or properly. The latter principle Taylor does not wish to universalize, and he still hopes that one may use one's liberty to refuse the courses forced by fear:

> He that is taken by a Tyrant and an unjust power and put amongst the troups [sic], is not innocent though in that fear and against his will he fight against his Prince. [Greek text, *which we omit*]...said *Dio Cocceius, They went willingly to warre, if at least they may be said to be willing who are constrained by fear.* It is an unwilling willingnesse, and therefore it is a sin almost against their will.[105]

Taylor, then, rests upon two statements of principle. One is an expression of belief, his principles emanating from his belief. The second principle appears to be, though it is not unambiguously expressed or developed, an acceptance that fear can overpower a person, and in such a state a person can commit heinous acts. The tension, however, which Taylor expresses is to suggest that there is something contradictory in the concept of a free act to say, at once, an act can be free because one's will is at liberty to choose as it may, *yet* one may be commanded or compelled against one's will. Taylor appears to argue that the concept of "free will" is a concept which admits either of no contrary (i.e., one is either free or not free, and both states cannot, potentially, co-exist in principle in one person), or, if it admits of "degrees of freedom," the act done is always, in some way, an expression of a degree of freedom, and it is not, as an act, an expression of non-free agency.*

To cite what appear to be rigorous texts concerning action done through fear does not mean that the period (*circa* 1640-80) was devoid of any examination of the passion. Edward Reynoldes, a Preacher at Lincoln's Inn at the time Hale practiced law in the Inn, wrote at some length upon the human passions and faculties,[106] and one can assume that his large work was known to Hale. The value of Reynoldes' work is that it does demonstrate to us that there did exist serious discussion during Hale's lifetime of the nature and operations of the soul, and that chief in those discussions was to present some coherent theory of Will and Intellect in relation to human actions

* It may be noted that Edward Reynoldes senses the same puzzle about the Will, but, in this instance, it is in regard to God's prescience: "but yet hee [God] doth not so worke his Will out of mens, as thereby to constraine and take away theirs (for indeed the constraint of a liberall and free Faculty, is (as it were) the extinction thereof)" (*A Treatise*, p. 545).

(among other human operations). Reynoldes stressed the liberty of the Will, which he thought to be absolute, and the action (or motion) of the Will was to assent to rational propositions and evidence provided it by the understanding. However, during his development of his argument concerning human passions and faculties, Reynoldes did discuss *fear* in itself as a passion, and the body of his discussion was to advance the understanding that fear simply could overpower man. It could be an object which infested human action so that all action done was done out of and because of fear. Of the case where death may cause one to fear inordinately, Reynoldes uses the language of "error" to discuss such an example, and it does have bearing here:

> For as Errour hath a property to produce and nourish any Passion, according to the nature of the subject matter which it is conversant about: so principally this present Passion: because Errour it selfe is a kinde of *Formido Intellectus*, a Feare of the Vnderstanding: and it is no great wonder for one Feare to beget another. And therefore when Christ would take away the Feare of his Disciples, he first removes their prejudice: Feare not those that can kill the Body onely, and can doe no more. Where the overflowing of their Feares seems to have been grounded on the overriding of an adverse power. Thus much for the Root and Essential cause of Feare.[107]

It may be suggested that Reynoldes transfers the emphasis from speaking of the Will being compelled to speaking about the understanding being misinformed. To act from compulsion would therefore mean to act from an improper estimation of the circumstances, or out of an improper estimation for ends. It would be natural, by use of this language, to suggest that one would excuse what was done out of fear because one was incapable of making a proper estimation of how to proceed. Reynoldes, therefore, preserves the liberty of the Will. The Will has not been compelled; it has acted because one could not form a proper judgment or estimate as to what ought to be done under the circumstances. His broad depiction of "fear" permits such a reading which precludes the somewhat curious objection: But how is liberty obviated in a faculty which, by necessity, directs itself? The passage may show that Reynoldes saw "fear" to be a complicated passion, not given over to simple "object of the will" or "object of the intellect" depictions:

> The opposite Passion to this of Hope is *Feare*: which being an Equivocall Passion, and admitting of many different kinds, can scarse have any whole and simple definition to explaine it.[108]

In the following chapter Reynoldes asks the question as to what are the effects of fear, having granted that it is a passion, and, as a passion, can dominate one. It clouds our understanding by magnifying an evil.[109] Once a man is gripped by fear, "the minde of man is drawne to a neerer sense of its weaknesse, and to a more prejudicate apprehension of the adverse power."[110] Reynoldes continues,

> *Tacitus*...speaks [of] *Inclinatis ad credendum*. So I may say, *Inclinatis ad timendum animis loco omnium, etiam Fortuna*, When the minde is once dropping, things which before passed away as matters of course and casualty, are now drawne within the compasse of presages and Emphaticall evils.[111]

This leads Reynoldes to make a coherent observation near the end of his work on the operations of the Will:

> In some cases it [i.e., the Will] worketh *Naturally* and *Necessarily*, as in its Inclination unto *Good* in the whole latitude, and generall apprehension thereof. For it cannot will any thing under the general and formall notion of Evill. In others *Voluntarily*, from it selfe, and with a distinct view and *knowledge* of an End wherunto [sic] it worketh [*Ethics*, 1.3.c.1.]. In other *freely*, with a *Liberty* to one thing or another, with a power to elicite, or to suspend and suppresse its owne Operation. In all *Spontaneously*, without violence or compulsion. For though in some respects the Will be not free from Necessity, yet it is in all free from *Coaction*. And therefore though *Ignorance & Feare* may take away the complete *Voluntarinesse* of an Action proceeding from the Will (because without such Feare or Ignorance it would not have been done. As when a man casteth his goods into the Sea to escape a shipwracke...) yet they can never force the Will to doe that out of violence, which is not represented under some notion of *Good* thereunto.[112]

We have, then, sufficient evidence from the period that the nature of the Will was subject to serious discussion by English writers. A broad faculty psychology committed Christian writers to a division that in matters intellective, one spoke of reason or of understanding, but with regard to actions, means, and ends, one spoke of the will. A difficulty which looms at large in such a distinction as was given between the sphere of the intellect and the sphere of the will was how to account for coactive actions, when, it will be appreciated, both faculties were described as possessing certain necessary properties, i.e., the mind necessarily knew, while the will necessarily elected to direct itself. Was it not to propound a contradiction in terms to speak of the will being moved by other than itself?

Hale borrowed from the third book of the *Nicomachean Ethics*, to the effect that the fear of death, either to oneself or to some other, ought not to justify a man's commission of a heinous act, and the law, therefore, he held, would never admit the defense of compulsion. But there were models at law – e.g., compulsion under contract which served to vitiate consent – which could serve as examples to justify the defense of compulsion. Hale, along with such other Christian writers as Reynoldes, Baxter, and Taylor, were aware of the contract examples; why then not advance the principle to cover compulsion?

It would appear that the Aristotelian and Christian assumptions about the Will, and about the moral content of certain actions, made the extension of the principle difficult, if not impossible. The Aristotelian tradition from the *Nicomachean Ethics*, Book III, part 1, made choice a choice of some good, and the "good" itself had to be circumscribed by the limits of propriety. Therefore, some actions in and of themselves were evil, and would admit of no justification; one would seek death rather than do them. The Christian tradition, drawing upon the *Ethics*, grafted the Aristotelian Will onto the concept of Christian creation to produce a hybrid of this kind. If God is good, and if God holds man responsible for the moral content of his actions owing to the nature of the human will, its essential and necessary freedom, how then could a class of actions be permitted to exist in the universe, caused by man, which were both *materially* heinous but *formally* neutral, i.e., wrongful actions produced as a result of compulsion? What then, the question might be framed, was the object which directed the Will to seek other than the good which was God? The Christian then would have the difficult task of justifying that God was the highest good to which all men, whatever their troubles and sufferings, ought to turn. There would come to exist that class of actions which produced harm, as do natural events and disruptions in Nature, but which were produced by man, who himself was to be above Nature, and, therefore, culpable, which Nature was not. There was the further paradox which both traditions could not relieve if appeal was made to their presuppositions about the Will: How can an essentially free faculty, *at times*, become a determined faculty? If free will admits of no contrary, then lack of freedom had to be one of degree, and not of kind, or not admit of a transmutation from a free faculty into a determined faculty. Hale solved it by denying compulsion as a grounds for a defense to the charge of murder done under compulsion. In this way he was consistent according to his religious tradition, and to the tradition of the *Ethics*. Whether he was correct is another problem.

Prescientific *apriorism*, of the kind which Hale evidenced, seemed unwilling to admit that, even within the language of faculty psychology, one would be able to speak of the Will being immobilized. Reynoldes came close when he depicted the various effects of fear, and Taylor was willing to admit that fear could paralyze (as the passages above showed). But the vision – if that is not too extravagant a word – of an ordered universe, made by God, total and perfect to its smallest parts, with man made in the image of God, seemed not to permit or to countenance that man could apparently fall again after the grand Fall. An action done under compulsion held the implication that man could fall from himself, and that such a fall could be greater in nature than the original fall from Paradise. The first fall left man with moral faculties; but a second fall, as caused by an action done through compulsion, would leave man bereft of moral responsibility because, it would be argued as a defense, those moral faculties were, or had become, immobilized.

Such reasoning, or such a vision, was the logic of prescientific centuries. An understanding of man began with an *a priori* conception of what a man should be, and when the facts did not fit the *a priori* vision, then the facts had to be wrong. It was the prescientific innocence, if you will, of an age which explained some forms of insanity by appeal to satanism and witchcraft, and which could not have had knowledge of brain dysfunction caused by an absence of tracer elements in the human system. We say this without any sense of cultural arrogance given by our living in this time.

There were the seeds, within Hale's own time, for understanding action done through compulsion, but the Christian rationalism of the period could not have seen it. We know this from history, and not from any disassociated consideration of logical truth. Hale saw by means of his assumptions, and if one sees the universe as a rational organism which reveals the rational workings of a God, then it is unreasonable to assume that any set of deistic assumptions will permit vast areas of moral neutrality to be permitted, especially if those areas produce harmful consequences. Put into the terms of a rationalist theology, how could a God permit man, or any man, to be so immobilized? Would that not mean that evil had triumphed, and that God had failed; the proof being this poor Jack, looking like a man, moving like a man, but deprived of that quality which made him a man – his ability to author voluntary actions? An argument which might serve to justify compulsion, and thus to arrest responsibility for the heinous consequences of an action done under compulsion, must have sounded like the arguments of Satan himself: moral harm but no moral responsibility. Hale could not and did not accept the defense. If the Devil himself could not control the Will of man, save by permission of a man, how then could an external threat, or, even the more removed, an immoral force, control the Will of man, and, to such an extent, cause one to perform wicked actions, consciously, but inculpably? It must have been seen by him to have been a complete contradiction in terms, or a wrongful assumption at the very least.

Hale had reiterated the dictum of Plowden: *Ignorantia eorum, quae quis scire tenetur, non excusat.*[113] When one looks to the case in which the proposition occurs, *Brett v. Rigden* (1568) 1 P1 343, one discovers that it was a truism advanced by Sergeant Roger Manwood, at the time a newly called Serjeant at Law of Inner Temple, in his argument of the case:

> For, he said, it is to be presumed that no Subject of this Realm is misconusant of the Law whereby he is governed. *For Ignorance of the Law excuses none* [italics ours]. And forasmuch as in indifferent Matters every one shall be presumed to know the Law according to his Duty, from thence it follows that in a last Will it shall be presumed that every Man is conusant of that which the Law has ordained touch the same.[114]

Hale extracted the sentence which we have placed into italics. What is of interest is that Hale does concede that *ignorantia facti* may excuse:

> For such an ignorance many times makes the act itself morally involuntary.[115]

The example which he gives to illustrate this proposition is an example taken from an incident of war, and one would assume that it is an extreme example used to justify a questionable position at law. He states:

> It is known in war, that it is the greatest offense for a soldier to kill, or so much as to assault his general: suppose then the inferior officer sets his watch, or sentenels[sic], and the general to try the vigilance or courage of his sentinels comes upon them in the night in the posture of an enemy, (as some commanders have too rashly done) the sentinel strikes, or shoots him, taking him to be an enemy; his ignorance of the person excuseth his offence.[116]

The example which Hale gives is compressed, but it does, we believe, adequately convey what may be the necessary elements to show what it means for an action to be done in ignorance, and how the consequences which arise from such an action may be excused.[117] One should note that Hale speaks of an act, "itself morally involuntary." He appears to assume that an action out of ignorance is a moral category which may, possibly, excuse for legal purposes. The word "act" is, we suggest, used by Hale both to describe the action *D* brought about (i.e., intending to kill an intruder, and setting into action causes which may kill the intruder) and to describe the consequences of *D*'s act (i.e., the intruder actually having been killed). Hale works from within an accepted framework regarding ignorance which had a strong medieval background.

What, then, does the example suggest? It is assumed that a human act, to be voluntary, and to which culpability may be attributed, must possess certain logically distinct features if it is to be seen as a moral act. It is assumed that *D* knew what he wanted to do, and that when he consented to elect the means to achieve what he wanted to do, that his object would be achieved, barring the introduction of some novel or intervening cause not of his own devising. An act could be rendered morally involuntary when there was an ignorance of the nature of the object, because it could be claimed that had *D* known what the object in fact truly was, he would have elected to have refrained from his undertaking.

In this case *D*, under military command, repelled an intruder. It was not *D*'s intention (for the sake of argument) to kill an innocent person; and, as a subset of that notion, it was certainly not *D*'s intention to kill his own commanding officer. It was the intention of *D* to thwart an intruder. What this analysis yields is that a moral act was seen to possess two broad elements. It possessed a *formal element*, which could be described as that which an agent intended to do, bring about, cause, etc., and it possessed a *material element*, that object of an intention which was a contingent fact. In this case the example Hale constructs shows one that there was not a relationship between the formal and material elements of the moral act. *D* had intended to repulse an intruder (the formal aspect of his action), but the intruder he repulsed was, unbeknown by him, his own commanding officer (the material aspect of his action). It had been a truism of the scholastic period that the definition of "x" was a combination of the material cause and formal cause; or, strictly put, a definition presented the matter and form of an object. For *D*'s act to have been wrongful, these components would have to be present in any description of *D*'s act: 1) that *D* had intended to kill his commanding officer, 2) and that at the time of his firing he knew that the alleged intruder was actually his commanding officer. There, one has a clear offense.

But the case could be altered. *D* could intend to shoot an intruder, and this we would state was *D*'s intention. When the intruder appeared *D* might have thought it was his commanding officer – for whatever reason – but then have acted without caring, shooting, and, at the same time, hoping that it was not his commanding officer whom he had killed. But if the facts of this example obtained, then one could not describe *D*'s act as a morally involuntary act. It would have been an act at fault in two ways: intentionally, because *D* could foresee that he might reasonably produce a harm or wrong; and materially, because if it were his commanding officer, then an innocent man would die. Hale wishes to convey by the force of his example that what *D* intended was free of moral culpability; and if realized through action, no moral harm would follow. If that were the case, the act of *D* would then be a moral act. But if harm arose at the material level – i.e., the intruder (unknown to all) is actually the general – then that harm or that wrong could not be attributed to *D*'s intending and willing it to be the case. Rightfully, then, Hale says of his example that the act of *D* is itself morally involuntary.

D did not intend to bring about a moral wrong, *and*, given the material facts surrounding the episode, *D* did not act carelessly, recklessly, or negligently.

Older language–which would have been acceptable to Hale, even though awkward to our ears now–would have said that *D*, when he formed an intention, was not wrongfully ignorant of the material facts of the moment prior to his willing, concurrent with his willing, or posterior to his willing. We may simplify the description now to state that *D*, when he had made up his mind and acted, took a reasonable stance with regard to the facts of the case, and that he proceeded reasonably. It was reasonable for *D* to thwart an intruder; the command to thwart intruders was a reasonable command; to expect intruders was a reasonable expectation; and to fire at one who acted like an intruder was reasonable military conduct by *D* under the circumstances.

There is no need to prolong the analysis of excuses by means of ignorance. Hale is correct to cite it as a moral category. It is questionable, as we stated (*ubi supra*, endnote 7), if the proposition can be generalized to be made into a legal proposition. Some actions, at law, done through ignorance may excuse; others may not. When they do not, it is generally the case that an offense has been made, one of strict observance through statute, e.g., one may not assault an arresting officer, even though one did not, in fact, know that *P* was an arresting officer [e.g., did not wear his uniform, and the like]. Some actions, though devoid of criminal *mens rea*, may nevertheless produce harm, and it may be thought that should be held responsible, or answerable, for the harm which he produces or causes, e.g., in tort law, and the law of defamation and slander, and in trespass, one does not advert to the mind or will of the accused. Strict liability statutes to which a criminal penalty may attach do permit their strict interpretation to be challenged; did they not, then guilt would rest in the simple accusing of *D* of having committed the proscribed act when an arresting officer filed a criminal information. Such a process would circumvent the function of the courts.

However, may the excuse of ignorance, which is a moral category, be an acceptable legal category as a defense? As a rule one would have to consider the facts of the case. As a category whereby to excuse for harms *D* caused, ignorance is open to abuse; every accused would plead it. It may diminish responsibility, and it may absolve one of criminal guilt. It could be argued that if certain conditions were found to obtain, e.g., that *D* did not entertain an intention in conjunction with an unlawful act (constructive malice, felony-murder rule, constructive manslaughter), *D* did not voluntarily seek to bring about a wrong or a proscribed state of affairs, and that the material conditions surrounding the act were such that a reasonable man could not have perceived them to be other than what *D* thought them to be, *then* it would be reasonable to argue on behalf of the accused before the court that the elements necessary for a criminal wrong to be found of *D* are not present, and that therefore 1) either there is not a case to answer, or 2) a verdict of not guilty should be returned. One doubts if the court would accept, let alone understand, a medieval analysis of ignorance in terms of a relationship to the intellect, to the will, and to the material conditions surrounding an act. A conditional analysis might obtain if one were to say that no fault could be predicated of *D*'s knowledge of "y"; that what was willed, or deliberately brought about, was not tainted by any sense of wrong nor maliciousness of will; and that the consequences of *D*'s act bore no material relationship to what *D* willed and intended. One can see that the analysis comes close to presenting the consequences as an accident. *D*, lawfully, was intending to *phi*, and *phi* is permissible at law. In no way related to or caused by *D*, *psi* results. *D* neither willed nor intended *psi* to be the case, and he had no knowledge that *psi* would be the case. To exclude the odd case, e.g., the mad doctor who wants the heart of *P*, but hopes *P* will not die *sans* his heart, one has to state that what *D* intended and willed was either reasonable or lawful, or both. The mad doctor case is neither.

When speaking about the killing of oneself[118] Hale uses the term voluntary in this Way:

> What a *voluntary killing*
> If a man voluntarily give himself a mortal wound...he is *felo de se*.
> It must be simply voluntary, and with an intent to kill himself.

The language suggests that the object of the intention must also be the object of the will, and this leads to the conclusion that an intentional act – in one sense – is predicated both of the will and of the intellect. "[I]ntention" may be used in other connotative senses, as: *What does D intend*? but we wish to suggest that "intention" is not restricted to a mentalistic usage only, i.e., to speaking only about purpose, or end, or aim, or plan. An "intention" may be that voluntary act D brings about *intentionally*, (even if a depiction of this kind is linguistically awkward), and the double sense of "intention" is conveyed: that of mind and that of will.

Hale advances a standard definition of murder which is familiar:

> *Murder* is a killing of a man *ex malitia praeçogitata*; *homicide* is killing a man without forethought malice.[119]

Hale overcomes the problem of time of death by concluding that if gives P a serious blow, and the blow produces an injury, and then during a year and a day (the length of time in which legal murder can be charged) P dies from that wound, then D may be charged with murder or manslaughter. The principle extracted is a doctrine of consequences: if D creates a serious risk, and, as a consequence of that risk, P dies, then D is criminally responsible for the death of P. There is a causative relationship between the proscribed act of D and the subsequent death of P.

But Hale does make a careful distinction which some writers today have failed to observe.[120] What if P dies because D has cast a spell upon P? Is this murder or manslaughter in D? The distinction Hale makes is sound:

> If a man either by working upon the fancy of another, or possibly by harsh or unkind usage put another into such passion of grief or fear, that the party either die suddenly, or contract some disease, whereof he dies, tho as the circumstances of the case may be, this may be murder or manslaughter in the sight of God, yet *in foro humano* it cannot come under the judgment of felony, because no external act of violence was offerd [sic], whereof the common law can take notice, and secret things belong to God.[121]

It is certainly acceptable to state that *actus reus* incorporates the external elements which the concept of *mens rea* precludes, and that, therefore, no external act of violence having been offered, no *actus reus* was evident to support the *mens rea* for the crime of murder or manslaughter. Such a rejection of witchcraft, or voodoo, or conjuration deaths, unless forbidden by statute, may stem from the other side of Hale's refusal to permit compulsion to be a defense for murder. Is it not theoretically consistent to maintain that if the Will of man cannot, in the end, be coerced against itself, then should it not be a corollary of such an assumption that the mind of man cannot be invaded by suggestion or conjuration or curse so that one might die simply as a result of a curse, or the like, having been uttered? But if a resolution to the question is to be had for the criminal law, the matter becomes then a question of determining the relationship, if any, between a supposed criminal intention and the event, i.e., the death of *P*. The law will permit theft by menaces, just as the law admits of an assault without a battery; but the *actus reus* of murder or manslaughter, perhaps out of consideration of the sheer difficulty of disproving counterexamples or of definitely proving examples, may not be words in themselves, just as a defense to provocation is not that the words provoked *D* to strike *P*. The force of these considerations must have been known to Hale when he rejected conjuration, etc., as a cause of murder because "no external act of violence was offer'd." He admitted that a statute could forbid and could punish acts of conjuration, but that was an example of the power and logic of a statute, and not because of any latent principle or logic of the common law in itself.

Hale maintains that commanding, counselling or abetting of a murder or manslaughter makes the accessory as guilty as the principal, but he does permit exceptions through appeal to intention.[122] Though modern law might appeal to a criminal conspiracy to analyze this case (which Hale did not), Hale believed that the dis-exercise of criminal intent relieved one of criminal intent:

> And therefore I have always taken the law to be, that if A. and B. 'have a design' to fight one with another upon premeditation or malice, and A. take C. for his second, and B. take D. for his second, A. kills B. in this case C. is principal, as present, aiding, and abetting, but D. is not a principal, because he was of the part of him, that was kild, and yet I know, that some have held, that D. is principal as well as C. because it is a compact.... [T]ho it be, I confess, a great misdemeanour, yet I think it is not murder in D.[123]

The second example again takes a killing in pursuit of an unlawful act.[124] Hale excuses, or offers as a principle of an excuse, the action of A. for being outside of the criminal design of the complices, giving expression to a proposition for the defense that a criminal intent must have, or may be presumed to have – the force of the phrases is different – limits. Those limits, as it were, are given by the object of the intention:

> A. meets with D. or some other, with whom he had a former quarrel, or that by reason of some *collateral provocation* [italics ours] given by D. to A. A. kills him without any abetting by any of the rest of his company, this doth not make all the party of A. tho present, to be therefore aiding and abetting, and consequently principal in this murder or manslaughter, which was accidental,* and not within the compass of their original intention.[125]

If however, any of the party joined in by words or actual resistance, then their overt acts will be read by the law to express the malice needed for the finding of murder or manslaughter.

Hale takes a third case, but in this instance the design of all the parties is a lawful design (contrary to the second case which was a poaching in which a murder occurred). In this case all pursue a lawful design:

> and one of the company kill another of an adverse party without any particular abetment of the rest to this act of homicide, they are not all guilty, that are of the company, but only those, that gave the stroke, or actually abetted it.[126]

It appears to be a common-sense principle, but, to take an example from the law of criminal conspiracy, some writers did not realize that to commit an unlawful conspiracy there had to be proved that an agreement had taken place, and that a simple conjunction of A and B was not sufficient to prove that a conspiracy had taken place.[127] In reasoning which predates discussions of criminal conspiracy, Hale used the same kind of reasoning to show that association or presence was not a sufficient ground to charge D_2, $D_3 ... D_n$ as being accomplices in a crime. A criminal intent must be demonstrated; and to the charge that the associates or companions must be guilty because they were present when the crime occurred, the presumption of guilt may be rebutted by showing that a common intention did not exist between the parties. Reasoning of this kind is especially of importance when one attempts to rebut the charge of criminal conspiracy, especially when, in a charge of that kind, proof for guilt is not rigorous, or admits of broad judicial discretion as to what evidence may be admissible.[128]

When Hale came to treat of the nature of murder, and of manslaughter, he used the standard phrase, "malice prepense," and variants,

---

* Note: "accidental" is used to mean: *not essential to, or necessary part of.*

to describe murder, and the latter offense of manslaughter was devoid of malice prepense but usually came about because of a sudden provocation or falling out, as the case law till then generally recorded of manslaughter cases. When he came to analyze malice prepense in murder he divided it into two kinds: "1. Malice in fact, or 2. Malice in law, or *ex praesumptione legis*."[129]

"Malice in fact" he linked to the notion of corporal harm, as these extracts will show:

> Malice in fact is a deliberate intention of doing some corporal harm to the person of another.
>
> Malice in fact is a deliberate intention of doing any bodily harm to another, whereunto by law he is not authorized.
>
> The evidences of such a malice must arise from external circumstances discovering that inward intention, as lying in wait, menacings antecedent, former grudges, deliberate compassing, and the like, which are various according to variety of circumstances.
>
> It must be a compassing or designing to do some bodily harm.[130]

One can appreciate that the conjunction of "intention" with "doing bodily harm" paved the way for the easy identification, at law, of the two distinct propositions, "to intend to kill *P*" and "to be reckless towards *P*" as when causing grievous bodily harm may be considered indictable as murder.[131] Hale is careful to state that "malice" has to it an element of rational control, putting the concept into the family of, "*D* knows what he is about to do." The knowledge need not extend to the full range of the circumstances, e.g., *D*, when making a murderous assault on *P*, does not have to realize that *P*, though at time t_n is wounded, will, in fact, die at time t_m (which might be months later).[132] Hale is willing to mitigate an offense if, when wounding does occur, the death is a result not of the wounding but is clearly the result of medical treatment, but the principle is advanced with great caution.[133]

Coupled to the notion of plan, or design, or preconsideration, is the notion of "voluntary" or "wilfully," as in, "When one voluntarily kills another without provocation, it is murder,"[134] or, "He that wilfully gives poison to another, that hath provoked him or not, is guilty of wilful murder, the reason is, because it is an act of deliberation odious in law, and presumes malice."[135]

The object of an intent determined the nature of the malice at law. Hale said, and it can pass without commentary, that malice is of several kinds:

> 1. In respect of the manner of the homicide, when without provocation. 2. In respect of the person kild [sic], *viz.*, a minister of justice in execution of his office. 3. In respect of the person killing.[136]

The *manner* would encompass the nature of the evidence to demonstrate the alleged seriousness of the criminal intention (e.g., long-standing grudge, or sudden saloon fight). Hale draws upon the example of a master correcting his servant where "the deliberate purpose thereof is not *ex malitia praecogitata*." But Hale continues, stating:

> But if the master design an immoderate or unreasonable correction, either in respect of the measure, or manner, or instrument thereof, and the servant die thereof, I see not how this can be excused from murder, if done with deliberation and design, nor from manslaughter, if done hastily, passionately, and without deliberation; and herein consideration must be had of the manner of the provocation, the danger of the instrument, which the master useth, and the age or condition of the servant, that is stricken, and the like of a schoolmaster towards his scholar.[137*]

By citing such an example as this (dating from 1666 per Kelyng's statement of the case, *infra*) Hale has suggested that "intention" also involves *practical wisdom* because it is a matter of practical estimation to fit the proper means to the end. Knowing "how" to do an act is not, in the language of ordinary philosophical discourse, thought to be within the province of the Will. The observation should provide little difficulty because, as we have argued, "intention" is a cluster concept, and is predicated jointly of the Will and of the Intellect. If, on the other hand, one argues that volition is blind, then one creates a logical difficulty as to how to explain a wrongful act. Every act would then be impulsive, *qua* act, because it could be advanced for

---

* Note: Reference is made in the 1736 edition of *Hale's P.C.* at the end of the extraction (*supra*) to Kelyng. The case in question occurs in that section of Kelyng's Reports which concerns "Murder and other Offences," and refers to *Grey's Case* 1 Kel. 64-65 (1666). Grey, without provocation, struck his apprentice with an iron bar to chastise him. On special verdict it was adjudged to be murder, "For if a Father, Master, or Schoolmaster, will correct his Child, Servant, or Scholar, they must do it with such things as are fit for Correction, and not with such Instruments as may probably kill them" (p. 64).

hypothetical consideration that if "knowledge" and "intention" apply only to the intellect, or reason, or mind, and may not be predicated of the will or of volition, then the execution of every human act would be impulsive, and its merit would depend upon the fortuity of its outcome, i.e., if harm ensued, it would be judged to be a wrongful act, and if benefit was produced, then it would be judged to be a proper act. If the Will (or whatever language one uses to speak of voluntary action) is thought to be non-rational, when then would one be held responsible for what, non-rationally, one did? If the reply were that the intellect embraced the sphere of rational choices, the objection would be that one had either transferred volitional functions to the intellect (and thus made a distinction without a difference, or made a confusing use of names), or that one had confused "to know" with "to select," i.e., one may know that a number of alternatives exist, but how does one put into act one of the alternatives, or make one choice from among many options, if, at the same time, this is not precisely what is meant by the voluntary, or, to will? If, on the other hand, "to will," etc., entails "to be aware of the rationality of," then the execution of an intention is not, or need not solely be, an impulsive act.* One gets more mileage from describing Will as a rational appetite than as a necessary appetite devoid of rationality.

The inconsistency between strict liability and actions done through ignorance shows itself for Hale when he holds that to kill an officer of the law is murder, the law therefore imputing malice to *D*.[138] We have dwelt at length on this problem earlier. The logical paradox it presents is a conflict between legal policy and legal theory. One can construct a case where *P* lawfully must arrest, but *D* could not know that *P* was an arresting officer (and, to complicate the case, *D* might be an innocent third party whom *P* is seeking to arrest). Earlier we saw that Hale wanted to excuse the sentinel who shot the intruder, even though the intruder was the commanding officer

---

* We make this qualification because a person may act knowing what he is doing, but his act is an impulsive act. But one leaves fact and enters theory when one speaks about impulsive acts done knowingly but at the same time done impulsively, e.g., the psychopath who states that he knows he might kill a person, and then, a short while later, does kill that person. Is such a deliberate act done voluntarily but out of malice? Or is it an act knowingly done but indeliberately so?

of the sentinel. We also saw that Hale quoted from Plowden of the innocent youth who set down poison for *C.* unknowing that it be poison, and Hale approved of the excuse of ignorance to prevail. Technically, one attacking a police officer must claim that he, *D*, acted in self-defense against whom he believed to be a criminal third party,[139] or, if an offense under a statute, a defense may be that the statute was ambiguous as to requiring that an officer make himself known to *D* (at the time of, or just prior to the attack).[140] Although the courts will generally impute malice to *D* over the death of *P* (who was an unrecognized officer of the law), the imputation is rebuttable, though difficult, by *D*. If it is clearly demonstrated to the court that *D*'s intention was not a criminal intention, that *D*'s action, in and of itself, was not unlawful, then *D* has discharged the burden of proof which strict liability statutes tend to cast upon him. Certainly it is general common law theory that an accused need not prove his innocence; it is a curious feature of strict liability statutes and offenses that they required *D* to *disprove* the charges of the Crown or the prosecution by showing that the elements of the statute or offense have not been established, and this often requires that *D* take the witness stand on behalf of himself. Strict liability legislation has to it an evidential ease. Much like trespass it need only demonstrate the fact and from the fact impute an intention (as with strict licensing law).

Our suggestion that a burden is thrown upon *D* to declare his state of mind is not a novel suggestion. If one adverts to a book on evidence close to the period one will read the following:

> On an indictment for murder, self-defence ought to be given in evidence, and not pleaded, because nothing can justify one private man's killing another (citing Co. Lit. 283 a. as authority to be consulted).
>
> ---
>
> Indictment for murder *ex malitia praecogitata*, and the evidence is of killing without provocation; the killing an officer; or that the party was committing an unlawful act, and that death ensued to somebody, upon that action; if the act was deliberate, and tended to the personal hurt of any one, this is proof of *murder*, for in these cases, the law implies the circumstances of *malice*; this implication of law, is for the defence of its officers and of mankind; for all *malice* is a secrect quality of the mind, and it is the fact only appears, and is able to be brought to proof, and it is from the circumstances

> of fact that a man must collect the offence of the mind; now when one man kills another, that is *prima facie* so ill-natured and bloody an action, that it is presumed to be malicious, and therefore the offender, to cover himself from the supposition that the law has made in tenderness to mankind, must shew some *provocation*, or some *accident* in excuse of the fact; and if he cannot thus mollify or excuse the actions, the supposition of law remains, and he ought to be punished with death.[141]

Abstracting from the rules of evidence which suited that period in history, one can extract the legal principle that intention is a defense to a charge of strict liability if *D* can demonstrate that his intention was lawful (i.e., to defend himself) and that it was based upon reasonable grounds (i.e., it was reasonable for *D* not to have known that *P* [for instance] was an officer rather than an assaulter). Implicit in the defense by appeal to *D*'s intention is the *reasonableness* of the intention, and that would have to be adduced from the surrounding circumstances. The danger inherent in the reasonableness test is this: although *D*'s intention may have been lawful (at the time), it may also have 'been unreasonable (e.g., he should have known the customs and mores of the community, or *D*'s was an innocence beyond belief, etc.).*

The controlling case regarding arrest was *Mackalley's Case* (1611) 9 *Co. Rep.* 66. Simply put, *D* resisted arrest, and *D* struck the Sergeant, who died as a result of the blow. The court did not press *how* the murder happened; it was content with a general statement of facts:

> And I moved all the Judges and Barons, if in this case of killing of a Minister of Justice in the execution of his office, the Indictment might have been general, *Sc.*, that the prisoners *felonice, voluntarie, & ex malitia sua praecogitata, &c. percusser*, without alleging any special matter....[68] So in the case at barr: And in this case of a Sergeant, the Indictment might have been general, That he feloniously and of his forethought malice killed the said *Fells*....The 2. cause was,...That the said *John*

* Note: A simple example can be given from Tort law to show the nature of the distinction between the lawfulness of an action and the unreasonableness yet lawfulness of an action. A motorist is permitted to drive within the posted speed limits down a thoroughfare, stopping only when a signal obliges him to stop. That is both lawful and reasonable driving. But the same case could be made unreasonable, by *D* driving at a proper speed through a traffic light in his favor, but closing his eyes when so doing. It would not be a defense to his hitting a pedestrian who crossed against the traffic signals that he, *D*, did not see the pedestrian. Strictly, the pedestrian should not have been walking against the traffic signals; strictly, the driver legally was permitted entrance into the crossways; unreasonably, *D* was incautious, however.

> *Mackalley, &c. eundum Richard Fells, &c. felonice, voluntarie, & ex militia sua praecogitata, &c. percussit & inforavit, &c.* so that above the special matter which implieth malice, it is expresly [sic] contained in the Indictment, that he feloniously and of his forethought malice killed the said Fells...[and also proved] that [all] the prisoners killed the said Fells of their forethought malice; and so well maintaineth the Indictment. And that in the end was the opinion of all the Judges and Barons of the Exchequer.[142]

Discharging any objection that the indictment was tainted (for form or substance) *D* and his accomplices were found guilty of having murdered Sergeant Fells. The Prisoner, Mackalley, had urged upon the court that he could not know truly if Fells were an officer or minister because it was night when the arrest occurred (5 to 6 pm in November). But the court replied that he could have had recourse to a legal remedy of false imprisonment had it been a wrongful arrest. From the facts of the case it appears that the arresting officer did identify himself, but either it was not a complete identification, or it lacked in some technical finesse. To this the court said,

> 2. It was Resolved, That if any Magistrate or Minister of Justice, in execution of their office, or in keeping of the peace according to the duty of his office be killed, it is murder, for their contempt and disobedience to the King, and to the Law,...and therefore, if a Sheriff, etc., or any one who commeth in their aid be killed in doing of their office, it is murder...: for when the Officer or Kings Minister by process of Law (be it erroneous or not) arresteth one in the Kings name, and they notwithstanding disobey the arrest or Commandment in the Kings name, and kill the officer...reason requireth that this killing and slaying shall be an offence in a higher nature than any offence of this nature; and the same is voluntary, felonious, and murder of forethought malice. And a Watchman by the Law may arrest a Night-walker, 4 H.7.2. and if a Watchman arresteth such a one, and he killeth him, the same is murder. *Vide Heydons case* in the 4th part of my *Reports*.[143*]

* Note: *Heydon's Case*, Trinit. 28 Eliz. in K. B. [1586] 4 *Co. Rep.* 41. Jacobus Heydon killed Edward Savage, watchman, wounding him in August, with death following in the following December. Since Savage was, it was presumed, in the course of his duty as a watchman, *D*'s killing of him was murder. Coke also cites *Seymayne's Case* (1604) 5 *Co. Rep.* 91b, as authority that a sheriff may arrest at night, but with a caution: "3. In all Cases when the King is party, the Sheriff (if the doors be not open) may break the parties [sic] house, either to arrest him, or to do execution of the Kings process, if otherwise he cannot enter. But before he breaks it, he ought to signifie the cause of his coming, and to make request to open the doors" (91-b).

The force of the authority, then, seems to indicate that legal authority is absolute, but an arresting officer, etc., ought to take prudent measures, and that *D*, if he does resist, ought *not* to be resisting to avoid arrest (which would then make *D*'s resistance an unlawful act) but resistance for the purpose of self-defense (which would then raise the question of self-defense and ignorance of fact). Hale's treatment of resisting (and/or killing) one not known to *D* to be an officer affirmed the position developed by Coke and the Bench in *Mackalley's Case*. One may extract as *obiter dictum* that an arresting officer, or the like, must act reasonably in the discharge of his office. When he does not, then he may place himself into the category of the lawful but foolish motorist whose car strikes the pedestrian wrongly crossing against the traffic signal, but the driver was unobservant, having closed his eyes. The duty, then, of *D* in the charge of resisting arrest (and/or killing) must be to show that his intention as the defendant was not in the entertaining of an unlawful purpose, that his action or response was, in the circumstances, reasonable; and also that the action of the victim was unreasonable, in addition to showing the court that the lawful identity of the victim could not, at that moment, be ascertained. Hale accepts the reasonableness test:

> 5. But whether it be in the day or night, it is sufficient notice, if he declare himself to be the constable, or command the peace in the king's name, and the like for any, that come in his assistance, or for a watchman, &c., and therefore, if any of them are kild [sic] after such a notification, it is murder in them, that kill him. 9 *Co. Rep.* 68.b. *Mackalley's case*.[144]

Hale continues in his acceptance of the traditional doctrine of transferred malice, but, from the example, it appears that the object of a wrongful intent must lie within boundaries the class of object proscribed by the law:

> If A. by malice fore-thought strikes at B. and missing him strikes C. whereof he die, tho he never bore any malice to C. yet it is murder, and he *transfers the malice* [italics ours] to the party slain; the like of poisoning.[145]

When Hale discusses manslaughter the distinction is simply made as a legal act which is voluntary but which is devoid of malice, be it expressed or implied.[146] The logical assumption which is preserved is not that *D* acts unintentionally (he may, but one must carefully qualify how the term "unintentional" is being used so as to avoid an ambiguity), but that the intention *D* entertains does not fulfil or meet the *mens rea* required for a finding of murder. One may establish a logical distinction between classes. One class may read, "If 'X,' then *phi*," and a contrary class may read, "If 'Y,' then *psi*," giving as a rule of interpretation that if class "*phi*" = "a," and class "*psi*" = "b," then a class distinction obtains if and only if "a" < = / = > "b." Intentional actions may fall into both classes, but the *object* of an intentional action (*arguendo*) can fall only into one class or the other.[*]

The confusion which sometimes arises in discussions of manslaughter is to confuse what function "intention" has for *D*, and in the definition of the crime *per se* as an act devoid of intention. What the law holds is that nothing which *D* intends happens to fall within the intentional class of objects proscribed by the law. Drawing upon the simple equation (*supra*), it is as if the law says that in order for murder to be found, what *D* did intend must have been some intentional object within the class "*phi*." If the defendant succeeds in showing to the court that he did not *phi*, but, in fact, was *psi*-ing, it then follows of course that "to *psi*" is not to entertain an object which is a member of a forbidden legal class; furthermore, it may then follow that *D* either is not guilty, or may be guilty of a lesser offense (depending upon the nature of the charge and the facts surrounding the case).

From what we have said one might feel safe to assume that Hale then used only the vocabulary of intention to describe lesser forms of killing. In fact, he did not. He moves to the language of the voluntary to speak about some forms of killing.[147] When he does so he establishes this proposition as a general definition of such killings:

> Involuntary homicide is the death or hurt of the person of a man against or besides the will of him that kills him.[148]

Given this general statement, Hale proceeds to divide it then into categories:

---

* This simple exercise is not helped by arguing about null classes or null sets. The assumption entertained here is, If an act, then an object, and "act" may be broadly interpreted to include omission, as in, "He may not attempt to dissuade his accomplice from firing the pistol at P." D_2 here has not acted positively; he has omitted to act, but his omission (for the law) is taken as the positive act of being an accomplice or confederate to a wrongful act.

> This involuntary homicide is of two kinds, *viz.*, either, 1. When it is purely involuntary and casual, as the killing of a man *per infortunium*, or, 2. When it is partly involuntary, and partly voluntary, but occasiond [sic] by a necessity, that the law allows, which is commonly called homicide *ex necessitate*, as killing a man in his own defense, or the like.[149]

The cases which he instances to depict the categories are common cases, and need not concern us. What does deserve some question at least is: why the language of the will to categorize non-intentional killings?

A consideration one could suggest, with regard to the text could be this. When a person is entertaining a lawful intention, and then sets about to execute his intention, the language of Hale's period might describe the act in this way. The intellect entertains an object, and the will, when moving the person to execute or reach or achieve that object, is said to act voluntarily when it attains or effects union with the object presented to it by the intellect. Now this is stick language for us, and it seems to be a creaky way to depict acts of intention and willing. At the bottom, however, is a sensible enterprise: namely, how to distinguish what one intended to do from what one did not intend to do.

This can be shown in a number of ways, of course. One can say that he did not intend to do "X" because he did not know that "X" possessed the properties or qualities that it did. For instance, one may say that he intended to give *P* a tablet for his headache, whereupon he discovered that the tablet was a diuretic. The reply of *D* might be then to say that he did not know the tablet possessed this property, and from that reply one can ask, Should *D* have known this (i.e., was *D* careless or reckless or negligent)? or was this a blameless inadvertence on the part of *D* not to have known this property of this tablet? However the case is resolved, one is appealing to some form of "ignorance" on the part of *D*. This is not to speak of the act as voluntary or not. It is only to speak of the act in terms of knowledge, or its lack.

Although a case could be made that Hale could have used this kind of language to depict lesser forms of killings, he did not. He seems aware that some confusion could arise between the distinctions of murder/manslaughter and involuntary killing, as this example shows:

> Regularly he that voluntarily and knowingly intends hurt to the person of a man, tho he intend not death, yet if death ensues, it

> excuseth not from the guilt of murder, or manslaughter at least, as if A. intends to beat B. but not to kill him, yet if death ensues, this is not *per infortunium*, but murder or manslaughter, as the circumstances of the case happen.[150]

It may be good, at this point, to stop here and deal with the common example. Why does it not support a claim for death *per infortunium*?

It may be what we said earlier, that the example takes as a category of the unlawful *either* "to intend to kill" *or* "to hurt in a grievous way." Truly, a logical distinction can be maintained between "intending to kill" and "intending to hurt the body of *P*." But for the law this has been (at some times[151]) a difficult distinction to support realistically. What Hale has assumed in his example (*supra*) is that *D* has entertained an unlawful intention (i.e., to kill *P*, or to harm *P* grievously), *and if*, because *D* effected that unlawful intention, further consequences follow as a result of *D*'s wrongful intention, then *D* may be held not simply accountable for hurting *P*, but, in event of *P*'s death, actually for having caused the death of *P*. Though *D*, by one portion of the example, did not intend to kill *P*, the unlawful actions of *D* were the *sine qua non* for the subsequent death of *P*. Bodily harm, being an occasion for a possible death, the law treats as if it were the occasion of actual death.

Without embarking upon an attempt to solve whether "intending to kill" should be taken to be logically equivalent to "causing grievous bodily harm" in the crime of murder, one may extract from Hale's example this guide. *D* both knowingly and voluntarily intended to hurt *P*. When the hurt was brought about it was not some state of affairs *D* did not want to know of, nor some state of affairs which *D* did not seek to cause. With regard to the object of his intention ("to cause harm to *P*") *D* was of single purpose both in mind and in will. That the consequences exceeded what *D* had intended and executed can be said to be a risk inherent in *D*'s intention and act. To seek deliberately and voluntarily to harm a person under the protection of the King's peace is to seek deliberately and voluntarily to violate the law, and the unlawful risk which *D* causes will be held to embrace the consequences within the scope of the unlawful risk. Three ingredients are put forth: 1) the initial act was unlawful, 2) the intention of *D* was unlawful, 3) *D* voluntarily pursued his wrongful intent in the act of causing grievous bodily harm to *P*.

The classic ingredients of *versari in re illicita* are present, save to argue for a strong form of *versarii* which held that the wrongful consequences must stem directly from the wrongful intention. Hale, in one sense, has argued for a diminished form of *versarii* (in this example) by holding that the offense could be either murder or manslaughter, depending upon the surrounding circumstances of the case.*

The *per infortunium* example assumes that *D* is not intending an unlawful object. Thus the "intellectual" requirement for an object, at law, is that what *D* knows and intends, as a result of his knowledge, is to achieve a lawful object or end. The will of *D*, therefore, sets in action – if we may be permitted recourse to stick language – to achieve a good end, but, *somehow*, a harm results. What answer is given to how the harm occurred will also be an answer as to whether *D*'s act, and its consequences, were involuntary, and thus were lawful.

The class of "*per infortunium*" is that class of actions done, in some respect, through ignorance. The ignorance is established by putting a question about the consequences to the will of the agent. Did *D* seek voluntarily to harm *P*? If the answer is, No, then the further question is, How then did the harm issue forth? Having discharged the "lawful" requirement – i.e., *D* was engaged in, or intending to bring about a lawful act – one turns to the nature of the voluntary (in what was done). How is it that *D* voluntarily sought to *phi*, but, in effect, *psi*-ed?

Two replies may be given. *Psi* may either be related to what *D* voluntarily did, or it may be unrelated to what *D* voluntarily did.

An example of the first leg of the disjunct is that *D* is engaged in a lawful sport, but *P* is hurt, or even injured grievously (e.g., wrestling, sword play [Hale gives the case of Sir John Chichester],** etc.). If, contrary to the

---

* Note: Strong form would hold that only if *D* intended to kill *P*, could murder then be found. Weak form would argue that though *D* may not have intended to kill *P* ("murder"), an assault which produced death would, at the very least, constitute an assault which was manslaughter, i.e., causing a wrongful death at criminal law but lacking of murderous intent.

** Note: Of the case, Hale says, "the end of the rapier prickt the servant in the groin, whereof he died: Sir John Chichester was for indicited of murder...and it was ruled, 1. that it was not murder tho the act itself was not lawful, because there was no malice or ill will between them. 2. That it was not barely chance-medley, or *per infortunium*, because the act,

Chichester case, the sport is lawful, then the harm which comes about is not a harm which *D* wills, and properly it is then said that *D*'s action was involuntary. He did not try rationally to execute a harm. The harm was caused by *D*, in that to explain the harm causally one would have to appeal to the actions *D* brought about; but that harm could not be attributed either to what *D* knew or intended, or to what *D* willed, or what voluntarily he wished to do. By excluding a class of predicates (i.e., voluntary, intentional, wrongful, deliberate) one excludes attribution of the harm to *D*, and, as it were, moves the act from the sphere of criminal responsibility to tortious responsibility. No class of criminal predicates apply to describe what *D* caused or brought about. The relationship which obtains between *P*'s death and *D*'s act is causative; what does not obtain between *D*'s act and the resultant harm was that *D* intended to harm *P*, or that *D* set about to harm *P*, or that *D* was engaged in unlawful conduct when the death of *P* happened.

From a simple relation of cause, there may be a second relationship which makes *D* even farther removed from harmful consequences. *D*, lawfully, is chopping down his own tree, and, as the tree falls over, it falls upon sleeping *P*, killing him. In the simplest of language, the lines of causality have intersected, i.e., but for the tree falling, and but for *P* sleeping (unnoticed) nearby at the same moment, no harm would have resulted. *D* is in no way involved with *P* (as, to the contrary, *D*, is involved with *P* in the first example). One has here only a happening.

In the first example other than what *D* sets about to do happens; in the second case, *D*'s doing of something inadvertently is the cause of harm because *P* intersects himself, or is there, when one course of action begins, harmless in its objective, but harmful if some other element is introduced. Both are involuntary harms (or classes of involuntary harms) because *D* had not willed to cause a harm. The intention which he sought to realize was a lawful intention; therefore, the object of his will was a lawful good. In seeking voluntarily to bring about, he was not seeking to create a risk, or

---

which occasiond [sic] the death, intended no harm, nor could it have done harm, if the chape had not been stricken off by the party kild [sic], and tho the parties were in sport, yet the act itself, the thrusting at his servant, was unlawful" (1*PC*473).

harm, or danger. That a risk, or harm, or danger resulted or ensued was an involuntary result or consequence.

We have, then, just the reverse of what we depicted earlier. What we have here is: 1) the initial act of *D* is a lawful act, 2) *D*'s intention is lawful, and 3) *D* is voluntarily intending to bring about a lawful act. The harm or injury which ensues is neither intended nor willed by *D*, and the elements surrounding the act are lawful. The harm which results is either one of pure accident (i.e., *P* walks out in front of *D*'s oncoming vehicle, etc.) or one in which the consequences are said neither to have been intended or willed by *D* in the course of lawful conduct (i.e., the hunting accident, the sports accident, or forms of relationships where *D* is lawfully involved with *P*, but as a consequence of the relationship *P* is harmed unintentionally). *D*'s act is then, for the purpose of the law, described as an involuntary act because the harm to *P* was not a harm which *D* would have sought to have brought about had the circumstances been other than they were. It is as if *D* had answered, "I would not have willed to do this if I had known, beforehand, that harm would have resulted from what I had done." Because *D* did not seek voluntarily to cause this harm, his act is said to be involuntary. The object of his willing was not the object willed.

Hale's understanding of criminal intention applied variously to the mind and to the will of *D*. *D* could be said to entertain an unlawful intent; *D* could also be said to have acted deliberately against the law. In the first instance, "intent" is predicated of the mind, reason, intellect, understanding; in the second instance, "intent" is predicated of the will, pertains to the voluntary, or is deliberate (as in "a deliberate act"). To do an unlawful act from malice prepense implied that one could know that his act was unlawful, could set about to do the unlawful act, and that what was done could be described as being unlawful, giving rise to three conditions surrounding the act of *D* at law: that the law had defined an action to be lawful or unlawful; that *D* had the capacity to know that his act was unlawful; and that *D* could voluntarily have brought about the unlawful act. To alter these conditions could, in theory, alter *D*'s guilt or innocence, or degree of responsibility for his actions.

A clear distinction regarding "malicious" and "wilful" is given to us by Hale when he treats of the crime of Arson.[152] It was a crime which consisted in the wilful and malicious burning of a house of another by day or by night. The definition of the crime provides for its maliciousness, as where *D* sets out to burn the house of another *and* the law has forbidden this kind of conduct by proscribing it; and *D*, in setting fire to the house, provides the element of the "wilful" in the offense:

> But if A. have a malicious intent to burn the house of B. and in setting fire to it burns the house of B. and C. or the house of B. escapes by some accident, and the fire takes in the house of C. yet in law it shall be said the malicious and wilful burning of the house of C. and he may be indicted for the malicious and wilful burning of the house of C.[153]

The three elements for a criminal offense are present: the definition of the crime (as proscribed by law); the object of the intent, i.e., to burn the house of *B*; and the voluntary execution by *D* of his intent, i.e., actually setting fire to the house of *B*. Since the intentional action is proscribed by law, the consequences of *D*'s act are viewed as criminal consequences, and they are proscribed by law. Hale would reject that the consequences are involuntary because they were foreseeable, although he does not use the term "foreseeable." He reasons to that position by this statement:

> An infant of about fourteen years of age or under may be guilty of malicious burning of houses, if by circumstances it can appear he knew it to be evil.[154]

One may assume that if the Crown or prosecution could demonstrate that it was reasonable for *D* to know of the possible consequences of his act, or that it was reasonable for it to be known (by a reasonable man) of the consequences of setting fire to a house (i.e., that it could burn down other houses because of the danger of a fire once started being such as to be outside of control), this would be much the same as asking of a youth if he *knew* that what he did was wrong. Hale invites a knowledge test, part of which may mean: if one knew when he was causing a harm, surely it would be reasonable to assume then the harm could be larger or wider in scope than anticipated. The test of "reasonableness," like the test for wrongfulness with a fourteen year old, would be to advert to the circumstances of the case, and make deductions from those circumstances.

Since we are not dealing with abstract categories in and of themselves, it should not be overlooked that the court will seek to ascertain what was the state of the accused's mind at the time of the commission of the offense. We have taken as a corollary of "Ought *D* to have known that 'y' might have happened?" that the court could inquire if it were reasonable to assume that greater harm might have ensued than what *D* intended by inquiring after the state of mind of the accused. Hale provides just such an example of a knowledge test.

He had tried a boy at Norfolk who was near the age of fourteen, and who was charged with malicious arson. In the facts we are told,

> when none were in the house but a child in the cradle, [the boy] carried fire out of the kitchen into a room of furzes, and set fire in it and went out, and thus burnt a second house, and the child in the cradle. For both these he was questioned, and at length confessed freely the whole circumstances of both facts...and upon his trial craftily insisted that he was under fourteen years of age; but I directed the jury, that it appeared by the circumstances, that his malice supplied his age, for it appeared, that he understood the evil of the first offense when he did it so secretly [i.e., the first arson], and yet charged another wrongfully....[155]

The force of the example is to show that the Court will seek to know what is reasonable to expect in the circumstances. In modern language we speak of foreseeability.

We wish to move now from this period of late medieval reasoning in law into our own century. With Hale, the scholastic mind in the common law had come to an end.

Endnotes Chapter 6

1. The standard bibliography and biography of Matthew Hale is that from which we have taken earlier extractions: *Matthew Hale* by Edmund Heward (London: Robert Hale, 1972). Master Heward, of the Royal Courts of Justice, gives a full account of both published and unpublished works of Hale. The *Tract on Natural Law* is unpublished, and is held by the British Museum in its Harlean Collection as HARL. MS. 7159 (and it is also listed on p. 184 as manuscript #5 by Heward [Appendix B, Hale Manuscripts at British Museum]). We shall cite the manuscript as: *Natural Law*, giving both the manuscript number, and the page of the folio.

2. "But he that incites a *Mad-man* to kill another, is a principal Murtherer." The *Summary* (London: 1694), "Murther," p. 43.

3. *Pleas of the Crown, or, A Methodical Summary of the Principal Matters relating to that Subject*, by Sir Matthew Hale, Knight, Late Chief Justice of the King's-Bench (London: printed by the Assigns of Richard Atkyns and Edward Atkyns...for William Shrewsbury and John Leigh, 1694).

4. *Ibid.*, *cf.*, "The Table: Notes used by the Author in his References."

5. *Ibid.*, "Heresie," pp. 3-5; "Witchcraft," pp. 6-8; "High Treason," pp. 9-22; "Of Felonies...," pp. 26-59.

6. *Ibid.*, "Manslaughter," pp. 56-57.

7. *Ibid.*, p. 225

8. *Ibid.*, p. 119.

9. *Ibid.*, "Murther," p. 4.

10. *Ibid.*, p. 23.

11. The first edition of the *Pleas* was in 1678, two years after Hale's death. Save for this edition of the *Summary* (which was the first authorized edition, an unauthorized edition appearing, also, in 1678), we have only his *Preface* to *Rolle's Abridgment* (London: 1668). The book is, therefore, an early book, and the use of "intent" throughout the work is, subsequently, early within the corpus of Hale's writings.

12. *Summary*, p. 6.

13. *Ibid.*, p. 7.

14. *Ibid.*, p. 83.

15. *Ibid.*, p. 67.

16. *Ibid.*, p. 58.

17. *Ibid.*, p. 51.

18. *Ibid.*, p. 50.

19. *Ibid.*, "High Treason," p. 13.

20. *Cf.*, *The Third Institute*, the title, "High Treason," cap. 1., paragraph (5).

21. *Summary*, "Murther," p. 53.

22. *Ibid.*, "Misprision of Treason. The Negative Misprisions," p. 127.

23. *Ibid.*, "High Treason," p. 21.

24. *Cf.*, *infra*, note 60.

25. *Ibid.*, "Murther," *cf.*, the body of the question, "What said *Malice*?" pp. 44-45.

26. *The Primitive Origination of Mankind, Considered and Examined According to the Light of Nature*, by Sir Matthew Hale (London: 1677).

27. *De Homine* occupies pp. 1-70 of the first edition of 1677 (*supra*).

28. The theory of "double truth" was one extreme position, espousing that one degree of truth applied for philosophy, and another degree of truth applied for theology, and that one sphere could contradict another sphere. *Cf.*, Boetius of Dacia, "On the Supreme Good," in *Medieval Philosophy*, edited by John F. Wippel and A. B. Wolter, O.F.M. (New York: The Free Press, 1969), pp. 367-375. Also, *cf.*, "On Faith and Reason," by John Duns Scotus, in *Medieval Philosophy*, edited by Herman Shapiro (Modern Library, 1964), pp. 441-480.

29. "So *the impure and Corrupted angels* haunt and flock about a man given over to vice, till they have wholly corrupted and putrified his soul; and those good men whom they cannot win over to them, they pursue with as much malice and envy as they can possibly; and although they cannot come within them, yet as far as they can, watch opportunities to ensnare or blemish them, though the vigilancy of a better guard, and their own prudence and circumspection, do for the most part disappoint and prevent them." At p. 361 of "Motives to Watchfulness in Reference to the good and evil Angels," from *The Works, Moral and Religious* of Sir Matthew Hale, edited by Rev. T. Thirlwall, M.A. (London: for J. White, 1805), volume two.

30. *De Homine*, p. 46.

31. *Ibid.*

32. *Ibid.*

33. *Ibid.*, pp. 46-47.

34. Two recent authors would reject Hale's assumptions outright. In J. L. Mackie's, *Ethics, Inventing Right and Wrong* (Penguin Books, 1977), and in Gilbert Harman's, *The Nature of Morality, An Introduction to Ethics* (New York: Oxford University Press, 1977), both scholars would argue generally that moral standards are not grounded upon natural perceptions of a necessary order to be found in the world. Moral rules are more conventions and agreements, akin to contracts, and not necessary natural perceptions of an inner moral sense, akin to some notions of natural law and natural moral order. A contrary view can, however, be found which is espoused by an English moralist. In *Authority in Morals*, by Gerard J. Hughes, S.J. (London: Heythrop Monographs, Heythrop College, 1978), its author argues that moral authority is derived both from natural law and from a consistent natural theology (*cf.*, Chapter IV of his text, "Authority in the Christian Community," pp. 91-121).

35. One may refer to the following treatise which will bear out how much Hale was a voice of standard moral perceptions of the period: *A Treatise of the Passions and Facvlties of the Soule of Man*, by Edward Reynoldes (late Preacher to the Honorable Society of *Lincoln's Inne*), (London: Robert Bostock, 1640). Hale was called to the Bar of Lincoln's Inn in 1628, and remained at the Bar until 1651. There is little doubt, with his interest in theology and philosophy, that Reynoldes would have been known to Hale, and, therefore, that Reynoldes' large work, *A Treatise*, would have been known to Hale. *A Treatise* is a very compelling work of the philosophy of mind which thoroughly presents the accepted wisdom of the period, and is deeply indebted to the Aristotelian corpus for its fundamental assumptions in psychology and epistemology.

36. *De Homine*, p. 47.

37. *Ibid.*, p. 52.

38. *Ibid.*, p. 54.

39. *Ibid.*, p. 55.

40. *Ibid.*, pp. 57-58.

41. *De Homine*, p. 58.

42. *Ibid.*

43. *Ibid.*

44. *Ibid.*, pp. 58-59.

45. *Ibid.*, p. 59.

46. *Ibid.*

47. *Ibid.*, pp. 59-60.

48. *Ibid.*, p. 60.

49. *Ibid.*, *cf.*, p. 46 ff.

50. *Ibid.*

51. *Ibid.*, *cf.*, pp. 54-55 ff.

52. *Ibid.*, p. 59.

53. *Leviathan*, by Thomas Hobbes of Malmesbvry (London: printed for Andrew Crooke, 1651), *Of Man*, Part I, Chapter VI, "Of the Interiour Beginnings of Voluntary Motions; commonly called the Passions," pp. 28-29.

54. *De Homine*, p. 58.

55. An aspect of Hale's theory of behavior is that a wise man must learn to control the objects of his desire. In part, then, what objects a person entertains will reveal if one is a virtuous person or not. This sentiment is expressed in his essay, "Of The Moderation of The Affections," to be found in volume two, pp. 363-372, of *The Works, Moral and Religious of Sir Matthew Hale*, edited by Rev. T. Thirlwall, M.A. (London: for J. White, 1805). In the essay, "Of Wisdom and The Fear of God," to be found in *Contemplations Moral and Divine* (London: printed by William Godbind for William Shrowsbury, 1676), pp. 17-52, Hale advances the general notion that a proper fear and reverence of and for God will direct a man's passions properly–which is to advance a standard Christian teaching. The same sentiment is consistent with what is expressed in *Primitive Origination*: "Man hath in the peculiarity of his nature these two great Powers and receptive Faculties, whereby he is rendred [sic] amply capable of a great enjoyment, namely his Understanding, whose proper Object is Truth, and the noblest Truth that is, and its proper action is directed to that Object, namely, Intellection and Will, whose proper Object is [Good,] and the greater and more sovereign the Good is, the more suitable it is to this power, and the proper act of this power is to reach after, and desire, and embrace, and delight in its Object: and the filling of these two receptive powers with the chiefest intellectual Truth, and with the chiefest and intellectual Good, is that which perfects, advanceth, and enableth these Faculties or Powers" pp. 377-378, Section IV, Cap, VIII, "A farther Enquiry touching the End of the Formation of Man, so far as the same may be collected by Natural Light & Ratiocination." Hale closes the logic of the argument in the same chapter by stating, "And this doth lead us to a just discovery of what that end of fruition is, for which Man was designed by his beneficent Creator, namely, such as is suitable, answerable, and proportionate to those Powers or Faculties in Man whereby he excells all inferior Animals, his Understanding and his Will; and herein consists his happiness, his end of fruition or enjoyment" p. 378. This is a form of the traditional Christian argument that the proper object of the

Will and of the Intellect is God: for the Will, God as the ultimate good; for the Intellect, God as ultimate truth. And, within the tradition of transcendentals, truth and goodness, when applied to God, are convertible. The unity of man is affirmed through his faculties of understanding and of will exercised upon an eternal, personal object: God as good and God as true.

56. Section IV, Cap, VIII, "A farther Enquiry touching of the End of the Formation of Man, so far as the same may be collected by Natural Light and Ratiocination" of, *The Primitive Origination of Mankind*, pp. 378-379.

57. *Cf.*, for instance, any of the following works discussing the Will: *The Darkness of Atheism Dispelled by the Light of Nature*, by Walter Charleton (London: printed by J. F. for William Lee, 1652), esp. Chapter VII, "Of the Liberty Elective of Mans (sic) Will" pp. 257-288. Also, *cf.*, both of Kenelm Digby's works, 1) *Two Treatises: The Nature of Bodies*, and *The Nature of Man's Soul* (London: printed for John Williams, M.DC.LVIII). The second Treatise, "The Nature and Operations of Man's Soul," was printed in London, 1657. [The Wing number is: W-1450.] In the *First Treatise* (Bodies) *cf.*, chapters 33, 34, 35, 36 and 37, pp. 346-419, which discuss the human faculties in general. In the *Second Treatise* (Souls), *cf.*, chapter two, "Of Thinking and Knowing," pp. 14-27, and chapter four, "How a man proceedeth to actions," pp. 41-49. Also, *cf.*, *A Discourse of the Freedom of the Will*, by Peter Sterry (London: printed for John Starkey, 1675). Also, *cf.*, *The Use of the Passions*, by J. F. Senault, and put into English by Henry, Earl of Monmouth (London: 1649), esp., chapter five, *The Fifth Treatise*, "Of the Power the Passion have upon the Will of Man," pp. 157-192. A general text which concerned human *self-control* and perfection was *Miscellanea Spritualia* or, *Devovt Essaies*, [by] Walter Montagu, Esq. (London: printed for W. Lee, D. Pakeman, and G. Bedell, M.DC.XLVIII), where one may refer to the book at large for its discussion of the will in relation to human passions and perfection. Joseph Truman argued for the freedom of the will in his *A Discourse of Natural and Moral Impotency* (London: printed for Robert Clavel, 1671), and one may argue that the book expressed the sentiment of the time which Hale himself reflected. Much of this general sentiment could also be related to the spiritual problem of the period of the relationship between action and belief, i.e., liberty of conscience. One may refer to the practical spiritual problem posed by will and differing beliefs. *Cf.*, *Tracts on Liberty of Conscience and Persecution, 1614-1661*, edited for the Hanserd Knollys Society by E. B. Underhill (London: for J. Haddon, 1846), the body of the volume. One of the strongest statements as to the rationality of will is to be found in Bishop John Bramhall's, *A Defence of True Liberty From Antecedent & Extrinsecal Necessity* (Dublin: M.DC.LXX.V.), which occupies pp. 647-729, as Tome III, found in the collected works (Dublin: 1676). One may assume, too, that Hale was familiar with Bramhall's other rejoinder to Thomas Hobbes: *Castigations of Mr. Hobbes, His Last Animadversions in The Case concerning Liberty, and Universal Necessity* (Dublin: 1658).

58. *Tract on Natural Law*, by Lord Chief Justice Hale, Harlean Manuscript 7159, British Museum, folio page 95a, beginning with, "Fifthly...." The manuscript is fairly well preserved, but the script is difficult to decipher.

Where we have had difficulties we have put into brackets, "[ ]," portions which are unclear, or portions which seem to require additional words to make sense of the text.

59. *Ibid.*, 95a.

60. *Ibid.*, 97a-97b.

61. *Ibid.*, 98a.

62. *Ibid.*

63. *Ibid.*, 3a.

64. *Ibid.*, 6a.

65. Taken from page 126 of *Principality and Polity* by Thomas Gilby, O.P. (London: Longmans, Green and Co., 1958), Chapter V, section 2, "The Concept of Law."

66. *Tract*, 5b-6a.

67. *Ibid.*, 6b-7b.

68. *Ibid.*, 90a-92a ff.

69. *Ibid.*, 196b.

70. *Ibid*, 197a-197b.

71. *Ibid.*, 14a-15a.

72. *Ibid.*, 142a. Also, *cf.*, *De Vera Obedientia oratio* by Bishop Stephen Gardiner (Thomas Berthelet, 1535) [STC Number: 11584], who permits such dissent for similar reasons.

73. *Cf.* endnote 70 (*supra*).

74. 1 *Hale P.C.*, pp. 14-15, Chap. II, "Concerning the several incapacities of persons, and their exemptions from penalties by reason thereof."

75. *Ibid.*

76. 1 *Hale P.C.*, p. 25, part '1' of section II of Chap. III, "Touching the defect of infancy and nonage."

77. 1 *Hale P.C.*, p. 30, Chap. IV, "Concerning the defect of Ideocy, Madness and Lunacy, in reference to criminal offenses and punishments."

78. *Ibid.*

79. 1 *Hale P.C.*, p. 34 ff.

80. 1 *Hale P.C.*, pp. 36-37. Note: If one cannot knowledgeably commit a felony, then, by parity of reasoning, one cannot commit treason so knowingly to be a betrayer ["*proditorie*"]. In this excerpt Hale distinguishes an action done wilfully ("*per electionem*") from an action done with the guidance of knowledge ("*intentionem*"). It is to be remembered, from his own observations on the nature of the will and the intellect, that *each* are reasonable faculties, but with regard to the Will its reasonable nature does not, of necessity, compel its motion–and, as we have remarked earlier, an appetite *in se* as an appetite (and thus a proper object for the Will) does not, out of logical necessity, compel the Will to it as an object necessarily to be willed. An appetite *may* direct the Will; it would not, to use Hobbesean language, for Hale, compel the Will or necessarily direct the Will in its election.

81. 1 *Hale P.C.* pp. 38-41, Chap. V, "Concerning casualty and misfortune, how it excuseth in criminals."

82. *Ibid.*, p. 38.

83. *Cf.*, *De Homine*, Sect. 1, Cap. 2, p. 50 ff.

84. *De Homine*, p. 55.

85. *De Homine*, Sect. 1., Cap. II, "Touching the Excellency of the Humane Nature in general," pp. 50-51.

86. *Cf.*, *Willing, Trying and Doing*, by Michael Gorr (*Australian Journal of Philosophy*, Volume 57, Number 3, September 1979 [published by: Bundoora, Melbourne, Victoria, Australia: La Trobe University, 3083]), pp. 237-250, for a modern statement of expressing the relationship between volition, intellection, and action. Representative examples of his position may be seen in these excerpts: "Volitions are mental events or processes which function to *explain* the intentionality or purposiveness that is characteristic of action; consequently they can never be rightly analysed *as* actions (or even as *parts* of actions)" (p. 237). "'Volition'...denotes a mental state or process which expresses a propositional attitude and which tends to initiate behavioural episodes corresponding to the content of that propositional attitude" (*ibid.*). "An important objection that might be raised...is that my suggestion leaves quite mysterious the exact nature of the relationship between volitions and intentions. If the two are as alike as I have supposed, considerations of simplicity would seem to dictate that they be identified with one another. Standing in the way of such an identification...is the fact, in general, volitions appear much more closely tied to actions than do intentions. If...I will to reach out with my hand and pick up the pencil on my desk, my reaching out and picking up the pencil is almost always what actually follows. If...I merely form the intention of going to Chicago next week, it is nowhere near as likely that such an intention will in fact be fulfilled" (p. 248).

87. 1 *Hale P.C.*, Chap. V, "Concerning casualty and misfortune, how far it excuseth in criminals," p. 39.

88. *Ibid.*

89. 1 *Hale P.C.*, p. 49 ff., Chap. VIII, "Concerning the civil incapacities by compulsion and fear."

90. *Ibid.*, p. 51.

91. *Ibid.*

92. *The Laws* (of Plato), translated by A. E. Taylor (New York and London: Everyman's Library, 1969), Book 1, section 647 to 648, p. 25.

93. *N.E.*, Bk. III, part 1, "Limitations of moral consent," p. 124 (of the Hatch edition, *op. cit.*), "On the other hand there are deeds, consent to which, even under compulsion, is inconceivable: death itself, under the direst tortures, is to be preferred thereto."

94. 1 *Hale P.C.*, p. 434.

95. *Op. cit.* (*infra.*, endnote 144), pp. 122-123.

96. *A Holy Commonwealth, or Political Aphorisms, Opening The True Principles of Government*, by Richard Baxter (London: printed for Thomas Underhill and Francis Tyton, 1659), Chap. VII, "Of Forced Consent," p. 181 [Wing number: B-1281].

97. *Ductor Dubitantium, or The Rule of Conscience, In all her generall measures; Serving as a great Instrument for the determination of Cases of Conscience* in four books, by: Jeremy Talor, D.D. (London: 1660).

98. *Op. cit.*, The Fourth Book, Of The Nature And Causes Of Good And Evil, Rule VII, p. 511.

99. *Ibid.*

100. *Ibid.*

101. *Ibid.*

102 *Ibid.*, pp. 511-512.

103. *Ibid.*, pp. 512-513.

104. *Ibid.*, p. 513.

105. *Ibid.*

106. *A Treatise of the Passions and Facvlties of the Soule of Man*, by Edward Reynoldes (London: printed by R. H. for Robert Bostock 1640). [S.T.C. number: 20938.] It is a voluminous work spanning 553 pages, richer in detail and examination of authors than *De Homine*, which comprised the first part of Hale's *Primitive Origination*.

107. *A Treatise*, p. 278, Chap. XXI, "Of the Passion of Feare: the Causes of it; Impotency, Obnoxiousnesse, Suddennesse, Neerenesse, Newnesse, Conscience, Ignorance of an Evill."

108. *A Treatise*, p. 274.

109. *A Treatise*, p. 291, which is from Chapter XXVIII, "Of the Effects of Feare, suspition, Circumspection, Superstition, 'Betraying the succours of Reason,' Feare Generative, Reflecting, Inward, Weakening the faculties of the Minde, Base Suspition, Wise Caution" (pp. 290-299).

110. *A Treatise*, p. 292.

111. *Ibid.*

112. *A Treatise*, pp. 548-549, which is Chapter XLII, "Of the Will: its Appetite: with the proper and chiefe Objects thereof, God. Of Superstition and Idolatry. Of its Liberty in the Electing of Means to an End. Of its Dominion Coactive and Perswasive. Of Fate, Astrology. Satanicall Suggestions. Of the manner of the Wils [sic] Operation. Motives to it. Acts of it. The Conclusion" (pp. 537-553).

113. *Cf.*, 1 *Hale P.C.*, p. 42, Chap. VI, "Concerning ignorance, and how far it prevails, to excuse in capital crimes."

114. *Cf.*, *Brett v. Rigden* (1568) 1 *Pl.* 340 at 343.

115. *Cf.*, 1 *Hale P.C.*, p. 42.

116. *Ibid.*

117. Also, *cf.*, 1 *Hale P.C.*, p. 431, re "ignorance": "If A. gives poison to B. intending to poison him, and B. ignorant of it give it to C. a child, or other near relation of A. against whom he never meant harm, and C. takes it and dies, this is murder in A. and a poisoning by him, (*Plowd. Com.* 474 a. *Dalt.* cap. 93), but B. because ignorant, is not guilty."

118. 1 *Hale P.C.*, p. 412, Chap. XXXI, "Concerning homicide and first of self-killing or *felo de se*."

119. 1 *Hale P.C.*, p. 425, Chap. XXXIII, "Of *homicide*, and its several kinds, and first of those considerations that are applicable, as well to *murder* as *manslaughter*."

120. *Cf.*, *Freewill and Responsibility*, by Anthony Kenny (London: Routledge & Kegan Paul, 1978), Chapter One: "The mind and the deed," pp. 1-21, where the author puzzles over a witchcraft case, *Nyuzi and Kudemera v Republic* [1967] African L.R. 249, thinking that the death of V may constitute a criminal offence. We have stated that the analysis given by Kenny is in error, as (here) the citation from Hale would support.

121. 1 *Hale P.C.*, p. 429, Chap. XXXIII.

122. *Cf.*, the body of: "Concerning commanding, counselling or abetting of murder or manslaughter," which is Chap. XXXIV, pp. 435-446, in 1 *Hale* P.C.

123. 1 *Hale P.C.*, p. 443.

124. *Ibid.*

125. *Ibid.*

126. 1 *Hale P.C.*, p. 444.

127. *Cf.*, *Criminal Law*, by Glanville Williams (London: Stevens & Sons Ltd., 1961), wherein he states: "A conspiracy is not merely a concurrence of wills but a concurrence resulting from agreement," Chapter 15, "Conspiracy," pp. 663-713, at p. 667, section 212: *Acts constituting conspiracy*.

128. *Cf. State v. Cooper, et alii*, 1976(2) S.A. 875 *re* "Conspiracy." In the typescript, p. 10, the Court said, "It is a significant feature in this case that the allegation of a conspiracy widened the ambit of initially admissible evidence."

129. 1 *Hale P.C.*, p. 451.

130. *Ibid.*

131. *Cf. Hyam v D.P.P.* [1974] 2 AllE.R. 41 at 43j-44a, Lord Hailsham: "It is acknowledged that intention to achieve the result of death or grievous bodily harm...is enough to convict" for the crime of murder. In *R v. Hyam*, CA [1973] 3 All ER 842 at 844j we read, "It was conceded on her [Hyam's] behalf that her acts had been reckless and she pleaded guilty to manslaughter...."

132. 1 *Hale P.C.*, p. 428, Chap. XXXIII, "Of homicide...."

133. *Ibid.*

134. 1 *Hale P.C.,* p. 455, Chap. XXXVII, "Concerning murder by malice implied presumptive, or malice in law."

135. *Ibid.*

136. 1 *Hale P.C.*, p. 451, Chap. XXXVI, "Touching murder, what it is, and the kinds thereof."

137. 1 *Hale P.C.*, p. 454, Chap. XXXVI.

138. 1 *Hale P.C.*, p. 460. *D* need not know that *P* be an officer he killed.

139. *Cf.*, *Kenlin v. Gardiner* [1966] 3 All.E. R. 931, Winn, L. J. stating, "knowledge that the man attacked is a police officer is unnecessary, but a genuine mistake of fact as to the character of the person concerned, e.g., genuine and reasonable belief that he was a thug and not a police officer, would be highly material in judging the scope of reasonableness and the degree of force falling within the liberty of justification of self-defence," allowing the appeal against the charge of assaulting a police officer in the execution of his duty contrary to s. 51 of the *Police Act*, 1964.

140. *Cf.*, *Sherras v. De Rutzen* [1895] 1 Q.B. 918, quashing D's conviction of having sold liquor to to a constable on duty contrary to section 16 (2) of the *Licensing Act*, 1872. D argued that he did not know that P was a constable on duty, and the court held that this was a reasonable defense, Mr. Justice Day stating," There must in general be guilty knowledge on the part of the defendant...in order to constitute an offence."

141. Essays upon *The Law of Evidence*, by John Morgan [in three volumes] (London: J. Johnson, 1789). *Cf.*, Volume One, "(11) Of the General Issue in Criminal Proceedings ," "(a) Of the Plea of Not Guilty," p. 420 ff., esp. pp. 422, and 424-425.

142. *Mackalley's Case* (1611) 9 *Co. Rep.* at 67b and 68.

143. *Mackalley's Case* (1611) 9 *Co. Rep.* at 68.

144. 1 *Hale P.C.*, p. 461.

145. *Ibid.*, p. 466.

146. *Ibid.*, p. 466, Chap. XXXVIII, "Of manslaughter...."

147. *Ibid.*, Chap. XXXIX, "Touching involuntary homicide, and first of chance-medley or killing *per infortunium*," pp. 471 ff.

148. *Ibid.*, p. 471.

149. *Ibid.*

150. *Ibid.*

151. *Hyam v. D.P.P.* [1974] 2 All E. R. 41 ff., will show how the House of Lords divided [3-2] on what must be the intentional requirement for the offense of murder. *Cf.* the dissent of Lord Diplock at 63h ff., rejecting the grievous bodily harm test in the charge of murder.

152. 1 *Hale P.C.*, p. 566, Chap. XLIX, "Of arson, or wilful burning of houses."

153. *Ibid.*, p. 569.

154. *Ibid.*

155. *Ibid.*, pp. 569-570. Hale found some relief of conscience when he learned that the boy's true age was near to fifteen years of age.

CHAPTER SEVEN

Intention in an Age of Reform

With the twentieth century nearly concluded, one would have thought that the problems which the concept of criminal intention had presented to legal minds would have been solved and put aside, once and for all, and that, like the Sea Captain whom Viola addressed in the *Twelfth Night*, the character of the concept would have been clear and so easily within the comprehension of any man:

> There is a fair behavior in thee, captain,
> And though that nature with a beauteous wall
> Doth oft close in pollution, yet of thee
> I will believe thou hast a mind that suits
> With this thy fair and outward character.
>
> (Act. 1, ii, 47)

Alas, the concept of criminal intention was not as simple as the smile on a girl's face. To the contrary, it was more akin to the lines which follow those above, when Viola continues:

> I prithee (and I'll pay thee bounteously)
> Conceal me what I am, and be my aid
> For such disguise as haply shall become
> The form of my intent...
> What else may hap, to time I will commit;
> Only shape thou thy silence to my wit.
>
> (Act. 1, ii, 52)

Criminal intention seemed to have to it that magician's quality, "Now you see it, now you don't," and it served to perplex this century. The concept did not bear an easily determined or determinable outward character, and, because of its elusive and (possibly) linguistically unframeable character, those who were paid bounteously in its cause were defense attorneys. As recently as

1978, two legal worthies in England did battle over what exactly criminal intent meant.[1] A little over a decade earlier two very great minds crossed swords, each to suggest that the other did not know what he was talking about (as if Plato and Aristotle were to accuse each other of deliberately misunderstanding central philosophical concepts).[2] As if enough had not been written about the concept in the nineteenth century, with its many Reports – and they in turn spawned other Reports in the common law world – minds of this century turned again to the task of making clear and of defining comprehensively what criminal intention meant. To some of those Reports we would now like to turn.

The belief persisted that if only the concept were defined clearly, and given precise limits, then the problems it engendered because of its vagueness or open texture might be solved. Through definition might come progress. Every other science and art had seemingly progressed because of the lucidity of linguistic analysis – physics, philosophy, theology, literary criticism, and, in general, the sciences – why then should not an equal amount of conceptual progress be attending criminal jurisprudence? Had the wrong question been asked? Or was it purely that the wrong answer had been given? It was as if the process of the criminal law had been trapped between the horns of the dilemma which Virginia Woolf vouchsafed on her deathbed: to, "What is the answer?" came the reply, "But what is the question?"

In twentieth-century England, scholars of law internecinely attacked each other through the columns of *The Times*, law journals and reviews, and books on law, with the 1960's and 1970's ablaze as to the meaning of "intention" in criminal law.[3] But not only academics engaged in such conceptual warfare. The appellate process itself presented internal disagreements, with verdicts being modified, remanded, overturned or quashed on appeal. One needs but to look at the central cases of the period to appreciate how the judiciary disagreed among itself. One case, perhaps the most bitterly disputed in judicial and legal circles this century, when it reached the Court of Criminal Appeal, *R. v. Smith* [1960] 2 All E.R. 450, composed of Byrne, Sachs and Winn, J.J., reduced the verdict of the Central Criminal Court, tried by Donovan, J., from murder to manslaughter, arguing that the verdict given in the first court for capital murder ought not to be allowed to stand because the jury instructions given by Donovan, J., were not clear as to the meaning of "intent." The trial judge's instructions, in part, read: "if you are satisfied that...he must, as a reasonable man, have contemplated that grievous bodily harm was likely to result to that officer still clinging on...then the accused is guilty of capital murder." The jury returned a verdict of capital murder *re*/s. 5 (1) (d) of the (then) *Homicide Act*, 1957. On appeal the Court of Criminal Appeal found the instruction on intent to be a misdirection, and therefore it reduced the verdict to one of manslaughter.

Leave to appeal to the House of Lords was given by the Attorney General on May 31, 1960, by granting a certificate under s.1(6) of the *Criminal Appeal Act*, 1907. The Director of Public Prosecutions did appeal the case, while the House of Lords in *D.P.P. v. Smith*, [1961] A.C. 260; [1960] 3 All E.R. 161, reversed the Court of Criminal Appeal, and reinstated the verdict of murder, holding that the direction of the trial judge, Donovan, J., was indeed correct with regard to intent. The progression is well known: the Home Secretary extended clemency, and the verdict of the House of Lords was put aside. Some years later the *Criminal Justice Act*, 1967, was instated, purposely enacted by Parliament to override the decision of the House of Lords in *Smith*.

Shortly after the decision by the House of Lords in *Smith*, the High Court of Australia, in a reserved [sic] verdict, refused to be bound in law by *D.P.P. v. Smith*, [1961] A.C. 260, when it decided *Parker v. The Queen*, [1962-63] 111 C. L. R. 610. Dixon, C.J., stated, "There are propositions laid down in the judgment [*Smith*] which I believe to be misconceived and wrong." He held that *Smith* should not be used as authority in Australia at all.

The echo from the nineteenth century and its proposed criminal codes in which the "meaning" of an act could be determined if the nature of the act were defined with care proved that "meaning" and "nature" could be poles apart. The (relatively) clear language of the *Homicide Act*, 1957, divided common law jurisdictions as to how "intent" ought to be interpreted:

> Sec. 1.-[1] Where a person kills another in the course or furtherance of some other offence, the killing shall not amount to murder unless done with the same malice aforethought (express or implied) as is required for a killing to amount to

> murder when not done in the course or furtherance of another offence.

All were distinguished courts, both in England and in Australia, but each disagreed strongly as to how *Smith* ought to have been decided. If one adverted to Section 1 of the Act (*supra*), then the position of the Court of Criminal Appeal seems to be consistent with the Act. But if one adverted to Section 2 of the same Act, where,

> (2)...a killing done in the course or for the purpose of resisting an officer of justice, or of resisting or avoiding or preventing a lawful arrest, or of effecting or assisting an escape or rescue from legal custody, shall be treated as a killing in the course or furtherance of an offence,

then the verdict of the trial court, and the decision of the House of Lords in *Smith* seemed to be consistent with the language of the Act. The difficulty, however, was that the Act itself supposedly abolished constructive malice. Such being the case, then one must advert to the actual intention of the accused at the time when the offense was committed. Therefore, Section 8-(a) and (b) of the *Criminal Justice Act*, 1967, became the remedy. But again, a leading Solicitor in the field of criminal law cautioned,

> The section [s-8(a) & (b)], however, does nothing to clarify whether, and to what extent in particular crimes, intent or foresight is required to be proved.[4]

Had any real progress been made as to understanding what criminal intent meant, and whether or not its meaning could be clearly expressed so that a court or jury could both understand and then use the concept to make a finding of criminal guilt in a criminal trial? Would the *ad hoc* findings of case law have to be abandoned, and in their place would the criminal courts have to be guided by proposed criminal codes akin to those of the *Fourth Report* (1839) or the *Criminal Code* [Proposed] of 1879? In addition to these questions may be added that the tension lay in the common law system of law itself. The accused is charged with having violated the law, either a statutory offense or a common law offense. The accused is not charged with having violated the law as Professor So-and-So may have viewed the law. The power of making a judicial finding rests ultimately with the Courts themselves, and, as a corollary of that position, the accused himself has the right to be charged with having violated the law in its existing state. No easy solution appeared at hand.

One further problem is to be seen by the proliferation of case law in this century in its regard to intention: namely, the concept, apart from its apparent lack of resolute definition and limits, began to bear too much. It was predicated both of the agent and his nature, and of the agent and his action, and of an action, with its consequences, itself. In the last edition of Kenny's *Outlines of Criminal Law*,[5] its editor suggested five different meanings for the definition of malice aforethought in murder. The general concept of criminal intention expressed a state of mind as to the following possibilities:

> 1. *D* has an intention to kill a particular person, and that person in fact was killed by *D*.
>
> 2. *D* has an intention to kill a particular person, but kills some other than he envisaged.
>
> 3. *D* has an intention to kill, but he has no particular person in mind.*
>
> 4. *D* intends only to hurt *P*, and not to kill him, but realizes that the hurt could quite possibly kill *P*.
>
> 5. *D* does an act, and the act possibly could kill *P*, but *D* has neither the intention to kill or to hurt *P*.[6]**

This simple set of possibilities hardly exhausts the range of possibilities intention might take for a legal philosopher. Turner's desire was to show a reader of criminal law what the case law had indicated; as an editor he did not propose to create logical puzzles. But it is difficult not to consider what puzzles a concept central to the understanding and operation of the criminal law may present. When a single concept begins to bear most of the weight in a legal system, the concept must either be clear, given over to a precise application, or general enough to permit expansion to novel situations. Some of the hard cases in modern criminal law have blurred the qualities of both worlds.[7] Rigidity can be mistaken for clarity, and ambiguity of meaning can be mistaken for application to novel situations. One wants to avoid, as Mr.

---

* Termed "universal malice" by Blackstone in *4 Bl. Comm. 200.*

** *R. v. Smith* [1960] 2 All E.R. 450.

Justice Cardozo said in *Hynes v. New York Central R. R.*, 231 N.Y. 229 at 235, a jurisprudence of *a priori* conceptions in which one extends a maxim or a definition with a relentless disregard for the consequences. The problem then remained: how to define *mens rea*, showing it then to be a simple concept which would serve the interest of justice in criminal law to the benefit both of the accused and of the State through pristine impartiality and logic.

But the problem did not end with a simple definition of "intention." A further problem, (as noted in footnote 6, *supra*), has been to define what kind of relationship must obtain between a criminal intention and the other elements of a criminal offense. We saw this earlier on when "ignorance" was discussed in its relation to a human action. For the medieval mind, ignorance could be prior to an act, it could be contemporaneous with an act, or it could be subsequent to an act; furthermore, each discrete element of the abstract relationship could admit either that one was culpable or non-culpable with respect to the presence or absence of ignorance. Both the kind of ignorance, and its quality, were evident in medieval discussions of moral theory.[8] It is not unusual then that Dean Marston in his fine article in the *Law Quarterly Review* raised similar issues with respect to what relationship *mens rea* and *actus reus* must bear one to the other. If a harm ensues – for instance, *P* dies – but the requisite elements of *mens rea* and *actus reus* are not connected in time, who is to bear the harm? Does one leave the world of logical considerations and then enter into the sphere of *policy* considerations, the reasoning being that the logical consistency of a coherent theory of intention will not permit the court to dispose of complicated criminal cases if that logic be adhered to rigorously? But "policy" is very close to being another way of introducing "constructive malice."[9] It is a simple academic exercise to multiply odd examples wherein one element of a criminal offense is separated by time from another element, but a positive harm does ensue: *P* dies.

As the criminal law has progressed two qualities have begun to appear. As a system of thought it has sought to free itself from former moral presuppositions, and it has also sought to become consistent and clear in relation to the core concepts of the system. Each brings with it problems. To be freed from older moral notions then entails that the legal system itself will have to offer a rationale for the sanctionative elements within itself; and, if to be consistent and clear as a set of axioms, then it must purge its ordinary terms of the confusion latent in them. The latter requires that key concepts be subjected to logical analysis. The criminal sanction has seldom taken with natural affection to the demanding rigors which attend logical inspection.

Prior to the enactment of the *Criminal Justice Act*, 1967, the Law Commission issued a paper on the subject of imputed criminal intent.[10] The Right Honourable The Lord Gardiner was, at the time of the report, Lord High Chancellor of Great Britain. It was apparent to him, as well as to the greater body of the judiciary of the United Kingdom, that the final decision of the House of Lords in *D.P.P. v. Smith* [1961] A.C. 290 had caused much unrest in the legal community, both in England and in other common law countries. It was proposed that he appoint a body of distinguished legal worthies to examine *Smith*, and to make proposals for the reform of the law of criminal intent in murder.[11] The specific recommendation the Law Commission was to make was: "That an examination be made of the effect and implications of the decision in *D.P.P. v. Smith*."[12] The resolution of the questions which criminal intent posed were seen by the Commission to fall into two broad categories, and these were: ought the test for criminal intent be an objective test, or ought it to be a subjective test?

In section 4 of the *Introduction* to the report, the Commissioners set down a tripartite division of the elements of the general question for them to solve, portions of which are cited herewith:

> 4. The main issues raised by the decision in the House of Lords appear to be the following:
>
> (a) Where murder is alleged, should the jury be found to infer the intent to kill or to inflict grievous bodily harm, which is under the present law necessary for a killing to amount to murder, if 'an ordinary man capable of reasoning' (Viscount Kilmuir L.C. on p. 331 of...*Smith*) would in the position of the alleged murderer have foreseen death or grievous bodily harm as the natural and probable consequence of his act? Alternatively, should the requirement of intent necessitate proof of the actual intent...[of D], and should the natural and probable consequence of his act only provide a basis from which such intent may be inferred?

> (b) Apart from its application to intent in murder should the objective or subjective approach to intent, or, where relevant, to foresight, be adopted in the criminal law generally?
>
> (c) Should the requirement of intent in murder, whether ascertained subjectively or objectively, be satisfied by either an intent to kill or an intent to inflict grievous bodily harm?[13]

Upon examination one can appreciate that the Commission had not strayed far from the standard presentations of the question of criminal intent in common law. With the existence of the great reports from the nineteenth century, any familiar with the language from those reports will appreciate that the Commission of 1967 had not framed any novel propositions. Any of them can be found well stated in any of the nineteenth-century reports on criminal law pertaining to indictable offenses.

But one problem can be extracted from the statement of the general issues, and it is this. What is meant by "objective" and by "subjective," when applied to criminal intent? It must be remembered that the Commission (1967) was studying the question of "imputed" criminal intent. Knowing that full well, the Commission (1967) chose to take a direction from an earlier Commission:

> The degrees of likelihood or probability being in truth infinite, it is clear that no assigned degree of likelihood or probability that an injurious consequence will result from any act can serve as a test of criminal responsibility. Such a degree of likelihood or probability admits of no legal mode of ascertainment, and it would, if capable of being ascertained, afford no proper test of guilt, for it is not the precise degree of likelihood or probability in such case, but the *knowledge or belief* that the thing is likely or probable which constitutes the *mens rea*, although the greater or less degree of probability may afford important evidence as to the real intention of the party.[14]

The same sentiment was reinforced by a citation from a later Commission's report: "Persons ought not to be punished for the consequences of their acts which they did not foresee."[15] The latter Commission (1949-53) was succinct in its estimation of constructive malice, while the *Seventh Report* (1834) framed the logical problem clearly with regard to predicting consequences from an act; namely, that from the concept of "to predict" possible consequences, knowledge of those consequences would then be attributed to *D* as if they were really and necessarily the case. The confusion is old to philosophers and theologians. It concerned the logical status of the claim of the verb, "to know," when applied to God's knowledge of future contingents, a question of impending concern both to medieval and Renaissance thinkers. One thinker, Socinus,[16] refuted the standard arguments for God's omniscience by making a modal distinction; namely, to assert that there is an epistemic difference between a claim which states, "A knows *that p*," from a claim of the form, "A knows *that p may possibly be the case*." For Socinus there was not the same epistemic import in statements, one which made an actual claim to actual knowledge, and the other which made a claim to future knowledge. His objection took the form that to know what is actually the case, is actually to know; to know what may be the case is to know the possible as possible. Actual knowledge and possible knowledge, therefore, were distinct and different modal states. By parity of reasoning, law courts make a pragmatic distinction in the degrees of knowledge when the courts frame different rules of evidence, e.g., holding that "hearsay" evidence has not the same force as "direct" evidence.* The *Seventh Report* (1834) had clearly appreciated that a difference did exist between actual intent, and the knowledge it embraced, from imputed intent, and the possible knowledge it embraced.

There is a problem which was not considered, and it may serve to illustrate why imputed intent, based upon what a reasonable man ought to expect to be the case, is not logically compelling of itself. Any of us have checks which we record in our checkbook. Any of us have concentrated when adding up the columns to determine the monthly balance in our account. Any of us have been surprised to be advised by the Bank that we were either overdrawn or had a larger balance than we had calculated. Any of us, therefore, have done our calculations seriously, only to be advised that we were in error. It is a universal human experience. But the simple case illustrates one problem: although there may be an "objective" answer to a mathematical problem, one may not "subjectively" have been aware of the correct (and, hence, objective) answer. To deliberate and cause an error does not entail that one has deliberated in bad faith. Hence the flaw in the

---

* American courts, however, hold that direct evidence and circumstantial evidence have equal weight in determining a verdict.

claim that objective knowledge is knowledge that any reasonable man would be expected to possess. There may be an objective state of affairs; it is a further, and different, claim to assert that therefore, one must know that objective state of affairs. And it is a positive *non sequitur* to assert that if one attends deliberately to what could be an objective state of affairs, one will necessarily know such an objective state of affairs.

The Commissioners were led to this understanding of intent in a criminal finding:

> [T]he inferences as to a man's intent to be drawn from the natural and probable consequences of his actions should be *permissible* only; they should not be *mandatory*, either in a conclusive or qualified sense.[17]

It would not be an extravagant claim to suggest that the force of the citation from the *Seventh Report* (1834) helped to form the reasoning of this Commission (1967). The Commission was also aware that a body of common law reasoning was developing which either rejected *Smith* outright, or circumvented its understanding of intent.[18] As to the question of whether an intent to murder ought also include an intent to inflict grievous bodily harm, the Commission made this distinction. If one is to be assumed to be guilty of murder, the element to mandate that assumption is that a finding was made that *D* had a willingness to kill; however,

> where it was not his [i.e., *D*'s] purpose to kill in any event, the essential question on a charge of murder should be whether, at the time when he took the action in fact resulting in death, he was willing by that action to kill in accomplishing some purpose other than killing. A man may hope that he will not kill, or he may be indifferent whether he kills or not, but if he is willing to kill, and does in fact kill, we think he should be guilty of murder.[19]

The commission used the concept of "willingness" in this way, and we wish to cite the usage fully because of the peculiar problems which it creates:

> So long as a distinction between murder and manslaughter is to be maintained, there must be a defensible criterion for distinguishing between them. In our view the essential element in murder should be willingness to kill, thereby evincing a total lack of respect for human life. A man who drives a car at an excessive speed down a crowded street, thereby killing a pedestrian, may know that by his reckless folly he runs the risk of killing that pedestrian, but, although he is aware of the risk, he may not be willing to kill him. He may be guilty of

> manslaughter because he has run an extreme risk; he is not guilty of murder if he was not willing to kill On the other hand, it is desirable to bring within the definition of a murderer a man who...plants a powerful time-bomb in an aeroplane in order to blow it up in flight with the aim of recovering the proceeds of insurance on the cargo. Although he has a purpose other than killing (namely, the recovery of the insurance money) it is clear from the circumstances that at the time when he planted the bomb, he was willing to kill those in the aeroplane in accomplishing his purpose of recovering the insurance money.[20]

Other cases might be more difficult to decide, the Commission admitted, but it maintained that when one was accused of a crime as serious as murder, an inquiry into his state of mind must be attempted, however daunting may be the difficulties of such an inquiry.

When the extract (*supra*) is unravelled, is there little more being presented by the Commission than a "*but for*" condition as to why *D* did not kill *P*? The object may have been unrealized but for some external happening over which *D* did not have control. Was not the Commission presenting an example based upon a hypothetical in which the objective *D* wished to obtain could be obtained in two ways? First, *D* could gain his objective directly without causing death: *D phi-s* and "x" is the case, but death does not ensue: therefore, "Phi and -(killing) but 'x'" = *D* accomplishes his aim ("x") without the need of wrongfully killing. Secondly, the equation, if "willingness" is realized, would simply read: "*D phi-s* but kills and accomplishes his aim ('x')." The *willingness* is present in each example. In the first case had not "x" been directly achieved, *D* would have killed; in the second case in order to achieve "x," *D* had first to kill. The stress in the commissions' test is not an objective test. The test is to unravel the conditions present in the will of the offender as to what he would do, or did do, to reach "x." It is an appeal not to a cognitive test, i.e., did *D* know what was the case? but is an appeal to the plan, and its elements, which D entertains. If the plan has to it that *D* would kill in order to achieve "x," then, for the Commission, *D* is a murderer (if an unintended death ensues). The Commission appeared to be speaking of motive.

The dangerous driver example rather muddies the water. From motive (what *D would* do, whether or not he actually *did* do) one is transported to objective conditions: the speeding motorist who knows that he could kill if he drove at dangerously high speeds down the crowded thoroughfare. Why would this not be murder if he hit *P*? It certainly fits any of the older examples used by Elizabethan writers of the man who throws bricks down from a roof onto a pathway where passersby may be, or the case of the man who rides fast into a crowd not caring whom his horse may injure. What the example shows which the Commission constructed is that *D was* willing to achieve his end (high speed) at any cost (even killing pedestrians) but, because of fortune, no pedestrians (or others) were present to be injured. The mere act of *D* driving at excessive speed means that if an accident or death does not come about it is through power or circumstances other than *D*–save for *D* braking dramatically in order to avoid a collision with a person or an object. If the case is intended to prove that *if D* did attempt to stop, *then* he could not have had an intent or willingness to kill, that is a *post hoc propter hoc* example. From the fact of high speed in itself either conclusion can be yielded: *D* may be willing to cause death, *D* may not be willing to cause death; we do not know unless *D* attempts to stop or avoid a collision. The Commission *assumed* that high-speed drivers do not intend to kill; they wish only to drive fast. If a logical form, it appears to take this form. Given that *D phi-s*, unless the objective is known, *phi-ing* in and of itself will not tell us whether or not *D* would kill. If, however, *phi-ing* in and of itself is dangerous, then we may defer to the objective *if* harm is not produced, i.e., *D* does plant the bomb aboard the aeroplane, but the bomb fails to explode. *D* is presumed to have had the requisite willingness, but circumstances or conditions thwarted his willingness to kill.

The trouble with this exercise is that it is reasoning based upon example, and examples may confuse or be tenuously extended. What the Commission did do which linked its reasoning to older reasoning, certainly medieval reasoning, was to stress the element in murder to be the "willingness" to cause death unlawfully. To be willing to kill imports with itself that *D* is not only thinking about or considering to do, but actually moves himself fully to kill. The shift in the concept of intent began slowly to move back to the volitive and away from the purely cognitive. It was not, *Did D know*? but, *Would D kill* (either as an end in itself, or as an adjunct to some further end)? To "intend" was now transformed into a volitive object, bringing the concept back into line with older reasoning which saw intentional action as action springing from character, disposition, and the will. A willingness to kill, in order to achieve an end, truly would be an example of "malice aforethought."

The Commission, in paragraph 20 of the report, dwelled upon "willingness." It said,

> We have had particularly in mind the objections of the judges of the Queen's Bench Division...to an earlier proposal which we made....In that proposal we included in the intent to kill the state of mind of a man who both foresaw that he might and was prepared to kill. We recognize that the concept of 'preparedness to kill' might be taken to apply only to a previously planned killing; we think that 'willingness to kill' is not so limited in its application, while still emphasizing what we have made the central point in our proposal, namely, a total lack of respect for human life. And, in so far as a man cannot will in the abstract but must at least envisage the subject matter of his will, we consider that the reference to foresight was unnecessary and perhaps misleading, in laying too much emphasis on the likelihood of, rather than on the willingness to cause, death.[21]

Paragraph 22 (a)-(c) set down the final proposals of this new legal voluntarism. Paragraph 22 (a) indicated that the Commission believed that a jury should not be bound to draw the necessary inference that *D* would see the natural and probable consequences of his act because, in theory, they might be depictable. A jury ought to consider all circumstances surrounding an act. This reference was incorporated into the *Criminal Justice Act*, 1967, as section 8(a) and (b). Paragraph 22(b) of the Law Commission's report held that a subjective test should be applied to determining intent or foresight. A court or tribunal or jury ought to strive to appreciate what was *D*'s actual intent when he acted, contrary to *Smith*.[22] The movement of the Report (1967) was away from a mathematical model or statistical model of intention, i.e., natural or probable circumstances; foreseeability, and a return to the older model of intent as an expression of a willingness to commit a legal wrong (in which death might ensue). It was a compressed but clear return to a position having its roots in a medieval tradition (as we have discussed in earlier portions of this study). The concept of "intent" was to be defined in its relation to the "will." If we advert to Paragraph 22(c) of the report under discussion we read of this relationship:

> 22(c): An intent to inflict grievous bodily harm should no longer be retained as an alternative to an intent to kill in the crime of murder. A killing should not amount to murder unless there is an intent to kill. But it should be made clear that, where a man does not have the purpose to kill in any event, he may nevertheless have the intent to kill, if, at the time when he takes the action in fact resulting in death, he is willing by that action to kill in accomplishing some purpose other than killing.[23]

If actions in themselves concern the class of the particular, and if actions are particular productions brought about by an agent through himself, then it would seem to follow logically that a finding of murder – a particular offense brought about by the agent – should reflect the particular volitional state of the agent who caused such an action.[24] To make a finding of other than what the agent had intended is then to have made a constructive finding. By stating that if an agent was willing to kill in order to achieve either a collateral or direct effect disposes of the possible problem that *D* might not have willed to kill *this* man rather than an unknown person. Being possessed of a willingness to kill wrongfully satisfied the intentional requirement for murder; it need not be further specified as to who will be the victim. The inclusion of "willingness" also disposes of the problem case in which a result might or might not be harmful,[25] but the will of the offender incorporates both conditions. If the harm does ensue it is different in classification if *D* willed the harm, or the means to cause the harm, than if the harm simply happened and was not intended by *D*.[26]

The report of the Law Commission (1967) on the subject of imputed criminal intent was not a philosophical paper, and one must read its case examples with a certain degree of leniency. However, the report did re-establish the dominance of the will in an act, making the cognitive elements of intention into a sub-class of the voluntary, a position the authors of the current study would accept. A willingness to do what could be harmful seems to have wider logical scope than a foresight of possible harms.

A leading paper in its set of *Working Papers*, samples of scholarship of the members of the Law Commission circulated for the purpose of receiving scholarly comment upon their proposals for the various reforms of the common law, was that paper concerned with the codification of the criminal law.[27] We will refer to this long-titled report as: *The Mental Element in Crime* (31). One of the members of the working party for this report was Professor Glanville L. Williams, Q.C., LL.D., F.B.A. (who, at the time, was also a member of the Criminal Law Revision Committee), who shortly before had published a set of lectures bearing the same title, and whom, it may be assumed, lent considerable scholarly weight to shaping some of the conceptual outcomes of *Working Paper 31*.[28] The membership of the working party, as they then were, constituted distinguished judges and practitioners who were richly acquainted with the Criminal Bar.[29] The Working Paper which was circulated was modest in size, some 65 foolscap pages, but direct in purpose, listing seven propositions to be considered, and then following such propositions with separate discussions of these categories: "intention," "knowledge," "intention and knowledge," "recklessness," "negligence," and "the place of mistake in relation to the mental element."

The paper set out to explore what was the relationship between *mens rea* and statutory offenses, "whether the language used in the creation of a statutory offence imports full *mens rea* (intention, knowledge or recklessness), some fault element short of *mens rea*, i.e., negligence, or some form of 'absolute' or 'strict' liability."[30] Their difficulty was framed in Paragraph (3) of the Paper:

> 3. We take the view that it has become essential to identify with precision those areas where the legislature has created offences without a requirement of fault (offences of strict liability), as well as those areas where fault is a prerequisite of liability only to the extent that the offender must have unreasonably failed to attain an objective standard of conduct (offences of negligence). By this means we seek to further the attainment of certainty in the criminal law.[31]

But the difficulty which was not expressed, and which a legal philosopher would note, was the broadness in which their aim was cast. For instance, were they seeking to set down rules for the interpretation of a legal proposition, as one might set down rules for the clear understanding of a proposition in logic or mathematics? Was a problem in linguistic construction to be solved for? Or was a broader problem to be explored:

namely, the relationship which an agent may bear to the understanding of a linguistic proposition? The logical reply would be simple. If a proposition is to supply or state the elements of an offense, then that proposition should state those elements clearly and precisely. If ambiguous, then the ambiguity should favor the innocence of the accused at the expense of the power of the State. The State could, after all, always redefine a statutory offense to make it more precise.[32] The working party admitted that past case law was of little help in determining what degree of fault should obtain in particular statutory offenses.

The working party saw their problem in terms of language, but not in the same way as might a linguistic philosopher. They were not composing a logical treatise on how to interpret key concepts. Yet they were concerned that key concepts could be employed ambiguously:

> Thus 'maliciously,' although in general a *mens rea* word, can, apparently, have a different meaning in two closely related sections of the same Act [*R. v. Mowatt* [1968] 1 Q.B. 421, on ss. 18 and 20 of the Offences against the Person Act 1861]. Again, it appears that the expression 'with intent to defraud' may include recklessness, although it is generally accepted that the expression 'with intent to inflict grievous bodily harm' does not [*R. v. Sinclair* [1968] 1 W.L.R. 1246].[33]

The Commission wanted to be guided by a general principle:

> that the fundamental assumption underlying the proposition is that fault, whether consisting of *mens rea* or of negligence, should be the normal requirement of the criminal law, and that strict liability should be exceptional,[34]

no doubt remembering what difficulties had been engendered when *Sweet v. Parsley* had been argued a few years earlier.[35] The problem, then, appeared to be a simple one: what relationship did key concepts in the criminal law bear to those statutory constructions which may either have embodied those conceptions, or may have *assumed* that such key concepts were pellucid, easy both to be understood and applied?

Seven legal propositions to apply to general principles of the criminal law were set forth. The first six of these were:

> 1. Subject to proposition 2, in every offence created after [a date to be prescribed] the fault required is a mental element consisting of intention, knowledge or recklessness on the part

of the defendant in respect of all the other elements of the offence, unless the requirement is expressly excluded.

2. Where an offence is an offence of omission or is defined so as to include an omission, the fault required is negligence in the defendant as to the omission, unless a mental element is expressly or impliedly required or the offence is expressly stated to be of strict liability or otherwise to be independent of fault in the defendant.

3. Where the requirement of intention, knowledge or recklessness is expressly excluded from some or all of the elements of an offence, the offence requires negligence in the defendant as to such elements, unless the offence is stated to be of strict liability or otherwise to be independent of fault in the defendant in respect of such elements.

4. Unless otherwise expressly provided, in all offences where negligence is required by reason of proposition 2 or 3 above, negligence may be treated as established in the absence of any evidence to the contrary.

5. Where the fault proved by the evidence is of a higher degree than that required for the offence the fault required shall be taken as established.

6. Subject to any specific exceptions, where the existing law does not require a particular degree of fault in respect of an element of the offence, that offence nevertheless requires negligence in the defendant as to that element.

In such cases, unless otherwise expressly provided, negligence may be treated as established in the absence of any evidence to the contrary.

Where the fault proved by the evidence is of a higher degree than negligence, negligence shall be taken as established.[36]

The Paper proceeded to discuss each proposition, setting forth examples and case law which pertained to each proposition. The Paper used an older term, "fault," to depict the wrongful element of an act (as "*culpa*" did in church law, when a penitent would assert, "*mea culpa, mea culpa, mea maxima culpa*"[*]), and it spoke of the consequences of wrongful conduct as "events." The case law selected to illustrate each proposition we have set down in the endnotes.[37]

---

* We do not wish to suggest that the Commission drew upon church law when it spoke of "fault" in reference to an offense. But the language of ('fault') does not have a long history in Western culture, and the comparison is not far-fetched or misleading.

The first proposition is *post hoc propter hoc* reasoning because it does not relate *D*'s actual knowledge of his act to *D* knowing that a law has been violated. The "fault" in question is attributed to *D*. The other categories, "knowledge" and "recklessness," the *Paper* defines at the close of the propositions (as will be done here). The logical fallacy consists in this: to know that *D* intends *phi* does not entail that *D* intends to commit a wrong. The presupposition of the use of *intent* in the first proposition is that *D* knows that he is intending a wrong prohibited by law, and also that in knowing that he is commiting a legal wrong he actually desires or wants to commit that very wrong. To know what I am doing does not entail that I want to do what I am doing.

The second proposition broadly concerns omissions for which *D* may be liable; for instance, a bankrupt obtaining credit, failure to comply with traffic signs, and the like.[38] The *Paper* argues that "negligence" ought to be the test for "fault" in omission cases, unless a statute imports *mens rea* (i.e., "implies") into the offense. All that such offenses seem to do is to cast the burden upon the accused to explain why his conduct should not be faulted, and says little, if anything, about mental elements. If *D phi-s* not knowing it to be a legal wrong, then *D*, under strict liability for an omission, is required to demonstrate that his ignorance was reasonable. If this does not absolve *D*, then one has only an example that statutory offenses may be strictly constructed (which does not address the mental element in a crime).[39] The power of a statute is distinct from the logic of a statute.[40]

Proposition three simply imposes the fault element, but chooses two conflicting examples to illustrate it. The first example is of one who makes an untrue declaration:

> (a) A law makes it an offence to make an untrue declaration irrespective of intention or recklessness in that regard. The defendant made an untrue declaration, but he did not know, and had no reason to suspect, that it was untrue. He will be not guilty (*cf.* Proposition '4').[41]

Any set of examples can be given. Essential to the example is that *D* asserts (or does) *phi*, which he believes to be "x," but which the law knows to be "y" (with "x" < = / = > "y"). But is this little more than to say that conviction should follow guilt? or that some forms of ignorance are excusable? If *D* could not know that *phi* was "y" (hence prohibited by law), what 'criminal knowledge' could *D* have possessed to be guilty of a crime?

The second example chooses the classic adulterated milk case, a rather unsatisfactory example. In *Tesco Supermarkets Ltd. v. Nattrass*, [1972] AC 153, the defendant manager was charged with a violation of the Trade Descriptions Act 1968, s. 11 (2), for advertising a good for sale but not having the good for sale. Ordinarily this would have been an offense of strict liability by way of agency. The House of Lords accepted as a defense to the charge that *D* could not have known of the offense because his employee had not taken proper care to stock the store shelves with the product, and the product was not in stock, which absence was unknown to *D*, a manager. It would appear that the House of Lords imported "reasonableness" into the concept of "to be strictly liable for," and that one would have to inspect such cases one by one. The same defense (in theory) could obtain against the seller of adulterated milk. It would be a matter only of credibility if the judge or jury accepted *D*'s reasons for his actions.

The fourth proposition simply places an evidential burden upon *D*. For example, if *D* does *phi*, believing it to be an innocent act, but the Crown claims that the act is a wrong, and then argues that because a wrong, therefore *D* must have intended a wrong (thus linking *mens rea* and *actus reus*), it will again be left to *D* to explain why he *phi-ed*, and to demonstrate why he did not know it to be a legal wrong. The tests may be both "reasonableness" and "ignorance." We have excluded "compulsion" from this category, as when *D*, because of addiction, possesses forbidden drugs, yet cannot control himself.[42]

The fourth proposition, however, serves to become an arm of State power, as with narcotics enforcement.[43] The matter there, it would seem, is that legislation embodies the general knowledge of the community that those who use narcotics generally know that they are using narcotics, and that such actions are by general knowledge forbidden. The logic of the statute is to appeal to "custom," and to say very little about legal logic. Furthermore, strict liability is often a policy matter, and addresses itself more to government and its police powers.

Proposition five assumes a standard of conduct, and that it is known to *D*. If a statute proscribes the selling of intoxicating liquor during certain hours, and if *D* sells "x," knowing it to be intoxicating liquor, during those forbidden hours, it is assumed he has violated the law. Proposition five holds that any state will satisfy guilt, whether *D* acted negligently or recklessly.

The sixth proposition requires the defendant to rebut the charge that he, *D*, acted negligently. *In R. v. Salter* [1968] 2 Q.B. 534, section 157 of the Bankruptcy Act 1914 required a bankrupt to furnish a reasonable explanation as to why his estate was lost. *D*, who did not fulfill this requirement, was permitted to show that he was non-negligent in that regard. The trial judge ruled that *D* had to be shown by the Crown to have possessed an intent to deceive. The Commission, in its *Commentary* on proposition six, felt that this was too lenient to the defendant. They wished the fault element to be constructive, thus changing the burden of proof from the Crown to the defendant.

In its commentary on proposition six at C-(2) (a), the Commission enunciates what appears to be a strange understanding of *mens rea*, suggesting that a negative statement of belief is a statement made outside of the boundaries of intention, knowledge or recklessness. The statement reads:

> *Mens rea* may, however, not always be expressed in terms of intention, knowledge or recklessness. For example, under section I of the Perjury Act 1911 a false statement must be made '...which [the defendant] knows to be false *or does not believe to be true....*'[44]

With respect, to utter a statement which one may not know to be true, but which one is willing to utter in spite of possible harmful consequences, is not to reck a rule; in short, it is to be reckless, which may be an intentional act. That there may not be a material correspondence between "*D* believes *that 'p'*" and the truth or falsity of "*...that 'p'*" in no way affects the liability of *D* under the terms of the Perjury Act 1911, section 1. The intentional object of the proposition, "*D* believes...," is taken by "or does not believe to be true." To satisfy that object is to have intentionally made a statement, and that statement is the intentional object for the belief of *D* (in that circumstance). The Commission appears to have confused material implication with logical implication. The contingent truth or falsity of a statement does not affect the intentionality of the statement with regard to the maker of the statement. A statement may be intentionally made, *and* be materially false; a statement may be intentionally made, *and* be materially true. In either case (barring defenses), *D* intentionally has made a statement.[45]

Proposition seven in *Working Paper 31* concerns definitions. The statements are short enough to reproduce, and we set them down:

INTENTION AND KNOWLEDGE

7. A. (1) A person intends an event not only

(a) When his purpose is to cause that event but also

[First alternative] (b) When he has no substantial doubt that that event will result from his conduct.

[Second alternative] (b) When he foresees that that event will probably result from his conduct.

(2) A person is not by reason only of Proposition 7A (1) (b) to be taken to intend the wrongdoing of others.

(3) A person knows of circumstances not only when he knows that they exist but also when

[First alternative] He has no substantial doubt that they exist.

[Second alternative] He knows that they probably exist.

RECKLESSNESS

B. A person is reckless if,

(a) knowing that there is a risk that an event may result from his conduct or that a circumstance may exist, he takes that risk, and

(b) it is unreasonable for him to take it having regard to the degree and nature of the risk which he knows to be present.

NEGLIGENCE

C. A person is negligent if he fails to exercise such care, skill or foresight as a reasonable man in his situation would exercise.[46]

One will observe that "intend" is defined with regard to consequences. Were one to borrow from Aristotelian terminology, for sake of parallel reasoning, action has been defined in terms of its "final cause," deleting reference to "formal cause," "efficient cause," or "material cause." Proposition 7.A. (1) appears to require a reading with both (a) and (b) (either alternative "b" reading) because the definition is framed with a conjunctive, "but also;" thus to intend an event the necessary conditions must be that *D* purposes that event (only?) *and also* that he has no doubt that the event will occur, *or also* that *D* foresees that the event will occur because of what he had done. We seem to have been given a schoolmaster's test by the Commission. What standard is to apply for measuring 7.A. (1) (b_1) and (b_2)? Will it be an objective test? or will it be a subjective test? Certainly it may be argued that the courts will appeal to a reasonable man test; but the language of Proposition seven seems not to appeal to that test. It frames its definition of intention as an event which *D* purposes and also either which *D* has no substantial doubt will occur, or foresees that the event probably will occur. These are difficult propositions to test. They import a standard of knowledge which the "willingness" test does not import. Both the dullard and the genius may have a "willingness" to kill; but the dullard may be unable to foresee or to determine how to effect the killing, while the genius is able to measure and foresee like an Archimedes.

Take the first example given on page 33 of *Working Paper 31*:

> (a) The defendant shot at A at long range hoping to kill him, but knowing that the chances of hitting him were extremely small at that range. He killed A. He is guilty of intentionally killing A.

But assume that D_1 is a gunsmith, and D_2 is firing a gun for the first time (in this hypothetical). D_1 *knows* that he can kill P, but D_2 does not; D_2 "hopes" that he might kill *P*. The second case is less one of intention, and more one of recklessness, while the first is one of intention (if "intend" is defined in terms of "to know that 'x' will result"). But take the same example and reverse it. D_1, who has a specialist's knowledge of rifles, intends only to "frighten" *P*, and therefore fires, only to his amazement to see that he has actually killed *P*. In terms of the above definition the intention of D_1 was other than what he had expected. If an "objective" test were appealed to, then it could be argued that D_1, who should have known, did not know that his shot would kill the victim. But if a "subjective" test were taken to determine what was D_1's *actual intent*, it could be argued that he did *not* intend the result. What of D_2, who has *no* specialist knowledge of the effectiveness of a rifle? He fires only to frighten, but *P* dies. Do we want to say that D_2 is reckless, while D_1, who possessed specialist knowledge, *either*, (a) intended to kill *P*, because any specialist would know that the rifle shot would kill a person under those conditions, or (b), D_1 was negligent only, arguing that because of his knowledge and belief he would not have wanted to kill *P*, nor would he have wanted to be reckless with regard to possible consequences?

What is missing in the use of "know" (i.e., "intends," "purpose," "no substantial doubt," "foresees") is a failure to make the old distinction between knowledge by description and knowledge by acquaintance; or, to employ a term used by Jacques Maritain to depict artistic knowledge, "knowledge by connaturality,"[47] knowledge in which the knower is "poetically" one with what he knows. The Greek "*poesis*" means: *to make*, *produce*, *create*; and, in a second sense, *to create*, *to beget*, *to bring into existence*; thirdly, *to produce*; lastly, *to compose* or *to write*.[48] What the verb and its cognates carries over is a sense of personal attachment to, knowledgeable ability to do or cause. One knows that not only may something be done, but one knows how properly to produce that something–as a chef knows how to produce a delicate hollandaise sauce well. Knowledge in these instances indicates knowledge of a personal kind.

The definition of "intend" in the *Working Paper 31* puts its full stress upon agent as predictor, while "willingness," in the earlier report of the Law Commission on imputed criminal intent (1967), puts its stress upon the fact that an agent would move himself to act, whether death were caused by his actions or not, or even collateral to his actions. *D*, who may be a criminal sociopath,[49] may have no doubt that his actions will cause certain (criminal) events, may have a sense of substantial certainty that the end will be achieved, and may even foresee the consequences of his act, *yet* may not intend to do what he did because he was privately compelled, by an aspect of himself that he could not control or understand, to act. The earlier report (1967) could deal with such a case because it would deduce that *D* did not have a willingness to act, however clear the consequences of his action (as contemplated, or mentally beheld in his compulsive state) were to him. If, however, "intend" is defined without any reference to any other possible cause, or relationships, and is defined only as a conceptual entity in and of itself (without reference to how it, as an intention, was produced), then, in a curious sense, a sociopath does intend, even though he cannot control what he intends.

It is trivially true if we wish to argue that *D*, who does *phi*, and knows that he *phi-s*, may be guilty of a wrong by force of statute, whether *D* intended to violate the statute or not. All that such reasoning reveals is that the State may, by its police powers, or for sake of policy, proscribe certain acts. Strict liability will permit defenses, but they will be rigorous.* Strict liability, which is mandated by statute, says little to nothing about *mens rea*. It is, as we have suggested, an example of legislative power, and the use or expression of that inherent power may or may not be fair and logical and coherent. It has been our contention that strict liability statutes are outside of the scope of this study, unless those statutes reveal some peculiar or difficult dimension about *mens rea* and its relationship to compliance with the said statute.

Proposition seven,[50] in an illustration and commentary, includes the ancient case, *Beatty v. Gillbanks*, (1882) 9 Q.B.D. 308, and it is also to be found anthologized in the casebooks on criminal law. It presents the simple distinction between one intending the consequences of his own acts (active sense) and one engaging in a situation in which one is likely to cause a

---

* For instance, take statutes which forbid one to expose his person. The purpose of such a statute is to forbid lewdness, as defined by law. Such statutes are generally vague, i.e., one does not know if genital display is prohibited, or nakedness is forbidden (in whatever degree of disrobing *D* may be). Case law is ambivalent on the point. But one can construct a case in which *D*, because of a fire in his heater, is forced to flee unrobed. Has *D* violated the statute? Strictly, he has; but the defense of necessity applies. One can multiply the examples, e.g., the milkman who is forced to deliver milk as if nothing had happened, while, in fact, he is being robbed. The milk he delivers is adulterated (i.e., the robber forced *D* to turn off the refrigeration unit). Has *D* violated the statute which prohibits the sale of adulterated milk?

disturbance but not intend it. In an illustrative case, the Salvation Army had staged a march through an area (the streets of Weston-super-Mare) in which their presence would provoke rioters. The march occurred; the riot occurred, but the Court of Queen's Bench, Field, J., held:

> Now I entirely conceded that every one must be taken to intend the natural consequences of his own acts, and it is clear to me that if this disturbance of the peace was the natural consequence of acts of the appellants they would be liable, and the justices would have been right in binding them over. But the evidence set forth in the case does not support this contention; on the contrary, it shews that the disturbances were caused by other people antagonistic to the appellants.

If, however, (as had happened in London in 1979 and 1980) the organization had been refused a permit to march because the area through which the organization proposed to march was an area in which a riot was likely, then the same facts would have yielded a different conclusion. In *Beatty*, the marchers were peaceful, and had not violated any law which would have forbade their marching.* This case will, however, permit a further analysis. It is this. One may very well "intend" to cause others to attack one, but such an intentional act is not proscribed by law; therefore, one's intentional act does not come within the legal domain.**

The section on "knowledge" (endnote 46) admits of differentiations. If evidence is adduced which shows that *D* knew he had committed a criminal wrong, then the conclusion is obvious. The examples given in the *Working Paper 31* (1970), on page 37, take that of explosives. In (a) *D* possessed a package for a long time which he did not know to be an explosive; not guilty. In (b) he received a package from a third party. If the first alternative is

---

* The conditions which existed in England throughout the late 1970's only serve to show that the police may deem it wise to require a permit to march. The National Front, a political organization accused of extreme right wing and racist tendencies, carried out various marches to protest against Jews, and against African and Indian immigration into the United Kingdom. In certain areas where the National Front carried out its demonstrations, riots did occur, and lives were lost. The police, in order to prevent riots, would, in some cities, not issue a permit to march; therefore, to march without a police permit would be a legal violation.

** If, however, *P* decided to sue in Torts for injuries he suffered, it may be a defense available to the tortfeasor that the actions of *P* were a contribution in negligence to the harm which resulted, i.e., *P* knowingly assumed a risk from which harm most likely would ensue. Reasoning of this kind leads to the world of provocation.

permitted, *D* is guilty of an offense if he knows that he received explosives; if the second alternative is adopted, "knows they probably exist," the Commission holds that he would also be guilty. But one would have to remark that the difference (if it is to obtain, otherwise there is no need for the alternative propositions given in 7.A. (3)) is a matter of degree. What "degree" of certitude must obtain for *D* to claim that "x" probably exists, as opposed to *D* has not substantial doubt that "x" exists? The latter case seems to be a definition which strongly favors the Crown because it incorporates the first alternative of "no substantial doubt." The first position excludes an appeal to the balance of probabilities, and requires the defendant to be possessed of certitude in order to convict, where the second position requires only some diminution of doubt in order to convict. Case (c) concerns suspicion of explosives only, and holds that *D* would not be guilty unless "apt words [were] used in the legislation..." and either alternative would fit the example.

As to intention and knowledge, the Working Party put forward two distinct views. One view favored that consequences would be part of *D*'s intention, and thus the word "purpose" was wide enough to embrace that concept; the other view was that intention involved the foresight of the probability of consequences, or the knowledge that such a probability could exist (a rather fine distinction). The latter, perhaps, was to dispose of bomb cases where *D* only wished to achieve his purpose, at the same hoping that no one would be hurt (or that all would act upon *D*'s warning, and thus the third parties would expectedly act to preserve their own self-interests). It is probable to foresee that some might not act accordingly, and thus the possibility of harmful consequences is not remote. The Working Party favored the definition of knowledge which was enunciated by the Court of Appeal in *R. v. Woods* [1969] 1 Q.B. 447, a Theft Act case in which *D* was charged under section 22 of the Act for handling stolen goods knowing or believing them to be stolen.

The second formulation, 7.A. (1) (b), involves the foreseeing of probable results to constitute an intention. The Working Paper wanted to avoid cases of the kind of *Warner v. Commissioner of Police for the Metropolis* [1968] 2 All E.R. 356 (*D* unknowingly drives onto and remains on a police officer's toe) when *D* might deliberately shut his eyes to a possible harm. The "probable test" entailed that *D* took efforts to know of the likelihood of the risk of danger.

In its commentary upon the category of recklessness the Commission developed a degrees of knowledge approach to the concept, but was careful to note, in its extended commentary,[51] that should *D* turn a blind eye to that state of affairs from which he would gain knowledge of the seriousness of his risk, recklessness could be imputed to *D*. The Commission added, "We all share the view of Devlin, J., [*Roper v. Taylor's Central Garage (Exeter)* [1951] 2 T.L.R. 284, 289] that, in principle, constructive knowledge has no place in the criminal law."[52] The four illustrations which accompany the test on "recklessness" are modestly helpful, but not conclusively so. The first illustration, (a),[53] concludes that *D* is not reckless when he implants jagged broken glass into his fence to impede trespassers. We cannot see how this differs much from putting spring guns in a garden, also with the intent to stop trespassers. It will be recalled that the illustration to accompany Proposition 7.A. (1) (a) and (b_1) and (b_2), forbade the spring gun for this reason:

> (b) The defendant set a spring gun in his woods, where he knew that trespassers might pass. Apart from being guilty of the specific offence relating to spring guns [s.31, Offences against the Person Act, 1861], he is guilty of intentionally killing if a trespasser is killed by the gun.[54]

It is difficult to separate out what degree of difference exists for that example, used to illustrate "intention," from the jagged glass example. The jagged glass adds the palliative that *D* is not guilty of recklessness, "if the step he has taken is reasonable for the protection of his property,"[55] which is rather much a circular argument. "[R]easonable," under what set of circumstances? If the spring gun or the jagged glass fence do equal harm, i.e., kill a victim, was one weapon less or more harmful than the other?

The second example, (b), is the standard surgeon example: There is a risk, but *D* evaluates it, takes it, but *V* dies. The surgeon is not guilty because he did not take an unreasonable risk. Again, a tautologous proposition: "p" is not harmful if "p" is not harmful. But the example can be altered. *D* plans to operate, and tells the patient there are three possible consequences, one of which is slightly risky, but unlikely. *D* operates, but a fourth consequence ensues; the patient dies. Expert knowledge is the category to which one must appeal for (1), *D* may not have known that a fourth consequence was possible,[56] or (2), *D* may have been culpably ignorant of the fourth category as a probable outcome. What the (b) illustration seems to tell us is that a risk, in and of itself, is not a sign of *D*'s being reckless or not. One could argue that the illustrations are incomplete.

In (c) we are given the Russian roulette example. The example says of a death caused by a jesting *D*, "If, however, the defendant thought it impossible that the weapon would fire he is not guilty of recklessness, as he would not have known of the risk."[57] The final example, (d), is of the motorist who pulls out on a blind stop and causes an automobile fatality.[58] *D* is guilty if he appreciated the risk. But the solution to the problem is an intuitive solution which appeals to a notion of the probable. One is unclear if "probable" signifies "common knowledge that 'x' might occur," or if "probable" means that any person would know what must be done under the circumstances – two distinct and different meanings of "probable." In an additional commentary the commission relies upon *Ross v. Moss* [1965] 2 Q.B. 396 to fortify their position that if *D* should take a blind eye to knowledge which he possesses, "it will be for the court on the relevant evidence to draw the inference that the person in fact knew of the circumstances." Nelson's blind eye is as good as his good eye.

There is something unsatisfactory about these positions taken with regard to "recklessness," either by the majority position or the minority position of the Commission.[59] The problem seems to be to determine what are the conditions of mind which the defendant must appreciate with regard to the risk, and what must be the state of the objective conditions which he must appreciate. The commentary on "recklessness" tells us simply,

> The definition of recklessness regarding both events and circumstances imposes a double test. The first question is whether the defendant realized that he was running the risk. The second element is whether, having such knowledge, it was unreasonable for him to take the risk. We have thus endeavored to give effect to the common-sense view that the defendant who appreciates the existence of risks but conducts himself 'regardless' is reckless.[60]

There seems to an element within this category of "ought," a prudential ought that *D*, in the circumstances, ought not only to have done other than what he did (or omitted to do) but also that *D* himself should have perceived what was the correct course of action, and did not act knowledgeably. Unless one is arguing from a simple legal model of liability as defined (the traffic speeding example), one then posits a complicated set of conditions to determine what is meant by "reckless," especially when one wishes to make "reckless" a separate category of legal behavior.[61] Although the Commission disavows constructive attribution of a crime to *D*, it would seem that the definition posed of "recklessness" asks that a jury (or judge) disregard the state to intention and to knowledge, and substitute for what *D* appreciated, its own appreciation of a state of affairs, and then to attribute that appreciation to *D*. The definition is further fraught with practical difficulties. It says that *D* must "know" that he is taking a "risk" when he acts. But if *D* takes the risk, then it means that he has acted intentionally *with regard to a risk*. An intentional object of his behavior to produce behavior which courts deem to be a danger, is a harmful risk. By compressing the elements of (a) and (b) in the definition of "recklessness," is not what was stated little more than that to be reckless means that one intentionally produces an unlawful harm? Section B(b), "recklessness," begs the question when it then concludes that *D* is unreasonable to act in light of the risk he knew; B(a) had already answered the matter, *unless* one wishes to argue that there is an *objective* element in the concept of "risk" which even *D* himself did not comprehend. If that is the case, *D* is to be punished for an objective element he could not comprehend. Example: *D* intends to *phi*. "Phi" is to drive his car very fast down the roadway. He considers what he wants to do, then sets out to do it, and knows that it is risky. He drives his car fast; however, unknown to him the road is no longer a public roadway; therefore, no dangerous risk.

But it will be observed that to define *D*'s conduct, one has defined what *D* may do by use of intentional predicates. But recklessness, as the Commission depicts it, is other than "intention" or "knowledge." If it is argued that to be reckless does not mean a positive statement, "*D* intends to cause this harm," or that it does not mean a negative statement, "an attitude of mental indifference to obvious risks,"[62] then it must be defined in terms of a subset of intention, namely: "*D* primarily intends to *phi*, but in order to *phi* he may also, but not necessarily, have to *psi* [and '*psi*' is a risk which may result in unlawful harm]." At this point, however, "recklessness" is transformed into a sub-category of intentional objects: namely, objects which may or may not be achieved, and which are collateral objectives to a primary objective. But is this little more, also, than to say that *D* has a "willingness" to produce a harm, whether or not the harm is actually produced? But, further, if there exists a willingness to produce a harm, does this not mean that the harm must be defined by law, and that in the absence of a defined and proscribed category, "reckless" or "recklessness" is a vapid category? Is *D* reckless with regard to his intent to kill *V*, if, during the course of the attempt he steps on *V*'s flowers in the garden? Or is *D* reckless if, with very limited legal knowledge, he accepts a case destined for the House of Lords? The difficulty which the term presents is to grasp what it means, and then how to judge if it applies. When the whole impedimenta of conceptual calculation is brought along to define the term, it seems that an objective category is being established, that which *D* did not, or could not, perceive. This would satisfy the non-intentional aspect of the definition of "recklessness." But if *D* cannot perceive that his conduct courts a risk, then is that not to say that *D* perceives his conduct to be without risk, or without dangerous risk? For instance, is a child "reckless" when, in doing "x," he does so because he does not possess the knowledge to inform himself that "x" ought not to be done?

In the close of the paper the commission addressed the issue of "mistake" in its relation to mental element in crime. It stated:

> "[I]f intention, knowledge or recklessness is lacking in relation to some or all of the external elements of any offence which requires a mental element, the defendant should, in principle, escape culpability.[63]

Since the theory of criminal law espoused by the Commission was a fault theory, if a defendant be not at fault, then guilt ought not to be imposed.[64] Whether to excuse a mistake as "honest" or "reasonable," the Commission opted for "honest," incorporating the spirit provided by ss 2(1) and 21(1) of the *Theft Act* 1968.* No elaboration is given for why "reasonable" as a

* Note: These two sections of the *Theft Act* 1968 are themselves complex, and are not self-explanatory as to what "mistake" may mean.

category is rejected, nor is much stated as to what constitutes a mistake. A brief sentence, by way of example, states: "he is mistaken as to the existence or non-existence of a material circumstance."[65] This is elliptical, at best.

To the second kind of mistake, a mistake of fact, the Commission in part refers to *R. v. Levett* (1638) Cro. Car. 538, and likens its own example to Levett. The Commission wrote:

> [D]efendant would have had a defence if the victim had actually been B, as where B is seeking to take the defendant's life and he would have been acting in lawful self-defence if he had fired at B. Here, the mistake of identity forms part of the defence. Nor, in fact, need there be a mistake of identity. If the defendant shoots A, as he believes, in self-defence because he thinks that A is going to kill him, it does not matter that A has no such intention and there is no B who has....*Levett* was very like this.[66]

The Commission had responded to the consideration that no rational legal system could possibly permit the defense that *D* had shot the wrong victim, whereupon it stated that *Levett* was an exception to that broad statement.

It may be wise to set down the report of *Levett* for the reason that it is a case within a case, and the facts are mildly confusing. The report occurs in *Croke's Reports*, the third part,[67] as reference made within *Cook's Case*.[68] In *Cook's Case*, Cook had shot one Marshall, who was a bailiff who was serving writs, *Capias ad satisfaciend.* [i.e., a Writ for the recovery of debt], on Cook. The bailiff had hidden on Cook's property, hoping to serve him when Cook entered. But the bailiff, in order to serve Cook, actually broke into Cook's home, breaking a window to enter. Cook told the bailiff and his assistants to leave; they did not; Cook thereupon discharged his musket, the bailiff dying shortly thereafter. The Court found, because of the technicality of the breaking and entering of the bailiff, that Cook did not murder the bailiff, but committed manslaughter:

> Yet they all held, That it was Manslaughter: for he [Cook] might have resisted him [Marshall] without killing him; And when he saw him and shot voluntarily at him, it was Manslaughter.

At the close of the report, the Court said of *Cook's Case*:

> But here they held cleerly; That it is homicide, because he [Cook] seeing and knowing him [Marshall], shot at him

> voluntarily, and slew him; whereupon they all resolved, It was not murder, but homicide only.

Levett's case is cited by way of contrast to *Cook's Case*. The full report reads:

> But JONES (J.) said, That it was resolved by the chief Justice and himself, and the Recorder of London, at the last Sessions at New-gate, in the case of one *William Levet* [sic], who was endicted [sic] of the homicide of a woman called *Frances Freeman*, where it was found by speciall Verdict, That the said *Levett* and his wife being in the night in bed and asleep, one *Martha Stapleton*, their Servant, having procured the said *Frances Freeman* to help her about her house-businesse, about twelve of the clock at night going to the dores to let out the said *Francis Freeman*, conceived she heart theeves at the dore offering to break them open; whereupon she, in fear, ran to her Master and Mistrisse, and informed them she was in doubt, that theeves were breaking open the house dore. Upon that he arose sodainly, and fetched a drawn Rapier. And the said *Martha Stapleton*, least her Master and Mistresse should see the said *Frances Freeman*, hid her in the Buttry. And the said *Levett and Hellen* his wife, comming down, he with his sword searched the entry for the Theeves; And she, the said *Hellen*, espying in the Buttry the said *Frances Freeman*, whom she knew not, conceiving she had been a thief, crying to her husband in great fear, said unto him, Here they be that would undoe us. Thereupon the said *William Levett*, not knowing the said *Frances* to be there in the Buttry, hastily entred therein with his drawn Rapier, and being in the dark and thrusting with his Rapier before him, thrust the said *Frances* under the left breast, giving unto her a mortail wound, whereof she instantly died: And whether it were felony, they prayed the discretion of the Court. And it was resolved, That it was not a felony; for he did it ignorantly without intention to hurt the said *Frances*.[69]

The importance of the case, we would urge, is not that it confirms "mistake"; rather, that it arrives at its verdict by appeal to an act done through ignorance, buttressing that position by appeal to a third party who gave information gained in fear. Because Levett's judgment was formed in and through ignorance, which ignorance was neither a fault on his part, nor deliberately of his own making, the court resolved that *D* could not have formed an intent to kill; and, by reference to *Cooks's Case*, Levett's action would have been non-voluntary, i.e., a mixed action in which there were to be found both voluntary and involuntary elements. It might further have been argued that it was an action done out of fear, as well as of ignorance, which together would lend to an Aristotelian interpretation that the action of Levett was mixed (possessed both of the voluntary and involuntary). Given this interpretation of the case, the Law Commission appears to have left unstated major portions of what may have been needed to make a coherent theory of what "mistake" meant. *Levett's* case draws upon the causes of the action by *D*, as well as to incorporate a traditional appeal to the concept of ignorance as a category which may excuse an otherwise blameworthy action. The Commission, on the contrary, appeals to a conclusion, i.e., "mistake" as a *fait accompli*, without investigating the premises which produce the conclusion. It may be – said only in passing, and not as conclusive evidence – that had the Commission investigated the premises they may have discovered that a statement about the nature of volition would have been required to explain how a mistake can be produced which will justify exculpation. The Commission, however, tended more to cognitive statements about intention, and less to volitive statements about the causes of intentional action. It was a difference in emphasis. *Levett* was less a mistake of fact than an involuntary act caused by ignorance.

The Law Commission for *Working Paper 31* had given, one may say, the skeletal elements (or a bare, logical form) to the use of key terms in criminal law: namely, "intention," "knowledge," "recklessness," and "negligence." It had applied its definitions to how those terms ought to relate to statutory offenses, but not exclusively so, drawing as it did upon common law examples. The tone of the said Paper was definitional, not philosophical nor analytical. Other papers would follow, from other Commissions.

The first report of the Law Reform Commissioner,[70] Melbourne, 1974, concerned the law of murder. The questions posed in this first report were of the nature of philosophical questions about criminal law, and the report itself, though brief, reads more like a series of reflective proposals than solely as a series of bare definitions. The Commissioner had been asked to consider three questions, that he,

> enquire into and report upon the amendments of the law of murder which would be necessary –
>
> (i) To introduce degrees of murder – or
>
> (ii) To classify murders as capital murders and non-capital murders – or
>
> (iii) To reduce the width of the definition of murder.[71]

The Victoria Commissioner saw the crime of murder in the four following classes:

(a) Where he causes death intentionally.*

(b) Where he intentionally causes really serious bodily harm (commonly referred to as grievous bodily harm) and death results from that injury.**

(c) Where he causes death by an act of violence done in the course of, or in furtherance of, a felony involving violence.***

(d) Where he causes death by an act of violence done to a person whom he knows to be an officer of justice acting in the execution of his duty or a person assisting him, and done with the object of preventing lawful arrest or detention, (or done to a person known to be acting to suppress an affray or apprehend a felon).****

The classes of (a) and (b) (*supra*) were considered to be intentionally caused. Such being the case, "intentionally" embraced not only the object *D* aimed at, but even an unexpected and/or undesired result. To cause a death "intentionally," *D* must have the purpose to bring about the death (or injury), and *D* chooses to act in such a manner in which he realizes or believes 1) that the result is certain, or 2) "more likely than not to follow."

As for classifying murder into degrees because of the inherent heinousness of the act, the Commissioner found that such a classification was fraught with difficulties. A classification would be either too broad, and include too many murders; or it would be too narrow, and include too few. So also should the classification of murder into capital and non-capital murders not be introduced. The Commission did, however, wish to consider if the "artificial" extensions of the law of murder ought to continue in the law of Victoria. Should murder mean only a homicide in which the death was

---

* The case law referred to in the four situations is: *R. v. Jakac* (1961) V.R. 367; *Vallance v. The Queen* lll C.L.R. 56; *R. v. Hallett* (1969) S.A.S.R. 141, 153-155; *R. v. Sergi* (1974) V.R. 1, 10; *R. v. Hyam* (1974) 2 W.L.R. 607 (H.L.); *R. v. Hyam* (1973) 3 All E.R. 842 (C.A.)

** Compare *D.P.P. v. Beard*, 1920 A.C. 479.

*** *R. v. Ryan & Walker* (1966); Stephen, *Digest of Criminal Law*, 5th edn., p. 183.

**** *Archbold*, 33rd edn., Sec. 1672; *R. v. Scriva*, No. 2 (1951) V.L.R. 298.

caused intentionally, or ought murder to include the concept of constructive malice aforethought, or implied malice aforethought?

The Commissioner cited two strong cases, the import of which was to affirm the doctrine of intention in the law of criminal law. Sir Owen Dixon, in *Thomas v. The King*, 59 C.L.R. 279 at 309, had said that the element of intention was "the most fundamental element in a rational and humane criminal code." The second case, *Morisette v. U.S.*, 342 U.S. 241, on p. 250, had stated:

> The contention that an injury can amount to a crime only when influenced by intention is no provincial or transient notion. It is as universal and persistent in mature systems of law as belief in freedom of the human will and a consequent ability and duty of the normal individual to choose between good and evil.

The Commissioner noted that Holmes, in *The Common Law*, made the observation that "even a dog distinguished between being stumbled over and being kicked." The gist of the Commissioner's argument against the felony-murder rule was expressed by him in paragraph (40) of the Report:

> (i) [such a] ...rule transforms into murders accidental deaths resulting from applications of force which neither the offender, nor anyone else, would have supposed to carry the slightest danger to life.
>
> (ii) That a tacit assumption is made that the community may properly impose the severest of punishments upon a man for unintended and unforeseeable consequences of his acts, in order to deter others from the intentional taking or endangering of life.[73]

The Commissioner felt that no social statistics *re* felony-murder deaths commended the need for the rule, and also when such deaths did occur, they occurred in spite of the rule, e.g., out of the heat of passion or distraction of the moment so that the existence of the rule would not have deterred their happening in any case. Paragraph (50) of the said Report recommended that the felony-murder rule be abolished.

The Report then turned to *R. v. Hyam* (1974) 2 W.L.R. 607. It stated its view of the case to be:

> (53) The House of Lords [in *Hyam*] [stated]...that in law there are two bases upon which this third form of constructive murder rests. The intentional infliction of grievous bodily harm (i.e., any really serious bodily injury) is by statute a felony [Crimes Act 1958, Section 17]. Hence, if death results, the case

> is one of constructive murder under the felony-murder rule [*R. v. Hyam* (1974) 2 W.L.R. 607 per Lord Diplock on pp. 629-630]. But secondly, and independently of this statutory basis, it is a rule of the common law that, if death results from an intentional infliction of grievous bodily harm (as above defined) malice aforethought is implied [see the majority decision in *R. v. Hyam*...and *R. v. Vickers* (1957) 2 Q.B. 664]. The malice aforethought, in that case, is said to be "implied" rather than "constructive," but the implication is made by the law and cannot be negatived by any evidence. Accordingly this category of murder, upon its second as well as its first basis, is a form of constructive murder. As in the cases of felony-murder and escape-murder no actual intention to kill is required. Death need not to be shown to have been either an object aimed at or a result expected. And there need not even be a realization that so much as a mere risk or possibility of death is being created.[74]

It was to the legal fictions (b), (c) and (d) (*supra*, endnote 72) that the Report was addressed, and it noted that save for category (a), the other three categories did not require an actual intention to kill, nor even a realization that death might occur. The Commissioner believed that the objection to constructive murder was that it subjected an offender to the severest of punishments from the criminal sanction for consequences of acts which the offender in no way intended. It can readily be seen that the object of the Report was to connect punishment to an offense, and the "link" would occur through intention, whether or not the Report itself examined the concept of intention in minute detail. In one sense the Report had returned to a simpler notion known to us from medieval writers: namely, that the consequences of an act, if they are to be consequences for which the offender may be severely punished, ought to be consequences which the offender intended.

The Commissioner, in paragraph (56), also queried another category which, until then, seemed to stand as a self-justifying category, much as if it were a legal first-principle. What does it mean to speak of "any really serious bodily injury"? The Report stated:

> (56) These particular examples point to another serious objection to this third category of constructive murder, namely that under it a person's liability to the severest of penalties is made to depend on the meaning attached by the jury to the expression 'any really serious bodily injury'—an expression to which it is not possible to attach a precise meaning.[75]

The Report had, in paragraph (55), stated that medical science had removed the seriousness from chance deaths from infected wounds one might have received in an affray, so it was purposeless to imply malice aforethought that from any such injury *D* must have intended to kill *V*. What the Report noted was that the category through and by which malice is imputed is itself a variable and imprecise standard, and it found that other Commissions were unable to draft language precise enough to give precise legal meaning to the concept so as to make it workable in law. Even *Hyam*, when decided by the House of Lords, was ambiguous on the point, with its strongly divided set of opinions. The conclusion of the Victoria Report was that all forms of constructive murder ought to be abolished.

For purposes of legal reform, "intent" was therefore to be defined in the following ways in the Report:

> 1. (1) Where a person kills another, the killing shall not amount to murder unless done with an intent to kill.
>
> (2) A person has an "intent to kill" if, but only if, his purpose is to kill or he realizes or believes that his actions are certain, or more than likely than not, to kill.
>
> (3) The "intent to kill" may relate to the person in fact killed or to another, and need not relate to any particular person.[76]

The definition was simple and direct. Section (3) of the definition disposed of the class and its member problem, e.g., *D* killing *P* when intending to kill *V*. An "intent to kill" satisfied the requirement for criminal intention, and it was not extinguished if *D*, entertaining an unlawful intention, killed the wrong victim.

It is interesting to note that the Commissioner did not remove from his more narrow definition of murder that of mercy killing:

> Mercy killing, in the sense of an intentional killing the motive for which is to spare the victim a continuance of severe suffering. In my view...it would be unwise to make such a change. To do so would be likely to increase the number of cases in which persons who, even under a system of legalized euthanasia, would not be given authority to kill, would take upon themselves the responsibility for doing so. Moreover the motive for killing a sufferer must often be predominantly to relieve the killer from a burden that he has come to find

> intolerable. And it would be undesirable to place temptation in the way of persons who carry such burdens, to kill for their own relief, and then to seek to evade full responsibility by asserting that their motive was to relieve suffering. The fact that a person yielding to such a temptation would commonly be the only person able to give an account of what occurred, and of the motives for it, would render it difficult for the truth to emerge.[77]

Apart from addressing the problem itself, the passage may be taken to indicate that "motive" will not excuse a criminal intention. The mention of motive may have reference to a passage from the report of The Royal Commission on Capital Punishment, 1949-1953,[78] which, at Paragraph 179, page 63 of the said Report, made the following distinction between "motive" and "intention," an echo of which is caught in the Victoria Report:

> 179. They [i.e., witnesses appearing to give evidence to the Royal Commission] thought it would be most dangerous to provide that "mercy killings" should not be murder, because it would be impossible to define a category which could not be seriously abused. *Such a definition could only be in terms of the motive of the offender, but both English and Scottish law have always eschewed definitions in terms of motive, which is notoriously difficult to establish and cannot, like intent, be inferred from a person's overt actions* [italics ours].

The view of the Law Reform Commissioner in his first report was that intention should be interpreted in a strong sense, and in that regard he reflected the sentiments of the English report of The Law Commission (1967) on Imputed Criminal Intent. The Victoria Report did not dwell at length on what would be complex juristic problems latent in the concept of "intent" itself, but the Report did affirm that "intent" should be used in its simple and direct sense: namely, that to ascribe "x" to *D*, it ought to be demonstrated that *D* intended an act and its consequences. Although no historical mention was made, one could demonstrate that *versari in re illicita* had once again entered the common law, even if it returned uninvited and unrecognized. The crime of manslaughter remained an offense committed without intention to cause death, because of provocation, because of recklessness in the discharge of a duty of care, because of excessive physical injury, because of a breach of criminal law which risked physical harm or appreciable risk of harm.

Other jurisdictions were interested in the reform of their criminal law. Queensland had established a law commission and one of its earlier projects had been to recommend the abolition of the distinction between wilful murder and murder.[79] Under their code of criminal law, wilful murder was:

> [s.301]...a person who unlawfully kills another intending to cause his death or that of some other person, is guilty of wilful murder,

while murder was described to be:

> [s.302]...a person who unlawfully kills another...if the offender intends to do to the person killed or to some other person some grievous bodily harm...is guilty of murder.

Wilful murder carried the death penalty, murder did not. The commission found this difficulty with the distinction:

> It happens not infrequently that a jury acquits of wilful murder and convicts of murder in a case in which the evidence points overwhelmingly to wilful murder....Because the accused has been acquitted of wilful murder he cannot be tried again for that offence; on the second trial therefore he is tried for murder, that is, for an unlawful killing in which intention was not to cause death, but to cause grievous bodily harm. But the evidence upon the second trial remains the same as that upon the first; that is, it points unerringly to an intention to kill. It is almost impossible in such a case for a Judge to sum up convincingly to a jury; that is, to direct them that they must be satisfied beyond a reasonable doubt that the accused intended, not to kill, but to do grievous bodily harm.[80]

The distinction was appreciated to obtain because, at one time, the death penalty obtained for wilful murder, which penalty had since been abolished. If the distinction obtained merely because of punishment, the Commission thought that it ought to be abolished. In recommending the abolition of the distinction between wilful murder and murder, they followed Section 70 of the Draft Code for the Australian Territories (1969), which section defined murder in this way:

> (1) Except as hereinafter provided a person who kills another:-
>
> (a) intending to kill any person; or
>
> (b) intending to do grievous bodily harm to any person; or
>
> (c) whilst committing or attempting to commit any of the offences referred to in

> subsection (2) or whilst impeding the detection, apprehension, or prosecution of a person who has committed or attempted to commit any such offence, he being aware that there is at least a substantial risk of his killing or doing grievous bodily harm to any person; is guilty of the indictable offence of murder.[81]

(Subsection (2) embraced: Treason; Murder; Piracy; Robbery; Kidnapping; Abduction; Resisting lawful arrest; Escaping from lawful custody; Rape; Burglary; Arson; and Unlawful destruction of property by means of explosives.)

One will appreciate that the Queensland Law Reform Commission (1970) instated constructive murder, the very opposite of which the Victoria Law Reform Commission would recommend in its report some few years later. Their positions were exactly reversed. The Victoria Commission wanted murder to be punishable as murder only if the offender did intend (or will) to kill, a position abandoned by the Queensland Commission. With difficulty would salvation come through definitions! If the only forceful purpose for maintaining a distinction between murder and manslaughter (and their cognates as refined by various criminal codes) was for the sake of the punishment imposed, then one is easily led to the conclusion enunciated by Lord Kilbrandon in *Hyam v. D.P.P.* [1974] 2 All E.R. 42, 72:

> There does not appear to be any good reason why the crimes of murder and manslaughter should not both be abolished and the single crime of unlawful homicide substituted; one case will differ from another in gravity, and that can be taken care of by variation in sentences downwards from life imprisonment.

When one comes to consider the *Report on Culpable Homicide* issued in 1976 by the Criminal Law Reform Committee of New Zealand,[82] one can sense how some jurisdictions were deciding to turn from solving conceptual problems about the law, and were turning to sentencing problems, assuming that one solved a complicated legal problem by adverting to the penalties which the law ought to impose. Lord Kilbrandon, in *Hyam*, gave expression to that frame of mind, a judicial pragmatism akin to the psychological pragmatism of behavioral psychologists. If there is thought to exist a difference between categories only because consequences are differently weighed, if the consequences are made identical, why then worry about distinctions between antecedents if each will produce the same consequence, or a consequence of equal merit or value? Why worry about the reason why one wets a bed if one extinguishes bed-wetting behavior by means of conditioned reflex therapy?

A greater portion of Criminal Law Reform Committee of New Zealand is not of concern here. Its purpose was to recommend what modifications or deletions ought to be made with regard to the law regarding murder, manslaughter, provocation, suicide pacts, and negligence which caused death or injury. The Committee had taken four to five years to deliberate upon such questions in relation to the criminal code of New Zealand, and the product of its deliberation was a Report a little in excess of one hundred pages. The gist of a portion of the Report was that greater sentencing powers should be given both to the Court and to the Minister of Justice, permitting the Court to give indeterminate sentences, and permitting the Minister of Justice to terminate a person's liability for recall to prison if so deemed. The system seems to have been little more than an extended system of parole, with an offender (if guilty of a serious offense) liable to an extended and indefinite sentence for a lifetime, (as is the case in many common law jurisdictions when a felon is paroled, but the conditions of his parole are that they can be revoked at any time, the felon thereupon being required to return to prison to complete the duration of his prison sentence).

A great deal of discussion in the Report (N.Z.) dealt with provocation, the resolution of which was to abolish provocation as a plea which would mitigate an offense from murder to manslaughter, with the question of provocation itself being transformed into a question of what circumstances ought to mitigate an offense. The Report (N.Z.) consistently turned from legal concepts, to legal consequences, and dealt chiefly with consequences in relation to punishment.[83] How consequences were to be dealt with was left always in the realm of practical judicial wisdom and discretion, a realm which appeared to be both sacred and beyond the realm of principles, and their requisite analysis, for the Commission (N.Z.). One objection to provocation was to determine what kind of a concept it was, and its status. Was it an objective standard by which the concept was to be judged? or was it a flexible standard, measured more by the foot of him who rules, than by rules? The Report (N.Z.) seemed to express dissatisfaction with various English attempts to address themselves to provocation.[84] The Committee (N.Z.) thought that the law on the subject of "provocation" was complex, confusing, and something which the ordinary man might not understand.[85] One case was discussed, its purpose to illustrate that, *at times*, because there existed no clear and precise line between what was and what was not provocation, injustice could and did come about. The case which served to illustrate this flaw was the Canadian case: *Perrault v. The Queen*, (1970) 12 D.L.R. (3d) 480.

In *Perrault* the Court concluded that a defendant could not combine the categories of "provocation" and "drunkenness" to yield a defense for non-capital murder. The difficulty with the case, as the dissent demonstrated, was that the two concepts, impartially inexact, were attempted to be mixed, which mixture was to yield an acceptable defense to the charge. *D*, thought the court, was neither drunk enough, nor so provoked, that *each*, in itself, would be an adequate defense to the charge of non-capital murder; but, thought the trial court, the two concepts taken together would yield an adequate defense. This was found to be a mistake of law by the Supreme Court of Canada. The New Zealand Commission (1976) dwelt upon this case because, as a difficult case, it showed that if an offense of unlawful killing were permitted – as was advocated by the Commission (N.Z., 1976) – then the gymnastics of law through which the Canadian Court tumbled could all have been avoided; it would, under the offense of unlawful killing, be only a question of what non-capital penalty to assess, and not be a question of (also) assessing what legal principles were, or were not, involved – in the case of *Perrault*, whether *D*'s intent had been negatived or not.

The New Zealand report may illustrate a trend growing in the criminal law: namely, to dismiss complicated discussion of further complicated mental concepts, and to stress, instead, all concentration upon consequences and effects.* It is easy to appreciate how much Baronness Wootton's own *Crime and The Criminal Law*,[86] must have affected this

* Modern Sentencing Reform Act legislation, which creates fixed and determinate jail penalties, shows this new frame of mind.

Commission. If criminal law is thought to be a necessary connection of "elements of a crime" *and* "punishment," if the punishment is made both non-capital and variable, why then bother with the nature of the conceptual elements of the offense, especially when those conceptual elements can be erased? A rebuttal would be: certainly an offense can be simply defined, as was the proposed statutory amendment which would abolish the defense of provocation.[87] But then how does one differentiate degree within punishment? It had been seen, in our earlier chapters, that Church law, after the dissolution of the Roman Empire, when the Church instructed its spiritual ministers on the matter of dispensing holy absolution, distinguished between the nature of transgressions, and that in all cases when a practical judgment had to be made by a priest or bishop about what penance to impose, and, if absolution should be given to the penitent, the priest or bishop had to inquire as to the nature of the sin, how it was committed, and to what degree was the penitent both intellectually and volitionally responsible for the commission of the sin. Legal consequentialism does not relieve one of inquiry into mental concepts and their conceptual elements, as the Report seemingly assures when it reduces all killings to unlawful killings, adverting then only to punishment to determine how serious was the offensive act in the eyes of the court. To return to practical judgment as a measure whereby an act and its heinousness is understood does not relieve one from the need to understand the nature, and its dispositions and elements, from which the act sprung.

In a peculiar way, although the Commission (N.Z.) avoided use of *mens rea*, the commission (N.Z.) reinstated an older notion of intention when it came to discuss manslaughter. The Commission perceived that *D* can act dangerously, and no harm can ensue; or that *D* can act dangerously, and harm can ensue. A disjunction was introduced between the concept of an act dangerous in itself, and the possible consequences of an act, but which consequences were seen as non-necessary. The Report stated,

> If there is, however, a significant element of danger in the accused's acts, it is that element of danger that ought to be taken into account in proscribing such conduct and setting a penalty in respect of it. The potential harm rather than the actual harm provides the proper measure of liability. It is

> recognized that the actual harm may be cogent evidence of the degree of risk created. For the reasons given we are unanimously of the opinion that the criminal law in this area should be directed against dangerous conduct, and that liability should be neither increased nor decreased according to chance results.[88]

Medieval Christian moral theologians would have been extremely pleased by such a principled statement of theory which held that wrong ought to be attributed to him who did it, and not what was done.

Endnotes Chapter 7

1. *Cf.*, The *Criminal Law Review*, January, 1978, 1) "Intent," by Mr. Justice J. H. Buzzard, pp. 5-13, and the rejoinder, 2) "Intent: A Reply," by Professor J. C. Smith, pp. 14-21.

2. *Cf.*, *Responsibility Before the Law*, by Lord Denning, MR (Magnes Press, 1961), and the reply to it, *The Mental Element in Crime*, by Glanville Williams, FBA (Magnes Press, 1965).

3. *Cf.*, *Reshaping the Criminal Law: Essays in Honour of Glanville Williams*, edited by Peter Glazebrook (London: Stevens & Sons, 1978), the index of Professor Williams' published writings which does show how intense correspondence was with *The Times* and other journals regarding differences betwixt scholars as to the meaning of "intent," pp. 449-468.

4. *A Guide to Law & Practice under the Criminal Justice Act 1967*, by [Sir] David Napley (London: Sweet and Maxwell, 1967), Chapter 3, "Proof," "1. Proof of Criminal Intent (Section 8)," p. 29. Sections 8(a) (b) read: A court of jury,

"(a) shall not be bound in law to infer that he intended or foresaw a result of his actions by reason only of its being a natural and probable consequence of those actions; but

(b) shall decide whether he did intend or foresee that result by reference to all the evidence, drawing such inferences from the evidence as appear proper in the circumstances (s. 8)."

5. Kenny's *Outlines of Criminal Law* [Nineteenth Edition, 1966], by J. W. Cecil Turner (Cambridge: At the University Press, 1966), Book II, "Definition of Particular Crimes," Chapter VII, "Homicide," Section 1, Introductory, paragraph 107, "Suggested definition of malice aforethought," pp. 151-154.

6. *Cf.*, "*In re*: Intention," *Aristotelian Society* (Suppl. vol. LI), 1977, pp. 187-220, esp. pp. 197-199.

7. There exists a line of cases in which cherished assumptions about the nature of the relation of one element to the other – *mens rea* to *actus reus* – in a criminal offense have been stretched to the extreme. The cases which, in part, show this tension are: *Fagan v. Metropolitan Police Commissioner* [1969] 1 Q.B. 439; *Lett v. R.* 6 West Indian Reports 92; *Thabo Meli v. R.* [*sub nom*: *Meli v. The Queen*] [1954] 1 W.L.R. 228; [1954] 1 All E.R. 373 (Privy Council); *R. v. Chiswibo*, 1961 (2) S.A. 714; *R. v. Church* [1966] 1 Q.B. 59; *State v. Masilela*, 1968 (2) S.A. 558. *Cf.*, "Contemporaneity of Act and Intention in Crimes," by Geoffrey Marston, 86 L.Q.R. 208-238 [April, 1970]. Dean Marston discusses a wide range of cases in which "act" and "intention" are separated, with the resulting question then: what relationship must obtain between "act" and "intention" for *D* to be guilty of an offense which

requires "act" and "intention"? If "act" = time bn, and "intention" = time bx, and (bn)< =/= >(bx), what relationship in time must (bn) bear to (bx) for *D* to have had the requisites present for a criminal act to be attributed to him?

8. *Cf.*, *Ignorance, Faith and Conformity*, by Kenneth E. Kirk (Longmans, 1925), Chapter 1, "*Ignorance*," pp. 1-43.

9. For instance, consider the crime of "constructive manslaughter" and the conceptual problems which attend both its definition and application. *Cf.*, *U.S. v. Jewell*, 532 F.2d 697 (1976) *re*: "knowingly," *re*: the meaning of "knowingly" in relation to deliberate ignorance, contrived with conscious purpose so as to avoid learning the truth. *Cf.*, also "Manslaughter by Unlawful Act: The "Constructive" Crime Which Serves no Constructive Purpose," by W. T. Westling, *The Sydney Law Review*, Volume 7, Number 2 (September, 1974): 211-223. Of the logic of the felony-murder rule, the author observes: "It is submitted that the bulk of the cases which have purportedly been decided on the basis of an 'unlawful' act can truly be decided on the basis of intentional infliction of harm or on the basis of criminal negligence" (p. 212). "[I]f we concentrate our inquiry on the dangerous character of the act in question it becomes clear that an act which is unlawful because it is dangerous must either be intended to inflict some harm or negligent. If it is intended to inflict harm it will give rise to liability for involuntary manslaughter when death results. If it is negligent the accused's conduct should be measured in criminal negligence terms to decide whether it is manslaughter when death results. The intentional infliction of harm principle is a subjective one: did the accused intend some more than trivial harm? The negligence principle is an objective one: would a reasonable man in the accused's position have recognized the risk and acted as he did? Anything which does not fall into one of these categories ought not be criminal homicide at all. If a third category of involuntary manslaughter is created, outside these first two, it is surely constructive. The unlawful and dangerous act principle must be either subjective or objective, and once it is thus identified it must be completely redundant when considered alongside the two basic principles. Recognition of this would effectively do away with the 'constructive' manslaughter which has been so long deplored" (p. 223).

10. *The Law Commission: Imputed Criminal Intent (Director of Public Prosecutions v. Smith)*, [Laid before Parliament by the Lord High Chancellor pursuant to section 3(2) of the Law Commissions Act 1965] (London: Her Majesty's Stationery Office, 1967 [reprinted: 1968]).

11. The distinguished body of Commissioners were, as of 12th December, 1966, these men, whose status of the period is given: The Honourable Mr. Justice Scarman, O.B.E., Chairman; Mr. L. C. G. Gower, M.B.E.; Mr. Neil Lawson, Q.C.; Mr. N. S. Marsh; Mr. Andrew Martin, Q.C.; Mr. H. Boggis-Rolfe, C.B.E., Secretary.

12. *The Law Commission: Imputed Criminal Intent* (1967), p. 5.

13. *Ibid.*, pp. 6-7.

14. *The Royal Commission on Criminal Law of 1834, Seventh Report* (Parliamentary Papers 1843, vol. xix: command Paper 448), p. 23.

15. *The Royal Commission on Capital Punishment, 1949-1953, Report* (London: Her Majesty's Stationery Office, 1953 [reprinted:1973], Command Paper 8932), paragraph 107, p. 40. The language of the *Report* read: "107. We have no doubt that, as a matter of general principle, persons ought not to be punished for consequences of their acts which they did not intend or foresee. The doctrine of constructive malice clearly infringes this principle and in our view it ought to be abolished."

16. It is a long and detailed debate which is far outside the scope of this study, but one may refer to these authors who have given detailed analysis to the modal differences imported by the verb, "to know." Variously, *cf.*, *The Divine Relativity*, by Charles Hartshorne (Yale, 1948). Professor Hartshorne speaks at length to the logic of Socinus' arguments concerning foreknowledge. *Gersonides*: *The Wars of the Lord*, *Treatise Three*: *On God's Knowledge*, A translation and commentary by N. M. Samuelson, Pontifical Institute of Mediaeval Studies (Toronto, Ontario, Canada: 1977); *The Foundations of the Articles of Faith,* by Al-Ghazzali, translated by Nabih Amin Faris (Kashmiri Bazar, Lahore [Pakistan]: Sh. Muhammad Ashraf, 1974).

17. *The Law Commission: Imputed Criminal Intent* (1967), p. 9.

18. Contrary to *Smith* were: *Reg. v. Sharmpal Singh* (P.C.) [1962]A.C. 188; *Parker v. The Queen* (1963) 111 C.L.R. 610, with approval of *Stapleton v. The Queen* (1952) 86 C.L.R. 358 at 365, "The introduction of the maxim...that a man is presumed to intend the reasonable consequences of his act is seldom helpful and always dangerous."

19. *The Law Commission*: *Imputed Criminal Intent* (1967), p. 14.

20. *Ibid*., pp. 14-15.

21. *Ibid*., p. 15.

22. *Ibid*., p. 11, paragraph 10, "*C*. Proof of intent and foresight in the criminal law generally." "[I]t is desirable, in the interests of the clarification of the law, to put on a statutory basis a rule that, where intent and foresight is required in the criminal law, such intent or foresight must be subjectively proved; that is to say, the matter in issue should be the actual state of mind of the accused."

23. *Ibid*. p. 16, "E. Summary of Proposals...22 (c)."

24. *Cf*., *The Nicomachean Ethics*, Bk. III, i, 1110b2, "...for actions are in the class of particulars...["*ai gar pragzeis hen tow prattonti*"]. The observation of Professor John Burnet, *The Ethics of Aristotle* [Methuen, 1900], may be added: "This is fundamental. There is no such thing as an act which is not this particular act in these particular circumstances....An act performed is

always *this* act. Hence too the difficulty; for there can be no scientific rules about particulars" (p. 116).

25. Such an example is the case of *R. v. Desmond* (1868) 11 Cox 146. The actual report of the case, *R. v. Desmond and Others*, is to be found recorded in *The Times*, London, at various dates: January 7th, 14th, 21st, 29th; February 5th, 12th, 19th, 26th; March 4th; with a report of the opinion of the court on Tuesday, April 28th, 1868, p. 11. The deceased in the case, one Mary Ann Hodgkinson, was killed as a result of a bomb blast which occurred on the 13th of December, 1867. Desmond, and others, were attempting to rescue a prisoner, and, in the prosecution of a felonious intention [sic] setting off a bomb to bring about his escape, glass was shattered in the victim's house, which pieces pierced her subclavian artery, causing a great hemorrhage, from which she died. If we advert to the Law Commission's concept of "willingness," one can see that it applies to *Desmond*: namely, although the defendants did not wish to kill, they were prepared to cause conditions the consequences of which may have been an unlawful death.

26. *Cf.*, *The Mental Element in Crime*, by Glanville Williams, LL.D., F.B.A. (Jerusalem: At the Magnes Press, The Hebrew University, 1965), pp. 10-12, in which four hypothetical cases are put. The fourth example, of inadvertent negligence, shows how a different classification of responsibility arises from the same case. Williams says (p.12), "The word 'intention' must be taken in relation to a particular consequence, and when an act has two or more consequences (as an act always has), it may be intentional as to one of those consequences and not as to another."

27. *The Law Commission, Published Working Paper No. 31, Second Programme Item XVIII, Codification of the Criminal Law, General Principles, the Mental Element in Crime*, [issued] 16 June 1970, by J. C. R. Fieldsend, Esq., Secretary, The Law Commission, Conquest House, 37-38 John Street, Theobald's Road, London, WC IN-2BQ, [paper number: 17-26-04].

28. *Ibid.*, endnote 26, *supra.*

29. Mr. Neil Lawson, Q.C.; Mr. Norman Marsh, Q.C.; The Hon. Mr. Justice Scarman, O.B.E.; Mr. T. R. Fitzwalter Butler; The Rt. Hon. Lord Justice Edmund Davies; The Common Sergeant, Mr. J. M. L. Griffith-Jones, M.C.; Mr. J. H. Buzzard; Mr. A. E. Cox; Mr. J. N. Martin O.B.E., Mr. Michael Walker; Professor Williams, with alternate members from the Home Office.

30. *Working Paper 31: The Mental Element in Crime* (L. C. 1970), pp. 1-2. In a footnote to their own statement, the Commission added: "Throughout this Paper, we use the world 'fault' to include the traditional terms 'intention,' 'knowledge,' 'recklessness' and 'negligence.' When we use the term, 'the mental element' or *mens rea*, we exclude negligence which, in contrast to recklessness, does not require actual advertence to the risk of the results or circumstances of conduct."

31. *Ibid.*, p. 2.

32. "The legislature may wish to provide for a different degree of fault in different elements of the same offences. The propositions, therefore, are subject to any specific provision the legislature may take in relation to the fault element in any particular offence" (p. 3, *Working Paper 31*).

33. *Ibid*., p. 3.

34. *Ibid*., p. 4.

35. *Sweet v. Parsley* [1969] 1 All E.R. 347 (H.L.), quashing *D*'s conviction for the possession of drugs, section 5(b) of the Dangerous Drugs Act 1965.

36. *Working Paper 31*, pp. 6-7.

37. Proposition One drew upon: *R. v. Cunningham* [1957] 2 Q.B. 396, "malice" = the foresight of a prohibited consequence, as defined by statute; *Bullock v. Turnbull* [1952] 2 Ll. L.R. 303, *D* boards a quarantined vessel unknowingly; *R. v. Cohen* [1951] 1 K.B. 505, did *D* knowingly evade custom's duty; *Cotterill v. Penn* [1936] 1 K.B. 53, *D* kills a house pigeon honestly believing it to be a wood-pigeon; *R. v. Forbes & Webb* (1865) 10 Cox C.C. 362; *R. v. Maxwell* (1909) 2 Cr. App. Rep. 26, unknowingly, *D* obstructs a police officer in performance of his duty.

38. The second proposition was supported by: *R. v. Salter* [1968] 2 Q.B. 793 (bankruptcy); *Rees v. Taylor*, 14 Oct. 1939 (unrep.) from *Stone's Justices Manual* [100th ed., p. 2404, note (d)], traffic violation in which *D* unwittingly proceeds through unseen signals.

39. The model case for an example of sheer statutory power was *R. v. Larsonneur* (1933) 97 J.P. 206.

40. *Cf*., *Lambert v. California* (1957) 355 U.S. 225; 78 S. Ct. 240; 2 L.Ed. 2d 228, *D* inadvertently violates a felon's registration law. Mr. Justice Douglas reversed the conviction. Also, *cf*., *Morissette v. United States*, (1952) 342 U.S. 246; 72 S. Ct. 240; 96 L.Ed. 288.

41. *Working Paper 31*, p. 17.

42. *Cf*., the illuminating dissent of Wright, J. (joined by Bazelon, C.J., and Tamm and Robinson, J.J.) in *United States v. Moore*, (1973) 486 F.2d 11239 [United States Court of Appeals, District of Columbia Circuit].

43. *Cf*., *United States v. Balint* (1922) 258 U.S. 250, removing common law *scienter* requirement in order to effect narcotics prosecutions. Also, *cf*., *United States v. Behrman* (1922) 258 U.S. 280; S. 42 Ct. 303. *D*, a physician, wrongfully prescribes narcotics. "[W]rongfully" is defined by statute, and not by medical practice.

44. *The Law Commission, Working Paper 31*, pp. 25-26.

45. Note: Proposition 7 (B) both (a) and (b), Recklessness, [*Working Paper 31*], would appear to negate the Commission's statement concerning perjury (*supra*, endnote 44), pp. 30-31. *Cf.*, endnote 46, (*infra*).

46. *Ibid.*, pp. 30-31.

47. *Cf.*, *Creative Intuition in Art and Poetry* [The A. W. Mellon Lectures in the Fine Arts, National Gallery of Art, Washington], by Jacques Maritain (Bollingen Series XXXV. 1), (New York: Pantheon Books, 1953), Chapter Four, "Creative Intuition and Poetic Knowledge," pp. 106-145, esp., pp. 117-125, "*Nature of Poetic Knowledge*." Also, *cf.*, *The Range of Reason*, by Jacques Maritain (New York: Scribners, 1952), Chapter III.

48. 'Poien,' col. 1, p. 1291, *A Greek-English Lexicon* (Oxford: Liddell and Scott, 1864).

49. *Cf.*, *State v. White*, 374 P.2d 942, 965 (Wash., 1962).

50. *The Law Commission, Working Paper 31*, (1970), p. 35.

51. *Ibid.*, p. 47, "*Further commentary on Proposition 7.A (3).*"

52. *Ibid.*

53. *Ibid.*, p. 49.

54. *Ibid.*, p. 33, "*Intention.*"

55. *Ibid.*, p. 49.

56. *Cf.*, *Roe v. Minister of Health, C.A.*, [1954] 2 Q.B. 66; [1954] 2 All E.R. 131.

57. But long ago we saw that, *The State v. Hardie*, Supreme Court of Iowa (1878), 10 Runnells 647, plainly rejected this test, i.e., the sport itself was a "reckless sport, and they should be held liable for the consequences of their acts."

58. A recent case on the matter would find *D* guilty, willy-nilly. *Cf.*, *Worsfold v. Howe* [1980] 1 All. E.R. 1028.

59. It will be remembered that the Commission put forward two distinct views regarding "intention and knowledge." It said, "*The first* [definition] of these equates intention as to consequences or knowledge of circumstances with states of mind in which the defendant has no substantial doubt that the consequences will result or that the circumstances exist. *The second* equates them with foresight of the probability of consequences or knowledge of the probable existence of circumstances." From, "Intention and Knowledge: Commentary," p. 39. We have carried over those distinctions for "recklessness," since recklessness involves some appreciation and some deficiency of knowledge. "[T]he majority would wish clearly to distinguish

intention and knowledge from recklessness and to keep the two former concepts as near to their ordinary meaning as possible" (para. 5, p. 43, *idem.*). The minority view favored a probability test for foresight of consequences. "[A]n alleged handler of stolen goods should be convicted if his state of mind, having regard to all the circumstances, is found to be that, when he handled the goods, he thought that they were probably stolen. This, they argue [as the minority], is not by any means the same thing as saying that the accused could be convicted if he thought that the goods *might* be stolen. In these circumstances, he has been no more than reckless, and the present law does not punish reckless handling of stolen property. The minority also see practical difficulties arising from the words 'no substantial doubt' which the majority prefer. What is a 'substantial doubt'? How are juries to be directed?" (para. 7, p. 45, *Idem.*).

60. *Commentary, Working Paper 31*, p. 53.

61. "[W]e are conscious of the fact that a concept of recklessness sometimes figures in the present law in contexts which it has a special meaning distinct from that provided in our definition, which is merely aimed at following the traditional common law. Recklessness is sometimes given a special meaning in offenses such as manslaughter [*Andrews v. D.P.P.* [1937] A.C. 576] and reckless driving [ss. 1 & 2, Road Traffic Act 1960], where the term is most nearly equated with 'gross negligence' or with what has been described as 'an attitude of mental indifference to obvious risks.'...We think that it is necessary to make clear that recklessness does not merely mean negligence, even gross negligence. Recklessness in deception offences seems, in most existing laws, to require foresight of risk [...(A)n exception in the Prevention of Fraud (investments) Act 1958, s. 13, by which false statements made knowingly or recklessly though not necessarily dishonestly are made punishable in certain circumstances. We do not regard this as a satisfactory use of the word 'recklessly' in a wider context. See...the Protection of Depositors Act 1963, s.1.," pp. 55-57, *Commentary*, para. 4.

62. *Working Paper 31*, *Commentary*, para. 4, p. 55.

63. *Working Paper 31, The Place of Mistake in Relation to the Mental Element*, para. 1, p. 63.

64. *Cf.*, "Fault, Threat and The Predicates of Criminal Liability," by Graham Strong (1980), 441 *Wisconsin Law Review* for a criticism of the fault model in its reliance upon knowledge and volition.

65. *Working Paper 31*, *The Place of Mistake in Relation to the Mental Element*," para. 1, p. 63.

66. *Ibid.*, p. 65.

67. The Third Part of the *Reports* of Sr. George Croke Kt. [London: 1661], collected by Sir Harbottle Grimston Baronet, Master of the Rolls.

68. *Cook's Case*, Termino Paschae, anno decimo quinto Caroli Regis, pp. 537-539, of *Croke's Reports* (*supra*, endnote 67).

69. *Levett's case* (1638), *Cro. Car.* 538.

70. *Law Reform Commissioner, Report No. 1, Law of Murder*, August, 1974, prepared by T. W. Smith (Law Reform Commissioner), 155 Queen Street, Melbourne, Victoria, Australia, 3000 (cited as *L.R.C. Report No. 1*, 1974).

71. *L.R.C. Report No. 1*, 1974, p. 1.

72. *Ibid.*, pp. 2-3.

73. *Ibid.*, 1974, pp. 12-13.

74. *Ibid.*, pp. 15-16.

75. *Ibid.*, p. 16.

76. *Ibid.*, p. 18, *Form of Amendment for Implementing the Recommended Reductions in the Width of the Definition of Murder.*

77. *Ibid.*, p. 20.

78. *Royal Commission on Capital Punishment 1949-1953 Report* (London: H.M.S.O., 1953 [1973], Cmd. 8932).

79. Report of the Queensland Law Reform Commission (Q.L.R.C.2.) on "Abolition of the Distinction between Wilful Murder and Murder," The Hon. Mr. Justice, W. B. Campbell (address - P. O. Box 312, North Quay, Brisbane, Queensland, Australia, 4000).. A second report was also issued, 19 December 1969, by the same Chairman, with the short title: Q.L.R.C.W.3, "Queensland, Law Reform Commission, Confidential, Working Paper on the proposed abolition of the Distinction between Wilful Murder and Murder." Both papers are substantially the same, and are listed here for sake of reference.

80. Q.L.R.C.2., p. 6.

81. *Ibid.*, p. 7.

82. *Report of [the] Criminal Law Reform Committee on Culpable Homicide*, July, 1976 (address - Private Bag, Postal Centre, Wellington, New Zealand).

83. *Culpable Homicide* (N.Z., 1976), Part 1, "Provocation," pp 3-23, esp. paragraphs, 5, 6, 8, 13, 29, and 42; also, *cf.*, Appendix 11, "Working Paper on Homicide under Provocation," Part 1, pp. 13-20. (Note, this is a separately appended "Paper," with pagination distinct from the Report.)

84. *Culpable Homicide* (N.Z., 1976), para. 34, p. 18.

85. *R. v. McGregor* [1962] NZLR 1069.

86. London: Stevens and Sons, 1963.

87. *Culpable Homicide* (N.Z., 1976) p. 42, para. 42 (1) (d) to revoke ss. 169 & 170 of the Crimes Act 1961.

88. *Culpable Homicide* (N.Z., 1976), para. 48, pp. 28-29, Part II, "Manslaughter, The effect of 'chance'."

CHAPTER EIGHT

Philosophy and Law:
Exploratio Intentionis

In his inaugural lecture, Professor Thompson said of the concepts *mens rea* and *actus reus*,

> *Actus non facit reum nisi mens sit rea* is one of the great maxims of criminal law. As with most of the Latin tags which are the lawyer's staple diet, it does not help us very much even when it is translated. *Mens rea* has come to mean that kind or degree of mental blameworthiness that is necessary in order to make conduct criminal. The term *actus reus* has come to mean conduct forbidden by law and the term *mens rea* the mental aspect of such conduct. Unfortunately scholars are not yet agreed on the meaning of these terms and as a result there is confusion in the cases. One can with some difficulty draw distinctions between various cases but one cannot deduce from them a consistent doctrine of criminal liability.[1]

Since these sentiments were expressed as recently as 1965, law commissions have abounded, and writing which is concerned with the meaning and clarification of the meaning of intention and its elements has abounded. What one commission affirms, another commission denies. New, however, to the old controversy as to what is the precise meaning of intention, *mens rea* and *actus reus*, is the legal philosopher, who looks not at the concepts as if he were a lawyer, but who looks into the concepts with a philosophical sense of detachment. He must see not only the law and what it means, but also if its meaning makes sense and is subject, at the same time, to justification. The sense of detachment from a need to support any legal system at all lets the philosopher appreciate that "intention," and its adjunct elements, is not to be solved, just as "existence" is not to be solved. The fact that the art of the philosopher may begin with his wondering at existence, may also carry over to existence of legal systems and their elements; in this case, that a concept so flexible and broad as is intention is not subject to a confined and restricted analysis, like morbid anatomy, but is more akin to the family of living and adventuresome sciences, like recombinative microbiology, which looks both to the *fons et origo* of life itself, and to novel and creative patterns which possibly may emerge or be created, given greater insight in genetic recombinations.

As to "intention" itself, whatever its verbal clothing, it appears to be a concept which grows and does not diminish in its complexity and intensity. The literature produced by various law commissions throughout the common law world is staggering, and is now enough in quantity that a legal philosopher could devote himself fully to considering and analyzing those productions.[2]

In criminal law, intention functions as the representative concept whereby human actions, and the reasons for them, are understood in relation to a criminal system. If no law, then no punishment; but, if a law, what then? How is *D* supposed to be understood in his relation to that body of criminal law? One is very much aware that the criminal law, as it is presently conducted, generally pits the smallness of an individual against the corporate greatness and might of the state. What ought to serve to balance, or to redress the balance, between these obvious imbalances?

In any exploration one hopes to return to the sources. In this extended legal exploration the sources have been wide and varied and, at times, rare and difficult to obtain. There have not been any clear and precise links of one moment of legal history to another; one has been required to make educated guesses, thoughtful assumptions, and infer what seemed to be reasonable links from one epoch into the next. Our own reading of our sources has suggested for us that intention had been seen mostly as a volitive concept, and, for that reason, its roots and beginnings as "malice aforethought" suggested that *D* had been moved to break the law (a law which was believed to have a moral foundation) because of his own disruption of character and moral disquietude. One did the deed, one did not think the deed.

But to break a law, which had a moral foundation, led one to ask further questions about both law and morals. Might it be that there was a common link between an ability to break a social law, and an ability to break a moral law? One will remember how both Bracton and Fleta admitted how both dimensions could surround a human act, choosing as their example the wicked judge who justly sentenced a man to death, but who took delight in the shedding of the defendant's blood. Law and morals had distinct spheres. At times they overlapped, and at other times they coursed independently one of the other. Common, however, to each sphere was the ability and capacity of a man to move in those spheres, and this led into the old and common effort: to inquire as to the nature of man.

That man possesses a nature is, no doubt, a truism; but that his nature can be deciphered, decoded, and put into well-defined, non-ambiguous sets of linguistic propositions has been and is the rub. Our common law was deeply indebted to our common prevailing modes of thought about human nature whereby the two broad differences found in our natures were cast into terms of intellect and will, and these broad conceptual differences themselves, for centuries, seemed to take on concrete forms of their own. One's Will, and one's Intellect, seemed to be reified in moral and theological writings, as if each were homunculus, possessed of its own distinct identity, acting for its own distinct ends. Added to this reification of concepts and operations, one further distinction was labored: that something about man's nature put him both into a world of matter (mass and extension) and of spirit (energy and infinitude). Could any more contradictory sets of postulates have been added to a growing legal system?

By reading the ancient sources with an imaginative mind one can discard, jettison even, much of the conceptual impedimenta which accompanied the early postulates from which common law notions of criminal responsibility evolved, and which they absorbed. If there be any wisdom in our own age it may be this: to appreciate that no single sentence or algorithm or formula can be generated which will both be a substitute for, and full explanation of, human nature. The problem of synonymity presents itself: namely, if "x" can be redefined by "y," then both "x" and "y" can be redefined by any further term. That redescription, or its possibility, is much like the number line: it is unbounded, and can, by itself, generate infinite redescriptions of elements of itself. If this applies to natural languages, it may be argued that it applies to objects which those natural languages seek to explain. If a relationship is to obtain between this sentence, and this object, that relationship will be an analogical relationship: partly described, partly indescriptive. It is not a paradox which, for the law, creates skepticism; it is a fairly honest depiction of the human condition, the endless movement from ignorance into intellectual light and knowledge. The broad categories which have been seen to describe human nature have been thought and volition. Since the common law could not effect a criminal sanction to control thought and volition *in se*, both had to be expressed in some form of action which was forbidden and which brought the person under the power of the law. "Action" need not be solely interpreted as some form of visible movement; were it so, then the concept of a criminal omission, or of a duty to act, would be a logical puzzle.

But if the law, then, is a hierarchy of concepts, each with its distinct elements, then the legal philosopher can ask questions about the nature of those concepts, and he can also ask how their application is justified. The broad concepts of "volitive" and "intellective" call for explanation and justification. It is a dual task: asking why *phi* obtains, and if *phi* should obtain. "*Phi*" may be any key legal concept. But the art of the legal philosopher is conceptual analysis of concepts *qua* concepts, and of concepts *qua* legal concepts.

Analyzing intention then was to analyze a complex relationship. It was to realize and appreciate that one was discussing some view of human nature, and it was to be aware that one was applying concepts, generally conveyed through ordinary language, to aspects of human behavior. Common law minimized many of the difficulties. It would not, as we saw, embrace skepticism or pyrrhonism. It assumed that an accused who came before the court would be found either guilty or not guilty, or, as in the case of Scottish verdicts, not proven. There seems to have run the consistent, common-sense assumption that legal findings can be set down in simple sentences; and, as a principle coeval with that assumption, that the requirements of the law can be set forth in declarative sentences with certainty. The assumption of the common law has been that language can make clear what the law requires and demands. Law, therefore, is a set of propositions which are both knowable and coherent. The parallel assumption for the Western philosopher has been that the world is knowable. While common law embraced a linguistic realism, it was certainly in harmony with the accepted philosophy of the West, that of philosophical realism.

A legal philosopher, however, need not be persuaded by these mutually supportive propositions. This sets him not against the assumptions embodied in the law–here, the criminal law–but in a state of pre-selection, as it were, much like Adam before the Fall, having neither to avow or disavow treasured postulates and their equally treasured corollaries. Because many conceptual and theoretical borrowings were at work in the shaping of the common law and its criminal sanction, one, in analyzing aspects of that great body of accumulated legal wealth, proceeds with reserve and caution. The slapdash, lasso statement has no place in such sustained analysis. One is forced by the nature of the subject to move through its monumental past slowly.

Amidst this vast pantheon it can be determined why one element sustained another. The common law, common to its Christian and Greco-Roman heritage, held an offender responsible for his actions. If action was simply attributed to *D*, but not originated by *D*, then *D* did not come into the control of the criminal law (save for curious statutory anomalies which simply attributed wrongdoing to *D*, whether or not *D* actually did a wrong).[3] The roots of the criminal sanction rested in transgression; but transgression had to flow from the conduct of *D*. Certainly, and it can be dismissed just as easily, any legal proposition can be constructed which attributes guilt to *D*. This is law strictly in the imperative mode. But our common law took over the older confessorial notions that guilt had to flow from knowledge, and knowledge had to be an expression of the free assent of the penitent. If *D* merely "knew," but did not consent to knowing, then any movement of his senses would have been described as knowledge fully and completely; but it was not.[4] Animal motions or sense impressions were never given the status or pedigree of knowledge gained in reflection. Once again, one returned to considering what was human nature, and what was embraced by the concepts and operations of mind and will?

Is there an ideal model for what relationship ought to obtain between the person and the criminal law? From the standpoint of the criminal law such an ideal relationship might view the law itself to be a vast body of well-defined propositions; the propositions, in theory, would be potentially knowable by any knower (excluding from the set of knowers infants, the insane, or any class of which it could be said that they were incapable of cognitive life); and, as a potentially knowable body of legal propositions, they could be converted by any knower into knowledge, and would thus function as reasons for one's legal actions. To know the law would mean to observe the law. Deducible from this model as a corollary of it would be the further claim that if the law is, in theory, knowable, then not to follow the dictates of the law would mean that one knowingly violated the canons of his legal knowledge. Not to obey the law would be viewed as a rational act. It could almost be converted into a simple machine model: if *P* follows the law, there is a law for him to know in order for him to follow it. But if *P* violates the law, there is a law for him to follow, but he himself knowingly creates propositions counter to those of the law, and knowingly violates the law. Is our simple model of the criminal law a complete model?

If one is assuming that a machine model, or a simple cognitive model, states the relationship which ought to obtain in the criminal law in a complete way, then the model, seemingly, is complete. A person is viewed somewhat like a computer without a program. Once the program is inserted, the computer operates. When it operates, according to the language of the program, it may be said to be operating "legally"–if the program is one of legal language. Raised to a higher, but simpler, level of abstraction, action in accord with the criminal sanction could be reduced to one simple, beatific vision: a comprehensive legal proposition converted into knowledge by a knower, and that knowledge converted into action by appropriate conduct. It would be as if one, in law, had converted the criminal sanction into "$E=MC^2$." One would, at this level of abstraction, be reducing the criminal sanction into a simple but comprehensive proposition which was knowable. Other legal systems have known of such a formulation: Christian theologians who posited an all-knowing God assumed that such a being would have perfect knowledge without the need for propositions. Our simple vision of the criminal sanction as a universal proposition potentially knowable by any person is hardly as complicated.

But is this an adequate model? If the side of the argument advances only from the side of the criminal law, and hence from the governing and police powers of the state, it may be thought to be a complete model. Theories of intention which stress only its cognitive aspect, which dwell exclusively upon the "mental elements" of intention, which speak of intention as if it were a set of propositions in a programmer's code, may be viewed as theories which advance the state's interest in not only control of the subject, but an easy control of the subject. Models of constructive attribution fall into such a view, as constructive malice, or constructive manslaughter, or felony-murder rules.

Justification for the acceptance of such cognitive models may rest in the belief that the criminal law is a construction of, and prerogative of, the state, and, as such, the state should make laws which it can enforce easily. One finds the increasing feature of modern criminal law – as well as other areas of the law, especially Tort law – that many decisions are justified on the grounds of "policy," in a word, the willingness of the state to resort to its police powers to effect conduct without appeal to logic.[5]

It has about it an appealing simplicity. Clear definitions of the law suggest that the law can be easily enforced, and, on occasion, when legal clarity is in dispute, the state may then enforce strained interpretations by an appeal to policy. Where the model begins to show signs of strain is when one questions both the nature of a legal proposition, and to whom, or what, it is to be applied. Take as a very simple case, obvious child neglect. Under section 1 of the Children and Young Persons Act 1933 if one is found guilty of wilful neglect of a child in one's custody one is subject to a fine, or, alternatively, to two years' imprisonment. The relevant portions of the Act are placed in the endnotes below.[6]

In *R. v. Sheppard and another*[7] the House of Lords was called upon to decide this point of law:

> What is the proper direction to be given to a jury on a charge of wilful neglect of a child under s. 1 of the Children and Young Persons Act 1933 as to what constitutes the necessary *mens rea* of the offence?

The facts were simple and human. The parents had a child who was sick. They failed to appreciate the gravity of the child's sickness since they were, unfortunately, possessed of low intelligence. Their child, an infant boy of 16 months of age, perished from hypothermia and malnutrition. The trial judge ruled that the offense under the Act was one of strict liability. The test for the defendants' guilt was to be an objective test: namely, an appeal to a reasonable parent test who would have been able to form a reasonable estimate of the objective seriousness of the infant's plight, and who would have obtained the requisite medical attention and treatment. The jury having been so directed, they found the defendants (who were the appellants in the present appeal) guilty. The Court of Appeal affirmed the conviction of the trial court, but signified that there was matter of geniune legal importance to be settled upon appeal by the House of Lords.

Although this was an appeal from a conviction arising because of an Act, the common law had known the offense for failing to provide food and medical necessities, and the like, for one under the care of another and unable to take care of oneself.[8] In most common law countries the criminal offenses are enumerated in a code, or sets of acts, and few of the older, purely common law offenses remain. To object that a finding under an act differs from the finding under a common law offense is of no moment.

The question in *Sheppard* was taken by the various Law Lords as to what would be the definitional range of the adverb, "wilfully." There would be its ordinary meaning; there would also be its meaning as it was used in an Act. As can be gathered from the learned opinion of the House of Lords, "wilfully" was not a simple adverb, or as simple as any might think. When a key word functions as a pivot in a legal proposition, upon which balances innocence or liability, one begins to see that a simple cognitive model which assumes that key words can be (or are) simply used, and therefore just as simply understood, is to mistake hope for reality. A key word, in relation to a key element of human nature (or a conception of human nature), does not yield up its treasure simply, as *Sheppard* may demonstrate.

Lord Diplock stated that the defendants' real defense was that they were parents who did not realize the gravity of their infant's illness. From the very beginning he introduced a division in his opinion between "fact," which is objectively the case, and an appreciation that such a fact is objectively the case by the defendant. Granting this division between what *D* knows to be the case, and what truly is the case, he proceeded to frame his theory of the case thusly:

> My Lords, the language in which the relevant provisions of the 1933 Act are drafted consists of ordinary words in common use in the English language. If I were to approach the question of their construction untrammelled (as this House is) by authority I should have little hesitation in saying that where the charge is one of WILFULLY NEGLECTING [caps ours] to provide a child with adequate medical aid, which in appropriate cases will include precautionary medical examination, the prosecution must prove, 1) that the child did in fact need medical aid at the time at which the parent is charged with having failed to provide it and, 2) EITHER [caps ours] that the parent was aware at that time that the child's health might be at risk if it were not provided with medical aid OR [caps ours] that the parent's unawareness of this fact was due to his not caring whether the child's health were at risk or not.[9]

He further stated that the presence of the adverb, "wilfully," in the Act indicated that the accused was required to possess *mens rea* for an offense under the Act, and that *mens rea* meant

> a state of mind on the part of the offender directed to the particular act or failure to act that constitutes the *actus reus* and warrants the description 'wilful.'[10]

One will take careful note that Lord Diplock views "*mens rea*" as a state of mind which bore to a *particular*. That *particular* would be those elements of the offense to which the description "*actus reus*" would rightly apply. If one wished to "re-convert" his language into an appropriate philosophical turn of mind, one might suggest, when speaking of statutory offenses (or, for that matter, crimes in general), that the offense with which an accused is charged consists of the adequation of the mind of the accused to the element of the offense, and the subsequent production of the offense, i.e., the proscribed act. How this adequation is brought about is moot, leaving room for the evident disagreements among (any variety of) cognitivists, voluntarists, behaviorists, or determinists.

Lord Diplock advanced one caveat: that the concept of a "reasonable man" was a standard from the civil law, especially from the law of negligence in Tort law; [and that]

> the obtrusion into criminal law of conformity with the notional conduct of the reasonable man as relevant to criminal liability, though not known (e.g., in relation to provocation sufficient to reduce murder to manslaughter), is exceptional, and should not lightly be extended: see *Andrews v. Director of Public Prosecutions* [1937] 2 All E.R. 552 at 556, [1937] AC 576 at 582-83. If failure to use the hypothetical powers of observation, ratiocination and foresight of consequences possessed by this admirable but purely notional exemplar is to constitute an ingredient of a criminal offence it must surely form part not of the *actus reus* but of the *mens rea*.[11]

To direct, as did the trial judge, that an offense under the Act assumed that actions of the reasonable parent were assumed, was an error:

> It does not...seem to me that the concept of the reasonable parent, what he would observe, what he would understand from what he had observed and what he would do about it, has any part to play in the *mens rea* of an offence in which the description of the *mens rea* is contained in the single adverb 'wilfully.'[12]

Given then these pre-conditions, what then was it for *D* "wilfully" to *phi*?

Lord Diplock thought that "wilfully" could bear a "narrow meaning" or a "natural meaning." These two meanings could bear upon the doing of a positive act "wilfully." What did this distinction mean?

> In the context of doing to a child a positive act (assault, ill-treat, abandon or expose) that is likely to have specified consequences (to cause him unnecessary suffering or injury), 'wilfully,' which must describe the state of mind of the actual doer of the act, may be capable of bearing the narrow meaning that the *wilfulness required extends only to the doing of the physical act itself which in fact results in the consequences described, even though the doer thought that it would not and would not have acted as he did had he foreseen a risk that those consequences might follow* (italics ours). Although this is a possible meaning of 'wilfully,' it is not the natural meaning even in relation to positive acts defined by reference to the consequences to which they are likely to give rise; and, in the context of the section, if this is all the adverb 'wilfully' meant it would be otiose.[13]

Lord Diplock's prose seems to indicate that one sense of doing something "wilfully," a positive act, is to do that from which circumstances do flow, but not, as an agent, to entertain the thought of what circumstances may flow. From Tort law one may draw an example, even though tort principles are not involved in *Sheppard*. In *Garratt v. Dailey* (1955), 46 Wash. 2d 197, 279 P.2d 1091, the Supreme Court of the State of Washington was called upon to determine if a minor, nearly six years of age, could be held responsible for battery. It was a problem presented to the Court for the first time.

The facts were relatively simple in *Garratt*. An infant had pulled away a chair from where an older person was beginning to sit. The chair absent, the adult fell backwards to the ground and was injured. The question for the Court to decide was one of responsibility: could an infant, nearly six years of age, be held responsible for the harm he had, if he had, occasioned? The Court accepted that the act of pulling away the chair was a volitional act. But whether *D*'s act was intentional led the Court to draw upon this early statement about an actor's intention from *1 Restatement, Torts 29, § 13*:

> It is not enough that the act itself is intentionally done and this, even though the actor realizes or should realize that it contains a very grave risk of bringing about the contact or apprehension. Such realization may make the actor's conduct negligent or even reckless but unless he realizes that to a substantial certainty, the contact or apprehension will result, the actor has not that intention which is necessary to make him liable under the rule stated in this section.

By subtraction, therefore, one may paraphrase the instant quotation to read: *D*, without an intention, nevertheless wilfully *phi-ed*, either not knowing that "x" would result, or not intending "x" to occur, or not foreseeing that "x" would occur; *yet,* D*'s act was a wilful act, but not a wrongful act*. Lord Diplock, in his characterization of one meaning of "wilfully," appears to have taken "to will" in the sense of meaning, simply, "to bring about," but *not* "knowingly to bring about intended or foreseeable consequences." We have drawn attention to *Garratt* purely to show that if a minor did not have knowledge of what he was doing, or if he lacked the requisite intention for legal wrongfulness, his act was, therefore, a voluntary act *simpliciter*. By removing the predicates, "malicious" and "intentional," one removes both a legal object and the legal category of wrong, and is left with the residue: to have acted wilfully. This may yield the odd sentence form of, "*D* willed," indicating that *D* did not have an object in mind, and further adding that because *D* did not have an object in mind *D* was not, however, at fault for not having an object in mind when he willed. Lord Diplock depicts this sense of willing as a narrow sense, and excludes this sense from his understanding of "wilfulness" under the Children and Young Persons Act, 1933.*

What kind of wilfulness then must be predicated of *D* for an offense under the Act? Lord Diplock held that the *actus reus* of the offense of wilful neglect is the failure to provide the prescribed care. But then he goes on to describe "wilful" in this fashion:

> Such a failure as it seems to me could not be properly described as 'wilful' unless the parent *either* (1) had directed his mind to the question whether there was some risk (though it might fall far short of probability) that the child's health might suffer unless he were examined by a doctor and provided with such curative treatment as the examination might reveal as necessary, and had made a conscious decision, for whatever reason, to refrain from arranging for such medical examination, *or* (2) had so refrained because he did not care whether the child might be in need of medical treatment or not.[14]

The second disjunct invited a finding of recklessness. But what of the first? Can one wilfully intend what one does not know? If one does not know of the existence of a risk, and the lack of knowledge is through or because of no fault of one's own (thus excluding that *D* may be "reckless"), what state of mind must *D* possess to be found to have "wilfully" *phi-ed* at criminal law? It had been stated (at 904-f) that negligence was a civil concept, and that the conditions which governed the use of that concept were not to be imported into the criminal law. At this point, Lord Diplock introduced a further distinction between "neglect" and "negligence":

> The danger of the statement** is that it invites confusion between...neglect and...negligence, which calls for consideration not of what steps should have been taken for that

---

* It is quite beside the point that the case was remanded for a further hearing, affirmed on a second appeal that the minor was liable for injuries he caused: *Garratt v. Dailey* (1956) 49 Wash.2d 499, 304 P.2d 681.

** *R. v. Senior*, [1899] 1 QB 283 at 290-91; [1895-99] All ER Rep 511, 514: "'Wilfully' means that the act is done deliberately and intentionally, not by accident or inadvertence, but so that the mind of the person who does the act goes with it. Neglect is the want of reasonable care – that is, the omission of such steps as a reasonable parent would take, such as are usually taken in the ordinary experience of mankind."

> purpose in the light of the facts as they actually were but of what steps would have been appropriate in the light of those facts only which the accused parent either knew at the time of his omission to take them or would have ascertained if he had been as mindful of the welfare of his child as a reasonable parent would have been.[15]

The complicated distinction is made in reference to *R. v. Senior* (excerpted above). The criticism Lord Diplock makes of Lord Russell, C.J., is that "wilfully" as described by the victorian Chief Justice seemed to explain "wilfully" in terms of positive acts only, acts which, thought Lord Diplock, would now be described as "voluntary." But he then proceeds to make this observation as a criticism of Lord Russell, C.J.'s definition of "wilfully":

> Lord Russell C.J.'s brief explanation of the meaning of 'wilfully' is confined to positive physical acts. In relation to these he equiparates wilful acts with acts that would now be described as voluntary. I do not myself think that this was right even in relation to positive physical acts of which the statutory definition included the characteristic that they were likely to have certain consequences; but its meaning in relation to positive acts is clear. *I find its meaning obscure, however, in relation to a failure to do a physical act where the failure is not deliberate or intentional in the sense that consideration has been given whether or not to do it and a conscious choice made not to do it. To speak of the mind going with the act is inappropriate to omissions*, but the contrast drawn between 'deliberately and intentionally' and 'by inadvertence' is at least susceptible of the meaning that if the accused has not addressed his mind to the question whether or not to do the physical act he is accused of omitting to do his failure to do the act is not to be treated as 'wilful' [italics ours].[16]

Neglectful conduct is not a novel category, nor is it a novel category that harmful consequences may flow from neglectful conduct. That conduct, as Lord Diplock appreciated, may be subject to civil and/or criminal classifications, but, he stated, the categories must not be confused. The measure of responsibility in civil law is not that of criminal law (904e). But it will be apparent to one on reflection that "neglect" and "harmful conduct" can admit of a number of logical and epistemic qualifications, and in *Sheppard* the mind of the majority was to explore those qualifications.

In the preceding passage, Lord Diplock appears to be arguing that the contrast between "deliberately and intentionally" and "by inadvertence" does not exhaust the ways in which fault or harm may come about. For example, assume that *D* is under an obligation to *P* (which obligation is defined by statute, just as an Act defines the obligation in *Sheppard*), and if the obligation is not *correctly* discharged, harm may come to *P*. Do the polarities, "deliberately and intentionally" and "by inadvertence" exhaust the logical ways in which *P* may be harmed by *D*? What of the logical possibility that *P* is harmed, but *D*, to the best of ability, either did not know that such harm could come about, or would come about? In the first edition of his *Criminal Law*, Glanville Williams stated: "*Wilfulness in criminal law implies knowledge of the circumstances that are relevant to the offense*."[17]

The possible confusion in the passage (905f-h) is that "by inadvertence" could admit of two distinct meanings. On the one hand it may simply mean, "not knowingly"; on the other hand it may mean, "not knowingly" but the omission was a culpable omission. In each case there is no appeal either to intention or to deliberation. Both are omissions, one of which is a wrongful omission. In one sense fault may be predicated of *D* for his inadvertence because the condition of his having omitted to do (or observe, know, anticipate, realize, etc.) is a wrongful omission. An early example in the texts was the Elizabethan statute compelling church attendance.[18] It read, in part,

> And that from and after the said Feast of the Nativity of Saint *John Baptist* next coming, all and every person and person inhabiting within this Realm or any other the Queens Majesties Dominions, shall diligently and faithfully, having no lawful or reasonable excuse to be absent, endeavor themselves to resort to their Parish Church or Chappel accustomed...upon every *Sunday* and other day ordained and used to be kept as holy-days; and then and there to abide orderly and soberly during the time of the Common Prayer...there to be used and ministered upon pain of punishment.

D certainly could, by inadvertence, not know that one day of the week was a Holy Day of obligation; and was the inadvertence supported by a lawful excuse, no penalty would lie upon him under the statute; but if the inadvertence were not supported by a lawful excuse, he would be subject to penalty. An unwilful and indeliberate omission may either be excused because of non-culpable ignorance, or be punished because of culpable ignorance. This simply reinstates an old position from moral theology on the nature of ignorance in relation to an act (and "act" may be that which *D* does, or that which *D* refrains from doing – reminiscent of the position adopted by Thomas Aquinas that to refrain from doing could be viewed as a positive act of the Will, or, in modern language, the positive act which one enunciates when one says, "No").*

If, then, the language of the Act required a "wilful neglect," and not simply a "neglect" of the well-being of a child, to explain "wilfully" has involved an agreed-upon understanding of a relationship which obtains between acts of willing and acts of understanding. If "to will" is a concept distinct in features from "to know" (or "to deliberate," etc.), then it is possible to consider that if knowledge is absent when one wills, and if the absence of the knowledge is not a fault, then one cannot at once be innocently wilful and wrongly knowledgeable. To be able wilfully to neglect, if one has not the conditions to satisfy "neglect," "wilfully" then functions solely as an adverb modifying nothing – it modifies no state of knowledge of the agent.

Placing these conditions in logical order then led Lord Diplock to conclude that the proper instruction concerning the Act would be:

> The proper direction to be given to a jury on a charge of wilful neglect of a child under s 2 of the Children and Young Persons Act 1933 by failing to provide adequate medical aid is that the jury must be satisfied (1) that the child did in fact need medical aid at the time at which the parent is charged with failing to provide it (the *actus reus*) and (2) either that the parent was aware at that time that the child's health might be at risk if it was not provided with medical aid or that the parent's unawareness of this fact was due to his not caring whether his child's health was at risk or not (the *mens rea*).[19]

By answering the general point of law in this way, Lord Diplock felt confident that parents would not be encouraged to neglect their children:

> It would involve the acquittal of those parents only who through ignorance or lack of intelligence are genuinely

---

* Note: The difficulty may be one of grammatical form by which to characterize a negative act. When one utters or states, "No, I will not go, or do this...etc.," it is not a statement about ability; it is a statement about what one will not do, even though one is capable of doing. A pianist, after giving a recital, demonstrated that fact; he now no longer wishes to play further. It may be that negative statements, in some fashion, must be understood. They are not simply statements which report perceptive states. But some, of course, may report a perceptive state, as when a mule will not move, and one can actively perceive that the animal will not move by noting its resistance.

> unaware that their child's health may be at risk if it is not examined by a doctor to see if it needs medical attention.[20]

Lord Edmund-Davies, of the majority, believed that the long series of cases from *R. v. Senior* [1899] 1 QB 283; [1895-9] All E.R. Rep. 511 down to *R. v. Lowe* [1973] 1 All E.R. 805; [1973] QB 702, had all made one central mistake when elaborating upon crimes of wilful neglect – to wit: "By attaching no importance to the mental ingredient of wilfulness, *R. v. Lowe* and all similar decisions must, in my respectful judgment, be regarded as wrongly decided."[21] And, if it is not appreciated that the adverb, "wilfully," qualifies "neglect," then the offense would be read as one of strictest liability wherein one would be guilty of the offense if the harm occurred by inadvertence, without regard for those qualifications which would excuse the inadvertence.[22] And, as Lord Diplock had seen, this would be to have imported the standards of the civil law for negligence into the criminal law.

Lord Keith put the matter in simpler language on behalf of the majority. He agreed that the Act in question deemed an offense of wilful neglect to require the adequate *mens rea* on the part of *D*. Here is what he said of "wilful":

> The primary meaning of 'wilful' is deliberate. So a parent who knows that his child needs medical care and deliberately, that is by conscious decision, refrains from calling a doctor, is guilty under the subsection [of the Act]. As a matter of general principle, recklessness is to be equiparated with deliberation. A parent who fails to provide medical care which his child needs because he does not care whether it is needed or not is reckless of his child's welfare. He too is guilty of an offense. But a parent who has genuinely failed to appreciate that his child needs medical care, through personal inadequacy or stupidity or both, is not guilty.[23]

This is further reinforced when, at 914e-f, of the same opinion he stated in criticism of R. Downes (1875) 1 QBD 25:

> Lord Coleridge CJ said (on page 30): 'By wilfully neglecting, I understand an intentional and deliberate abstaining from providing the medical aid, knowing it to be obtainable.' I have difficulty in understanding how the abstention could be intentional and deliberate if the accused did not appreciate that medical aid was needed. It seems clear that the court proceeded wholly on the irrelevance of the accused's motive for not providing medical aid. None of these cases show any trace of an attempt to face up to the proper application of the law to the situation where no question of motive is in issue, but

> where the accused's failure to provide medical care is due to inability, through stupidity or ignorance, to appreciate the need for it. So in my opinion it is an error to treat anything decided or said in these cases as authoritative in that situation. I consider that the Court of Appeal fell into that error in *R. v. Lowe*.

It does not require damaging paraphrasing to suggest that the House of Lords, in this opinion of its majority, had returned to older concepts of an act done or omitted to be done owing to ignorance, which state of ignorance is without fault, and also of a concept of the Will in which it was assumed that unless the Will was qualified, or related to knowledge one could not predicate of *D* that he had wilfully *phi-ed*. The movement of the opinion of the majority was carefully to rule out intentional states, recklessness, and maliciousness, and to concentrate solely upon this problem and an answer to it: Can *D* be said to have committed an unlawful act of wilful neglect if *D* could not, at the same time, have "wilfully neglected" to *phi*? The reasoning of the majority had gone beyond the concept of, "to have a lawful excuse." The reasoning of the majority was to affirm that unless the logical conditions were present in *D*, the offense could not then be attributed to *D*. One can, with some ease, apply the older theological notion[24] that some forms of ignorance excuse:

> 1. The first sort of ignorance, which is *involuntary, invincible* and *antecedent*, that is, is *the cause of an action*, so that the thing would not be done but by that ignorance, does certainly make the action also itself involuntary, and consequently not criminal. In this sense is that of the law, *Errantis nulla voluntas, nullus consensus*. They that know nothing of it, consent not. This is meant of ignorance that it is involuntary in all regards, that is, such as is neither chosen directly nor indirectly, but is involuntary both in the effect and in the cause. Thus what fools and mad-men and infants doe is not at all imputed to them, because they have no understanding to discern good from evil, and therefore their appetite is not deprav'd or malicious which part soever they take.

With some qualifications, Taylor's statement admirably fits *Sheppard*. Since the defendants seemed ignorant of the arts of the medical needs required, they suffered the fate of a death: "he who in arts erres willingly, can mend it when he please; but so cannot he that erres ignorantly. Ignorance is the only disparagement of his art, and malice is the only disparagement of our manners."[25]

The minority in Sheppard, Lord Scarman and Lord Fraser, dissented. Lord Scarman held that the neglect by the parents in *Sheppard* to provide needed medical care was a fact in the case:

> The parents knew that a doctor was available and would come, if called. They also knew that their child was ill, off his food, and that he was totally rejecting food for the two days before his death. *Failure in such circumstances to obtain any medical aid was clearly a neglect of the child.* The live issue in the appeal is whether the neglect was 'wilful.'[26]

Lord Scarman thought that the instruction of the trial judge was correct in law with reference to s 1 of the Children and Young Persons Act 1933. He laid this foundation in support of his dissent:

> In my judgment, the conduct must be intentional. But the word does not impart into the statutory offense the requirement of foresight or recklessness as to the consequences of what was done or not done (as the case may be).[27]

In his survey of the history which led to the first enactment of a statute to protect children from neglect (the Poor Law Amendment Act 1868 [royal assent, 31st July]), Lord Scarman believed that the purpose of the nineteenth-century statute was to defeat the finding in *R. v. Wagstaffe* (1868) 10 Cox CC 530, in which the jury acquitted the accused.

The facts of the case are simple, but bear mention. A religious believer, whose child was ill, did not call a physician to examine the child. It would have been against the faith to have done so. Elders of the religious sect were called in to pray for the child. The child died. At the trial, Willes, J. submitted instructions to the jury for the crime of manslaughter because of neglect. Lord Scarman offered this paraphrase, which we cite:

> In directing the jury Willes J said that to make out the offense 'gross and culpable negligence' had to be proved; and he left to the jury the defence that these affectionate parents had done what they honestly believed was best for the child.[28]

One will recall that the majority in *Sheppard* would have taken this kind of instruction to be an appeal to "motive."

The history, then, was that the 1868 statute had been passed. Then came the case of *R. v. Downes* (1875) 1 QBD 25. We have turned to the report of the case itself for fuller details. It was a reserved case, alternatively reported in 13 Cox . . 111 for 1875. The prisoner had been indicted in

Central Criminal Court for the manslaughter of Charles Downs, his son. Once again the prisoner was a member of a religious sect. In paragraph 7 of the reported decision it was stated that the prisoner

> consulted the witness Hurry as to what was the matter with the child, and as to what should be given to it. They thought it was suffering from teething; and he advised the parents to give it port wine, eggs, arrowroot, and other articles of diet which he thought suitable for a child suffering from such a complaint, all of which were supplied accordingly.
>
> ***
>
> 10. It was admitted on the part of the prosecution that the child was kindly treated, kept clean, furnished with sufficient food, and nursed kindly by the mother and the women of the sect.
>
> ***
>
> 15. I told the jury [i.e., Blackburn, J.] that the law casts on the father who has the custody of a helpless infant a duty to provide according to his ability all that is reasonably necessary for the child, including, if the child is so ill as to require it, the advice of persons reasonably believed to have competent medical skill, and that if death ensues from the neglect of this duty it is manslaughter in the father neglecting the duty.[29]

Written instructions and questions were submitted to the jury by Blackburn, J., for the sake of making clear their verdict, and for protecting the status of the prisoner who had appeared without the benefit of counsel.

The jury convicted. Paragraph 16 is of interest:

> 16. Did the prisoner neglect to procure medical aid for the helpless infant when it was in fact reasonable so to do, and he had the ability?
>
> –YES.
>
> Was the death caused by that neglect?
>
> –YES.

If one looks at this case carefully, adverting to its language, one will find that it does not *precisely* sustain the minority reasoning in *Sheppard*. First of all, after the judgment of Blackburn, J., one reads the other opinions appended. Mellor, J. stated, "The words of the section 'wilfully neglect' mean intentionally or purposely omit to call in medical aid," and then he adverted both to *Wagstaffe* and *R. v. Hines* (n. d.), 13 Cox . . 114, as a note.[30]

It had been observed by Mellor, J., that Baron Pigott had not had called to his attention the statute of 31 & 32 Vict. c. 122, s.37. It may be asked, that had the statute been called to his attention, would it have altered his reasoning in the matter?

Coleridge, C.J., in *Downes*, said that but for the statute (to which reference was just made) he would have desired further argument in the case, and added: "Perhaps it is enough to say that the opinions of Willes, J., and Pigott, B., are deserving of grave consideration." He said that he understood the statute to require conviction if any parent wilfully neglected to provide (*inter alia*) needed medical aid, stating:

> That enactment I understand to mean that if any parent intentionally, i.e., with the knowledge that medical aid is to be obtained, and with a deliberate intention abstains from providing it, he is guilty of the offense. Under that enactment upon these facts the prisoner would clearly have been guilty of the offense created by it. If the death of a person results from the culpable omission of a breach of duty created by the law, the death so caused is the subject of manslaughter. In this case there was a duty imposed by the statute on the prisoner to provide medical aid for his infant child, and there was the deliberate intention not to obey the law; whether proceeding from a good or bad motive is not material.[31]

But it takes little appreciation to realize that *Sheppard* did not involve "motive," nor did it involve one who intentionally disobeyed the law. Lord Diplock's minute analysis of the case disposed of this course.

Following directly upon Coleridge, C.J.'s opinion was that of Bramwell, B., who viewed the statute as one which

> has imposed a positive and absolute duty on parents, whatever their conscientious or superstitious opinions may be, to provide medical aid for their infant children in their custody. The facts show that the prisoner thought it was irreligious to call in medical aid, but that is no excuse for not obeying the law.

Once again it may be observed that in *Sheppard* the accused did not wish to disobey the law; furthermore, the statute (1933) imposed criminal liability, but not absolute liability for neglect. Lord Diplock showed that the standards of liability from Tort law were not, nor ought to be, applicable in the case. Bramwell, B., it may be remarked, had not analyzed so much as he had affirmed or stated. The locution, "to impose an absolute duty upon," is more reminiscent of early Tort theories.

R. v. Senior, which the majority in *Sheppard* disaffirmed, was another religious sect case in which the father did not provide needed medical aid for a dying child, knowing the child to be in aid of medical care and attention. The father of the child, who died from diarrhea and pneumonia, believed that the New Testament passage in James, c. 5, verses 14-15, forbade seeking physicians to cure the ill, believing, instead, that prayer alone was sufficient to cure physical ills. The parent did not realize that the verse pertained to "moral" illness and not physical illness.

Lord Russell of Killowen, C.J., thought that the prisoner was rightly convicted, and stated that he dissented entirely from the view expressed by Pigott, B. in *Hines*. The meaning of "wilfully neglects" was:

> 'wilfully' means done deliberately and not by inadvertence, and 'neglect' the omission to do something for the benefit of the child – in other words, intentional failure to take those steps which the experience of mankind show to be generally necessary.[32]

He proceeded to sketch two hypothetical cases: What if the child had a broken thighbone and needed an operation? or, What if an infant needed a tracheotomy to prevent its suffocating? Were a parent to deny medical aid in either case it would then be a clear case of wilful neglect on the part of the parent.

Again, the examples do not address the problem in *Sheppard*. *Senior* provided an analysis of 'wilful neglect' which flowed from *D* having been aware that medical aid was needed, and *D* consciously refused to provide such medical aid. The facts in *Sheppard* did not show that the parents were aware that medical aid was needed, they believing that the child's illness was slight or passing. Lord Diplock's objection (905g) that Lord Russell, C.J.'s analysis of omission was incorrect. Lord Scarman seemed not to appreciate the force of this distinction, preferring to state that if a harm ensued (the death of a child) it must be taken as a neglect, and that neglect then must impute that it was a wilful neglect. With respect, the logical analysis is faulty, and it seemed not to address itself to distinction concerning "wilful" which Lord Diplock had advanced. It may also be seen that Lord Scarman assumed that a statute could have the force of "policy," and that as a policy it would teach parents how to obey, drawing upon Johnsonian language that penalties sharpen one's wits:

> I do not share the view expressed by my noble and learned friends Lord Edmund-Davies and Lord Keith that parents who though not reckless or indifferent to their child's welfare yet fail through stupidity or immaturity to appreciate the need for medical aid will not be deterred by a criminal sanction. They underrate, with respect, the deterrent power of the law. The existence of a penalty can concentrate and sharpen the minds of men and women. It is for this reason that in some exceptional areas the law accepts strict liability.[33]

Lord Fraser, in a vigorous dissent, also thought that the Act (1933) imposed strict liability based upon objective evidence. He cautioned,

> If the offense required proof that the particular parents were aware of the probable consequences of neglect, then the difficulty of proof against stupid or reckless parents would certainly be increased and so I fear might the danger to their children....Especially in these times when parental responsibility for children tends to be taken all too lightly, such a sharp change towards relaxation of the law on the subject seems to me appropriate only for the legislature and not for the courts.[34]

What this excursion into linguistic analysis of a central concept, that of "wilful neglect," may reveal is that legal analysis when it pursues the logic of a concept may show a hitherto unperceived logical ground in the concept. Lord Diplock, by pursuing a model that "wilfully," as an adverb, cannot modify an omission when the omission is the result of non-culpable ignorance, revealed a new dimension to the term "wilfully." He drew upon a much older notion that some forms of ignorance can negative both intent and wilfulness. He also demonstrated how, if properly understood,[35] the language of *mens rea* is still a proper language in which to cast discussions about omissions, and the logic peculiar to omissions. The obviousness of statements about "wilful," and their cognates, is not, after all, so obvious at all. And, in another sense, he demonstrated that the reasoning in *R. v. Hines*, though not mentioned in the body of his speech, was sound.

One may advert to a recent case to show that from inadvertence one may not necessarily deduce recklessness: *R. v. Stone*, and *R. v. Dobinson*.[36] Neither was cited in *Sheppard*. Both show that sound law is based upon a sound and logical analysis of concepts, not upon the mere foisting upon the members of a polity a policy (because the logic of the law would so prevent the policy) to achieve social ends. Reason, we would wish to argue, creates equals; policy creates ranks and subordinates.

The facts in *Stone* and *Dobison* were these. *A* and B lived together. *A* was a man aged 67, of low but average intelligence; *B* was his mistress, aged 43, who was an inadequate and ineffectual person. To this household comes *F*, sister of *A*, to live with them. *F* was a woman in her fifties who was morbidly afraid of gaining weight; thus, *F* was not wont to eat food or to care for herself. The village in which these parties resided knew that *F* resided with *A* and *B*, and all of the locals worried that *F* might become ill through self-neglect, and thus urged *A* and *B* to care for her (*F*). *A* and *B*, however much aware of the deteriorating condition of *F*, failed nevertheless to attend to and for her in any materially significant way. *F* died in squalid conditions in the house of *A* and *B* to whence originally she had come to lodge.

In dismissing the appeal of the joint appellants, the Court of Appeals let stand the convictions for manslaughter. In their appeal the defendants had, jointly, contended that they had not undertaken a duty to care for *F*, or, if a duty were found by the court, they contended that they had not been reckless in their discharge of the duty. As to the first footing of the defense, the Court said that the circumstances of the case demonstrated that *F* had come to them as a helplessly infirm person, and that *A* and *B* could have discharged themselves of that duty either by summoning outside social agencies, or by themselves caring for *F*. The Court found that they had assumed the duty of care, and that the model from standard Tort law, i.e., of not having to rescue a drowning swimmer, did not apply. *A* and *B* had undertaken some duties with regard to *F*; furthermore, *F* was a blood relation of *A*.

To prove recklessness, the Court turned to the words of Lord Atkin in *Andrews v. D.P.P.* [1937] 2 All E.R. 552 at 556; [1937] AC 576 at 583:

> Simple lack of care such as will constitute civil liability is not enough. For purposes of the criminal law there are degrees of negligence, and a very high degree of negligence is required to be proved before the felony is established. Probably of all the epithets that can be applied 'reckless' most nearly covers the case. It is difficult to visualize a case of death caused by 'reckless' driving, in the connotation of that term in ordinary

> speech, which would not justify a conviction for manslaughter, but it is probably not all-embracing, for 'reckless' suggests an indifference to risk whereas the accused may have appreciated the risk and intended to avoid it, and yet have shown in the means adopted to avoid the risk such a high degree of negligence as would justify a conviction.

Drawing upon this statement of legal principles, the Court of Appeal in *Stone* and *Dobinson* then described why such reasoning ought to apply jointly to *A* and *B* in the instant case:

> It is clear from that passage that indifference to an obvious risk and appreciation of such risk, coupled with a determination nevertheless to run it, are both examples of recklessness. The duty which a defendant has undertaken is a duty of caring for the health and welfare of the infirm person. What the Crown has to prove is a breach of that duty in such circumstances that the jury feel convinced that the defendant's conduct can properly be described as reckless. That is to say a reckless disregard of danger to the health and welfare of the infirm person. Mere inadvertence is not enough. The defendant must be proved to have been indifferent to an obvious risk of injury to health, or actually to have foreseen the risk but to have determined nevertheless to run it.[37]

Leave was given to appeal to the House of Lords on the question:

> Whether in a case of manslaughter it is necessary to prove that the defendant was reckless as to whether the victim would suffer death or serious bodily harm,

but the appeal was not argued.

It may be remarked, and in no way do we wish to be paradoxical, that all of the criminal law concerns omissions: namely, of *D* omitting to follow the law. To suggest that there is something inherently unresolvable about the logic of legal discourse which surrounds criminal omissions is to entertain a misperception of the criminal law itself. One may have some difficulty in relating a duty, as defined by the criminal law, and the failure of *D* to carry out that duty. *Sheppard*, in Lord Diplock's acute analysis, did show that a duty may lie, but that there may also be conditions or capacities which *D* must possess in order for the duty to obtain of which it is charged that *D* wilfully neglected. It is not that *D*, somehow mysteriously, performs a "negative act." One could rightly wonder what such a locution signified, just as much as Bertrand Russell, decades ago, wondered about negative facts, and was rightly puzzled over them. By violating the law, *D*, in the first instance, brings about an omission: namely, he omits to follow the law. In omitting to follow the law he may, in the act of transgressing the law, do so by a further omission. He may omit (say), were he a doctor, to administer his skills with proper care; he may omit (say), were he a parent, to care for his family; he may omit (say), were he a stockbroker, to furnish proper information required by the Securities and Exchange Commission (S.E.C.) about the nature of his stockbroking activities – was he inflating stock, was he gaining by "insider" dealing, was he requiring proper credit margins of his clients, and the like? The instances can be multiplied with ease in which *D* omits, and by omitting, he commits a crime. The problem for the legal analyst is to determine if some classes of omissions are culpable omissions, and this may take careful and rigorous analysis. But the category is not a new category, as moral theologians know so well. The novelty of the category at law may be to state the conditions and requirements for a wrongful omission in clear and understandable legal language, *Sheppard* being a clear example that the task, at times, may be difficult to achieve. It is not, however, unachievable.

Throughout this study it may have become apparent to a reader that legal discourse is different from, but also borrows from, other forms of discourse, such as theology, moral philosophy, and, broadly, philosophy itself. Unless one has in front of one case law to analyze, legal discourse can become vapid, arid, tautologous, and senselessly abstract. The common law especially does not lend itself to empty systematizing. In this way, discourse about the common law is both restricted – the need to draw upon the great wealth of recorded cases – and protected – by use of the case law one concentrates the mind upon (generally) a particular problem. To extract common principles from this vast body of law requires that one work with that vast body of law. Economy of expression is not the mark of common law jurisprudence.

There are broad areas into which we have not ventured, and one of which specifically we would like to mention. We have not discussed what may be called "psycho-chemistry" and the relation research in such an area would bear to human action in its relation to the criminal law. We have chosen to remain silent on the area because it is an area not within our competence. It does not seem impossible in theory that much of human action in its relationship to serious matters of concern is action which is not intentional. The counter-set of intentional, in this instance, is not unintentional. The counter-set is that human action may be so controlled by behavioral states, which result from bio-chemical activities, that what may seem to be an intentional action under a legal description is, in fact, a bio-chemical action brought about because of the bio-chemical nature possessed by the agent in whom such a bio-chemical state occurs. It becomes especially trying for the law when it says to *D*, "Listen here, you knew that you had this condition, why then did you not take the proper precautions, or exercise proper judgment, to prevent harm being caused to another because of your unhealth?" It is not only that one is raising a question about criminal responsibility and mental illness,[38] but one is raising a far broader and far more wide-ranging question: What of human actions in general in their relationship to the criminal law in which it is posited that *D* was not responsible because *D* could not be responsible, given the genetic state of *D* at time t_n when the offense occurred?

It is at this point that how one understands the concept of intention to be will bear upon how one will treat an offender. If, for instance, one believes that there is no problem between "intention" and "free will," but assumes that one can dismiss the latter as a problem worthy of consideration, but stress the former, then one can produce such obvious oddities as: Yes, *D* was determined, but he intended to *phi*, nevertheless; ergo, *D* is legally guilty because, at law, *D* legally intended. The assumption underlying such a position would be that if *D* had the requisite intention, *D* offended; how the requisite intention came about would be precluded from inquiry, just as one might state that deposit banks are generally concerned only with the money deposited, not with the origins of the money deposited – a Swiss bank principle.* If it means that to have a requisite intention that one can generate a description of a proscribed act in which an intentional phrase is used, and then that such an intentional phrase can be attributed to *D*, then the use of such an intentional phrase indicates that *D* is guilty. The contrary would be assumed equally to be the case: namely, if an intentional phrase could not be used of *D*, *D* would not be guilty. As one recent moral philosopher wrote:

> It is hard to see why a man who does something inexplicably does not really *do* it. Let us suppose that the hardened criminal's action [i.e., of not robbing a poor box] really is inexplicable; we can only say, 'He just turned away,' and not why he did so; this does not mean that he did it by accident, or unintentionally, or not of his own free will....In any case, to explain an action is not necessarily to show that it could have been predicted from some fact about the agent's character–that he is weak, greedy, sentimental, and so forth. We may if we like say that an action is never *fully* explained unless it has been shown to be covered by a law which connects it to such a character trait; but then it becomes even more implausible to say that an action must be explicable if we are to admit it as something genuinely *done*. In the ordinary sense we explain the criminal's action if we say, for instance, that a particular thought came into his mind; we do not also have to find a law about the way such thoughts do come into the minds of such men.[39]

It may, indeed, for the sake of theoretical consistency be most important to explain how thoughts do originate. The model which the common law has accepted for centuries has been a model which was derived from Christian theism in which, because of a particular understanding of what was volition and intellection, responsibility could be predicated of an agent if certain conditions were fulfilled: namely, if the agent could freely will, and if the agent could be shown to have the capacity to know. It has been a very simple but very persuasive model, and the common law embraced it. If, however, only the cognitive aspects of intention are stressed when expounding criminal liability, in theory it is possible that cognition, as a description of human action and as an element of human nature, could be predicated of non-volitional acts. To make necessary formal deductions in a

* One excluded the "laundering" of money knowingly.

syllogism, or in a propositional argument, is not impredicable of an agent unpossessed of free will (or of the voluntary); it may simply convert to this statement that an agent necessarily made necessary deductions. If the consequences of an act are thought to be the measure of an act, there is no contradiction in terms to assert that an agent necessarily reached correct deductions, or that an agent freely reached necessary deductions, if, in each case, the necessary deductions were the correct deductions.

There is a great temptation, if one may personalize the criminal law, for the criminal law to disregard clear statements of personal intent and principles, and to fly to policy and to principles borrowed (unknowingly, often) from Tort law to justify convictions – even to hasten them. One aim of the criminal sanction is to control behavior, even, at times, when the principles of fairness and justice indicate abatement. In the gray areas of the criminal law – what relationship pertains, or ought to pertain, between it and theories of mind – we have witnessed a great hostility on the part of the criminal law to accept less than a cognitive model of human nature and human actions.[40] As Professor Whitlock had remarked,[41] the English criminal law, and the common law in general by implication, assumes that one is responsible for one's acts notwithstanding, and evidence or theory to the contrary is often times treated without sympathy.

What we wish to suggest – and we are fully aware that it is a suggestion only, and not a theory or a postulate or an hypothesis – is that it is possible to view human action as, in part, an expression of bio-chemical activity. Even if one is fond of philosophical dualism, it yet admitted that an area of darkness was the material substratum. The hylemorphic* theories about what relationship obtained, and how, between matter and form left the area of "matter" dark and unexplainable. Matter, it will be recalled, was explainable only in its relation to form because "form" was the natural object of the human intellect. Matter, however, was the condition for dualistic existence. In language from our own scientific milieu one would speak of one's (possible) genetic predisposition to development. The dative phrase, "to development," may be taken to indicate not only a phylogenous development

---

* *Note:* How 'matter' and 'form' were joined to make up an object or being.

of a member of a species, it may also be taken to indicate what may be the reasons which cause a member to act as it does.

It must be remembered that the common law grounds its explanations of intentional actions in the agent himself; psycho-chemical theory may argue that "agent" is not a predicative stop; that "agent" is itself a term in need of explanation. Common law discourse uses the term "agent" as if it were the ground upon which all predications are to be founded. To have reached agency is to have stopped the explanatory process, i.e., the agent acted; *full stop* – or, the agent intended; *full stop*. To suggest that one could have the concept of an agent, but not at the same time that an agent is responsible because of his status as an agent, is heresy, for the most part, to the common law.[42] It may also be, it is certainly to be remembered, that traditional theories of human action divided actions into those which sprang from within the individual himself, and those which were predicated of the individual as caused from without. In either case, "individual" (or "agent") is the substratum upon which responsible action or volition is predicated. Psycho-chemical theories do not accept that "agent" or "individual" is a first principle from which other explanations derive.

Our suggestions here are only at the level that it is not inconsistent with human behavior to search for a newer or different base for human action and behavior other than in the language of traditional, cognitive models which divided behavior into mental and voluntary. It is not inconsistent to suggest that human behavior is a mode of action far wider than the traditional linguistic categories which have been used to depict it. To the charge that *D* could have acted other than he did, there may rest the reply: But I could not. And that reply may be a genuine report of *D*'s human state. It does not, presently, explain why *D* acted as he did; it reports only that he did act as he did. The disturbing element in such a report is that it reports a form of behavior counter to accepted mentalistic and affective models. It also lets in a notion which has been found repelling to the common law: that *D* may have been determined to do what he did.

A counter model is not that *D* may have been determined *to* do what he did, but was determined *in* that he did. The concept of "to" suggests the model of the divine playwright who has first written the play, and every scene of it, and all the actor then does is to fill in the role and the steps. Used in this way, "to" suggests that the object has been knowingly forecast. But to argue that bio-chemical determination may direct an agent *in* what he does, does not give one the divine playwright who has scripted every contingent feature in a finite series. Given a genetic predisposition (and given our ignorance of a language at present to unravel the code of a genetic predisposition) it is not unusual that *D* would act in this way rather than in that way. Genetic predisposition suggests preferences. There may be a wide range of "choices" that *D* could make, without in any way involving the objects of a genetic predisposition, just as there may be a wide range of colors which may be seen without appealing to a spectrum outside of that wide range which only a specially disposed eye could see. One is speaking about a range and possibilities, and that there may be sets of possibilities (or the concept of other possibilities) outside of a range.

It may also be suggested that conditions are required in which to exercise both volition and rationality. Criminal defenses, in some ways (but cautiously), admit this. It is not to cause a logical disparity to suggest, in theory, that it is possible to think that unless conditions are present for the proper exercise of rational volition, *D* may be acting, but neither rationally nor of his own volition. How, after all, does one report that he acted rationally, and of his own volition, unless he is able to believe that he has done so? It is truly a Rylean puzzle to consider that one of the conditions of the voluntary is to act at liberty or without restraint, yet not know that one's genetic disposition predisposes one to act as one did.[43] A psycho-chemical analysis of human action does not turn the agent into a complicated chemical set necessarily; what a psycho-chemical analysis of human action may indicate is that many conditions, which have been assumed to be the case about human action, and have been unreflectively assumed, are not the case. Who, for instance, would have thought that lithium salts would ever have been a cure for manic depressive disorders? By use of a common and abundant pharmaceutical a patient, who may either have alternating moods of uncontrollable mania – unusual energy, grandiose plans – alternating with uncontrollable depression, hopelessness, despair – or, in some cases, only the manic or only the depressive phases may occur, lithium will help such patients to attain stability of mood, avoiding, for the most part, the highs and lows of alternating mood swings, and permitting them to function successfully in their business pursuits and in their private lives.

One may rejoice that one has left the realm of theory and has entered the realm of the experimental. It may be the case that our modes of common law criminal trial procedure force a legal system to resolve its tensions and conflicts on a rational model. To suggest that rational or mental behavior can be expressed in terms other than a simple dualism is a phase of intellectual and legal development which the criminal law will have to undergo. That the law takes cognizance of diminished behavior, or that certain common law jurisdictions are rethinking the nature of the insanity defense in light of present discoveries about the function and operation of the brain,[44] may signal that the traditional procedures of the criminal law process are attempting to accommodate the findings of behavioral and neurological science within the ancient advocacy model. The Court itself has shown signs of being puzzled by the relationship which the law dictates must obtain between an offender, the crime he committed, and the punishment he must receive if it can be said of *D* that he intended *phi*, and *phi* was a prohibited act,[45] when it seems clearly the case from a medical and therapeutic point of view that what *D* did should better be seen in terms of patient and ailment than in terms of offender and crime. On the other hand, the willingness of the criminal sanction to accept an extended form of duress while under stress has met with a chilling coldness and rejection.[46]

If there can be difficulties about what it means "willingly" or "wilfully" to do a criminal act, or if there can be difficulties about the tenability of criminal responsibility itself being predicated of an agent when some suggest that an agent was genetically predisposed to do what he did, the difficulties concerning a general theory of criminal responsibility do not stop there. There can be difficulties just as serious to consider when one comes to reflect upon knowledge and a criminal act. The general assumption about the common law and human responsibility was ably put by Professor Whitlock, when he stated:

> In English law it is assumed that all persons are of sound mind and responsible for their actions unless it can be shown that

> there is sufficient mental abnormality to exonerate them from responsibility. Should he commit acts or omissions contrary to the law he is liable to punishment or to make restitution unless it can be shown that certain special circumstances were operative at the time of the offence which either exonerate him completely or diminish the degree of responsibility.[47]

We wish to offer an extended example of a case at law which struggled to free one from a criminal charge. The case involved a curious understanding of "know," and its cognates. The case also demonstrates how the criminal law grows and gives new turns and meanings to accepted linguistic usages.[48]

The defendant was a practicing attorney. He had been charged with multiple counts of theft of client funds. The trial was a jury trial for multiple felonies of theft. The defendant pleaded not guilty. Through counsel he argued that the thefts did occur, but he raised the defense of diminished mental capacity due to his own addiction both to cocaine and to alcohol. The *facts* of the charges were admitted; but the defense would be that the facts, as stated, and if understood properly in light of his defense, would not constitute legal facts needed to bring about a criminal conviction for theftous activity.

When one turns to the Criminal Code for the State of Washington, one reads RCW 9A.56.020, which states:

> *THEFT – Definition, defense.*
> (1) "Theft" means: (a) To wrongfully obtain or exert unauthorized control over the property or services of another or the value thereof, with intent to deprive him of such property or services; or (b) By color or aid of deception to obtain control over the property or services of another or the value thereof, with intent to deprive him of such property or services.

The defense argued for his client that the crime of theft requires the prosecutor or the state to prove that the defendant intended to deprive an owner of the property permanently. An appeal was made to a recent case in which such a general statement of the crime was given: *State v. Burnham*, 19 Wn.App. 442, 444-445 (1978). It was further stated that to deprive an owner of property permanently was a crime of *specific intent*. But to have the specific intent to deprive an owner permanently of his property, an accused had to be shown to do such *knowingly* at the time when the accused committed the crime. The burden, then, upon the prosecutor was to show, (1) that the defendant intended permanently to deprive his clients of funds, and that this was an act of specific intent; (2) that the accused knew his actions would result in such a deprivation of funds from his clients, and that this second element constituted the criminal knowledge needed to find him guilty under the statute.

The facts of the case showed the defendant to be a successful lawyer. His specialty at law was to represent injured parties before Workman's Industrial Tribunals. The function of these Tribunals was to assess the injury a worker may have, and to make a monetary award to the worker as compensation for the injury he had suffered. The award was in the nature of an insurance award for injuries, the amount of which was to be determined by the evidence, and its force, upon the Tribunal. When the Tribunal made its award, it would send a check to defense counsel, who, in turn would disburse those funds awarded to his clients. However, on a number of occasions, defense counsel in this case illegally deposited the client funds to his own account for his own purposes, thus depriving the client of the monetary award the Tribunal had made.

When a police investigation was made it had discovered this defalcation. The accused was charged and brought to trial. The trial lasted for one week. It had been assumed in the legal community where the trial was held that the accused would be found guilty straight away. The state had in evidence the endorsed and stolen checks. At the trial the prosecutor was able to have the accused admit that the signature on the back of each and every cashed check was, in fact, the signature of the accused. The checks, which were presented for payment, were not the property of the accused; hence, it would seem, the charge of theft on many counts was easily proved.

But one needed to remember that the accused was charged under the new Criminal Code of the State of Washington, a Code which had been in effect less than ten years at the time of this trial (1984). The new Code had introduced degrees of culpability, and had displaced, so it thought, older concepts of criminal intention. The new Code stated in RCW 9A.04.020:

> *Purposes – Principles of construction.*
> (1) The general purposes of the provisions governing the definition of offenses are:
> (a) To forbid and prevent conduct that inflicts or threatens substantial harm to individual or public interests;

> (b) To safeguard conduct that is without culpability from condemnation as criminal;
> (c) To give fair warning of the nature of the conduct declared to constitute an offense;
> (d) To differentiate on reasonable grounds between serious and minor offenses, and to prescribe proportionate penalties for each.

To give an accused fair warning of what he is charged means, under the Code, *to spell out* the elements of the crime with which he is charged. Since the Code represents the mind of the state, and the prosecutor speaks for the mind of the state, the duty upon the prosecutor before a Tribunal of the state – i.e., Superior Court in which a criminal cause is heard – is to make clear whether or not the accused did commit the crime with which he was charged. The crime is expressed in sentences of the Code, and the duty of the prosecutor is to show, if it can be shown, that each element of the crime, as expressed in the sentences which state the crime is proven to be the case.

If one will look again at the language of theft (RCW 9A.56.020), nowhere does one find the terms of art of "specific intent" nor of "knowledge" nor of "knowingly." The Code does in a separate title declare what are the principles of liability. In RCW 9A.08.010 one reads the following,

> *General requirements of culpability*. (1) Kinds of Culpability Defined.
> (a) *Intent*. A person acts with intent or intentionally when he acts with the objective or purpose to accomplish a result which constitutes a crime.
> (b) *Knowledge*. A person knows or acts knowingly or with the knowledge when:
>
> > (i) he is aware of a fact, facts, or circumstances or result described by a statute defining an offense; or
> > (ii) he has information which would lead a reasonable man in the same situation to believe that facts exist which facts are described by the statute defining an offense.
>
> (c) *Recklessness*. A person is reckless or acts recklessly when he knows of and disregards a substantial risk that a wrongful act may occur and his disregard of such substantial risk is a gross deviation from conduct that a reasonable man would exercise in the same situation.
> (d) *Criminal negligence*. A person is criminally negligent or acts with criminal negligence when he fails to be aware of a substantial risk that a wrongful act may occur and his failure to be aware of such substantial risk constitutes a gross deviation from the standard of care that a reasonable man would exercise in the same situation.

> (2) Substitutes for Criminal Negligence, Recklessness, and Knowledge. When a statute provides that criminal negligence suffices to establish an element of an offense, such element also is established if a person acts intentionally, knowingly, or recklessly. When recklessness suffices to establish an element, such element also is established if a person acts intentionally or knowingly. When acting knowingly suffices to establish an element, such element also is established if a person acts intentionally....
>
> (4) Requirements of Wilfulness Satisfied by Acting Knowingly. A requirement that an offense be committed wilfully is satisfied if a person acts knowingly with respect to the material elements of the offense, unless a purpose to impose further requirements plainly appears.

Counsel for the defendant was to argue that the crime of theft had to be bound by RCW 9A.08.010 (1) (b) (i), which made theft a crime which required knowledge, and that a person act knowingly, which indicates that one acts with awareness of the facts, etc., described by the statute defining the offense.

A crime of specific intent, as understood by counsel for the defendant, indicated that one intended to do a particular act: namely, permanently to deprive an owner of his property. Two elements were then to be presented by the state: (1) specific intent, and (2) knowledge. Was this an example of an intricate simplicity? Counsel for the defendant drew upon a case of recent standing to urge the distinction upon the Superior Court. The case cited was *State v. Edmon*, 28 Wn.App. 98, 103-104 (1981). That Appellate Court said:

> (2) Our analysis to this point has been within the terms of the traditional rule that only *specific intent* can be negated by this type of evidence. The rule must be modified because RCW Title 9A was designed to replace concepts like specific and general intent with the four levels of culpability in RCW 9A.08.010. Wherever 'intent' as defined in RCW 9A.08.010 (1) (a) is an element of a crime, it may be challenged by competent evidence of a mental disorder that causes an inability to form 'intent' at the time of the offense. Premeditation, of course, can still be negated by this defense. See *State v. Carter* [sic: which was cited in the body of the opinion].
>
> 'Knowledge' also is subject to this defense. RCW 9A.08.010 (a) (b) (i) reads: 'A person knows or acts knowingly or with knowledge when: (i) he is aware of a fact, facts, or circumstances or *result* described by a statute defining an

> offense...' [italics ours]. The concept of specific intent involves an intent in addition to the intent to do the physical act. *State v. Nelson*, 17 Wn.App. 66, 561 P.2d 1093 (1977). Thus, an intent to produce a certain result from the act would be specific intent. The fine distinction between the intent to produce a result (specific intent) and the awareness of a result of one's conduct (knowledge) should not determine the admissibility of expert medical evidence of a mental disorder. We have previously recognized the relevance of voluntary intoxication to the existence of 'knowledge' *State v Norby*, 20 Wn.App. 378, 579 P.2d 1358 (1978). It would be incongruous to allow a defense to 'knowledge' where the defendant was responsible for his mental state (voluntary intoxication) and to reject it where the defendant was not responsible for his mental state (mental disorder).

What was slowly evolving in the defense of the accused was that certain acts were done, but, for reasons yet to be specified, such were not full-fledged human acts to which criminal responsibility ought to attach. Underlying the theory the defense was advancing was that the intentional object required for criminal guilt did not exist. The defense would argue that *D* had no *specific intent* to commit the crime as charged, and also that the elements of *actus reus* were lacking (even though defense counsel did not employ such words).

Such an approach was not new at law. One may turn to the speech of Thomas Erskine, in his defense of James Hadfield, *R. v. Hadfield* (1800) 27 *St. Tr.* 1281. In his remarkable speech to the court, Erskine argued that to be insane did not mean that one had to suffer the total deprivation of memory and understanding, for if that was what insanity meant, then few had ever been insane. What was wanted for a finding of insanity in 1800 was that an accused lacked the capacity to form right intentions at law, and Hadfield had suffered from such mal-organization of mind, as the facts of that case demonstrated.

To return to *Rentel*, defendant's counsel argued that *D* lacked the ability to form a specific intent, and such was caused by a mental disorder not amounting to insanity in this case. The accused had become totally dependent upon cocaine. Case law permitted them to argue this dependency, and such inability to form a specific intent: *St. v. Ferrick*, 81 Wn. 2d 942, 506 P.2d 860, *cert. denied sub nom: Gustav v. Washington*, 414 U.S. 1094, 38 L.Ed. 2d 552, 94 S.Ct. 726, (1973); *St. v. Martin*, 14 W.App. 74, 538

P.2d 873 (1975). Counsel also argued that the cause of the inability to form a specific intent must be a mental disorder, and not emotions like jealousy, fear, anger, or hatred, citing *St. v. Moore*, 61 Wn.2d 165, 377 P.2d 456 (1959), and *St. v. Upton*, 16 Wn. App. 195, 556 P.2d 239 (1976). The mental disorder must be causally connected to the lack of specific intent, and it must not be just a reduced perception, or an overreaction, or some other irrelevant mental state. The inability to form the specific intent must occur at the time relevant to the offense, citing *St. v. Craig*, 82 Wn.2d 777, 514 P.2d 151 (1973). And if it is found, from the evidence, that the accused did suffer from mental disorder (even of a temporal nature), then that mental disorder must substantially reduce the probability that the defendant formed the alleged criminal intent, citing *St. v. White*, 60 Wn. 2d 551, 374 P.2d 942 (1962), *cert denied*, 375 U.S. 883, 11 L.Ed. 2d 113, 84 S.Ct. 154 (1963), and *St. v. Carter*, 5 Wn.App. 802, 490 P.2d 1346 (1971).

What defense counsel had skillfully done was to argue to the court that the forming of a criminal intention in the Criminal Code was an example of an exercise of a capacity, and one could not be said *to intend* at law under that Code if one could not exercise that capacity in a specify way to a specific end. In this case, *D* had to have the specific intent to commit the crime described by the Code. *D* was intending only "b" and not "a" or "c." The train ticket was, as it were, for Cambridge, and not for Oxford or London. The defendant would argue that he had developed a chemical dependence upon both cocaine and alcohol, but the nature and full extent of his dependence upon these chemicals was a dependency he could not fully appreciate. It is the paradox of addiction: in point of fact the addict is addicted to some chemical, but the self-awareness of that addiction is not appreciated by him. The old apothegm expressed this of the sin of pride, "Pride goeth before a fall," meaning the proud man does not know that he himself is proud. In like fashion, the addict *in this case* was unaware of the extent of addiction and of his debilitating dependence upon cocaine and alcohol. Because such a dependence could be diagnosed by means of psychiatric testimony and evidence, it could then be argued by the defense that the mental capacity of *D* was reduced, and such a reduction entailed the finding that *D* could not, and thus did not, form the specific intent required for the crime with which he was charged under the Code. The jury then was asked to consider the actions of the defendant in light of his own diminished mental capacity.

Two very heavy evidential burdens were placed upon the prosecution in this case. In the first instance, the State had to prove every element of the crime of theft. Then, as a further positive obligation, the State had to prove, *beyond a reasonable doubt*, that the defendant was not suffering from any relevant form of diminished capacity. This meant that the State had to establish for the jury that the defendant *both* specifically intended permanently to deprive his legal clients of their funds given to him by the Industrial Tribunal as workers' compensation for their injuries, *but also* when the accused acted so as to deprive them of these insurance funds the accused *knew* that his actions would so permanently deprive those persons of their funds. (It had the echo to it of the old penitential requirement that in order for one to commit a grave or mortal sin, one had to do so with full knowledge of what one was doing.) At the time of the trial this was a novel extension of the defense of diminished capacity. It had been part and parcel of common law assumptions* that one who had himself induced himself to take illegal drugs could not then plead as a defense to a felonious charge that one's drug-taking had become a pernicious and dependent habit, and that the habit had therefore deprived one of lucidity of mind: *ergo*, one's crimes are to be excused. The prosecution assumed that it had an easy case to prove. How could any wrongdoer benefit from his own wrongdoing, or seek a plea in mitigation because of his own wrongdoing and the unfortunate consequences it brought about?

The stumbling block for the prosecution came in the form of *Jury Instruction No. 27.* In American courts of law, when an issue goes to a jury for its deliberation, counsel in both tort and criminal cases are allowed to submit to the jury sets of instructions which the jury must follow in forming its decision as to liability, or as to guilt or innocence. The printed jury instructions are submitted to the judge by both counsel, and each has the chance, out of the presence of the jury, to argue for or against a putative jury

---

* "*Qui peccat ebrius lüat sobrius*," He who offends when drunk shall be punished when sober.

instruction. The judge makes the final decision as to what jury instructions he will allow to go to the jury.*

> *Jury Instruction No. 27* read as follows:
> When a person is charged with a crime, it is the burden of the State to prove beyond a reasonable doubt that the defendant did not have diminished capacity.
>
> A defendant has a diminished capacity if, at the time of the commission of the crime, as a result of a mental disorder, the defendant was not capable of acting intentionally as that term is defined in these instructions.
>
> If, after considering all of the evidence in this case, the State has not proven beyond a reasonable doubt that the defendant did not have a diminished capacity, you must find the defendant Not Guilty.

One is aware, therefore, that a set of legal sentences in which offenses were described was to be applied, in some fashion by a jury, to the acts or the omissions of an accused. The sentences were not "value free," as the jargon of sociology at times puts the matter. But, in a like fashion, the legal sentences were not sets of instructions (as one might find on a road map). The function of the jury, further, was to represent the mind of the community, to present, in some manner, the fashion and feelings of the community at large. But none on the jury were schooled philosophers, or lawyers, or semanticists. They were all average people, akin to the riders (in the past) of that famed Clapham omnibus. Yet we recognize that the language of the Code was meant, somehow, to apply to what the accused had done; either to find him Guilty, or to find him Not Guilty. The form of the language was realistic; it could be used. When "know," in any of its cognate forms was employed, it was assumed that "knowing" was something over which the accused had control and could in some way focus. The verb was not used at law here as if that same verb could be used of "sense knowledge," which has little, if any, indication of the voluntary in its use. The eyes "see," the ears "hear," and the senses report what is presented to them, independent of one's wanting to see or hear or sense. As used in the Criminal Code, "know," and its cognate forms, imported control and selection and the

---

* It is grounds for reversal if the judge rejects certain jury instructions without good reason, and counsel may lodge a motion for appeal if it believes that certain jury instructions were wrongly excluded by the judge.

exercise of a capacity. But under the Criminal Code, an accused, and by extension any citizen of ordinary status, is assumed to know the Code, or to know that there is a Code by which they are bound.* It would be an exceedingly rare defense for one to plead ignorance of the law and to have the court accept that defense, as if one were to say, "I knew some parts of the Code, but not all of it, and this part under which I was charged I did not, I am sorry to say, know."

It may be a separate question of great logical interest to ask whom does a Criminal Code address? The simplest answer may be from the law itself. A criminal code addresses those who may find themselves within the jurisdiction of the Code. If an accused is determined to have standing in a court of criminal law, then he is within the jurisdiction of the criminal code. It is a functional answer, as are most answers in criminal procedure. If, however, a legal philosopher wishes for an *a priori* answer as to whom the criminal code addresses, then a reply, at law, would fairly much be those whom the law deems capable of following that Code. The language, for instance of RCW.9A.04.030, "State Criminal Jurisdiction," gives five classes of addressees:

> (1) A person who commits in the state any crime, in whole or in part.
> (2) A person who commits out of state any act which, if committed within it, would be theft and is afterward found in the state with any of the stolen property.
> (3) A person who being out of the state, counsels, causes, procures, aids, or abets another to commit a crime in this state.
> (4) A person who, being out of the state, abducts or kidnaps by force or fraud, any person, contrary to the laws of the place where the act is committed, and brings, sends, or conveys such persons into this state.

---

* It is not our intention to argue curious exceptions to the general rule that ignorance of the law does not excuse one from the sanctions of the law. There is case law to show that the courts will excuse one from the penalties of the law because one truly did not know of the existence of the law, or, when the law was made, it was impossible for one to have known that such a law was actually in force: *R. v. Bailey* (1800) R. & R. 1, 168 E.R. 651. There *D* was at sea when a new law was introduced, and there was no way in which *D* could have known the law at the time he was charged. The court found him guilty, but avoided the logical embarrassment which such guilt entailed by mitigating the sentence.

> (5) A person who commits an act without the state which affects persons or property within the state, which, if committed within the state, would be a crime.

This is a very broad audience, and it would be very hard to determine what would be the limits beforehand as to whom the Code may apply. Further speculation brings one into questions more at home in the Conflict of Laws.*

The common-sense assumption is that the Code addresses itself to a community of common language users. Further embodied in this assumption is that an agent, by knowing himself through the power or capacity of self-knowledge, is able to control the manner of his actions, and it is therefore to the element of knowledgeable control to which the Code addresses itself. One may argue that it is the broad, primitive, unanalyzed assumption at work in the Code. The Code both assumes a community of common language users, and a community composed of those who can exercise self-control. But assumptions of this nature (or, if one prefers, statements of first principles put in that way), carry other possible problems which are of interest to philosophical analysis, and these problems appear when one tries to make sense of key terms under a Code, such as "wilfulness," or of a strained use of "know." To have acted wilfully is, it appears, also to have acted knowingly. But we do have a strong and long-enough tradition in the common law to show that these terms are not necessarily interchangeable as to meaning and scope. What in actuality we are encountering is the power of the legislative (the law-making power) to make terms mean what they wish those terms to mean, probably out of the assumption that broad terms will not permit of tricky defense exceptions or exemptions. But, as *Rentel* itself did show, precisely because the rubric governing "know" and its cognates under the Code was not clear or precise, the defendant was permitted to engage in broad and ingenious defense theory.

What may serve to make the concept of intention especially difficult to understand is that the concept seems to lead a dual life. On the one hand it may have the non-legal use when it is predicated of human actions in

---

* It is a truism of the subject of the Conflict of Laws that no *a priori* answer can be given as to the extent of a legal rule over some putative subject. What the legal study of this subject shows is how difficult it is to arrive at satisfactory answers as to the extent of jurisdiction.

general, or when it is used to give moral explanations of human actions. On the other hand the concept has a definite legal use, and the language which embodies that legal use may itself not be clear as to how the concept is to be used and extended. Or, as with so much of our language, the usage may seem to embody all levels of language, both legal and non-legal, and for the philosopher these various uses combined into one term may produce varying conclusions, one part of which may be in opposition to another part.

When one is attempting to account for the distinct acts of the agent *qua* agent, but also when one is attempting to account for those acts under a legal system which embodies intentional language and limits, the intertwining of purposes may yield other difficulties. The agent may protest that his aims are disparate to those of a legal system under which his aims are to be described. An interweaving of the purposes of the agent with the purposes of the legal system does not safely occur. There, as we know too well, the law resorts to legal fictions, as with constructive malice. This appeal to fiction, however, does force the law (as it did in the *Smith* case, [1961] AC 290), when an occasion presents itself, to reconsider questions of logical refinement. For instance, are intentional acts and intentional objectives to be understood from the eyes and mind of the agent, or from the logical structure of the legal language itself which sets down a standard known as the reasonable man or as an objective standard? Two sets of powerful self-interests become evident; one, that an agent be understood fairly and, as far as possible, correctly; the other, that the law be obeyed. One interest is that of the person, the other interest is that of the state.

Other issues spring forth from newer problems which criminal law needs to address. How much should the habits of a culture affect the basic distinctions in the law between voluntary and knowing acts, with regard to guilt for crimes? As a culture grows more and more irrational – certainly, as in our own culture which places heavy emphasis upon immediate gratification and change – must the criminal law faithfully reflect the habits of a culture? American industrial culture has spawned a vast world which appeals to the will: namely, a world which stresses "personal satisfaction" very often devoid of concerns for responsibility, or, in much milder language, a world devoid of any concern for social manners and civility. Must a cultivated cultural weakness which appeals to instant credit, video images (as with rock-video imagery used to promote rock music, in which images are moved across a video screen without any order or plot to them, but do appeal to underlying violence), easy bankruptcy, short-term marriages which may end in instant no-fault divorces, must a criminal law reflect a culture which tends increasingly to aspects of will and character and the subjective when that law sentences, or when that criminal law moves through the process of determining guilt? It will be remembered that the *1976 Report on Culpable Homicide* from New Zealand suggested that one may have to take national character into mind when forming theories of criminal responsibility, but that was a *Report* only which did not have the force of law or judicial decision. However, it does touch a question as to how far a theorist may propose national habits and customs as a way to temper the law. The ultimate question, however, comes to how such formulations could be made to be workable and fair in any judicial finding, and it does appear that the problems far outweigh the benefits of such a theoretical incorporation. A criminal theorist may believe that an indulgent culture may be required to pay dearly for its acts of indulgence.

Our research was undertaken much like a journey into an unknown and forgotten land of the mind. Our subject, human action itself under the criminal law, is far vaster and far more complicated than our writing about that subject. We do not delude ourselves into believing that we have exhausted the possible legal combinations which human action can devise to escape, or to establish, a finding of guilt under the criminal law.

We are aware, too, that we began this work as philosophers interested in the law, and, quite by accident and because of a great passage of time, each of us also became practising lawyers. We can feel the natural tensions between the roles of philosopher and lawyer, and how each sets about to solve legal problems and issues. Our concern, when combining both of those roles within ourselves, was to concentrate upon, and to explore and to investigate, a category which we found to be cardinal to the common law: its use and its understanding of intention in the criminal law. We tried to use case law itself which showed the internal tensions[49] nearly always at work in trying to refine this subject concept of intention, and by use of case law we came to see for ourselves that the concept, having strong roots in both the camps of the will and of the intellect, was difficult to capture.

In attempting to be or become a legal philosopher one does not have at one's disposal a simple handbook of instruction to state in what the art or discipline may consist. In like fashion, when speaking about legal terms such as *intention* or *mens rea*, and the like, one does not have a handy "Fowler's Correct Legal Usage" at one's fingertips to indicate what is the ordinary usage as distinguished from the extraordinary usage of the terms. There have been no clear rules for the use of key terms in the law in which responsibility is ascribed to or predicated of an agent by their use. One legal philosopher recently stated that law is a parasitic science, and it borrows its vocabulary (often) from the fashion and styles of the times.[50] There is no easy rule which cleanly marks off "legal usage" from "ordinary usage" in law. Common law reasoning is especially elastic. Its use of language tends more to an analogical use of words than it does to a strict and restricting univocal use of words. The legal philosopher often finds himself moving in two worlds. From one world he brings in the habit of mind of the philosopher, who hopes to set conceptual boundaries upon the use of a term (or, at least, to discover what may be those boundaries), but he also must have the mind and the feeling of a legalist, who appreciates that law does not use language in a way mathematically precise.

There is another feature of legal language, and we are not trying to sound especially clinical, in which one assays the key terms of that language: namely, the past, and how those terms came to be used in the way they are used. The intuition which sparked our interest in this topic was that key legal terms, such as the various forms of intention, had to them a rich linguistic past, but like anything rich and detailed, that past could easily be forgotten; or, which is a graver fault, those key terms could be used without regard for their past. One is indebted to the commonplace spirit which Wittgenstein gave to twentieth-century philosophy when he argued that we are directed, in good part, by the logic of ordinary language which is embedded in common linguistic use. The logic directs one to conclusions, the logic of which eludes us oftentimes as to why *this* conclusion rather than *that*. But because one is not attendant to the logical force embodied in, and submerged within, a language, it must needs then occasion logical errors by a user of that language when the user does not appreciate, or is not aware of, the logic of the language.

The warning is not new to lawyers. Lord Coke had an insight much akin to Wittgenstein's when, in the sixteenth century, Coke spoke of the "artificial reason" of the law, going to such an extent, even, as to rebuke a monarch, telling him that the art of making legal decisions took a long time to learn because one had to be especially sensitive to the nuances which legal language contained. The metaphor of "artificial reason" can be taken to mean that the set of legal sentences which so compose the law at any moment are a set of sentences which also contain that logical usage whereby the law is made and formed. For one to be ignorant of this kind of linguistic and logical history which legal terms embody is to fail to appreciate what law fully is.

A reading through the legal history of the common law will show one, we believe, that no doctrine of intention issued forth from the mind of Zeus reflective of godly purity or clarity. What has come forth through the slow development of the law is a concept which is at once flexible, rich, intricate, simple, but whose pedigree and logical elements are elusive, contrary, difficult and complex. Following the mind and habit of the law, the chosen method of our research has been, wherever possible, to document a claim by an appeal to a legal citation of some kind or other. The reason for this style is to protect both the reader and ourselves against inadvertent manufacturing of evidence and against making claims beyond the purview of the evidence. It is not to do history or to write historiography. As a legal philosopher one is beholden to the legal historian for providing one with documents so that one's investigation may be done. The legal philosopher is concerned with the logical form of arguments, with the logical consistency of a concept, with linguistic expression whereby a logical concept is expressed, or a rule or code embodied, and the like, and he uses some of the matter common to history, but as a philosopher and not as an historian.

What is not our intention in this work is to delve too deeply, or too long, into what ought to be a proper theory of legal language. For the most part, legal sources of the common law did not doubt the power of language.

Language was used, and by its use it was also refined. Criminal law, however, did not have the fineness of use which property law had. The metaphysics of the common law was its property law; criminal law, alas, required centuries of use and practice before any kind of conceptual refinement occurred in it. The subject borrowed from other disciplines, from commonplace morality and social notions of right and wrong. There was a general acceptance in the law over centuries that men had a common nature, that there was a common sense of what was right and what was wrong, and that the ordinary man, Everyman, knew in his heart of what right conduct consisted and of what wrong conduct consisted. Lord Chesterfield embodied the conventional wisdom in his essay on men and manners, at one point clearly and simply writing,

> In order to judge the inside of others, study your own; for men in general are very much alike; and though one has one prevailing passion, and another has another, yet their operations are much the same; and whatever engages or disgusts, pleases or offends you, in others, will, *mutatis mutandis*, engage, disgust, please, or offend others, in you. Observe, with the utmost attention, all the operations of your own mind, the nature of your passions, and the various motives that determine your will; and you may, in a great degree, know all mankind.[51]

But the reason for this linguistic detour is to advise the reader that the aim of this study will be to support its claims and findings, and possible conclusions, by an appeal to the language of the common law tradition. One should reflect on how legal language operates; and one poses a legitimate enterprise when one seeks to investigate and to find out what may be the latent assumptions controlling the legal language of the common law. The spirit of such a direction has taken philosophers of all ages, and it is by no means a new pursuit. The pursuit, however, is not moved onwards by the force of the cautions of the linguistic philosophers of this century who wisely have advised and warned us that language is not a limpid pool of unobstructed clarity. To the contrary, language is itself a difficult form of art, with numerous levels of logic controlling its use. Like human nature itself, the possessor is perplexed by his possession.

There is another reason, too, for dwelling at length upon the language of the law. Charles Richardson saw it – but not in relation to law* – when he wrote his little book, *On The Study of Language*, in 1854.[52] Whether one wishes to call him an early linguistic philosopher is not important here. What is of importance was the warning he spelled out in some detail that terms are not terms pure and simple. Terms are metaphors oftentimes, and over the course of time the use of certain terms brings about confusions because the metaphorical roots and origins of the terms have been lost to us. Two simple samples may illustrate his thinking. First,

> WILD is willed, will'd (or self-willed), in opposition to animals, etc., tamed or subdued to the *will* of others or of Societies.

And, for our second example,

> WILE, GUILE...The Anglo-Saxon Wigl-ian, ge-wigl-ian, be-wigl-ian, means to conjure, to divine, consequently to practise cheat, imposture, and enchantment.
>
> WILE (from Wigl-ian), and *guile* (from ge-wigl-ian), are that by which any one is *deceived*.
>
> GUILT, is Ge-wigled, guiled, guil'd, guilt; the past participle of *ge-wigl-ian*. To find *guilt* in any one, is to find that he has been *guiled*, or, as we now say, beguiled; 'that is,' says Mr. Trench, 'instigante diabolo – as is inserted in all indictments for murder, the forms of which come down to use from a time when men were not ashamed of tracing evil to his inspiration.'**
>
> WICKED means witched, or bewitched; and to pronounce *guilt* is to be pronounced *wicked*.[53]

This does not set one solely on a lexical course, but it does advise one that a sentence, and in this case a legal sentence, may require greater conceptual analysis than simply to understand (say) what holding it advances in the law. One may be required to analyze, or to attempt an analysis of, the key terms which convey the holding at law, and this may involve one in more than legal analysis.

Not only may a term mask a complex but unperceived metaphor, but the sentence in which the term occurs may raise a further issue as to whom

---

* Richardson did discuss legal and moral terms in Chap. 1, "Of the Rights of Man," Vol. II, Chap. 1., pp. 86-101, but in a general way, and not as would a law book.

** On the Study of Words, Lec. 6.

the term is addressed. One will recall *D.P.P. v. Smith*, 1961 A.C. 290 (H.L.), which troubled itself over the question whether intention was to be measured by a subjective or by an objective standard. Did the language and tradition of the common law address the perception of the agent in his doing of an act, or did the language of the common law address a class of reasonable actions, their reasonableness something akin to the reasonable man standard of tort law? One need not exhume the legal commentary here upon *Smith*, but the case demonstrated how difficult it was to ascertain a clear and simple standard by which to judge criminal intent. A next step may be to ask, not only whom a term addresses, but what is the proper referent of a term? One will recall the decision from the United States Supreme Court, *Roe v. Wade*, 410 U.S. 113, *rehearing denied*, 410 U.S. 959 (1973), in which the Court itself, during the period of oral argument, asked counsel for the defendant, who had been charged with procuring an illegal criminal abortion, whether or not the term "person," as used both in the Texas statute forbidding abortion, and the use of the word "person" in the Fifth and Fourteenth Amendments of the United States Constitution, applied to an unborn child? *Was an unborn child a person at law?*

The transcript of the case, as published in the series of leading Supreme Court cases by the University of Chicago, shows that the Justices of the Court were asking *both* for a philosophical use and understanding of the word "person," and a legal use and understanding of the word "person." The question, however, as the transcript shows, was never answered at oral argument; and the lengthy decision of the case left more verbal and conceptual difficulties about the nature of the word and concept, "person," than it resolved. (The case itself is not within the boundaries of our research.)

The simple Latin phrase, *Actus non facit reum nisi mens sit rea*, appears late in common law literature in the case of *Fowler v. Padget* (1798), 7 T.R. 509, *per* Lord Kenyon, C.J. Like so much of English law, it was far from original. But the maxim – for that is what it was – borrowed from a latinate literature long forgotten, served less to explain than it did to confuse. What did the maxim express? Did it express an empirical truth about human nature and behavior? Was it a rule whereby a finding could be made under the rule? How was the maxim to be read? Was it (say) a preamble to a larger code or set of rules? Was it a maxim to which no exception at law should be allowed, unless a law-making or law-declaration power so affirmed? Like a piece of metal which, after careful inspection one ascertains to be some kind of ancient implement or tool, was this maxim some arcane rubric indicating some use which had been lost in the past? Like an ancient tool one could surmise that it was used for something, but what its specific use was time has erased for us. The maxim, however, had not reached that state of desuetude; it was used, now and again, at law; and, like a solar battery on an outer-space vehicle, it was still sending back to us some kind of signal, even if not as clear as one wished. Some, however, have taken a very hard attitude and have moved for the abandonment of the maxim on the grounds that its use has caused such unlimited confusion no further good can be gained from continuing its legal use. These, as the 1960's and the 1970's have shown us, are the modern codifiers of the criminal law.[54]

Try as some jurisdictions have to rid themselves of legal confusions in the criminal law by making into supposedly clear codes what must be the specific elements of a crime, the logical primitives of the voluntary and the involuntary, the intent and purpose of an act, are not to be removed. One is not arguing that a law-making or law-declaration power could not remove difficulties, or could not so construct a code of criminal law that only the effects of an act were censored and punished; but, in a strict sense, this would be to graft on to the criminal law the principles which seem to govern tort law (when not concerned with intentional torts), and this kind of a hybrid would produce a criminal law heretofore unknown to common law jurisdictions. It is not impossible to imagine (as if one were constructing a game theory) some legal universe in which the law-making powers ruled out any appeal to the personal state of an agent, or to his testimony as to why he did what he did. Criminal law could be seen as a fixed system of tariffs, like traffic infractions. But for the sake of consistency one would have to declare the absolute rule that no further testimony by the defendant could be given. As with the car improperly parked, the offense would be that *act* as apprehended: namely, the car improperly parked.* One would be strictly liable for one's actions, and one would proceed at one's peril.

But this has not been the history of the common law of crimes, save for that period of time when the accused could not give evidence on his own behalf because it was assumed that he could not be impartial in his testimony because of his direct self-interest in the outcome of the trial. That period is long behind us. For good or ill, intention is used as a concept whereby guilt or innocence is determined in the common law system of criminal law, and it is with that long system of law that we are concerned. The sum of human experience under liberal democracy indicates that when one is accused of a crime, one wishes to have a chance to affirm one's innocence, to explain why one is not guilty.** The system of criminal law which appears to have evolved in the common law countries is one which affords the right to an accused to explain his actions if he so wishes. As long as a legal system has a right of reply or of rejoinder, it will not be comprised of a strict list of crimes of strict liability.

The legal process whereby the common law is exercised is, at best, a fragile and shifting process. It is fragile because its practitioners are human, and to be human is to be capable of error. The consequences of error in a legal process can be harmful in the extreme. To deprive a person of his liberty, or even of his life, is to make a serious deprivation, and it should be done with all precautions for an accused. The machinery of justice which the state can move is a mighty engine, and when wrongly or unwisely moved, it destroys most about it, including itself. Whether one speaks of the witchcraft trials over which Lord Justice Hale presided,*** or the trials which

---

* And this example is hardly free from logical difficulties or exceptions.

** One need not cavil about the modern rules of evidence in their various jurisdictions. The common law rule is followed that the Crown, or the State, must prove the elements of the crime charged, and if such is not proven by the State, one may move for a directed verdict to have the case discharged. Common law rules of evidence do not require one as the accused to defend oneself affirmatively. What may happen, however, is that once the State has discharged its burden of proof, the burden then shifts upon the defendant and he may choose to give evidence in his own behalf or not.

*** The English statutes which governed the witchcraft trials were: 5 Eliz., c. 16 (1562), and 1 Jac. 1, c. 12 (1604), late repealed by 9 Geo. 1, c. 5 (1736). An argument could be made

embodied modern political witchcraft when a whole nation found many to be Communists in the 1950's with but the slightest pretext, how the accused is to be found guilty, and what are the legal elements of guilt are questions constantly to be reviewed, and canons which constantly are to be evaluated.

The style of philosophical analysis we embraced in this monograph has been analytical analysis of texts and concepts. The analytical method is a style which is helpful because it creates a tension of the text against a question. What, for instance, is meant by "will" (when one speaks about the human will); or what is meant by "action" (when one speaks of human action); or what is meant by "know" (when it is stated that one must know the quality or the nature of one's acts)? In the past, judicial thinkers seemed either to gloss over any sustained analysis of such questions as these, or blindly to assume that such sustained analysis and questioning need not be put against a legal text. There was the confident tone that any man who rode the Clapham omnibus home in the evening would easily know how to answer puzzling legal questions. But one finds that such confidence is self-defeating; the hard problems do not go away. St. Augustine, when asked by a child what was meant by the Trinity, is the paradigm case for us that what may be simple may not simply be answered or avoided. Analytical philosophy, as a method of asking and solving questions, underwrites the assumption that what may seem obvious is not, after all is said and done, obvious.

One may find that a concept, or a notion, admits of various degrees, or interpretations, or meanings. How does one choose between this or that? Here, it may be that one transcends simple speculation to enter into a realm of preferences. One may list various applications of a concept; one may say it should mean this, another that, or a third yet different from both – but which is absolute? Which wins the day? It may very well be that one must look and see. One may have to admit that this is a limit to analyticity as a

---

that such statutes were examples of law-making power which created for *D* a "no win" situation, and that properly speaking this is not a question of the intentions of a defendant, but is a question of what defense a legal system will, or will not, permit whatever may be the real intentions of *D*. In theory, law-making powers may exclude defenses for any class of victims (*Roe v Wade*) or any class of accused (Jews in Nazi Germany who were declared to be non-persons, and hence did not have rights of defense under the criminal system).

method of investigation. One leaves a world of logic and one enters into a world of aesthetics. If *A* can do a proof in ten steps, while *B* can do the same proof in twenty steps, which is to be preferred? One proof may be concise; the other proof may be charmingly clear. No method can finally protect one against deciding and what the problem of choice entails. One hopes that if one has been clear and lucid, then what one has decided will itself also be clear and lucid. The shortest distance between two points may be a straight line, but for the road engineer it may mean that he must permit the destruction of miles of countryside for the planned extension of a dual carriage-way, while for some other engineer such would offend the overall aesthetic he has of road building. Each engineer embraces certain values on how the roadway is to be built; but who is the better of the two, which is the better choice, brings in far more values than the distance between two points.

One perceived such a state of legal tension when the House of Lords struggled to decide *Hyam*. Three of the law lords believed that the verdict of murder should stand; two of the law lords believed that manslaughter should have been substituted for the verdict of murder. One set of assumptions or one set of legal facts, if held, led to one conclusion; but if differently held, then to another conclusion. There comes that moment when one must step outside of the protective environment which the formality of an analytic system will give to one, and that stepping outside is the moment or act of judgment. The child, after all of his practice and reading, finally must sit down at the piano and play the piano, or put on his ice skates and actually skate on the ice, in both cases taking the chance that the perilous will occur – a wrong note out of sequence, a fall when trying to execute a delicate turn on the ice. At law, judgment seems to be more than the sum of its preceding steps. How one chooses a jural fact from among the facts of a case is one of the mysteries of legal reasoning. When James I and VI, as both King of England and Scotland, tried his hand at judging law cases it was said of him that when he first heard one side of a case, he could decide for it; but when he had to hear the other side of the case, he could decide in its favor too; and was reported to have abandoned being a King who judged actual law cases because he found the art too difficult.

There is no simple logical form to a legal decision. One may move from the very simple reports of early cases which Brooke or Fitzherbert state from the mid-1500's, to extremely complicated statements of great length which compose a judicial judgment, as was the decision in *Pacific Acceptance Corporation v. Forsyth and Others* (1970), of the New South Wales Supreme Court, which report is printed over 359 pages and is concerned with a new area of the law, actions against professional advisers. No legal philosopher claims that legal decisions are the model of logical conclusions. Some decisions at law are confused, and one is driven to madness when trying to locate the *ratio decidendi* of the judgment. As with such a state of affairs (as can be found often in administrative law decisions) one is led to strive to make some connection between the sentences of the judgment, and the judgment itself. Reasons *may* lead to action, but not always so. One is, at that point, left to theorize, stating that the reason why the court did not state its reasons conclusively was to indicate that it did not wish to become further involved in cases of this kind.*

Not intending to give hostages to fortune, one should nevertheless appreciate – and we state it here – that a strict positivist theory of language, if adopted by the law, does yield serious difficulties. To hold that the terms of the law do not describe states of affairs is to enter upon some kind of *Alice in Wonderland* theory of language. If one holds that legal terms, *in strictu senso*, are purely nominative, or purely stipulative, then one finds oneself in a naming of the beasts problem without considering the nature of the beasts named. To call a rabbit a lion, and a lion a rabbit, without regard to the natures of either, is to become dinner for the rabbit if it enters your garden!** A legal language which has no respect for natures is no respecter of persons either. Although this is an issue of law-declaration power, the defense

---

* One assumes that a court acts in good faith and impartially. In such a case, there may be instances when the court has arrived at a decision, but the written judgment fails to give a solid justification for the holding in the decision. If the court has acted fairly, and has heard the evidence of the parties, then as a court of law it has discharged itself. That it may decide wrongly, or unclearly is an inherent risk.

** A serious proponent of a stipulative theory of language for the law may be found in "Language and the Law," by Glanville Williams, L.Q.R., 1945-1946.

against a faulty law which has been declared by a legislative power is to hold that the law does not apply to the natures it embraces. The quickest disposal of it as a theory was done by the late Governor Adlai Stevenson of the United States, who, when the legislature of his state, Illinois, sought to make a law prohibiting cats from prowling about at night, said, "Cats being cats, I don't expect they will follow the law." The legislature got the message; the law was never enacted.

In great part, then, our research attempted to investigate the origin, development, and changes which intention in the law underwent over many centuries. For purposes of readability and volume, we wanted to end the chief part of our research with what broadly were the medieval roots of the common law, and we saw Chief Justice Hale as the last great embodiment of those scholastic roots, and, by the same token, a springboard into the modern development of reasoning from case law from within the tradition and sources themselves of a developing common law. It would be to the later scholars, like Blackstone, Wooddeson, East, Foster, Kelyng, and the various Reports on the Criminal Law throughout the nineteenth century, along with Stephen, Wright, *et alii*, to develop a coherence of presentation of a developing common law without incessant return to its medieval roots. As the case law developed and progressed, it would become the basis, more and more, of how the common law of crimes would emerge and grow.

By moving from the time of Hale into our own century it was possible to demonstrate that theories of criminal liability had not changed unalterably from their ancient roots. We wanted to show that there persisted a relationship between the past and the emerging present, and that there was what seemed to be a consistent assumption about the nature of criminal liability which was expressed variously over time.

Our wish was to demonstrate in this book one central insight which we believe was inherent in the early Christian roots to which we traced intention. It was that action was within the province of the human will. The whole world of intention at criminal law is a world which deals with the will of man, and which attempts to depict how the will acts. We are aware that we no longer speak in this stilted way, but at the very bottom of our research was an awareness, which we tried to develop, that the will is the key faculty, or concept, to intentional analysis. This sentiment was well put at the time of Chief Justice Hale, and in closing, we wish to impress it upon our reader:

> § III.3. LASTLY, to render sin compleat and perfectly criminal, it is neither enough that for the matter of it, it be against some law, nor that such Law be known, but the act or omission must be voluntary; that is, not what a man was overborn into by some fatal necessity, or compelled to by the force of some violent impression, nor what he could neither help nor hinder; but what was so far subject to his own free choice, that he willingly did what he did, and could have done otherwise, or omitted doing if he had so pleased. For whatever is not of this nature is not properly an humane act, and therefore cannot involve him in the guilt of sin, no more then [sic] the effect and productions of natural causes can be esteemed vicious. And though men have understanding which those other causes are destitute of, yet that being onely the *Criterion* or Test of truth and falsehood, not of moral good and evil, therefore vertue and vice are not imputable to the understanding but to the Will, which being the Helm of the soul determines all its motions, and accordingly is accountable for them.[55]

When the Latin phrase entered into English law through its occurrence in *Fowler v. Padget* (1798) 7 T.R. 509, or 101 E.R. 1103, "*Actus non facit reum nisi mens sit rea*," it brought with it a concern for the will in human acts. Lord Kenyon's utterance of the dictum as a fundamental principle of the criminal crime was consistent with the respect paid to an understanding of will which could be found in the literature pre-existing *Fowler*. The Rector of Hadham (*supra*) certainly could have appreciated that the maxim embodied an appeal to the voluntary. One could also have turned to the law of Scotland, near that time, to see that its understanding of human action at law reflected common understandings about the voluntary which were later mirrored in English law. John Erskine wrote:

> 2. It is of the essence of a crime that there be an intention in the actor to commit it: for an action, in which the will of the agent has no part, is not a proper object, either of rewards or punishments: Hence arises the rule: *crimen dolo contrahitur*. Simple negligence does not therefore constitute a proper crime. 1.7 *ad leg. Corn. de ficar.* Yet where it is extremely gross, it may be punished arbitrarily or *extra ordinem*. See *1.11. de incend. ruin naufr.*- Far less can we reckon in the number of crimes involuntary actions, the first cause of which is not in the agent; or those committed by an ideot or furious person: But lesser degrees of fatuity, which only darken reason, will not

> afford a total defence, tho' they may save from the *poena ordinaria*. Actions committed in drunkenness are not, as to this question, to be considered as involuntary, seeing the drunkenness itself, which was the first cause of the action, is both voluntary and criminal.[56]

One will appreciate that a serious analysis of English laws did not emanate until Blackstone issued his *Commentaries* (1765). A sentiment of the same kind, but expressed in more Christian terms, is written by Blackstone:

> For as God, when he created matter, and endued [sic] it with a principle of mobility, established certain rules for the perpetual direction of that motion; so, when he created man, and endued [sic] him with freewill to conduct himself in all parts of life, he laid down certain and immutable laws of human nature, whereby that freewill is in some degree regulated and restrained, and gave him also the faculty of reason to discover the purpose of those laws.[57]

This passage plainly suggests that what a great legalist saw as the key to human action under the law was the human will.

We believe that the early Christian stress upon the will found its way into the common law, and that as the early common law developed it incorporated the models of the voluntary which the Christian environment presented. How this incorporation came about at each stage of legal development is difficult to say. More time, finer collections of early legal documents and sources, and one may be able to document how the legal and cultural osmosis may have occurred. Because there are only one or two endowed chairs of legal history, and then but a few more endowed chairs in jurisprudence, this is a problem still in need of research, scholars and a solution. Further, as in the United States, the great law schools are turning away from classical jurisprudence (with its emphasis upon the use of sources) and are turning to a jurisprudence founded mostly upon economic theory, seeing the workings of law as predominantly expressions of latent and patent theories of economics. Little understanding will be gained of the complications of intention from an economic jurisprudence.

Having presented what we believe to be our understanding of the roots of criminal intention, we do not think that one can simply hold that one has solved a problem–*full stop*. Intention by its very nature is open-textured, because it is a concept through which particular human actions are attempted to be understood. There is always that element in any human action which is particular to the person causing that action. There is the *particularity* of an act, and particulars have the logical feature of their particularity which does not lend them to easy comparison with other particulars. We do not mean to resurrect the metaphysics of *haecciety* ("thisness"), which John Duns Scotus espoused, and which was later expressed by the late nineteenth-century poet, G. M. Hopkins, but we should realize that human actions are selfsamely particulars. When we enter into law, and its relationship to the particular, we come into an area we cannot simply describe or predict. What the case will be is how the case will emerge. The understanding of this activity is made even more difficult because one of the particulars to a legal decision (namely, this-case-yet-to-be-decided) is itself not yet a particular legal entity. It is an example of an assortment (all of the action and detail which the legal process of a trial incorporates) yet-to-be-the-case. It is not even a fetal state, which seems to imply that some kind of determined identity will emerge, even though that identity is not yet the case. In the world of the putative legal particular, however, one does not know what identity will emerge.

In a world populated simply by objects, one may appeal to various general categories (shape, size, quality, and the whole mode of accidents which surround a particular) by which to come to know the particular, but in human actions, with their human histories, one does not have a simple particular. Although human action may be considered a natural event (from the point of view of some other person or perspective), we know, to the contrary, that a human action taken from the viewpoint of the agent (who deliberates or may deliberate) is not a natural event. In bringing about a deliberative act, no particular yet exists. Intention was a way in which religious thinking, moral thinking, and legal thinking tried to comprehend the agent in relation to himself as one who produced an action. The world of the law was like a general map about human action, yet like all maps it could be unclear, or it could fail to give insight into territory which was unknown to it. How complete a map to human action the law, which embraced intention, might be, only case-by-case analysis would tell. We believed the relationship between what the criminal law was mapping, and what occurred when an agent acted or omitted to act, lay in developing some understanding of what the voluntary meant, and might entail. As case law developed, it embodied assumptions about human nature and behavior, and we had read those sets of assumptions (which were both consciously and unconsciously incorporated into a developing body of criminal law) to be assumptions about the nature of the voluntary. The key (to us) between the world of the legal map of the criminal law, and the particular actions of this and that person, lay in understanding the will in its relation to intelligent action.

The decided case, just as the past action of some person, underneath its obviousness, i.e., this case printed out, or this action which is now a past action, to be of help in deciding forthcoming cases, or to be of help in understanding further human actions, must embody some level of generality, which in turn can be understood and, somehow, applied to further cases and actions. One finds that one must be able to rise to some level of generality, and to be able to pick and choose similar features (or to see that similar features are present, or obtain) from a case (or a human action), and then enter into a world of qualities so that, at law, *stare decisis* can function. Equally, if one chooses to neglect what may be the common elements present in cases, or in human actions, then one absolves oneself from having to use a past case as a binding precedent. This very loose and *ad hoc* nature of the common law prevented it from revealing any simple organizing principles. It is painfully commonplace for a lawyer to be frustrated by the court's decision, especially when no simple organizing principle is revealed in the decision whereby *this case* was decided: Courts, whether they choose to give reasons to support their decisions, nevertheless have the power to decide, and that power may be raw judicial power devoid of the insulating material which reasons for a decision may provide.

Too, there came with the parasitic nature of common law its habit of using a vocabulary, but not freeing that borrowed vocabulary from past meanings, or from the richness of past use. "Will," "nature," "soul," "mind," are not simple terms like "wrench," "screwdriver" or "hammer." When one borrows terms from another vocabulary, especially from a well-formed and diffuse vocabulary as existed in the writings of theology and philosophy, one brings into the law a vocabulary which carries with itself meanings, both overt and hidden, from that original vocabulary. Unless a term is given a precise legal sense, one has a range of nuances to consider when the term is used.

Like a successor corporation, a borrower inherits the strengths and weaknesses of what one has borrowed. But not only does one borrow the terms from other vocabularies, one uses the concepts which those terms express, and which may have taken centuries to develop and then to refine. Key terms used to describe human actions and behavior bring with themselves vast philosophical and theological *impedimenta* to which the legal philosopher must attend when he seeks to understand the operations of a legal concept. The impurity of legal language constantly calls for its refinement and purification.

Intention as a concept in common law reaches way back to the Hellenic world in its moral philosophy, and then slowly works its way through Roman law, through early Church law, into medieval philosophy and theology, and then slowly, near to the end of the eighteenth century, begins to take upon itself a legal shape from out of its own legal resources. The development of the concept is slow and tedious, and so much of its development is open to conjecture. The links along the way of the course of the legal development of intention are less than clear and direct. The vocabulary of the criminal law came from far and wide, and how that vocabulary functioned in conveying what intention meant, has been the subject of this research. As philosophers we worked with that vocabulary, and as philosophers we put questions to the criminal law about what we believed to be its key concept: intention. It has been the spirit of the philosopher which impelled us to write as we have, girded in the belief that philosophical analysis is always timely, and is never destroyed by time, no matter from what age.

Endnotes Chapter 8

1. *Criminal Law Reform, An Inaugural Lecture*, by D. Thompson, LL.B., Ph.D., Barrister-at-Law, Professor of Law, in the University of Keele, 22nd February 1967 (published by the University of Keele), pp. 4-5.

2. *Cf.* for instance, these few examples. [The] *Fourth Report*: *The Substantive Criminal Law*, [published by] Criminal Law and Penal Methods Reform Committee of South Australia [July, 1977], Supreme Court, Victoria Square, Adelaide, S.A. 5000, pp. (xlviii) + 460. The American Law Institute has recently issued, in three volumes, its massive: *Model Penal Code and Commentaries* (Official Draft and Revised Comments), edited by Herbert Wechsler, published by The American Law Institute, 1980, Philadelphia, Pennsylvania, U.S.A. One may also consult the various papers issued by the *Criminal Law Revision Committee*, and published by Her Majesty's Stationery Office, London. Some of the papers were: *CLRC: Working Paper, Section 16 of The Theft Act 1968* (London: HMSO, August, 1974); *CLRC: Working Paper on Offenses against the Person* (London: HMSO, August,1976). There are, also, the various "Working Papers" issued, from time to time, by *The Law Commission*, and published by HMSO. Some were: *WP No. 50: Inchoate Offenses, Conspiracy, Attempt and Incitement* (London: HMSO, 5 June 1973); *WP No. 55: Codification of the Criminal Law, General Principles, Defences of General Application* (London: HMSO, 1974); *WP No. 56: Criminal Law, Conspiracy to Defraud* (London: HMSO, 1974); *WP No. 57: Codification of the Criminal Law, Conspiracies relating to Morals and Decency* (London: HMSO, 1974); *WP No. 63: Conspiracies to effect a public mischief and to commit a civil wrong* (London: HMSO, 1975). The work of both Commissions is a continuing enterprise. One may also encounter various Home Office papers, for example: *Report of The Advisory Group On The Law of Rape* (London: HMSO, December 1975 [Cmnd. 6352]). Then there exist the published reports of *The Law Commission*, after deliberation and criticism of their "Working Papers," and some of these final reports have been in the field of criminal law: Law Com. No. 55, "Report on Forgery and Counterfeit Currency" (London, HMSO, 1973 (320)); Law Com. No. 89, "Report on the Mental Element in Crime" (London: HMSO, 1978 (499)); Law Com. No. 76, "Report on Conspiracy and Criminal Law Reform" (London: HMSO, 1976, (176)); Law Com. No. 102, "Attempt, and Impossibility in Relation to Attempt, Conspiracy and Incitement" (London: HMSO, 1980 (646)). All are vast reports.

3. *R. v. Larsonneur* (1933) 97 J.P. 206.

4. *Cf., Jaggard v. Dickinson* [1980] 3 All E.R. 716, *re*: "belief" induced by intoxication.

5. One may observe the tension which can exist between the logic of the law and the policies of the state in its use of law. An interesting class of cases are those dealing with criminal attempts, the object of which act is itself not a

criminal wrong. One class of cases will hold that the object of a criminal attempt must itself be criminal, reasoning that one, normally, cannot steal one's own watch (or possession). *Cf.*, *People v. Jaffe*, N.Y.C.A., 1906, 185 N.Y. 497, 78 N.E. 169, "Bartlett, J., The crucial distinction between the case before us...lies not in the possibility or impossibility of the commission of the crime, but in the fact that...the act, which it was doubtless the intent of the defendant to commit would not have been a crime if it had been consummated." Contrary reasoning may be cited from, *The Queen v. Whitchurch, and Others*, (1890) 24 Q.B.D. 420, in which *D*, not herself pregnant, was found guilty of attempting to procure an abortion (contrary to the statute, 24 & 24 Vict. c. 100, s. 58 (1)). Lord Coleridge reasoned that if three persons combine to commit a felony, "they are guilty of conspiracy, although the person on whom the offense was intended to be committed could not, if she stood alone, be guilty of the intended offense" (p. 422). Hawkins, J., found her in the instant case guilty: "What she did was a conspiracy to commit a criminal act" (p. 422). The literature on Attempt and Impossibility is rich, and confusing. One may confer: "Criminal Attempts at Common Law," by E. R. Keedy, U. Penn. L.R. [Vol. 102, 1954], pp. 464-489; "One Further Footnote on Attempting the Impossible," by Graham Hughes, *N.Y.U.L.R.* [Vol 42, December 1967, No. 6], pp. 1005-1034; also, *cf.*, *The Law Commission*. (Law. Com. No. 102), "Criminal Law: Attempt, and Impossibility in Relation to Attempt, Conspiracy, and Incitement" (London: H.M.S.O., 25 June 1980 (646)), which took the general position, "2.99 - Our conclusion is that the fact that it is impossible to commit the crime aimed at should not preclude a conviction for attempt" (p. 53, s.4). A "policy" justification was advanced.

6. "(1) If any person who has attained the age of sixteen years and has the custody, charge, or care of any child or young person under that age, wilfully assaults, ill-treats, neglects, abandons, or exposes him, or causes or procures him to be assaulted, ill-treated, neglected, abandoned, or exposed, in a manner likely to cause him unnecessary suffering or injury to health (including injury to or loss of sight, or hearing, or limb, or organ of the body, and any mental derangement), that person shall be guilty of a misdemeanour, and shall be liable – (a) on conviction on indictment, to a fine, or alternatively, or in addition thereto, to imprisonment for any term not exceeding two years....

"(2) For the purposes of this section – (a) a parent or other person legally liable to maintain a child or young person shall be deemed to have neglected him in a manner likely to cause injury to his health if he has failed to provide adequate food, clothing, medical aid or lodging for him, or if, having been unable otherwise to provide such food, clothing, medical aid or lodging, he has failed to take steps to procure it to be provided under enactments applicable in that behalf.

It may be noted, from the case which is to be discussed, that the provisions of s.1(1) have been familiar to the common law since 1889 in the Prevention of Cruelty to, and Protection of, Children Act. Case law which was decided from it, as well as its later enactments, is to be found in *R. Senior* [1899] 1 QB 283, [1895-1899] All ER Rep 511, and in *R. v. Petch* (1909) 2 Cr App R 71. A statutory offense of this kind is nearly a century old.

7. *R. v. Sheppard and another* [1980] 3 All E.R. 899. The House of Lords divided 3 to 2 in allowing the appeal of the appellants, James Martin Sheppard and Jennifer Christine Sheppard, against the decision of the Court of Appeal, Criminal Division (Lord Widgery, C.J., Bridge, L.J. and Woolf, J.). Allowing the appeal were Law Lords Diplock, Edmund-Davies, and Lord Keith of Kinkel; dismissing the appeal were Law Lords Fraser of Tullybelton and Scarman.

8. *Cf.*, Archbold's *Pleading, Evidence and Practice in Criminal Cases* (40th Edn., 1979, page 2, para. 3, and the cases cited therein).

9. *Sheppard*, [1980] 3 All E.R. 899, at 902j-903a-b.

10. *Ibid.*, 903c-d.

11. *Ibid.*, 903h-j.

12. *Ibid.*, 904a.

13. *Ibid.*, 904a-c.

14. *Sheppard*, 904d-e.

15. *Ibid.*, 905e-f.

16. *Ibid.*, 905f-h.

17. *Criminal Law, The General Part*, by Glanville Williams (London: Stevens & Sons Limited, 1953), Chapter 5, "*Mens Rea* as Affected by Ignorance of Fact," at §s-(39), "Application of the rule to statutory crimes requiring wilfulness," p. 115. In a footnote upon this sentence, Professor Williams added: "In civil proceedings for maintenance it has been assumed that there may be a wilful refusal to maintain if the refusal is based upon reasonable mistake: see *Chilton v. Chilton* [1952] p. 196. "But this point has not been expressly decided, and whatever may be the civil law it is submitted that the reasonableness of the mistake is not in issue in criminal proceedings." Cp. *Dept. of Agriculture v. Burke* [1915] 2 I.R. at 140: "'Wilfully' means 'intentionally,' 'not by inadvertence or mistake.'" The observation remained substantially the same in the 2nd, enlarged edition of his work (1961), as Chapter 5, §-(53), p. 142.

18. Stat. 1, *Eliz*, cap. 2., Sect. 8, in: *The Laws...Explained*, by William Cawley (London: for John Wright, MDCLXXX), p. 16. [Wing No.: C-1651c.]

19. *Sheppard*, 906j-907-a.

20. *Ibid.*, 906g-h.

21. *Ibid.*, 908g.

22. *Ibid.*, 908b.

23. *Ibid.*, 914a-b.

24. *Ductor Dubitantium, or The Rule of Conscience*, by Jeremy Taylor, D.D. (London: printed by James Flesher for Richard Royston, 1660), "Of The Nature and Causes of Good and Evil...The Fourth Book, Chap.1., Rule VI, Ignorance does always excuse the fact, or diminish the malignity of it, or change the kind and nature of the sinne" (p. 500).

25. *Ibid.*, "What is probable ignorance?" para. 16, p. 499.

26. *Sheppard*, 915a.

27. *Ibid.*, 915a.

28. *Ibid.*, 916f.

29. *Downes*, 13 Cox. C.C. 111; (1875) 1 QBD 25.

30. *Hines* is a long note, but its reasoning bears upon *Sheppard*, and we wish to cite a great portion of *Hines*. "Reg. v. Hines was an indictment against Hines for unlawfully endangering the life of his child, aged two years, by omitting to provide proper and sufficient medicine." Pigott, B., after hearing the argument, and the citations to cases [*Reg. v. Smith*, 8 C&P; *Reg. v. Hurry*, Central Criminal Court Reports, vol. 76, p. 63] said, "I am of opinion that there is no case to go to the jury of any crime; I think it is one of those cases in which a parent, instead of being guilty of anything like culpable negligence, has done everything that he believed to be necessary for the good of his child. That he may be one of those who have very perverted views and very superstititious views...may be perfectly true; but that there is anything in the nature of a duty neglected, that is, a duty which he believed or knew to be such...does not show. On the contrary, he believed his duty to be in the direction in which he acted, and he carried out that duty to the utmost of his ability. He may altogether have mistaken what his duty was; still I believe it was an honest mistake. It may be an ignorant mistake, in all probability it is the result of ignorance and superstition, but certainly there is not a trace of anything like an intentional omission of duty or a culpable omission of duty within the meaning of that expression as used in the criminal law....But I am clearly of opinion that no judge sitting in a Criminal Court, without any direction or enactment of the Legislature, would be justified in saying that a parent who exercised his best judgment, though a perverted one, in dealing with his child by nursing and care instead of calling in a doctor...was guilty of criminal negligence."

31. *Downes*, 13 Cox C.C. 114; (1875) 1 QBD at 29.

32. *R. v. Senior*, [1895-99], All E.R. Rep., C.C.R. 514.

33. *Sheppard*, 918c.

34. *Ibid.*, 913a-c.

35. In his searching article, Professor Graham Hughes argued that the language of the law in which the logic of omissions was understood was not compelling, and was often confusing. He felt that *mens rea* was a notion inappropriate to the logic of omissions. With his statement we would disagree, however helpful we found his research to be. The opinion of Lord Diplock in *Sheppard* is strong proof for our position. *Cf.*, *Criminal Omissions*, by Graham Hughes, *The Yale Law Review* [Vol. 67: 1958, pp. 590-637].

36. [1977] 2 All E.R. (C.A.) 341, heard as one case.

37. *Stone* and *Dobinson*, 347f-h.

38. *Cf.* the thoughtful discussion of the matter by F. A. Whitlock in his *Criminal Responsibility and Mental Illness* (Butterworths, 1963).

39. *Cf.*, "Free Will as Involving Determinism," Chapter iv, pp. 62-73, in *Virtues and Vices*, by Philippa Foot (Oxford: Basil Blackwell, 1978), pp. 65-66.

40. *Cf.*, *R. v. Rivett* (1950) 34 Court of Criminal Appeal 87; *R. v. Windle*, [1952] 2 Q.B. (C.C.A.) 826; *R. v. Walden* [1959] 1 W.L.R. 1008; 3 All E.R. 203; 43 C.A.R. 201 (C.C.A.); *Roberts and others v. Ramsbottom* [1980] 1 All E.R. (QBD) 7; *R. v. Spratt* (1980) 2 All E.R. (C.A.) 269; *State v. Crenshaw*, 27 Wn. App. 326.

41. *Op. cit.*, Chapter 5, "Mens Rea, Determinism, Free Will and Responsibility," pp. 54-71.

42. *Cf.*, the essay by Lord Devlin, "Mental Abnormality and the Criminal Law," to be found in *Changing Legal Objectives*, edited by R. St. J. MacDonald (Toronto, Canada: University of Toronto Press, 1963), pp. 71-85.

43. In Chapter iv, "The Will," in *The Concept of Mind*, by Gilbert Ryle (London: 1949), most of the remarks could be accommodated to a psycho-chemical theory of action: namely, of any action one did it could be said, "He did it." Also, *cf.*, *The Mind Possessed*, by William Sargant (Heinemann: 1973).

44. *Cf.*, *The Insanity Defence in New York: A Report to Governor Hugh L. Carey [from the] New York State Department of Mental Hygiene* (February, 17th, 1978) [obtainable from: State of New York Department of Mental Hygiene, 44 Holland Avenue, Albany, New York, 12229]. Also, *cf.*, *Burden of Proof of Insanity in Criminal Trials* (Chief Justice's Law Reform Committee, 6th April, 1965) [obtainable from: University of Melbourne (Australia), Law School, Professor H. Luntz, Secretary, C.J.L.R.C.].

45. *Cf.*, "*Mens Rea* Reconsidered...," by G. V. Dubin [*Stanford L. R.*, Vol. 18, No. 2, January 1966], pp. 326-395, esp. "2. *The conformity principle in the Supreme Court*," pp. 380-392, *re*: crimes because of addiction.

46. In *Hearst*, both the trial court, and the appellate court, rejected the defense of Duress.

47. *Criminal Responsibility and Mental Illness*, by F. A. Whitlock (London: Butterworths, 1963). Citation taken from chapter 5, "Mens Rea, Determinism, Free Will and Responsibility," pp. 54-55.

48. *State of Washington v. Gary W. Rental* (1984), a case argued in Superior Court of the State of Washington in and for the County of Pierce, Cause number: 83-1-01538-5.

49. One may read *Hyam v. D. P. P.*[1974] 2 All ER 41, [1975] A.C. 55, a divided decision of 3-2 from the House of Lords. The speeches for the majority give one impression as to the meaning of *mens rea*, while the speeches of the minority give a contrary meaning as to the elements and extension of the concept at law. One may also read the recent report issued by the Scottish Law Commission in which the Commission shows its disagreements with the ruling in *Hyam*, as well as with certain definitional proposals as to how the concept ought to be expressed in various draft Bills and by various law revision committees. *Cf. Scottish Law Commission*, "The Mental Element in Crime," published by H.M.S.O., Edinburgh (November, 1983). One may also read some of the modern cases which attempt to connect "recklessness" and "intention," and then so define "recklessness" to mean a vacuousness of mind. *Cf.*, *R. v. Caldwell* [1982] A.C. 341 (H. L.), and also *R. v. Lawrence* [1982] A.C. 510 (H. L.). It may be advanced that the two cases go a long way from any common understanding of intention, but also as case law, they give no clear rules as to how the concept should be applied, or to what extent it may be applied. *Cf.*, the strong criticism expressed of the two decisions: "Recklessness Redefined," by Glanville Williams, 1981 C.L.J. 252.

50. Readings in the *Philosophy of Law*, edited by Ronald Dworkin (Oxford University Press), from *The Preface*.

51. Lord Chesterfield's *Advice To His Son* (London: M.DCC.XCII), "Knowledge of the World," pp. 56-74, esp. p. 61.

52. (London: George Bell, 1854), Vol. II, Chap. 11, "Of Abstraction," p. 101 ff.

53. *Ibid.*, p. 120, and pp. 168-169, "Of Abstraction."

54. One example from among many will suffice. In the State of Washington, on the 1st of July, 1976, a revised Criminal Code was to come into force. One would be charged under that Code: RCW 9A, and then a further number after 9A which would indicate the named offense under the Code. RCW 9A.16.030 would indicate: "*Homicide – When excusable.*

Homicide is excusable when committed by accident or misfortune in doing any lawful act by lawful means, without criminal negligence, or without any unlawful intent." However, one would have to keep in mind a direction under the Code: RCW 9A.04.060 "*Common law to supplement statute*. The provisions of the common law relating to the commission of crime and the punishment thereof, insofar as not inconsistent with the Constitution and statutes of this state, shall supplement all penal statutes of this state and all persons offending against the same shall be tried in the courts of this state having jurisdiction of the offense." As in the common law, rules for interpretation, in good part, emerge from the developing case law, and many of the same conceptual difficulties would obtain.

55. *The Penitent Pardoned*, by John Goodman, D.D., Rector of Hadham, [London], 1679 [First edition], [Wing number: W-1115]. We have preserved the original spelling, and this passage was taken from Chapter III, "Of the Nature of Sin, and of the divers States of Sinners," section III, "All sin is voluntary...," p. 56.

56. *Cf., The Principles of the Law of Scotland* (3rd edition), by John Erskine (Edinburgh: John Balfour, M.DCC.LXIV (1764)), *Title 4*, "Of Crimes," pp. 469-470.

57. 1 *Bl. Com.* 39 and 40, Sect. 11 (Fourth edition; Dublin: MDCCLXXI.)

INDEX

G

H

J

K

L

S

Z

TORONTO STUDIES IN THEOLOGY

1. Robert R. N. Ross, **The Non-Existence of God: Linguistic Paradox in Tillich's Thought**
2. Gustaf Wingren, **Creation and Gospel: The New Situation in European Theology**
3. John C. Meagher, **Clumsy Construction in Mark's Gospel: A Critique of Form-and Redaktionsgeschichte**
4. Patrick Primeaux, **Richard R. Niebuhr on Christ and Religion: The Four Stage Development of His Theology**
5. Bernard Lonergan, **Understanding and Being: An Introduction and Companion to *Insight***, Elizabeth A. Morelli and Mark D. Morelli (eds.)
6. John D. Godsey and Geffrey B. Kelly (eds.), **Ethical Responsibility: Bonhoeffer's Legacy to the Churches**
7. Darrell J. Fasching, **The Thought of Jacques Ellul: A Systematic Exposition**
8. Joseph T. Culliton (ed.), **Non-Violence - Central to Christian Spirituality: Perspectives from Scripture to the Present**
9. Aaron Milavec, **To Empower as Jesus Did: Acquiring Spiritual Power Through Apprenticeship**
10. John Kirby and William M. Thompson (eds.), **Voegelin and the Theologian: Ten Studies in Interpretation**
11. Thomas I. Day, **Dietrich Bonhoeffer on Christian Community and Common Sense**
12. James Deotis Roberts, **Black Theology Today: Liberation and Contextualization**
13. Walter G. Muelder *et al.*, **The Ethical Edge of Christian Theology: Forty Years of Communitarian Personalism**
14. David Novak, **The Image of the Non-Jew in Judaism: An Historical and Constructive Study of the Noahide Laws**
15. Daniel Liderbach, **The Theology of Grace and the American Mind: A Re-presentation of Catholic Doctrine**
16. Hubert G. Locke (ed.), **The Church Confronts the Nazis: Barmen Then and Now**
17. M. Darrol Bryant (ed.), **The Future of Anglican Theology**
18. Kenneth Cauthen, **Process Ethics: A Constructive System**
19. Barry L. Whitney, **Evil and The Process God**
20. Donald Grayston, **Thomas Merton: The Development of a Spiritual Theologian**
21. John J. McDonnell, **The World Council of Churches and The Catholic Church**
22. Manfred Hoffmann (ed.), **Martin Luther and the Modern Mind: Freedom, Conscience, Toleration , Rights**

23. Eric Voegelin, **Political Religions,** T. J. DiNapoli and E. S. Easterly III (trans.)

24. Rolf Ahlers, **The Barmen Theological Declaration of 1934: The Archeology of a Confessional Text**

25. Kenneth Cauthen, **Systematic Theology: A Modern Protestant Approach**

26. Hubert G. Locke (ed.), **The Barmen Confession: Papers from the Seattle Assembly**

27. Barry Cooper, **The Political Theory of Eric Voegelin**

28. M. Darrol Bryant and Hans R. Huessy (eds.), **Eugen Rosenstock-Huessy: Studies in His Life and Thought**

29. John Courtney Murray, **Matthias Scheeben on Faith: The Doctoral Dissertation of John Courtney Murray,** D. Thomas Hughson (ed.)

30. William J. Peck (ed.), **New Studies in Bonhoeffer's** *Ethics*

31. Robert B. Sheard, **Interreligious Dialogue in the Catholic Church Since Vatican II: An Historical and Theological Study**

32. Paul Merkley, **The Greek and Hebrew Origins of Our Idea of History**

33. F. Burton Nelson (ed.), **The Holocaust and the German Church Struggle: A Search for New Directions**

34. Joyce A. Little, **Toward a Thomist Methodology**

35. Dan Cohn-Sherbok, **Jewish Petitionary Prayer: A Theological Exploration**

36. C. Don Keyes, **Foundations For an Ethic of Dignity: A Study in the Degradation of the Good**

37. Paul Tillich, **The Encounter of Religions and Quasi-Religions: A Dialogue and Lectures,** Terence Thomas (ed.)

38. Arnold A. van Ruler, **Calvinist Trinitarianism and Theocentric Politics: Essays Toward a Public Theology,** John Bolt (trans.)

39. Julian Casserley, **Evil and Evolutionary Eschatology: Two Essays,** C. Don Keyes (ed.)

40. J. M. B. Crawford and J. F. Quinn , **The Christian Foundations of Criminal Responsibility: A Philosophical Study of Legal Reasoning**

41. William C. Marceau, **Optimism in the Works of St. Francis De Sales**

42. A. James Reimer, **The Emanuel Hirsch and Paul Tillich Debate: A Study in the Political Ramifications of Theology**

43. George Grant, *et al.*, ***Two Theological Languages* by George Grant and Other Essays in Honour of His Work,** Wayne Whillier (ed.)

44. William C. Marceau, **Stoicism and St. Francis De Sales**

45. Lise van der Molen, **A Complete Bibliography of the Writings of Eugen Rosenstock-Huessy**

46. Franklin H. Littell (ed.), **A Half Century of Religious Dialogue, 1939-1989: Making the Circles Larger**

47. Douglas J. Davies, **Frank Byron Jevons, 1858-1936: An Evolutionary Realist**

48. John P. Tiemstra (ed.), **Reforming Economics: Calvinist Studies on Methods and Institutions**

49. Max A. Myers and Michael R. LaChat (eds.), **Studies in the Theological Ethics of Ernst Troeltsch**

50. Franz G. M. Feige, **The Varieties of Protestantism in Nazi Germany: Five Theopolitical Positions**

51. John W. Welch, **A Biblical Law Bibliography: Arranged by Subject and by Author**

52. Albert W. J. Harper, **The Theodicy of Suffering**

53. Bryce A. Gayhart, **The Ethics of Ernst Troeltsch: A Commitment to Relevancy**

54. David L. Mueller, **Foundation of Karl Barth's Doctrine of Reconciliation: Jesus Christ Crucified and Risen**

55. Henry O. Thompson (ed.), **The Contribution of Carl Michalson to Modern Theology: Studies in Interpretation and Application**

56. David G. Schultenover (ed.), **Theology Toward the Third Millennium: Theological Issues for the Twenty-first Century**

57. Louis J. Shein, **The Philosophy of Lev Shestov (1866-1938)**

checked 3/8/91 cb